WILLS, TRUSTS, AND ESTATE ADMINISTRATION

EIGHTH EDITION

Options.

We understand that affordable options are important. Visit us at cengage.com to take advantage of our new textbook rental program, which can be bundled with our MindTap products!

Over 300 products in every area of the law: MindTap, textbooks, online courses, reference books, companion websites, and more – Cengage Learning helps you succeed in the classroom and on the job.

Support.

We offer unparalleled course support and customer service: robust instructor and student supplements to ensure the best learning experience, custom publishing to meet your unique needs, and other benefits such as Cengage Learning's Student Achievement Award. And our sales representatives are always ready to provide you with dependable service.

Feedback.

As always, we want to hear from you! Your feedback is our best resource for improving the quality of our products. Contact your sales representative or write us at the address below if you have any comments about our materials or if you have a product proposal.

Accounting and Financials for the Law Office • Administrative Law • Alternative Dispute Resolution • Bankruptcy Business Organizations/Corporations • Careers and Employment • Civil Litigation and Procedure • CP Exam Preparation • Computer Applications in the Law Office • Constitutional Law • Contract Law • Criminal Law and Procedure • Document Preparation • Elder Law • Employment Law • Environmental Law • Ethics • Evidence Law • Family Law • Health Care Law • Immigration Law • Intellectual Property • Internships • Interviewing and Investigation • Introduction to Law • Introduction to Paralegalism • Juvenile Law • Law Office Management • Law Office Procedures • Legal Research, Writing, and Analysis • Legal Terminology • Legal Transcription • Media and Entertainment Law • Medical Malpractice Law • Product Liability • Real Estate Law • Reference Materials • Social Security • Torts and Personal Injury Law • Wills, Trusts, and Estate Administration • Workers' Compensation Law

---

CENGAGE
Learning®

5 Maxwell Drive
Clifton Park, New York 12065-2919

For additional information, find us online at: **cengage.com**

WILLS, TRUSTS, AND ESTATE ADMINISTRATION

EIGHTH EDITION

DENNIS R. HOWER
Professor Emeritus
University of Minnesota

EMMA R. WRIGHT, J.D.
Assistant Professor
University of Cincinnati

JANIS L. WALTER, J.D.
Professor
University of Cincinnati

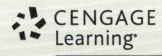

CENGAGE
Learning·

Australia · Brazil · Mexico · Singapore · United Kingdom · United States

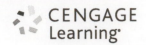
CENGAGE
Learning·

Wills, Trusts, and Estate Administration, Eighth Edition
Dennis R. Hower, Janis L. Walter, Emma R. Wright

SVP, GM Skills & Global Product Management: Dawn Gerrain

Product Director: Matthew Seeley

Product Manager, Katie McGuire

Senior Director, Development: Marah Bellegarde

Senior Product Development Manager: Larry Main

Senior Content Developer: Melissa Riveglia

Senior Product Assistant: Diane Chrysler

Vice President, Marketing Services: Jennifer Ann Baker

Marketing Manager: Scott Chrysler

Senior Production Director: Wendy Troeger

Production Director: Andrew Crouth

Senior Content Project Manager: Betty L. Dickson

Managing Art Director: Jack Pendleton

Software Development Manager: Joe Pliss

Cover image(s):
Monkey Business Images/ShutterStock.com
wavebreakmedia/ShutterStock.com
Ocskay Bence/ShutterStock.com
ptnphoto/ShutterStock.com

> For product information and technology assistance, contact us at
> **Cengage Learning Customer & Sales Support, 1-800-354-9706**
>
> For permission to use material from this text or product, submit all requests online at **www.cengage.com/permissions**. Further permissions questions can be e-mailed to **permissionrequest@cengage.com**

Library of Congress Control Number: 2015948464

ISBN: 978-1-305-50625-1

Cengage Learning
20 Channel Center Street
Boston, MA 02210
USA

Cengage Learning is a leading provider of customized learning solutions with office locations around the globe, including Singapore, the United Kingdom, Australia, Mexico, Brazil, and Japan. Locate your local office at: **www.cengage.com/global**

Cengage Learning products are represented in Canada by Nelson Education, Ltd.

To learn more about Cengage Learning, visit **www.cengage.com**

Purchase any of our products at your local college store or at our preferred online store **www.cengagebrain.com**

Notice to the Reader

Publisher does not warrant or guarantee any of the products described herein or perform any independent analysis in connection with any of the product information contained herein. Publisher does not assume, and expressly disclaims, any obligation to obtain and include information other than that provided to it by the manufacturer. The reader is expressly warned to consider and adopt all safety precautions that might be indicated by the activities described herein and to avoid all potential hazards. By following the instructions contained herein, the reader willingly assumes all risks in connection with such instructions. The reader is notified that this text is an educational tool, not a practice book. Since the law is in constant change, no rule or statement of law in this book should be relied upon for any service to the client. The reader should always refer to standard legal sources for the current rule or law. If legal advice or other expert assistance is required, the services of the appropriate professional should be sought. The publisher makes no representations or warranties of any kind, including but not limited to, the warranties of fitness for particular purpose or merchantability, nor are any such representations implied with respect to the material set forth herein, and the publisher takes no responsibility with respect to such material. The publisher shall not be liable for any special, consequential, or exemplary damages resulting, in whole or part, from the readers' use of, or reliance upon, this material.

Printed at CLDPC, USA, 02-19

Unless otherwise noted, all items are © Cengage Learning

I dedicate this book to my husband, Roger Wright, and my parents, Rosalind Walter and Julius Walter. Without their patience, support, and understanding, but most importantly, their love, the ability to even undertake the writing of this book would have been impossible. Thanks for always being there!   *–JW*

To Mom and Dad—for always seeing the best in me; to Pete—my constant inspiration and the greatest little brother there ever was; to Andrew—for the love and laughter you bring to my life. May you all have the great amount of joy in your lives that you have brought to mine.   *–EW*

BRIEF CONTENTS

CONTENTS

PREFACE

Over the past few decades, the performance of qualified and competent paralegals has raised their status as legal professionals. The economic benefits paralegals bring both to their employers (supervising attorneys) and to the firm's clients have proven their need and value. Therefore, it is no surprise that their vocation has grown rapidly over the last 10 years. Although the current national market for paralegals remains strong, it will be competitive. Students who choose quality programs for their education and certification will have the best employment opportunities.

The goal of this edition of *Wills, Trusts, and Estate Administration* Eighth Edition is to continue to provide a textbook that explains the basic, practical, everyday duties of a paralegal in the fields of law and prepares paralegals, such as yourself, to confidently undertake and successfully accomplish these tasks. After using the text and obtaining work experience, you will attain the level of competence that will enable you to perform your work with confidence and continue the success and uphold the standards that your profession demands.

The text is written primarily for paralegals, but others such as trustees and personal representatives appointed to administer the estate of a deceased person may find it useful. The text identifies the responsibilities and duties that a paralegal can perform under the supervision of an attorney when drafting a will or trust or assisting with the administration of a decedent's estate. The text provides a review of the terminology and general principles of law that are the bases for drafting wills and trusts, or planning and administering an estate, and identifies the participants and the duties they must perform in these legal areas. New material has been included updating the discussion of inheritance rights for same-sex couples, estate tax changes, and the disposition of digital assets. A chronological treatment of the step-by-step procedures required to complete the will and trust drafts and the administration of a decedent's estate is presented, including sample drafts and the executed forms needed to administer the estate. Current federal and state tax information and the appropriate tax forms are also discussed.

CHAPTER ORGANIZATION

To help students obtain confidence and proficiency, each chapter of the eighth edition contains the following features.

- *Objectives*. The objectives focus students on what they will learn upon completion of the chapter.
- *Scope of the Chapter*. The scope identifies and lists, in order, the topics to be discussed within the chapter.

- *Terminology*. Key terms are printed in boldface type and are defined in the margin at their first appearance. Key terms are also listed at the end of each chapter and defined in a comprehensive end-of-text glossary.

- *Examples, hypothetical situations, sample state statutes, legal forms, exhibits, checklists, drafted documents, and actual cases*. These are interspersed throughout the chapters to help students understand the concepts and procedures discussed.

- *Assignments*. Frequent assignments within the chapters require students to apply the chapter's legal concepts or to perform tasks required of a practicing paralegal.

- *Checklists*. Checklists that collect relevant client data and information are included in the text, and "What You Do" lists and "You Must" notations in the Estate Administration chapter emphasize and clarify the actual procedures and specific tasks the paralegal student must master to attain confidence and competency.

- *Ethical Issues*. These issues are found throughout the text to call attention to important ethical concerns that are relevant to the procedures discussed within the individual chapters.

- *Review Questions*. Review questions are included at the end of each chapter and revised to correspond to the changes in content within the chapters.

- *Case Problems*. These actual cases and hypothetical problems are included at the end of the chapters to enable the students to verify what they have learned and apply it to a specific problem or task discussed in the chapter.

- *Points of Interest*. Real-life contemporary cases or issues are included to enhance student understanding.

- *Practical Assignments*. Additional practical assignments have been added to the end of chapters to provide students with more hands-on type skills required in the law office. Many incorporate the Internet as a research tool to familiarize students with situations they will encounter as a practicing paralegal.

CHANGES IN THE EIGHTH EDITION

- *New legal topic*. The eighth edition includes a discussion of the disposition of digital assets. This topic is being overlooked by many practitioners in estate planning and administration despite the prolific use of social media, email, and digital accounts. Sample forms addressing these issues have been included.

- *Reorganization of chapters*. Chapters have been reorganized to match the order in which a paralegal instructor is more likely to cover the materials. A student must understand the basic concepts of property before being able to determine what one would include in an estate. Once we have completed the discussion of estate administration and taxation of the estate, the focus switches to trusts and their classifications. The eighth edition concludes with estate planning and issues regarding long-term care.

- *Statutes*. State statutes that identify the variations in state laws and emphasize the need for paralegals to master the statutes of the state in which they live and practice have been added or updated.

- *State-by-state charts*. All charts have been updated where appropriate.
- *Legal forms*. Legal forms have been updated within the chapters, and essential newly executed estate administration forms, including selected tax forms, are included in Appendix A.
- *Surviving spouse*. The definition has been expanded and a discussion added to reflect changes in state laws as they apply to same-sex conjugal couples; new information includes a state chart.
- *Checklists*. The checklists used for collecting data and information for drafting wills, trusts, or an estate plan have been revised where necessary.
- *Tax laws*. Chapter 11 on taxes and pertinent charts have been updated to reflect current tax regulations.
- *Uniform Probate Code*. The Uniform Probate Code is available at law libraries; state versions can be accessed online.
- *Points of Interest*. Information regarding current issues and cases has been added to allow the student to reflect on real-life situations and how they might affect an estate practice.
- *Practical Assignments*. More practical assignments have been added to increase the marketability of the student.

SUPPLEMENTAL TEACHING AND LEARNING MATERIALS

Instructor Companion Site

The online **Instructor Companion Site** provides the following resources:

Instructor's Manual and Test Bank

The **Instructor's Manual and Test Bank** have been greatly expanded to incorporate changes in the text and to provide comprehensive teaching support. They include the following:

- Chapter overviews
- Case briefs
- Answers to text questions
- Test bank and answer key

PowerPoint Presentations

Customizable Microsoft PowerPoint® Presentations focus on key points for each chapter. (Microsoft PowerPoint® is a registered trademark of the Microsoft Corporation.)

Cengage Learning Testing Powered by Cognero is a flexible online system that allows you to:

- author, edit, and manage test bank content from multiple Cengage Learning solutions
- create multiple test versions in an instant
- deliver tests from your LMS, your classroom, or wherever you want

Start right away!

Cengage Learning Testing Powered by Cognero works on any operating system or browser.

- No special installs or downloads needed
- Create tests from school, home, the coffee shop—anywhere with Internet access

What will you find?

- Simplicity at every step. A desktop-inspired interface features drop-down menus and familiar intuitive tools that take you through content creation and management with ease.
- Full-featured test generator. Create ideal assessments with your choice of 15 question types (including true/false, multiple choice, opinion scale/Likert, and essay). Multi-language support, an equation editor, and unlimited metadata help ensure your tests are complete and compliant.
- Cross-compatible capability. Import and export content into other systems.

To access additional course materials, please go to login.cengage.com. Use your SSO (single sign on) login to access the materials.

Please note that the Internet resources are of a time-sensitive nature and URL addresses may often change or be deleted.

ACKNOWLEDGMENTS

The authors would like to thank former product manager Paul Lamond and current product manager Katie McGuire for trusting in us to complete this revision of *Wills, Trusts, and Estate Administration,* Eighth Edition. We have enjoyed the process and the challenge. Special thanks go to Melissa Riveglia, senior content developer, for her patience, thoughtful comments, and exemplary guidance. We couldn't have completed this work without you!

Special thanks go to the reviewers of the text for their ideas and suggestions:

Hannah Barnhorn
National College
Kettering, OH

Michele Bradford
Gadsden State Community College
Gadsden, AL

Beverly Woodall Broman
Everest Institute
Pittsburgh, PA

THE CONCEPT OF PROPERTY RELATED TO WILLS, TRUSTS, AND ESTATE ADMINISTRATION

1

Outline

Objectives

After completing this chapter, you should be able to:

- Identify, explain, and classify the various kinds of property, such as real and personal property or probate and nonprobate property.

- Recognize and understand the terminology associated with property law.

- Distinguish the various forms of ownership of real and personal property and explain the requirements for their creation and function.

- Understand and explain why courts do not favor the creation of joint tenancies between parties other than spouses.

- Identify the community property states and differentiate between community and separate property.

- Explain the kinds, methods of creation, and characteristics of estates in real property.

SCOPE OF THE CHAPTER

Everyone owns some kind of property, e.g., a home, car, savings and checking accounts, appliances, clothes, jewelry, websites, or stocks and bonds. While alive, the owner of certain property called probate property (discussed below) has the opportunity to transfer it by gift, sale, or the creation of an *inter vivos* (living) trust. After the owner dies, probate property can pass by will, testamentary trust, or **inheritance** according to state law. Without property, a will is unnecessary, and a trust cannot be created. Thus, property is the essential component that establishes the need for and purpose of wills and trusts. You must fully understand the law of property and its terminology before you can draft wills or trusts and assist with the administration of a decedent's estate. This chapter introduces the terminology of the law of property; explains its association with wills, trusts, and estate administration; and discusses related statutes and court decisions. Also introduced are ways or forms in which property can be owned; each form of ownership is identified, defined, and explained. Estates in real property (freeholds and leaseholds) are also covered.

inheritance
Property that descends (passes) to an heir when an ancestor dies intestate.

PROPERTY: TERMINOLOGY AND CLASSIFICATION

Property is anything subject to ownership. It is classified as either real property or personal property.

Real Property

Real property (also called realty or real estate) is property that is immovable, fixed, or permanent. It includes the following:

- Land
- Structures affixed to land such as houses, apartment buildings, condominiums, and office buildings
- Objects attached to land and buildings called fixtures
- Things grown on land except those for the purpose of sale (see below)

Owners of real property also have rights to airspace above their land and to the earth below it, including any minerals in the earth.

Fixtures

fixture
Something so attached to land as to be deemed a part of it, e.g., real property that may have once been personal property but now is permanently attached to land or buildings.

A **fixture** is real property that may once have been personal property but now is permanently attached to land or buildings. An example of a fixture that grows on land is a tree; however, growing crops that are annually cultivated for sale like corn, wheat, and vegetables are not fixtures. They are considered to be personal property. Carpeting nailed to the floor and a built-in dishwasher are examples of fixtures in buildings.

State courts apply three tests—annexation, adaptation, and intention—to determine if personal property has been converted into a fixture.

1. Annexation means that the personal property has been affixed or annexed to the real property.

2. Adaptation means that the personal property has been adapted to the use or purpose of the real estate. The court asks whether the property is necessary or beneficial to the function or enjoyment of the real estate.

3. In most states, however, the intention of the person who annexed the personal property to the real property has been the controlling test that determines the existence of a fixture.

Courts throughout the country vary substantially on what constitutes a fixture, but generally, though not always, doors, fences, windows, stoves, refrigerators, electric lights, wall-to-wall carpeting, and the like are held to be fixtures. Compare the following cases.

- *Mortgage Bond Co. v. Stephens,* 181 Okl. 419, 74 P.2d 361 (1937), in which the court held that a refrigerator was a fixture, as it was built into the cabinets.
- *Elliott v. Tallmadge,* 207 Or. 428, 297 P.2d 310 (1956), in which the court held that a refrigerator was personal property since by simply unplugging it, it could be moved at will.

Tenants often install fixtures on property they rent. A tenant farmer who raises chickens may build a shed to shelter them or install gasoline tanks to avoid long drives to town for fuel; a tenant who rents an apartment may add carpeting, bookshelves, and a doorbell for comfort and convenience. Previously, any such items a tenant attached to the real estate could not be removed when the tenant vacated. Today, however, tenants may remove property they have attached to real estate if the property falls under one of three exceptions, known as tenant's fixtures.

1. *Trade fixtures.* Property placed on the land or in a building to help the tenant carry on a trade or business.

   EXAMPLES: Smokehouse, machinery, barber chairs, greenhouse, pipe organ.

2. *Agricultural fixtures.* Property annexed by the tenant for farming purposes.

   EXAMPLES: Wooden silo, toolshed, henhouse, hay carrier, irrigation plant.

3. *Domestic fixtures.* Property attached by the tenant to make an apartment more comfortable or convenient.

   EXAMPLES: Carpeting, dishwasher, clothes dryer, gas stove, bookshelves.

ASSIGNMENT 1.1

Henry recently sold his movie theater to Helma. Which of the following items are fixtures (real property) that now belong to Helma? Give reasons for your answers.

Seats in the auditorium	Popcorn machine	Furnace in the building
Computers in the office	Movie projector	Framed movie poster
Carpeting in the theater	Movie film	Mirrors in the restrooms

deed
A writing signed by the grantor whereby title to real property is transferred or conveyed to the grantee.

Transfers of Real Property

When real property is transferred by gift or sale, the title or ownership is conveyed to the donee or buyer by a formal written document called the **deed**. Some of the more important terms associated with transfers of real property include the following:

- *Transfer*. An act by which the title to property is conveyed from one party to another. A party may be a person, a corporation, or the government.
- *Conveyance*. Any transfer by deed or will of legal or equitable title (see below) to real property from one person to another.
- *Disposition*. The parting with, transfer, or conveyance of property.
- *Grant*. A transfer of title to real or personal property by deed or other instrument.
- *Grantor*. The person who conveys (transfers) real or personal property to another. In the law of trusts, the creator of a trust, also called the settlor or trustor.
- *Grantee*. The person to whom real or personal property is conveyed.

  EXAMPLE: Cody conveys Blackacre, a farm, by deed to his friend, Noah. Cody is the grantor; Noah is the grantee. The act of conveyance of Blackacre to Noah is a disposition.

- *Deed*. A written, signed, and delivered legal document that transfers title or ownership of real property such as land or buildings from a grantor to a grantee.
- *Title*. In the law of property, the right to and evidence of ownership of real or personal property.
- *Legal title*. A title that is complete, perfect, and enforceable in a court of law, granting the holder the right of ownership and possession of property. In the law of trusts, the trustee receives legal title that provides the right of ownership and possession but no beneficial interest in the property that exists in another, i.e., the holder of the equitable title who is the beneficiary of the trust.
- *Equitable title*. In the law of trusts, a party who has equitable title has the right to have the legal title transferred to him or her. The person, i.e., beneficiary, who holds the equitable title has the beneficial interest, which includes the right to the benefits of the trust, and is regarded as the real

POINT OF INTEREST

Use Technology to Access Real Estate Records

Land record offices and for-profit companies are making real property records, including deeds, mortgages, and tax information, accessible through the Web. Information about a parcel of property may be accessed by owner's name, street address, or tax identification number.

owner although the legal title is placed in possession and control of the trustee.

- *Interest.* The terms *interest* and *title* are not synonymous. An interest entitles a person to some right in the property, but that right may be less than title or ownership.

- *Vest.* To deliver possession of land. At death, state law automatically vests title to the decedent's real property in beneficiaries of the will or in heirs if the decedent dies without a will "subject to" the right of the personal representative to devest or take away the property in order to pay claims of the decedent's creditors (see Cal. Prob. Code § 7000 and Tex. Prob. Code Ann. § 37).

- *Devest or divest.* To withdraw or take away title from the possessor.

The following example illustrates the use of these and earlier terms.

EXAMPLE: Keisha agrees to buy Malik's cottage. At the closing, Malik *transfers title* to the cottage by the *conveyance* of a *deed* to Keisha. Since Malik is the person (seller) who transfers *real property* (the cottage) to another (Keisha, the buyer), Malik is also the *grantor*. Keisha is the *grantee*. Clearly, Keisha has an *interest* in the cottage, and in this case, her interest is the *ownership (title)* of the cottage. One year later, Keisha dies in a car accident without having made a will.

Title to real property (cottage) owned by the decedent (Keisha) *vests* in her heirs the moment she dies. If Keisha had substantial debts, her personal representative may have a right to *devest* (*take away*) the property from the heirs and sell it to pay creditors' claims. However, title to Keisha's *personal property* passes to her *personal representative,* who uses the property, if necessary, to pay taxes due and creditors' claims or transfers it to *beneficiaries* of the will or to *heirs* if there is no will.

In another scenario, Keisha creates an *inter vivos* (living) trust and names her friend Gabe as *trustee.* The trust property is an apartment building, which is conveyed by deed into the trust and splits title to the apartment so that Gabe, the trustee, holds legal title and Keisha's daughter, Naomi, the *beneficiary,* holds the *equitable title.* As trustee, Gabe has *fiduciary duties* to manage and maintain the apartment for Naomi's benefit until the trust terminates when he transfers the apartment building to Naomi according to the terms of the trust.

Personal Property

Personal property is movable property. It is everything subject to ownership that is not real estate and includes such items as clothing, household furnishings, stocks, money, contract rights, digital assets, and life insurance. A **chattel** is an item of personal property.

chattel
Generally, any item of personal property.

At death, title to a decedent's real property vests directly in the decedent's beneficiaries or heirs. Title to the decedent's personal property passes to the personal representative (executor or administrator) appointed to handle the administration of the decedent's estate. If creditors must be paid, the decedent's personal property is generally used first to obtain the necessary funds and real property is the last asset used to pay estate debts.

Personal property can be subdivided into two categories.

1. *Tangible personal property.* Property that has a physical existence, i.e., it can be touched and is movable.

EXAMPLES:

Merchandise	Animals	Tools
Clothing	Household goods	Furniture
Appliances	Jewelry	Works of art
Books	China	Stamp/coin collections
Television sets	Cars	Boats
Airplane	RVs	Computers

2. *Intangible personal property.* Property that has no physical existence, i.e., it cannot be touched. Although such property has little or no value in itself, it establishes and represents the right to receive something of value. The ownership of intangible property is established by various documents, such as bank statements, stock or bond certificates, and written contracts for life insurance and annuities.

chose in action
A right to bring a civil lawsuit to recover money damages or possession of personal property.

Intangible personal property also includes a **chose in action**, a right to bring a civil lawsuit to recover possession of personal property or receive money damages, e.g., payment of a debt. An important, yet often overlooked, area that qualifies as intangible personal property includes digital assets. Digital assets are those that are stored electronically, either locally or in the cloud. In addition to images, photos, music, and videos, digital assets include reward points, electronic mail, electronic money, social media accounts, online accounts, websites, video gaming accounts, intellectual property, and domain names.

EXAMPLES: A 10-dollar bill is just a piece of paper; however, it represents the right to receive property worth 10 dollars. A promissory note by itself has no value, but it represents the right to receive payment from a debtor. The 10-dollar bill and the promissory note are intangible personal property. Examples of intangible personal property include the following:

Cash	Savings and checking accounts
Profit-sharing plans	Shares of corporate stock
Annuities	Corporate and government bonds
Pension plans Life insurance proceeds Patent rights	Negotiable instruments (checks and promissory notes) Government benefits such as Social Security and veterans' benefits
Copyrights	Individual retirement accounts
Trademarks Royalties	Claims against another person for debts, property damage, personal injury, or wrongful death
Bitcoins	Frequent flier miles
Podcasts	Online poker account
Blogs	Electronic mail

ASSIGNMENT 1.2

Classify each of the following items by placing a mark (X) in the most appropriate column.

Item	Real Property	Tangible Personal Property	Intangible Personal Property
Car			
Cash in checking account			
Right to renew apartment lease			
Hotel loyalty points			
House			
Life insurance proceeds			
Furniture			
eBay account (for sale of your property)			
Stocks and bonds			
Furnace			
Personal injury lawsuit			
Clothing			
Dishwasher (built-in)			
Dishwasher (portable)			
Mobile home on wheels			
Houseboat			
Tax refund check			
Television roof antenna			
Bookcase			
Trees on land			
Gun collection			
Corn growing on farm			
Online blog			

Your major role, as part of the legal team, will be to help the personal representative find, collect, preserve, appraise, and liquidate or distribute the decedent's personal assets. These tasks will be discussed in more detail in future chapters. In addition, you will have to list all the decedent's assets and classify them as real property or tangible or intangible personal property. Since an accurate classification is essential to the administration of the estate, you must learn to distinguish the different types of property and *be sure to verify your classification with your supervising attorney.*

⚖ *Ethical Issue*

Probate Property or Probate Estate

Most decedents own one or both of the two types of property (real and personal). Together, these assets are often called the decedent's estate. An **estate** (also called a gross estate) is all the property, real and personal, owned by any living person, or all the assets owned by a decedent at the time of death.

> **EXAMPLE:** Oxana Drosdov is single. She owns her home, furniture, household goods, and clothes. She has money in savings and checking accounts, stocks and bonds, and valuable jewelry. She maintains a blog and has electronic email, along with a social media account. She also owns a lake cottage with a boat and motor. All these property items, real and personal, constitute Oxana's estate or gross estate.

Not all property owned by the decedent can be passed by will, however. The only type of property a decedent can distribute through a will or by intestate succession, if there is no will, is **probate property**, which is also referred to as probate assets, the probate estate, or simply the estate.

Probate property is all real or personal property that the decedent owned either individually as a single or sole owner, called ownership in **severalty (tenancy in severalty)**, or as a co-owner with another person or persons in the form of ownership called tenancy in common. Probate property is subject to estate administration by the personal representative (executor or administrator) according to the terms of the will or, if the decedent died intestate, without a will, according to the appropriate state intestate succession statute.

> **EXAMPLE:** Kiara Morgan owns her house, car, furniture, social media accounts, email account, and savings account in severalty; i.e., she is the sole owner of each of these items of property. Kiara also owns a boat and condominium equally with her best friend, Breana, as tenants in common. If Kiara dies and her debts and taxes due are paid, all of this property, including her one-half interest in the boat and condominium as a tenant in common, would be probate property and would pass to her named beneficiaries or devisees if she has a will or to her heirs if she died intestate.

Probate property includes the following:

- Real property owned in severalty (single ownership) or in a tenancy in common
- Personal property owned in severalty or in a tenancy in common.
- Life insurance proceeds payable to the estate
- Monies owed the decedent for mortgages, promissory notes, contracts for deed, loans, rents, stock dividends, income tax refunds, interest, royalties, and copyrights
- Gain from the sale of a business (traditional or online)
- Social Security, Railroad Retirement, and Veterans Administration benefits
- Civil lawsuit for money damages
- Testamentary trusts

Probate property is subject to creditors' claims and federal and state death taxes (see below).

Nonprobate Property or Nonprobate Assets

Some of the real and personal property owned by the decedent at the time of death cannot be transferred by will or inheritance; therefore, it is not subject to probate. This is the decedent's nonprobate property and includes the following:

- Real and personal property owned and held in joint tenancy, tenancy by the entirety, or, in certain states, community property with the right of survivorship
- Real and personal property transferred into an *inter vivos* (living) trust prior to the settlor's death
- Real property subject to transfer under a transfer-on-death deed or beneficiary deed
- Money placed in a bank account as a **Totten trust**, or as a pay-on-death (POD) account
- Securities, including brokerage accounts, registered in transfer-on-death (TOD) form
- Proceeds of a life insurance policy payable to a named beneficiary (recipient of the money) and not to the decedent's estate as long as the decedent retained the **incidents of ownership** (see discussion in Chapter 14) .
- Employment contract benefits that contain a named beneficiary (not the estate) such as profit-sharing plans, pension plans, group life insurance, 401(k) plans, employee stock ownership plans (ESOPs), and self-employed retirement plans
- Annuity contracts with a named beneficiary (not the estate)
- Individual retirement accounts (traditional and Roth IRAs) with a named beneficiary (not the estate)
- U.S. savings bonds payable on death to a named beneficiary (not the estate)
- Property owned in *tenancy in partnership* (see glossary)

Totten trust
A bank deposit of a person's money in the name of the account holder as trustee for another person.

incidents of ownership
An element or right of ownership or degree of control over a life insurance policy.

Each of these types of nonprobate property goes directly to the named beneficiary or to the surviving joint tenant(s) or partners by **operation of law**. If the decedent's entire estate consists of nonprobate property, there is no need for estate administration (probate).

Nonprobate property is real or personal property that is not part of the decedent's probate estate. Therefore, this property is

operation of law
Rights pass automatically to a person by the application of the established rules of law, without the act, knowledge, or cooperation of the person.

- not distributed according to the decedent's will.
- not distributed according to intestate succession statutes if there is no will.
- not subject to estate administration (probate) of the decedent's estate.
- not subject to a surviving spouse's claims.
- not subject to claims of the decedent's creditors.

However, nonprobate property is part of the decedent's *gross estate* for federal and state death tax purposes; i.e., it is subject to federal and state estate taxes and state inheritance tax, and, therefore, you must identify and keep accurate records of each property item for the preparation of required tax returns. See Exhibit 9.10 and Chapter 11.

Digital Assets and Their Effect on Estate Planning

Historically, information was stored using a variety of physical resources, e.g., photo albums, letters, journals. There has been a major shift in how we preserve our data with much now being stored electronically through email, photos, music, blogs, social media accounts, software licenses, and financial management accounts. Combined, these digital assets make up one's digital estate. Unfortunately, there is no common

In light of the problems that have arisen with accessing and transferring digital data, companies have sprung up that offer to manage and transfer your "virtual legacy." They allow you to store your digital assets in an online version of a safety deposit box. Upon proof of death and verification of your beneficiaries, they will manage the process of passing your digital assets in accordance with your wishes. However, problems have also arisen with this process. The first is that the software only works if the testator has entered all of the requisite date prior to death. Secondly, the assets pass via will, revocable trust, or other type of transfer. These online companies may transfer the asset to the wrong beneficiary, potentially resulting in a lawsuit. And lastly, the selected online company may no longer be in business at the time of death.

definition of what constitutes a digital asset. The Uniform Fiduciary Access to Digital Assets Act (UFADAA), states that digital assets "mean a record that is electronic." The UFADAA goes on to define electronic as "technology having electrical, digital, magnetic, wireless, optical, electromagnetic, or similar capabilities." Simply put, a digital asset is any digitally stored content, including online accounts, owned by an individual. With the proliferation of digital technology, a major portion of an estate may include digital assets. The problem is the lack of access to these assets. Most are password protected, and accessing them may violate federal felony laws under the Electronic Communications Privacy Act. With the passage of the UFADAA, fiduciaries may have the legal right to gain access to these accounts. Unfortunately, the UFADAA has only been adopted by a few states. Assuming the personal representative has the right to access the account, the next hurdle is to find the digital assets. Testators should be encouraged to maintain an inventory of accounts with access information. It should include the physical location of each account, username and password access, and their selected beneficiary for each asset. However, caution should be used to protect the information contained in the inventory. If the information is included in the will, it becomes public with the publication of the will. If the testator uses a password-manager program, the access information to that account can be shared with the personal representative. While it remains impossible to ameliorate the potential legal problems associated with accessing the account in most states, some form of written permission would be advisable.

STATUTES THAT GOVERN THE PASSAGE OF PROPERTY

The law of property is mostly statutory law. States have the power to enact statutes that govern the passage of property from one generation to another or from the deceased to someone in his or her own generation. The states derive such power from their right, under the U.S. Constitution, to levy and collect taxes and from their duty to protect the citizenry.

EXAMPLE: If Mariana Garcia dies with a will and owns property that includes her house and items of personal property such as household furniture, savings and checking accounts, and automobiles, what are the respective rights of her beneficiaries, heirs, and creditors? As an owner of an estate, Mariana Garcia may distribute her property as she wishes, as long as her plans do not conflict with the statutory rights of others, e.g., a spouse, children, or creditors. Generally, a spouse cannot be disinherited, and although children can be disinherited, minor children are entitled to support. Also, all creditors have the right to be compensated for their valid claims; states establish statutory procedures whereby creditors may make claims against the decedent's estate whether or not the decedent has made a will.

Each state requires careful recording of all activity during the administration of a decedent's estate so it can fairly and accurately calculate the amount of tax that may be due from the estate of the decedent. Thus, the state becomes another "creditor" (see Chapter 11).

The state protects the decedent's rights by enacting statutes to ensure that each person will be allowed to make a will. If someone dies without a will, the state's statutes also provide for distribution of the property to those whom the decedent would probably have chosen if the decedent had made a will. These are the laws of **descent and distribution**, more commonly called *intestate succession statutes*. Exhibit 1.1 is the intestate succession statute of New York (for further discussion, see Chapter 3).

descent and distribution
Refers to the distribution by intestate succession statutes.

ASSIGNMENT 1.3

1. Define the following new words contained in the New York statute (Exhibit 1.1) by using the Glossary at the end of this book (all these terms will be defined and discussed in later chapters): *dower, right of succession, distributee, issue, distributive share, per capita,* and *half blood.*

2. List seven types of property interests that are not part of the decedent's probate estate.

FORMS OF PROPERTY OWNERSHIP

Various forms of property ownership exist. They range from one person who owns or holds the entire interest in an item of real or personal property to situations where two or more persons share concurrent ownership rights as co-owners, also called co-tenants. The most common forms of property ownership are *tenancy in severalty* (individual ownership) and *concurrent ownership* (joint tenancy, tenancy in common, tenancy by the entirety, and community property). The term *tenant* or *tenancy*, which is used to describe severalty and some of the types of concurrent ownership, is synonymous with "owner" or "ownership." Exhibit 1.2 summarizes the forms of property ownership.

Tenancy in Severalty—Ownership by One Person

Tenancy in severalty (ownership in severalty, or individual ownership) means that one person is the sole owner of real property, such as land, or personal property, such as a car. As an individual, the owner in severalty has absolute ownership of the real or personal property with exclusive rights, privileges, and interests. The owner may voluntarily dispose of the property while living, either by gift or sale, or may dispose of it at death through a will. If no such **disposition** has taken place

disposition
The parting with, transfer of, or conveyance of property.

EXHIBIT 1.1 New York State's Intestate Succession Statute

N.Y. Estates Powers and Trusts Law § 4-1.1
Descent and Distribution of a Decedent's Estate

The property of a decedent not disposed of by will shall be distributed as provided in this section. In computing said distribution, debts, administration expenses and reasonable funeral expenses shall be deducted but all estate taxes shall be disregarded, except that nothing contained herein relieves a *distributee* from contributing to all such taxes the amounts apportioned against him or her under 2–1.8. Distribution shall then be as follows:

(a) If a decedent is survived by:

(1) A spouse and *issue*, fifty thousand dollars and one-half of the residue to the spouse, and the balance thereof to the issue by representation.

(2) A spouse and no issue, the whole to the spouse.

(3) Issue and no spouse, the whole to the issue, by representation.

(4) One or both parents, and no spouse and no issue, the whole to the surviving parent or parents.

(5) Issue of parents, and no spouse, issue or parent, the whole to the issue of the parents, by representation.

(6) One or more grandparents or the issue of grandparents (as hereinafter defined), and no spouse, issue, parent or issue of parents, one-half to the surviving paternal grandparent or grandparents, or if neither of them survives the decedent, to their issue, by representation, and the other one-half to the surviving maternal grandparent or grandparents, or if neither of them survives the decedent, to their issue, by representation; provided that if the decedent was not survived by a grandparent or grandparents on one side or by the issue of such grandparents, the whole to the surviving grandparent or grandparents on the other side, or if neither of them survives the decedent, to their issue, by representation, in the same manner as the one-half. For the purposes of this subparagraph, issue of grandparents shall not include issue more remote than grandchildren of such grandparents.

(7) Great-grandchildren of grandparents, and no spouse, issue, parent, issue of parents, grandparent, children of grandparents or grandchildren of grandparents, one-half to the great-grandchildren of the paternal grandparents, per capita, and the other one-half to the great-grandchildren of the maternal grandparents, *per capita*, provided that if the decedent was not survived by great-grandchildren of grandparents on one side, the whole to the great-grandchildren of grandparents on the other side, in the same manner as the one-half.

(b) For all purposes of this section, decedent's relatives of the *half blood* shall be treated as if they were relatives of the whole blood.

(c) *Distributees* of the decedent, conceived before his or her death but born alive thereafter, take as if they were born in his or her lifetime.

(d) The right of an adopted child to take a *distributive share* and the *right of succession* to the estate of an adopted child continue as provided in the domestic relations law.

(e) A distributive share passing to a surviving spouse under this section is in lieu of any right of *dower* to which such spouse may be entitled.

Source: State of New York

EXHIBIT 1.2	**Forms of Property Ownership**

Real or personal property can be owned:

By one person (individual ownership)	or	By two or more persons (concurrent ownership)
• Tenancy in severalty		• Joint tenancy • Tenancy in common • Tenancy by the entirety • Community property

at the time of death, the property remains in the owner's estate and passes to certain specified takers under intestate succession statutes.

EXAMPLE: Juan buys Joe's car. The title is transferred to Juan. Juan is the sole owner of the car. He owns it in severalty.

EXAMPLE: Kennedy is given a ring by her aunt. Once delivered, the ring belongs to Kennedy, solely. She owns it in severalty.

EXAMPLE: Uncle Hiroki died. In his will, he left his lake cottage to his niece, Yumako. Yumako owns the real property in severalty.

EXAMPLE:

Blackacre—a farm		No person, other than Joel, has any ownership right or interest in the property. He owns the property in a tenancy in severalty (or simply referred to as *in severalty*).
Joel	Tenancy (ownership) in severalty	

Forms of Concurrent Ownership—Ownership by Two or More Persons

Concurrent ownership is a right of ownership in real or personal property shared by two or more persons. The most common forms of such multiple ownership are joint tenancy, tenancy in common, tenancy by the entirety, and community property.

Joint Tenancy

Joint tenancy is the ownership of real or personal property by two or more persons (called the **joint tenants**) who obtain an equal and undivided interest in the property by gift, purchase, will, or inheritance. The unique and distinguishing characteristic of a joint tenancy is the **right of survivorship**. On the death of one joint tenant, the right of survivorship passes the decedent's interest in the property automatically to the surviving joint tenants by operation of law, *without the need for probate* and with the last surviving joint tenant entitled to the whole property in severalty.

joint tenants
Two or more persons who own or hold equal, undivided interests in property with the right of survivorship.

right of survivorship
Passes the decedent joint tenant's interest in property automatically to the surviving joint tenant(s) by operation of law without the need for probate.

EXAMPLE:

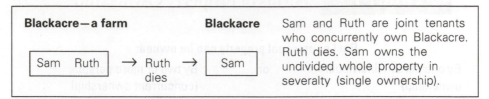

| Blackacre—a farm | | Blackacre | Sam and Ruth are joint tenants who concurrently own Blackacre. Ruth dies. Sam owns the undivided whole property in severalty (single ownership). |
| Sam   Ruth | → Ruth dies → | Sam | |

The farm goes directly to Sam *without* passing through Ruth's estate. The farm is nonprobate property. Even if Ruth has a will, it does not affect property owned as joint tenants since she cannot pass joint tenancy property through a will.

In order for a joint tenancy to be created, common law requires "four unities": unity of time, unity of title, unity of interest, and unity of possession. According to common law, a simple conveyance of property that uses the words "to two or more persons as joint tenants" does not necessarily create a joint tenancy unless the four unities also exist. The decision in *Cleaver v. Long*, 69 Ohio Law Abs. 488, 126 N.E.2d 479 (1955), supports the common law rules for the creation of a joint tenancy; in the case, the court said all joint tenants must

- have the same interest in land with respect to duration of the estate (unity of interest).
- acquire their interest by the same title (unity of title).
- receive their interest at the same time (unity of time).
- take their right to possession of the estate at the same time (unity of possession).

Cleaver involved a quitclaim deed, a deed without any warranties of the owner's rights, to which husband and wife were both grantors and grantees; the deed created a joint tenancy for them with the right of survivorship. The court ruled that the deed was valid as long as the four unities under common law were present. The next paragraphs discuss the common law definitions of these "unities" in more detail.

Unity of Time

For unity of time to exist, joint tenant owners must receive or take their interests in the property together, i.e., at the same time.

EXAMPLE: In most states, a single conveyance of property from Mia to Lucy and Audrey as joint tenants dated July 15, 2015, creates a joint tenancy. If, however, Mia conveys the property to Lucy and Audrey as joint tenants in a single transfer that takes effect on different dates, Lucy receives an interest on July 15, 2015, and Audrey receives an interest a day later, the conveyance fails in its attempt to create the interest desired, and a tenancy in common exists between Lucy and Audrey. Some states require an express statement to create a joint tenancy and avoid a tenancy in common (see the discussion below).

ASSIGNMENT 1.4

Howard conveys a farm, Blackacre, by deed to "Brown and Jones as joint tenants and not as tenants in common." What form of ownership is presumed in your state by this conveyance?

Unity of Title

For unity of title to exist, the tenancy must be created and the tenants must receive their title (ownership rights) from a single source, e.g., the same will or deed.

> **EXAMPLE:** When Mia, in a single deed, transfers real property to Lucy and Audrey as joint tenants, unity of title exists and a joint tenancy is created. However, if Mia transfers property to Lucy and Audrey by will *and* deed, respectively, or by more than one deed, the use of multiple instruments of transfer fails to meet the unity of title requirement, and a joint tenancy is not created.

Some states do not allow the creation of a joint tenancy wherein the grantor names himself or herself and another or others as joint tenants. For example, if Brown conveys a farm, Blackacre, which he inherited and now solely owns, to "Conrad and himself (Brown) as joint tenants with the right of survivorship," a joint tenancy, generally, does not result because of the lack of unities of time and title. The parties do not receive their interest in the property simultaneously since Brown already owned the farm, nor do they receive their title from one document since Brown received his title through inheritance.

To create a joint tenancy between an existing owner of the property (Brown) and one or more persons, Brown must first transfer a deed to the property to a third person, called the **straw man** (Jones); then, by a second deed, Jones, the straw man, immediately reconveys the property back to the original owner (Brown) and the new co-owner (Conrad) as joint tenants with the right of survivorship. The prevailing view in the majority of states today, however, is that, as in the *Cleaver* case, Brown can convey the farm from himself to "himself and Conrad" and create a valid joint tenancy.

straw man
A person used to create a joint tenancy of real property between the existing owner of the property and one or more other persons.

Assignment 1.5

Determine whether your state statute would allow an existing owner to create a joint tenancy as Brown did in the last example by conveying the farm to "himself and Conrad as joint tenants."

Unity of Interest

For unity of interest to exist, each tenant must have an interest in the property identical with that of the other tenants; the interests must be of the same quantity and duration.

> **EXAMPLE:** If Mia conveys property to Lucy, Audrey, and Carol as joint tenants with the right of survivorship, a joint tenancy is created. If instead, Mia gives both Lucy and Carol one-sixth shares of the ownership rights and Audrey a two-thirds share, the unity of interest requirement is not met, and Lucy, Audrey, and Carol own the property as tenants in common, although the conveyance specifies they are joint tenants.

Unity of Possession

For unity of possession to exist, each joint tenant must own and hold the same undivided possession of the whole property held in joint tenancy. As part of the group that owns all the property, each joint tenant has an equal right to possess the entire property and share equally in the profits and losses derived from the property, e.g., the sale of crops or livestock.

EXAMPLE:

Blackacre—a farm	Alice, Roy, and Vera are joint tenants, and each has the right to possess the whole property concurrently with the other co-tenants. None has the right to exclude the others from possession of all or any part of the property, and each has the right to share in profits derived from the use of the farm.
Roy Alice Vera	

EXAMPLE: A conveyance of a farm, Blackacre, from Mia to "Lucy and Audrey as joint tenants with the right of survivorship" with no restrictions on the amount of their respective possession rights creates a joint tenancy. However, if Mia attempts to limit the possession rights of either Lucy or Audrey and states "to Lucy and Audrey as joint tenants, but only Audrey has the right to possess Blackacre," the transfer fails to create a joint tenancy for lack of the unity of possession.

SUMMARY EXAMPLE: Neil conveys a farm to Rohan, Jay, and Vishnu as joint tenants on June 1, 2015 (unity of time), by a single deed (unity of title). Each co-owner receives a one-third undivided interest (unity of interest) of the whole property, and each has an equal right to possession of the whole (unity of possession). All four unities are present. Therefore, a valid joint tenancy is created if Neil complies with other state statutory requirements, e.g., uses language that indicates he desires to create a joint tenancy, such as "to Rohan, Jay, and Vishnu as joint tenants and not as tenants in common." If any of the four "unities" is not included in the conveyance of the property, the form of ownership created is *not* a joint tenancy but may be a tenancy in common (see the discussion below).

ASSIGNMENT 1.6

1. If Efrain Gonzalez owned a farm in your state and died leaving by will the farm to "my three sons, Elias, Manuel, and Javier as joint owners with equal shares," what form of ownership would the three sons have in your state?

2. If Efrain Gonzalez in the problem above had devised the farm "to my three sons, Elias, Manuel, and Javier as joint tenants and not tenants in common," would a joint tenancy be created according to the laws of your state?

3. Joyce, age 21, and Ellen, age 20, are sisters. When Aunt Sandra dies, she leaves her country home "to Joyce immediately and to Ellen on her 21st birthday, as joint tenants with the right of survivorship." What form of ownership has Aunt Sandra created?

The legal document in Exhibit 1.3, a deed, is executed to illustrate the creation of a joint tenancy with the required four unities. The type of ownership a person has in real property is determined by an examination of the deed to the property. Notice that the conveyance reads "to Roger L. Green, and Elizabeth R. Green, husband and wife, grantees as joint tenants" and not as tenants in common. In some states, this language is necessary to create the joint tenancy. Since Roger and Elizabeth receive their co-ownership at the same time (August 1, 2015—the date on the deed); by the same legal document (the deed); with the same undivided interest in the whole (equal interest); and with the right to possess the entire property (equal possession), all four unity requirements are satisfied.

ASSIGNMENT 1.7

Assume you own the house in which you now live. Using your state form, draft an unsigned deed conveying the house to your two best friends as joint tenants. Draft a second unsigned deed conveying the house to your friends as tenants in common.

Besides the four unities, certain other characteristics distinguish joint tenancy from tenancy in common and other forms of co-ownership. They include the following:

- Right of survivorship
- **Undivided interest**
- **Severance**

Right of Survivorship

When a joint tenant dies, the surviving joint tenants receive the interest of the deceased, i.e., the equal and undivided part, with nothing passing to the beneficiaries, heirs, or devisees of the decedent. The deceased joint tenant's ownership rights pass automatically to the other living joint tenants under the *right of survivorship*. Each joint tenant has this right of survivorship, which prevents a joint tenant from transferring property by a will. If all the joint tenants die except one, the surviving joint tenant owns the property *in severalty*, which means that the joint tenancy is destroyed and the lone survivor owns the property solely.

Undivided Interest

Joint tenants are entitled to the equal use, enjoyment, control, and possession of the property since they have an equal and undivided identical interest in the same property. Each joint tenant is considered to be the owner of the whole property and also of an undivided part. The undivided interest means that no joint tenant owns a specific or individual part of the property. If a joint tenant did own a particular portion of the property, it would be owned as a single owner, *in severalty*, not as a co-owner, *joint tenant*. (See the example and further discussion under Tenancy in Common.)

Undivided interest
A right to an undivided portion of property that is owned by one of two or more joint tenants or tenants in common before the property is divided (partitioned).

Severance
The destruction of a joint tenancy by one of the joint tenants transferring while alive his interest in real property to another person by deed, thereby creating a tenancy in common with the new owner and the other remaining joint tenant(s).

ASSIGNMENT 1.8

1. Which of the following items of property can be owned in a joint tenancy?

Stocks	House
Bonds	Cottage
Bitcoins	Boat
Art	Condominium
Jewelry	Online gambling account
Car	Contents of a safe deposit box

2. Conchita and Emilio are not related by blood or marriage. All of the items in Question 1 are given, sold, or willed to Conchita and Emilio as joint tenants with the right of survivorship. Emilio dies and owes many debts. Do his creditors have any claim against the property? Can Emilio transfer by will any of the property to his spouse and family? When Emilio dies, who owns the property? What form of ownership is created by Emilio's death?

EXHIBIT 1.3   Sample Deed Showing Creation of a Joint Tenancy

No delinquent taxes and transfer entered: Certificate of Real Estate Value ( ) filed ( ) not required
Certificate of Real Estate Value No. _____
_____, 20_____

_____
County Auditor

By _____
Deputy

)
)
)
)
)
)
)
)
)
)
)

------------- reserved for recording data -------------

STATE DEED TAX DUE HEREON: $ 282.70

Date: August 1, 2015

GENERAL WARRANTY DEED

FOR AND IN CONSIDERATION OF ONE DOLLAR ($1.00) AND OTHER VALUABLE CONSIDERATION, Henry J. Smith and Sarah M. Smith, husband and wife, hereinafter referred to as "Grantors" of Hamilton County, Ohio grants and conveys with general warranty covenants, to Roger L. Green and Elizabeth R. Green, husband and wife, hereinafter referred to as "Grantees," as joint tenants with right of survivorship whose tax-mailing address is 1463 Main Street, Cincinnati, Ohio 45202, the following real property:

SITUATED IN THE CITY OF CINCINNATI, HAMILTON COUNTY, OHIO:
BEING LOT NO. 11 AND THE EAST EIGHT (8) FEET OF LOT NO. 10, OF JOSEPH HECKINGER'S ADDITION TO THE TOWN OF CINCINNATUS, NOW KNOWN AS CINCINNATI, AS SHOWN ON PLAT RECORDED IN PLAT BOOK 1, PAGE 234.
THE TRACT HEREIN CONVEYED, MEASURED FORTY (40) FEET IN WIDTH FROM EAST TO WEST AND FRONTS ON THE NORTH SIDE OF SECOND STREET (NOW MAIN STREET) BY ONE HUNDRED FORTY (140) FEET IN DEPTH, TO A TWENTY (20) FOOT ALLEY.

Permanent Parcel No.: 593-0004-0163-00

Property Address: 1463 Main Street, Cincinnati, Ohio 45202

SUBJECT to all existing taxes, assessment, liens, easements, rights-of-ways, covenants and mineral, oil or gas reservations of record, if any, the Grantors hereby covenant that they are seized in fee simple of the above-identified premises and have the right to sell and convey the same; and that Grantors, their heirs and assigns shall warrant and defend the title unto the Grantees, their heirs and assigns against any lawful claims.

TO HAVE AND TO HOLD same unto Grantees as joint tenants with right of survivorship, their heirs and assigns forever, with all appurtenances thereunto belonging.

Prior Instrument Reference: Volume 10, Page 27.

Executed this 11th day of April, 2015.

/s/ Henry J. Smith
HENRY J. SMITH, Grantor

/s/ Sarah M. Smith
SARAH M. SMITH, Grantor

COUNTY OF HAMILTON
STATE OF OHIO

This instrument was hereby acknowledged before me on the 11th day of August, 2015 by Henry J. Smith and Sarah M. Smith to be true and accurate.

My Commission Expires:

_____

_____
NOTARY PUBLIC

This Instrument Prepared by:

Rachel Hensley, Attorney at Law
944 Ravine Street
Cincinnati, OH 45202

Severance

While alive, each joint tenant has the right of severance, i.e., an act of severing, separating, or partitioning real property. Severance occurs when a joint tenant owner conveys his or her equal interest in the property during his or her lifetime, thereby destroying one of the four essential unities and terminating the joint tenancy. Such an "*inter vivos*" conveyance, i.e., a transfer of interest by gift or sale while the joint owner is alive, is the *only* way a joint tenancy can be severed. Severance of real property is accomplished when a deed is conveyed. After a joint tenancy is severed in this manner, the remaining joint tenants and the new tenant are tenants in common, and the new tenant has no right of survivorship. (See the examples below.)

EXAMPLE: To illustrate joint tenancy ownership, suppose X dies and gives by will a farm to A and B as joint tenants. If during their lifetimes neither A nor B conveys (gives or sells) his interest in the farm by deed to another person and A dies, B becomes the sole owner *(in severalty)* of the farm through right of survivorship.

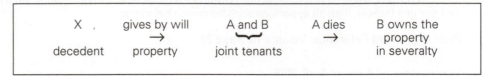

Assume that X dies and gives by will the farm to A, B, and C as joint tenants. C later conveys, by deed, his undivided one-third interest in the farm to D. This conveyance, as a severance, terminates the joint tenancy between (A and B) and (C) and creates a tenancy in common form of ownership between (A and B) and (D). Since they have done nothing to change (sever) their form of ownership, a joint tenancy still remains between A and B. Thereafter, if A dies and has made no conveyance of his interest, B would receive A's interest in the farm through right of survivorship. The result: B and D own the farm as tenants in common, i.e., B owns a two-thirds interest and D owns a one-third interest in the property. The unities of time, title, and interest have been destroyed and only the unity of possession remains.

EXAMPLE:

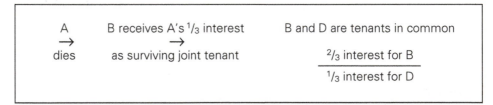

Result: A and B own a two-thirds interest in the farm and remain joint tenants (each owns a one-third undivided interest). A tenancy in common now exists between (A and B) and (D), who owns the other one-third.

Later:

As tenants in common, on the death of either B or D, the decedent's interest in the farm passes by will or inheritance to his beneficiaries, heirs, or devisees (see the discussion of tenancy in common below).

ASSIGNMENT 1.9

Apply the previous illustration to the following cases and then answer the questions.

Case 1. Alice dies. In her will she leaves her farm, Blackacre, to her three nephews, Able, Baker, and Charlie, as joint tenants. Able is married and has 11 children; Baker is divorced and has two children; and Charlie is a bachelor. Able dies. His will leaves all his property to his wife, Agnes. Who owns Blackacre? What form or forms of ownership exist between the owners?

Case 2. Continue with the facts of Case 1; however, Able sold and deeded his interest in Blackacre to Dolan, and Charlie gave and deeded his interest to Elaine, his girlfriend. Who owns Blackacre? What form or forms of ownership exist between the owners? What happens to Baker's interest in the property when he dies? Does Able's wife, Agnes, have any interest in Blackacre?

Creation of a Joint Tenancy

Today, state statutes determine whether a joint tenancy is legally created. Most states recognize joint tenancy, but they vary in the express language they require to create it. Proper use of the mandatory words and the intent of the creator of the joint tenancy determine whether a binding joint tenancy is established. For example, if Alex Huang wants to give his lake cottage to his two children, Phillip and June, he may satisfy the statutes in most states by writing in the deed of conveyance, "to my two children, June Huang and Phillip Huang as joint tenants." Other states require more, such as "… as joint tenants with the right of survivorship" or, as some documents are written today, "… as joint tenants with the right of survivorship and not as tenants in common" (see the Illinois statute below). Louisiana has no joint tenancy with survivorship rights. See the forms of ownership by state in Exhibit 1.4.

EXHIBIT 1.4	Forms of Ownership by State			
By One Person	**By Two or More Persons**			
Tenancy in Severalty	**Tenancy in Common**	**Joint Tenancy**	**Tenancy by the Entirety**	**Community Property**

All states	All states	All states except as follows:
		   Alaska—for personal property only
		   Louisiana— not recognized
		   Ohio—called survivorship tenancy
		   Oregon—equivalent only if language reads "tenancy in common with the right of survivorship"
		   Texas—for real property owners must sign a joint tenancy survivorship agreement
			Arkansas, Delaware, Florida, Kentucky, Maryland, Massachusetts, Michigan, Missouri, Montana, Oklahoma, Pennsylvania, Tennessee, Vermont, Virginia, Wyoming
			   Alaska, Illinois, Indiana, Mississippi, New Jersey, New York, North Carolina, Oregon—for real property only
				Arizona*, California*, Idaho, Louisiana, Nevada*, New Mexico, Texas, Washington
				   Wisconsin*— recognizes marital property equivalent of community property
				   Alaska*—recognizes community property but is a voluntary system available to residents and nonresidents
				*These states allow spouses to hold community property with right of survivorship.

Another variable among the states is their preference for certain forms of co-ownership of property. At one time, common law preferred the creation of a joint tenancy over a tenancy in common whenever a conveyance was unclear regarding which of these two interests was intended by the grantor. Today, in most states, the reverse is generally true, and by statute, when the intention of the parties is not clear, tenancy in common is presumed and preferred over a joint tenancy since the legislatures believe the decedent's property should pass to beneficiaries, heirs, or devisees and not to surviving joint tenants. An example of one such statute is Minn. Stat. Ann. § 500.19(2), *Construction of grants and devises*. The decision in *In re Christen's Estate*, 238 Cal. App. 2nd 521, 48 Cal. Rptr. 26 (1965), illustrates the current preference. In this case, the court stated, "To create a joint tenancy interest by will or transfer, the instrument must expressly declare the interest to be a joint tenancy." Notice the words that are required and preferred for the creation of concurrent ownership in the states of Rhode Island and Illinois.

R.I. Gen. Laws § 34-3-1
The law provides that conveyances made to two or more persons, whether they be husband and wife or otherwise "… create a tenancy in common and not a joint tenancy, unless it be declared that the tenancy is to be joint…."

Ill. Compiled Stat. Ann. Ch. 765 § 1005/1
The law states that the deed of conveyance must expressly provide that the property interest is granted "… not in tenancy in common but in joint tenancy…."

ASSIGNMENT 1.10

Using your state's codes, find and cite appropriate statutes, if any, that determine the form of ownership that would be created by the following conveyances by deed: (1) "to A and B jointly," (2) "to A and B as joint owners," (3) "to A and B equally," (4) "to A or to B," (5) "to A and to B." If your statutes or case law do not address this problem, find a statute from another state that does. Find and cite your state statute that determines the required words to create a joint tenancy or a tenancy in common.

Advantages and Disadvantages of Joint Tenancy

Ethical Issue

When working with clients, you will discover they frequently have created joint tenancies with spouses and others. When you discuss the following advantages and disadvantages with the client, *you must be careful not to attempt to respond to questions that seek legal advice or interpretations*. All such questions must be referred to your supervising attorney.

Advantages of a joint tenancy

- On the death of a joint tenant, title passes automatically to the surviving joint tenant(s) by right of survivorship.
- It avoids probate. No corresponding expenses and delays are necessary or required for the surviving joint tenant(s) to acquire title.
- Title passes to the surviving joint tenant(s) free of the claims of the decedent's creditors unless the joint tenancy was created to defraud creditors. The decedent's real estate is subject to certain unpaid debts, such as mortgages, property taxes, and liens, e.g., a mechanic's lien for work or improvements to the property.

- If the joint tenants are spouses (but see tenancy by the entirety below), no federal gift tax is owed because of the unlimited marital gift tax deduction (this may also be true for state gift tax concerns). See discussion in Chapters 11 and 14.

- If real property located in other (foreign) states is in a joint tenancy, ancillary administration may be avoided (see discussion in Chapter 7).

- Joint tenancy of bank accounts, which include checking, savings, certificates of deposit, Totten trusts, and POD accounts, that are properly and legally created to establish the right of survivorship for the named co-owners or beneficiary, can avoid probate and provide immediate cash for family needs on the death of a spouse or parent. You must be careful to ensure the account is correctly created, e.g., all signature cards executed and state statutory requirements met.

- Creation of a joint tenancy is fast and inexpensive, whereas probate and the creation of a trust are expensive.

Disadvantages of a joint tenancy

- The person who creates the joint tenancy no longer has complete control of the property.

   EXAMPLE: Shirley is a single parent who has a teenage son, Zachary. Shirley buys a house in joint tenancy with Zachary. A wonderful job opportunity becomes available in another state, and Shirley must immediately sell the house. Since Zachary is a minor and cannot convey real property, a court must appoint a guardian (Shirley) to represent and protect Zachary's interest in the house. However, this loss of control and subsequent delay may cause Shirley to lose the employment opportunity.

- Any joint tenant can terminate (sever) the joint tenancy without the agreement of the other joint tenant(s).

   EXAMPLE: The mother of Andre and Rachael dies and leaves the family farm to them as joint tenants. Rachael wants to live on the farm. Andre wants to sell his interest. If Rachael cannot afford to buy Andre's interest, the farm *may* have to be sold to a third party since it is Andre's right to terminate the joint tenancy.

- The surviving recipient of the property previously held in joint tenancy may not have been the intended beneficiary.

   EXAMPLE: In the preceding example, if Shirley died after creating the joint tenancy with Zachary, he would own the house. If Zachary was killed in a car accident a year later while still the owner of the house, the house will pass to his only heir, his father, if living, which may not be a result that Shirley intended.

- The stepped-up basis for full value of the proceeds is lost. See the discussion and example in Chapter 14.

- Other examples of problems created by joint tenancy follow.

   EXAMPLE: Prakash, age 19, wants to buy a car but is unable to obtain a loan to finance the purchase. His parents agree to cosign the promissory note required by the bank for the loan. The parents also list themselves as joint tenancy owners with Prakash on the title of the car. While driving the new car, Prakash is the sole cause of an accident in which the driver of the other car is seriously injured. The injured driver sues Prakash and his parents. If the injured driver wins the case and receives a judgment of $450,000 in damages, the driver can collect money damages from the personal assets of Prakash or his parents if they are not adequately insured.

EXAMPLE: A married couple, Sofia and Luis, want to avoid probate and see no reason to have individual wills, so they place all their real and personal property (including their home, cars, checking and savings accounts, stocks and bonds) in joint tenancy. When one of them dies, the title to all of the property will go to the surviving spouse by right of survivorship. However, if both spouses die in a common disaster, for example, in a plane crash, the property will have to go through probate, and since they have no wills when the accident occurs, their property will be transferred to their heirs according to their state's intestate succession laws, which may be a distribution very different from what they wanted or intended.

Tenancy in Common

Tenancy in common is a form of concurrent ownership of real or personal property by two or more persons called tenants in common. Each tenant owns separate undivided interests in the property with the "unity" of possession. The tenants' interests may be equal or unequal. The "unity" of possession establishes each tenant's right to take and possess the whole property with the other co-tenants, and each is entitled to share proportionately in the profits derived from the property. A tenancy in common differs from a joint tenancy in several important ways, including the following:

- The undivided interest of the joint tenants *must be* equal; for tenants in common, it may be equal or unequal. Thus, when there are two tenants in common, each may own one-half of the property, i.e., an equal interest, or one may own three-fourths of the property and the other one-fourth, i.e., an unequal interest. Neither owns a specific portion of the property, because each has an undivided interest in the entire property.

  EXAMPLE: X may expressly create a tenancy in common in the following way.

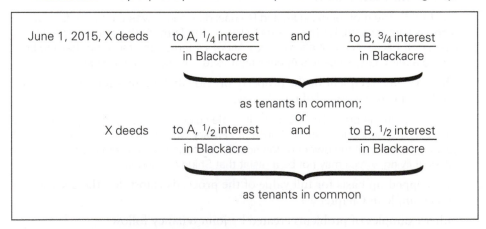

- The creation of a joint tenancy must include the "four unities" (time, title, interest, and possession); a tenancy in common requires only "unity of possession."
- Property held in joint tenancy is nonprobate property; property held in a tenancy in common is probate property.
- The distinguishing characteristic of a joint tenancy is the right of survivorship; there is *no* right of survivorship in a tenancy in common. Therefore, unlike a joint tenancy, when a tenant in common dies, the

decedent's interest goes to an heir or as directed in a will, and it is subject to estate administration (probate).

EXAMPLE: Jeff Morrow dies with a will. In the will, he gives a one-half interest in his original Picasso painting to his only living relative, his nephew Charles Morrow. Jeff gives the other half of the ownership rights in the painting to his two close friends, Aidan Byrne and Anthony Trotta, equally. Charles, Aidan, and Anthony are co-owners of the Picasso painting as tenants in common. If Aidan Byrne dies, his one-fourth interest in the painting is transferred according to his will, if he has one, or to his heir (closest blood relative, if he is not married) according to state law.

Not only may tenants in common own different interests in terms of quantity and duration, but they may receive their interests from different parties through different instruments of conveyance at different times. Nevertheless, they retain an undivided interest in the property unless it is merged or severed.

Creation of a Tenancy in Common

A tenancy in common may be expressly created as in the deed in Exhibit 1.5, but as previously mentioned, a tenancy in common is also created when a grantor makes a conveyance and fails to use the terminology required to establish a joint tenancy. In addition, once a joint tenancy is validly established, if one of the joint tenants makes an *inter vivos* conveyance by deed to another person, the joint tenancy is severed, and a tenancy in common is created for the new owner (see the examples below).

EXAMPLE: Most states today prefer the establishment of tenancy in common over a joint tenancy. Therefore, if Simon Ackerman dies and provides in his will that Blackacre is to go "to my sons, Cameron and Joel jointly in equal shares," the real property will pass to the two sons as tenants in common in states with such a preference. Note that the conveyance did not contain an explicit statement saying that a "joint tenancy" was to be created.

EXAMPLE: In another case, suppose Simon Ackerman creates a valid joint tenancy in his will that states that Blackacre goes "to my sons, Cameron and Joel, as joint tenants with the right of survivorship and not as tenants in common." Simon dies. Cameron and Joel are joint tenants. Joel, by deed, sells his interest in Blackacre to Thurston Brown. The result is the original joint tenancy is severed by Joel's *inter vivos* conveyance and a tenancy in common is created between Cameron and Thurston.

ASSIGNMENT 1.11

1. If Kaimi conveys one-third of his farm, Blackacre, to Craig on August 15, 2015, and the remaining two-thirds to Danny on September 20, 2015, what form of ownership will Craig and Danny have according to the statutes or case law in your state?

2. If Ashley and Eric are joint tenants, and Eric gives his interest in the property to Tim by a valid conveyance, what form of ownership exists according to your state law?

The state of New York, by statute, handles the transfer of property to two or more persons in the following way.

N.Y. Estates Powers and Trusts Law § 6-2.2
When Estate Is in Common, in Joint Tenancy or by the Entirety.

EXHIBIT 1.5   Sample Deed Showing Creation of Tenancy in Common

No delinquent taxes and transfer entered: Certificate of Real Estate Value (   ) filed (   ) not required
Certificate of Real Estate Value No. _____
_____, 20_____

_____
County Auditor

By _____
Deputy

)
)
)
)
)
)
)
)
)
)
)
)

------------ reserved for recording data ------------

STATE DEED TAX DUE HEREON: $_____282.70_____

Date: _____September 12, 2015_____

WARRANTY DEED

FOR AND IN CONSIDERATION OF ONE DOLLAR ($1.00) AND OTHER VALUABLE CONSIDERATION, Sally J. Jones, an unmarried woman, hereinafter referred to as "Grantor" of Hamilton County, Ohio grants and conveys with general warranty covenants, to William L. Jackson, an unmarried man, hereinafter referred to as "Grantee," whose tax-mailing address is 1463 Main Street, Cincinnati, Ohio 45202, the following real property:

> SITUATED IN THE CITY OF CINCINNATI, HAMILTON COUNTY, OHIO:
> BEING LOT NO. 11 AND THE EAST EIGHT (8) FEET OF LOT NO. 10, OF JOSEPH HECKINGER'S ADDITION TO THE TOWN OF CINCINNATUS, NOW KNOWN AS CINCINNATI, AS SHOWN ON PLAT RECORDED IN PLAT BOOK 1, PAGE 234.
> THE TRACT HEREIN CONVEYED, MEASURED FORTY (40) FEET IN WIDTH FROM EAST TO WEST AND FRONTS ON THE NORTH SIDE OF SECOND STREET (NOW MAIN STREET) BY ONE HUNDRED FORTY (140) FEET IN DEPTH, TO A TWENTY (20) FOOT ALLEY.
>
> Permanent Parcel No.: 593-0004-0163-00
>
> Property Address: 1463 Main Street, Cincinnati, Ohio 45202

SUBJECT to all existing taxes, assessment, liens, easements, rights-of-ways, covenants, encumbrances, restrictions and mineral, oil or gas reservations of record, if any, the Grantor hereby covenants that she is seized in fee simple of the above-identified premises and has the right to sell and convey the same; and that Grantor, her heirs and assigns shall warrant and defend the title unto the Grantee, his heirs and assigns against any lawful claims.

TO HAVE AND TO HOLD same unto Grantee, his heirs and assigns forever, with all appurtenances thereunto belonging.

Prior Instrument Reference: Volume 10, Page 27.

Executed this 11th day of April, 2015.

/s/ __Sally J. Jones
SALLY JONES, Grantor

COUNTY OF HAMILTON
STATE OF OHIO

This instrument was hereby acknowledged before me on the 11th day of August, 2015 by Sally J. Jones to be true and accurate.

My Commission Expires:

_____   _____
                                 NOTARY PUBLIC

This Instrument Prepared by:

Rachel Hensley, Attorney at Law
944 Ravine Street
Cincinnati, OH 45202

(a) A disposition of property to two or more persons creates in them a tenancy in common, unless expressly declared to be a joint tenancy.
(b) A disposition of real property to a husband and wife creates in them a tenancy by the entirety, unless expressly declared to be a joint tenancy or a tenancy in common.
(c) …
(d) …
(e) A disposition of property to two or more persons as executors, trustees or guardians creates in them a joint tenancy.
(f) Property passing in intestacy to two or more persons is taken by them as tenants in common.

EXAMPLE: Jin-Sang, a resident of New York, dies without a will. Her husband, Yejoon, died a year earlier. She leaves a house, which is in her name only, and no debts. Her children, Yi and Min-soo, are entitled to the house in tenancy in common under the law of descent and distribution of the state of New York.

ASSIGNMENT 1.12

1. Susan Sowles, a resident of New York, dies without a will. If she has a lakeshore cottage in New York and her heirs are her three children, what form of ownership of the cottage results for their benefit?

2. If Holly Simpson, also a resident of New York, dies with a will that transfers her homestead to her two nephews, who are the executors of her estate, what form of ownership exists between the nephews in New York and in your state?

Transfer of an Interest

Each tenant in common may transfer an interest by gift, will, or sale or may pledge it as security for a loan. When a tenant in common dies without having conveyed his or her share of the property, it passes to the beneficiaries, heirs, or devisees. The *right of survivorship* that accompanies a joint tenant interest does not exist with a tenancy in common.

EXAMPLE: A, B, and C each own an undivided one-third interest in property as tenants in common. If A dies *intestate*, A's interest in the property will pass by descent to his heirs and not automatically go to B and C.

Concurrent Ownership of Blackacre			
A, B, and C are tenants in common			
A	B	C	A dies
1/3 interest	1/3 interest	1/3 interest	

Result: A's heirs receive one-third interest (by descent). (A's heirs and B and C are tenants in common.)

If A died testate (with a will) in the above example, his will determines how and to whom his interest in Blackacre will be distributed. Such a testamentary transfer is not possible in a joint tenancy since the property held in joint tenancy is automatically transferred to the surviving joint tenant.

ASSIGNMENT 1.13

Abner, Boswell, and Clarence are owners of Blackacre as joint tenants. Clarence sells his interest and delivers a deed to Boswell. Abner gives his interest to Ruth by delivering a deed. What form of ownership exists? Name the owners and the amount of their interests. Explain what would happen to Boswell's interest if he died testate or intestate.

When a tenant in common disposes of an interest by gift, sale, or will, the new owner is also a tenant in common with the remaining co-tenants. Tenancy in common is destroyed by merger when the entire ownership rights pass to one person or by severance when the property is partitioned (see below).

EXAMPLE: A and B are tenants in common. A purchases B's interest by deed. A now has merged the property and is the sole owner of the property *in severalty*.

Undivided Interest

As mentioned previously, an undivided interest is a right to an undivided portion of property that is owned by two or more *tenants in common* or joint tenants before the property is divided (partitioned). The ownership of a farm (buildings, machinery, livestock, and land) in joint tenancy or tenancy in common creates an *undivided interest* for each co-tenant. In a practical sense, this means that each co-owner has a right or interest in the entire farm, but cannot claim a specific portion of the property, e.g., the house or the livestock, as the co-owner's own individual property. After partition, each person (co-owner) owns the apportioned part of the property in severalty, i.e., in single ownership. (See the examples below and discussion of partition.)

EXAMPLE:

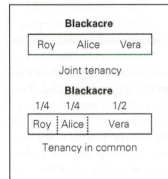

Each of the three joint tenants has a onethird *undivided interest* in the whole property. Each has the equal right to use and possess the whole property and to share equally the profits from the crops, buildings, and livestock.

The dotted lines are used to show that the interests of tenants in common may be unequal. Roy and Alice each have a onefourth *undivided interest* in the whole property; Vera has *a* one-half *undivided interest* in the whole property. Each has a right to use and possess the whole property.

Partition

One way to cause severance is for a joint tenant or tenant in common to ask the court to **partition** the property. Partition is the division of real property held by joint tenants or tenants in common into distinct and separate portions so that the individuals may hold the property in severalty. The parties may want a partition as their relationship may have deteriorated and they are no longer able to reach agreements regarding the use of the property. A partition can occur by a voluntary agreement of the co-owners, or it can be made by the court. If the co-owners cannot agree on a division, any one of the owners can petition the court for partition, which, in most cases, can force the sale of the property. The owners then split the proceeds. In some states, a court-ordered partition is not allowed for property in joint tenancy.

Once joint tenancy or tenancy in common property has been partitioned, severance results, and the former co-tenants each own a portion of the property in severalty. Joint tenancy property is partitioned into equal parts; tenancy in common property is partitioned into equal or unequal parts. (See the example below.)

EXAMPLE: If a concurrently owned farm, Blackacre, is partitioned, it is divided into separate parts.

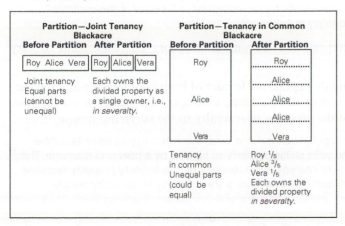

partition
The division of real property held by joint tenants or tenants in common into separate portions so that the individuals may hold the property in severalty, i.e., in single ownership.

Tenancy by the Entirety

Tenancy by the entirety is an estate available only to spouses, which must be created in writing and is nonprobate property. It is essentially a special form of "joint tenancy" modified by the common law theory that spouses are one person. Therefore, in addition to the four unities of time, title, interest, and possession required for joint tenancy, tenancy by the entirety requires a fifth unity—the unity of person, i.e., a spouses are one.

Tenancy by the entirety has most of the same advantages and disadvantages of joint tenancy. However, unlike joint tenancy, neither spouse in a tenancy by the entirety can mortgage, sell, or give the property to another or sever the tenancy while alive or by will or trust without the written and signed consent of the other spouse. Unless both spouses join in (i.e., sign) the conveyance, it is invalid. This characteristic distinguishes tenancy by the entirety from joint tenancy since joint tenants can transfer their interest (by deed) without obtaining the permission of the other joint tenants. Since it imposes such restrictions on the transfer of property, some states have abolished tenancy by the entirety as being against public policy. Consequently, tenancy by the entirety is not recognized in all states (see Exhibit 1.4).

The states that allow tenancy by the entirety differ in the wording they require in the deed or will that creates the tenancy. In some states, unless the deed or will provides differently, a conveyance to both spouses automatically creates a tenancy by the entirety. Other states require that the conveyance include explicit language, e.g., to husband and wife "as tenants by the entirety with the right of survivorship." Any conveyance without the exact words may result in the creation of another form of co-ownership, e.g., a tenancy in common, or simply fail to create the desired result.

> **EXAMPLE:** A will states, "I hereby give and devise my farm, Blackacre, to Javier and Ana Sofía Lozano, husband and wife, in tenancy by the entirety." However, if the will had been worded "I hereby give and devise my farm, Blackacre, to Javier and Ana Sofía Lozano, husband and wife, with the right of survivorship," the devise might have been interpreted to be a tenancy by the entirety in some states or a joint tenancy in other states. In the latter case, it could be severed and individually transferred by one of the joint tenants.

> Most statutes concerning tenancy by the entirety are worded like the Indiana statute (Ind. Code Ann. § 32-17-3-1).

> The law states that a written contract in which a husband and wife purchase real estate "… creates an estate by the entireties …" except if the contract "… expressly creates a tenancy in common…."

However, court interpretations of similar statutory language seem to vary among the states.

The predominant and distinguishing feature of both joint tenancy and tenancy by the entirety is the *right of survivorship*, which, on the death of one spouse, passes sole ownership of the property in severalty to the surviving spouse.

> **EXAMPLE:** Liam and Sigrid, husband and wife, own property as tenants by the entirety. Liam dies and wills all his property to his son by a previous marriage. The son does not receive any interest in the tenancy by the entirety property because of Sigrid's right of survivorship. Sigrid owns the property in severalty (single ownership).

A creditor of one spouse cannot foreclose on property held in tenancy by the entirety or enforce a judgment (court decision) against it, and a judgment against one spouse is not a claim (lien) against the property. However, a judgment against both spouses can become a lien against the property, and a creditor can foreclose.

In most states, the unity of person in a tenancy by the entirety is terminated by a divorce (dissolution). The divorced couple become tenants in common of the property with each former spouse owning a one-half interest in the property. Unlike a divorce, a legal separation does not terminate a tenancy by the entirety in most states.

Some commentators have argued that the common law tenancy by the entirety should be abolished for policy reasons. First, property owned in this form is not subject to the claims of creditors of a deceased tenant (spouse); second, the specific language that creates this form of ownership is not always clear; and finally, when marital problems and disagreements arise, the mutual consent required to transfer property held in tenancy by the entirety may be difficult to obtain.

ASSIGNMENT 1.14

1. Amanda and Warren are married and live in your state. The deed conveying their property states, "to Warren F. Grossen and Amanda M. Grossen, husband and wife, as joint tenants and not as tenants in common." (a) Would this conveyance create a tenancy by the entirety in your state? (b) Cite your state statute, if any.
2. What five unities are necessary for the establishment of a tenancy by the entirety? Explain each one.
3. Which unity exists in tenancy by the entirety but not in joint tenancy?
4. Select a state that recognizes tenancy by the entirety (possibly your own state) and identify the type of tenancy created by the following conveyances according to the courts of that state. Each conveyance is to spouses with wording as indicated.

	Joint Tenancy	Tenancy by the Entirety	Tenancy in Common
• "as tenants by the entirety"			
• "as tenants by the entirety with the right of survivorship"			
• "with the right of survivorship"			
• "as joint tenants"			
• "as tenants in common"			
• no other words, just to "husband and wife"			

Community Property

Two classifications of marital property law systems exist in the United States: community property law and common law. Originally eight southern and western states (Arizona, California, Idaho, Louisiana, Nevada, New Mexico, Texas, and Washington) adopted by statute the form of ownership by spouses known as **community property**. Wisconsin adopted provisions of the Uniform Marital Property Act (UMPA), which is essentially the same as the community property system, and joined the other eight states in 1986. Alaska, in 1998, enacted the Alaska Community Property Act, which is also based on the UMPA, but differs from the

community property
All property, other than property received by gift, will, or inheritance, acquired by either spouse during marriage is considered to belong to both spouses equally in the nine community property states and Alaska if community property is elected.

other community property states by being a voluntary system that can be elected by residents and nonresidents (see Exhibit 1.4). The other states are classified as common law jurisdictions, and this marital property law system will be discussed under Dower and Curtesy below and in Chapter 3. The theory behind community property ownership is that both spouses should share equally in the property acquired by their joint efforts during marriage. Therefore, each spouse is considered to own an undivided half interest in all property acquired during their marriage even though one spouse may have earned considerably less than the other or even nothing at all. Also, both spouses have the right to convey by will their individual half of the community property to whomever they choose, but each spouse has no control over the other spouse's half of the property (see discussion below). Community property law is set entirely by state statutes, which vary considerably among the 10 states.

Community property states recognize two kinds of property: **separate property** and community property. Separate property includes the following:

separate property
Property that a spouse owned prior to their marriage or acquired during marriage by gift, will, or inheritance.

- Property individually owned by that spouse prior to their marriage
- Property acquired by an individual spouse during marriage by gift, will, or inheritance
- Property that is currently separate property and is traded, replaced, or sold for other property and becomes "new" separate property
- Social Security, railroad retirement, and veterans' benefits

Note: All of the above property will remain separate property if it is kept separate and not combined (commingled) with community property (see discussion below).

Caveat: Income earned during the marriage by the spouses' property, such as rents or interest, is treated as follows.

- Income produced by community property of the spouses during their marriage is community property.
- Income produced by a spouse's separate property during the marriage is treated in one of two ways.
- In Idaho, Louisiana, Texas, and Wisconsin the income is community property.
- In Alaska, Arizona, California, Nevada, New Mexico, and Washington the income is separate property.
- In all community property states, appreciation in the value of separate property is separate property. A right to be reimbursed for labor or community funds used to acquire or improve the separate property may exist for the other spouse. It is necessary to check the statutes of the individual states.

Although income earned by the individual spouses' employment during their marriage, as mentioned above, is classified as community property, it is possible for this income to be classified as separate property, e.g., if the spouses sign a written agreement, such as a premarital agreement, in which they approve the separate property classification and place the employment income in their own separate bank accounts.

Separate property is entirely under the management and control of the spouse who owns it no matter how it is acquired, and it is free from all interests and claims of the other spouse. Without the consent of the other spouse, either spouse may dispose of separate property by gift, sale, or will as stated in the following statute.

Cal. Prob. Code § 6101 Property Which May Be Disposed of By Will
A will may dispose of the following property:
(a) The testator's separate property.
(b) The one-half of the community property that belongs to the testator under Section 100.
(c) The one-half of the testator's quasi-community property that belongs to the testator under Section 101.

Community property includes the following:

- Property obtained during the marriage by gift, sale, or will that names both spouses as the recipients.

- Income earned or acquired during the marriage by either spouse's employment, except by gift, sale, will, or inheritance to just one spouse; however, compare comment above on income produced by separate property during the marriage in the six states listed.

- Property obtained from community property income during the marriage.

- Property owned by the spouses in partnerships, stocks and bonds, and as tenants in common.

- Property that was originally separate but is now transformed into community property by a gift from one spouse made to both spouses during their marriage, e.g., one spouse transfers her individual bank account into an account in both spouses' names, or a spouse who owns real property signs a deed naming both spouses owners of the property as "community property."

If the spouses agree in writing, they can change separate property into community property. All other property acquired by either spouse during the marriage in any manner is *presumed* to be *community property* (see La. Civ. Code Ann. art. 2340). The presumption may be rebutted by valid evidence that proves the property is separate property.

To determine whether a married couple's property is separate or community property, the following factors should be considered.

- Whether the property was acquired by either spouse before or after their marriage

- The language and date of the conveyance (deed or will)

- The intent of the grantor, if the conveyance was made by deed, or of the testator (trix) if made by will

- Whether the property was given as a gift to one or both spouses

- Whether the property was inherited by one or both spouses

- Whether separate property of a spouse was sold or exchanged for other separate property, or whether the purpose of the sale was to use the proceeds for community purposes

- The purpose and use of property acquired or obtained by the married couple

- The provisions of a prenuptial or postnuptial agreement regarding property characterization

EXAMPLES:

1. In a community property state, if a deed conveys real property to the spouses, it is community property.

2. However, a deed that expressly states the real property is separate property of either of the spouses creates a conclusion that it is separate property.

3. A married woman's father dies and conveys community property in his will to her. The property is the woman's separate property.

4. If a married woman's father dies intestate and she is his only heir, she will inherit his community property as her separate property.

5. An employer gives $1,000 to a married man living in California. The man's husband claims the money is a salary bonus. The employer testifies in court that the $1,000 was a gift. The court disagrees. Therefore, it becomes part of the spouses' community property. Conversely, if the court agrees the $1,000 was a gift, it becomes the husband's separate property.

Characteristics of Community Property

Formerly, a husband had sole control over community property and could convey or mortgage it without his wife's consent. Today, the community property states have enacted statutes requiring the signatures of both spouses on any transfer or mortgage of community property.

Since each spouse owns one-half of the community property, on the death of either (in the majority of the community property states), the surviving spouse is entitled to his or her one-half of the community property (see Cal. Prob. Code § 100). The decedent's will, if one exists, or the state's intestate succession statutes determine the disposition of the decedent's remaining half. Under no circumstances can either spouse dispose of more than one-half of the community property by will.

The statutes of the community property states differ on the division and distribution of property in cases involving intestacy, divorce, community property with right of survivorship, community property agreements, creditors' claims, commingling, and a category of property created by these statutes called "quasi-community property." Each topic is discussed in more detail in the following paragraphs.

Intestacy

In some community property states, depending on the length of the marriage, when a spouse dies intestate, all of the decedent's community property passes to the surviving spouse and only a smaller share of the separate property (see Cal. Prob. Code § 6401 (a) & (c), but compare Tex. Prob. Code Ann. § 45 where a surviving spouse may not be entitled to all of the property and La. Civ. Code Ann. art 890). See also the case *In re Salvini's Estate*, 65 Wash. 2d 442, 397 P.2d 811 (1964), in which the court ruled a gift of store property to the deceased and her husband prior to her death was community property and, after her death, passed to her husband.

Divorce

In a divorce, the division of community property varies. If a married couple is divorced, the court generally divides the community property so that each party receives an equal share (see Cal. Fam. Code § 2550). Other states, such as Arizona, allow the court to use its discretion in deciding how to divide community property "equitably" (see Ariz. Rev. Stat. Ann. § 25-318). In most community property states, even without divorce, spouses may at any time enter into an agreement that dissolves the community relationship and divides the property. The share each spouse receives is his or her separate property.

Community Property with Right of Survivorship

A form of ownership of community property that allows a surviving spouse to automatically receive the property and avoid probate on the death of the other spouse is through right of survivorship. This form of community property is permitted in Alaska, Arizona, California, Nevada, and Wisconsin.

Community Property Agreements

A separate signed document called a community or marital property agreement that allows spouses to create a right of survivorship in community property in Alaska, Idaho, Texas, Washington, and Wisconsin (see Tex. Prob. Code Ann. §§ 451 and 452). These agreements may include other matters, if provided for by statute, such as mutual rights and obligations of the spouses; selection of what property is to be considered separate or community property; management and control of the property; gifting and sale of the property; division of property upon divorce; nontestamentary distribution of property to named persons or entities upon the death of either spouse; and the terms and conditions of revocation or the termination date of the agreement.

Creditors' Claims

The classification of property as community or separate also affects claims of creditors. In some community property states, e.g., Arizona and Washington, a creditor of one spouse can attach only that spouse's separate property (see *Nationwide Resources Corp. v. Massabni*, 143 Ariz. 460, 694 P.2d 290 [App. 1984], and *Nichols Hills Bank v. McCool*, 104 Wash.2d 78, 701 P.2d 1114 [1985]).

In the *Massabni* case, the court acknowledged that in community property states, all property acquired by either spouse during marriage is presumed to be community property and a spouse's separate property can be transmuted (changed) into community property by agreement, gift, or commingling. In this complex case, however, the court held the property in question was the husband's separate property and, therefore, a judgment creditor of the husband could **garnish**, make a claim against the husband through a **garnishment** proceeding, only his separate property to satisfy the debt, but could not make a claim against the spouses' community property for the husband's individual debt.

In the *Nichols* case, the court ruled, "although one spouse's interest in community property can be reached (and used) to satisfy a tort judgment," a bank (the creditor) could not enforce a loan guaranty agreement signed only by the husband against his interest in the community property since the wife had neither signed nor ratified the agreement. The state of Washington statute requires consent of both spouses before a gift or transfer of community property can be legally enforced.

Other community property states allow creditors with community debts to satisfy their claims against the community property of the spouses and creditors with separate debts to satisfy their claims first against the individual spouse's

garnish
Make a claim against.

garnishment
A three-party statutory proceeding in which a judgment creditor may demand that someone who owes money to or possesses property of a judgment debtor pay the money or transfer the property to the creditor to satisfy the creditors claim against the debtor.

separate property and then, if the debt is not paid in full, to collect the remainder of the debt from community property.

Commingling

Another concern of spouses in community property states is the problem of commingled separate and community property. When extensive **commingling** occurs and it becomes impossible to identify the separate property, the presumption is that the commingled property is community property. To overcome this presumption, each spouse must keep complete and accurate records of how the property was obtained, as well as its purpose and use.

Quasi-Community Property

Property that is acquired in a common law state and then moved into a community property state or that is owned by spouses who have moved into a community property state is called **quasi-community property**. If the newcomer dies *domiciled* in the community property state, the presumption discussed earlier still stands; i.e., all of the decedent's property that is not separate property as defined by the current domicile state is community property. However, if the newcomer's domicile is considered to be the former, the common law state, the presumption can be rebutted and reversed. Conversely, when spouses move from a community property state to a common law state, the community property obtained while they lived in the community property state is not automatically converted into separate property solely by the change of domicile. However, all property acquired by either spouse after both spouses move to the common law state is considered separate property when purchased by a spouse with his or her own funds. When your clients are spouses seeking your assistance, *you must not forget to inquire about their state residences throughout their marriage.*

⚖️ *Ethical Issue*

Community property states have abolished the form of co-ownership called a tenancy by the entirety, except for Alaska, which recognizes tenancy by the entirety for real property only. Joint tenancy is usually allowed except for Louisiana. Alaska recognizes joint tenancy for personal property only. Review Exhibit 1.4 and see Exhibit 1.6 for a summary and comparison of forms of concurrent ownership.

ASSIGNMENT 1.15

1. Casey and Adam Burns live in a community property state. They own the following property: a house in joint tenancy; two cars in both names; a camper given to Adam by his father; savings and checking accounts in both names; a boat purchased by Casey before their marriage; and furniture and household goods, a stereo, and television sets purchased during their marriage. Adam dies. Identify the property Adam can convey in his will.

2. If possible, obtain your family documents and determine the forms of ownership in which your family property is held, e.g., house, stocks, bonds, savings account.

ESTATES IN REAL PROPERTY

The law divides estates in real property into two categories: **freehold estates** and nonfreehold or leasehold estates. The categories are distinguished by the extent and duration of the individual's interest. In other words, freeholds and leaseholds in real property are classified according to how long and how much an interest a person has in realty. Exhibit 1.7 illustrates the classification of estates that will be discussed.

Freehold Estates

Fee Simple Estate or Fee Simple Absolute

The vast majority of all real property, including houses, apartment and office build-ings, and farms, is owned as a fee simple estate. A **fee simple estate**, also known as a fee simple absolute, an estate in fee, or simply as a fee, is the largest, best, and most extensive estate possible. An individual holding a fee estate has an absolute, unqualified, and unlimited interest in the real property. This means the fee estate is not subject to any restrictions, and the owner is entitled to all rights and privileges

fee simple estate
An estate in real property that is the largest, best, and most extensive estate possible. Also known as a fee simple absolute, an estate in fee, or simply a fee.

EXHIBIT 1.6	Summary and Comparison of Forms of Concur[rent] Ownership—Two or More Persons			
Form of Ownership	**Joint Tenancy**	**Tenancy in Common**	**Tenancy by the Entirety**	**Community Property**
Formation: By deed—gift or sale or by will	Yes	Yes	Yes	No—by operation of law
Owners: Two or more named in conveyance	Yes	Yes	Two only—must be spouses	Two only—must be husband and wife by operation of law
Right of survivorship	Yes	No	Yes	No*
Unity of interest: Undivided and equal shares	Yes	Undivided but shares may be equal or unequal	Undivided but spouses as a unit own the property	Yes—of the community property
Unity of possession	Yes	Yes	Yes	Yes
Right of partition	Yes—but not in all states	Yes	No—except if spouses divorce	No—except if spouses divorce
Probate or nonprobate	Nonprobate	Probate	Nonprobate	Probate**
Co-owner's right to sell or give by deed his or her interest in the property	Yes	Yes	No—spouses must agree to transfer in writing	No—of the community property
Creditors of individual co-owner may attach co-owner's interest	Yes	Yes	No—only creditors of both spouses	Yes—but only separate property in Arizona and Washington

 * In some states, spouses can hold the property as community property with the right of survivorship or create right of survivorship with a community property agreement.
** Except community property with the right of survivorship.

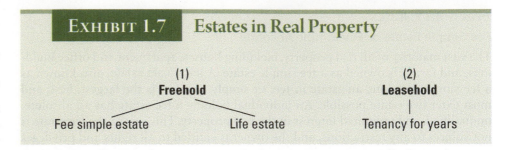

EXHIBIT 1.7   Estates in Real Property

(1)	(2)
Freehold	**Leasehold**
Fee simple estate Life estate	Tenancy for years

associated with the property, i.e., there is no limit on the estate's duration or on the owner's method of disposition. The owner has the unconditional power to dispose (sell or make a gift) of the property during his or her lifetime by deed and after death by will; if the owner dies intestate, the property descends (passes) to the heirs (see the statute and discussion below). Section 44-6-20 of the Georgia Code Annotated defines the estate as follows.

> An absolute or fee simple estate is one in which the owner is entitled to the entire property with unconditional power of disposition during his life and which descends to his heirs and legal representatives upon his death intestate.

In most states no special language is needed to establish a fee simple estate. Every conveyance is presumed to create a fee simple estate unless the conveyance expressly states an intent to create another type of estate such as a smaller estate or an estate of limited duration (see discussion below).

Characteristics of a Fee Simple Estate

The following are characteristics of a fee simple estate in real property.

- *A fee simple estate is transferable during life by deed.*

    EXAMPLE: Jane Doe owns a farm, Blackacre, in fee simple. While alive, she can sell the farm or give it away by the transfer of the title to the real property as a fee simple estate to another person by conveying (delivering) a deed. Jane Doe sells Blackacre by deed to Tom Brown.

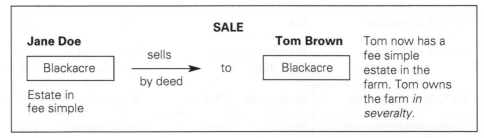

Jane Doe gives Blackacre to Tom Brown by delivering the deed to the farm to Tom.

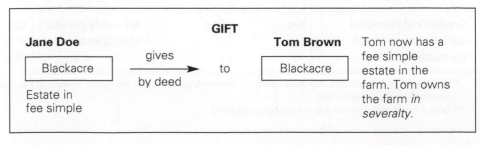

- A fee simple estate is transferable after death by will.

  EXAMPLE: Jane Doe owns Blackacre in fee simple. In her will she gives the farm, Blackacre, to her niece, Sheila Johnson. When Jane dies, Sheila will own Blackacre as a fee simple estate.

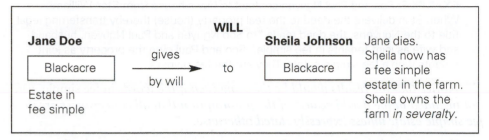

- *A fee simple estate descends to heirs if not transferred through a will.*

  EXAMPLE: Jane Doe owns Blackacre in fee simple and dies intestate. The state in which the farm is located will determine which of Jane's heirs are entitled to the farm in fee simple.

ASSIGNMENT 1.16

Assume that Blackacre in the above example is located in your state. Caitlin Meyer owns Blackacre, the family home, in her name only and dies intestate. She is survived by a husband, three children, her father, and two brothers. According to your state law, who owns Blackacre?

- *A fee simple estate is subject to the rights of the owner's surviving spouse.*

  EXAMPLE: Jane Doe owns Blackacre. She dies. Whether Jane dies testate or intestate, her surviving spouse, Janet, is entitled to an interest in Jane's property. The current rights one spouse has in the decedent spouse's estate are discussed below.

- *A fee simple estate is subject to claims of creditors of the fee owner both before and after the owner's death.*

  EXAMPLE: Jane Doe owns Blackacre in fee simple. Jane owes Sam Bender $10,000, which is now due for payment. If Jane cannot pay this debt to Sam using her other assets, she may have to sell or mortgage Blackacre in order to satisfy the debt.

Creation and Transfer of a Fee Simple Estate

Under common law, a fee simple estate could be created in only one way. The fee owner was required to convey the title to real property by deed or will using the words "to A *and his heirs.*" (The letter A stands for the name of a person.) The words "and his heirs" create a fee simple absolute estate for A and were the only words allowed by common law to create this estate. Times have changed, however, and currently, the words "to A and his heirs" are infrequently used to create a fee simple estate. Today a fee simple estate can be created by any words that indicate an intent to convey absolute ownership, e.g., "to A in fee simple," "to A forever," or simply, "I give the land to A." Generally, whenever any real estate, e.g., a house, is purchased, the buyer becomes the fee owner.

  EXAMPLE: Elliot Hagan buys a business including the land and building in which the business operates. When the current fee owner, Miranda Jennings, transfers the deed to Elliot, he becomes the sole owner of the property *in severalty* and holds the real property in a *fee simple estate.* The transfer of the deed accomplishes the following: (1) Elliot now holds legal title to the property; (2) Elliot, as sole owner, owns the property *in severalty*—single ownership; (3) Elliot receives a *fee simple estate* in the realty since this is the estate Miranda held and transferred to Elliot by deed. All the rights associated with a fee owner are now Elliot's.

EXAMPLE: Soo and Paul Nguyen contract to buy a house from Stan Williams. When Stan delivers the deed to the real property (house) thereby transferring legal title to the Nguyens, the deed reads "to Soo Nguyen and Paul Nguyen, husband and wife as joint tenants in fee simple." Soo and Paul own the property as joint tenants with a fee simple estate. They are the fee owners.

Notice that the results would be the same even if the words in fee simple *were not included in the deed because of the presumption that all conveyances create a fee simple estate unless expressly stated otherwise.*

Keep in mind the characteristics of joint tenancy ownership and a fee simple estate while you review the following summary that explains the application and relationship of these different principles of property law, i.e., estates in real property versus forms of ownership.

- A fee simple estate allows the fee owner, while alive, the right to sell or give the property to another. However, since the property is held in joint tenancy by a spouses, or in some states, tenancy by the entirety, both types of joint owners must join in the conveyance (sale or gift) to pass the title to the new owner(s). Thus, both Soo and Paul (in the previous example) must sign a deed that transfers their house to another as part of a sales contract or as a gift.

- Although another characteristic of a fee simple estate allows a fee owner to transfer the property through a will, neither Soo nor Paul can transfer by will her or his interest in the house, unless severed, to another since they are joint tenants or tenants by the entirety and have the right of survivorship; therefore, if Soo dies first, her interest automatically passes to Paul by operation of law. Thus, the survivor, Paul, would hold a fee simple estate as a single owner and could, subsequently, transfer the estate by will. While both Soo and Paul are alive, neither can pass the property by a testamentary disposition until after the death of the first joint tenant or tenant by the entirety.

ASSIGNMENT 1.17

Jackson, a Montana farmer, deeds 20 acres of his land to his daughter, Grace, in fee simple when she becomes engaged to Ian. Grace marries Ian, and they have two children. Upon Grace's death, Ian claims that he, and not the children, is the owner of the land as a joint tenant with the right of survivorship. Is Ian's claim correct? Explain.

Life Estate

A **life estate** in real property is another type of freehold estate in which an individual, called the **life tenant**, holds an interest in the property that lasts either for the lifetime of that individual or for the life of another person. If the life estate is created for the life of a person other than the life tenant, then it is known as an estate *pur autre vie*.

The next paragraphs discuss the characteristics of life estates and examine some property law concepts associated with them including future interests (reversion and remainder), dower and curtesy, a spouse's elective rights, and waste.

life estate
A freehold estate in which a person, called the life tenant, holds an interest in real property during his own or someone else's lifetime.

life tenant
The person holding a life estate.

pur autre vie
An estate lasting for the life of a person other than the life tenant.

Characteristics of a Life Estate

The characteristics of a life estate can be summarized as follows.

- *A life estate may last for the lifetime of the original owner (the person who conveys the estate).*

  EXAMPLE: Sam conveys Blackacre by a deed to "Marcela for the life of Sam." Marcela has a life estate based on Sam's lifetime. Marcela is the life tenant. Since real property is being conveyed, Sam is the grantor and Marcela is the grantee.

- *A life estate may last for the lifetime of the person enjoying the estate (the person to whom the estate is conveyed).*

  EXAMPLE: Sam conveys Blackacre by a deed to "Marcela for life." Marcela receives a life estate based on her own lifetime.

- *A life estate may last for the lifetime of a third person, called an estate* pur autre vie.

  EXAMPLE: Sam conveys Blackacre by a deed to "Marcela for the life of Julie." Marcela has a life estate based on Julie's lifetime.

- *A life estate can be created by deed or will.*

  EXAMPLE: Sam sells Blackacre to "Marcela for life" and delivers a deed to her at the closing.

  EXAMPLE: Sam gives Blackacre to "Marcela for life" in his will.

- *Unlike a fee simple estate, a life estate cannot be transferred by will.*

  EXAMPLE: Marcela, a life tenant, cannot transfer her life estate to another person through her will.

- *Life tenants while living may convey their interests in the property by sale or gift to a third person, however.*

  EXAMPLE: Marcela, a life tenant, sells her lifetime interest in Blackacre to Laverne. When Marcela gives a deed to Laverne, Laverne becomes the new life tenant and holds the property until Marcela dies. Marcela can sell only her interest in Blackacre, i.e., her life interest or life estate. Since a life tenant's death is inevitable but uncertain and it terminates the life estate, finding a buyer for a life estate is difficult and uncommon.

- *On the death of the life tenant, the life estate terminates, and no interest remains to be passed to heirs or by will; nor can it be probated or be subject to creditors' claims.* The property returns (reverts) to the grantor who created the life estate by conveying the property by deed.

  EXAMPLE: Sam conveys Blackacre by a deed to "Marcela for life." Marcela dies. The property is returned to Sam (see the discussion below).

Future Interests—Reversion and Remainder

Whenever a grantor, who owns a fee simple estate in real property, creates a life estate, one of two results occurs.

1. At the time of the creation of the life estate, the grantor retains a reversion or reversionary interest.

2. Alternatively, at the time of the creation of the life estate, a future remainder interest can also be created within the same conveyance. The person who receives the future remainder is called the remainderman.

   Each of these possibilities is discussed in the next paragraphs.

Reversion

reversion or reversionary interest
The interest in real property that a grantor retains when a conveyance of the property by deed or by will transfers an estate smaller than what the grantor owns, e.g., when the grantor has a fee simple estate and conveys to the grantee a life estate. At some future time the real property reverts back to the grantor.

grantor
The person who makes a conveyance (transfer) of real or personal property to another.

grantee
The person to whom a conveyance of real or personal property is made.

A **reversion or reversionary interest** is the interest or right a **grantor** alone has to the return of real property, at present in the possession of another (the **grantee**), on the termination of the grantee's preceding estate. A reversion exists only when the grantor holding a fee simple estate conveys an interest in property by deed or will that is less than the entire fee simple estate.

When a life estate is created and a reversion is retained, the following rules apply.

- The grantor is the only person entitled to a reversion.
- The grantor is entitled to the reversion (return) of the property, when the grantee's estate terminates, i.e., when the grantee dies.
- The grantor, while alive, can transfer the reversion by deed or will.
- If the grantor dies before the grantee, the reversion is not lost because the right to the reversion can be transferred by the grantor's will to beneficiaries; or if the grantor dies without a will, the right to the reversion can be inherited by the grantor's heirs.
- The real property that reverts (returns) does not go through the probate process of the life tenant's estate and is not subject to tax or creditors' claims.

The following example explains the grantor's right to a reversion or reversionary interest.

EXAMPLE: Peter Nokamura owns a farm, Blackacre, in fee simple. Peter conveys (transfers) the farm by a deed to "Reiko Yoshida for life." Peter is the grantor who retains a reversion in the farm. Reiko receives a life estate and is both the grantee and life tenant. Reiko's life estate gives her the right to use and possess Blackacre or to convey her life estate to another for her own lifetime. When Reiko dies, the life estate ends, and the farm, because of the reversion, automatically reverts (returns) to the grantor, Peter, without going through probate. If Peter dies before Reiko, then his reversion in the property passes (reverts) to Peter's estate, and Peter's will, if he has one, or his state intestate succession statute, if he has no will, determine which of Peter's beneficiaries, heirs, or devisees will receive the property. Exhibit 1.8 diagrams a reversion of this example.

ASSIGNMENT 1.18

Jane Smallwood owns a lake cottage. In a deed she conveys the cottage "to my father, Brent Smallwood, for life, then to my sister, Sue Smallwood for life." Jane outlives her father but dies before her sister, Sue. Is Brent a life tenant? Who gets the property when he dies? What interest does Sue have at the time of Jane's conveyance? Explain what will happen to the property, and why, after the death of Sue.

Remainder

remainder
A future estate in real property that takes effect on the termination of a prior estate created by the same instrument at the same time.

A **remainder** is a future estate in real property that will take effect on the termination of a prior estate created by the same instrument at the same time. A grantor who owns a fee simple estate in real property can create a life estate for one person and, in the same conveyance and at the same time, transfer the future fee simple

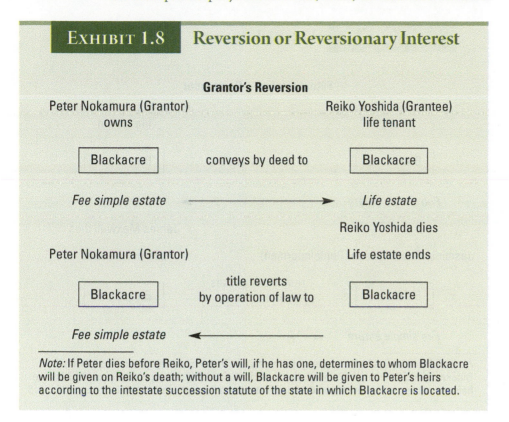

EXHIBIT 1.8   **Reversion or Reversionary Interest**

Grantor's Reversion

Peter Nokamura (Grantor)
owns

Reiko Yoshida (Grantee)
life tenant

Blackacre   conveys by deed to   Blackacre

Fee simple estate ———————————————➤   *Life estate*

Reiko Yoshida dies

Peter Nokamura (Grantor)   Life estate ends

Blackacre   title reverts
by operation of law to   Blackacre

Fee simple estate ◀———————————————

Note: If Peter dies before Reiko, Peter's will, if he has one, determines to whom Blackacre will be given on Reiko's death; without a will, Blackacre will be given to Peter's heirs according to the intestate succession statute of the state in which Blackacre is located.

estate to another person by deed. When the life tenant dies, the property passes to the future fee owner who is called the **remainderman**. This term is used for any person (man or woman) who receives the future estate.

> **EXAMPLE:** Bill Maxwell conveys Blackacre by deed "to James Maxwell for life, then to Jasmine Wilson and her heirs" or "to James Maxwell for life, then to Jasmine Wilson." Result: By the same conveyance and at the same time, James receives a life estate and Jasmine receives a future fee simple estate. When James dies, the property does *not* revert to the grantor, Bill, but instead passes as a fee simple estate to Jasmine. Since he has a fee simple estate and conveys the property by deed, which gives a future fee simple estate to Jasmine, Bill terminates his grantor's right to a reversion in Blackacre. Once Jasmine becomes the fee owner, she is entitled to do with the property as she pleases, i.e., sell it, give it to another, or convey it after death through her will. The same result would have occurred if Bill had conveyed Blackacre "to James Maxwell for life, then to Jasmine Wilson forever," or "to Jasmine Wilson in fee simple." In such cases, where a person, other than the grantor, is entitled to the remainder of an estate in real property after another prior estate has expired, the person (Jasmine) is called the remainderman. Exhibit 1.9 presents a diagram of this example.

remainderman
A person entitled to the future fee simple estate after a particular smaller estate, e.g., a life estate, has expired.

ASSIGNMENT 1.19

According to your state laws, what kind of an estate in real property would Jasmine Moore receive if her Uncle Charles deeded a farm to her in the following ways? (1) "to Jasmine"; (2) "to Jasmine and her heirs"; (3) "to Jasmine in fee"; (4) "to Jasmine forever"; (5) "to Jasmine for life"; (6) "to Jasmine for the life of Ania"; (7) "to Jasmine for as long as I live."

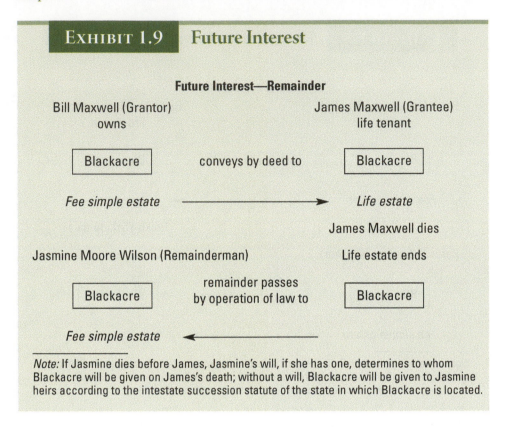

EXHIBIT 1.9   Future Interest

Future Interest—Remainder

Bill Maxwell (Grantor)
owns

Blackacre   conveys by deed to

Fee simple estate

James Maxwell (Grantee)
life tenant

Blackacre

Life estate

James Maxwell dies

Jasmine Moore Wilson (Remainderman)

Blackacre   remainder passes
by operation of law to

Fee simple estate

Life estate ends

Blackacre

Note: If Jasmine dies before James, Jasmine's will, if she has one, determines to whom Blackacre will be given on James's death; without a will, Blackacre will be given to Jasmine heirs according to the intestate succession statute of the state in which Blackacre is located.

Dower and Curtesy

dower
At common law, the right of the surviving wife to a life estate in one-third of all real property her husband owned during the marriage.

curtesy
The right of the surviving husband to a life estate in all of his wife's real property owned during the marriage, but only if the married couple had a child born alive.

Property law in America is derived from the English common law. The rights of spouses in each other's real, but not personal, property, called rights of **dower** and **curtesy**, developed through the common law system. Under common law, at the time of marriage, and to protect her from disinheritance, a wife was given dower rights to provide her with the means of support after her husband's death. Specifically, dower was the surviving wife's (widow's) right to a life estate in one-third of all the real property her husband owned during the marriage. Similarly, the husband was given curtesy rights to his wife's real property.

Curtesy was the right of the surviving husband (widower) to a life estate in all of his wife's real property owned during the marriage, but only if the married couple had a child born alive. In the past under common law, the wife's dower right terminated if

- she was divorced from her husband when he died; a legal separation did not terminate dower, however.
- her husband held his real property in joint tenancy with another person; however, if the real property was held by the husband in a tenancy in common, his share was subject to his wife's dower right.

Dower and curtesy applied whether or not the decedent died testate. The surviving spouse had a right to a life estate in real property.

Both dower and curtesy have undergone numerous changes in every state. Most states (including Uniform Probate Code states) have abolished or materially altered dower and curtesy and replaced them with statutes establishing a surviving spouse's right to a share, often called an elective or forced share, of the entire estate (both real and personal property) in cases where the decedent spouse's will makes unreasonable or inadequate provisions or attempts to disinherit the surviving spouse. Some states have replaced dower and curtesy with marital property rights established by community property statutes (see Exhibit 1.4). Other states have retained their own versions of dower and curtesy rights, though with major modifications. A few states grant equivalent rights or shares to both spouses under the term "dower" (see Ohio Rev. Code Ann. § 2103.02). Other states have enacted "statutory" dower and curtesy where dower is not available if the decedent spouse dies intestate since the surviving spouse is an heir (see 20 Pa. Stat. Ann. § 2105). In these states, a conveyance of real property owned by one spouse requires written consent by the other spouse to release the statutory dower or curtesy interest in the property. Despite these variations, today, the few states that retain dower and curtesy agree on the following:

- Dower and curtesy occur only on the death of a spouse.
- Dower and curtesy provide the same rights to an interest in land to both spouses.
- Dower and curtesy apply even if the decedent died testate.
- Dower and curtesy are terminated by a divorce and the common law rules on real property owned in joint tenancy are retained.
- Dower and curtesy rights in property can be released by spouses only with their written consent.
- Dower and curtesy cannot and do not exist in community property states where the surviving spouse generally receives at least one-half of the community property.
- Dower and curtesy are exempt from the claims of the creditors of the decedent spouse or the decedent spouse's estate except for liens and encumbrances such as mortgages and judgments (see Ohio Rev. Code Ann. § 2103.02).

Policy reasons for replacing dower and curtesy include (1) the inadequate support they provide a surviving spouse under the common law rules; (2) the complications that occur in the transfer or clearance of title to real property for the benefit of prospective purchasers or for future beneficiaries, heirs, or devisees; (3) the fact they transfer only real property, and many estates contain only personal property, such as cash, stocks, and life insurance; and (4) the fact a surviving husband was treated more favorably than a surviving wife under common law rules.

Spouse's Right to Election or Elective Forced Share

With the demise of dower and curtesy, most states, except community property states, give a surviving spouse the statutory right to avoid being disinherited by the will of the decedent spouse. The right is established by a statute that allows the surviving spouse to choose between the provisions made by the deceased spouse's will or the prescribed share set by state statute. This choice is called the spouse's right to an election. The statute granting the *right of election* to take "against the will" is the *elective* or *"forced share" statute*, and the property acquired by the selection is called the spouse's *forced share, elective share*, or *statutory share. Note:* The elective (forced) share statute is only applicable to cases in which the decedent spouse dies with a will. For a complete discussion on the elective (forced) share of the spouse, see Chapter 3.

Waste

While in possession of real property, a life tenant has the absolute right to possess and use the property. However, due to the future reversion and remainder interests of grantors and remaindermen, the life tenant is under a duty to exercise reasonable and prudent care to protect and preserve the property and is required by law not to cause or commit "**waste**." *Waste* is a legal term that refers to "any act or omission that does permanent damage to the real property or unreasonably changes its character or value." Therefore, waste occurs when a life tenant permits any unreasonable or unauthorized use or neglect of the real property that causes permanent physical damage, decreases the property's value, and detrimentally affects the persons entitled to the future interest, i.e., reversion and remainder interests. Specific examples of waste include the following:

- To fail to make necessary building repairs
- To harvest and sell all trees on timberland
- To strip-mine, remove, and sell excessive minerals from the land
- To neglect to heat a house in winter causing major damage to the plumbing

If guilty of waste, the life tenant may be subject to a lawsuit for damages, an injunction from an equity court, or—the extreme remedy—forfeiture (termination) of the tenant's life estate. Unless the facts are obvious, most courts are reluctant to find waste. In addition, state court decisions are inconsistent in determining what constitutes waste. A case involving waste that illustrates the limits placed on a life tenant concerning mineral rights is *Nutter v. Stockton*, 626 P.2d 861 (Okl. 1981).

Leasehold Estates

Various types of **leasehold estates** exist including tenancy at will, tenancy at sufferance, and tenancy from month to month. This text will examine only one example, however, a tenancy or estate for years.

Tenancy for Years

A tenancy or estate for years creates an interest in real property that will last for a fixed period of time, e.g., a tenancy for 10 years. Such a tenancy is created and terminates according to its own terms. No notice to terminate is required.

> **EXAMPLE:** John Kellar owns a farm, Blackacre, in fee simple. John conveys the farm by deed to "Maude Owens for 20 years." Maude holds Blackacre as a tenancy for 20 years. She has the right to use, possess, or even to sell her *interest* in the property. At the end of the 20-year period, however, Maude's interest ends, and the property reverts to John because of the grantor's reversionary interest. A tenancy for years may include a lease, but it must be clear that interest in real property is conveyed for the stated period and not just rights to possession.

ASSIGNMENT 1.20

On the basis of the above discussion, and after reviewing freehold estates, answer the following questions.

Amy conveys by deed her lake cottage to "Clare for life, then to Maxine for 20 years, then to Elizabeth and her heirs."

1. What kind of estate does Clare have?
2. Who receives the property when Clare dies?
3. If Maxine dies before Clare, who receives the property on Clare's death?
4. Does Amy have a reversionary interest in the property? Explain.
5. What interest does Elizabeth hold?
6. Two remaindermen are involved in the conveyance. Who are they and why are they so classified?
7. Do Elizabeth's heirs have any interest in the property by this conveyance?

Leaseholds, such as a tenancy for years, also include the standard landlord-tenant relationships. If Harold signs a lease, i.e., a contract to take possession of real property for a specified time and agrees to pay rent while in possession, such a contract creates the estate called a tenancy for years. It is not the function of this text to review in depth this area of contract and property law, but it is important to understand the association of the landlord–tenant relationship with the terminology and legal concepts previously discussed. Confusion between such terms as *landlord–tenant* and *joint tenancy*, *tenancy in common*, *tenancy by the entirety*, and *tenancy for years* must be avoided.

Key Terms

inheritance	right of survivorship	life estate
fixture	straw man	life tenant
deed	undivided interest	*pur autre vie*
chattel	severance	reversion or reversionary interest
chose in action	partition	grantor
estate	tenancy by the entirety	grantee
probate property (estate)	community property	remainder
severalty (tenancy in severalty)	separate property	remainderman
Totten trust	garnish	dower
incidents of ownership	garnishment	curtesy
operation of law	commingling	waste
descent and distribution	quasi-community property	leasehold estate
disposition	freehold estate	
joint tenants	fee simple estate	

Review Questions

1. How does real property differ from personal property?

2. In whom and when does the real and personal property of the decedent vest (pass)?

3. What are the three tests state courts use to determine if property is a fixture?

4. What are trade fixtures? List three examples.

5. Write out your own definition of each key term in this chapter. Are your definitions essentially the same as those in the text?

6. How do tangible and intangible personal property differ?

7. What items of property are classified as probate property and what items are nonprobate property?

8. What is the significance of property being classified as probate or nonprobate property in terms of the need for probate, creditors' claims, and payment of federal estate and state estate and inheritance taxes?

9. What are the four common law "unities" required for the creation of a joint tenancy?

10. How does a joint tenancy differ from both a tenancy in common and a tenancy by the entirety?

11. How many states are community property states? List them.

12. In a community property state, what property is separate property and what is community property?

13. What is a fee simple estate and what are its characteristics?

14. Concerning future interests in real property, what are the differences between a reversion and a remainder?

15. How does dower differ from curtesy and why have most states replaced them with a spouse's right to elect "against a will"?

16. What responsibilities does a life tenant have concerning the problem of "waste"? Give an example of waste.

Case Problems

Problem 1

A client of the law firm where you work as a paralegal, and with whom you have become acquainted, calls you at your home to discuss and ask your advice about the following matter. The client wants to change the form of ownership in a cottage she currently owns in severalty to either a joint tenancy or a tenancy in common with her two adult children and herself. She tells you her main concern is that she does not want her children's spouses to "ever have any interest in the cottage," and she wants your advice as to how she can obtain this result. Due to your experience, you feel you know the answer to the question. How should you respond to her request? Is this an ethical issue or concern for you as a paralegal? Find and cite the Rule of Ethics for your state.

Problem 2

When he died, Abner Huntington owned a magnificent and expensive home well known for its beautiful landscaping and flower gardens. In his will, he gave his children "all household furnishings, equipment, decorations, and appliances." The home was sold to a famous entertainer who claimed the children had improperly removed certain fixtures from the house and the premises. The property removed included garden statues, lighting fixtures, a pipe organ, metal decorative birds around the swimming pool, and inside the house, a large statue of Pegasus, the flying horse. Most of these property items could be easily removed.

A. In your opinion, are these items fixtures? Explain.

B. Read the case *Paul v. First National Bank of Cincinnati*, 52 Ohio Misc. 77, 369 N.E.2d 488 (1976). In that case, the court ruled that items similar to those in the example were fixtures. Do you agree?

Practical Assignments

1. Determine where you can find information regarding the property where you reside. Who is the owner of record?

2. Make a list of property that you own that would qualify as part of your probate estate.

3. Review the list of property that you made in Question 2. Is there any property on that list that you can convert to nonprobated property? If so, how could you accomplish this?

THE ESTATE PLAN AND THE PURPOSE AND NEED FOR A WILL

2

Outline

Objectives

After completing this chapter, you should be able to:

- Explain the need for and purpose of an estate plan and the procedures and documents used to create a plan.

- Understand and explain the reasons why many Americans die without a will.

- Begin to identify and become familiar with the basic terminology of wills and trusts.

- Recognize and explain the function and purpose of wills.

- Begin to identify and contrast the procedures and outcomes when property is passed by testacy versus intestacy.

- Begin to recognize the terms used to identify the persons who make, manage, administer, or benefit from wills, trusts, and a deceased person's estate.

- Identify and understand the functions of fiduciaries including guardians, conservators, trustees, and personal representatives.

- Identify examples of instances where a person may not need a will.

SCOPE OF THE CHAPTER

This chapter begins with a general discussion on the need for an estate plan and the legal documents, e.g., wills and trusts, required for its creation. After a brief explanation of the reasons people in this country die without wills, the terminology associated with the law of wills, trusts, and estate administration is introduced as you begin the process of mastering the terms and legal concepts essential to the practice of law in these areas. A discussion of the purpose and use of wills and the necessity of having a will, also called a **testament**, concludes this chapter.

testament
Another name for a will.

THE ESTATE PLAN

Estate planning is the determination and utilization of a method to accumulate, manage, and dispose of real and personal property by the owner of the property during life and after death and to minimize the income, gift, inheritance, and estate taxes due. The purpose of estate planning is to identify, preserve, and increase the assets owned and provide for distribution of these assets, with the least possible tax expense, to family members and institutions the owner wishes to benefit. If estate planning is properly performed, the intent and desires of the owner will be accomplished, and the beneficiary-recipients (primarily family) will receive the maximum benefit and enjoyment of the property.

Unfortunately, most people are so involved in their daily activities that they give little thought to the consequences of their deaths. As people grow older, they do give thought to their mortality, and many realize the importance of purchasing life insurance to protect their dependents. However, people often die prematurely and fail to provide through a valid will or an appropriate trust for those for whom they care. The consequences of these acts of procrastination can be financially devastating.

The following chapters in this book explain in detail how you can assist in the creation and use of trusts and wills to resolve and avoid these unfortunate consequences. It is also important that you are prepared to assist those who have the responsibility for estate planning and administration, i.e., your supervising attorney and the personal representative of the decedent's estate.

In addition to the attorney, numerous other individuals are qualified to give estate planning advice. They include trust officers from banks and trust companies, accountants, investment advisers, financial planners, and life insurance agents. Acting as a team, many of these advisers will take an active role in the development of an appropriate estate plan for each client. The attorney you assist will give advice on legal matters; the accountant will handle tax concerns; the financial planner will advise on investments; and the life insurance agent may play a key role in the formation of an insurance policy to ensure financial security for the client's family. While you assist these estate planners, your tasks will be to gather information, maintain records, and communicate by phone or letters to update and keep the client and planners informed of the plan's progress. *Such tasks require you to neither divulge confidential information nor submit or propose unauthorized legal advice even in response to a specific request.*

⚖️ *Ethical Issue*

These assets and their value create a need to formulate a sound and appropriate financial plan—called an **estate plan**. The estate plan is an arrangement of a person's estate that takes into account the laws of wills, property, trusts, insurance, and taxes in order to gain maximum financial benefit of all these laws for the **disposition** (distribution) of the property during life and after death. If the plan is properly formed and executed, it should produce the best possible economic security for the individual and the family. The estate plan encompasses the creation of the estate, its maximum growth and conservation, and, ultimately, its distribution. It necessitates active planning strategies during the individual's life and important postmortem decisions after death. If designed appropriately, the estate plan should meet all the individual's objectives and provide (1) a comfortable retirement income; (2) financial protection for the family; (3) proper custodial care if incompetency or any serious physical or other mental health problem occurs; (4) a minimum of taxes and expenses throughout the implementation of the plan; and (5) expedient, efficient, and harmonious distribution of the estate according to the individual's wishes after death.

The development of an estate plan for the client commences once the client reaches a "comfort level" with the supervising attorney and paralegal, which allows the paralegal to accumulate the personal and financial data.

After information has been obtained from interviews and questionnaires and reviewed with the client, an estate plan is created using legal documents, e.g., wills

estate plan
An arrangement of a person's estate using the laws of various disciplines, e.g., wills, trusts, taxes, insurance, and property, to gain maximum financial benefit of all the laws for the disposition of a person's assets during life and after death.

disposition
The distribution, transfer, or conveyance of property.

and trusts, and devices that save estate tax either by an increase in the deductions from the gross estate or by reducing the gross estate itself.

The next sections discuss the role the will plays in the development of an estate plan.

AN INTRODUCTION TO WILLS

will
The legally enforceable written declaration of a person's intended distribution of property after death.

Unfortunately, many people in the United States die without a valid **will**—the written declaration of a person's intended distribution of property after death. The result is they have no say in the way property they have accumulated over a lifetime will pass after they die.

Most young adults (over 18) have few possessions and dying is not their everyday concern. Correspondingly, in their view, neither is the need for a will. However, every adult owns some property, and most individuals want to determine to whom this property will be distributed after they die. Why then do so many people fail to make a will?

In the first place, almost everyone under 18 and adults who have a mental deficiency cannot make a will because legally they are either too young or they lack the mental health (sanity) required to create a valid will. Currently, financial planners nationwide recommend individuals make a will as soon as they reach the age of majority, if only to give sentimental property to a favorite relative or friend. Some people fail to make a will because they are reluctant to discuss their property and finances with "strangers"; others procrastinate, then die prematurely due to an accident or unexpected illness; some do not want to discuss or face their mortality; others cite cost as their reason (although attorneys generally charge minimal fees for preparing simple wills); and, finally, many people are aware that each state has laws that determine the passage of their property to family and blood relatives if they die without a will, so they allow their state to "make a will" for them. It seems no matter how much effort is spent to encourage Americans to make a will, many are not convinced or motivated to act.

statutes
Laws passed by state and federal legislatures.

legal capacity
Age at which a person acquires capacity to make a valid will, usually 18.

testamentary capacity
The sanity (sound mind) requirement for a person to make a valid will.

testator (male)/testatrix (female)
A man or a woman who makes and/or dies with a valid will.

sound mind
To have the mental ability to make a valid will. The normal condition of the human mind, not impaired by insanity or other mental disorders.

Statutory Requirements for a Will

As mentioned, one reason why the young and some adults die without a will is that not everyone can legally make a will. To begin with, state laws impose restrictions on the makers of wills and on the procedures for creating a valid will. Through its legislature, every state passes laws, called **statutes**, that determine the **legal capacity** (age) and **testamentary capacity** (sanity) requirements for a person to make a will. The maker or **testator (male)/testatrix (female)** must be old enough (usually 18) and be of **sound mind** (sane) at the time the will is made.

In the case of *Matter of Yett's Estate*, 44 Or.App. 709, 606 P.2d 1174 (1980), a will was challenged on the basis that the testator lacked testamentary capacity. The court held that to determine whether the maker of a will had testamentary capacity, great weight is accorded the testimony of attesting witnesses who were present at the execution of the will. It is the testatrix-decedent's capacity at that time, not her general condition over a span of time, that determines testamentary capacity. In this case, the evidence indicated she had this capacity even though she suffered from a malignant brain tumor. The court also ruled the evidence failed to establish her illness, i.e., the tumor, had caused insane delusions that resulted in a decreased share of her estate passing to the contestant of the will. Consequently, the court ruled that the will was valid.

State statutes also establish formal requirements for the creation and **execution of a valid will**; e.g., most wills must be written, signed, and dated by the maker and attested and signed by two or three witnesses. To be properly executed, a will must conform to the laws of the state in which it is made. Each state enacts (passes) laws on the execution of wills, and these laws are not always the same. Laws differ, for example, on the method of writing that may be used (e.g., whether the will may be handwritten or **holographic**, typewritten, computer generated and printed, audiotaped, or videotaped) and on the placement of the testator's signature (e.g., whether it must be on every page, only at the end of the will, or simply anywhere on the will). Individuals who are unfamiliar with the laws of their state and try to create their own wills often make mistakes or omissions concerning their property, naming their **beneficiaries**, or attempting to satisfy the statutory requirements for a will. The result may be an unintended, incomplete, or invalid will. To become a well-trained and experienced paralegal, you need to learn and master the laws of your state so you can explain the statutory requirements, terminology, and procedures associated with wills and help clients execute a valid and meaningful will that accurately fulfills their intent and desires. *However, always be careful not to provide legal advice!*

Basic Terminology Related to Wills

Before proceeding further, it will be helpful to present some basic terminology related to wills and estates. Exhibit 2.1 explains the terms that are used to indicate whether a person died with or without a valid will.

The following terms relate to the actual making of a will.

- *Execute.* To perform or complete, i.e., to write and sign a will.
- *Attest.* To bear witness; to affirm or verify as genuine, e.g., the witness who attests the testator's intent, capacity, and signature on a will.

---

execution of a valid will
The acts of the testator who writes and signs the will and the two or more witnesses who attest and sign it to establish the will's validity.

holographic
A completely handwritten, signed, and usually dated will that often requires no witnesses.

beneficiaries
A person who is entitled to receive property under a will or to whom the decedent's property is given or distributed.

⚖️ *Ethical Issue*

> ## EXHIBIT 2.1   Testacy versus Intestacy
>
> **Decedent**
> (the deceased or person who dies)
>
> *With a valid will*
>
> - Testacy. Death with a valid will.
> - Testate. Any person who makes and/or dies with a valid will. The decedent's property is distributed to beneficiaries and devisees.
> - Testator. A man who makes and/or dies with a valid will.
> - Testatrix. A woman who makes and/or dies with a valid will.
>
> *Without a valid will*
>
> - Intestacy. Death without a valid will.
> - Intestate. Any person who dies without a valid will. The decedent's property passes to heirs according to state laws called intestate succession statutes.
>
> ─────────
> *Note*: Today, common practice often uses the term *testator* for both sexes. In most cases, this text will refer to any person (man or woman) who makes and dies with a valid will as a *testator*.

- *Subscribe.* To sign one's name generally at the end of a will.
- *Witnesses.* Two or more persons who attest and subscribe (sign) the will.

  Other important terms relate to the administration of the decedent's estate.

- *Estate.* Also called *gross estate*. The property accumulated during a person's lifetime and owned at the time of death.
- *Property.* Anything subject to ownership; classified as real property or personal property.
  - *Real property.* Land, buildings, and things permanently attached to them.
  - *Personal property.* Any property that is not real property.
- *Estate administration.* The process of appointing a personal representative (executor or administrator) to collect, preserve, manage, and inventory the decedent's estate; notifying creditors to present their claims; paying all the decedent's debts and death taxes due; and distributing the remaining estate property to beneficiaries named in the will or heirs according to state law if the decedent died intestate, i.e., without a will.
- *Probate.* Court procedure by which a will is proved to be valid or invalid. Probate has been expanded to include the legal process of the administration of a decedent's estate. The term is often used synonymously with estate administration. For example, the phrase "to avoid probate" means to avoid the process and procedures of estate administration. The probate process is required to legally establish the beneficiary's or heir's title to a decedent's property. The **formal probate** (estate administration) or **informal probate** is performed by the personal representative, e.g., executor or administrator, of the estate under the supervision of the appropriate court, often called the probate court.
- *Probate court.* The general name for the court that has jurisdiction (authority) over the handling or administration of a decedent's estate and

formal probate
A court-supervised administration of a decedent's estate.

informal probate
A court proceeding of a decedent's estate with limited or no court supervision.

the distribution of the property; also may be called chancery, surrogate, or orphans' court, depending on the state.

- *Personal representative.* The person (man or woman) who is appointed by the probate court to manage the estate of the decedent and either distribute the estate assets according to a will or a state's intestate succession statute when there is no will. A personal representative includes the following:

  - *Executor/executrix.* The man or woman named in the will to carry out its provisions, i.e., administer the decedent's estate.

  - *Administrator/administratrix.* The man or woman appointed by the probate court to administer the decedent's estate when there is no will.

Other specialized types and titles of personal representatives are discussed in Chapters 7 and 8.

The following terms are used to refer to the recipients of the decedent's property.

Will Terms

- *Beneficiary.* Traditionally, a beneficiary is a person who is entitled to receive property under a will or a person who has already received the property. Under common law, a beneficiary received the personal property of the decedent by will, but today, the term is used to describe a person entitled to any gift (real or personal property) under a will. Therefore, a beneficiary can include a devisee or legatee. This definition for beneficiary will be used throughout the text.

- *Devisee.* A person who receives a gift of real property under a will; or as defined by the **Uniform Probate Code (UPC)**, the person who receives a gift of either real or personal property. Throughout the chapters of the book, relevant sections of the Uniform Probate Code will be cited.

- *Legatee.* A person who receives a gift of personal property under a will.

Uniform Probate Code (UPC)
A uniform law available for adoption by the states to modernize and improve the efficiency of the administration of a decedent's estate.

Intestate Terms

- *Heir.* Under common law, an heir was a person entitled by statute to receive the real property of a decedent who died intestate. Today, an heir includes persons who are entitled by statute to receive or have already received any gift (real or personal property) of the intestate. In addition, although technically incorrect, the popular use of the word *heir* has also been expanded to include persons who receive any gift through a decedent's will. However, throughout the text, the term *heir* will include persons who receive any gifts by intestate succession statutes. See comparison chart on terminology, Exhibit 3.1.

- *Distributee.* A person who is entitled to share in the distribution of an estate of a decedent who dies intestate, or as defined by the UPC, any person who has received property of a decedent from the personal representative other than a creditor or purchaser.

- *Next of kin.* The nearest blood relatives of the decedent; or those who would inherit from a decedent who died intestate, whether or not they are blood relatives, e.g., a spouse.

THE PURPOSE OF WILLS

The primary function of a will is to allow individuals to distribute their property any way they choose. A will gives the testator the opportunity to accurately describe the property owned at death and to designate to whom that property is to be distributed. Since **probate courts** (see Exhibit 7.2) closely scrutinize the language of the will to determine the testator's true intent, it is of paramount importance that no word or sentence within the will create a contradiction, ambiguity, or mistaken interpretation that could cause confusion that would change the testator's plan or, worse, invalidate the will.

> **EXAMPLE:** In an early provision of her handwritten will, Selena Parker leaves "all my antique furniture to my best friend, Maeve Thompson." Later in the will, Selena states that she wants the furniture to go to her only daughter, Carissa. In the final clause of the will, she selects five pieces of this furniture to be given to her housekeeper. The court could declare the will invalid because of these and other contradictions.

Since the context of the general language and particular words in a will is a major factor used to determine the testator's intent, it is essential the will be carefully constructed to ensure the testator's plan for the distribution of the estate property is clearly understood. The court in the case of *Richland Trust Co. v. Becvar*, 44 Ohio St.2d 219, 339 N.E.2d 830 (1975) stated, "The function of the court in a will construction case is to determine and apply the testatrix's intention, as expressed in the language of the whole will, read in the light of the circumstances surrounding its execution."

Without a will, the statutes of the decedent's **domicile** (home state) will determine to whom the decedent's property will be distributed with the exception that **real property**, i.e., land, buildings (house, cottage, apartment, or office building), and the like, will be distributed according to the laws of the state in which the property is located. One of your major tasks and responsibilities will be to prepare drafts of the will and review them carefully with the client *to ensure that the final draft contains complete, accurate, and clearly understandable language to enable readers, especially the probate court, to agree on the meaning of the will and the client's intent.*

Since all wills are **ambulatory**, i.e., subject to change and revocation anytime before death, a will takes effect only after the testator dies. While living, the testator can review and modify the will whenever he wishes by the addition, deletion, or modification of gifts, beneficiaries, clauses of the will, or fiduciaries (see further discussion below under Appointment of Fiduciaries). Also, the testator can sell or dispose of any property listed in the will before death. In the past, if the modification was a simple change, e.g., adding a new gift, a **codicil** or amendment to the will was sufficient. Today, codicils have become obsolete. With the change from typewriter to word-processing software, which rapidly and easily produces legal documents, a "new will" is the preferred and more appropriate choice for *any* needed modification. Also, the use of a computer-generated and printed new will eliminates the serious potential problem of locating two or more documents, i.e., a will and multiple codicils. For further discussion see Chapter 4.

In no particular order of importance, the next paragraphs discuss the testator's essential letter of instructions and some of the reasons for making a will.

---

probate courts
The court that has jurisdiction (authority) over the probate of wills and the administration of the decedent's estate.

domicile
The location (state) of a person's true and legal home.

real property
Land, buildings, and things permanently attached to them.

 *Ethical Issue*

ambulatory
Subject to change and revocation anytime before death; e.g., a will is ambulatory.

codicil
A written amendment to the will that changes but does not invalidate it.

Funeral and Burial Plans and the Letter of Instructions

The best and most appropriate method for individuals who preplan their funeral and burial arrangements is to include the plans in a **letter of instructions** and *not* in a will or codicil. One of the valuable uses of the letter of instructions is to provide a written document that identifies and explains a person's funeral and burial plans and is readily accessible for the testator's review and modification. After planning the funeral with a mortician (including costs and arrangements for a casket, church service, and reception) and purchasing a burial plot, individuals can insert these plans into the letter of instructions and make them known to their family, physician, religious adviser, and future personal representative by giving them copies of the letter. Thus, the letter avoids a frequently unpleasant, and sometimes painful, problem the family faces when a loved one dies, often suddenly and unexpectedly, and the will or codicil cannot be found or obtained before the decedent-testator's burial. The letter should not be kept in a safe deposit box.

Preplanning and prepaying the costs of the funeral and burial takes a heavy burden off the grieving family, both economically and emotionally. Alternately, if the individuals prefer to be cremated and want to ensure that their wishes will be followed without revealing the contents of the will, they can review the letter containing the cremation plans with family members; and, if there are any concerns or objections, they can be resolved prior to the person's death.

Unfortunately, if a testator places funeral and burial arrangements only in the will, all such preplanning may be an exercise in futility, either because the will is not found until after the testator has been buried, or because the family simply disregards or disobeys the instructions. Since statutes in most states allow the desires of a surviving spouse and next of kin to legally supersede the plans of the testator, often the family makes the final decisions concerning the disposal of the testator's body and the type of funeral or service. The following persons generally have priority in deciding on funeral and burial arrangements including cremation: the **surviving spouse**, an adult child, a parent, an adult sibling, the decedent's guardian, and any other authorized or obligated person, e.g., a personal representative or medical examiner. All too frequently, serious disagreements arise over such questions as whether there should be a burial of the body or cremation, a denominational or nondenominational religious service, an open or closed casket, and the like.

EXAMPLE: Nathan has told his family he wants to be cremated when he dies. After his death, Nathan's family, for religious reasons, decides to have a traditional service without cremation. Often the decedent's wishes are not followed, as in this example.

Sometimes the testator's family disregards the funeral plans outlined in the will because the arrangements are too elaborate, too expensive, or unreasonable.

EXAMPLES: Xavier wants to be cremated and have his ashes flown to Paris and spread from the top of the Eiffel Tower. Anthony wants a horse-drawn carriage, a hundred-member band, and an all-night party. Honoring such requests may deplete the estate and create additional hardships for survivors.

The above problems can best be alleviated by preplanning and prepaying the funeral and burial arrangements, discussing them with family and the funeral director, and placing them in the letter of instructions. *Caveat:* Copies of the letter must be given to the family and the future personal representative.

letter of instructions
A document that specifies the testator's instructions for organ donation and funeral and burial plans. It can also be an all-inclusive checklist of various personal and estate information to help the family and personal representative locate and identify property and documents necessary to administer the estate.

surviving spouse
A spouse who outlives the other.

Even though the funeral and burial arrangements are often made by someone other than the personal representative (such as a surviving spouse or other family member), the cost of all "reasonable" expenses is paid as a priority debt of the decedent's estate according to state law, as will be discussed in detail in later chapters. It will be your job to keep accurate records of the costs and *remind the personal representative that these expenses remain "reasonable."* Personal representatives are liable to the estate if they allow these costs to become excessive due to their neglect.

⚖ *Ethical Issue*

If an individual intends to donate organs or remains for transplant or medical research, the donation instructions must also be included in the letter instead of a will, which may not be discovered in time to make a "useful" organ donation. Although most states recognize donor designation on a driver's license or other organ donor documentation, it may not be enough, as many organ procurement organizations and hospitals continue to seek consent from the donor's next of kin. Some states have passed legislation that seeks to avoid complications arising from a donor's next of kin opposing the organ donation. These laws generally provide that a properly executed organ donation statement, not revoked by the donor, must be enforced and cannot be overridden by any other person. Minn. Stat. Ann. § 525.9212(2) (h) is typical, providing that, upon the donor's death, an unrevoked organ donation designation is enforced and does not require the approval of, nor can it be opposed by, any other person. Even in states that call for such protection of the donor's wishes, it may still be advisable to inform the family to ensure the donor's wishes will be honored. Many states have established organ donor registries. For the most part, they are operated in participation with the Department of Motor Vehicles and provide for donor designation on the driver's license. For further discussion of funeral and burial arrangements and organ donation by the testator, see Chapter 6.

ASSIGNMENT 2.1

1. Does your state have an organ, tissue, and eye donor registry?

2. Does your state provide for donor designation on the driver's license?

3. Is online registration available for your state's donor program?

4. What policy does your state have in place for informed consent to organ donation?

5. Does your state have legislation requiring that the organ donor's wishes be carried out?

The letter of instructions is potentially a multipurpose document, but it is not legally enforceable. It is, therefore, not a substitute for a will. The letter's purpose can range from a document limited to funeral and burial plans, to an all-inclusive checklist that identifies the testator's personal and family history; assets and liabilities; various insurance policies; financial advisers; health and service providers; location of legal and personal documents; and many other matters. A checklist may be drafted from a list such as that shown in Exhibit 2.2. The subject matter list enables testators to select and create appropriate schedules for their personal letter of instructions.

EXAMPLE: A sample schedule in the letter of instructions containing assets such as pension/retirement plans of the testator might appear as follows.

Pension/Retirement Plans   **Date** _____

Plan	Location Home safe/ File cabinet	Designated beneficiary	Present value
1. IRA—Traditional/Roth	_____	_____	_____
2. Self-Employed Retirement Plan	_____	_____	_____
3. 401(k) Plan—Traditional/Roth	_____	_____	_____
4. Profit-Sharing Plan	_____	_____	_____
5. Pension Plan	_____	_____	_____
6. Stock Bonus Plan/ESOP	_____	_____	_____
7. Other	_____	_____	_____

EXAMPLE: Another common schedule identifies insurance policies.

Insurance Policies   **Date** _____

Type	Location Home safe/ File cabinet	Insurer	Policy number
1. Life	_____	_____	_____
2. Health	_____	_____	_____
3. Accident	_____	_____	_____
4. Disability	_____	_____	_____
5. Homeowners	_____	_____	_____
6. Automobile	_____	_____	_____
7. Umbrella	_____	_____	_____
8. Other	_____	_____	_____

A third potential schedule could include a list of securities (stocks and bonds) within the letter of instructions to enable the investor to review and regularly update the entries so that necessary changes, e.g., number of shares, date acquired, purchase price, date sold, sales price, and stockbroker, can be made. If the letter is on a computer, assets such as securities can be evaluated daily for future investment strategies.

By keeping the letter of instructions current and distributing copies to family members to inform them of its contents, especially funeral, burial, and organ donation plans, the letter becomes the ideal method for the documentation of this information in place of a will or codicil. Most importantly, it allows the testator's organ donation and funeral plans to be implemented when time is of the essence.

EXHIBIT 2.2   Letter of Instructions—Subject Matter

Personal Information
Name/ (a/k/a)
Address
Prior Residences (Past 10 Years)
Telephone Number (Home/Work)
Date/Place of Birth (Certificate)
Social Security Number
Religion
Date of Marriage (Certificate)
Date of Divorce (Decree)
Education
Employment History
Military Record
Other

Organ Donation/Funeral Plan
Organ Donation
    Donor Card
    Driver's License Provision
    Registry
    Health Care Directive
Body Donation
Funeral Plan
    Prepaid Funeral/Burial Contract
    Funeral Service
    Burial/Cemetery Plot
Other

Family Information
Relationship (Spouse, Children,
    Grandchildren, etc.)
Name
Address
Telephone Number (Home/Work)
Date/Place of Birth
Marital Status
Date of Death
Other

Fiduciaries
Personal Representative
    Successor
Guardian (Minor or Incapacitated Persons)
    Personal Guardian
    Property Guardian
    Conservator
    Successor
Trustee
    Successor
Other

Family Financial Advisers
Accountant/Tax Adviser
Appraiser
Attorney
Banker/Trust Officer
Financial Planner
Insurance Agent (Broker)
Real Estate Agent (Broker)
Stockbroker
Other

Liabilities
Automobile Loan
Business Debts
Charge Accounts
Contract for Deed Payments
Credit Card Charges
Installment Purchases
Loans on Insurance Policies
Mortgages on Real Property
Pledges to Charities,
    Religious Organizations, etc.
Promissory Notes
Taxes
Other

Assets
Automobile, Boat, etc.
Bank Accounts
Business (Family) Ownership
Furniture/Household Goods
Notes, Contracts for Deed, etc.
Pension/Retirement Plans
Real Property
Royalties/Patents & Copyrights
Securities
Trusts
Other

Additional Topics
Credit Cards
Insurance Policies
Legal & Personal Documents
Location of Documents
Medical & Dental Providers
Service Personnel
Spiritual Advisers
Safe Deposit Box
Tax Returns
Other

Apportionment for Death Taxes

By adding an appropriate **apportionment clause** to the will, the testator can determine the source from which death taxes (federal and state estate taxes and state inheritance taxes) will be paid. If the apportionment clause is explicit and included in the will, it determines the method of apportionment. However, if the will has no apportionment clause or is ambiguous, the statute of the testator's domicile determines the method of apportionment. The following is an example of an apportionment clause from West's McKinney's Forms, ESP, § 7:387.

> I direct that all estate, inheritance, succession and transfer taxes and other death duties, including any interest or penalties thereon, imposed or payable by reason of my death upon or in respect of any property passing under my will and required to be included in my gross estate for the purpose of such taxes, shall be paid out of my residuary estate as an administration expense and shall not be apportioned. Source: Thomson/West from West's McKinney's Forms.)

Many states place the burden of estate and inheritance taxes on the **residuary estate** of the will, which is also the source of payment of creditors' claims. Other states apportion federal and state death taxes among the various persons (**legatees** or beneficiaries) on a **pro rata** basis (see N.Y. EPTL § 2–1.8).

The advantage of having the testator make the apportionment decision rather than leaving it to state law is that customarily the property included in the will's residue clause, often a substantial portion of the estate, is left to the surviving spouse and children. If this property is the primary or sole source of payment of creditors' claims and death taxes, *these family members may be unintentionally placed in a hardship situation by this major oversight.* It is your responsibility to recognize this mistake and bring it to your supervising attorney's attention. The attorney will explain its significance to the client and obtain permission for you to redraft appropriate provisions of the will for the attorney's approval.

The Uniform Estate Tax Apportionment Act of 2003, which apportions federal and state death taxes among all beneficiaries on a pro rata basis, has been adopted in some states and is incorporated in the UPC § 3–916. *Remember:* An apportionment clause in a will overrules any apportionment method established by state statute.

Property Distributions

With a will, the testator can avoid many ill-advised and awkward property distributions. Consider the following example.

> **EXAMPLE:** Jacob Weizman dies intestate. His only heirs are five unmarried daughters. Jacob's estate assets consist of three farms (each farm is located in Jacob's home state (domicile) and is worth $200,000) and a total of $100,000 in various banks. Jacob's state statute, like the law in most states, divides his assets equally among his five daughters. Dividing the money is easy—each daughter receives $20,000. The three farms, however, go to the five daughters in the form of co-ownership called **tenancy in common**, which creates for each co-owner (each daughter) an undivided, equal interest in each farm and the right to equal possession of the entire premises of each farm. As a **tenant in common**, each daughter, on her death, can pass her $20,000 and her equal interest (one-fifth) in each farm to the beneficiaries she names in her will; if she dies intestate, the law of the state where the farms are located will determine who receives her one-fifth interest and her $20,000.

apportionment clause
A clause in a will that allocates the tax burden among the residuary estate and the beneficiaries of the will.

residuary estate
The remaining assets (residue) of the decedent's estate after all debts have been paid and all other gifts in the will are distributed.

⚖ *Ethical Issue*

legatees
A person who receives a gift of personal property under a will.

pro rata
According to a certain rate or percentage.

tenancy in common
The ownership of an undivided interest of real or personal property by two or more persons without the right of survivorship, which allows each owner's interest to be passed to his or her beneficiaries or heirs upon death.

tenant in common
One of two or more persons who own property in a tenancy in common.

This situation becomes more complicated if, for example, two of the daughters want to live on one of the farms; the others want to sell them; or one or more of the daughters marry. The point is clear: Even if serious personality conflicts do not occur, the occupation and management problems of the property could create numerous and unfortunate consequences. This unpleasant situation is avoided if Jacob discusses his assets with his daughters, so that, as a family, they identify possible options and arrive at a compromise acceptable to all. In this way, Jacob's original plan to treat the daughters fairly is accomplished harmoniously, and the solution could be included in his will.

ASSIGNMENT 2.2

Review the facts in the Jacob Weizman example above. Draw up three different plans that may be used as part of Jacob's will to transfer the three farms and the $100,000 to his five daughters in equal shares.

Provisions for Family Members

With a will, the testator can appropriately provide for a surviving spouse and the special needs of individual children. In most cases, the surviving spouse receives the majority of the testator's estate. If the testator's estate plan includes lifetime gifts and specific provisions in wills and trusts, death taxes, especially federal and state estate taxes, can be reduced, thereby maximizing the portion of the estate family members receive. These tax reductions may be lost if the decedent dies intestate. For a complete discussion of these problems and tax concerns, see Chapter 14.

intestate succession statutes
Laws passed in each state establishing the manner in which a decedent's property will be distributed when death occurs without a valid will.

When a spouse and minor children survive a decedent who failed to make a will, the **intestate succession statutes** of most states pass the estate property to the spouse individually, or for life, and to the children equally as tenants in common. Since the children are minors, a probate court needs to appoint a **guardian** (see Appointment of Fiduciaries below) to handle any property in which they have an interest. In such a case, the surviving spouse is appointed guardian, but the appointment may cause additional expense and needless delay if the property has to be sold promptly, e.g., to provide funds for the family's necessary living expenses or if the family needs to relocate. For this reason, it is often best to leave the decedent's estate solely or as a life estate to the surviving spouse without minor children becoming the co-owners. This can be accomplished using a will and/or a trust.

guardian
The person or institution named by the maker of a will or appointed by the court when there is no will to care for the person and/or property of a minor or a handicapped or incompetent person.

spouse's statutory, forced or elective share
The spouse's statutory right to choose a share of the decedent spouse's estate instead of inheriting under the provisions of the decedent's will.

The only person a testator cannot disinherit is a surviving spouse since the spouse has a statutory right to a share of the decedent spouse's estate. This is called the surviving **spouse's statutory, forced or elective share**. Every state has a statute with a provision for the benefit of the surviving spouse that makes it impossible for the deceased to leave the surviving spouse nothing. However, a decedent who dies testate can disinherit children. Of course, this happens at times, but more commonly, the testator wants the children to receive the estate equally. Due to special circumstances, the testator may grant unequal shares of the estate to meet the children's different needs (see the examples below).

EXAMPLES: In her will

1. Kristin Neilsen leaves the entire estate to her three children equally.

2. Kristin Neilsen leaves the majority of the estate to her child with special needs and smaller shares to her other two children.

3. Kristin Neilsen intentionally and specifically states that one, two, or all three of her children (naming them) are not to receive any assets of the estate.

In the above examples, if the decedent, Kristin Neilsen, dies intestate, the children's special needs will not be met, but none of them will be disinherited. If the children are Kristin's only heirs, they will receive equal shares.

Numerous other problems concerning family members' inheritance rights are discussed in detail in Chapters 3 and 5.

Appointment of Fiduciaries: Guardians and Conservators

With a will, a testator can appoint guardians for a **ward** (minor or **incompetent person**). Guardians appointed by the court are either **personal guardians** or **property guardians**. Both guardians are a type of **fiduciary**, a person in a position of trust and confidence who controls and manages property exclusively for the benefit of others and owes the highest duty of obedience, diligence, and good faith to those the person represents. Fiduciaries include guardians who act for minors or incompetent persons, trustees who act for beneficiaries of a trust, and personal representatives who act for beneficiaries of a will or for **heirs** when there is no will. The fiduciary is required to give absolute loyalty to the beneficiary or minor while performing **fiduciary duties**, i.e., all transactions that concern the property held in trust.

A personal guardian is an adult who has custody, control, and responsibility for the care and supervision of the minor child until the child reaches the age of majority, usually 18. If the decedent-testator is survived by the other natural or **adoptive parent**, that parent by law immediately becomes the personal guardian of the minor. An attempt by the testator to appoint some other person as the minor's guardian is not valid or binding, see Tex. Prob. Code Ann. § 676(b). This situation frequently occurs when married couples divorce, and one of the former spouses is given custody of the minor children of the marriage. If the custodial spouse dies while the children are still minors, the attempt in a will to name a personal guardian who is not the other natural parent (the former spouse) would fail.

When there is no other surviving natural parent, the appointment of a personal guardian in the custodial parent's will is generally upheld by the court, and any further hearing on custody is unnecessary, see Mass. Gen. Laws Ann. ch. 201 § 3. The appointment of a personal guardian is discussed in detail with examples and cases in Chapters 6 and 9.

When parents die without a will or fail to appoint a guardian in a will, the probate court must select both a personal and a property guardian based on what is "in the best interests of the child." Godparents are not legal guardians. Although they acknowledge responsibility to help raise a child by reason of a religious ceremony, they do not have legal standing, i.e., they are not recognized as having the legal authority of parents. Usually, the court appoints a family member who may

ward
A minor or incompetent person placed under the care and supervision of a guardian by the probate court.

incompetent person
A person under legal disability, e.g., a mentally incapacitated person.

personal guardians
An individual or trust institution appointed by a court to take custody of and care for a minor or an incompetent person.

property guardians
An individual or trust institution appointed by a court to care for and manage the property of a minor or an incompetent person.

fiduciary
A person, such as a personal representative, guardian, conservator, or trustee, who is appointed to serve in a position of trust and confidence and controls and manages property exclusively for the benefit of others. By law the fiduciary's conduct is held to the highest ethical standard.

heirs
Traditionally, a person, including a spouse, who is entitled by statute to the real property of an intestate. Today, a person entitled to any gift (real or personal property) of the intestate or in the decedent's will.

fiduciary duties
A duty or responsibility required of a fiduciary to act solely for another's benefit that arises out of a position of loyalty and trust.

adoptive parent
A person who legally adopts another individual, usually a child.

conservator
A fiduciary; an individual or trust institution appointed by a court to care for and manage property of an incompetent person.

testamentary trust
A trust created in a will. It becomes operational only after death.

***inter vivos* or living trust**
A trust created by a maker (settlor) during the maker's lifetime. It becomes operational immediately after the trust is created.

trust
A right of property, real or personal, held by one person (trustee) for the benefit of another (beneficiary).

settlor
A person who creates a trust; also called donor, grantor, creator, or trustor.

legal title
The form of ownership of trust property held by the trustee, giving the trustee the right to control and manage the property for another's benefit, i.e., the holder of the equitable title.

trustee
The person or institution named by the maker of a will or a settlor of a trust to administer property for the benefit of another (the beneficiary) according to provisions in a testamentary trust or an *inter vivos* trust.

beneficiaries
The person or institution who holds equitable title and to whom the trustee distributes the income earned from the trust property and, depending on the terms of the trust, even the trust property itself.

equitable title
A right of the party who holds the equitable title or beneficial interest to the benefits of the trust.

or may not have been the choice of the decedent. Without a will, the appointment of a guardian can lead to a time-consuming and expensive contest in probate court between relatives. Unfortunately, the dispute often has lasting harmful effects on the children.

> **EXAMPLE:** Tal Anderson dies intestate. Tal had often talked to Katherine and Joe Merrill, Tal's close friends, about his desire to have them "take care of my children if I should die." Even though Katherine and Joe inform the probate court of Tal's wishes and their willingness to be the guardians, the probate court will most likely appoint blood relatives of Tal who agree to be the guardians.

> **EXAMPLE:** The only blood relative of Ana Herrera, age 27, is her grandmother, age 70. Due to her grandmother's age and uncertain health, Ana asked her close friend, Rosie Cooper, if she would be the guardian of her 8-year-old daughter. Rosie agrees, but Ana dies intestate. The probate court will likely appoint as guardian, the grandmother, if she is willing to serve, even though she was not Ana's choice.

Unlike the case of the personal guardian, the surviving natural or adoptive parent or the person appointed by the testator's will is not automatically appointed the property guardian for the decedent's minor or incompetent children. Such people may be appointed and often are, but the decision is made by the probate judge, who appoints the guardian.

The property guardian can be a natural person or a legal person such as a corporation, bank, or trust department, which happens infrequently. The property guardian's responsibility is to take exclusive control of and manage the property inherited by a minor or incompetent person in order to preserve and increase its value. The guardian must perform the management and investment functions according to strict standards set by the court and state law. These standards cannot be changed, broadened, or made less rigid by the terms of a will even if that was the testator's intent.

A property guardian for an incompetent person whom the probate court has found to be incapable of managing property is, in a few states, called a **conservator**, another type of fiduciary. Typically, conservators are appointed for individuals who, due to advanced age or an illness such as Alzheimer's disease, are under a legal disability that makes them mentally incapable of managing their property. States usually require that a conservator or guardian be appointed whenever an incompetent person owns property obtained through gifts or inheritance. Property guardians or conservators are discussed further in Chapters 6 and 9.

Creation of Testamentary Trusts

A testator can create either a **testamentary trust**, i.e., a trust within the will, which becomes operational only after the testator's death, or an ***inter vivos* or living trust**, which takes effect immediately after the trust is created. A **trust** is a legal agreement in which one person (the **settlor**) transfers **legal title** (ownership) to one or more persons (the **trustee** or co-trustees) who, as a fiduciary, holds and manages the property for one or more **beneficiaries** who receive the **equitable title**, which gives them the right to the benefits of the trust. The settlor gives up possession, control, and ownership of the property to the trustee who is specifically instructed by the trust terms how the trust is to be managed and the trust property invested so that income produced (profits) can be distributed to the beneficiaries. All three positions (settlor, trustee, and beneficiary) can be held by the same person, but the fundamental characteristic of a trust is the trust splits title of the trust property into legal title (transferred to the trustee) and equitable title (given to the beneficiary), and requires that no one person can be the sole trustee and the sole beneficiary since that person would hold both titles, merging them and invalidating the attempt to create a trust. The solution to this problem is to have either co-trustees or co-beneficiaries so the "split title" requirement is satisfied.

EXAMPLES:

1. A trust is not created if the settlor, Kevin Ford, names himself as both the sole trustee and the sole beneficiary.

2. A trust is created if the settlor, Kevin Ford, names himself sole trustee and Carly Hamilton and himself as co-beneficiaries.

3. A trust is created if the settlor, Kevin Ford, names Carly Hamilton and himself as co-trustees and himself as sole beneficiary.

All trusts, whether testamentary or *inter vivos* (living), are either revocable or irrevocable. A revocable trust may be changed, amended, or canceled by the settlor while living, but, generally, revocable trusts become irrevocable when the settlor dies. Irrevocable trusts are final from the moment of their creation. They cannot be changed or revoked. *Caveat:* Unless the trust document contains a clause that expressly reserves the right or power of the settlor to revoke the trust, the trust is irrevocable. The significance and consequences of revocable or irrevocable trusts are discussed in Chapters 12 and 13. One of the most common uses of a testamentary trust is the **bypass trust** (also called Trust B of an A-B trust, credit shelter trust, family trust, and residuary trust) established for the benefit of a surviving spouse. By limiting the surviving spouse's right to a life estate in the **principal** of Trust B, the property is not included in the estate of the surviving spouse when that spouse dies; thus, it avoids **federal estate tax**. By reducing federal taxes in this manner, more of the estate property is free to pass to future beneficiaries, usually the children (see the detailed discussion in Chapter 14). If a person dies without a will (intestate), this tax advantage would be lost.

Another common reason for creating testamentary or *inter vivos* (living) trusts is to counter and avoid the rigid control and considerable expense of a property guardian for minors or a conservator for incompetent persons. The following examples illustrate the advantages of trusts.

EXAMPLE: In a trust, trustee Maurice Benson can be given discretion to choose among accumulating trust income, distributing **income**, or even distributing the principal of the trust for the benefit of one or more beneficiaries. The stricter regulations imposed on a property guardian or conservator would not grant this freedom.

EXAMPLE: After reviewing the pros and cons of wills, trusts, and guardianships, Joshua and Taylor Price, who have two minor children, decide on the following: Since he has a terminal illness, Joshua drafts and executes his will, which leaves his entire estate to his surviving spouse, Taylor. He is confident that she will provide for their minor children and eventually transfer the balance of the property to them in her own will. Since no property is left to the minor children, guardianships (with their corresponding control and expense) are avoided. In the event that Taylor dies first, Joshua adds a contingent testamentary trust, which leaves his estate to the trust for the benefit of his minor children.

---

bypass trust
An estate planning device whereby a deceased spouse's estate passes to a trust as a life estate for the surviving spouse rather than entirely to the surviving spouse, thereby reducing the likelihood that the surviving spouse's estate will be subject to federal estate tax.

principal
In trust law, the capital or property of a trust, as opposed to the income, which is the product of the capital.

federal estate tax
A tax imposed on the transfer of property at death.

income
Interest, dividends, or other return from invested capital.

Other reasons for the creation of trusts include the following:

- Trusts are used to provide professional management of the trust property for those beneficiaries (including a settlor-beneficiary) who do not have the time, inclination, or skill to manage the property themselves or, because of illness or incapacity, are no longer able to do so.

public (charitable) trusts
A trust established for the social benefit either of the public at large or the community.

- Trusts known as **public (charitable) trusts** can be established for religious, scientific, charitable, literary, or educational purposes under IRC § 170(c)(4).

- Trusts can prevent spendthrift beneficiaries, including children, from recklessly depleting the trust fund and can also prevent their creditors from obtaining the trust principal on demand for the payment of debts.

- Trusts can save taxes and avoid probate expenses if properly established.

A complete discussion of the formation, drafting, and types of trusts, including the popular living trust, is included in Chapters 12 and 13.

Selection of Personal Representative

personal representative
The person who administers and distributes a decedent's estate according to the will or the appropriate intestate succession statute. It includes executor and executrix when there is a will and administrator and administratrix when there is no will.

executor or executrix
A man or woman named in the will by the maker to be the personal representative of the decedent's estate and to carry out the provisions of the will.

administrator or administratrix
The man or woman appointed by the probate court to administer the decedent's estate when there is no will.

The **personal representative** is a UPC term that identifies the man or woman who manages, administers, and distributes a decedent's estate according to the terms of a will or the appropriate state intestate succession statute if the decedent dies without a will; see UPC § 1–201(35). A personal representative includes an **executor** (man) **or executrix** (woman) who is selected by a testator to carry out the terms of a will or an **administrator** (man) or **administratrix** (woman) who is appointed by the court to administer the estate of a decedent who dies intestate. Consideration by the testator should be given in the selection of the personal representative, especially if the estate contains digital data. A personal representative who is competent to handle an estate that includes digital data may require special skills and responsibilities. Throughout the remaining chapters of the text, the words *personal representative* will be used to identify any person who has the responsibility to administer the estate of a decedent who dies either testate or intestate. The various types of personal representatives and the important role they play in administering the decedent's estate are discussed in Chapters 7, 8, and 9.

Like trustees and guardians, the personal representative is a fiduciary who owes fiduciary duties (acts of trust, loyalty, and good faith) to the recipients of the decedent's estate, e.g., beneficiaries, heirs, and devisees. To acquire the authority and powers of the position, a personal representative must be appointed by the appropriate court, often called the probate court. Generally, in testacy cases, the court appoints the person nominated in the testator's will unless that person is not qualified under state law. Whether a person dies with or without a will, states usually have statutes that list the persons who are not qualified to be personal representatives (see Tex. Prob. Code Ann. § 78). The Texas list includes the following:

1. An incapacitated person, e.g., minors or incompetent persons

2. A person convicted of a felony

3. A nonresident (natural person or corporation) who has failed to appoint a resident agent to accept service of process

4. A corporation that is not authorized to act as a fiduciary in the state

5. A person whom the court finds "unsuitable"

EXAMPLE: Leslie Powell's will names Aaron Shroeder to be the personal representative. Due to previous associations, Leslie's family and heirs feel extremely hostile toward Aaron. The hostility of beneficiaries toward a nominated personal representative does not ordinarily or automatically disqualify the person as "unsuitable." However, see *Matter of Petty's Estate*, 227 Kan. 697, 608 P. 2d 987 (1980), where the court refused to appoint the will's nominee to be personal representative, because the hostility between the beneficiaries and nominee could lead to unnecessary difficulties and expenses for the estate.

Caveat: If a testator selects a personal representative and also in the will names an attorney to assist the personal representative with the estate administration, the estate is not legally bound to this selection. Personal representatives have the right to select an attorney of their own choice to represent the estate. *It is a violation of the Code of Ethics for the attorney or paralegal to suggest that they be named in the will for such purpose.*

 **Ethical Issue**

Chapter 3 of this text discusses death with a will (testacy) and death without a will (intestacy) in more detail.

WILL SUBSTITUTES

In some cases it may not be necessary to have a will. However, the decision should be made *only* after consultation with an attorney knowledgeable about estate planning. It may be possible, especially with small estates, to employ "will substitutes" instead of a will to distribute a decedent's estate. Examples of will substitutes include (1) joint tenancy, (2) life insurance, (3) *inter vivos* trusts, (4) *inter vivos* gifts, (5) community property agreements, and (6) **transfer-on-death deeds or beneficiary deeds.** The value and kinds of property owned by the client and the needs of the beneficiaries generally determine whether a will should be executed.

- Joint tenancy

  EXAMPLE: Jean and her fiancé, Darnell, own a house in **joint tenancy** valued at $90,000. They also have $1,200 in a checking account and $4,000 in a savings account, which are both joint tenancy accounts. They each own other separate property. Both Jean and Darnell are salaried employees and contributed equal sums to purchase the home and to the checking and savings accounts. Jean dies without a will. As the sole surviving joint tenant, Darnell will receive all the joint tenancy property, which was the couple's intent. Jean's individual or separate property has to go through probate. The tax consequences in such cases will be discussed in the tax chapter (see Chapter 11). A more complex problem could result, however, if the unmarried couple were to die in a common disaster and both die intestate.

- Life insurance

  EXAMPLE: As another example of a will substitute, assume that Tierra, a single parent, had only one major asset, a $100,000 life insurance policy through a group plan with premiums paid equally by Tierra and her employer. Her son, Christian, is named as sole beneficiary. If Tierra dies testate or intestate, Christian will receive the proceeds of the life insurance policy, which do not go through the probate process. Under current tax law, the proceeds are not taxable income or a gift to Christian, so no income or gift taxes are owed (see Chapter 14).

transfer-on-death deed or beneficiary deed
A type of deed, properly executed and recorded, that allows the transfer of real property to a designated beneficiary without probate. The transfer does not take effect until the death of the owner.

joint tenancy
Ownership of real or personal property by two or more persons with the right of survivorship.

- *Inter* vivos (living) trust

  EXAMPLE: Serena owns an apartment building valued at $300,000. During her lifetime she places this property in an *inter vivos* (living) trust, naming her brother, Garrett, trustee, and two friends, Vaughn and Renee, beneficiaries. In the trust instrument, Serena directs the trustee to pay the income from the trust property—the apartment building—to the beneficiaries, Vaughn and Renee, during their lifetimes and, at the death of the last of the two to survive, to convey the apartment building and land to the children of Renee (Jayden and Cody) as tenants in common. Even if Serena dies testate or intestate, the distribution of the trust income and the trust property will be determined by the trust instrument. Any remaining property in Serena's estate at her death will be distributed according to the provisions of her will or according to the state intestate succession statute. For a more complete discussion of the use of an *inter vivos* (living) trust as a substitute for a will, see Chapter 13.

- *Inter vivos gift*

  EXAMPLE: Anyone may dispose of property while alive by gift. During his lifetime, Sherman gives to his relatives and friends $100,000 in cash, $50,000 in stocks and bonds, a pickup truck, and his collection of Chinese figurines. Once these gifts are delivered (executed) Sherman has no legal right to demand their return. Gift taxes may be due and payable on the *inter vivos* gifts if Sherman exceeds the current $ $14,000 per donee annual exclusion. The exclusion is indexed annually for inflation and may change. Annual gifts over a lifetime can reduce the size of the donor's estate and result in death tax savings. For a complete discussion of the gift tax laws, see Chapters 11 and 14.

- *Community* property agreement

  EXAMPLE: The state of Washington has a document authorized under its community property law called the "community property agreement." The agreement acts as a will substitute and is often used by a married couple domiciled in Washington to transfer, at the death of the first spouse, all the community estate to the surviving spouse without the necessity of probate. These agreements, with varying provisions, are also used in Alaska, Idaho, Texas, and Wisconsin.

- Transfer-on-*death* deed or beneficiary deed

  EXAMPLE: Missouri authorizes the use of a beneficiary deed to avoid probate. This type of deed conveys an interest in real property to a designated beneficiary that does not take effect until the death of the owner. It is legal only if executed and recorded with the recorder of deeds where the real property is located (see Mo. Rev. Stat. § 461.025). In addition to Missouri, the states of Arkansas, Arizona, Colorado, Kansas, Nevada, New Mexico, and Ohio have authorized the use of either a transfer-on-death deed or beneficiary deed (see Exhibit 2.3). Several other states are considering the use of these deeds.

CHECKLIST TO DETERMINE THE NEED FOR A WILL

To determine whether a client needs a will, the following questions should be answered.

1. What property does the client own?

2. Where is the property located? Will a **domiciliary administration** be the only one required?

domiciliary administration
The administration of an estate in the state where the decedent was domiciled at the time of death.

EXHIBIT 2.3	Transfer-on-Death Deed

TRANSFER-ON-DEATH DEED

_____, (marital status) as owner, transfers on death to

_____ as grantee beneficiary (beneficiaries) the following

described interest in real estate located in _____ County, Kansas:

Except and subject to:

THIS TRANSFER-ON-DEATH DEED IS REVOCABLE. IT DOES NOT TRANSFER ANY OWNERSHIP UNTIL THE DEATH OF THE OWNER. IT REVOKES ALL PRIOR BENEFICIARY DESIGNATION BY THIS OWNER FOR THIS INTEREST.

This TOD is made pursuant to K.S.A. 59-3501 _et seq._

_____
Grantor

_____
Grantor

Dated: _____

STATE OF _____)) SS. COUNTY OF _____) This Transfer-on-Death Deed was acknowledged before me on _____, _____, by (marital status) dated _____, _____. (SEAL) _____ Printed Name: _____ Notary Public My Appointment Expires: _____ Pursuant to K.S.A. 79-1437e, a real estate validation questionnaire is not required due to Exception No. _____ (complete if applicable).	Reserved for Register of Deeds

017D-10/97

3. In what form of ownership, e.g., severalty (sole ownership), joint tenancy, or tenancy in common, is the property held?

4. Is the client aware of the intestate succession statute that determines who would take the property if the client died without a will? Would the client be content with these persons receiving the property, or does the client desire to leave the property to someone else, e.g., a close friend or institutions such as a church or a charity?

5. Are specific items of real or personal property to be given to certain beneficiaries or devisees?

6. Does the client wish to establish a testamentary trust for the purpose of maintaining an income for a surviving spouse, elderly parent, minor child, or spendthrift relative?

7. Is there a need for a guardian to be appointed for property or the person of minor children or incompetent persons?

8. Does the client want to select a personal representative (executor or executrix) to handle the administration of the estate?

9. Has the client considered the possible tax consequences to the estate, with or without a will, and to the beneficiaries, devisees, or heirs?

10. Does the client want any taxes owed, including state inheritance taxes, to be paid out of specific estate assets?

11. What powers and authority does the client wish to bestow on the personal representative (executor), guardian, conservator, or trustee?

12. If married, and the client and spouse were to die in a common disaster, have the consequences to their respective estates been considered?

13. Does the client want to avoid the probate process and its corresponding expenses and delays?

14. Is the client aware that probate files may be open to the public?

BASIC REQUIREMENTS FOR A LEGAL WILL—A REVIEW

The testator must have the following:

- Legal capacity—generally age 18 or older
- Testamentary capacity—be of sound mind (sanity)

The will must

- be written, i.e., typewritten, computer generated and printed (today's method), or handwritten (allowed in some states).
- be signed by the testator usually in the presence of witnesses.
- be dated (in most states).
- be attested and signed by two witnesses.
- select a personal representative (executor or executrix) to administer the decedent's estate.

See a detailed discussion of these requirements in Chapter 4.

THE NEED FOR A WILL—A CONCLUSION

In summary, there are numerous reasons why so many Americans die without a will. They include the following:

1. Some people, by statute, cannot make a valid will, e.g., minors and incompetent persons.

2. Everyone does not need a will. Some people have limited or no property; others have no heirs (and believe they have no need); and some are satisfied with the "will" their state makes for them, i.e., the intestate succession statute.

3. Some attempt to create a will, but it is declared invalid by the probate court due to improper execution.

4. Some people, concerned about the cost of a will or their reluctance to discuss their finances, procrastinate too long and die prematurely. Others simply do not bother.

5. Some use "will substitutes" instead of wills to distribute the decedent's estate.

As Chapter 1 explains, the need for a will is determined by the kind of property the individual possesses and the form of the possessor's ownership.

Key Terms

testament	surviving spouse	*inter vivos* or living trust
estate plan	apportionment clause	trust
disposition	residuary estate	settlor
will	legatee	legal title [of a trust]
statutes	pro rata	trustee
legal capacity	tenancy in common	beneficiary [of a trust]
testamentary capacity	tenant in common	equitable title [of a trust]
testator (male)/testatrix (female)	intestate succession statutes	bypass trust
sound mind	guardian	principal
execution of a valid will	spouse's statutory, forced or elective share	federal estate tax
holographic will		income
beneficiary [of a will]	ward	public (charitable) trust
formal probate	incompetent person	personal representative
informal probate	personal guardian	executor or executrix
Uniform Probate Code (UPC)	property guardian	administrator or administratrix
probate court	fiduciary	transfer-on-death deed or beneficiary deed
domicile	heir	
real property	fiduciary duty	joint tenancy
ambulatory	adoptive parent	domiciliary administration
codicil	conservator	
letter of instructions	testamentary trust	

Review Questions

1. Explain the reasons why many Americans die without wills.

2. What does it mean to say the maker of a will has testamentary capacity? How does it differ from legal capacity?

3. List your state's statutory requirements for the execution of a will. How do your state's requirements for a valid will differ from those of other states?

4. Since the terminology included in this chapter is essential to your understanding of legal concepts and procedures presented in future chapters and your practice in the fields of wills, trusts, and estates, write out your own definition of each key term in this chapter. Are your definitions essentially the same as those in the text?

5. Can a will be changed or revoked? Explain.

6. List and explain the various reasons or purposes for making a will.

7. Identify six examples of "will substitutes" and discuss how each might possibly be used to eliminate the need for a will.

Case Problems

Problem 1

Cho Wang handwrote a three-page will in pencil. At the end of the business day, he took the will to an attorney and asked that it be typed. Since Cho mentioned that he was leaving on a vacation and would be out of state for one week, the paralegal for the firm asked if he would like to sign the hand-written (holographic) will. Cho did sign the will, but he also stated that he would return after his trip to sign "his will," i.e., the typed will. While on vacation, Cho became ill and died. Answer the following:

A. Is a signed holographic will a valid will in your state?

B. Are witnesses required for a holographic will?

C. Should the executed holographic will operate as Cho's will pending the execution of the typewritten will? Explain. See and compare *In re Teubert's Estate*, 171 W.Va. 226, 298 S. E.2d 456 (1982).

Problem 2

Raj Gupta died testate. He was survived by 27 nieces and nephews. Raj had little formal education and had not learned how to write his signature; therefore, he signed his name with a mark, i.e., an "X." Raj's nieces and nephews challenged the validity of his will. They claimed the will had been improperly executed because he signed with an "X."

A. Is a testator's mark, i.e., an "X," sufficient to satisfy the signature requirement for a valid will in your state? Cite the statute or case law.

B. In your opinion, if there is no statute or case law on this issue in your state, how should your state court decide this issue? See and compare *In re Hobelsberger's Estate*, 85 S.D. 282, 181 N.W.2d 455 (1970).

Practical Assignments

1. Draft a clause that would be included in a Letter of Instruction that contains instructions regarding the donation of your organs upon death.

2. Locate your state statute regarding intestate succession. Apply the statute to your estate to determine who would inherit from you if you died without a will.

3. Examine the Last Will and Testament of Elvis Presley, which can be found at http://www.ibiblio.org/elvis/elvwill.html. Who did Elvis appoint as the executor of his estate? Did Elvis name an alternate executor? If so, who?

Outline

Objectives

After completing this chapter, you should be able to:

- Recognize, understand, and explain the basic terms, including the difference between orthodox (traditional) and UPC terminology, associated with testacy and intestacy.

- Read a will and identify the parties and gifts using both orthodox (traditional) and UPC terminology.

- Recognize and identify lineal and collateral relationships and determine who is entitled to receive a decedent's property under state intestate succession statutes.

- Understand the difference between the right of heirs of an intestate to take their share of the estate per capita or per stirpes.

- Explain the process of escheat.

- Explain the intestate succession statutory rights of family members versus the spouse's election rights when a decedent spouse dies with a will.

- Identify the advantages and disadvantages of a will.

SCOPE OF THE CHAPTER

Chapters 1 and 2 defined the basic terms associated with death with a will (testacy) and death without a will (intestacy) and identified the fiduciaries (personal representative, executor, administrator, trustee, and guardian) who are named in a will or appointed by the probate court. By now you are familiar with these and other terms such as decedent, intestate, and testator or testatrix. If your memory needs refreshing, review these terms in the opening chapters.

succession
The act of acquiring property of a decedent by will or by operation of law when the person dies intestate.

Before wills and trusts are drafted and the required forms for the administration of a decedent's estate are identified and executed, you need to add more terms to your basic vocabulary. This chapter defines the terms associated with the individuals and proceedings involved in the law of **succession**. The law explains how and to whom a decedent's property is distributed whether a person dies with or without a will. This acquired knowledge and the guidance of your supervising attorney will prepare you to perform your future tasks of drafting preliminary wills, trusts, and the numerous forms required for estate administration. Two sets of terminology, orthodox (traditional) and the Uniform Probate Code, used in the practice of law and by legal writers are identified, defined, and discussed. Both will be included throughout the remainder of the text.

First to be discussed are terms related to testacy—death with a will. A sample will is included with an illustrative review of the terminology. Next, terms that relate to death without a will—intestacy—are discussed, and the use of intestate terminology is also illustrated. The chapter concludes with a list of the advantages and disadvantages of wills.

DEATH WITH A WILL—TESTACY

When death occurs, it is necessary to determine whether the decedent died testate or intestate. These terms refer to death with a valid will (**testacy**) or without a valid will (**intestacy**). The difference in the way and to whom property is distributed between testacy and intestacy is significant whenever the decedent's will is challenged, for example, in a will contest. If the challenge is successful and the will is declared invalid, the state intestate succession statute or a previous will determines who receives the decedent's property. These recipients may be entirely different from those individuals named in the contested will.

testacy
Death with a valid will.

intestacy
Death without a valid will.

When a will exists, your training, experience, and investigatory skills should enable you to determine, with verification by your supervising attorney, if the will is valid, e.g., whether it was properly drafted and executed. If it is not valid, you must analyze and accurately apply your state's intestate succession statute to determine to whom the property will be distributed. Even when a will exists, its distribution provisions may not dispose of some probate property; for example, the will may not include a residuary clause. In such cases, the forgotten, overlooked, or excluded property not disposed of by the will passes by the state's intestate succession statute. To learn how to collect the requisite information and prepare the preliminary draft of a client's will, you must understand certain basic terms.

Terminology Related to Wills

In general, two different types of terminology are used for wills.

- *Orthodox or traditional terminology.* Orthodox terminology refers to the traditional words related to wills and probate matters that were used universally before the adoption into law of the **Uniform Probate Code (UPC)**.

The purpose of the UPC is primarily to

- *simplify* and clarify the law, terms, and procedures in estate administration.
- *lessen* the expense and time for the administration.
- *provide* an alternative system, which, if adopted by the states, establishes uniform law.

States are not required to adopt the Code, although they are free to adopt it individually through their legislatures.

- *UPC terminology.* The Code presents for adoption an alternative plan for probate procedures and new terminology for wills and estate administration. Many states have either adopted or modified the UPC or use the terminology it recommends. States that have adopted the UPC, or a modified version, include the following:

Alaska	Idaho	Montana	South Carolina
Arizona	Maine	Nebraska	South Dakota
Colorado	Massachusetts	New Jersey	Utah
Florida	Michigan	New Mexico	
Hawaii	Minnesota	North Dakota	

Most states use a combination of UPC and orthodox terminology. Exhibit 3.1 lists both the traditional and UPC terms used in testacy and intestacy cases.

Wills are divided into four basic types and a separate document called a living will.

Holographic (Also Called an Olographic) Will

A holographic will is written in the maker's own handwriting. About half of the states and the UPC allow holographic wills; generally, such wills do not require witnesses or that the will be dated in order to be valid (see UPC § 2–502 and Exhibit 3.2). Compare Nev. Rev. Stat. § 133.090 and Okla. Stat. Ann. tit. 84 § 54, two states that require a date. In the case of *In re Mulkins' Estate,* 17 Ariz. App. 179, 496 P.2d 605 (1972), the court held the handwritten words by the decedent on a publisher's will form was a valid holographic will. Many states require some or all of the following for a holographic will to be valid.

- The will must be "entirely" handwritten by the testator.
- The testator must have a clear intent to make a will.
- The testator's signature must be placed in a specific part of the will, e.g., at the "foot" or end of the will.
- The will must be dated.

Valid holographic wills have been written on envelopes, cabinet tops, and even petticoats. Audiotape or audio videotape recordings and typewritten wills are

Uniform Probate Code (UPC)
A uniform law available for adoption by the states to modernize and improve the efficiency of the administration of a decedent's estate.

Exhibit 3.1   Orthodox (Traditional) and UPC Terminology Compared

Testacy Terminology	Orthodox	UPC
Person appointed to administer an estate when there is a will	Executor (man) Executrix (woman)	Personal representative
Gift of money by will	Legacy	Devise
Gift of personal property by will (other than money)	Bequest	Devise
Gift of real property by will	Devise	Devise
Recipient of money by will	Legatee	Devisee
Recipient of personal property by will (other than money)	Beneficiary	Devisee
Recipient of real property by will	Devisee	Devisee

Intestacy Terminology	Orthodox	UPC
Person appointed to administer an estate when there is no will	Administrator (man) Administratrix (woman)	Personal representative
Person entitled by statute to real property of intestate	Heir or heir at law	Heir
Person entitled by statute to personal property of intestate	Distributee or next of kin	Heir
Passage of an intestate's property to the state when the decedent has no surviving blood relatives (kin)	Escheat	Escheat

Testacy or Intestacy Terminology	Orthodox	UPC
Person, other than creditors, entitled to the real or personal property of a decedent by will or through intestate succession	No all-inclusive word	Successor
Person, other than a creditor or purchaser, who has actually received real or personal property from the decedent's personal representative	No all-inclusive word	Distributee

generally not recognized as valid holographic wills. See *Matter of Reed's Estate*, 672 P. 2d 829 (Wyo. 1983).

Nuncupative (Oral) Will

nuncupative will
An oral will.

A **nuncupative will** is an oral will spoken in the presence of witnesses; the will is valid only under exceptional circumstances, such as the imminent death of the person "speaking" the will. Nuncupative wills are prohibited in the majority of states (see Exhibit 3.2). However, when they are allowed, they must be probated within a statutory period and can generally pass only a limited amount of personal property of the speaker-testator (see Kan. Stat. Ann. § 59-608 and Tenn. Code Ann. § 32-1-106). Some states allow nuncupative (oral) wills, such as soldiers' and sailors' wills made during military service in time of war; however, a few states do not require formal hostilities; see Va. Code Ann. § 64.1-53, and N.Y. EPTL § 3-2.2(b). The Code does not allow oral wills (UPC § 2–502).

| EXHIBIT 3.2 | Types of Valid Wills by State |

	Holographic	Nuncupative	State's Statutory Will Form	Uniform Statutory Will Act
Alabama	(2) (6)	(6)		
Alaska	Valid	Prohibited		
Arizona	Valid	Prohibited		
Arkansas	Valid	Prohibited		
California	Valid	Prohibited	X	
Colorado	Valid	Prohibited		
Connecticut	(2) (6)	Prohibited		
Delaware	(6)	Prohibited		
Florida	Prohibited	Prohibited		
Georgia	(2)	Prohibited		
Hawaii	Valid	Prohibited		
Idaho	Valid	Prohibited		
Illinois	(2)	Prohibited		
Indiana	(2) (6)	(4) (5)		
Iowa	(2) (6)	Prohibited		
Kansas	(2) (6)	(3) (5)		
Kentucky	Valid	Prohibited		
Louisiana	Valid	(7)	X	
Maine	Valid	Prohibited	X	
Maryland	(1)	Prohibited		
Massachusetts (8)	(2) (6)	(1)		X
Michigan	Valid	Prohibited	X	
Minnesota	(6)	Prohibited		
Mississippi	Valid	(3) (5)		
Missouri	Prohibited	(4) (5)		
Montana	Valid	Prohibited		
Nebraska	Valid	Prohibited		
Nevada	Valid	(3) (5)		
New Hampshire	Prohibited	(1) (3) (5)		
New Jersey	Valid	Prohibited		
New Mexico	(6)	(6)		X
New York	(1)	(1)		
North Carolina	Valid	(3) (4) (5)		
North Dakota	Valid	Prohibited		
Ohio	Prohibited	(3) (5)		
Oklahoma	Valid	(1) (4) (5)		
Oregon	Prohibited	Prohibited		
Pennsylvania	(2)	Prohibited		
Rhode Island	(1) (6)	Prohibited		
South Carolina	(6)	Prohibited		
South Dakota	Valid	(1) (4) (5)		
Tennessee	Valid	(4) (5)		
Texas	Valid	Prohibited		
Utah	Valid	Prohibited		
Vermont	Prohibited	(5)		
Virginia	Valid	(1)		
Washington	(6)	(3) (5)		
West Virginia	Valid	(1)		
Wisconsin	(2) (6)	Prohibited	X	
Wyoming	Valid	Prohibited		

(1) Prohibited except for mariners at sea or for military exceptions, e.g., armed forces members in actual service or during armed conflict.
(2) Prohibited unless it meets execution requirements, e.g., witnesses.
(3) Applies to anyone during their last illness.
(4) Applies to anyone in imminent peril of death and who dies from that peril.
(5) Prohibited unless declared in the presence of witnesses, reduced to writing, and/or probated within statutory periods.
(6) Prohibited unless valid where executed.
(7) See La. Code of Civ. Proc. Art. 2884 and Art.150 et. Seq.

Statutory Will

statutory will
A fill-in-the-blank will that is created and authorized by statute in a few states.

A **statutory will** fulfills all the state's mandatory formal requirements for a will, which include the following: the will must be written or typed; signed and dated by the testator; and attested and signed by at least two witnesses. A statutory will is a fill-in-the-blank will and is an official legal document printed in the state statute for exclusive use in the testator's domiciliary state.

Some states, including California, Maine, Michigan, and Wisconsin, have developed their own unique statutory wills (see Exhibits 3.2, 3.3, and 5.7). Other states, like Massachusetts and New Mexico, have adopted the Uniform Statutory Will Act (see N.M. Stat. Ann. § 45-2A-17). Louisiana refers to its statutory wills as "notarial testaments" (see La. Stat. Ann. C.C. 1576). Statutory wills are inexpensive and easy to execute. *However, the options provided in a preprinted statutory form are often limited.* Most of the decedent's property must go to spouses and children since the form has few, if any, options for close friends or charitable and religious organizations and they cannot be amended to comply with alternative or additional estate plans. Therefore, spouses and children are the primary individuals for whom statutory wills are appropriate.

Joint and Mutual (Reciprocal) Wills

joint will
A will for spouses that consists of a single document signed by them as their will.

mutual (reciprocal) wills
Separate and identical wills made by spouses that contain reciprocal provisions and agree that neither spouse will change his or her will after the death of the first spouse.

When one document is made the will of two persons (usually spouses) and signed by them, a **joint will** is created. The joint will is probated twice—on the death of each spouse. **Mutual (reciprocal) wills** are usually the separate and identical wills of spouses who make reciprocal provisions in each will and agree that neither spouse will change his or her will after the death of the first spouse. Many problems are created by these two types of wills, especially if the spouses divorce or one dies and the other spouse remarries and decides to make a different will or wishes to revoke the original joint or mutual will. An additional problem is created for spouses with mutual wills. After the death of the first spouse, the problem emerges if the surviving spouse decides to make substantial gifts of their combined estate assets to beneficiaries other than those named in the mutual wills. This may not change the terms of the mutual will, but it most assuredly changes the distribution of the estate. Most attorneys do not recommend or use joint or mutual wills.

living will
A document, separate from a will, that expresses a person's wish to be allowed to die a natural death and not be kept alive by artificial means.

Living will. A **living will** is a separate legal document from the standard will. When the maker of a living will is no longer able to make decisions regarding medical treatment, the living will governs withholding or withdrawal of life-sustaining treatment in the event of an incurable or irreversible condition that will cause death within a short time. For further discussion and an example of a living will, see Chapter 6.

Types of Dispositions—Gifts Made in a Will

A will's dispositions are the various ways property is conveyed by the will. Dispositions include gifts that are called bequests, legacies, or devises.

Bequest, Legacy, or Devise

According to traditional terminology, a bequest or legacy is a gift of personal property, and a devise is a gift of real property. When gifts are made by a will, they are called a specific legacy or a specific devise. In cases in which a testator has mistakenly used the wrong term in connection with the transfer of real or personal estate property, e.g., "I *bequeath* my home to my daughter, Sarah," or "I *devise* my books and paintings to my son, Benjamin," the courts have consistently upheld such gifts

EXHIBIT 3.3 Wisconsin Basic Will

Signature of Testator ....

WISCONSIN BASIC WILL OF

....
(Insert Your Name)

Article 1. Declaration.

This is my will and I revoke any prior wills and codicils (additions to prior wills).

Article 2. Disposition of My Property

2.1 PERSONAL, RECREATIONAL AND HOUSEHOLD ITEMS. Except as provided in paragraph 2.2, I give all my furniture, furnishings, household items, recreational equipment, personal automobiles and personal effects to my spouse, if living; otherwise they shall be divided equally among my children who survive me.

2.2 GIFTS TO PERSONS OR CHARITIES. I make the following gifts to the persons or charities in the cash amount stated in words (. . . . . . Dollars) and figures ($ . . . . . .) or of the property described. I SIGN IN EACH BOX USED. I WRITE THE WORDS "NOT USED" IN THE REMAINING BOXES. If I fail to sign opposite any gift, then no gift is made. If the person mentioned does not survive me or if the charity does not accept the gift, then no gift is made.

FULL NAME OF PERSON OR CHARITY TO RECEIVE GIFT. (Name only one. Please print.)	AMOUNT OF CASH GIFT OR DESCRIPTION OF PROPERTY.	SIGNATURE OF TESTATOR. ....
FULL NAME OF PERSON OR CHARITY TO RECEIVE GIFT. (Name only one. Please print.)	AMOUNT OF CASH GIFT OR DESCRIPTION OF PROPERTY.	SIGNATURE OF TESTATOR. ....
FULL NAME OF PERSON OR CHARITY TO RECEIVE GIFT. (Name only one. Please print.)	AMOUNT OF CASH GIFT OR DESCRIPTION OF PROPERTY.	SIGNATURE OF TESTATOR. ....
FULL NAME OF PERSON OR CHARITY TO RECEIVE GIFT. (Name only one. Please print.)	AMOUNT OF CASH GIFT OR DESCRIPTION OF PROPERTY.	SIGNATURE OF TESTATOR. ....
FULL NAME OF PERSON OR CHARITY TO RECEIVE GIFT. (Name only one. Please print.)	AMOUNT OF CASH GIFT OR DESCRIPTION OF PROPERTY.	SIGNATURE OF TESTATOR. ....

(continued)

EXHIBIT 3.3   (continued)

2.3 ALL OTHER ASSETS (MY "RESIDUARY ESTATE"). I adopt only one Property Disposition Clause in this paragraph by writing my signature on the line next to the title of the Property Disposition Clause I wish to adopt. I SIGN ON ONLY ONE LINE. I WRITE THE WORDS "NOT USED" ON THE REMAINING LINE. If I sign on more than one line or if I fail to sign on any line, the property will go under Property Disposition Clause (b) and I realize that means the property will be distributed as if I did not make a will in accordance with Chapter 852 of the Wisconsin Statutes.

PROPERTY DISPOSITION CLAUSES *(Select one.)*

(a) TO MY SPOUSE IF LIVING; IF NOT
LIVING, THEN TO MY CHILDREN
AND THE DESCENDANTS OF ANY
DECEASED CHILD BY RIGHT OF
REPRESENTATION.   ....

(b) TO BE DISTRIBUTED AS IF I DID NOT
HAVE A WILL.   ....

Article 3. Nominations of Personal Representative and Guardian

3.1 PERSONAL REPRESENTATIVE. *(Name at least one.)*
I nominate the person or institution named in the first box of this paragraph to serve as my personal representative. If that person or institution does not serve, then I nominate the others to serve in the order I list them in the other boxes. I confer upon my personal representative the authority to do and perform any act which he or she determines is in the best interest of the estate, with no limitations. This provision shall be given the broadest possible construction. This authority includes, but is not limited to, the power to borrow money, pledge assets, vote stocks and participate in reorganizations, to sell or exchange real or personal property, and to invest funds and retain securities without any limitation by law for investments by fiduciaries.

FIRST PERSONAL REPRESENTATIVE

SECOND PERSONAL REPRESENTATIVE

THIRD PERSONAL REPRESENTATIVE

3.2 GUARDIAN. *(If you have a child under 18 years of age, you should name at least one guardian of the child.)*
If my spouse dies before I do or if for any other reason a guardian is needed for any child of mine, then I nominate the person named in the first box of this paragraph to serve as guardian of the person and estate of that child. If the person does not serve, then I nominate the person named in the second box of this paragraph to serve as guardian of that child.

FIRST GUARDIAN

SECOND GUARDIAN

Signature of Testator ....

EXHIBIT 3.3 (continued)

3.3 BOND.
My signature in this box means I request that a bond, as set by law, be required for each individual personal representative or guardian named in this will. IF I DO NOT SIGN IN THIS BOX, I REQUEST THAT A BOND NOT BE REQUIRED FOR ANY OF THOSE PERSONS.

I sign my name to this Wisconsin Basic will on ....(date), at ....(city), ...(state).

....
Signature of Testator

STATEMENT OF WITNESSES *(You must use two adult witnesses.)*

EACH OF US DECLARES THAT THE TESTATOR SIGNED THIS WISCONSIN BASIC WILL IN OUR PRESENCE, ALL OF US BEING PRESENT AT THE SAME TIME, AND WE NOW, AT THE TESTATOR'S REQUEST, IN THE TESTATOR'S PRESENCE AND IN THE PRESENCE OF EACH OTHER. SIGN BELOW AS WITNESSES, DECLARING THAT THE TESTATOR APPEARS TO BE OF SOUND MIND AND UNDER NO UNDUE INFLUENCE.

Signature...................................
Print Name
Here:...

Residence Address: ....
....

Signature...................................
Print Name
Here:...

Residence Address: ....
....

....
Signature of Testator

Source: Wisconsin Legal Blank Co., Inc. Reprinted with permission.

because of the unmistakable intention of the testator. Therefore, the terms can be used interchangeably or applied to either real or personal property if the context of the will clearly indicates that such was the testator's intent. The states that have adopted the UPC use one term, *devise*, to include the transfer of all gifts of real or personal property by will. The next paragraphs define and explain the categories of dispositions of a will: specific legacy, specific devise, demonstrative legacy, general legacy, and residuary legacy or devise.

Specific Legacy

specific legacy or bequest
A gift of a particular item or class of personal property in a will.

A **specific legacy** (also called a **specific bequest** or, in states that have adopted the UPC, a specific devise) is a gift of a particular item or class of personal property in a will.

> **EXAMPLE:** In his will, Kevin Williams states
>
> 1. "I give my Buick to my daughter, Marilyn Williams, if she survives me."
>
> 2. "I give my gun and stamp collections to my son, Ian Williams, if he survives me."
>
> 3. "I give my grand piano and all my sheet music to my niece, Theresa Anderson, if she survives me."
>
> 4. "I give one half of all the rest of my tangible personal property, that has not otherwise been specifically mentioned heretofore in this will, to my spouse, Elizabeth Williams, if she survives me. If my said spouse, Elizabeth Williams, does not survive me, I give the above-mentioned property to my children, Marilyn Williams and Ian Williams, in equal shares." (This is an example of a gift of a class of property.)
>
> 5. I give my blog and all revenue earned from the advertising to my daughter, Daphne Christian.

A specific legacy is the only type of testamentary gift subject to ademption (see discussion below).

Specific Devise

specific devise
A gift of real property in a will. Under the UPC, a gift of real or personal property in a will.

A **specific devise** is traditionally a gift of real property in a will. In states that have adopted the UPC, a specific devise includes a gift of real or personal property in a will.

> **EXAMPLES:** In his will, Kevin Williams states, "I give my homestead at 4645 Fair Hills Lane, City of Kendallville, County of Noble, State of Indiana, and legally described as 'Lot 7, Block 4, of Hillstrom's Addition to Stone Valley' to my spouse, Elizabeth Williams, if she survives me. If she does not survive me, I give the hereinbefore described homestead to my son, Ian Williams, if he survives me."

Demonstrative Legacy

demonstrative legacy
A gift or bequest of a specific monetary amount to be paid from the sale of a particular item of property or from some identifiable fund.

A **demonstrative legacy** is a gift of a specific monetary amount to be paid from the proceeds of the sale of a particular item of property or from some identifiable fund.

> **EXAMPLES:** In his will, Kevin Williams states
>
> 1. "I give $2,000 to be paid from the *sale* of my U.S. savings bonds to my nephew, Aaron Anderson, if he survives me."
>
> 2. "I give $5,000 to be paid out of my savings account on deposit in First State Bank, 1204 Main Street, City of Astoria, County of Clatsop, State of Oregon, to my niece, Theresa Anderson, if she survives me."

A demonstrative legacy differs from a specific legacy as follows: If the fund from which the demonstrative legacy is to be paid has diminished or is nonexistent when the testator dies, the payment can come out of other estate funds the same as a general legacy. A demonstrative legacy differs from a general legacy as follows: It does not *abate*, i.e., it is not subject to unpaid debts as is a general legacy, but is instead used to pay debts like a specific legacy (see discussion of abatement below).

Since demonstrative legacies are similar to both specific and general legacies, the distinction between them can be difficult and lead to confusion. Therefore, drafters seldom include demonstrative legacies in wills. The court in the case of *In re Jeffcott's Estate*, 186 So.2d 80 (Fla.App. 1966), identifies and distinguishes general and demonstrative legacies.

General Legacy

A **general legacy** (also called a pecuniary bequest) is a gift of a fixed amount of money from the general assets of the testator's estate or an amount of money derived from a source established in the estate by a calculated formula.

> **EXAMPLES:** In his will, Kevin Williams states
>
> 1. "I give the sum of $20,000 to my niece, Theresa Anderson, if she survives me."
>
> 2. "I give one-half of all the value of the stock I own at the time of my death to my daughter, Marilyn Williams, if she survives me." (Calculations are necessary to determine the actual amount Marilyn will receive.)

general legacy
A gift of a fixed amount of money from the general assets of the estate.

Residuary Legacy or Devise

A gift of all the testator's personal property not otherwise effectively disposed of by a will is a **residuary legacy** and a gift of all the real property not disposed of is a **residuary devise**.

A residuary clause distributes the remaining assets (the residue) of the decedent-testator's estate after all other gifts in the will have been distributed. A residuary clause is the most important clause in a will because it generally passes the bulk of the decedent's estate after the payment of debts, taxes, and costs of administration and the distribution of specific, demonstrative, and general legacies. It is essential that every will include a residuary clause; otherwise all remaining assets, whether inadvertently overlooked, omitted, forgotten, or acquired after execution of the current will, pass through intestate succession statutes. Clearly, this would not reflect the intent of the will's maker since it defeats the will's purpose.

residuary legacy or devise
A gift of all the testator's personal property not otherwise effectively disposed of by a will is a residuary legacy, and a gift of all the real property not disposed of is a residuary devise.

> **EXAMPLE:** In his will, Kevin Williams states, "I give all the rest, residue, and remainder of my estate, including all real and personal property wherever located that is not previously disposed of by this will, to my wife, Elizabeth Williams, if she survives me. If she does not survive me, I give this, my residuary estate, to my children, Marilyn Williams and Ian Williams, in equal shares."

If the decedent does not include any specific, demonstrative, or general legacies in the will, a gift by Kevin Williams that states "I give all my real and personal property to my daughter, Marilyn Williams" acts as a residuary clause.

If any beneficiaries of the will, especially those named in the residuary clause, predecease the testator, the will should be reviewed and new or successor beneficiaries added to avoid passage of the property through intestate succession.

These changes, even if minor, can best be accomplished by the creation of a new will using word-processing computer software.

Another important function of the residuary clause is that after any intestate property of the decedent, it serves as the next, and generally the major, source of payment of the decedent's debts, death taxes, and funeral, burial, and administration expenses. If property (funds) from the residue is insufficient to pay these debts and taxes, other gifts in the will are used to satisfy these obligations (see Abatement below).

Ademption, Lapses, and Abatement

The gifts (legacies or devises) distributed by will can be affected by ademption, lapses, and abatement.

Ademption

Whether a legacy, bequest, or devise, gifts of property made in a will may not be available for transfer to the named beneficiaries or devisees because the testator no longer owns the property at the time of death. After execution of the will, the testator, by an intentional act of **ademption**, has the right to

ademption
The intentional act of the testator, while alive, to revoke, recall, or cancel a gift made through the will or deliver the gift or a substitute to the beneficiary.

- revoke or cancel any testamentary gift.
- deliver the gift to the beneficiary or someone else before the testator's death.
- substitute a different gift for the original one.

As a result, the beneficiary or devisee does not receive the original gift through the will, and other property of the estate passes to the beneficiary or devisee as a substitute for the **adeemed** gift, *only if* the testator so indicated in the will or delivered the substitute gift before death. Of the three types of legacies, only the specific legacy is subject to ademption; however, in some states, a specific devise can be adeemed if the intention is expressed by the testator in writing as required by a state statute.

adeem
To take away, extinguish, revoke, or satisfy a legacy or devise by delivery of the gift or a substitute to the beneficiary by the testator before death.

Ademption can occur by extinction or by satisfaction. Ademption by extinction occurs when the property is either nonexistent (destroyed by storm, fire, and the like) at the time of the testator's death or is given or sold by the testator to someone other than the person named in the will.

EXAMPLES:

1. In her will, Chandra leaves Alfonso her champion thoroughbred racehorse, Secretary. Secretary dies before Chandra. The gift of the horse is "adeemed" by extinction.

2. In her will, Chandra leaves Alfonso the horse, but she sells or gives the horse to another person before she dies. Again, the gift of the horse is "adeemed" by extinction.

See *Shriner's Hospital v. Stahl*, 610 S.W.2d 147 (Tex. 1980), in which the court ruled that a specific devise of property was "adeemed" when the testatrix sold the property before her death, and the proceeds of the sale passed under the residuary clause of her will.

Ademption by satisfaction occurs when the testator, while living, gives the gift in the will to the named beneficiary with the stated intent in writing that the gift will not be replaced with a substitute or additional gift.

EXAMPLE: In her will, Chandra leaves Benedict her Renoir painting. Chandra decides to give Benedict the painting on his birthday. When she delivers the painting to him, Chandra adeems the specific legacy by satisfaction.

Lapses

A **lapse** is the failure to pass or distribute a gift in a will because the beneficiary or devisee dies before the testator. The beneficiary's death causes the gift in the will to lapse or fail and fall into the residue of the estate *unless* the will designates an alternate beneficiary or a statute provides for the gift's distribution. Such a state statute, called an **antilapse statute,** passes the gift to the decedent beneficiary's children or heirs who survive the testator. The antilapse statutes of Illinois and Mississippi only pass the gift to the decedent beneficiary's heirs if the beneficiary is the descendant of the testator. Most states' antilapse statutes have expanded the eligible heirs who can receive the gift, but no state includes, as an heir, the spouse of the decedent beneficiary. If a testator wants to avoid the application of an antilapse statute, the words in the following clause accomplish that objective.

"I give my Picasso painting to my daughter, Irene Benson, if she shall survive me."

If Irene dies before the testator, an antilapse statute would not apply for the benefit of Irene's children or heirs because of the above clause, "if she shall survive me." Instead, the Picasso painting becomes part of the residue of the estate and is passed to the persons named as beneficiaries in the residuary clause of the will.

However, if the testator wants a successor to receive the gift if the beneficiary predeceases the testator, the clause would state

"… to Irene Benson, if she shall survive me, if she does not survive me, to my son, Howard Benson, if he shall survive me."

Abatement

Abatement is the proportional reduction of the legacies and devises in a will because of inadequate available funds from the assets of the testator's estate. Abatement determines the order in which gifts (legacies and devises) made by the testator in the will shall be applied to the payment of the decedent-testator's debts, taxes, and expenses. If required, such payments can and most assuredly will cause the gifts made in the will to be reduced or even eliminated. Abatement occurs whenever there are insufficient assets in the testator's estate to pay all the death taxes, funeral, burial, and administration expenses, and other creditors' claims that must be paid before the remaining estate is distributed to beneficiaries and devisees. State statutes list the order in which the various assets and categories of gifts (legacies and devises) are used to pay these debts and taxes. Usually, the order is: first, any intestate property not disposed of by the will; second, residuary assets (legacies and devises); third, general legacies and devises; fourth, demonstrative legacies; and last, specific legacies and devises.

EXAMPLE: In the examples earlier in this chapter, Kevin Williams made specific legacies (his car, gun and stamp collections, piano and sheet music, and all of the rest of his tangible personal property); a specific devise (his home); demonstrative legacies (sums of money from the sale of bonds or from an identifiable fund); general legacies (cash and money from a calculated source); and a final residuary gift. Kevin dies. Before any of the property listed in the will can be distributed,

---

lapse
Failure to distribute a gift in a will because the beneficiary or devisee dies before the testator.

antilapse statute
A statute that prevents a lapse (termination) of a clause in a will that would otherwise occur if the beneficiary who was to receive property under the clause dies before the testator.

abatement
The process that determines the order in which gifts made by the testator in the will shall be applied to the payment of the decedent-testator's debts, taxes, and expenses.

Kevin's debts, expenses, and taxes due must be paid. The gifts made in the will, with the exception of the homestead, are used according to the priority order of payment listed in the preceding paragraph.

marshaling of assets
The arrangement or ranking of testamentary gifts into a certain order to be used for the payment of debts.

This arrangement or ranking of testamentary gifts into a certain order to be used for the payment of debts is called **marshaling of assets** of the estate, and the assets used for payment are said to "abate." Generally, personal property is the source of the funds used to pay debts and taxes, but, if necessary, real property must be devested, or taken away, from devisees or heirs by the personal representative and sold to pay the decedent's creditors. In a few states, the decedent's personal property in all categories must be used first before any real property is used to pay debts and taxes due (see Mass. Gen. Laws Ann. ch. 202 § 1). Other states only require that all personal property in each category be used for payments prior to the use of real property within the category (see Tex. Prob. Code Ann. § 322B). Today, the prevailing trend is to use gifts of real and personal property within the same category equally; see Cal. Prob. Code § 10000; N.Y. EPTL § 13-1.3(b); and UPC § 3–902. When property within each category "abates" to pay decedent's debts, the gifts are used for payment on a *prorated basis*.

EXAMPLE: Gemma makes the following testamentary gifts: $2,000 cash to Ayda, a homestead valued at $45,000 to Ralph, and the residue (valued at $8,000) to Sebastian. Expenses, debts, and taxes amount to $12,000. The residue assets would first be applied to payment of expenses, debts, and taxes. Thus, Sebastian would lose all his $8,000. Second, the general gift, i.e., the sum of money left to Ayda ($2,000) would be applied. Ayda would lose all her $2,000. Third, Ralph would be required to pay the remaining deficiency of $2,000, or, depending on the state, the homestead may have to be sold and $2,000 of the proceeds of the sale used to pay the deficiency. Ralph would get the remainder of the proceeds of the sale. If a spouse survives the decedent, however, the spouse will receive the statutory (elective) share of the decedent's estate before any of the other named devisees receive their gifts through the will.

EXAMPLE: Oscar dies and leaves an estate valued at $175,000. It consists of a homestead owned in his name valued at $100,000, $30,000 in cash in a savings account, $30,000 in stocks and bonds, and $15,000 in household furnishings. Oscar leaves his home and $10,000 in cash to his spouse, Evelyn. He leaves $10,000 in cash to his nephew, Alfred, and $10,000 to his niece, Ruby. His administration and funeral expenses, death taxes, and creditors' claims (debts) amount to $60,000. Since these obligations must be paid first (have priority), only $115,000 remains to be distributed among the named beneficiaries and devisees.

In the example above, since insufficient assets remain in the estate to distribute them as Oscar intended, the domiciliary state statute on abatement determines which beneficiaries or devisees lose their gifts. If Oscar's estate is probated in New Jersey, it would have to adhere to the New Jersey abatement statute. This statute is similar to other state laws that determine the order of payment when the decedent's assets are insufficient.

N.J. Stat. Ann. § 3B: 23-12
Abatement for Purpose of Paying Claims and Debts Except as otherwise provided in a decedent's will, the property of a decedent's estate shall abate for the purposes of paying debts and claims, without any preference or priority as between real and personal property, in the following order:
(a) Property passing by intestacy;
(b) Residuary devises;
(c) General devises; and
(d) Specific devises.

USE OF TESTATE TERMINOLOGY

To better understand the meaning and usage of the terms discussed above, read the following facts and the will in Exhibit 3.4.

The Facts

Evonne Bookins has a will. In the will, she leaves a fur coat and her other clothing to a sister, Jade Johnson. Evonne also gives $20,000 to each of her children living at her death. To a cousin, Isaiah Stewart, Evonne leaves her one acre of land in Kennebec County. The sum of $100,000 is left in trust for her surviving grandchildren, to be administered by Glen Howard of the Fullservice Bank. The rest of her estate is given to her husband, Gabriel; however, if he does not survive her, then her surviving children receive the property in equal shares. In the event that Evonne and her husband die in a common disaster before her children are adults, she nominates her sister, Jade, to be their guardian. Viola Larson is named personal representative to manage and distribute the estate according to the will, which is signed and witnessed by Charles Larson and Althea Gibbons.

Review of Terminology

Since Evonne Bookins has a will, on her death, she will die *testate*. For her will to have validity, it must be *executed* carefully to comply with the requirements of state statutes that establish *testate succession*. The fact that Mr. Larson and Ms. Gibbons are required to *attest* and *subscribe* the will is an example of such statutory control.

Evonne Bookins, the *testatrix*, can change her mind and dispose of her estate prior to death in any manner she chooses. She also retains the option to cancel or destroy the will and either substitute a new will in its place or decide not to make a new will, in which event she would die *intestate*.

The *beneficiaries* in her will are Evonne's children and grandchildren living at her death, her sister Jade, cousin Isaiah, and husband Gabriel; these are the persons to whom she intends to leave her estate. Before any of the assets pass to these recipients, the will must be *probated*, i.e., declared by a *probate court* to be a valid testamentary disposition. This procedure for approval of a will and *estate administration* is discussed in detail in later chapters.

The following discussion illustrates the use of both orthodox and UPC terminology. The first term listed is the orthodox term; the corresponding UPC term, if different, is placed in parentheses (review Exhibit 3.1).

Distribution of Evonne's one acre of land is a *specific devise,* a gift of real property by will, and its taker, cousin Isaiah, is a *devisee* (or *successor*). Evonne devised the land to him. The $20,000 to be received by each of Evonne's surviving children, a gift of money, is a *general legacy (devise)*. Evonne's children are *legatees (devisees* or *successors)* of the money. Since she receives personal property under the will, Jade is a *beneficiary (devisee* or *successor),* but distribution of the fur coat and other clothing to her, since it is not money, is known as a *specific legacy* or *specific bequest (devise)*. Evonne bequeathed (devised) the clothing to her. Although it is important to keep the latter distinction in mind, in modern practice the terms *bequest* and *legacy* are used interchangeably. Generally, if orthodox terms such as *bequeath* or *bequest* are used in a will, they stand for a gift of any personal property, including money. In preparing wills today, however, most attorneys prefer to use the phrase *I give* in place of the words *I bequeath* or *I devise*.

EXHIBIT 3.4   Last Will and Testament of Evonne Bookins

I, Evonne Bookins, of the City of Winslow, in the County of Kennebec, and State of Maine, being of sound mind and memory, and not acting under duress, menace, fraud, or undue influence of any person whatsoever, do make, publish, and declare this instrument to be my Last Will and Testament. I do hereby cancel, revoke, and annul all former wills and testaments or codicils made by me.

First: I direct that all my valid debts, last illness, funeral, burial, and estate administration expenses be paid out of my estate as soon as possible after my death;

Specific legacy →

Second: I give my fur coat and all other personal clothing to my sister, Jade Johnson;

Specific devise →

Third: I give my one acre of land with the following legal description, "Lot 1, Block 4, Brauer Addition," located in Kennebec County to my cousin, Isaiah Stewart, and his heirs;

General legacy →

Fourth: I give $20,000 to each of my children living at my death;

Demonstrative legacy →

Fifth: I give $100,000 from the sale of my Picasso painting entitled "Self Portrait" to Glen Howard of the Fullservice Bank to hold in trust for the benefit of my grandchildren. See attached testamentary trust.

Residuary legacy or devise →

Sixth: All the rest, residue, and remainder of my estate, real, personal, or mixed of any kind, and wherever located, of which I die possessed or to which I am entitled at the time of my death, I give to my husband, Gabriel, if he survives me, and if he does not survive me, or we die in a common disaster, I give this, my residuary estate, to my children that survive me in equal shares;

Seventh: In the event of a common disaster in which both my husband and I die, I nominate and appoint my sister, Jade Johnson, to be the personal and property guardian over any of my minor children living at the time of our deaths;

Eighth: Finally, I nominate and appoint Viola Larson to be the personal representative of this my last will and testament and direct that she not be required to give any bond or security for the proper discharge of her duties.

IN TESTIMONY WHEREOF I hereunto set my hand on this *10th* day of *March, 2014.*

[Signature] *Evonne Bookins*
[Address] *11712 Sundown Avenue*

The foregoing instrument, consisting of two pages, including this page, was, on the date hereof, signed, published, and declared by Evonne Bookins, the testatrix above named, at the City of Winslow, County of Kennebec, State of Maine, as and for her last will and testament, in our presence, who, in her presence, at her request, and in the presence of each other hereunto set our names as witnesses.

Names	Addresses
Althea Gibbons	*4656 Gaywood Drive*
Witness	
Charles Larson	*401 Elm Street*
Witness	
	[Signed by two witnesses]

The $100,000 earmarked for the grandchildren is a *demonstrative legacy (devise)* that constitutes a *testamentary trust* (i.e., a trust created by will) and Glen Howard of the bank is its administrator, the *trustee*. Since Viola Larson has been named to manage the estate, she is its *executrix (personal representative)*. Had Viola's husband, Charles, been given the responsibility instead, he would be the *executor (personal representative)* of the estate. Evonne's sister, Jade, has a role beyond that of a *beneficiary (successor)*. As the person designated to care for the testatrix's minor children at her death, if Evonne's husband, Gabriel, is also deceased, Jade is a *guardian* for Evonne's children.

Exhibit 3.5 Last Will and Testament of Adrian Munez

LAST WILL AND TESTAMENT OF ADRIAN MUNEZ

I, Adrian Munez, of the City of <u>St. George,</u> in the County of <u>Washington</u> and State of <u>Utah,</u> being of sound and disposing mind and memory, and not acting under duress, menace, fraud, or undue influence of any person whatsoever, do make, publish, and declare this instrument to be my Last Will and Testament. I do hereby cancel, revoke, and annul all former wills and testaments or codicils made by me at any time.

First: I direct that all my just debts, last illness, funeral, burial, and estate administration expenses be paid out of my estate as soon as possible after my death.

Second: I give to my son, Ignacio, my diamond ring and all my other personal jewelry.

Third: I give to my son, Ignacio, the sum of five thousand dollars.

Fourth: All the rest, residue and remainder of my estate, real, personal, or mixed, of whatsoever character and wheresoever situated, of which I die seized or possessed or to which I am in any way entitled at the time of my death, I give to my wife, Rosa Maria, if she survives me, and if my said wife is not living at the time of my death or we both should die in a common disaster, I give this my residuary estate to my son, Ignacio.

Fifth: I nominate and appoint Richard Leon to be the personal representative of this my last Will and Testament, and I direct that my said personal representative shall not be required to give any bond or security for the proper discharge of his duties.

IN TESTIMONY WHEREOF I hereunto set my hand on this *15th* day of *June, 2014*.

[Signature] _____ *Adrian Munez* _____
[Address] _____ *798 Village Drive* _____

The foregoing instrument, consisting of two pages, including this page, was, on the date hereof, signed, published, and declared by ADRIAN MUNEZ, the testator above named, at the City of St. George, County of Washington, State of Utah, as and for his Last Will and Testament, in our presence, who, in his presence, at his request, and in the presence of each other have hereunto set our names as witnesses.

Tauhna Rios _____ *1054 South Shore Drive*

Regina Dias _____ *917 Hillcrest Street*

[Signed by two witnesses]

Read the Adrian Munez will (Exhibit 3.5) and then answer the following questions.

1. Who is the testator?
2. Is there a testatrix?
3. Did Adrian Munez die testate or intestate?
4. Does the document name a guardian or trustee?
5. Is the document a will or a codicil?
6. What is the diamond ring given to Ignacio called according to the UPC?
7. Is a devisee named in the will?
8. Who are the beneficiaries named in the will?
9. Who is the personal representative?
10. Is there an executrix?
11. Does the document contain a testamentary trust?
12. Has the will been attested and subscribed?
13. Is this an example of a nuncupative or holographic will?
14. How many witnesses are required to sign this will according to your state statute?

DEATH WITHOUT A WILL—INTESTACY

A person who dies without a will dies intestate. He or she is called the intestate. In all states, the distribution of an intestate's estate is determined by state law called the intestate succession statute. Such statutes, in effect, write the will the decedent failed to make and determine the distribution of the intestate's property to the heirs. Each state has its own specific statutes and court decisions that cover and control intestacy. These laws and decisions vary substantially from state to state and identify the heirs, rights of family members, guardianship of minor children, procedures and rules for the administration of the estate, appointment of the personal representative or administrator, and the disposition of the estate property to the surviving spouse and blood relatives of the intestate. The controlling statutes are those of the state in which the intestate was domiciled *and* the states where any *real property* is located.

> **EXAMPLE:** Keola lives in Nebraska, where she owns a house, is registered to vote, has her driver's license, and pays state income tax. Collectively, these factors determine that Nebraska is Keola's true legal home—her domicile. She also owns real property in other states, i.e., a cottage in Wisconsin and a condominium in Florida. If Keola dies intestate, Nebraska's statutes will determine how and by whom her house and personal property will be inherited; however, Wisconsin's statutes will decide who receives the cottage, and Florida's law, the condominium.

Through study, research, and experience, you must become knowledgeable of your state's intestate statute so that you can accurately explain and apply its provisions to the estate of the deceased.

Terminology Related to Intestacy

The following terms are associated with the persons and proceedings involved in the law of intestate succession.

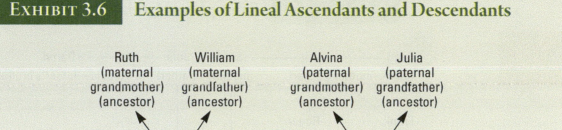

EXHIBIT 3.6   Examples of Lineal Ascendants and Descendants

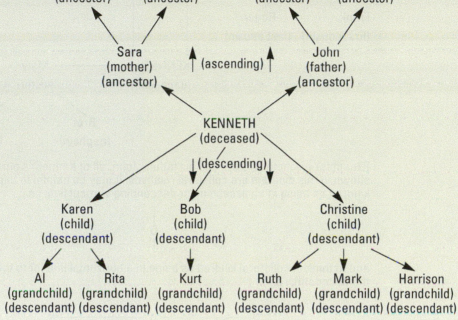

- *Kindred.* Kindred refers to persons related to one another by blood. The persons are also referred to as kin or next of kin.
- *Consanguinity.* Consanguinity refers to persons who are related by blood through a common ancestor.

  EXAMPLE: A child, grandchild, grandparent, aunt, uncle, and cousin are related to the decedent through a common ancestor and are kindred. Janice Rule is the granddaughter of Elliot Sanderson. She is related to her grandfather by consanguinity (blood) and is his kin.

- *Affinity.* Affinity refers to persons who are related by marriage. They include stepchildren, father- or mother-in-law, and brother- or sister-in-law. Since only blood relatives can inherit from the intestate's estate, none of the individuals related by affinity (except for a surviving spouse) can inherit from the intestate under the laws of intestate succession.

  EXAMPLE: In Exhibit 3.8, Nathan's wife, Ann, is related to Joe by affinity. She cannot inherit from Joe under intestate succession laws. The decedent and the person related to him by affinity have no common blood ancestor. This rule, of course, does not apply to the spouse of the decedent even though spouses are usually related solely by marriage (by affinity).

- *Ascendant or ancestor.* An ascendant or ancestor is a claimant to an intestate's share who is related to the decedent in an ascending lineal or collateral blood line.

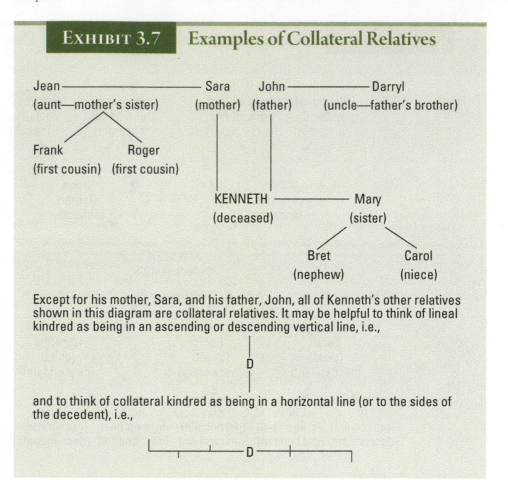

| EXHIBIT 3.7 | Examples of Collateral Relatives |

Except for his mother, Sara, and his father, John, all of Kenneth's other relatives shown in this diagram are collateral relatives. It may be helpful to think of lineal kindred as being in an ascending or descending vertical line, i.e.,

and to think of collateral kindred as being in a horizontal line (or to the sides of the decedent), i.e.,

EXAMPLE: The parent of a decedent is a lineal ancestor. The sister of a decedent is a collateral relative.

- *Descendant.* A descendant is a claimant to an intestate's share who is related to the decedent in a descending lineal or collateral blood line.

  EXAMPLE: The child of a decedent is a lineal descendant. A niece is a collateral descendant.

- *Lineal.* As a noun, a lineal is an heir or relative related to an intestate decedent in a direct line either upward in an ascending bloodline (e.g., parents, grandparents, or great-grandparents) or downward in a descending bloodline (e.g., children, grandchildren, or great-grandchildren). See Exhibits 3.6, 3.8, and 3.10. Lineal consanguinity exists between persons when one is descended (or ascended) in a direct line from the other, e.g., a father to a son or daughter.

- *Collateral.* As a noun, in intestate terminology, a collateral is an heir or relative, not in a direct line of lineal ascent or descent, who traces a kinship relationship to an intestate decedent through a common ancestor (e.g., brothers, sisters, aunts, uncles, nieces, nephews, cousins, and other such relatives), forming a collateral line of relationship (see Exhibits 3.7, 3.8, and 3.10). Collateral consanguinity exists between persons who have the same ancestors, but who do not descend or ascend from each other, e.g., brother, uncle, or nephew.

EXHIBIT 3.8	Examples of Lineal and Collateral Relationships

Joe (deceased) ┌───┴───┐ Keith David Molly	Joe's three children are in his direct line—also called descending lineal bloodline.
Mother—Father (parents) ┌─────┴─────┐ Joe Brenda (sister) ┌──┼──┐ ┌──┴──┐ Keith David Molly Fran Larry (niece) (nephew)	Joe's lineal ancestors are his mother and father. Joe's sister, Brenda, and her children, Fran (niece) and Larry (nephew), are Joe's collateral kindred.
Mother—Father ——————— Nathan—Ann ┌──┴──┐ (uncle) (aunt) Joe Brenda	Nathan, Joe's uncle, is Joe's collateral kin. Nathan's wife, Ann, is not a direct lineal or collateral relative, i.e., she is not related to Joe *by blood.*

Mother—Father ——————— Nathan—Ann
┌──┴──┐   ┌──┴──┐
Joe   Brenda   Susan   Sally
                       (first (first
                       cousin) cousin)
	Nathan, Joe's uncle, has two children, Susan and Sally, who are Joe and Brenda's first cousins (see Exhibit 3.10) and are collateral kindred.

Great-grandparents
┌────────┴────────┐
Grandmother—Grandfather Sam—Shirley
┌────────┴────────┐   (great
                          uncle)
Mother—Father Nathan—Ann Mary—Sue
┌──┴──┐   ┌──┴──┐
Joe Brenda   Susan Sally (first cousins
                            once
                            removed)
	Sam is the son of Joe's great-grandparents and is Joe's great uncle who has two children, Mary and Sue. They are Joe's first once cousins removed (see Exhibit 3.10). Sam, Mary, and Sue are collateral kindred. Sam's wife, Shirley, is not a collateral relative. She is not related to Joe by blood.

- *Half blood.* Half blood is the degree of relationship that exists between persons who have the same mother or the same father in common, but not both parents.

EXAMPLE: Oliver and Antoine are half brothers. They are related to each other through only one common ancestor, i.e., they have the same father but not the same mother. Most state statutes, including the UPC § 2–107, allow half blood and whole blood kindred to receive an equal share of the intestate's estate (see Cal. Prob. Code § 6406; Iowa Code Ann. § 633.21 9; Mass. Gen. Laws Ann. ch. 1 90 § 4; Mich. Comp. Laws Ann. § 700.21 07; N.J. Stat. Ann. § 3B: 5-7; and N.Y. EPTL § 4-1.1 [b]). Other states give the half blood kindred only half as much as a whole blood (see Fla. Stat. Ann. § 732.1 05 and Va. Code Ann. § 64.1–2).

Intestate Succession Laws

Each state has enacted its own intestate succession statute. These statutes vary considerably from state to state. They provide rules for descent and determine distribution of the probate property of the decedent. An important distinction exists, however, between real and personal property that involves the application of the intestate succession statute. Generally, the law of the intestate's domiciliary state determines the inheritance of personal property regardless of where the property is located. However, real estate passes according to the intestate succession statute of the state where the real property is located.

> **EXAMPLE:** Fernanda Navarro owns a house in South Dakota, her domiciliary state, and a cottage in Minnesota. She has furniture in both the home and the cottage and savings accounts in banks in both states. If Fernanda dies intestate, the intestate succession statute of South Dakota will determine the recipients of her house and all of her personal property, including her furniture and savings account in Minnesota. The real property in Minnesota—the cottage—however, will pass to the recipient according to Minnesota's intestate succession law.

Nonprobate property, such as property held in joint tenancy and tenancy by the entirety, is affected neither by a will nor by intestate succession statutes but instead passes automatically, by right of survivorship, to the surviving co-owners.

Some of the terms used in intestate statutes to identify heirs and methods of distributing the intestate's property include *issue, per capita, per stirpes,* and distribution *by representation.* The term *issue* refers to all of the lineal descendants from a common ancestor. The law of intestate succession rests on these basic principles.

1. The intestate's property passes first to the surviving spouse who is entitled to his or her intestate share; then issue (children and other blood relatives) receive the remaining estate.

2. The intestate's property does not pass to all members of the class of persons defined as "issue" but only to persons closest in line to the intestate, e.g., generally children take before grandchildren and parents before grandparents.

3. The heirs can only be persons who survive the intestate; they must be living at the time of the intestate's death. A deceased person's "estate" cannot be an heir. Thus, if an intestate's child dies before the intestate, neither the child nor the child's estate is an heir. However, the deceased child's children living at the time of the intestate's death would be heirs. See the discussion and examples below.

An intestate's estate is distributed by one of two statutory methods: *per capita distribution* or *per stirpes distribution.*

Per Capita Distribution

per capita distribution
A method of dividing an intestate estate; if a member of the identified group predeceases the decedent, then his or her share would pass to the other members of the group rather than to his descendants.

Per capita means "equal to each person" or "by the heads." **Per capita distribution** is a method of dividing an intestate estate by giving an equal share to a number of persons all of whom are related to the decedent in the same degree of relationship (same-generation ascendants or descendants).

> **EXAMPLE:** Howard dies intestate. Since his wife predeceased him, his only heirs are his children, Betty, Sue, and Joe. The three children receive equal shares in Howard's estate per capita.

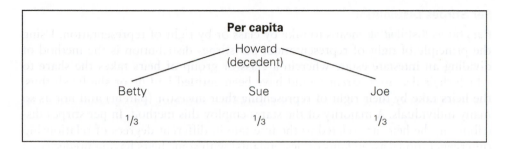

Per capita

Howard
(decedent)

Betty — Sue — Joe

$1/3$ — $1/3$ — $1/3$

EXAMPLE: Continuing with the above case, suppose not all of the heirs are of the same generation because one or more heirs in a class (generation) has predeceased Howard. Under per capita, all the living members of an identified group will receive an equal share of the decedent's estate. However, if a member of the identified group predeceases the decedent, then his or her share would pass to the other members of the group rather than to his descendants. For example, suppose Betty dies before Howard and has two surviving children, Bob and Sally, Howard's grandchildren. Per capital distribution in this case would be determined by counting the members of the identified group. Since Betty predeceased Howard, Howard's entire estate would be divided equally between Sue and Joe.

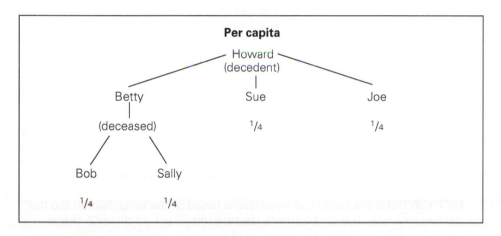

Per capita

Howard
(decedent)

Betty — Sue — Joe

(deceased) — $1/4$ — $1/4$

Bob — Sally

$1/4$ — $1/4$

EXAMPLE: Continuing with the above case, suppose again that not all of the heirs are of the same generation because one or more heirs in a class (generation) has predeceased Howard. If the testator specified **per capita by representation**, each living "head" of a descendant's line takes equally, per capita. If Betty dies before Howard and has two surviving children, Bob and Sally, Howard's grandchildren, per capita by representation, distribution in this case would be determined by counting the number of heirs that "head" each descendant's line (since Betty is dead, Bob and Sally "head" her line; Sue and Joe "head" their lines); therefore, there are four heirs, and each would receive an equal one-fourth of Howard's estate per capita.

Right of Representation

When Betty died and was survived by her two children, Bob and Sally, the principle of **right of representation** gives Betty's children, Bob and Sally, the share in Howard's estate that Betty would have taken if she had survived Howard. All states allow distribution by right of representation, although some states limit it among collateral heirs, see and compare UPC § 2–103.

per capita by representation
A method of dividing an intestate estate; if the members of the identified group are not of the same generation, then the younger generation will only be entitled to the that portion of the estate that the older generation would have received had they survived.

right of representation
The right of a child to receive the share of an intestate's property the child's deceased parent would have received if the parent were still living.

Per Stirpes Distribution

Per stirpes distribution means to take by class or by right of representation. Using the principle of right of representation, per stirpes distribution is the method of dividing an intestate estate wherein a class or group of heirs takes the share to which their deceased parent would have been entitled had he or she lived; thus, the heirs take by their right of representing their ancestor (parent) and not as so many individuals. A majority of the states employ this method. In per stirpes distribution, the heirs are related to the intestate in different degrees of relationship (intergenerational ascendants or descendants) with some heirs having predeceased the intestate. The descendants of such persons receive their shares through the predeceased heir by representation. Using the per stirpes method, the intestate's estate is divided into as many equal shares as the decedent has children (1) who are living or (2) who are already dead but have living descendants. The living children of any deceased parent take their parent's share per stirpes, by right of representation.

EXAMPLE: Returning to the previous example, a per stirpes distribution would be as follows.

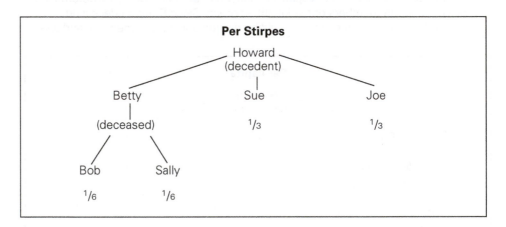

METHOD Divide the estate into equal shares based on the living children and the children who have died but have living descendants. There are three (3) shares. Thus, Sue and Joe each receive one-third of the estate, and Bob and Sally receive their mother's (Betty's) one-third share equally by right of representation. Bob and Sally each receive a one-sixth share.

An example of a statute regulating per capita and per stirpes rights to an intestate's estate is Idaho Code § 15-2-103 on the share of heirs other than a surviving spouse.

The part of the intestate estate not passing to the surviving spouse under section 15-2-102 of this part, or the entire intestate estate if there is no surviving spouse, passes as follows:

(a) To the issue of the decedent; if they are all of the same degree of kinship to the decedent they take equally [per capita], but if of unequal degree, then those of more remote degree take by representation [per stirpes].

EXAMPLE: Mary, a widow, has three children—Jim, Nora, and Kathryn. Jim is married and has two children—Matt and Colleen. Nora is single. Kathryn also was married and had three children—Charles, Darlene, and Elaine. Kathryn died two years ago. Now Mary dies. (Refer to Exhibit 3.8.) If Mary dies intestate, leaving an estate valued at $225,000 after payment of debts, taxes, and all other expenses, and her only surviving relatives are two of her three adult children and her five grandchildren (three of whom are the children of her deceased daughter, Kathryn), her estate would be distributed according to the Idaho statute as follows.

- $75,000 to Jim (son) per capita—a one-third interest

- $75,000 to Nora (daughter) per capita—a one-third interest

- $25,000 to Charles (grandchild) per stirpes—a one-ninth interest

- $25,000 to Darlene (grandchild) per stirpes—a one-ninth interest

- $25,000 to Elaine (grandchild) per stirpes—a one-ninth interest

If Kathryn had been alive at her mother's death, she would have taken a per capita share of $75,000 (one-third of the total estate). Since Kathryn died before her mother, Kathryn's children receive her share per stirpes (by right of representation), i.e., they "represent" their mother. This means Kathryn's share is divided equally among her children and each child receives a third of their mother's share. The other two grandchildren of the decedent receive nothing because their father, Jim, who is the son of the decedent, Mary, survived his mother. If Mary had died with a will and left her estate to her then living children and to the issue of any deceased child of hers per capita, then Mary's estate would be distributed as follows: Jim, Nora, Charles, Darlene, and Elaine would each receive $45,000. See Exhibit 3.9.

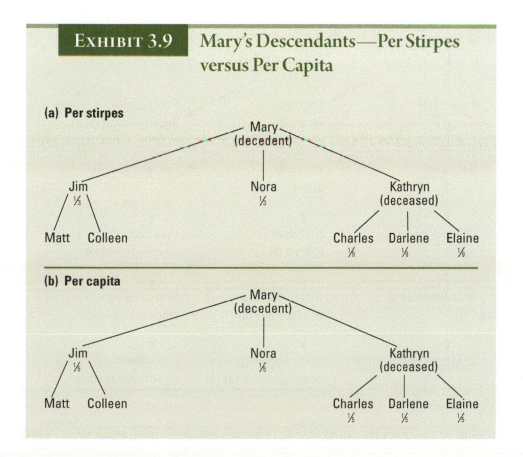

EXHIBIT 3.9 **Mary's Descendants—Per Stirpes versus Per Capita**

(a) Per stirpes

(b) Per capita

Degree of Relationship

The **degree of relationship** is a method of determining which **collateral relatives** or **heirs** will inherit from an intestate with the use of a **degrees of kindred** genealogy chart (see Exhibit 3.10). When a person dies intestate, most state statutes and the UPC pass the decedent's estate in the following order.

1. First to a surviving spouse and lineal descendants (children), but if none, then to

2. Other lineal descendants such as grandchildren or great-grandchildren, but if none, then to

3. Lineal ascendants (ancestors) such as parents or grandparents, but if none, then to

4. Collateral relatives who are lineal descendants of the decedent's parents such as brothers and sisters and their children who come before aunts, uncles, and cousins, and whose degree of relationship determines their inheritance rights.

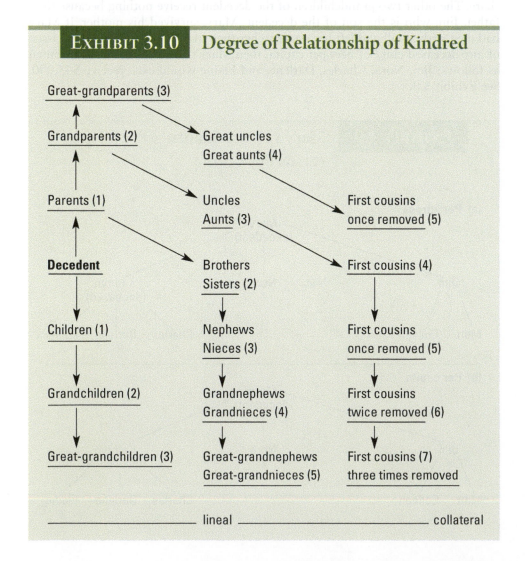

EXHIBIT 3.10   Degree of Relationship of Kindred

5. Other next of kin, blood relatives of the decedent.

6. If there are none of the above, the decedent's property passes to the state by escheat, the right of the state to title of an intestate's property when no spouse or kindred survive the intestate. Reminder: Real property would pass by escheat to the state in which the real property is located.

To determine which collateral heirs receive the intestate's property to the exclusion of other collateral heirs, it is often necessary to ascertain the degree of relationship between the decedent and the particular collateral heirs in question, i.e., which relative is most closely related to the decedent by blood. Most states and the UPC limit collateral heirs to the next of kin, i.e., to the collateral relatives of the decedent who are lineal descendants of the decedent's grandparents. These potential heirs are determined according to either the civil law or the common law as follows.

- *Civil law computation.* Obtain a genealogy (degrees of kindred) chart. See Exhibit 3.10. The chart illustrates the summary history of a family and assigns a degree of relationship number to each relative of the decedent to show how closely the persons listed are related to each other. Each degree (number) represents one generation, e.g., parents are related to the decedent in the first degree, grandparents in the second degree, etc. Under the civil law method, the degree of relationship of a relative is calculated by first counting up from the decedent-intestate to the *closest common ancestor* to both the decedent and the possible heir, and then counting down to the heir. When counting, the decedent is excluded, and the possible heir is included. See Ga. Code Ann. § 53-2-1.

  EXAMPLE: Using Exhibit 3.10 to determine the degree of relationship of a grandnephew, Jeffrey, to the decedent-intestate, Marilyn, count up to her parents (1), the closest common ancestor to both Marilyn and Jeffrey, and then down through brothers and sisters (2) and nephews and nieces (3), to Jeffrey, the grandnephew (4). Thus, the grandnephew, Jeffrey, is related to the decedent in the fourth degree. Similarly, Marilyn's first cousin, Lisa, is also related in the fourth degree, i.e., parents (1), grandparents (2), uncles and aunts (3), to first cousins (4).

In states that follow the civil law computation, the collateral heir who is related to the decedent-intestate in the lowest degree (smallest number) receives the property to the exclusion of the other collateral heirs. If several collateral heirs are related in the same degree, they share equally; thus, in the example above, Jeffrey and Lisa would receive equal shares. However, some states specify that in case of a degree tie (same number) between collateral heirs, those related through the closest common ancestor take to the exclusion of the others; see Cal. Prob. Code § 6402(f); Mass. Gen. Laws Ann. ch. 190 § 3(6). Thus, in the example above, although Jeffrey and Lisa are both in the fourth degree, Jeffrey would receive Marilyn's property since he is related through her parents while Lisa is related through Marilyn's grandparents.

- *Common law computation.* This method computes the degree of relationship by first counting up from the decedent-intestate to the closest common ancestor to the decedent and the possible heir and, next, starting a new count down to the heir. The greater or higher this second number is in comparison with other possible collateral heirs determines who receives the inheritance.

EXAMPLE: Using the Marilyn–Jeffrey–Lisa example above, the closest common ancestor between Marilyn and Jeffrey is Marilyn's parent. Counting from Marilyn to the parent is (1), and, starting the new count, from the parent to Jeffrey, the grandnephew, is (3). Thus, (3) is the degree of relationship between Marilyn and Jeffrey. However, calculating the degree of relationship between Marilyn and Lisa using their common ancestor, the grandparent, leads to the degree of (2); i.e., counting from Marilyn to the grandparent is (2) and, starting the new count, from the grandparent to the first cousin is (2). Therefore, since Jeffrey has the higher number, he receives the inheritance.

No matter which system, the civil law or common law method, is used for determining degrees for collaterals, the decedent-intestate's property usually goes to the "nearest surviving kin" as established by state statutes. Most states give preference to descendants over ancestors, e.g., children over parents; brothers and sisters over grandparents; and nephews and nieces over first cousins. Since the variations in individual state laws are numerous, *you must carefully review your state's laws with the supervising attorney if they must be applied to determine a client's interest in an intestate's estate.*

Escheat

escheat
The passage of an intestate's property to the state when there are no surviving blood relatives or a spouse.

Escheat is the passage of property to the state when an intestate leaves no surviving spouse or blood relatives (kindred) entitled to inherit the intestate's estate. Real property of an intestate escheats to the state in which it is located. For example, see Maryland's escheat statute (Md. Estates and Trusts Code Ann. § 3-105), which passes the intestate's property to the county board of education to be used in public schools of the county. Since heirs are generally found, escheat rarely occurs.

EXAMPLE: Tariq dies intestate, leaving an estate valued at $100,000. There are no surviving relatives. The property "escheats" to the state; the state enjoys complete ownership and can use the property as it sees fit; it can sell or lease the property just as an individual owner could do.

Note: If a legitimate surviving heir is discovered after the intestate's property escheats to the state, the heir can usually claim the property or its value if the claim is made within the statute of limitations period.

ASSIGNMENT 3.2

Armond died in Great Falls, Montana. Either by choice or through oversight, he had neither married nor drawn a will. At his death, Armond had the following blood relatives surviving him.

- A brother, Niles, living in Sacramento, California
- A sister, Lorraine, living in London, England
- A niece, Francine, living in Fridley, Minnesota, and a nephew, Frank, living in Albany, New York, both children of Armond's deceased brother, Harry
- A mother, Lila, who lived with Armond
- A grandfather, Alonzo, Lila's father, living in Cleveland, Ohio
- An aunt, Rose, Lila's sister, living in Bangor, Maine
- A first cousin, Judy, Rose's daughter, living in Lawrence, Kansas

Answer the following questions.

1. Who of Armond's surviving blood relatives are lineal descendants?
2. Who of Armond's surviving blood relatives are lineal ascendants?
3. Who of Armond's surviving blood relatives are collaterals? What are their degrees of relationship?
4. What is the order of inheritance of Armond's surviving relatives in your state? Which heir receives property to the exclusion of others?
5. Do any of Armond's kindred receive his property per stirpes or per capita?
6. If Francine and Judy are Armond's only surviving relatives when he dies intestate, who receives his property according to your state statute? If Francine is dead but her son, Fred, and Judy are living when Armond dies, who receives the property?
7. Beginning with Alonzo, diagram a family tree for Armond's family.

General Rules of Distribution under State Intestate Succession Statutes

As we have emphasized throughout this discussion, intestate succession statutes vary from state to state. Nevertheless, many states do have similar rules on which surviving relatives will inherit an intestate's estate. The following scenarios illustrate some of these general rules of distribution. If the decedent-intestate is survived by

- a surviving spouse and no blood relatives: The spouse receives the entire estate.

- a surviving spouse and children all born to the surviving spouse and the deceased: In some states, the spouse receives the entire estate; in other states, the spouse receives a lump sum of money (ranging from $7,500 to $150,000 depending on the state) and/or a portion (usually one-half) of the estate; the children receive the remainder of the estate equally.

- a surviving spouse and children, some or all of whom are not the children of the surviving spouse: The spouse receives a lump sum of money (ranging from $7,500 to $150,000 depending on the state) and/or a portion (usually one-half) of the estate; the children receive the remainder of the estate equally.

- a surviving spouse, no children, but surviving parents: In some states, the surviving spouse gets everything; in other states, the spouse receives a lump sum ranging from $7,500 to $200,000 plus one-half to three-fourths of the remaining estate, and the parents receive the balance.

- a surviving spouse, no children and no parents, but brothers and sisters: In the majority of states, the surviving spouse receives everything; in a few states, the spouse receives one-half of the remaining estate, and the brothers and sisters receive the other half equally.

- no surviving spouse and no children: The parents receive the property followed by brothers and sisters, and then their children and other collateral heirs.

- no spouse or kindred (blood relatives): The state receives the property by escheat.

ASSIGNMENT 3.3

Charlotte Martin dies intestate in your state. She had three children, Casper, Sophia, and Tobias. Casper and Sophia each have two children. Casper's two daughters are Lena and Lisa; Sophia's two sons are Florian and Fabian. Tobias died six months before Charlotte, and he had three children, Sienna, Sarah, and Simon. Answer the following according to your state statute.

1. Who receives Charlotte's property?
2. What portion does each recipient receive?
3. Is the inheritance per stirpes, per capita, or per capita by representation? Explain.
4. Does any of Charlotte's property escheat to the state?

RIGHTS OF FAMILY MEMBERS TO A DECEDENT'S ESTATE

On the death of the family "breadwinner," the surviving family members may face a financial crisis. This section examines the rights of a surviving spouse and children to the property of the decedent. **Caveat:** You must not confuse the following two state statutes.

- The intestate succession statute that determines the inheritance of an intestate's surviving spouse and heirs
- The spouse's elective (forced) share statute that, as an option, is granted if the decedent spouse dies testate

Rights of a Surviving Spouse

Surviving Spouse's Testate and Intestate Rights

When a married person dies testate, the rights of the surviving spouse to the decedent spouse's estate are usually determined by the will (but see section on elective share). When the decedent spouse dies without a will, the surviving spouse's rights to the intestate spouse's estate are determined by state statute and by which other family members, e.g., children, parents, brothers and sisters, and other kindred, survive the intestate. For an example of the rights of surviving spouses under state intestate succession statutes, see the New York statute in Exhibit 1.1. Exhibit 3.11 includes intestate succession statute citations for all states.

POINT OF INTEREST

Escheat Property

Most states have an Unclaimed Property program that publishes a decedent's name and heirs in a newspaper of general circulation in the county where the estate was probated. If you are identified as a potential heir, you might have a valid claim against the estate. However, if no claim activity has been made on an estate within the statutory period, the property will escheat to the state.

EXHIBIT 3.11 Intestate Succession Statute Citations for All States

Alabama	Ala. Code § 43-8-41; § 43-8-42
Alaska	Alaska Stat. § 13.12.102; § 13.12.103
Arizona	Ariz. Rev. Stat. Ann. § 14-2102; § 14-2103
Arkansas	Ark. Code Ann. §§ 28-9-203 to 28-9-206; § 28-9-214
California	Cal. Prob. Code § 6401; § 6402
Colorado	Colo. Rev. Stat. § 15-11 -102; § 15-11 -103
Connecticut	Conn. Gen. Stat. Ann. § 45a-437; § 45a-438; § 45a-439
Delaware	Del. Code Ann. tit. 12 § 502; § 503
Florida	Fla. Stat. Ann. § 732.102; § 732.103
Georgia	Ga. Code Ann. §53-2-1
Hawaii	Haw. Rev. Stat. § 560:2-102; § 560:2-103
Idaho	Idaho Code § 15-2-102; § 15-2-103
Illinois	Ill. Comp. Stat. Ann. Ch. 755 § 5/2-1
Indiana	Ind. Code Ann. §29-1-2-1
Iowa	Iowa Code Ann. § 633.211; § 633.212; § 633.219
Kansas	Kan. Stat. Ann. §§ 59-504 to 59-508
Kentucky	Ky. Rev. Stat. Ann. § 391.010; § 391.030; § 392.020
Louisiana	La. Civ. Code Ann. Art. 889 to 902; Art. 1493
Maine	Me. Rev. Stat. Ann. tit. 18-A § 2-102; § 2-103
Maryland	Md. Est. & Trst. Code Ann. §§ 3-101 to 3-112
Massachusetts	Mass. Gen. Laws Ann. ch. 190 §§ 1 to 8; ch. 190B: 2-101 to 114
Michigan	Mich. Comp. Laws Ann. § 700.2102; § 700.2103; § 700.2105
Minnesota	Minn. Stat. Ann. § 524.2-102; § 524.2-103
Mississippi	Miss. Code Ann. § 91-1 -3; § 91 -1 -7; § 91 -1 -11
Missouri	Mo. Rev. Stat. §474.010
Montana	Mont. Code Ann. § 72-2-112; § 72-2-113; § 72-2-115
Nebraska	Neb. Rev. Stat. § 30-2302; § 30-2303
Nevada	Nev. Rev. Stat. §§ 134.040 to 134.110
New Hampshire	N.H. Rev. Stat. Ann. § 561:1
New Jersey	N.J. Stat. Ann. § 3B:5-3; § 3B:5-4
New Mexico	N.M. Stat. Ann. § 45-2-102; § 45-2-103
New York	N.Y. EPTL§ 4-1.1
North Carolina	N.C. Gen. Stat. § 29-14; § 29-15
North Dakota	N.D. Cent. Code §30.1-04-02; §30.1-04-03
Ohio	Ohio Rev. Code Ann. § 2105.06
Oklahoma	Okla. Stat. Ann. tit. 84 §213
Oregon	Or. Rev. Stat. §§ 112.025 to 112.045
Pennsylvania	Pa. Stat. Ann. tit. 20 § 2102; § 2103
Rhode Island	R.I. Gen. Laws § 33-1 -1; § 33-1 -2
South Carolina	S.C. Code § 62-2-102; § 62-2-103
South Dakota	S.D. Cod. Laws Ann. § 29A-2-102; § 29A-2-103
Tennessee	Tenn. Code Ann. §31-2-104
Texas	Tex. Prob. Code Ann. § 38
Utah	Utah Code Ann. § 75-2-102; § 75-2-103
Vermont	Vt. Stat. Ann. tit. 14 § 551
Virginia	Va. Code Ann. § 64.1-1; § 64.1-11
Washington	Wash. Rev. Code Ann. § 11.04.015
West Virginia	W.Va. Code §42-1-2; §42-1-3
Wisconsin	Wis. Stat. Ann. §852.01
Wyoming	Wyo. Stat. §2-4-101

Legal Meaning and Significance of Surviving Spouse

Historically, a surviving spouse was defined as the husband or wife that out-lived the person to whom they were married. A valid marriage could only exist between a man and woman. This definition changed with the 2015 U.S. Supreme Court's milestone decision in *Obergefell v. Hodges*, 576 U.S. ____ (2015). In *Obergefell*, the highest court ruled that the Fourteenth Amendment requires a state to license a marriage between two people of the same sex and to recognize a marriage between two people of the same sex when their marriage was lawfully licensed and performed out-of-state. As a result, the definition of a "surviving spouse" expanded to include married couples of the same sex. This seminal ruling ends a legal battle that had brewed in the states for over 45 years, beginning with Minnesota in the 1970s to Hawaii in the 1990s and New England after the turn of the century. A critical point in the clash came in 2013, when the high court forced the federal government to recognize same-sex marriages and allowed them to resume in California. Although 37 states recognized same-sex marriages when *Obergefell* was decided, others had passed constitutional amendments refusing to give full faith and credit to same sex marriages recognized in other states. The ruling is not just about marriage. By allowing marriages throughout the United States, the decision guarantees the same rights and benefits as legally married, opposite-sex couples, including tax relief, emergency medical decision-making power, the ability to adopt children, albeit banned in some states, spousal benefits (including workers' compensation and Social Security), and inheritance rights. It has also made the terms "civil unions" and "domestic partners" obsolete.

Surviving Spouse's Elective (Forced) Share

In a will, a testator is permitted to specifically disinherit anyone *except a surviving spouse*. As previously mentioned in Chapter 1, most states offer a surviving spouse the choice or **right of election** to either take the benefits in the will or to *elect* a **statutory forced share** of the deceased spouse's estate established by state statute. Generally, the surviving spouse chooses whichever share is greater. In a few states, the **elective share** of the surviving spouse is the same amount the spouse would receive if the decedent spouse died intestate.

right of election
The right of a surviving spouse to choose to take, under the decedent's state law, his or her statutory share in preference to the provision made in the deceased spouse's will.

elective or forced share statute
The statute that grants the surviving spouse the election or choice. Also called statutory share.

The elective right has replaced common law provisions of dower and curtesy, which have been abolished or materially altered in most states (see UPC § 2–112). By statute, the spouse's election must be made within nine (9) months of death. If no election is made, the surviving spouse is required to take the share provided under the decedent spouse's will. The election is made when the spouse gives written notice to the personal representative and files the notice with the probate court. See Exhibit 3.12 for an example of a notice.

The amount of the decedent's property that passes to the spouse as the elective share, excluding a life estate interest, qualifies for the estate tax marital deduction (see the discussion in Chapter 14).

If the choice is to elect "against the will," the spouse waives the will, renounces it, and takes what the state provides, thereby forfeiting any further claims to property under the will. States vary substantially in the amount a surviving spouse receives by statute. A few states determine the amount by their version of "dower or curtesy"; some set the amount by their intestate

EXHIBIT 3.12   Notice of Election of Surviving Spouse

SURROGATE'S COURT: COUNTY OF _____

_____

In the Matter of the Estate of

_____ ,

_____ Deceased.

NOTICE OF ELECTION

File No. _____

To: [*Insert name of fiduciary and clerk of court*]

1. I,_____, am the surviving spouse of _____ , who died a domiciliary of the County of _____ , and the State of New York, on _____ , 20____ .

2. The said decedent left a certain Last Will and Testament dated the _____ day of _____ , 20____ , which was probated in the Surrogate's Court of the County of _____ , New York, on the _____ day of _____ , 20 _____ , and Letters Testamentary were issued to _____ as Executor on _____ , 20____ .

3. I, _____ , the surviving spouse of _____ , deceased, do hereby exercise the personal right of election given to me pursuant to the provisions of Section 5–1.1–A of the New York Estates, Powers and Trusts Law, and I do hereby elect to take my elective share pursuant to the provisions of the New York Estates, Powers and Trusts Law.

IN WITNESS WHEREOF, I have hereunto set my hand and seal this _____ day of _____ , 20____ .

[*Acknowledgement*]

_____   _____ L.S.

Source: Reprinted with permission of Thomson/West from West's McKinney's Forms, ESP § 7:482.

succession statute; others allow their method of "dower" and have an "elective right" statute; and the community property states grant each spouse one-half of the community property. Most states, however, grant one-third to one-half of the decedent's *augmented estate* to the surviving spouse. The augmented estate consists of the value of all property, whether real or personal, tangible or intangible, wherever situated, that constitutes the sum of four components (1) the decedent's net probate estate; (2) the decedent's nonprobate transfers to others; (3) the decedent's nonprobate transfers to the surviving spouse; (4) the surviving spouse's net assets and nonprobate transfers to others, reduced by funeral and administration expenses, homestead allowance, family allowances, exempt property, and enforceable creditors' claims, see UPC §§ 2–202 through 2–207.

The right of election does not apply if the surviving spouse has previously waived the right to the elective share by signing a prenuptial or postnuptial agreement. Also, in some states like New York, a surviving spouse can be prohibited from the election if the spouse "abandoned" the deceased spouse prior to the latter's death or failed to provide required support for the deceased spouse for any period before death (see N.Y. EPTL §§ 5-1.1 and 5-1.2).

Sections 2–202 and 2–203 of the Uniform Probate Code set the spouse's elective share at the amount equal to the value of the elective-share percentage of the augmented estate, determined by the length of time the spouse and the decedent were married to each other, in accordance with the following schedule.

If the decedent and the spouse were married to each other	The elective-share percentage is
Less than 1 year	Supplemental Amount Only
1 year but less than 2 years	3% of the augmented estate
2 years but less than 3 years	6% of the augmented estate
3 years but less than 4 years	9% of the augmented estate
4 years but less than 5 years	12% of the augmented estate
5 years but less than 6 years	15% of the augmented estate
6 years but less than 7 years	18% of the augmented estate
7 years but less than 8 years	21% of the augmented estate
8 years but less than 9 years	24% of the augmented estate
9 years but less than 10 years	27% of the augmented estate
10 years but less than 11 years	30% of the augmented estate
11 years but less than 12 years	34% of the augmented estate
12 years but less than 13 years	38% of the augmented estate
13 years but less than 14 years	42% of the augmented estate
14 years but less than 15 years	46% of the augmented estate
15 years or more	50% of the augmented estate

Note: In any situation, $50,000 minimum elective-share is granted for the support of the surviving spouse, see UPC §2–202(b). Exhibit 3.13 summarizes the spouse's elective share in all 50 states.

Effect of Divorce and Marriage on a Spouse's Rights

Divorce

If the testator obtains a divorce (or annulment) *after* executing a will, the effect on the will is determined by state law. In most states, by statute or case law, a divorce revokes only the provisions that benefit the former spouse, not the will itself, and any gift to the divorced spouse passes to the residuary beneficiaries or

EXHIBIT 3.13	Summary of Spouse's Elective Share by State
Alabama	Lesser of (1) all of the decedent's estate reduced by the value of the surviving spouse's separate estate; or (2) one-third of decedent's augmented estate (§ 43-8-70)
Alaska	One-third of decedent's augmented estate (§ 13.12.202)
Arizona	One-half of community property (community property law) (§ 14-2102; § 14-2301)
Arkansas	Dower or curtesy interest (§ 28-39-401)
California*	One-half of community or quasi-community property (community property law) (§100; § 101)
Colorado*	Up to one-half of the augmented estate determined by the length of time the spouse and the decedent were married to each other (§ 15-11-201)
Connecticut*	One-third of decedent's estate for life (§ 45a-436)
Delaware*	One-third of the elective estate (tit.12 § 901)
Florida	Thirty percent of the elective estate (§ 732.2065)
Georgia	One year's support from date of decedent's death (§ 53-3-1)
Hawaii*	Up to one-half of the augmented estate determined by the length of time the spouse and the decedent were married to each other (§ 560:2-202)
Idaho	One-half of augmented quasi-community property; one-half of community property (community property law) (§ 15-2-203)
Illinois*	One-third of estate if surviving descendants; one-half if no surviving descendants (Ch.755 § 5/2-8)
Indiana	One-half of net estate if surviving spouse is first spouse of decedent; if not, up to one-third of net estate (§ 29-1-3-1)
Iowa*	One-third of decedent's estate (§ 633.238)
Kansas	Up to one-half of the augmented estate determined by the length of time the spouse and the decedent were married to each other (§ 59-6a202)
Kentucky	Dower right (§ 392.020; § 392.080)
Louisiana	One-half of community property (community property law L.A.C.C. §980)
Maine*	One-third of the augmented estate (tit.18-A § 2-201)
Maryland	One-third of net estate if surviving issue; one-half if no surviving issue (§3-203; ET 3-203)
Massachusetts*	One-third of estate if surviving issue; $25,000 plus life estate in one-half of remaining estate if surviving kindred but no issue; $25,000 plus one-half of remaining estate if no surviving kindred or issue (ch. 191 § 15)
Michigan	One-half of intestate share, reduced by one-half of the value of all property received from decedent other than by testate or intestate succession; or dower right (§ 700.2202)
Minnesota	Up to one-half of the augmented estate determined by the length of time the spouse and the decedent were married to each other (§ 524.2-202)
Mississippi	Intestate share not to exceed one-half of the estate (§ 91-5-25)
Missouri	One-half of estate if no lineal descendants survive decedent or one-third if lineal descendants (§ 474.160)
Montana	Up to one-half of the augmented estate determined by the length of time the spouse and the decedent were married to each other (§ 72-2-221)
Nebraska	One-half of the augmented estate (§ 30-2313)
Nevada*	One-half of community property (community property law) (§ 123.250)

EXHIBIT 3.13   (continued)

New Hampshire*	One-third of estate if surviving issue; $10,000 of personalty and realty each plus one-half of remaining estate if surviving parent or sibling but no issue; $10,000 plus $2,000 for each year of marriage to decedent plus one-half of remaining estate if no issue, parent, or sibling (§ 560:10)
New Jersey*	One-third of the augmented estate (§ 3B:8-1)
New Mexico	One-half of community property (community property law) (§ 45-2-805)
New York*	The greater of $50,000 or one-third of net estate (§ 5-1.1-A)
North Carolina	Up to one-half of total net assets depending on the presence and number of descendants surviving decedent (§ 30-3.1)
North Dakota	One-half of the marital property portion of the augmented estate (§ 30.1-05-01)
Ohio	Up to one-half of net estate; one-third if two or more surviving children or their lineal issue (§ 2106.01)
Oklahoma	One-half of all property acquired during marriage by the joint industry of the spouses (tit. 84 § 44)
Oregon*	One-fourth of net estate (§ 114.105)
Pennsylvania	One-third of decedent's estate (tit. 20 § 2203)
Rhode Island	Life estate in real estate of deceased as provided by intestacy law (§ 33-25-2)
South Carolina	One-third of decedent's probate estate (§ 62-2-201)
South Dakota	Up to one-half of the augmented estate determined by the length of time the spouse and the decedent were married to each other (§ 29A-2-202)
Tennessee	Up to forty percent of the net estate determined by the length of time the spouse and the decedent were married to each other (§ 31-4-101)
Texas	All of the community property estate reduced to one-half if lineal descendants; P.C. §45
Utah	One-third of the augmented estate multiplied by a fraction (§ 75-2-202)
Vermont*	Entire intestate estate reduced to one-half if lineal descendants (tit. 14 § 11)
Virginia	One-third of the augmented estate if surviving children or their descendants; one-half if no surviving children or their descendants (§ 64.1-16)
Washington*	One-half of community property (RCWA §11.02.070)
West Virginia	Up to one-half of the augmented estate determined by the length of time the spouse and the decedent were married to each other (§ 42-3-1)
Wisconsin*	One-half of the augmented deferred marital property estate (§ 861.02)
Wyoming	One-half of estate if no surviving issue or if spouse is also a parent of any surviving issue; one-fourth if spouse is not the parent of any surviving issue (§ 2-5-101)

* In these states, surviving partners of an officially recognized, legally valid, same-sex domestic partnership, civil union, or marriage have the same survivor inheritance rights as those of heterosexual marital partners.

devisees of the will (see Exhibit 3.14 and UPC §§ 2–802 and 2–804). The decision in *Matter of Seymour's Estate*, 93 N.M. 328, 600 P.2d 274 (1979), illustrates this position (for further discussion, see Chapter 4). A legal separation that does not terminate the spouse's marital status does not revoke a will's provisions for the benefit of a spouse; see Cal. Prob. Code § 6122(d).

EXHIBIT 3.14	Consequence of Divorce on Preexisting Will

Does not affect provisions of the will
    Mississippi (unless implied revocation doctrine applies)
    Vermont
Revokes all the will provisions pertaining to the former spouse
    All remaining states not listed earlier

Marriage

In some states, a testator's subsequent marriage after creating a will may revoke the entire will (see R.I. Gen. Laws § 33-5-9 and Exhibit 3.15). Since the majority of states allow a statutory forced share to a surviving spouse who elects against a decedent spouse's will, most of these states often have no "marriage revocation law" since the new spouse is covered by the election right. Community property states automatically pass one-half of the decedent's community property to the surviving spouse. Numerous states and the UPC give the new (omitted) spouse an amount equal to the intestate share of the decedent spouse's estate unless it can be shown the omission was intentional or the testator provided for the surviving spouse by transfer outside the will and intended the transfer be in lieu of a testamentary provision (see UPC §§ 2–301 and 2–508). See also the discussion in Chapter 4.

Other Spouses' Rights before or after Marriage

Various methods allow widows, widowers, or divorcees, who are contemplating a second marriage, to transfer some of their currently owned assets to existing family

EXHIBIT 3.15	Consequence of Marriage on Preexisting Will

Revokes the entire will
Georgia	(marriage, birth, or adoption of a child by the testator)
Kansas	(marriage followed by birth or adoption of a child by the testator)
Maryland	(marriage followed by birth, adoption, or legitimation of a child by the testator, provided the child or the child's descendant survives the testator)
Massachusetts	
New Hampshire	(implied revocation doctrine applies)
Oregon	(if survived by a spouse)
Rhode Island	
Tennessee	(marriage followed by birth of a child by the testator)

Whether revoked or not, all states make provision for the surviving spouse (omitted spouse) to receive a statutory elective share or intestate share unless otherwise provided for.

members, e.g., children and grandchildren, by the elimination of these assets from the statutory elective share or intestate succession rights of their future spouse. Disclosure of the transfer of the property and its value to the future spouse is essential for approval by state courts. These methods can be created before or after the marriage.

Before Marriage

Creation of a Joint Tenancy

As discussed in Chapter 1, on the death of one joint tenant, the title to property held in joint tenancy automatically passes to the surviving joint tenant.

> **EXAMPLE:** Clara, a 62-year-old widow, and Nathan, a 65-year-old widower, plan to marry. Clara has two children from her first marriage; Nathan has one child. Clara owns a lake home, Tanglewood, that she and Nathan plan to use as a vacation home during the summer months after they marry. Clara wants Tanglewood to go to her children after she dies. Before the marriage, Clara creates a joint tenancy with equal interests in Tanglewood for herself and each of her two children. Clara tells Nathan about the joint tenancy, and he acknowledges and states, "It's the right thing to do." They marry. If Clara dies before Nathan and her children, Tanglewood will belong to the children, and Nathan will have no legal claim to the lake home.

Creation of a Revocable Living Trust

Prior to a second marriage, a revocable living trust can be established by a former spouse (widow, widower, or divorcee) for the benefit of his or her children for the purpose of transferring currently owned personal assets into the trust to avoid subjecting these assets to the statutory intestate succession or elective share claims of a future (new) spouse. Once the property is transferred, only the beneficiaries of the trust, i.e., the children, are entitled to it. Such a trust could be revoked during the lifetime of the spouse (settlor), but on that spouse's death, the trust becomes irrevocable. After the marriage, a claim by the new spouse that the living trust is an attempt to defraud said spouse from statutory rights would be declared invalid as long as disclosure of the trust's existence, value, and plan for property distribution was made to the new spouse prior to the marriage.

> **EXAMPLE:** Rosa and Hector plan to marry. Rosa and her first husband, Juan, who died in 2004, owned and managed a successful restaurant for 32 years. Rosa's three adult children also work at the restaurant, and she wants them to have it after she dies. Rosa transfers title to the restaurant into a revocable living trust, naming herself trustee and her children beneficiaries of the trust. She informs Hector of the trust, its value, and her plan for the property distribution. Later, they marry. Under these circumstances, if Rosa dies before Hector, an attempt by him to claim the living trust is fraudulent and would be denied.

Creation of an Antenuptial Agreement (Contract), Also Called a Prenuptial or Premarital Agreement

antenuptial (premarital) agreement
A contract made by the parties before their marriage or in contemplation of that marriage whereby the property rights of either or both of the prospective parties are determined.

Due to the increasing frequency of second marriages after a divorce or death of a spouse, the couple now contemplating marriage often wishes to pass their separate estates to the existing children of their earlier marriages free from claims of the new spouse. To accomplish these plans, mutual agreements called **antenuptial or premarital agreements** or contracts are created prior to the marriage. The provisions and validity of such agreements vary from state to state. See *In re Estate of Peterson*, 221 Neb. 792, 381 N.W.2d 109 (1986).

EXAMPLE: Julia and Robert have agreed to marry. Julia, a divorcee, has a son, Ryan; Robert has never married. Ryan has been raised and continues to live on Julia's ranch in Montana. Since she wants her son to own the ranch after her death, Julia tells Robert she will marry him only if they sign an antenuptial agreement legally transferring the ranch to Ryan on her death or if she and Robert divorce. Robert agrees. After Julia and Robert sign the agreement, they marry. Two years later, Julia is killed in an accident. Ryan is entitled to the ranch because of the antenuptial agreement.

After Marriage

Creation of a Postnuptial Agreement (Contract)

A **postnuptial agreement** is made after marriage between spouses while still married to determine the rights of each spouse in the other spouse's property in the event of death or divorce (see Ind. Code Ann. § 29-1-3-6 and UPC § 2–213). At death, postnuptial agreements allow a transfer of the decedent spouse's separate estate assets to children of a previous marriage and prevent the surviving spouse from making a successful claim for the property based on fraud.

> **postnuptial agreement**
> A contract made by spouses after marriage whereby the property rights of either or both spouses are determined.

EXAMPLE: Using the facts in the previous example, if Julia and Robert consented to create the identical antenuptial agreement for the benefit of Ryan after they were married, the executed contract would be a postnuptial agreement.

Some states, e.g., Kansas (see Kan. Stat. Ann. §§ 23-801 et seq.), have adopted the Uniform Premarital Agreement Act that establishes the standards for their courts to resolve the antenuptial agreement problems concerning the claims of the spouse who waives statutory intestate succession or elective share rights by signing such an agreement. The agreement is unenforceable against a party who did not execute the agreement voluntarily. It is also unenforceable if it is unconscionable and three factors are present when the agreement is signed: the challenging party did not (1) receive a reasonable disclosure of assets, (2) waive the disclosure voluntarily and in writing, and (3) have adequate knowledge of the assets.

Other states have similar provisions (see *Matter of Burgess' Estate*, Ok.Civ. App. 22, 646 P.2d 623 [1982]) and all states extend enforcement provisions to postnuptial agreements (see *In re Estate of Beat*, 25 Wis. 2d 315, 130 N.W. 2d 739 [1964]).

Rights of Children (Issue)

Issue

All persons who have descended from a common ancestor are the **issue** of the ancestor. Issue is a broader term than children and, as it is normally used in wills, includes all blood descendants of the ancestor, not just lineal descendants, such as children, grandchildren, and great-grandchildren; see *In re Wolf's Estate*, 98 N.J. Super. 89, 236 A.2d 166 (1967). Formerly, the term included only legitimate issue, but in *Reed v. Campbell*, 476 U.S. 852, 106 S.Ct. 2234, 90 L.Ed.2d 858 (1986), the U.S. Supreme Court prohibited unjustified discrimination against children born out of wedlock. In some states, such as New York, a nonmarital child shares in the intestate estate of the child's father; see N.Y. EPTL § 4-1.2. In trusts in Massachusetts, the word *issue*, which formerly meant legitimate children, today includes all biological descendants unless the settlor clearly expresses a different intent; see *Powers v. Wilkinson*, 399 Mass. 650, 506 N.E.2d 842 (1987). In addition, many states' intestacy statutes have established an adopted child is "issue" of the adoptive parents, which gives the child

> **issue**
> All persons who have descended from a common ancestor.

the same rights, including inheritance rights, as the adoptive parents' natural children. The next paragraphs discuss the rights of children in the following order: natural children, adopted children, nonmarital children, pretermitted (omitted) and posthumous children, and children who may be disinherited by statute.

Natural Children

A natural child is a child by birth of a mother and the biological father, as distinguished from a child by adoption. In addition, if a married woman gives birth to a child, her husband is presumed to be the father of the child. Although most testators leave all or most of their property to their surviving spouse, state intestate statutes differ sharply from those testamentary provisions. Under the statutes, whenever a spouse *and* child(ren) survive the intestate, the surviving spouse generally receives a lump sum amount of the estate plus half of the remainder, and the child(ren) receive the other half; alternatively, the spouse receives one-third to one-half of the estate with the remainder to the children. In either case, this distribution of a decedent's estate is substantially different from what the usual testator's will provides. Thereafter, except for specific bequests (gifts) to named children, most natural and, as we shall see, adopted children receive the estate of their parents when the second parent dies. Obviously, this is not the case in single-parent families, since the parent who dies testate generally leaves the entire estate to the children. When the single parent or the second parent-spouse dies intestate, the natural children are the first-in-line heirs and inherit the entire estate, except that a deceased child's share will pass per stirpes, by right of representation, to that child's issue. In all states, parents are not required to leave anything to their children. Excluding children from sharing in an estate can be accomplished by inserting a clause in the will to the effect that the testator or testatrix has intentionally made no provision for a certain named child. However, despite a testator's intention to disinherit, if no specific exclusion is stated in the will, the child may ultimately receive a share as a result of an omitted child statute (see discussion below).

Divorce and remarriage often have a detrimental effect on the rights and opportunities of natural or adopted children to inherit by will or by law. In divorce decrees, the spouses may agree by stipulation that the spouse who is obligated to pay child support will make a will leaving a portion of the estate to the child(ren) or name the child(ren) as beneficiaries of a life insurance policy.

Adopted Children

adoption
The legal process by statute that establishes a relationship of parent and child between persons who are not so related by nature.

adopted child
The person (child) adopted.

Adoption is a legal process whereby state statutes terminate legal rights and duties between children and their natural parents and substitute similar rights and duties between the children and their adoptive parents. The state statutes are inconsistent in determining the inheritance rights of adopted children or adoptive parents. The modern trend is to treat the **adopted child** as a natural child of the adoptive parents and not as the child of the former natural parents for all legal purposes including inheritance. The states that have adopted UPC §§ 2–115, 2–116 have followed this trend. Consider the following examples.

EXAMPLE: Karen Wilson's son, Ron, is adopted by Scott and Shirley Mikulski. The adopted child, Ron, has the right to inherit from either of the adoptive parents, Scott or Shirley, when they die intestate, and they have the right to inherit from Ron. However, Ron will no longer inherit from his natural mother, Karen, nor will she inherit from him. See *In re Estate of Fleming*, 21 P. 3d 281 (Sup. Ct. Wash.

2001), in which the court held that the biological parent severs all parental rights, including the right to inherit.

EXAMPLE: If, instead, Karen Wilson marries Fred Maxwell and Fred adopts his stepson, Ron, Ron will continue to have the right to inherit from his natural mother, Karen, and also from his adoptive parent, Fred, and they, in turn, have a right to inherit from Ron.

Note: Not all states follow the procedures described in these examples. Several states allow adopted children to inherit from their biological kindred; see Ala. Code § 43-8-48; La. Civ. Code Ann. art. 214; and Wyo. Stat. § 2-4-107. Since a testator can leave an estate to anyone, with the exception that a surviving spouse cannot be disinherited, the adoption rules apply only to intestacy cases. When a testator has an adopted child whom he wants to treat equally as a natural child, a clause, such as the following, should be added to the will to avoid confusion.

Sample Clause

For the purpose of this will, the words *issue, child,* or *children* used within this will describing the relationship of a person or class of persons to another shall refer both to persons who are related by blood and also to any person whose relationship is acquired by adoption.

Adults can also be adopted in some states. When this occurs, the purpose is generally to allow the adopted adult to inherit, or take by will, from the adopting person. The case *In re Adult Anonymous II,* 88 A.D.2d 30, 452 N.Y.S.2d 198 (1982), in which a gay lover was adopted, is an example of adoption for economic and inheritance purposes. This case predates the U.S. Supreme Court's decision granting gays the right to marry, which eliminates the purpose for such an adoption. Adult adoptions generally only affect the inheritance rights of the immediate parties.

Nonmarital Children

A **nonmarital child** is a child born to parents who are not married to each other. A nonmarital child's inheritance rights are governed by state statute. Generally, they hold that the child has the right to inherit from and through the child's mother, but the statutes vary about the rights of the child to inherit from the father. However, since the U.S. Supreme Court's decision in *Trimble v. Gordon,* 430 U.S. 762, 97 S.Ct. 1459, 52 L.Ed.2d 31 (1977) established that a nonmarital child has a constitutional right to inherit from a father, most states have amended their statutes to avoid unjustified discrimination against nonmarital children. Some states continue to control the right of inheritance from the biological parent by requiring either (1) an acknowledgment by the man that he is the father of the child or (2) convincing evidence in a civil paternity lawsuit that the man is the father of the child. Whenever either of these requirements is met, the nonmarital child has the right to inherit from the father; see Ark. Code Ann. § 28-9-209 and UPC § 2–114. Today, current DNA identification is an accurate method to establish paternity.

Reversing the roles, most states allow parents and their relatives to inherit from their nonmarital children who die intestate without issue (children). However, the father must establish appropriate proof of paternity; see Ga. Code Ann. § 53-2-4

nonmarital child
A child born to parents who are not married.

and Tex. Prob. Code Ann. § 42, and compare UPC § 2–114(c), in which the parent must have treated the child as his or hers and supported the child. Some states, like New York, have passed legislation preventing a parent from inheriting from a child whom the parent abandoned or failed to support during minority; see N.Y. EPTL § 4-1.4.

Pretermitted (Omitted) and Posthumous Children

preterminted (omitted) child
A child omitted in a parent's will.

Unlike a surviving spouse, children can be disinherited by their parents if the omission is intentional. A **pretermitted child** is a child omitted in a will by a parent. If a parent unintentionally does not mention a child or make a provision for a child in the will, and the child was either living at the date of the will's execution or was born thereafter, a statute may provide that the child, or the issue of a deceased child, shall receive a share in the estate as though the parent-testator had died intestate. The decision in *Crump's Estate v. Freeman*, 614 P.2d 1096 (Okl. 1980), illustrates this position. The court held that the omitted child (in the case) should receive the same share of the estate that the child would have taken if the testator had died intestate "unless the omission was intentional and not caused by accident or mistake." Most states have statutes that allow a child who is not named in the will to receive a share of the parent's estate. The UPC and other state statutes, however, include only children who were born after the will was executed; see UPC § 2–302, which limits the amount given to the omitted child to an equal amount that is given to other children. Other states cover children born before or after the testator's death; see Mass. Gen. Laws Ann. ch. 191 § 20. For an adopted child, the date of the adoption rather than the date of birth is controlling. An example of a state statute on the pretermitted child's right to inherit is Wis. Stat. Ann. § 853.25.

Under a pretermitted statute, a testator, while living, must (1) make some settlement or give an equal share of property to the omitted child (or grandchild, if the child is dead and there is a grandchild) by way of advancement; (2) after death, name the child as a beneficiary in the will; *or* (3) make it clear in the will that the omission of the child was intentional. Thus, a parent can give a child little or nothing through a will but must do so expressly; if the child is not mentioned in the will, the assumption is that the omission was inadvertent. The testator should include a specific clause in the will to establish a clear intent and avoid potential problems concerning pretermitted or omitted children.

> ### Sample Disinheritance Clause
> I have intentionally not provided in this will for my daughter, Elizabeth May Johnson, and for my son, Robert Jay Johnson, and these omissions are not caused by accident or mistake.

Section 2–101 (b) of the UPC officially recognizes the right of the testator to disinherit any heir, except a surviving spouse, by specifically excluding the named person or class of persons in the will.

posthumous child
A child born after the death of his or her father.

A **posthumous child** is conceived before but born after the death of his or her father. Under most state statutes, the child is given an intestate share of the deceased father's estate.

An emerging area of law involves the rights of a posthumously conceived genetic child—one where the child is conceived years after a parent's death with the help of frozen sperm or eggs. Although there are few cases in this area, several courts have ruled that a posthumously conceived child could be considered a "descendant" under certain circumstances and thus eligible to inherit from an estate. Other states have enacted laws that require a baby to be born within 36 months of the parent's death to have inheritance rights. In a Massachusetts case, genetically conceived twins born two years after their father's death were granted the right to have his name on their birth certificate. However, issues have arisen as to whether these children are entitled to Social Security benefits. The Social Security Commissioner refused to pay benefits contending that despite a state statute providing for posthumous children to be considered living at the death of their parent, the statute did not apply to posthumous "conception." In addressing the issue of Social Security benefits, the Supreme Court decided that deference should be given to state law. If state law provides that the child must be conceived in their father's lifetime in order to qualify for intestate succession, they would not be entitled to Social Security benefits.

⚖ *Ethical Issue*

It is important during an initial interview to discover whether the family has banked sperm and/or eggs. If so, it needs be very clear, in writing, how the eggs and/or sperm will be disposed of; and whether posthumously conceived children will inherit.

Disinheritance of Heirs (Children and Others) by Statute

All states, by statutes or court decisions, abolish the right of a convicted murderer, including a spouse or child, to inherit by will or intestacy the property of the victim. These state statutes are often called slayer or homicide statutes (see Cal. Prob. Code § 250; Ill. Compiled Stat. Ann. Ch. 755 § 5/2-6; Tenn. Code Ann. § 31-1-106; and UPC § 2–803). Often the slayer statute considers the killer to have predeceased the murdered victim, which may allow the inheritance to pass to the slayer's heirs, e.g., children. States have also passed legislation to abolish the inheritance rights of a beneficiary of a will who is convicted of killing other beneficiaries. Some states recognize mistreatment of a vulnerable or disabled testator or intestate by an heir as grounds for disinheriting the heir if convicted of financial exploitation, abuse, or neglect of the person from whom the heir could inherit (see Ill. Comp. Stat. Ann. 755 § 5/2-6.2).

Additional Rights or Protection for a Surviving Spouse and Children

In addition to the specific rights of a surviving spouse and children discussed above, these family members may receive benefits from a decedent spouse's estate that are not determined by the decedent's will or the state intestate succession statute. These benefits, established by other specific statutes, include the homestead exemption, homestead allowance, exempt property, and family support or allowance (sometimes called maintenance). They take priority not only over the decedent's will or the intestacy laws but also over creditors' claims against the decedent's estate.

Homestead Exemption

In some states, statutes protect a family that owns their house from eviction by creditors by allowing the **householder** or head of the family to designate a house and

householder
The head of the household or family who is entitled to the homestead exemption.

land as the homestead. The **homestead exemption** statute exempts the homestead from claims by creditors regardless of the amount of the householder's debt.

The **homestead** is defined as the house and adjoining land occupied by the owner as a home. The amount of land comprising the homestead may be limited in acreage by statute. For example, in Kansas a rural homestead is limited to 160 acres and an urban homestead to 1 acre. The following Minnesota statutes define a homestead, identify its area limits, and explain its descent to surviving family members.

Minn. Stat. Ann. § 510.01 **Homestead Defined; Exempt; Exception**
The house owned and occupied by a debtor as the debtor's dwelling place, together with the land upon which it is situated to the amount of area and value hereinafter limited and defined, shall constitute the homestead of such debtor and the debtor's family, and be exempt from seizure or sale under legal process on account of any debt not lawfully charged thereon in writing, except such as are incurred for work or materials furnished in the construction, repair, or improvement of such homestead, or for services performed by laborers or servants and as is provided in section 550.175.

Minn. Stat. Ann. § 510.02 **Area and Value; How Limited**
The homestead may include any quantity of land not exceeding 160 acres, and not included in the laid out or platted portion of any city. If the homestead is within the laid out or platted portion of a city, its area must not exceed one-half of an acre. The value of the homestead exemption, whether the exemption is claimed jointly or individually, may not exceed $300,000 or, if the homestead is used primarily for agricultural purposes, $750,000, exclusive of the limitations set forth in section 510.05.

Minn. Stat. Ann. § 524.2-402 **Descent of Homestead**
(a) If there is a surviving spouse, the homestead, including a manufactured home which is the family residence, descends free from any testamentary or other disposition of it to which the spouse has not consented in writing or as provided by law, as follows:
   (1) if there is no surviving descendant of decedent, to the spouse; or
   (2) if there are surviving descendants of decedent, then to the spouse for the term of the spouse's natural life and the remainder in equal shares to the decedent's descendants by representation.
(b) If there is no surviving spouse and the homestead has not been disposed of by will, it descends as other real estate.
(c) If the homestead passes by descent or will to the spouse or decedent's descendants, it is exempt from all debts which were not valid charges on it at the time of decedent's death except that the homestead is subject to a claim filed pursuant to section 246.53 for state hospital care or 256B.15 for medical assistance benefits. If the homestead passes to a person other than a spouse or decedent's descendants, it is subject to the payment of expenses of administration, funeral expenses, expenses of last illness, taxes, and debts. The claimant may seek to enforce a lien or other charge against a homestead so exempted by an appropriate action in the district court.
(d) For purposes of this section, except as provided in section 524.2-301, the surviving spouse is deemed to consent to any testamentary or other disposition of the homestead to which the spouse has not previously consented in writing unless the spouse files in the manner provided in section 524.2-211, paragraph (f), a petition that asserts the homestead rights provided to the spouse by this section.

It is common practice for spouses to hold title to their home in joint tenancy or tenancy by the entirety. When one spouse dies, the homestead automatically passes to the surviving spouse as a result of the right of survivorship.

If both spouses are living, most states provide that the homestead cannot be sold without the consent and signature of each spouse.

To illustrate the passage of a homestead upon the intestate death of its owner, consider the following assignment.

ASSIGNMENT 3.4

Felix and Ava have been married for the past 32 years. Felix owns their house, which he purchased before their marriage, in his name only. Felix dies without a will. He is survived by his widow, Ava; two children, Abby and Marie; and six grandchildren: Hannah and Elias, Abby's children; Mia and Max, Marie's children; and Leon and Johanna, children of Felix's deceased child, Stanley. The house in which Felix and Ava lived has a lien against it for partial nonpayment of 2014 property taxes and a 30-year mortgage with 5 years remaining. According to your state laws, how, to whom, and in what shares will the house descend? Is the descent of the homestead free from creditors' claims against it?

Homestead Allowance

Instead of a homestead exemption, some states provide a cash award called a **homestead allowance** for the benefit of a surviving spouse or minor children. This allowance is also not subject to creditors' claims and is a priority payment made to the surviving spouse or minor children in addition to any property passing to them by the provisions of a will, by intestate succession, or by a surviving spouse's right to an elective share; see UPC § 2–402.

homestead allowance
A statute that provides a modest cash award for the benefit of a surviving spouse or minor children; it is a priority payment to them and is not subject to creditors' claims.

Exempt Property

Many states and the UPC also exempt some of the decedent's personal property up to a specific dollar amount, which is given to the surviving spouse and/or children free from claims of creditors. The property is often limited to a selection of household furniture, appliances, furnishings, automobiles, and personal effects, and the number of items in the various categories that constitute the **exempt property** can also be limited, e.g., one car; see Ala. Code § 43-8-111; R. I. Gen. Laws § 33-10-1; Va. Code Ann. § 64.1-151.2; and UPC § 2–403. Under the UPC, the selected exempt property either goes to the surviving spouse or to the children equally if there is no surviving spouse. Sections 271, 272, and 278 of the Texas Probate Code allow minor or adult children to receive exempt property. In cases in which the decedent did not own any qualifying exempt personal property, state laws may provide for a modest cash allowance in place of the property; see Tex. Prob. Code Ann. §§ 273-277. Exempt property is identified in the following statute.

exempt property
The decedent's personal property up to a specific dollar amount that is given to the surviving spouse and/or minor children and is exempt from creditors' claims.

Minn. Stat. Ann. § 524.2-403 **Exempt Property**
(a) If there is a surviving spouse, then, in addition to the homestead and family allowance, the surviving spouse is entitled from the estate to:
    (1) property not exceeding $10,000 in value in excess of any security interests therein, in household furniture, furnishings, appliances, and personal effects, subject to an award of sentimental value property under section 525.152; and
    (2) one automobile, if any, without regard to value.
(b) If there is no surviving spouse, the decedent's children are entitled jointly to the same property as provided in paragraph (a), except that where it appears from the decedent's will a child was omitted intentionally, the child is not entitled to the rights conferred by this section.

(c) If encumbered chattels are selected and the value in excess of security interests, plus that of other exempt property, is less than $10,000, or if there is not $10,000 worth of exempt property in the estate, the surviving spouse or children are entitled to other personal property of the estate, if any, to the extent necessary to make up the $10,000 value.

(d) Rights to exempt property and assets needed to make up a deficiency of exempt property have priority over all claims against the estate, but the right to any assets to make up a deficiency of exempt property abates as necessary to permit earlier payment of the family allowance.

(e) The rights granted by this section are in addition to any benefit or share passing to the surviving spouse or children by the decedent's will, unless otherwise provided by intestate succession or by way of elective share.

Family Allowance

During the administration of the decedent spouse's estate, most states give the probate court the power to award the surviving spouse and/or minor children the exempt property (see previous discussion) *and* a monthly cash allowance for their maintenance and support; see Ariz. Rev. Stat. Ann. § 14-2404; Conn. Gen. Stat. Ann. § 45a-320; Or. Rev. Stat. § 114.015; and UPC § 2–404. The amount of the award varies and is determined by the probate court based on the assets and liabilities of the estate and the family needs. The award may be terminated by the death of the recipient(s) or remarriage of the surviving spouse, as illustrated by the case of *Hamrick v. Bonner*, 182 Ga.App. 76, 354 S.E.2d 687 (1987). The decedent's will cannot defeat this **"family" allowance** even if the decedent disinherited them, and it, too, is exempt from creditors' claims. In Tennessee, such an award is called the "year's support allowance."

> **"family" allowance**
> A statute that allows the court to award to the surviving spouse and/or minor children a monthly cash allowance for their maintenance and support.

The following statute provides an example of such an allowance.

Minn. Stat. Ann. § 524.2-404 Family Allowance

(a) In addition to the right to the homestead and exempt property, the decedent's surviving spouse and minor children whom the decedent was obligated to support, and children who were in fact being supported by the decedent, shall be allowed a reasonable family allowance in money out of the estate for their maintenance as follows:
   (1) for one year if the estate is inadequate to discharge allowed claims; or
   (2) for 18 months if the estate is adequate to discharge allowed claims.

(b) The amount of the family allowance may be determined by the personal representative in an amount not to exceed $1,500 per month.

(c) The family allowance is payable to the surviving spouse, if living; otherwise to the children, their guardian or conservator, or persons having their care and custody.

(d) The family allowance is exempt from and has priority over all claims.

(e) The family allowance is not chargeable against any benefit or share passing to the surviving spouse or children by the will of the decedent unless otherwise provided, by intestate succession or by way of elective share. The death of any person entitled to family allowance does not terminate the right of that person to the allowance.

(f) The personal representative or an interested person aggrieved by any determination, payment, proposed payment, or failure to act under this section may petition the court for appropriate relief, which may include a family allowance other than that which the personal representative determined or could have determined.

See also Chapter 9 on family allowances.

ASSIGNMENT 3.5

Lorenzo and Gianna, husband and wife, have been married for 10 years. They have three minor children, Mateo, Anthony, and Martina. Lorenzo is killed in an airplane mishap. He has no will, and his wife and children survive him. Gianna has been advised that probate might be lengthy. Lorenzo's estate includes (a) a $140,000 house; (b) household furnishings, clothing, and other like items valued at $25,000; (c) additional items of personal property amounting to $20,000; (d) a $15,000 family car. Gianna estimates that upkeep for the family during probate of her husband's estate will cost $1,400 per month. At death, Lorenzo's estate had $200,000 in assets and $5,000 in liabilities.

As an exercise in how to analyze a state statute, answer the following according to the family allowance and exempt property procedures under the Minnesota law, mentioned above.

1. From what source and how much can Gianna seek as the allowance and exempt property granted a surviving spouse?
2. Will Lorenzo's children be entitled to receive the allowance, and if so, when?
3. Does the family allowance or exempt property in this case include the car?
4. Will the family receive a sum of money to maintain it for the balance of the time it takes to administer Lorenzo's estate? If so, for how long? If not, why not?
5. Check to see if your state has a family allowance statute. If it does, answer the questions above according to your own state laws.

On the descent of other property, Minn. Stat. Ann. § 524.2-101 states that subject to the family allowances that are granted in cases of both testacy and intestacy, the items paid out of the estate are the expenses of probate administration, funeral expenses, expenses of the last illness, and taxes and debts under federal and state law (see UPC § 3–805). The balance of the estate, both real and personal property, descends and is distributed as follows.

Minn. Stat. Ann. § 524.2-102 Share of the Spouse
The intestate share of a decedent's surviving spouse is:
(1) the entire intestate estate if:
    (1) no descendant of the decedent survives the decedent; or
    (2) all of the decedent's surviving descendants are also descendants of the surviving spouse and there is no other descendant of the surviving spouse who survives the decedent;
(2) the first $150,000 plus one-half of any balance of the intestate estate, if all of the decedent's surviving descendants are also descendants of the surviving spouse and the surviving spouse has one or more surviving descendants who are not descendants of the decedent, or if one or more of the decedent's surviving descendants are not descendants of the surviving spouse.

Minn. Stat. Ann. § 524.2-103 Share of Heirs Other Than Surviving Spouse
Any part of the intestate estate not passing to the decedent's surviving spouse under section 524.2-102, or the entire intestate estate if there is no surviving spouse, passes in the following order to the individuals designated below who survive the decedent:
(1) to the decedent's descendants by representation;
(2) if there is no surviving descendant, to the decedent's parents equally if both survive, or to the surviving parent;
(3) if there is no surviving descendant or parent, to the descendants of the decedent's parents or either of them by representation;

(4) if there is no surviving descendant, parent, or descendant of a parent, but the decedent is survived by one or more grandparents or descendants of grandparents, half of the estate passes to the decedent's paternal grandparents equally if both survive, or to the surviving paternal grandparent, or to the descendants of the decedent's paternal grandparents or either of them if both are deceased, the descendants taking by representation; and the other half passes to the decedent's maternal relatives in the same manner; but if there is no surviving grandparent or descendant of a grandparent on either the paternal or the maternal side, the entire estate passes to the decedent's relatives on the other side in the same manner as the half;

(5) if there is no surviving descendant, parent, descendant of a parent, grandparent, or descendant of a grandparent, to the next of kin in equal degree, except that when there are two or more collateral kindred in equal degree claiming through different ancestors, those who claim through the nearest ancestor shall take to the exclusion of those claiming through an ancestor more remote.

Finally, if neither a spouse nor any kindred survives the intestate, the estate passes to the state by the process of *escheat*. Personal property *escheats* to the state of the decedent's domicile at death as does real property located in that state. Real property situated outside the state of the decedent's domicile escheats to the state of its location.

USE OF INTESTATE TERMINOLOGY

The following situation illustrates the meaning and use of the terminology used in cases of intestacy.

The Facts

Toby Smith dies without a will. His survivors are Sally Smith, Toby's present wife; Wylie Smith and Margo Smith Tyler, children by his marriage to Sally; John Smith, an adopted son; Bob Smith, his brother; Sue Smith, his sister; Doris Smith, his mother; Kay and Mary Tyler, Margo's children; Bert and Thad Smith, Wylie's nonmarital children; Rosey Thorn, Sally's daughter by a previous marriage; Tom Johnson, a foster child who lives with the Smiths; Jane Carson, a woman Toby had lived with, but not married; and Carol Stuart, Toby's former wife. Frank Malcolm is appointed administrator by the probate court to manage and administer Toby's estate.

Review of Terminology

Toby Smith dies *intestate* because he left no will directing the distribution of his estate at his death. His death without a will is known as *intestacy,* and Toby, the decedent, is the *intestate.* What, how, and to whom the various items of property in his estate pass on his death are controlled by *intestate succession statutes,* state laws that govern the process by which intestate estates are distributed. In effect, the state writes the "will" when a decedent fails to write one.

In addition to the decedent's spouse, various family members, ranked in the order of closest blood relative to the intestate, are the *heirs, distributees,* or *successors* who share in the distribution of the *intestate's* estate. Under the UPC, an heir may receive either real or personal property, or both. Confusion exists in the terminology used to describe the manner in which property passes from an intestate. Under the orthodox terminology, an *heir* is one entitled to inherit the decedent's real property, and a *distributee* or *next of kin* is one entitled to inherit the decedent's personal property. However, these words are frequently used interchangeably.

All persons mentioned in the facts above who survived Toby, including his adopted son John, are potential *heirs, distributees,* or *successors,* except Rosey Thorn, Tom Johnson, Jane Carson, and Carol Stuart, who are not blood relatives and do not trace their relationship to Toby through *consanguinity.* His mother, Doris, is an *ascendant* who possesses an interest in the estate through a direct upward bloodline as an ascending *lineal ancestor.* Wylie, Margo, Bert, Thad, Kay, and Mary, Toby's children and grandchildren, who are in a direct bloodline downward as descending lineals, are his *descendants.* Bob and Sue, his brother and sister, are not direct blood *lineals,* but instead trace their relationship to him through their mother, Doris, as a common ancestor. They are *collaterals* in a collateral relationship line to Toby.

Toby's *adopted* son, John Smith, would be entitled to share in the estate. Statutes entitle *adopted children,* such as Toby's son, John Smith, to inherit from their *adoptive parents* (Toby) on the same basis natural children (Wylie and Margo) have for inheritance—lineal descent. In some states, adopted children are precluded from inheritance from their natural parents. However, in a few states, the adopted child (John) can inherit from both his natural parents in all circumstances and from his adoptive parents (Toby) but the natural parents do not inherit from or through the adopted child (John) (see R.I. Gen. Laws § 15-7-17 and Wyo. Stat. § 2-4-107).

The inheritance rights of a child whose natural parent dies and whose surviving parent remarries and the new spouse legally adopts the child are sometimes delineated by statute.

Conn. Gen. Stat. Ann. § 45a–731 Effects of Final Decree of Adoption— Surviving Rights

A final decree of adoption, whether issued by a court of this state or a court of any other jurisdiction, shall have the following effect in this state: ...

(8) Notwithstanding the provisions of subdivisions (1) to (7), inclusive, of this section, when one of the biological parents of a minor child has died and the surviving parent has remarried subsequent to such parent's death, adoption of such child by the person with whom such remarriage is contracted shall not affect the rights of such child to inherit from or through the deceased parent and the deceased parent's relatives; ... [see UPC § 2–114(b)].

Depending on the statutes of Toby's *domiciliary state,* Wylie's *nonmarital children,* Bert and Thad, may or may not inherit from Toby, since their inheritance through intestacy is possible only if Wylie dies before Toby. Most state statutes would allow Bert and Thad to inherit their mother's share of Toby's estate *by representation.* Tom Johnson, the foster child living with the Smiths, would not inherit from Toby.

ASSIGNMENT 3.6

After Cameron's father died, his mother remarried; her second husband legally adopted Cameron. Three weeks later, the brother of Cameron's natural father died intestate, leaving no other surviving heirs. Cameron wishes to claim his uncle's estate. Is he entitled? Cite statutory authority from the state of Connecticut. If this situation had occurred in your state, what statute(s) would control it?

In most states, all the heirs in the same *degree of relationship* to the intestate share equally through *per capita* distribution. For example, if Toby dies and only his children survive him, then Wylie, Margo, and John would each receive one-third of his estate per capita, a distribution equally divided among the heirs standing in the same degree of relationship to the intestate.

EXAMPLE:

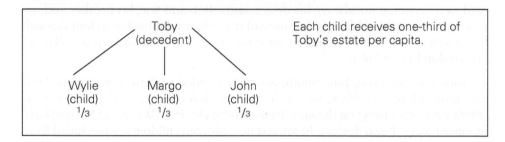

Each child receives one-third of Toby's estate per capita.

The same is true if only his grandchildren are living and Toby's domiciliary state statutes allow nonmarital children to inherit from their grandparent.

EXAMPLE:

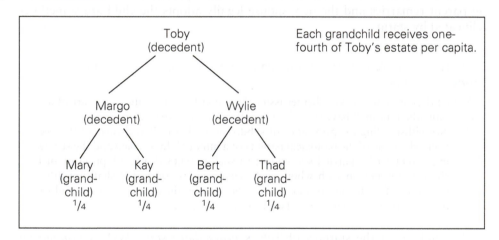

Each grandchild receives one-fourth of Toby's estate per capita.

The same is true if only his brother and sister survive his death.

EXAMPLE:

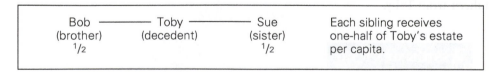

Each sibling receives one-half of Toby's estate per capita.

A different result is reached when a successor (heir) predeceases the intestate. If Wylie dies before her father, and later Toby dies, his grandchildren, Bert and Thad, would receive Wylie's share of their grandfather's estate by right of representation *(per stirpes)* to be divided equally between them.

EXAMPLE:

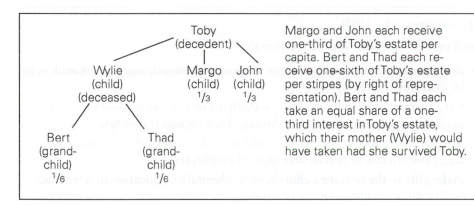

Toby
(decedent)

Wylie
(child)
(deceased)

Margo
(child)
¹/₃

John
(child)
¹/₃

Bert
(grand-
child)
¹/₆

Thad
(grand-
child)
¹/₆

Margo and John each receive one-third of Toby's estate per capita. Bert and Thad each receive one-sixth of Toby's estate per stirpes (by right of representation). Bert and Thad each take an equal share of a one-third interest in Toby's estate, which their mother (Wylie) would have taken had she survived Toby.

If Toby dies without the aforementioned persons surviving him, or any other relatives entitled to inherit his estate, the property *escheats*, i.e., the state acquires title to the intestate's property.

Since Frank Malcolm is appointed to manage and distribute Toby's estate, he is the *administrator* or *personal representative* who acts under the supervision of the *probate court.* If, however, Frank's sister, Karen (or any other woman), is appointed by the probate court, she would be the *administratrix* of Toby's estate.

ASSIGNMENT 3.7

Natalie Robinson dies without a will. The following relatives survive her: a husband, Len; an adopted daughter, Lana; a foster son, Thomas; two sisters, Faith and Nadine; a brother, Thor; her mother, Simone; her father, Ernie; her mother-in-law, Isla; Len's sister, Cynthia; an aunt, Rose; an uncle, Oscar; two nephews, Donnie and Kevin, sons of her deceased brother, William; a niece, Diane, daughter of her deceased sister, Sharon; a grandson, David, son of her deceased daughter, Denise; a granddaughter, Luella, daughter of her deceased daughter, Nancy; and Manny, a husband by a prior marriage whom she divorced.

1. Who is the intestate?
2. Who is the administrator or administratrix?
3. Name the laws that govern the passage of the decedent's estate.
4. Find and cite the state statute that would determine the passage of Natalie's estate in your state.
5. Name the decedent's lineal relatives who are ascendants and descendants.
6. Name the collaterals related to the decedent.
7. List all the potential successors (heirs) of the decedent.
8. Name the relationship that entitles the persons in question 7 to possibly share in the decedent's estate.
9. List persons who might be excluded from receiving any of the decedent's property.
10. How are the persons in question 9 related to the decedent?
11. Name relatives who might receive their share of the decedent's estate per capita.
12. Name relatives who might receive their share of the decedent's estate per stirpes.
13. What would happen if the decedent had no surviving spouse or relatives?
14. Diagram a family tree for Natalie and her relatives.

ADVANTAGES AND DISADVANTAGES OF A WILL

Advantages of a Will

A will makes it possible for the testator to

- designate how much and to whom all property owned, real or personal, is to be distributed after death.
- leave property to family members equally or in varying amounts based on need or the affection for or worthiness of the chosen recipients.
- leave property to someone who would not take under intestate succession, e.g., close friends or special and faithful employees.
- make gifts to the testator's church, or to charitable, educational, scientific, and health institutions or organizations.
- subject to the approval of the probate court, nominate a personal guardian to care for any minor or incompetent person and a property guardian to manage the property inherited by the minor or incompetent person.
- appoint a trustee and create testamentary trusts, which, through proper estate planning, can diminish death taxes, e.g., estate taxes.
- nominate a personal representative and grant the nominee special powers relating to the administration of the estate.
- avoid many legal problems that may accompany an intestate's estate administration, e.g., a will can waive the bond requirement for the appointed personal representative.

Disadvantages of a Will

Disadvantages include the following:

- The probate of a will is often time-consuming and expensive and can cause inconvenience to the decedent's family.
- In addition to the delays and costs, probating a will also causes bureaucracy (red tape) problems.
- A will does not eliminate complicated procedures, e.g., the problems that accompany the transfer of ownership from the decedent to the beneficiary.
- The loss of privacy and confidentiality concerning the decedent's property and named beneficiaries. All wills are filed in the county courthouse of the decedent's domiciliary state, and they are open to the public and the news media.
- If the will is ill-fitting, poorly drafted, outdated, or inadequate, having no will might be more acceptable.

ASSIGNMENT 3.8

1. Review § 1–201 of the UPC on general definitions. Does your state's code have a separate section on such definitions? Note any differences from those presented in this text.
2. Does every eligible member of your family have a will? Why or why not? If a member of your family has no will, list reasons why that person should have one.
3. Secure a copy of someone's will (e.g., spouse, parent) or a sample will from a law library and identify as many of the terms defined in this chapter as possible.

Key Terms

succession

testacy

intestacy

Uniform Probate Code (UPC)

nuncupative will

statutory will

joint will

mutual (reciprocal) wills

living will

specific legacy or bequest

specific devise

demonstrative legacy

general legacy

residuary legacy or devise

ademption

adeem

lapse

antilapse statute

abatement

marshaling of assets

per capita distribution

per capita by representation

right of representation

per stirpes distribution

degree of relationship

collateral heirs (relatives)

degrees of kindred

escheat

right of election

elective or forced share statute

antenuptial (premarital) agreement

postnuptial agreement

issue

adoption

adopted child

nonmarital child

pretermitted (omitted) child

posthumous child

householder

homestead exemption

homestead

homestead allowance

exempt property

family allowance

Review Questions

1. What is a will contest? If the contestant of a will is successful and the will is declared invalid, what law determines how and to whom the intestate's in-state and out-of-state real and personal property is distributed?

2. Review the comparison of orthodox and UPC terminology in Exhibit 3.1. How do the meanings of the terms *heir* and *devisee* differ between the two sets of terminology?

3. What are four types of basic wills? Define and explain each one.

4. Explain the differences between (A) a bequest and a devise; (B) a specific legacy and a specific devise; (C) a demonstrative legacy and a general legacy; and (D) a residuary legacy and a residuary devise.

5. What does it mean when a gift in a will is adeemed or lapses?

6. When there are insufficient assets in the testator's estate to pay all debts, taxes, and expenses, what is the order of abatement of the decedent's assets including legacies and devises?

7. How does per capita distribution differ from per stirpes distribution in intestacy cases?

8. Which computation method, the civil law method or the common law method, do you prefer to determine the degree of relationship of collateral heirs? Explain.

9. What does the term *escheat* mean? When does escheat occur?

10. Why is it generally impossible for a testator to disinherit his or her surviving spouse? Explain.

11. What effect does a divorce or a marriage have on a preexisting will?

12. What are the inheritance rights of an adopted child; a stepchild; a nonmarital child; and a pretermitted child?

13. How does a homestead exemption differ from a homestead allowance? How do family allowances differ from exempt property?

14. Review the provisions of Leona Helmsley's will as reported in the press. Which conditions, restrictions, or bequests do you find reasonable and appropriate? Which ones do you think are "quirky" and inappropriate? Explain why you reach those conclusions.

Case Problems

Problem 1

Emmett Tomas, a bachelor, makes the following testamentary gifts: a house valued at $110,000 to his best friend, Roxanne Rudin; furniture and household appliances worth $8,000 to Roxanne; a television and stereo system worth $2,500 to his nephew, Roland Tomas; a Toyota Camry worth $15,000 to his only brother, William Tomas; a gift of $10,000 to his sister-in-law, Sally Tomas, to be paid out of his savings account in Metro State Bank in his hometown; a gift of $5,000 to his church; and a residue gift of his remaining property, which is all personal property worth $22,000, to the American Cancer Society.

A. Place each gift in the appropriate disposition category.

Specific devise

Specific legacy

Residuary legacy

General legacy

Demonstrative legacy

B. After his death, Emmett's expenses, debts, and taxes amount to $50,000 and none of his assets pass outside his will as intestate property. Explain how Emmett's testamentary gifts are used to pay his obligations according to the abatement process.

C. If William dies before Emmett and no successor beneficiary is named to receive the Toyota before Emmett dies, what happens to this gift and how does it abate?

D. If the law in Emmett's domiciliary state "abates" a decedent's property within each disposition category and uses the property for payment of debts on a prorated basis, how much, if any, of the specific legacies does each beneficiary get to keep after the $50,000 obligation is paid? See *Matter of Estate of Wales*, 223 Mont. 515, 727 P.2d 536 (1986).

Problem 2

The following diagram shows the interest each descendant would receive in Howard's estate. All descendants are living except as noted.

A. Is the distribution method per capita, per capita by representation, or per stirpes? See *Warpool v. Floyd*, 524 S.W.2d 247 (1975), and *In re Morton's* Estate, 48 N.J. 42, 222 A.2d 185 (1966).

B. Explain how the shares of Abel and Barb are determined.

C. Eli, Fred, and Gary do not receive an interest. Why not? Explain.

D. Explain the calculation of the shares of Kathy and Lee.

E. If Debbie were married, would her surviving husband receive an interest? Explain.

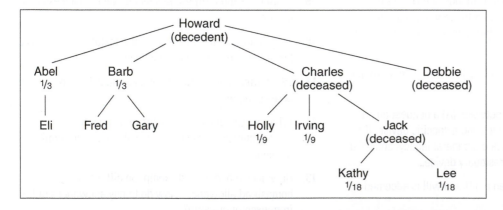

Practical Assignments

1. Using form 3.3, complete the will as if you were the testator and a resident of Wisconsin.

2. Draw a diagram of your family tree including descendants and ascendants through the second degree.

3. Determine who would inherit from you if you died intestate under your own state laws.

WILLS: VALIDITY REQUIREMENTS, MODIFICATION, REVOCATION, AND CONTESTS

4

Outline

Objectives

After completing this chapter, you should be able to:

- Use the terminology associated with the validity, modification, and revocation of wills.

- Recognize the formal requirements for a valid will and verify that a client's will has satisfied all those requirements.

- Interpret statutes and statutory language so that you can apply the statutes to problems presented by a client's will.

- Understand the legal requirements for modifying an existing will and know how to avoid errors in making modifications.

- Identify and describe the various methods of revoking a will.

- Explain the legitimate grounds for contesting a will.

SCOPE OF THE CHAPTER

The execution, modification, and revocation of a will must be done according to specific statutory guidelines. This chapter discusses the terminology and basic requirements for creation of a valid will. The ways an existing will can be changed or modified are covered next along with the procedures that demonstrate the intention of a testator or testatrix to revoke a will. The chapter concludes with a discussion of will contests—the proper persons to contest the legality of a will and the grounds for commencement of a will contest.

REQUIREMENTS FOR THE CREATION OF A VALID WILL

case law
Law made by judges' decisions.

A will is a legally enforceable, written declaration of a person's intended distribution of property after death. Since a will is "ambulatory," i.e., subject to change, the declaration is revocable during the testator's lifetime and is operative only upon death. Each state passes legislation that controls the right and power of a person to execute a valid will, and these statutes and subsequent **case law** (court decisions) establish the procedure that must be followed. The following state statutes are examples of the requirements for testamentary capacity and the proper execution of a will.

> *Ill. Compiled Stat. Ann. Ch. 755 § 5/4-1* **Capacity of Testator**
> Every person who has attained the age of 18 years and is of sound mind and memory has power to bequeath by will the real and personal estate which he has at the time of his death.

> *Ohio Rev. Code Ann. § 2107.03* **Method of Making Will**
> Except oral wills, every last will and testament shall be in writing, but may be handwritten or typewritten. Such will shall be signed at the end by the party making it, or by some other person in such party's presence and at his express direction, and be attested and subscribed in the presence of such party, by two or more competent witnesses, who saw the testator subscribe, or heard him acknowledge his signature.

ASSIGNMENT 4.1

Wyatt Hasper is 17 years old. He handwrites and signs a will, leaving all his property to his brother, Landen. There are no witnesses to the will. At age 23, Wyatt is killed while driving a car. Wyatt's only living relatives are Landen and their mother, Trinity. Answer the following questions according to your state law.

1. Is Wyatt's will valid? Explain.

2. Does Wyatt's holographic need witnesses? Must it be dated?

3. What formal requirements for the proper execution of a will are lacking?

4. If both Trinity and Landen claim Wyatt's estate, who prevails? Explain.

The importance of learning your state's requirements for making a valid will cannot be overstated. At the same time, even though state statutes that regulate the preparation and execution of wills are not uniform, they do share some basic similarities. All wills must meet specific formalities to prevent fraud and uncertainty.

Commonly, the requirements for a properly executed will are (1) the maker must have testamentary intent and capacity; and (2) the will must comply with certain formal requirements, e.g., the will must be written, signed, and dated by the testator and witnessed and signed by at least two persons.

Intent of the Testator

For a will to be declared a legal document that can transfer a decedent's estate after death, the maker must have **testamentary intent**; that is, the testator must establish that the written document currently operates as his last will. The document is a valid will only if the maker possesses the required *animus testandi*, i.e., the intention to make a will with the express purpose of disposing of property upon death—but not before, as illustrated by the case of *Faith v. Singleton*, 286 Ark. 403, 692 S.W.2d 239 (1985). The testator's intent is revealed from the form, general language, and particular words used in the will itself. Many courts, however, also look at the surrounding circumstances in determining testamentary intent, e.g., the comments and activities of a person who is terminally ill, the collection and placement of important papers in a safe location, and comments made by a person about distribution plans after death. The absence of the ceremonial declaration "this is my last will" often creates doubt about whether a will is intended (see *Matter of Griffin's Will*, 81 A.D.2d 735, 439 N.Y.S.2d 492 [1981], in which the court ruled that because the testatrix, Griffin, did not declare or publish to the witnesses that she intended a document they signed to be her will, the document was not entitled to be probated). Courts have often ruled, however, that a document need not be labeled a "will" to be a valid testamentary instrument. In the case of *Estate of Logan*, 489 Pa. 29, 413 A.2d 681 (1980), a paper stating "… I give all my monies and estates to my sister Lillian …" was declared a will and probated.

Caveat: With the exception of "statutory" wills, which have been adopted in a few states (see the detailed discussion in Chapter 5), writing one's own will or using preprinted will forms to avoid the expense of an attorney may be foolhardy. Even worse, it may end in the creation of a document that fails to satisfy the statutory requirements for a legal will regardless of the good intentions of the maker.

Capacity of the Testator

As explained in Chapter 2, **testamentary capacity** is necessary for the creation of a valid will. In all states, a testator must be of majority age (usually 18) and sane, i.e., have the required testamentary capacity to create a valid will (see UPC § 2–501). State statutes and court decisions have established, however, that a member of the armed forces or a married person can make a valid will even if under the age of majority (see Tex. Prob. Code Ann. § 57 and Iowa Code Ann. § 599.1). Sanity is the "soundness of mind" that enables a person to have sufficient mental capacity to create a valid will. In general, a testator must meet the following test for testamentary capacity (sound mind).

- The testator must remember and be aware of the persons who are the "**natural objects of the testator's bounty**"—usually family members but also persons for whom the testator has affection.
- The testator must know and be aware of the kind, extent, and nature of the property to be distributed.

testamentary intent
Requirement for a valid will that the testator must intend the instrument to operate as his/her last will.

testamentary capacity
The sanity (sound mind) requirement for a person to make a valid will.

natural objects of the testator's bounty
Family members and other persons (friends) and institutions (charitable or religious organizations) for whom the testator has affection.

- The testator must formulate a plan, e.g., a will, for distribution of the property to the intended beneficiaries, i.e., family and friends, and understand the effect of the dispositions of the plan.

The case *In re Lacy's Estate*, 431 P.2d 366 (Okl. 1967), illustrates the application of this test. The court stated, "A person has 'testamentary capacity' when his mind and memory are such that he knows, in a general way, the character and extent of his property, understands his relationship to the objects of his bounty and those who ought to be in his mind on the occasion of making a will, and comprehends the nature and effect of the testamentary act."

This test for "sound mind," which was formed in case law instead of statutes, relates to the testator's ability, not to his actual knowledge of details. Still a testator must be able to hold these facts in mind long enough to make a rational judgment. Such capacity is needed only at the time of making and executing the will. Even though a person has a low level of intelligence or suffers from a mental illness or senility, it does not mean the person necessarily lacks testamentary capacity. The individual case and circumstances must be investigated and judged on the basis of the test, as established in cases such as *Estate of Wrigley*, 104 Ill.App.3rd. 1008, 60 Ill.Dec. 757, 433 N.E.2d 995 (1982). Case law has consistently held that neither eccentricities or peculiarities of the will nor uncleanliness, slovenliness, neglect of person and clothing, and offensive and disgusting habits of a testator constitute an "unsound mind."

insane delusions
A person with a disordered mind imagines facts to exist for which there is no evidence.

A common question when determining testamentary capacity is whether a person suffering "delusions" lacks such capacity. Some courts have held that a testator suffering delusions is not mentally competent. Most have decided that the presence of **insane delusions** is consistent with testamentary capacity, if the delusions are of such a nature that they cannot reasonably have affected the dispositions made by a will. The testimony of witnesses to the will is often critical in court decisions on "delusions" as noted in *Yett's* case in Chapter 2. See also *Matter of Coleman's Estate*, 1 Haw. App. 136, 615 P.2d 760 (1980), in which the court held that during a "**lucid interval**," a mentally ill person can execute a valid will.

lucid interval
A temporary restoration to sanity during which an incompetent person has sufficient intelligence and judgment to make a valid will.

In will contest cases, Section 3–407 of the Uniform Probate Code places the burden of proof of the lack of the testator's capacity on the contestant—the person contesting the will (this was the decision in *Lacy's Estate*, cited above). Some states, however, place the burden of proof of the testator's "sound mind" on the proponent—the person who submits or delivers the will to the court—as in the case of *Croucher v. Croucher*, 660 S.W.2d 55 (Tex. 1983). The procedures generally followed to satisfy the burden of proof and establish testamentary capacity (i.e., sound mind) include the following:

- The filing of the will.
- The witnesses give testimony or affidavits are filed that acknowledge the proper completion of formal procedures required for a valid will and the testator's rational behavior and comments *at the time of the execution of the will.*
- The order of the probate court admitting the probate of the will.

Next, during the contest of the will, others, in addition to the witnesses, may testify concerning the testator's "sound mind." Family members, the testator's personal physician, and other medical care providers may testify, for example. Since the determination of testamentary capacity is a "fact issue," the decision of capacity or lack thereof is generally left to a jury or the court. As a paralegal, if you are asked to witness a will, you must make your judgment of the testator's capacity at the time of the execution of the will with the understanding that *if the testator obviously lacks capacity you should not sign the will.*

⚖️ *Ethical Issue*

ASSIGNMENT 4.2

1. Dylan Dalton, age 18, inherited an estate valued at $150,000 from his father. Dylan wants his property to go to his dog, Opie. Therefore, Dylan executes a formal written will that passes all his property to his best friend, Connor, to be used solely for the benefit of the dog and provides that when the dog dies, the remaining property is to be given to the Animal Humane Society. At age 20, while walking on the railroad tracks, Dylan is killed by a train. Dylan's only living relative, his mother, claims his estate. Was Dylan's will valid in your state when he died? Who would receive Dylan's estate according to the law in your state?

2. Bradford, age 85, is not married and has no heirs besides his sisters, Katherine and Layla, who live with him and are completely dependent on him for support. He dies and, in his will, gives his entire estate of $100,000 to the American Lung Association. Do Katherine and Layla have grounds on which to challenge the will by alleging that Bradford lacked the capacity to make a valid will? Answer the question according to your state's law.

Formal Requirements of a Will

In addition to testamentary intent and capacity to create a valid will, a testator must execute it with certain formal requirements.

A Written Will

By either statute or case law, a majority of the states require a will to be in writing to be valid (see UPC § 2-502). Generally, a will must be typed, printed, or handwritten to fulfill the requirement. *Note:* Today, the most common method is a computer-generated and printed will. One state, Nevada, recognizes wills and the associated signatures that are written in a completely electronic form (see Nev. Rev. Stat. Ann, § 133.085). A completely handwritten or holographic will is valid in many states, but it must meet the other formal requirements unless otherwise provided by statute. Section 133.090(1) of the Nevada Revised Statute provides the following:

> A holographic will is a will in which the signature, date, and material provisions are written by the hand of the testator, whether or not it is witnessed or notarized. It is subject to no other form, and may be made in or out of this state.

Currently, over half of the states allow holographic wills (see Exhibit 3.2), but the requirements for their validity differ from state to state. In the case *Matter of Estate of Cunningham*, 198 N.J.Super. 484, 487 A.2d 777 (1984), the court did not require a holographic will to be completely handwritten. Instead, the court held that all that is required to admit the writing to probate as a holographic will is that the signature and material provisions in the will be in the handwriting of the testator. Some states require the will to be signed and dated in the testator's handwriting, but compare UPC § 2–502, which does not require a holographic will to be dated. The courts have held that neither an audiotape nor an audio videotape recording of an oral statement can be probated as a will.

ASSIGNMENT 4.3

Carter Brown executed an instrument in his own handwriting in which he wrote, "To whom it may concern. When I die, I sign everything I own over to my best friend, Brehona Watson." Signed and dated: Carter Brown, August 13, 2014. Mr. Brown was a bachelor. Two witnesses also signed the instrument. Would this document be considered a valid will? Were the witnesses necessary for this will? Answer these questions according to your state statutes or case law.

As mentioned earlier, a few states allow oral wills under specific conditions. An oral will is called a nuncupative will. It is usually made during a terminal illness in the presence of witnesses or during military service in time of war. When allowed by statute, oral wills generally can pass only personal property (see North Carolina and Washington statutes below). If a nuncupative will is reduced to a writing by the still living testator or by disinterested witnesses (usually two are required) who can attest to the decedent's oral declaration within a statutory period (e.g., 10 to 30 days) after it was spoken, it may be probated. The following are examples of statutes that recognize nuncupative wills.

N.C. Gen. Stat. §31-3.2 Kinds of Wills

(b) Personal property may also be bequeathed by a nuncupative will which complies with the requirements of G.S. 31–3.5.

N.C. Gen. Stat. §31-3.5 Nuncupative Will

A nuncupative will is a will

(1) Made orally by a person who is in his last sickness or in imminent peril of death and who does not survive such sickness or imminent peril, and

(2) Declared to be his will before two competent witnesses simultaneously present at the making thereof and specially requested by him to bear witness thereto.

Wash. Code Ann. § 11.12.025 Nuncupative Wills …

any person competent to make a will may dispose of his or her personal property of the value … not to exceed one thousand dollars, by nuncupative will if the same be proved by two witnesses who were present at the making thereof, and it be proved that the testator, at the time of pronouncing the same, did bid some person present to bear witness that such was his will, or to that effect, and that such nuncupative will was made at the time of the last sickness of the testator, but no proof of any nuncupative will shall be received unless it be offered within six months after the speaking of the testamentary words, nor unless the words or the substance thereof be first committed to writing, and in all cases a citation be issued to the widow and/or heirs at law of the deceased that they may contest the will, and no real estate shall be devised by a nuncupative will.

Nuncupative wills play a minimal role in actual probate proceedings. The Uniform Probate Code and the majority of the states do not allow oral wills.

ASSIGNMENT 4.4

Ayiana Anderson is dying of cancer at the county hospital. In the presence of her doctor and two nurses, Ayiana, who has no written will, announces that it is her intent to leave her entire estate to her favorite niece, Cacie Marble. She asks those present to act as witnesses of her intention and oral declaration. Ayiana's only other living relative is another niece, Delia Bergen, whom Ayiana states she wishes to disinherit. Later that day, Ayiana dies. According to your state statutes, would Cacie be entitled to Ayiana's estate? Are nuncupative wills on the "deathbed" of the speaker-decedent valid in the majority of the states?

Signature of the Testator

A will must ordinarily be signed by its maker. However, because of illness or illiteracy, the mere making of a mark, e.g., an "X" or an initial, can suffice in some situations. See *Estate of Mangeri*, 55 Cal.App.3d 76, 127 Cal.Rptr. 438 (1976), where the court ruled that a signature by mark was permitted (but other statutory requirements were not met), and *Mitchell v. Mitchell*, 245 Ga. 291, 264 S.E.2d 222 (1980), where an "X" was allowed when it was directed and intended to be a signature, thereby authenticating the will. Also, a New York statute, N.Y. EPTL § 3-2.1, requires that a will bear the testator's signature or some mark that can be regarded as the testator's signature. Nevada recognizes electronic signatures (see Nev. Rev. Stat. § 719.240). In addition, in all states a person other than the testator may sign the maker's name to the will in his presence, but such signing must occur at the express direction of the maker, given in a clear manner. The express direction must precede the signing.

> **EXAMPLE:** If Sam's wife, Mary, signs his name on his will for Sam, her signing alone does not validate the will. Sam must direct or request that she sign for him. The case of *Matter of Kelly's Estate*, 99 N.M. 482, 660 P.2d 124 (App. 1983), illustrates this requirement. The court ruled that another person who signs the testator's name on the will must be directed by the testator and that two witnesses must attest to the request and the substitute's signature; since those requirements were not met in this case, the will was not admitted to probate.

Courts have also consistently held that subsequent ratification of a prior will signed by a substitute person is not sufficient to reinstate the prior will. However, at his request, the hand of the testator may be guided by another to aid in the signing. All wills should also be dated in the testator's handwriting, but it is somewhat perplexing that this is not a common requirement except in the holographic wills that are recognized in some states (see Mich. Comp. Laws Ann. §700.2502). In the case of *Randall v. Salvation Army*, 100 Nev. 466, 686 P.2d 241 (1984), the court ruled that "the fact that the instrument bears more than one date does not necessarily make its date uncertain or otherwise prevent it from being probated as a holographic will."

The placement of the testator's signature has created a lot of controversy. In most cases, the maker's signature need not be at the end of the will if it can be shown that the intention to authenticate the will was present. See *In re Estate of Carroll*, 192 Ill. App.3d 202, 139 Ill. Dec. 265, 548 N.E.2d 650 (1989), in which the Illinois court ruled it is immaterial where the signature is written in the will as long as there was intent to authenticate. However, some states insist that the testator's signature appear at the end of the will. Under New York law, the testator's signature marks "the end of the will"; see N.Y. EPTL § 3-2.1. The Pennsylvania court in the case of *In re Estate of Treitinger*, 440 Pa. 616, 269 A.2d 497 (1970), held the testator must sign at the end of the will. Therefore, testators domiciled in the state of Pennsylvania should not only sign the bottom of each page of their will, but also at the end of the document. The Kansas Supreme Court took a similar position in the case of the *Matter of Reed's Estate*, 229 Kan. 431, 625 P.2d 447 (1981), where the court held that a will must be signed at the end by the testator in order for it to be probated. However, compare the comment to UPC § 2-502, which states that if the testator "writes his name in the body of the will, and intends it to be his signature, this would satisfy the statute" and the will can be probated. Since the proper place for a signature varies from state to state, the statutes of the state that has jurisdiction over the decedent's estate must be checked.

A lengthy will of several pages must be carefully drafted and should be typed using computer technology to prevent unscrupulous persons from inserting additional words, names, or even pages into the will. To ensure that there is no opportunity to alter the will, each page should be numbered; no spaces on any page should be large enough for additions or modifications; and the total number of pages should be specifically identified in an attestation clause that states, "The foregoing last will and testament consisting of eight pages, including this page, etc...." In some states when a will consists of multiple pages, it might be wise for the maker to sign or initial each page; however, all states have routinely validated wills that are signed only on the last page (see Exhibit 4.1).

ASSIGNMENT 4.5

1. Jack Foster was 85 years old and suffered from arthritis. He asked that a will be drawn for him. The will was delivered to Jack's hospital room, and in the presence of three witnesses, he said, "This is my last will. I want my property to be distributed according to its provisions." Jack did not sign the will or direct anyone to sign for him. Does this document fulfill the requirements for a valid will in your state based on statute or case law? Compare your answer with Ky. Rev. Stat. Ann. § 394.040.

2. Viola Carter drew a will satisfying all other statutory requirements of her state, but she signed the eight-page document on the first page only. Would her will be valid in your state? Cite the controlling law and see UPC § 2-502, Tex. Prob. Code Ann. § 59, and Ga. Code Ann. § 53-4[0, and compare 20 Pa. Stat. Ann. § 2502.

3. If Viola had asked Jane to sign Viola's name for her on all eight pages, would her will be valid in your state? Cite the controlling law.

4. If Viola had a 20-page will and page 5 was missing when she signed the will, would the will or any part of the will be valid in your state? Cite the controlling law and review *Matter of Griffin's Will*, discussed previously, and compare it to *In re Beale's Estate*, 15 Wis.2d 546, 113 N.W.2d 380 (1962).

5. If Viola misspelled her name or used a nickname when she signed her will, would her will be valid in your state? Cite the controlling law. Compare your answer with 72 ALR 2d 1267 and 98 ALR 2d 841.

6. Viola writes, "I, Viola Carter, leave my property to Phyllis Meyer" but does not sign after the statement. Does the fact that Viola wrote out her name in the statement constitute a "signature"? See *Matter of Estate of Cunningham*, previously cited, *Burton v. Bell*, 380 S.W.2d 561 (1964), and *Clark v. Studenwalt*, 187 W.Va. 368, 419 S.E.2d 308 (1992).

Signatures of Witnesses

The purpose of witnesses is to validate that the document declared to be a will was freely and intentionally signed by a competent testator. As the court explained in *Gonzalez v. Satrustequi*, 178 Ariz. 92, 870 P.2d 1188 (1993), "the observatory function of the witnesses' subscription is the direct and purposeful observation of the testator's acknowledgment of signing the will," and by so doing, "seeks to prevent the perpetuation of a fraud against the testator" (see *Truitt v. Slack*, 137 Md. App. 360, 768 A.2d 715 [2001]). The witnesses are not required to read the will or even to be told its contents, but they must be made aware that what they are signing is the testator's will. Witnesses are required to perform two duties: **attest** and **subscribe** the will.

attest (a will)
To bear witness; to affirm or verify a will as genuine.

subscribe (a will)
To sign one's name at the end of a will.

Exhibit 4.1		Formal Requirements for a Valid Basic Will by State		
	Age	**Testamentary Capacity**	**Testator's Signature Required**	**Witnesses**
Alabama	18	(2)	Yes	Two
Alaska	18	(2)	Yes	Two
Arizona	18	(2)	Yes	Two
Arkansas	18	(2)	Yes (4)	Two
California	18 (1)	(2)	Yes	Two
Colorado	18	(2)	Yes	Two
Connecticut	18	(2)	Yes	Two
Delaware	18	(2)	Yes	Two
Florida	18	(2)	Yes (4)	Two
Georgia	14	(2)	Yes	Two
Hawaii	18	(2)	Yes	Two
Idaho	18 (1)	(2)	Yes	Two
Illinois	18	(2)	Yes	Two
Indiana	18 (1)	(2)	Yes	Two
Iowa	18 (1)	(2)	Yes	Two
Kansas	18	(2)	Yes (4)	Two
Kentucky	18	(2)	Yes	Two
Louisiana	16	(2)	Yes (5)	Two (6)
Maine	18	(2)	Yes	Two
Maryland	18	(2)	Yes	Two
Massachusetts	18	(2)	Yes	Two
Michigan	18	(2)	Yes	Two
Minnesota	18	(2)	Yes	Two
Mississippi	18	(2)	Yes	Two
Missouri	18	(2)	Yes	Two
Montana	18	(2)	Yes	Two
Nebraska	18	(2)	Yes	Two
Nevada (7)	18	(2)	Yes(7)	Two
New Hampshire	18 (1)	(2)	Yes	Two
New Jersey	18	(2)	Yes	Two
New Mexico	18	(2)	Yes	Two
New York	18	(2)	Yes (4)	Two
North Carolina	18	(2)	Yes	Two
North Dakota	18	(2)	Yes	Two
Ohio	18	(2, 3)	Yes (4)	Two
Oklahoma	18	(2)	Yes (4)	Two
Oregon	18 (1)	(2)	Yes	Two
Pennsylvania	18	(2)	Yes (4)	None
Rhode Island	18	(2)	Yes	Two
South Carolina	18 (1)	(2)	Yes	Two
South Dakota	18	(2)	Yes	Two
Tennessee	18	(2)	Yes	Two
Texas	18 (1)	(2)	Yes	Two
Utah	18	(2)	Yes	Two
Vermont	18	(2)	Yes	Two
Virginia	18	(2)	Yes	Two
Washington	18	(2)	Yes	Two
West Virginia	18	(2)	Yes	Two
Wisconsin	18	(2)	Yes	Two
Wyoming	18	(2)	Yes	Two

(1) Younger if: emancipated minor; member of the Armed Forces; or married.
(2) Sound mind; mentally competent; or legally competent.
(3) Not under restraint.
(4) Signature at end of will.
(5) Signature at end of each separate page of will.
(6) Notary required.
(7) Recognizes wills and signatures in electronic form.

Most state statutes provide that to be valid a will must be signed in the maker's presence by two competent witnesses (but compare UPC § 2-502, which also allows the testator to acknowledge to the witnesses that he signed the will). Pennsylvania is an exception. It does not require witnesses to the will at the time of the signing unless done by the testator's mark (signed with an "X"). However, witnesses are required during the probate proceeding to verify the maker's signature, which can be accomplished with their oath or affirmation. A written will is not valid without witnesses unless it is a holographic will. State statutes establish the required number of witnesses; currently, all states require two witnesses, (see Exhibit 4.1). In addition, the witnesses must be competent, i.e., capable of testifying as to the facts of execution of the will and the mental capacity of the testator. Various factors help determine the **competency of a witness**, although age does not appear to be one of them. The minimum age to be a witness is below the age of majority in some states. The following questions must be answered in order to assess competency. The list also helps identify who is and who is not an appropriate witness.

competent witness
A person who is legally capable and suitable to act as a witness to a will.

- *Is the witness capable of testifying as to the facts of the execution of the will?* (See the next example.)
- *Is the witness able, by legal standards, to testify as to the mental capacity of the testator?*

  EXAMPLE: Owen Ratliff attests (witnesses) and subscribes (signs) Logan Hartman's will. Owen is acquainted with Logan; knows the document is Logan's last will; remembers and can relate the facts of the execution of the will, i.e., declared and signed by Logan; and can testify to Logan's mental capacity. Thus, Owen is a competent (capable) witness.

- *When is the competency of the witness required?* The witness must be competent at the time of the execution of the will. If the witness is incompetent at the execution of the will and later becomes competent to testify, the will is invalid.

  EXAMPLE: Stephen Hart is intoxicated. He is asked to witness Kevin Hanson's will. Stephen signs his name, unaware of what he is signing. Later, when sober, Stephen is told he witnessed and subscribed Kevin's will. The witness's competence must exist at the time of the execution of the will. The will is not valid.

Conversely, if the witness is competent at the time a will is attested, subsequent incompetency does not invalidate the will. See Mass. Gen. Laws Ann. ch. 191 § 3.

  EXAMPLE: Stanley Novak attests and subscribes Allan Sheppard's will. Five years later Stanley becomes mentally ill and is hospitalized. Stanley's subsequent insanity would not affect the validity of Allan's will. The purpose of the statutory requirement that a will be witnessed by a competent person is that such a person might later be required to testify that the deceased testator was of sound and disposing mind and memory at the time of the will's execution.

- *Can the personal representative (executor) or trustee named in the will also act as a competent witness?* The prevailing view is that a person named as personal representative (executor) or trustee in a will, if *not* a beneficiary or devisee of the will, is qualified to act as a proper witness to a will. The basis for the rule is the opinion that an executor does not have a direct interest in the will by virtue of the duty to see that the testator's wishes are carried out, even though the executor claims a personal representative's fee from the estate. The fact that an executor's interest is not "pecuniary, legal and immediate," as is a beneficiary's, qualifies the executor to be a witness. However, it is preferable that a personal representative not be a witness.

EXAMPLE: Fred Johnson names Robert Olson executor of his will. Robert also attests and subscribes the will. Most states consider Robert a competent witness. (Check your state to see if it follows the majority view.)

- *Is a person disqualified as a competent witness because the testator owes the person a debt?* Generally, a creditor is competent to act as a witness as long as no bequest or devise other than the debt owed is mentioned in the will.

EXAMPLE: In her will, Janet Martin provides that all her approved debts, funeral expenses, and taxes should be paid out of assets of her estate. Marian Cooper is a creditor of Janet's. No other provisions in the will mention Marian. Marian is a competent witness.

- *Is an "interested witness," i.e., a person who is both a witness and a beneficiary, or devisee named in a will, a competent witness?*

EXAMPLE: In his will, Daniel Kane gives a valuable ring to his sister, Margaret Wilson. Margaret can testify to Daniel's mental capacity and is one of the witnesses and subscribers to the execution of his will. She is a competent witness. However, Margaret's act of attesting a will in which she is named a devisee may cost her the ring because she is an **interested witness**—a witness who is also a beneficiary of the will. If there are two other witnesses, the gift to Margaret is valid. If she is one of only two witnesses, however, the gift to Margaret is void, in some states, even though she remains a competent witness. Finally, under some state statutes such as the Tennessee statute below, Margaret may be able to retain the gift even if she is one of only two witnesses, because as an heir, she would receive her intestate's share within the limits of the value of the gift she was to receive through the will. See UPC § 2–505, which provides that a will is valid even if it is attested by an interested witness and allows the witness-beneficiary to receive the gift.

> **interested witness**
> A person who is a beneficiary and a witness of the same will.

The following is a state statute that addresses itself to this problem.

Tenn. Code Ann. § 32-1-103 **Witnesses—Who May Act**
(a) Any person competent to be a witness generally in this state may act as attesting witness to a will.
(b) No will is invalidated because attested by an interested witness, but any interested witness shall, unless the will is also attested by two (2) disinterested witnesses, forfeit so much of the provisions therein made for him as in the aggregate exceeds in value, as of the date of the testator's death, what he would have received had the testator died intestate....

This statute is typical in states that have not enacted the Uniform Probate Code.

Good legal practice dictates that a beneficiary or devisee, although competent to act as a witness, should never be a witness to a will from which the beneficiary or devisee benefits, since the bequest or devise (gift of real or personal property) may be voided or may possibly invalidate the entire will. It is also unwise for the attorney who drafts a client's will to act as a witness. Although no statute forbids an attorney from being a witness, this is seldom done since any challenge to the will could require the attorney to cease to represent the estate if the attorney is likely to be called as a witness in a will contest. *A paralegal who acts as a witness could run into the same ethical problem.* However, compare Rule 3.7 of the Model Rules of Professional Conduct, which appears to allow an attorney who is

⚖️ *Ethical Issue*

also a witness to turn the will contest over to another member of the law firm and resume acting as attorney for the estate after the will is proved (accepted).

In summary, a witness should be acquainted with the testator to establish competency but should not be a beneficiary of the will.

ASSIGNMENT 4.6

Answer the following according to your state laws.

1. Can an heir of an intestate, who becomes a beneficiary or devisee when the intestate makes a will, be a competent witness?

2. In such a case, can the heir-devisee or heir-beneficiary receive any property from the decedent testator?

3. Linda is Sara's daughter and only heir. Sara dies testate. In her will, she leaves Linda the following property: a diamond ring valued at $2,500; silverware worth $750; a fur coat worth $1,800; and a lake cottage appraised at $25,000. The rest of Sara's estate is given to charity. The total value of the estate after deducting expenses, debts, and taxes is $100,000. Linda and Sara's best friend, Sylvia, witness and sign the will. In Tennessee, is Linda a competent witness? In your state, is Linda competent? In your state, would Linda be entitled to receive any of her mother's estate? If so, how much? In your state, what effect does Linda's signature as a witness have on the validity of the will?

4. Determine whether the following persons can act as competent witnesses in your state: (a) a minor, (b) the attorney drafting the will, (c) the spouse of the testator, (d) the personal representative (executor) not named a devisee, (e) a parent of the testator, (f) a creditor of the testator, (g) the probate judge, (h) a spouse of a beneficiary or devisee named in the will.

5. If you are drafting your own will, should the age of an adult witness (person over 18) have any bearing on whether you choose a witness younger or older than yourself? Explain.

In most states the witnesses to the will must sign in the conscious presence of the testator (see Conn. Gen. Stat. Ann. § 45a-251, but compare UPC § 2–502 where presence is not required). In a few states, the witnesses do not necessarily have to sign in one another's presence so long as they both were present when the testator signed the will. In common practice, however, subscribing (signing) by witnesses is accomplished in the presence of both the maker of the will and each other. The signatures of the witnesses attest to the act of signing by the testator, his age and sound mind, and that they themselves signed in his presence. In addition, some states require the addresses of the witnesses be given. Although witnesses need not know the contents of a will, they usually must be aware that what they have subscribed is a will. To help resolve doubts that the testator and the witnesses were present together when all signatures were made, they all should sign with the same pen. For an example of a standard attestation clause used in drafting a will, see Exhibit 4.2.

In summary, the individual state's statutory requirements concerning the maker of the will (testator), witnesses, and signatures vary substantially and may or may not require any or all of the following:

- The will must be written.
- Two witnesses are required (see Exhibit 4.1).

EXHIBIT 4.2	Sample Signature and Attestation Clauses

Signature Clause

I, Jane C. Doe, have signed this my last will and testament consisting of ten (10) typewritten pages including this page, on June 15, 2014.

_____
Jane C. Doe, Testatrix

Attestation Clause

We certify that in our presence on the date appearing above the testatrix, [name], signed the foregoing instrument and acknowledged and declared it to be her will, that at her request and in her presence and in the presence of each other, we have signed our names below as witnesses, and that we believe her to be eighteen (18) years of age or more, of sound mind, and under no constraint or undue influence.

_____ residing at _____
(Witness) (Address)
_____ residing at _____
(Witness) (Address)
_____

Note: Although an attestation clause is not required, all states recommend its use.

- The testator must declare (publish) to the witnesses that the document is his will (this is called publication) and request they sign it (see N.Y. EPTL § 3-2.1[a], [2], [3], [4]). **Publication**, as the term is used in the law of wills, is the declaration or act of the testator at the time of execution of a will that manifests intent that the document is a will; any communication made to witnesses by word, sign, motion, or conduct is sufficient to constitute a publication. This was the definition of publication upheld by the court in the *Matter of Kelly's Estate* case cited previously. However, see and compare *Matter of Estate of Polda*, 349 N.W.2d 11 (N.D. 1984). Publication is becoming an unnecessary formality in many states, and it is not required under the Uniform Probate Code.

- The testator must sign the will in the presence of the witnesses.

- The testator's signature must be at the end of the will.

- The witnesses must see the testator sign the will, or the testator must acknowledge in their presence that the signature on the will is his (see Cal. Prob. Code § 6110[c] or N.Y. EPTL § 3-2.1 [a] [2]).

- The witnesses must sign (subscribe) in the presence of the testator and/or at the testator's request (see *Matter of Graham's Estate*, 295 N.W.2d 414 [Iowa 1980]).

- The witnesses must sign in each other's presence (see Ky. Rev. Stat. Ann. § 394.040 or Fla. Stat. Ann. § 732.502). However, the placement of the witnesses' signatures may vary according to individual state laws, as noted in the cases cited previously.

Note: The modern way to satisfy these requirements is to include signature and attestation clauses, which state that all the formalities listed above have been properly performed (see Exhibit 4.2). The most common method to resolve

Publication
In the law of wills, the formal declaration made by a testator at the time of signing a will that it is his last will and testament.

these requirements is the use of a self-proving affidavit of witnesses that creates a self-proved will (see Chapter 6). In some states, e.g., Indiana, a videotape may be used to verify that these formalities have been met to establish the validity of the document (see Ind. Code Ann. § 29-1-5-3.2).

For the most part, statutes have not established many qualifications for attesting witnesses; e.g., in many states, there are no age requirements for witnesses, but they must be competent as previously discussed. When choosing attesting witnesses, good practice would be to choose adult, mature, literate witnesses who are younger than the testator, especially if the testator is elderly, and someone acquainted with the testator. If not acquainted, such witnesses should engage in conversation with the testator prior to the execution of the will to establish some rapport and, most importantly, to reassure the attesting witnesses that the testator exhibits both testamentary intent and capacity should they later be asked to verify these requirements in court.

ASSIGNMENT 4.7

David Erickson executes a will and declares to three competent witnesses: "This is my last will and testament." In the will, Erickson leaves part of his estate to Allan Potter, who is also a witness to the will. Answer the following questions according to your state's law.

1. Must the witnesses know the contents of Erickson's will before they attest and subscribe their names to the document in order for it to be valid?

2. Can Potter receive his benefit from the will?

3. Is the will valid?

MODIFICATION OF A WILL— CODICIL V. NEW WILL

Since people are living longer, many years may pass between the date a will is executed and the death of the maker of the will. During that time, the testator's wishes concerning the beneficiaries or devisees of the estate assets may dramatically change, as may the potential beneficiaries themselves. For example, the testator's decisions may be influenced by the birth, death, adoption, marriage, divorce, legal separation, change of a minor's guardian, change of state of residency, or change in financial standing. The testator's property may no longer be the same due to additions, sales, gifts, losses, destruction, or a change in value. *Caveat:* As a result of such events or changes, it becomes absolutely essential to update and revise the testator's original will and estate plan.

The most appropriate way to accomplish these major and necessary changes in the will is to execute a "new" updated will that specifically states all earlier wills are revoked. *Therefore, when you are asked to prepare a codicil for a client, you should always discuss the reasons for drafting a "new" will as the preferred document.*

In the past, the most common method to change or modify provisions in a will was a codicil (see Exhibit 4.3). Today, codicils are almost obsolete. In this age of computers, modern practitioners agree that the use of codicils to modify or change existing wills is not sound judgment. Since today's will is on a computer disk, it is faster and easier to create a "new will" whenever any changes, whether minor or substantial, are necessary. Equally important, the computer technology eliminates the need and expense to create, revise, and eventually find and probate multiple documents, i.e., the will and one or more codicils, after the testator's death. Any will that has been substantially rewritten by one or more codicils is bound to be awkward and confusing.

To cross out terms or a clause of a will and write in new words or a provision (called **interlineation**) does not create a new will since the act does not meet the statutory requirements for a valid will. In other words, the will, prior to interlineation, was executed validly with respect to attestation, signature, and the like, but that validity does not apply to the will in its interlineated state. The will must meet the formal requirements of the maker's state statutes (see N.Y. EPTL § 3-4.1 [a]). Example clauses of wills are discussed in Chapter 6.

interlineation
The act of writing between the lines of an instrument.

ASSIGNMENT 4.8

On July 15, 2014, Colleen Shannon executes a will. In one of its provisions, she leaves a $50,000 diamond brooch to Susan Slade, a lifelong friend. Sometime afterward, Susan and Colleen have a falling out. No longer wanting Susan to receive the brooch, Colleen crosses out Susan's name from the will and writes in Diane Pylkas as the new beneficiary. A short time later, after having won $100,000 on a television quiz show, Colleen adds a page to her will giving the prize money to Patty Barron. According to your state's law, are the changes Colleen made to her will valid? Explain.

REVOCATION AND REJECTION OF A WILL

A will is operative only after the testator or testatrix dies. Until then, it is **ambulatory**, i.e., revocable and subject to change. A will can be changed or revoked at any time before death by methods authorized by statute or case law. Whenever the maker of the will changes the way estate property is to be distributed upon death, revocation results, and it terminates the existence of a will. Revocation may be accomplished in three ways.

ambulatory
Revocable and subject to change.

1. Revocation by physical act

2. Revocation by operation of law

3. Revocation by subsequent writing

Revocation by Physical Act

The following are examples of revocation by a physical act.

- Keri Wilson burns her will.
- Steven Wong tears his will in half.
- Kendra Espinoza writes the word "canceled" across each page of her will.
- Jack Miles uses a pen to cross out all clauses of his will.
- Vern Leong, who suffers from frostbite on both hands, asks Julie Adams to burn Vern's will. Julie, in the presence of her husband, Todd Adams, and under specific directions by Vern, burns the will.

EXHIBIT 4.3   Sample Codicil

[The facts: Henry Hamilton executed a will on June 1, 2008. One provision of the will gives his gun collection to his son, John; another gives his faithful employee, Joe Spencer, $10,000. In 2010, John lost an arm in a hunting accident. That same year, Joe Spencer died. Henry therefore executes the following first codicil to his will.]

CODICIL

I, Henry Hamilton, of River City, Cornwald County, State of A, do make, publish, and declare this to be the first codicil to my last will and testament executed June 1, 2008.

First: Whereas in Article IV in my said last will and testament, I gave my gun collection to my son, John; and whereas my said son is no longer able to use said gun collection, I hereby give said gun collection to my son, Edwin Hamilton, if he survives me.

Second: Whereas in Article V, I gave $10,000 to my employee, Joseph Spencer; and whereas my said employee has died, I give said $10,000 to his wife, Renee Spencer, if she survives me.

Third: Except as modified by this codicil, in all other respects, I ratify, confirm, and republish all of the provisions of my said last will and testament dated June 1, 2008.

IN WITNESS WHEREOF, I have hereunto set my hand to this, the first Codicil to my Last Will and Testament, dated this 26th day of February, 2011.

_____
Henry Hamilton
_____
2114 Oak Street

THIS INSTRUMENT, bearing the signature of the above-named Testator, was by him on the date there of willingly signed, published, and declared by him to be a Codicil to his Last Will and Testament, in our presence, who, at his request and in his presence, and in the presence of each other, we believing him to be of sound mind and under no constraint or undue influence, have hereunto subscribed our names as attesting witnesses.

Mary Ann Garsity	residing at	*9341 Silverman Avenue*
Lawrence Escrach	residing at	*87 Coronada Circle*

All these deliberate physical acts, i.e., burning, tearing, canceling, obliterating, or otherwise destroying a will or directing and consenting to have another person do the same, allow the maker to revoke the will. Once revoked, if the testator later changes his mind, he cannot revive or reinstate the original will unless he writes a new will. The case of *In re Bonner's Will*, 17 N.Y.2d 9, 266 N.Y.S.2d 971, 214 N.E.2d 154 (1966), illustrates a revocation of a will by deliberate act.

A will of Merritt Bonner that had been cut in two was found after his death. The executors named in the severed will offered it for probate, and the decedent's father opposed the petition to admit the will on the grounds that the will had been revoked. The court ruled that cutting a will in two was an act of revocation that canceled the will.

The destruction of a will by a person other than the testator must comply with the state statute that regulates revocation by destruction. Some states require such destruction to be witnessed by two persons, neither of whom is the destroyer; others require only that the destruction be at the direction and with the consent of the testator. The following Pennsylvania statute is typical of state statutes that outline procedures for the revocation of wills.

20 Pa. Stat. Ann. § 2505 **Revocation of a Will**
No will or codicil in writing, or any part thereof, can be revoked or altered otherwise than:

(1) *Will or codicil* By some other will or codicil in writing;

(2) *Other writing* By some other writing declaring the same, executed and proved in the manner required of wills; or

(3) *Act to the document* By being burnt, torn, canceled, obliterated, or destroyed, with the intent and for the purpose of revocation, by the testator himself or by another person in his presence and by his express direction. If such act is done by any person other than the testator, the direction of the testator must be proved by the oaths or affirmations of two competent witnesses [Compare UPC § 2–507].

When the testator's intent is not destruction but to delete or cross out specific words or clauses in the will, the deletions are allowed without the required witnesses' signatures if the testator's intent can be proven. That is the problem. Since the testator often dies before the deletions are discovered, the subsequent confusion often leads to an expensive will contest.

Lost Wills

Sometimes a will cannot be found even though individuals acknowledge it existed. A lost will that cannot be found is not necessarily considered to be a revoked will by a physical act. Many states have statutes or allow case law to decide whether a "lost will" can be probated. With or without a statute, courts require "clear and convincing proof" of a lost will, as in the case of *In re Thompson's Estate*, 214 Neb. 899, 336 N.W.2d 590 (1983), where a second will revoked the original but the second will could not be found. Thus, the required standard of "clear and convincing proof" was not met, and the original will was probated. State laws vary on the question of whether a "lost will" is revoked or can be probated. The decision is generally based on the following:

- Proof that the will was properly executed
- Proof that while the will was under the control of the decedent-testator, he did not expressly revoke it
- Proof of the contents of the will

One method of satisfying the "proof of execution" requirement is to have the two witnesses to the lost will, if available, testify that the "lost" will was acknowledged and signed by the testator. Depending on the circumstances, a true and complete copy of the lost will may or may not be admitted to probate. Consider the following examples.

EXAMPLE: Martina Martinez's will is properly executed and left in her attorney's office. Martina dies and her will cannot be found. The state statute requires two witnesses to testify concerning the "lost will," but only one witness is discovered. The result could be the same as in the famous lost will case, *Howard Hughes Medical Institute v. Gavin*, 96 Nev. 905, 621 P.2d 489 (1980). There the court denied probate because the statute governing lost wills required evidence from two witnesses and only one witness was found.

EXAMPLE: Peter Wheaton properly executes a will in 2005. During the last five years, Peter has frequently mentioned to his attorney, beneficiaries, and heirs that he is happy with his estate plans and keeps his will at home. He has shown his family the contents of his will. When Peter dies, the will cannot be found. Any statutory presumption that this will is revoked by physical act can be opposed and refuted by the facts, e.g., the will was under the control of the decedent-testator. See *Matter of Travers' Estate*, 121 Ariz. 282, 589 P.2d 1314 (App. 1978), in which the court ruled that the evidence supported the trial court's finding in a will contest that the will had been destroyed by the testator with intent to revoke. If the other issues, such as proper execution of the will and no expressed revocations by the testator while the will was under his control, are resolved, then a lost will can be probated if its contents are satisfactorily proved.

EXAMPLE: Boris Decker properly executed his will. When he died, his will could not be found. The attorney who drafted the will retained a photocopy of the original will. This copy could be used as evidence to prove the contents of the will (see *Matter of Wheadon's Estate*, 579 P.2d 930 [Utah 1978], but compare the case of *In re Sage's Will*, 76 Misc.2d 676, 351 N.Y.S. 2d 930 [1974], in which the court disapproved the use of a photocopy in place of the original will).

Case law has generally held that in will contests involving lost or misplaced wills, the burden of proof is on the proponent of the lost will to prove that the testator did not intentionally revoke the lost, misplaced, or destroyed will during his lifetime. This was the position of the Supreme Court of Nevada in the case of *Estate of Irvine v. Doyle*, 101 Nev. 698, 710 P.2d 1366 (1985). In *Barksdale v. Pendergrass*, 294 Ala. 526, 319 So.2d 267 (1975), another case in which the original will could not be found, the court stated that the burden was on the proponent alleging a lost will to establish (1) the existence of a will; (2) the loss or destruction of the will; (3) the nonrevocation of the will by the testatrix; and (4) the contents of the will. The court affirmed the jury's decision that the original will was lost, misplaced, or destroyed but not with the testatrix's intent.

Finally, a lost will may be found after the administration of a decedent's estate is completed. In that case, if the will is offered for probate and a request to reopen the administration is made, the following factors apply.

- The request may be barred by a statute of limitations. Some states like Texas have a four-year limit after death (see Tex. Prob. Code Ann. § 73[a] and [b]); others like California have no time limit (see Cal. Prob. Code § 8000, and compare UPC § 3-108, which provides for a three-year limit with some exceptions).

- Generally, creditors, banks, trustees or guardians of property, and "good faith" purchasers of estate property are exonerated and protected by the previous estate administration; see Tex. Prob. Code Ann. § 73 (b).

- In some states, however, beneficiaries, devisees, or heirs are subject to the distribution provisions of the lost will; see UPC § 3–108.

Revocation by Operation of Law

A will can be revoked wholly or partially by the following:

- By marriage
- By divorce

A will can be revoked by other than a deliberate physical act on the part of the maker or another person. A state statute may automatically revoke or amend a will without the testator's knowledge of or agreement to the revocation. For example, by **operation of law**, a will is often affected by the marriage or divorce of the testator or testatrix. If the testator marries after executing a will, it is revoked in some states by operation of law, and the testator's property passes by intestacy. Under UPC § 2–508 and a majority of the states, a subsequent marriage does not revoke a will. The surviving spouse receives an intestate share of the decedent spouse's estate, and the rest of the estate passes under the will (see UPC § 2–301). However, if a maker is divorced after executing a will, all provisions in favor of the maker's former spouse are revoked by operation of law in most states, leaving the rest of the will intact. This is especially appropriate because the divorce decree usually contains a property settlement between the spouses. For the effects of divorce and marriage on an existing will in all states, review Exhibits 3.14 and 3.15. An example of a state statute explaining the effect of marriage on an existing will follows.

operation of law
Rights pass to a person by the application of the established rules of law, without the act, knowledge, or cooperation of the person.

Or. Rev. Stat. § 112.305 **Revocation by Marriage**
A will is revoked by the subsequent marriage of the testator if the testator is survived by a spouse, unless:
(1) The will evidences an intent that it not be revoked by the subsequent marriage or was drafted under circumstances establishing that it was in contemplation of the marriage; or
(2) The testator and spouse entered into a written contract before the marriage that either makes provision for the spouse or provides that the spouse is to have no rights in the estate of the testator. [Compare UPC § 2–301.]

ASSIGNMENT 4.9

Harold and Maude are close friends. Maude has completed her will, leaving half her estate to Harold and the other half to charity. If, subsequently, Harold and Maude marry, would Maude's will be revoked by operation of law in Oregon? What would your answer be according to the laws of your state? Would the charity receive half of Maude's estate in your state?

The following Pennsylvania statute addresses itself to the effect of a divorce on an existing will.

20 Pa. Stat. Ann. § 2506 **Modification by Circumstances**
Wills shall be modified upon the occurrence of any of the following circumstances, among others:
(2) Divorce. If the testator is divorced from the bonds of matrimony after making a will, any provision in the will in favor of or relating to his spouse so divorced shall thereby become ineffective for all purposes unless it appears from the will that the provision was intended to survive the divorce…. [Compare UPC § 2–802.]

ASSIGNMENT 4.10

Frank and Eleanor are single and both have their own wills. Frank and Eleanor marry. Both execute new wills. Subsequently, the couple obtains a divorce. Answer the following according to the statutes of your state.

1. What effect did the marriage have on the wills Frank and Eleanor made before marrying?

2. What effect does their divorce have on the former spouses' wills?

Revocation by Subsequent Writing

Both of the following are examples of a revocation of a will by subsequent writing.

- Samantha Nguyen writes a new will.
- Lee Shapiro adds a codicil to her will.

A current will can be expressly revoked only by a written document executed with the same formalities required for a valid will. The law is well settled that the last will and codicil executed with these formalities is the valid will of the decedent. This is the decision of the courts whenever more than one will or codicil is discovered after the death of a testator. Today, in our computer world, codicils are rarely used and have been replaced by "new" wills.

A revoked will is usually destroyed, but it may be advisable to retain the former will when the testator's testamentary capacity is questioned or there is a possibility of a will contest. The reason for saving the will is that the revocation of the earlier will may turn out to be dependent on the validity of the later will. Possibly, too, the testator may change his mind and decide he prefers the terms of the earlier will. If the later will is held invalid, it may be possible and appropriate to probate the earlier will. An example of a statute concerned with the retention and validity of an earlier will is 20 Pa. Stat. Ann. § 2506.

> If, after the making of any will, the testator shall execute a later will which expressly or by necessary implication revokes the earlier will, the revocation of the later will shall not revive the earlier will, unless the revocation is in writing and declares the intention of the testator to revive the earlier will, or unless, after such revocation, the earlier will shall be reexecuted. Oral republication of itself shall be ineffective to revive a will. [Compare UPC § 2-509.]

EXAMPLE: In 2005, Richard makes a will and leaves $4,000 to his niece, Myrrha. In 2008, he revokes but does not destroy the first will and writes a second will, which gives $2,000 to Myrrha and $2,000 to her sister, Melisande. Later, Richard destroys the second will because he does not approve of the person Melisande marries. Although he intends to revive the first will, he dies before this task is accomplished. In the eyes of the law, Richard died intestate. Myrrha would not be entitled to the $4,000 since the first will was rendered ineffective by Richard's deliberate revocation of it. The second will was revoked when Richard destroyed it, but this revocation does not revive the first will. Compare *Kroll v. Nehmer*, 705 A.2d 716 (Ct.App., Mary., 1998), in which it was decided that the testator clearly intended to revoke an earlier will and, since the later wills were ineffective because they lacked the signatures of attesting witnesses, the testator died intestate.

ASSIGNMENT 4.11

1. In the above example, would Myrrha be entitled to the $4,000 in your state?

2. How could Richard, while living, revive the first will after he destroyed the second will?

WILL CONTESTS

A will contest is a lawsuit commenced in probate court that challenges the validity of an existing will. Very few wills are contested and most contests are unsuccessful. State statutes govern will contests, but they vary regarding when a hearing on a will contest must occur. In the *Tobin* case discussed below, the Illinois court allowed a niece, who was not given notice, to contest the will 18 years after the will was admitted to probate. As a rule, the hearing is prior to or shortly after a will is admitted to probate by the court. Before the hearing, the contesting party files an affidavit of objection to the petition for probate and lists the grounds for the objection.

Who Can Contest a Will

A lawsuit must be commenced by a person who has "standing" and, consequently, may make an objection to the probate court and request that a will offered for probate be rejected. A person with **standing** is someone who stands to lose a pecuniary interest, i.e., a share of the decedent's estate, if a will is allowed, such as a spouse, beneficiary, or heir of an earlier will. The person who contests the will has the burden of proving his objection by "clear and convincing evidence," a standard that is more than a mere preponderance of the evidence (the civil law standard) but less than beyond a reasonable doubt (the criminal law standard). Generally, creditors are *not* proper contestants since they can pursue their claims in a separate lawsuit in civil court; however, they must be given notice of the probate proceeding so they can pursue their claims. If probate is denied, i.e., the will is successfully contested and declared invalid by the probate court, then the decedent's estate passes according to intestate succession laws, and all belongings are distributed as if the decedent had left no will. This law is the reason an heir, who would inherit if the decedent is declared intestate, has standing, i.e., the right to contest the will, but creditors do not have standing.

Most states have a statute of limitations, i.e., a limited time during which the contestant must file the appropriate documents to contest the will. If the time limit is not strictly followed, the opportunity to contest the will is lost regardless of the validity of the contestant's challenge (but read and compare the *Tobin* case below).

standing
The requirement that a person stands to lose a pecuniary interest in a decedent's estate if a will is allowed.

POINT OF INTEREST

Who Gets the $1.6 Billion?

In 1994, Anna Nicole Smith married Texas billionaire oilman J. Howard Marshal, who died 18 months later on August 4, 1995, leaving an estate worth $1.6 billion. Shortly thereafter, Smith claimed a one-half interest in her late husband's estate, which was opposed by one of J. Howard's sons, Pierce Marshal. What legal doctrines or concepts did each side use to support its position? Over the next 19 years, the parties fought one another in a series of court cases. What were the rulings in each of the cases and on what grounds? Who were the parties to the dispute, and why? What is the current legal status of the dispute?

ASSIGNMENT 4.12

Harry is not mentioned in the will of his father, George. In their domiciliary state, Harry receives a share of his father's estate if George dies intestate. George's will provides that half his estate goes to his wife, Helen, and the remaining half goes to charity. As an heir, Harry contests the will and establishes his right to inherit the property in the case of intestacy. According to your state's laws, is Harry entitled to contest the will? Would this will contest succeed? If Harry wins the case, how much of his father's estate does he receive in your state?

ASSIGNMENT 4.13

Joan is named beneficiary in her Aunt Grace's will, dated April 10, 1999. In 2010, Grace executes a new will, which states that it revokes all prior wills and codicils. Joan is not mentioned in the new will. Joan establishes that the will dated April 1999 had been properly executed while the will written in 2010 was witnessed by two persons also named as beneficiaries. According to your state's laws, is Joan a proper will contestant? Would Joan's contest succeed? Explain.

Grounds for Contesting a Will

The probate court may refuse to accept a will for several reasons. In some of the cases, the court finds legitimate grounds for a successful will contest. The following are grounds for contesting a will.

- *The will is not properly executed.*

    EXAMPLES: (1) John writes but does not sign his will. (2) John writes and signs the will, but it is not witnessed. (3) John writes and signs the will, but the witnesses are not competent (review the discussion on competency in this chapter).

- *No notice of the probate of a will is given to heirs or creditors.*

    EXAMPLE: John's estate is administered and distributed without notice of the proceedings being given to one of John's sons or to a creditor. The requirement of notice is illustrated by *In re Estate of Tobin*, 152 Ill.App.3d 965, 105 Ill.Dec. 891, 505 N.E.2d 17 (1987). In that case, the court ruled that a niece, who was an heir of the decedent but did not receive notice, was entitled to contest the will even though 18 years had passed.

- *The will or the testator's signature is forged.*

    EXAMPLES: (1) John's signature is copied and written by another. (2) John's written (holographic) will is a forgery. Handwriting experts could be retained to determine authenticity.

- *The testator lacks testamentary capacity.*

    EXAMPLES: (1) John lacks legal capacity. He is a minor. (2) John lacks testamentary capacity. He is of "unsound mind." He has a mental illness or has mental retardation

POINT OF INTEREST

In this age of technology, a testator might think that a videotape would prove to the testator's family and friends that he was competent and acting independently. Courts have held that a homemade videotape could be introduced as evidence in support of the testator's will. However, this has appeared to backfire. In three recent cases from three different states, each court ruled that the videotape established that the testator was not competent to execute a will. If you are considering using a videotape in support of competency, you should weigh carefully the advantages and disadvantages to ensure that the testator can and will make the right impression.

and lacks knowledge and understanding of the nature and extent of his property and of the persons who are the natural objects of his bounty at the time of the execution of the will. In the case *In re Stitt's Estate*, 93 Ariz. 302, 380 P.2d 601 (1963), which involved a will contest, the court stated that "in determining testamentary capacity, the law is concerned only with the testator's state of mind at the time of the execution of the will." As previously discussed, the Uniform Probate Code places the burden of proof on the contestant to establish the testator's lack of mental or testamentary capacity, i.e., a sound mind; see UPC § 3–407.

- *The will has been revoked.*

  EXAMPLES: (1) John has written a new will. (2) John has destroyed or canceled his existing will. (3) John has married or been divorced since writing his will.

- *The testator is induced by fraud to write or change the will.*

  EXAMPLES: (1) John is tricked into leaving his estate to his nephew who causes John to believe erroneously that his only other heir is dead. (2) John disinherits his daughter after he was lied to by his son that the daughter hates John.

In order for a probate court to disallow a will on the grounds the testator was deceived into making it, the contestant must prove (1) a beneficiary of the will actually led the testator into an erroneous belief concerning the disposition of the property (as in the first example above, where John's nephew caused him to believe his only other heir was dead) and (2) the testator, who believed the false statement to be true, relied on it and wrote a will accordingly. (If John did not believe his nephew, but nevertheless wrote a will favoring the nephew over the other heir, the court would allow the will to be probated and disregard the claim of fraud. The testator's reliance on the beneficiary's willful misrepresentation is essential.)

- *The will contains material contradictions, ambiguities, or mistakes.*

  EXAMPLES: (1) John's will leaves the same items of property to different persons. (2) John's will is written so ambiguously it is impossible to determine his intent. (3) John did not know he was signing a will.

A material mistake is one that alters the substance or matter of the provision in which it appears. If John had given his automobile to Eugene and to Eloise in the same will, both gifts to take effect at the same time, John's mistake would be material; it would alter the bequest itself. Without further evidence to show which beneficiary John intended to have the automobile, the probate court would hold the gift invalid. Although a probate court does not have the power to rewrite the will in its entirety, the court may strike down individual provisions on the grounds that the testator's wishes concerning the bequests or devises therein cannot be determined; the remaining portions of the will would then be admitted. Sometimes a mistake may invalidate a will. If the mistake is material, e.g., a mistake as to the document signed, the entire will is invalid.

  EXAMPLE: John signs a document that he believes to be his will, when in fact it is his wife's will. This document is not valid.

However, if the mistake is a simple drafting error, e.g., the will lists the address of the testator as 4711 Fair Hills Avenue instead of 4771, this will is valid.

- *The testator is forced by duress or persuaded by undue influence to sign the will.* The contestant in this situation alleges the testator did not execute the will independently or voluntarily.

EXAMPLES: (1) John is forced by physical threats to himself or his family to sign the will. (2) John is influenced by another with whom John has a close personal (confidential) relationship to include that person in his will while excluding his rightful beneficiaries or heirs, e.g., his spouse and children. (3) John makes a will, leaving a substantial amount of his estate to his housekeeper, Mary, who also signs the will as one of the two required witnesses. As previously discussed, some states presume there was undue influence in this case, while other states declare the will invalid because Mary is an "interested witness" or at least deny her the benefits she would receive through John's will but do not invalidate the rest of the will.

In the above examples, John, at first glance, may have written and executed a proper will and satisfied the required formalities of the law of wills in his state, yet the probate court could hold the will invalid because John's free will to dispose of the property according to his own wishes has been denied. To create a valid will, the requisite testamentary intent must be present. A will is invalid if obtained through physical threats or mental influence that destroys the freedom of choice and intent of its maker. To threaten the maker or members of his immediate family with violence to force the execution of a will constitutes duress and physical coercion—factors that invalidate the will. To substitute by force someone else's wishes in place of the maker's is another example of the use of coercion in drafting a will. Although not physical in nature as with duress, nor apparent from the appearance of the will as with mistake, undue or extraordinary influence on the mind of the maker can also render the will invalid.

A will might be disallowed because of both fraud and undue influence, as illustrated by the case of *Cook v. Loftus*, 414 N.E.2d 581 (Ind.App. 1981), in which a beneficiary of a new will falsely told the testator that the beneficiaries under his prior will planned to put him in a nursing home. The court upheld the prior will.

The presence of undue influence is especially difficult to determine for there are as many kinds of undue influence as there are personalities. The probate court must consider the testator, the person who allegedly exerted the undue influence, and the circumstances. The court may infer undue influence if the testator ignores blood relatives and names, as beneficiary, a nonrelative who is in constant close contact with the testator and thus in a position to impose undue influence. Nevertheless, undue influence must still be proven.

EXAMPLE: An in-law or friend caring for the deceased at the time of death is named beneficiary to the exclusion of all family members. See *In re Estate of Price*, 223 Neb. 12, 388 N.W.2d 72 (1986), in which the court found that in this instance there had been no undue influence. See also the case of *Succession of Bacot*, 502 So.2d 1118 (La.App. 1987), in which the court upheld a devise of the decedent's estate to a gay lover instead of to the family.

In some states, a presumption of undue influence is raised if a contestant (opponent) of the will shows (1) a confidential relationship (doctor, attorney, legal assistant, caregiver, priest or minister, fiduciary) allowed the alleged influencer an opportunity to control the testamentary act; (2) the testator's weakened physical and mental condition easily permitted a subversion of free will; (3) the influencer actively participated in preparing the will; or (4) the influencer unduly profited as a beneficiary or heir under the provisions of the will. *Note:* In most states, not to mention the canons of professional ethics, *a lawyer or paralegal who is intended to be a beneficiary or heir under a will must refrain from drafting and designing the will.* See Rule 1.8(c) of the Model Rules of Professional Conduct.

However, see *In re Conduct of Tonkon*, 292 Or. 660, 642 P.2d 660 (1982), where the attorney (Tonkon) represented his client (testator) for many years and the client's final will left Tonkon a gift of $75,000. Even though Tonkon did not advise the client to consult another attorney, the Oregon Supreme Court held that he did not violate the Code of Professional Responsibility. As an attorney or paralegal in a situation like Tonkon's, the following are other procedures you could and should use to avoid this ethical problem.

1. Refuse to draft the will.

2. Insist that another attorney of the client's choice draft the will but not an associate or partner from your law firm. See Model Rule 1.10(a).

3. Fully disclose the Code of Conduct to your client.

4. Make sure you do not in any way suggest or encourage the gift and that the client originated the bequest.

5. Make sure the gift is not the major asset of the estate.

ASSIGNMENT 4.14

Review the resolutions of the ethical problem above and then answer the following:

1. You are asked to draft a client's will that includes a gift to you as in the *Tonkon* case. What should you do if the client is so near death there is no time to obtain another attorney?

2. Could you argue that the gift is appropriate because you are a "close personal friend" of the client and, therefore, "a natural object of the testator's bounty"?

The burden of proving undue influence, fraud, duress, mistake, or revocation is generally on the contestant and, as mentioned earlier, the proof must be "clear and convincing" (see UPC § 3–407). Once the contestant has established sufficient evidence of the truth of his contention, he has established a **prima facie** case. Now the burden of establishing evidence to the contrary that establishes the will's validity shifts to the proponent of the will. Exhibit 4.4 illustrates the method and legal form used to contest a will in the state of New York.

prima facie
At first sight; on the face of it. A fact presumed to be true unless disproved by evidence to the contrary.

In Terrorem or "No Contest" Clause—A Forfeiture Clause

People who have wills are concerned about will contests even though very few contests are successful. If the maker of a will fulfills all requirements for a valid will and executes it correctly, the probate court will uphold it. Nevertheless, any will is open to a will contest whether by legitimate persons or unscrupulous ones. Unfortunately, even though the will contest has no merit, the cost of the potential litigation may be so high that a settlement is reached and gives the contestants part of the estate even though this was not the intent of the testator.

In anticipation that an omitted family member or disgruntled heir may contest the will, the testator may attempt to prevent a will contest by such person by including in the will a "no contest" or **"in terrorem" clause**. Such clauses state that if a beneficiary or heir named in the will disputes the validity of the will, objects to

"in terrorem" clause
A clause in a will that if a beneficiary of the will objects to probate or challenges the will's distributions, that contestant forfeits all benefits of the will.

the probate of the will, or challenges the dispositions, i.e., the kind and amount of the gifts that pass to the named persons listed in the will, that contestant forfeits all benefits of the will. Some states, e.g., Indiana, declare such in terrorem clauses unenforceable; some, e.g., New York and Wyoming, strictly enforce the clause; others disregard the clause if the contestant had "probable cause" to commence the will contest. See N.Y. EPTL § 3-3.5 and *Dainton v. Watson*, 658 P.2d 79 (Wyo. 1983), in which the court ruled that "a no contest or in terrorem clause in the will, which required forfeiture of the bequest to the [beneficiary] as a result of the beneficiary's unsuccessful will contest, was valid and did not violate public policy." The following is an example of an in terrorem clause.

If a beneficiary or devisee under this will contests or challenges the probate of this will or any of its clauses in any manner, in such event the bequest or devise of my estate given to such beneficiary or devisee under this will is hereby revoked and forfeited, and said bequest or devise shall be distributed as part of my residuary estate.

EXHIBIT 4.4   Objection to Probating a Will

Surrogate's Court: County of _____

In the Matter of the Objections to Probate against   Objections to Probate
the Last Will and Testament of _____,   File No. _____
Deceased.

_____, a distributee objects to the probate of the instrument propounded herein as the last will and testament of _____, late of the County of _____, deceased, upon the following grounds:

First: That the alleged will was not duly executed by the said _____, deceased, that she did not publish the same as her will in presence of the witnesses whose names are subscribed thereto, that she did not request the said two witnesses to be witnesses thereto, and that the said alleged witnesses did not sign as witnesses in her presence or in the presence of each other.

Second: That on the _____ day of _____, 20 ____, the said decedent, _____, was not of sound mind or memory and was not mentally capable of making a will.

Third: That the said paper writing was not freely or voluntarily made or executed by the said _____, as her last will and testament, but that the said paper writing purporting to be her will was obtained and the subscription and publication thereof if it was in fact subscribed or published by her, were procured by fraud and undue influence practiced upon the decedent by _____ and _____, the principal legatees and devisees named in said paper, or by some other person or persons acting in concert or privity with them, whose name or names are at the present time unknown to this contestant.

Fourth: A trial by jury of the issues raised by this answer is hereby demanded.

Wherefore, the above named contestant prays that this proceeding may be dismissed, with costs.

_____
Attorney for Objecting Distributee
P.O. Address
Tel. No.

[*Verification*]

This form is used in New York when an interested party (beneficiary, distributee, or heir at law) objects to the acceptance and probate of a will.

Key Terms

case law	attest (a will)	ambulatory
testamentary intent	subscribe (a will)	operation of law
testamentary capacity	competent witness	standing
natural objects of the testator's bounty	interested witness	prima facie
insane delusions	publication	in terrorem clause
lucid interval	interlineation	

Review Questions

1. Who may make a valid will?

2. Can an attorney or a paralegal prepare and draft a will for a client who is of unsound mind? Explain.

3. What are the statutory or formal requirements for executing a will?

4. What are the signature requirements, e.g., types of signatures or placement of signatures, for testators and witnesses?

5. How is a witness determined to be competent?

6. Can an attorney or a paralegal be a competent witness to a will? Should they be witnesses?

7. Is an attestation clause required in every will? Explain.

8. In what three ways can a will be revoked? Explain.

9. Under what circumstances can a "lost will" be probated?

10. Only a person with "standing" can contest a will. What does this mean?

11. What are the appropriate reasons or grounds for contesting a will? Explain.

12. Are in terrorem clauses in a will enforced in your state? Cite the appropriate statute or case law.

Case Problems

Problem 1

Bill Jorgenson is terminally ill. Suppose Bill's son, Harold, convinces his father that Cheryl Jorgenson, Bill's wife and Harold's mother, is initiating institutional commitment proceedings against Bill. In fact, that is not true. Nevertheless, Bill changes his will because of this allegation and leaves everything to Harold. According to your state's law, what are the grounds for contesting a will? Which grounds can Cheryl use to contest Bill's will? What other rights does Cheryl have if the will is declared valid? See the Cook case previously cited.

Problem 2

A will was drafted for Melinda Wadsworth. Melinda's attorney, Malcolm Edwards, was present when she signed the will. Malcolm then signed as one of the attesting witnesses. It was Malcolm's intent to have Jaclene Morgan, a paralegal working for his law firm, be the second required witness. However, Jaclene was out of the office when Melinda and Malcolm signed the will. When Jaclene returned, Melinda had left the office. Malcolm showed the will to Jaclene, informed her that it was Melinda's will and signature, and asked Jaclene to witness and sign the will. Instead of immediately signing the will, Jaclene first called Melinda and verified that it was Melinda's will and signature. Then, Jaclene signed as a witness to the will.

A. Is the above procedure for executing a will proper? Explain.

B. Would this will be valid in your state? Cite the statute or case law. See *Matter of Jefferson's Will*, 349 So.2d 1032 (Miss. 1977).

Practical Assignments

1. A client comes to your office. She wants to disinherit her three children and leave her entire estate in trust for the benefit of her dog, Fifi. Develop a list of questions that could be used to determine whether the testator has the capacity to understand the consequences of her actions.

2. Prepare a sample signature and attestation clause that would meet the requirements for your jurisdiction.

3. A client comes to your office for a consult regarding his father's will. The father recently passed away and left client the sum of $100,000. The client is an only child and the father's estate is worth $8 million. The mother predeceased the father. The client believes he is entitled to the entire estate. In reviewing the will, you discover the following clause: If a beneficiary or devisee under this will contests or challenges the probate of this will or any of its clauses in any manner, in such even the bequest or devise of my estate given to such beneficiary or devisee under this will is hereby revoked and forfeited, and said bequest or devise shall be distributed as part of my residuary estate.

Review the law in your state and advise your client whether this clause is enforceable.

PREPARATION TO DRAFT A WILL: CHECKLISTS AND THE CONFERENCE WITH THE CLIENT

5

Outline

Objectives

After completing this chapter, you should be able to:

- Collect and assimilate the relevant facts in preparation for the preliminary draft of a will.

- Identify, explain, and interpret the sources of law, e.g., common (case) law and statutes that determine the validity of a will.

- Develop and use checklists to elicit the information necessary for the preliminary draft of a will.

- Ensure that all necessary pertinent information obtained from appropriate checklists is accurate and complete.

- Recognize when additional information is needed.

- Identify and follow guidelines used to prepare wills.

SCOPE OF THE CHAPTER

This chapter is concerned with the procedures prior to making a will. A will must be prepared with meticulous care and follow the standards prescribed by case law and state statutes. If not careful, a drafter can fail to execute a valid and appropriate will if essential information is not elicited from the client and certain rules of practice are not followed.

The chapter begins with the initial meeting with the client. It identifies the checklists that are created and used to gather facts to determine to whom the client's assets will be transferred, and how tax burdens and miscellaneous problems can be minimized or resolved. Definitions and examples of terms used in the checklists precede the individual lists. Sample checklists used to prepare a draft of the will are illustrated. You must learn to develop checklists and questionnaires appropriate for your client's needs. Next comes a discussion of some pitfalls in the preparation of the rough draft of a will. Guidelines to make the document a purposeful, legally enforceable, and unimpeachable testamentary disposition are presented.

THE CONFERENCE WITH THE CLIENT: INITIAL INTERVIEW, CHECKLISTS, AND OTHER MATTERS

When you and the attorney meet with a client to discuss preliminary matters prior to drafting a will, you must collect information about the client's finances and family. Checklists will be used or created to obtain the necessary data.

In order to assist the attorney to formulate an appropriate will for a client, you will need to develop interviewing, data-collecting, drafting, and counseling skills to help clients overcome the normal reluctance most people have when they discuss family relationships and financial matters. By being positive, cooperative, reassuring, informative, and professional in appearance and demeanor, you can help the client overcome this reluctance and understand that his or her best interests will be served by an open and frank discussion of complete financial data and information. *You should also assure the client that strict confidentiality of all matters will be maintained.* Once a client who seeks a will or an estate plan hires your supervising attorney, your work as a paralegal will commence.

⚖️ *Ethical Issue*

Initial Interview

The development of a will begins with an initial and lengthy interview of the client by the attorney. Assuming a "comfort" level has been reached and the client is willing to be open and frank about financial data in front of others, you will be asked to attend the interview. Your first task will be to help the client identify all facts, data, and information needed to create a draft of the will. You must develop checklists and questionnaires or expand, amend, or modify existing copies of these documents and thoroughly review them with the client to ensure they elicit the information necessary for the draft. Exhibits 5.1 through 5.6 are examples of the checklists that will enable you to obtain the requisite information.

You will need to collect information concerning the client's financial affairs and family members' names, addresses, domicile, and marital status. A chart showing

POINT OF INTEREST

Technology Advances May Mean Client Has Created His or Her Own Will

Will preparation kits are sold in office supply stores, bookstores, and in major retail outlets. These products can also be ordered from catalog companies and from e-commerce retailers. Some will forms are available for free on the Internet. The easy access to these forms may result in some attempts by clients to draft their own wills. It is questionable how adequate and valid these documents are. Rarely will clients fully understand the terminology used. It is doubtful that the will execution was properly performed. If a client has attempted to prepare his or her own will and is now seeking assistance from a law office, he or she should be commended for realizing that professional counsel is needed. Use the client's draft to assist with the interview. Some predict that will contests will be more prevalent with the use of these preprinted will forms.

the family tree should be drawn. It should identify adopted and nonmarital children and include the general health of all family members. Assets and liabilities should be listed. Beneficiaries, including charities, should be named, and the assets to be transferred to them should be identified and valued. All fiduciaries, e.g., personal representatives, trustees, guardians, or conservators, should be named. All known creditors and the amounts of the debts owed to them should be listed. Finally, the specific wishes of the client for disposition of the estate should be determined and carefully considered in order to anticipate, counter, or prevent potential will contests by disgruntled family members who may receive nominal gifts of the estate or be completely disinherited.

Once the checklists have been executed and the questionnaires answered, you will review them with the client to ensure they are complete and accurate. Then you can discuss how best to achieve the specific objectives of the client. In addition, one of the more important tasks the attorney undertakes is to help the client reduce death taxes. The attorney should familiarize the client with the taxes imposed on a decedent's estate and give legal advice, *something you must not do,* on how to minimize them. This can be accomplished by reducing the decedent's gross estate through lifetime gifts and increasing the potential deductions from the gross estate, such as the marital and charitable deductions. Finally, the client should be informed of the necessity of making decisions about how best to achieve an effective, valid distribution of the estate, at death, in a manner of his or her own choosing.

⚖ *Ethical Issue*

If it is obviously apparent that a person lacks testamentary capacity—a sound mind—the attorney and paralegal cannot accept employment. The lawyer and paralegal should not be judgmental about the client's plans for the will, even if they are eccentric. The paralegal should be helpful and encourage the client to carefully examine, analyze, and determine his or her true feelings toward beneficiaries and the distributions planned for them. The attorney and paralegal can help the client focus on whether the will should distribute the testator's estate (1) on the basis of a property distribution plan in which the closest family members

⚖ *Ethical Issue*

EXHIBIT 5.1   Family Data

CHECKLIST: FAMILY DATA

Client

Name and address:	_____ City, State _____
Alias or a.k.a:	_____
Telephone number: Home	_____ Other _____
Social Security number:	_____
Date of birth:	_____ City, State _____
Marital status:	_____ Maiden name _____
Date of marriage:	_____ City, State _____
Date of divorce:	_____ City, State _____
Date of death:	_____ City, State _____
Present health:	_____
Occupation/business:	_____
Name of employer:	_____ Telephone _____
Employer address:	_____

Family Members (use additional sheets as necessary) (spouse, children, grand-children, parents, other dependents, relatives, and beneficiaries)

Name:	_____
Relationship:	_____
Telephone number: Home	_____ Other _____
Address:	_____
Date of birth:	_____ City, State _____
Marital status:	_____ Maiden name _____
Date of death:	_____ City, State _____
Present health:	_____

Domicile of Client

	Address	City	County	State
Home:				
Other residences (homes, cottages, etc.):				
Prior residences over past 10 years, especially if in a community property state:				

Business

Name of business:	_____
Business address:	_____
Telephone number:	_____
Type of business (purpose):	_____
Form of ownership (interest):	_____
Sole proprietor:	_____
Partner:	_____
Limited partner:	_____
Corporation:	_____
Other:	_____

Family Concerns

Antenuptial or postnuptial agreements:	_____

EXHIBIT 5.1	**(Continued)**

Previous marriages: _____
   Children of
   previous
   marriages: _____
Divorce or legal
   separation: _____
Settlement information
   (child support,
   maintenance, etc.): _____
Special dependency
   cases:
     Handicapped child,
     parent, relative: _____
   Mental disability: _____
   Emotional problems: _____
   Other health problems: _____

Trusts
   Spendthrift child: _____
   Life estate to be
     transferred: _____
   Potential inheritance: _____

Persons to be disinherited (specific reasons listed below):
_____
_____

Advancements (property previously transferred before client's death):
_____
_____

Names and Addresses of Potential Fiduciaries and Successors
   Personal representative
     (executor/trix): _____
     Successor: _____
   Guardian for minor children: _____
     Successor: _____
   Trustees: _____
     Successor: _____

---

receive the greater share and other relatives and friends a lesser amount, (2) on the basis of family need, or (3) a combination of these two. Some clients may adopt an unduly submissive or subordinate attitude toward their attorney or the paralegal and may even suggest or request the attorney or you advise them as to what they should do with their estate property. *This request must be denied to avoid unethical consequences.*

⚖️ *Ethical Issue*

After the interview, you should prepare optional drafts of the will distribution plans for consideration and review by the client. The plans should include comparisons of their tax consequences and other expenses including attorney's fees. The drafts should be summarized and explained in plain language to the client so that any modifications can be noted and incorporated into the appropriate selected

⚖️ *Ethical Issue*

draft. Once the client is satisfied with the changes, the final will is prepared and properly executed. *While you must avoid improper solicitation,* you should recommend periodic reviews of the will whenever the client's marital status (divorce or marriage), domicile, or the law changes, or when additional children are born or adopted.

Use of Checklists to Obtain Basic Data

The following discussion illustrates the development and use of checklists, which help to assemble the data necessary to draft a will appropriate for the individual needs of the client. Definitions and examples of terms used within the checklists precede the individual lists. In addition to being used during the formation of the will, the information is helpful to determine the proper venue for probating the estate and the location of beneficiaries, devisees, and assets of the deceased.

⚖️ *Ethical Issue*

The client should be given a copy of each checklist before the conference so he or she can gather the information requested with the assistance of family members and financial advisers if necessary. You will also help obtain the information. *If an earlier will exists, obtain a copy from the client for review.*

The purpose of checklists is to ensure that accurate, complete, and requisite information is obtained. As you review each checklist, you need to analyze and interpret the collected data and recognize when supplementary information is needed.

The sample checklists in this chapter are (1) Family Data, (2) Family Advisers, (3) Assets, (4) Liabilities, (5) Life Insurance Policies, and (6) Locations of Important Documents. In Chapter 6 you will be asked to draft your own will from these sample checklists or from those you develop for yourself. The same or similar checklists will be used to establish an estate plan in Chapter 14. In specific instances, additional or supplementary checklists may be needed, and you will be asked to produce them.

Terminology Associated with Family Data Checklists

The following are terms you are likely to encounter when you prepare a family data checklist.

advancement
Money or property given by a parent while living to a child in anticipation of the share the child will inherit from the parent's estate and in advance of the proper time for receipt of such property.

- *Advancement.* An **advancement** is money or property given by a parent to a child in anticipation of the share the child will inherit from the parent's estate. Prior to the parent's death, it is given to the child and is intended to be deducted from the share of the parent's estate the child eventually receives after the parent's death.

  EXAMPLE: Trang Sasaki has 100 shares of valuable stock. Under intestate succession laws, Trang's only daughter is entitled to the 100 shares. While alive, Trang gives her daughter 50 shares. The 50 shares would be considered an advancement unless Trang dies testate or other evidence is presented that rebuts the advancement presumption. The laws of most states require a written confirmation of an advancement must exist on the date of the donor's death. The rule of advancement generally applies when there is no will.

- *Disinheritance.* Disinheritance by will is the act by which the testator of an estate specifically deprives another, who would otherwise be the testator's legal heir, from receiving the estate.

EXAMPLE: Rivka Mizrachi specifically states in her will, "I, intentionally and with full knowledge, leave nothing to my son, Asher, from the assets of my estate." *Note:* Compare this to the "no contest" (in terrorem) clause in Chapter 4.

- *Life estate.* A life estate is an interest in real property, e.g., land and buildings, for a lifetime, either the lifetime of the person holding the estate or of some other person. A person who holds a life estate, called the life tenant, possesses and is entitled to use the real property only during the lifetime of the person named in the will or deed that granted the life estate.

  EXAMPLE: Barack receives a life estate in a lake cottage through his uncle's will. Barack may use and possess the cottage until he dies.

- *Spendthrift.* A spendthrift is one who spends money unwisely and wastefully.

  EXAMPLE: Zaire wastes the estate left him by his father by drinking, gambling, idleness, and the like.

Checklist for Family Data

As a paralegal, part of your investigatory duties is to collect complete information concerning your client, the client's family, and the beneficiaries or devisees to be named in the will. You should obtain the following:

- *Full* names, addresses, and phone numbers of the participants: maker of the will; beneficiaries or devisees; executor (or executrix); witnesses; guardians; and trustee, if any
- *Age* and marital status of the maker, beneficiaries, and devisees
- *Relationship* of appropriate participants to the client
- *Mental* and physical health of the client, spouse, and other beneficiaries
- *Financial* status (worth) of the client, spouse, and family, and the nature of any business in which the client has an interest
- *Family* affairs, including tensions, possible mistreatment of the client and the source of such mistreatment, debts owed the maker by family members, advancements (property previously transferred) given to some members, spendthrifts, persons incapable of handling their own financial affairs who may need a trustee, and other pertinent matters

Using a checklist like the one in Exhibit 5.1, you can collect and organize the family data.

The Need for Supplementary Data

In some instances, information provided by the checklists will not be adequate to inform the attorney of all the client's needs or plans to dispose of estate property. As an observant paralegal, you should note situations likely to lead to problems with specific devises (gifts) and should further pursue these matters with the client after first bringing them to the attention of the supervising attorney. *You should not discuss any circumstances or suggest resolutions to problems that may involve giving legal advice.*

⚖️ *Ethical Issue*

EXAMPLE: Suppose Willie Tomkins, the client, indicated he had been previously married and had two children by that marriage. The paralegal would have to determine (1) whether the former spouse and children are still living; (2) whether a satisfactory property settlement and child support agreement were reached by all interested parties in the prior marriage, and the terms of those agreements; and (3) whether the client intends to leave any part of his estate to his former wife and children of the marriage.

EXAMPLE: Suppose the client, Willie, has an invalid mother who is 75 years old. He has supported his mother for the past 15 years and wants to continue this support for her lifetime. The original checklist only includes information that the client's mother is alive and currently an invalid. Questions you put to the client could obtain additional information about his mother and the method by which Willie wishes to maintain support for her in case he should die first, *but legal advice must come from the attorney.*

⚖️ *Ethical Issue*

EXAMPLE: Suppose Willie does not want any of his estate to go to his brother, Tion. The reasons for this decision and the manner in which Willie's intent can be manifested in his will must be discussed with the client under the supervision of the attorney.

EXAMPLE: Suppose that while he completes the checklist, Willie comes to the question of advancements and remembers he gave his youngest son $5,000 to buy a used automobile last year. Like most people, Willie is not sure what an advancement is. This concept must be reviewed and explained. You could explain this term and probable results or outcomes; *however, any counseling or legal advice must come from the attorney* during the conference with the client.

⚖️ *Ethical Issue*

The checklists help you to draw out general information and to clarify the client's intentions. If additional data about specific matters and details to be incorporated into the future will must be obtained, you perform that task.

Checklist for Family Advisers

A list of the names of the client's advisers is helpful to obtain information about the names of creditors or debtors and the location of the client's assets, personal records and documents, beneficiaries, successors, or previous will (see Exhibit 5.2).

Terminology Associated with Assets and Liabilities Checklists

The following terms may appear in your assets and liabilities checklist.

- *Dividend.* Dividend is the share of profits or property to which the owners of a business are entitled; e.g., stockholders are entitled to dividends authorized by a corporation in proportion to the number of shares of the corporation's stock owned by each stockholder.

- *Fair market value.* The fair market value is the monetary amount an item of property, e.g., a house, would bring if sold on the open market. Usually, it is the price agreed to by a willing seller and a willing buyer, neither party being compelled to offer a price above or below the average price for such an item.

  EXAMPLE: Reuben Bomar offers $120,000 to buy Ernest Waite's house. Houses of this type usually command a price of at least $120,000. Ernest accepts Reuben's offer. The fair market value of the house is $120,000.

- *Homestead.* A homestead is the family home and the adjoining land (within statutory limits) where the head of the family lives; it is the family's fixed place of residence. Most states allow the head of the family to exempt the homestead from claims by creditors.

EXHIBIT 5.2   Family Advisers

CHECKLIST: FAMILY ADVISERS

	Name	Telephone Number
Accountant:		
Address:		
Tax preparer:		
Address:		
Attorney:		
Address:		
Banker:		
Address:		
Physician:		
Address:		
Religious adviser:		
Address:		
Insurance agent:		
Address:		
Appraiser:		
Address:		
Financial planner:		
Address:		
Trust officer:		
Address:		
Stockbroker:		
Address:		
Computer Consultant:		
Address:		
Others:		
Address:		
Address:		

Terms associated with miscellaneous property include the following:

- *Copyright.* A government grant to an author of an exclusive right to publish, reprint, and sell a manuscript for a period of the life of the author plus 70 years after the author's death for works written after January 1, 1978
- *Patent.* A government grant to an inventor of an exclusive right to make, use, and sell an invention for a nonrenewable period of 20 years from the date of application
- *Royalty.* A payment made to an author, composer, or inventor by a company that has been licensed to publish or manufacture the manuscript or invention of that author, composer, or inventor

- *Receivables.* Debts (such as promissory notes) established in the course of business that are currently due from others or due within a certain time period

  The following terms describe liabilities you are likely to encounter

- *Contract for deed.* An agreement or contract to sell real property on an installment basis. On payment of the last installment, the title to the property is transferred by delivery of the deed to the purchaser.

- *Installment purchase.* The purchase of goods on credit whereby the purchaser pays for them over a period of time. The purchaser (in the case of a small-loan purchase) immediately obtains the title, or ownership, of the purchase; the seller retains a security interest until the purchaser has paid the full price.

- *Mortgage.* A mortgage is a contract by which a person pledges property to another as security in order to obtain a loan.

  EXAMPLE: Debra Bechtold obtains a $70,000 mortgage from her bank as a loan in order to finance the purchase of a house costing $90,000.

- *Mortgagor.* The mortgagor is the person who mortgages property; the borrower or debtor.

- *Mortgagee.* The mortgagee is the person to whom property is mortgaged; the lender, e.g., bank.

  EXAMPLE: Debra Bechtold in the example above would be the mortgagor (borrower), and the bank would be the mortgagee (lender).

- *Promissory note.* A promissory note is a promise in writing to pay a certain sum of money at a future time to a specific person.

Checklists for Assets and Liabilities

Lists of all assets and liabilities of the client are made, and the form of ownership of each asset is noted, e.g., whether the asset is solely owned or concurrently owned, such as a homestead in joint tenancy between spouses. The lists should include the following information.

- *Real property,* including the legal description and estimated fair market value of the homestead, all other land, and business buildings. Determine whether the property is owned individually in severalty or concurrently in joint tenancy, tenancy by the entirety, tenancy in common, or as community property (see Chapter 1). Check the location of the property. If it is outside the client's domiciliary state, ancillary administration might be necessary.

- *Tangible personal property,* including personal effects and clothing of considerable value, furniture and household goods, automobiles, boats, jewelry, antiques, art and stamp collections, and other miscellaneous items.

- Other items of personal property such as savings and checking accounts, safe deposit box, stocks and bonds, cash on hand, promissory notes receivable, digital assets, mortgages, patents, and copyrights.

- *Insurance* policies, including life, disability, health, accident, and annuities, must be scrutinized to determine how and to whom payments are to be made on the client's death.

- *Employee* benefits like Social Security, veterans' benefits, pension plans, profit-sharing plans, death benefits, stock options, and all other claims to which the client's estate or successors may be entitled.

- Business interests in a corporation, partnership, or sole proprietorship, with complete details about the client's interest, rights, and responsibilities therein.

- All debts owed by the client, including outstanding mortgages, promissory notes payable, business debts, payments owed on contracts for deed, and accounts with a stockbroker.

- Interest and duties in trust assets (property transferred, beneficiary, trustee, trust agreement) or estates of others, including powers of appointment (a power to dispose of property not owned by the holder of the power), which the decedent may hold by virtue of being given this power by another's will or trust. A general power of appointment held by the decedent is taxable to the decedent's estate (see Chapter 14).

Use checklists like those in Exhibits 5.3 and 5.4 to collect and organize the data on the client's assets and liabilities.

ASSIGNMENT 5.1

Your law firm's client is heavily invested in the bond and stock markets. As a paralegal for the firm, you have been asked to collect the necessary data concerning the extent and value of the client's holdings. Due to the client's extensive holdings, you will need a more detailed checklist than the one shown in Exhibit 5.3. You have been asked to include the number of shares, ownership, date of purchase and cost basis, and current market value for all stocks, bonds, and mutual funds owned by the client. Draft an appropriate checklist.

If the client has substantial stock holdings, separate lists of the holdings should be attached to the assets checklist. The value of assets such as patents, art and coin collections, hobby equipment, or business interests may be difficult to estimate accurately; therefore, it may be necessary to use appraisers to assist with the evaluation of these items. A separate list should be made of this information.

Terminology Associated with a Life Insurance Policies Checklist

The life insurance policies checklist may include the following terms.

- *Life insurance.* Life insurance is a contract, a legally binding agreement, by which one party (the insurance company) promises to pay another (the policyholder or designated beneficiary) a certain sum of money if the policyholder sustains a specific loss (e.g., death or total disability). For this protection the policyholder makes a payment called a premium on a regular basis, usually annually, to the insurance company. Life insurance includes term, ordinary (whole or straight) life, and universal life insurance (see Chapter 14).

- *Annuity.* An annuity is a fixed sum to be paid at regular intervals, such as annually, for either a certain or indefinite period, as for a stated number of years or for life.

EXHIBIT 5.3   Assets

CHECKLIST: ASSETS

List the item (by name), the estimated fair market value of the property owned, the location, the form of ownership, e.g., single ownership by identifying party (S-name), joint tenancy (J), tenancy by the entirety (E), tenancy in common (C), community property (CP) or Other (O) for each item, and the beneficiary or beneficiaries (Bene.).

Item	Value	Location	Form of Ownership (S-name/J/E/C/CP/O) Bene.

Cash
Cash and checking
    accounts: _____
Savings accounts: _____
Money market accounts: _____
Certificates of deposit: _____

Stocks and Bonds
Stocks (Name and no. of
    shares): _____
Stock options: _____
Brokerage accounts: _____
U.S. government bonds: _____
Municipal bonds: _____
Mutual funds: _____
Other: _____

Real Property
Residential (homestead): _____
Business building: _____
Recreational (summer
    cottage): _____
Rental property: _____
Timeshare: _____
Foreign real estate: _____
Other: _____

Personal Property
Furniture and household
    goods: _____
Furs and jewelry: _____
Automobiles (model and
    year):
    (1) _____
    (2) _____
    Collections (art, guns,
      coins, stamps,
      antiques, etc.): _____
Other vehicles (boats,
    trailers, campers,
    snowmobiles,
    motorbikes, etc.): _____
Digital Assets (Identify
    by name): _____
Wearing apparel and
    personal effects: _____
Other: _____

EXHIBIT 5.3	(Continued)

Business Interests
Sole proprietorship: _____
Partnership: _____
Limited partnership: _____
Corporation: _____
Buy-sell agreements: _____
Other: _____

Receivables
Accounts receivable: _____
Promissory notes
  (payable to client): _____
Contract for deed (client
  is seller): _____
Other: _____

**Employee, Corporate,
  and Other Benefits**
Pension plan: _____
Stock bonus: _____
Profit-sharing plan: _____
401(k) plan: _____
Self-employed
  retirement plan: _____
Individual retirement
  account (IRA)
    Traditional: _____
    Roth: _____
Insurance
    Accident: _____
    Health: _____
    Disability: _____
Social Security: _____
Union benefits: _____
Railroad retirement
  benefits: _____
Veterans' benefits: _____
Fraternal organization
  benefits: _____
Other: _____

Interests in Trusts _____
**Power of Appointment
(General or Special)** _____
**Insurance and Annuities
  (See Exhibit 5.5)**
Straight life, universal
  life, or term: _____
Endowment or annuity: _____
Group life insurance: _____

Miscellaneous Property
Patents: _____
Copyrights: _____
Royalties: _____
Other: _____

TOTAL ASSETS (value): _____

(continued)

Exhibit 5.4	Liabilities

CHECKLIST: LIABILITIES

List the item, the estimated value of each debt, its location, the parties indebted, i.e., husband (H), wife (W), or joint (J), and the creditor.

Type of Liability	Item	Value	Location	Form of Liability (H/W/J)	Creditor
Promissory notes (to banks, loan companies, individuals, etc.):					
Mortgages—on real property:					
Payment on contracts for deed:					
Charge accounts and installment purchases:					
Automobile loans:					
Credit card charges:					
Loans on insurance policies:					
Business debts:					
Enforceable pledges to charitable and religious organizations:					
Taxes owed:					
Other:					
TOTAL LIABILITES (value):					

- *Primary beneficiary.* A primary beneficiary is the person who has a superior claim over all others to the benefits of a life insurance contract. The policyholder selects the primary beneficiary.

- *Secondary (contingent) beneficiary.* A secondary beneficiary is the person selected by the policyholder as a successor to the benefits of a life insurance policy whenever the proceeds of the policy are not paid to the primary beneficiary.

- *Cash surrender value.* In ordinary (straight) life insurance, the cash surrender value is the cash reserve that increases (builds) each year the policy remains in force as a minimum savings feature. After the policy has been in force for a period specified by the insurer (company), the policyholder may borrow an amount not to exceed the cash value.

- *Premium.* The premium is the sum paid or agreed to be paid annually by the insured person (policyholder) to the insurance company (insurer) as the consideration for the insurance contract.

- *Settlement option.* A settlement option is one of a number of alternatives that parties to an insurance contract agree to follow to discharge their agreement.

  EXAMPLE: Ricardo Rivera is the named primary beneficiary of his deceased parent's life insurance policy. The policy gives Ricardo the option of receiving payment in a lump sum or in monthly payments over a period of years. The option selected by Ricardo acts as a present or eventual discharge of the contract.

ASSIGNMENT 5.2

Ted Whaley owns a straight life insurance policy with the Life Assurance Company of Kingstown with $50,000 as its face value. Ted names his wife, Shelley Whaley, as his primary beneficiary and his son, Nelson Whaley, as the secondary beneficiary. The cash value of the policy at the time of Ted's death is $8,700. The year before Ted's death, he obtained a $2,500 loan on his insurance from the insurance company at 5 percent interest. When Ted died, a $1,200 balance, including interest, was unpaid on the loan. To whom will the life insurance be paid? How much will the beneficiary receive?

Checklist for Life Insurance Policies

Exhibit 5.3 (Assets) includes basic information about the existence and types of life insurance owned by the client. If necessary, more detailed information about such policies must be compiled. This is an example of an instance in which you must develop a checklist within a checklist. Exhibit 5.5 is a checklist of information on the client's life insurance policies. Information on the insurance policies of the client's spouse and children should also be obtained.

Checklist for Important Documents

You collect all documents involving the client's property and business interests for review with the attorney. These documents may include stock certificates and options, contracts, deeds, receivables, insurance policies, gift tax returns, income tax returns for the past seven years (the Internal Revenue Service can challenge the accuracy of a taxpayer's income tax return for the three previous taxable years, although if fraud is involved, the statute of limitations does not apply; see IRC §§ 6501 and 6531), divorce decrees and alimony or child support payments or other property settlements from a previous marriage, antenuptial agreements, mortgages, *inter vivos* (living) trust agreements in which the client is either the donor or beneficiary, and any existing will the client may have. Exhibit 5.6 is a sample checklist to collect information about the existence and location of these important documents.

ASSIGNMENT 5.3

Using the checklists in this chapter as a guide, develop and fill in the checklists necessary to prepare a preliminary draft of your will or the will of some member of your family, e.g., a spouse, parent, brother, or sister.

PRELIMINARY TAX ADVICE AND OTHER MATTERS

At the conference with the client, in addition to eliciting information by means of the checklists, the attorney or the supervised paralegal should explain the tax consequences of death in terms understandable to the client. The resolution of tax problems under the supervision of an attorney is an important function of a paralegal. Chapter 11 of this text identifies and defines the various types of federal and state taxes, explains how the basic tax regulations are applied to analytical problems, and demonstrates the necessary tax calculations. Therefore, the chapter must be reviewed before you can perform the duties outlined below during the conference.

EXHIBIT 5.5	Life Insurance Policies

CHECKLIST: LIFE INSURANCE DATA

Policyholder (owner): _____

Insured: _____

Insurance agent: _____ Phone: _____

	Company 1	Company 2	Company 3	Company 4	Totals
Name/Policy no.					
Location of policy					
Type of insurance					
Face or death value					
Dividends					
Annual premium					
Cash (surrender) value					
Loan on cash value					
Primary beneficiaries					
Secondary beneficiaries					
Settlement option installment					
Annuity					
Others					

At the conference the following matters should be explained and discussed. The tax items are discussed in more detail in later chapters.

- For smaller estates, joint tenancy ownership can avoid additional administration expenses. You must guard against overemphasizing the advantages of this form of property ownership. Since the transfer of property into joint tenancy divides the ownership and control of the property, it becomes impossible to sell the entire property without the consent of both joint tenants.

- You must determine if the federal estate tax can be reduced by using the marital and charitable deductions to which a client's estate is entitled (see Chapter 14).

- The use of certain *inter vivos* gifts or trusts to lower administration expenses and death taxes by reducing the client's gross estate.

- Whether the client wants taxes on the estate paid from estate funds or whether the individual beneficiaries or devisees are to pay taxes on their shares.

During the conference you should clarify other pertinent matters for the client and determine the client's desires in a number of situations. Particularly important are the spouse's right of election and the children's right to inherit.

Spouse's Right of Election—A Review

The client should be reminded that a married testator cannot determine conclusively the disposition of the entire estate by will because a surviving spouse cannot be completely disinherited. Most states offer a surviving spouse the right to renounce the will and elect a statutory share of a certain minimum portion of the deceased spouse's estate, thus invalidating an exclusion from the will. Therefore, your state's right of election should be explained to the client. A typical state statute that addresses this matter is Ohio Rev. Code Ann. § 2106.01, which allows a surviving spouse to take an elective share equal to the intestate share not to exceed one-half of the net estate or one-third if two or more children or their lineal descendants survive (but compare UPC §§ 2–202 and 2–203).

For a review of this topic, see Chapter 3.

EXAMPLES: Klaus Gruenwald dies testate and leaves his surviving spouse, Brigitte, (1) *all* his property; (2) *some* of his property; (3) *nothing*—he disinherits Brigitte. In Case 1, Brigitte would receive through Klaus will all his property as his sole successor. In Case 2, Brigitte would have the election (statutory) right to take either through Klaus will or by statute. Usually, she would choose whichever was the greater. She cannot take both. In Case 3, Klaus would fail in his attempt to disinherit his wife since in most states she is entitled to the statutory elective share, which she would naturally choose.

ASSIGNMENT 5.4

If Jana Fredricks is domiciled in your state and attempts through her will to leave all, some, or none of her property to her surviving spouse, how would your state handle each conveyance? Cite and explain your statute.

EXHIBIT 5.6   Locations of Important Documents

CHECKLIST: RECORDS OR DOCUMENTS (COPIES)

List the applicable documents' location or comment on missing items. Use additional sheets as necessary. If any documents are kept in a safe deposit box, list its location.

Checklists   Location
    Checklists: _____

Personal Data (Client and Family Members)
    Birth certificate:
    Social Security card:
    Medicare card:
    Marriage certificate:
    Separation agreement:
    Divorce decree:
    Antenuptial agreement:
    Postnuptial agreement:
    Adoption papers:
    Naturalization papers:
    Passports:
    Military records:
    Death certificate:
    Cemetery deed:
    Other: _____

Real Property
    Abstracts of title:
    Deeds:
    Contracts for deed:
    Leases:
    Appraisals:
    Property tax valuation notices:
    Other: _____

Personal Property
    Titles/registrations for
        Automobiles:
        Recreational vehicles:
        Trailers:
        Boats:
        Airplanes:
    Other: _____

Cash, Stocks, and Bonds
    Bank account statements:
    Investment account statements:
    Certificates of deposit:
    Bonds and other debentures:
    Stock certificates:
    Inventory of digital asset:
    Other: _____

Miscellaneous Property
    Patent agreements:
    Copyright agreements:
    Royalty agreements:
    Promissory notes:
    Other: _____

EXHIBIT 5.6   (Continued)

Business Interests
Partnership agreements: _____
Limited partnership agreements: _____
Franchise agreements: _____
Buy-sell agreements: _____
Corporation documents
   Charter: _____
   Bylaws: _____
   Stock certificates: _____
   Stock options: _____
Other:_____ _____

Retirement Plans
Pension plan: _____
Profit-sharing plan: _____
Stock bonus plan/
   ESOP: _____
401(k)/403(b) plans: _____
Self-employed
   retirement plan: _____
Individual retirement
   account (IRA)
   Traditional: _____
   Roth: _____
Social security: _____
Veterans' benefits: _____
Other:_____ _____

Interests in Trusts
Trust agreements: _____
Declaration of trust: _____
Powers of appointment: _____
Other:_____ _____

Insurance Policies
Life insurance: _____
Annuity contracts: _____
Accident insurance: _____
Health insurance: _____
Disability insurance: _____
Title insurance: _____
Homeowners' insurance: _____
Mortgage insurance: _____
Automobile insurance: _____
Boat insurance: _____
Other:_____ _____

Liabilities
Promissory notes: _____
Mortgages on real property: _____
Contracts for deed: _____
Loans on insurance policies: _____
Installment purchases
   Automobile loans: _____
   Credit card charges: _____
Business debts: _____
Other:_____ _____

(continued)

EXHIBIT 5.6 (Continued)

Miscellaneous (specify)
　Credit cards: _____
　ATM cards: _____
　Other:_____ _____

Tax Returns
　Federal income tax (7 years): _____
　State income tax (7 years): _____
　Federal gift tax (all years): _____

Current Will or Trust
　Original (client): _____
　Original (spouse): _____
　Codicil: _____
　Trust documents: _____
　Letter of instructions: _____
　Memorandum of personal
　　property: _____

Advance Directives
　Living will: _____
　Durable power of attorney
　　for health care: _____
　Health care proxy or
　　appointment of a health
　　care agent: _____

Safe Deposit Box Location: _____

ASSIGNMENT 5.5

1. Stephen and Audrey Maxwell are husband and wife. They have no children. If on Audrey's death Stephen were to choose to take the surviving spouse's elective share according to your state's statute, how much of Audrey's property would Stephen receive?

2. In another example, Stephen and Audrey have five children—Marty, Micha, Marc, Minnie, and Michelle. Marc died in a childhood accident; all the other children are married and have two children. On Stephen's death, what would Audrey's share be if she elected against the will based on your state's statute?

3. In a third case, Stephen and Audrey have one child, Marty, who is married and has three children. Marty dies in an industrial accident. Stephen dies one year later. Audrey elects against the will. What will her statutory elective share be according to your state statute?

Children's Right to Inherit—A Review

It should be made clear to the client that parents are not required to leave anything to their children. Nevertheless, if children are to be excluded from a share of a parent's estate, it is best accomplished by the insertion of a clause in the will that states the parent has intentionally made no provision for a clearly identified child named in the will (see Chapter 3). When a child is not specifically excluded in the will, the child may ultimately receive a share as a result of a state's Pretermitted

(Omitted) Child Statute, despite the parent's intent to disinherit. Most parents, however, have no intention of disinheriting their children, but they may wish to pass their estates to their children in unequal proportions because of the children's different financial or health status.

ASSIGNMENT 5.6

In the completion of the family data checklist (see Exhibit 5.1), Dean Richardson, age 68, the testator, indicates that of his four adult children, Duane, Dwight, Amelia, and Amaryllis, and one minor child, Daphne, age 17, only Amelia has consistently shown an interest in her father's health and welfare. Therefore, Dean intends to leave his entire estate to Amelia. Answer the following according to your state laws.

1. Can Dean disinherit his three adult children other than Amelia? If so, how could this be done?

2. Can Dean disinherit his minor child, Daphne? Explain.

3. If Duane, one of Dean's adult children, is physically handicapped or has mental retardation, can William disinherit him? Explain.

4. Dean stated in a clause in his will, "I intentionally disinherit all my other children, Duane, Dwight, and Amaryllis, because of their mistreatment of me, and leave my entire estate to Amelia." Daphne is not mentioned, yet the words *all my other children* are included in the will. After Dean dies, Daphne and the other adult children, Duane, Dwight, and Amaryllis, contest their father's will. Who prevails according to your state laws?

GUIDELINES FOR PREPARATION OF A WILL

In addition to the collection of pertinent facts from the client for the creation of a first draft of a will, you should follow general guidelines to ensure the will's effectiveness and validity and to decrease the likelihood that persons who claim an interest in the decedent's estate might challenge it in a will contest. The following are guidelines for the creation of a valid testamentary document. They provide a convenient checklist of good construction habits to develop in preparation for the execution of a will. Actual drafts will be included in Chapter 6.

Guideline 1: Avoid the Use of Preprinted Will Forms

Preprinted will forms should seldom be used. They may not fill the special needs of the testator and can cause problems. For instance, if part of the form is printed, part is typed, and part is handwritten, a will contest based on forgery could result. An alteration of any kind in a will usually casts doubt on whether the altered section is the work of the testator or of some other person. *Note:* The state "statutory will" forms available in California, Louisiana, Maine, Michigan, and Wisconsin are an exception to the caveat on using printed or computerized forms. These are preprinted fill-in-the-blank forms with written instructions to the maker of the will, and they require choices that must be made on the form; see Cal. Prob. Code §§ 6220-6226 and Mich. Comp. Laws Ann. § 700.2519 and compare the California and Wisconsin statutory wills in Exhibits 5.7 and 3.3.

Another problem is that words on preprinted forms are often crossed out or deleted by ink or type. Sometimes corrections or changes called interlineation are written on the forms. In such cases, the question arises as to who made these changes and the reason for them. Thus, the validity of the will is in jeopardy.

A third problem is that preprinted forms are written in generalities and therefore do not address the specific problems or objectives of the testator. Property may be inadvertently omitted, intended beneficiaries or devisees may be excluded, and tax advantages may be overlooked.

> **EXAMPLE:** Louise Pendleton, using a preprinted will form, forgot to include a residuary clause to pass the residue or remainder of her estate to a named person. Louise had made a number of specific gifts to relatives and friends, but the bulk of her estate was in the residue. Since Louise used a preprinted form and no residuary clause was included, the residue of her estate would pass by intestate succession statutes.

ASSIGNMENT 5.7

In the example above, if Louise had only two relatives, Peter, a nephew, and Clara, a grandparent, how and to whom would Louise's residuary estate be transferred according to your state laws?

Guideline 2: Use the Same Word-Processing Software and Computer Printer Typeface

Among the good habits to develop in the creation of wills is to use the same word-processing software and typeface for the entire testament. The use of different typefaces makes it appear someone other than the testator's drafter has inserted provisions. In addition, the typist should not leave blank spaces in the will, which might make possible the addition of words or names or even an entire page. Such procedures help ensure that the decedent's heirs will be protected from persons who could change the will to benefit themselves.

> **EXAMPLE:** Jacques intends to leave the bulk and residue of his considerable estate to five friends—Helen Moscowitz, Adam Korkowski, Elmer Bartholomew, Jean Olson, and Stanley Weskoskowitz. Due to the length of Stanley's last name, the typist of the will left some space at the end of a line of the will and started Stanley's name on the next line.

Harley Wilker typed his name in the empty space left on the line after Jean Olson's name. Unless the addition is detected and deleted before Jacques's death, Harley may become a residuary beneficiary or devisee of Jacques's will.

> **EXAMPLE:** Dimitri has typed a six-page will. Before it is witnessed and signed, his brother, Dino, adds an extra page to the will in which most of Dimitri's estate passes to Dino. Even if Dimitri does not notice the additional page, he could have protected himself by signing each of the original pages and stating in the attestation clause that the will contained only six pages.

Another advantage of typing the entire will is that uncertainties so often found in holographic (handwritten) wills due to the illegible handwriting of the testator can be avoided. Computer-printed wills are easier to read and errors are more readily identified and corrected than in handwritten wills. However, typed wills prove disadvantageous if the will is contested because of forgery or undue influence, or if a question arises concerning the testator's knowledge of the contents of the will; if the testator had written a holographic will, it could avoid these contentions.

EXAMPLE: Rosalind is elderly and suffers from severe arthritis. She is concerned that her signature on the will may be contested as a forgery. What procedures might be followed to avoid a foreseeable will contest? (1) Rosalind could identify her affliction within the will's provisions so all interested parties have notice of her infirmity. A will contest on the grounds of forgery requires that many persons testify to the genuineness of the writing; the testatrix's own declaration as to the reason for her unusual signature would eliminate the need for calling a great number of witnesses and provide direct evidence in the matter. (2) A better procedure is to have Rosalind write in her own hand the testimonium clause so that, if necessary, a handwriting expert could compare and identify the validity of Rosalind's signature. (3) The best procedure would be to have her personal physician witness the will so that, if called to testify, the physician could explain the reason for the shaky signature.

Guideline 3: Use Words That Avoid Ambiguity

The will must be written so that the testator's intent is clear. Chapter 6 discusses the creation of a will and includes sample clauses or provisions to illustrate its step-by-step formation. Our immediate concerns are the uncertainties, ambiguities, and alterations the testator must avoid. The will should be clear and understandable.

EXAMPLE: Cari's will provides: (1) I give my diamond ring to my best friend, Florence Williams. (2) I give $5,000 to my faithful employee, Steven Newell. (3) *All my personal property* I leave to my beloved son and only heir, Jeremy. A conflict such as this in which the testator apparently leaves the same gifts to different persons may result in a will contest.

Guideline 4: Use Simple Language

As noted in Chapter 3, the UPC attempts to resolve confusion surrounding terminology used to identify gifts transferred through a will and the recipients of such gifts. Since the traditional terms *bequest, legacy,* and *devise* are used interchangeably, misunderstanding and confusion result. The proper way to solve this problem is to use the phrase "I *give* my diamond ring to my daughter, Corinne," rather than "I *bequeath* my ring, etc." The use of simple and more recognizable terms is the better practice in will construction.

Guideline 5: Place Small Estates in Joint Tenancy

In appropriate cases, small estates can be placed in joint tenancy, one of the most common ways to avoid probate, to diminish administrative procedures and expenses. On the death of a joint tenant, ownership rights pass automatically to the surviving joint tenant(s) by right of survivorship.

Guideline 6: Sign the Will According to State Statutes, but Do Not Sign Copies

The original will must be signed and should be dated. If the will consists of multiple pages, all pages of the original should be signed or initialed except in states such as New York that require the signature to be only at the end of the will. If copies are made, they should not be signed. To have many original executed wills in existence is a potential problem since it increases the possibility of will contests. All copies that are executed (signed and witnessed) must be presented in court, or the law presumes the will was revoked. *Therefore, you should make copies of*

EXHIBIT 5.7   California Statutory Will

THE CALIFORNIA STATUTORY WILL OF:

Print Your Full Name Above

1. **Will.** This is my Will. I revoke all prior Wills and codicils.

2. **Specific Gift of Personal Residence.** (Optional - use only if you want to give your personal residence to a different person or persons than you give the balance of your assets to under paragraph 5 below.) I give my interest in my principal personal residence at the time of my death (subject to mortgages and liens) as follows: (Select one choice only and sign in the box after your choice.)

   a) Choice One: All to my spouse or domestic partner, registered with the California Secretary of State, if my spouse or domestic partner, registered with the California Secretary of State, survives me; otherwise to my descendants (my children and the descendants of my children) who survive me.
   AUTOGRAPH

   b) Choice Two: Nothing to my spouse or domestic partner, registered with the California Secretary of State; all to my descendants (my children and the descendants of my children) who survive me.
   AUTOGRAPH

   c) Choice Three: All to the following person if he or she survives me: (Insert the name of the person):
   _____
   AUTOGRAPH

   d) Choice Four: Equally among the following persons who survive me: (Insert the names of two or more persons):
   _____
   _____
   _____
   AUTOGRAPH

3. **Specific Gift of Automobiles, Household and Personal Effects.** (Optional - use only if you want to give automobiles and household and personal effects to a different person or persons than you give the balance of your assets to under paragraph 5 below). I give all of my automobiles (subject to loans), furniture, furnishings, household items, clothing, jewelry, and other tangible articles of a personal nature at the time of my death as follows: (Select one choice only and sign in the box after your choice.)

   a) Choice One: All to my spouse or domestic partner, registered with the California Secretary of State, if my spouse or domestic partner, registered with the California Secretary of State, survives me; otherwise to my descendants (my children and the descendants of my children) who survive me.
   AUTOGRAPH

   b) Choice Two: Nothing to my spouse or domestic partner, registered with the California Secretary of State; all to my descendants (my children and the descendants of my children) who survive me.
   AUTOGRAPH

   c) Choice Three: All to the following person if he or she survives me: (Insert the name of the person):
   _____
   AUTOGRAPH

   d) Choice Four: Equally among the following persons who survive me: (Insert the names of two or more persons):
   _____
   _____
   AUTOGRAPH

4. **Specific Gifts of Cash.** (Optional) I make the following cash gifts to the persons named below who survive me, or to the named charity, and I sign my name in the box after each gift. If I don't sign in the box, I do not make a gift. (Sign in the box after each gift you make.)

Name of Person or Charity to receive gift (Name one only – please print)	Amount of Cash Gift
	Affix your Autograph in this Box to make this Gift

Name of Person or Charity to receive gift (Name one only – please print)	Amount of Cash Gift
	Affix your Autograph in this Box to make this Gift

EXHIBIT 5.7   (Continued)

| Name of Person or Charity to receive gift (Name one only -- please print) | Amount of Cash Gift |
| | Affix your Autograph in this Box to make this Gift |

| Name of Person or Charity to receive gift (Name one only -- please print) | Amount of Cash Gift |
| | Affix your Autograph in this Box to make this Gift |

| Name of Person or Charity to receive gift (Name one only -- please print) | Amount of Cash Gift |
| | Affix your Autograph in this Box to make this Gift |

5. **Balance of My Assets.** Except for the specific gifts made in paragraphs 2, 3 and 4 above, I give the balance of my assets as follows: (Select one choice only and sign in the box after your choice. If I sign in more than one box or if I don't sign in any box, the court will distribute my assets as if I did not make a Will).

   a) Choice One: All to my spouse or domestic partner, registered with the California Secretary of State, if my spouse or domestic partner, registered with the California Secretary of State, survives me; otherwise to my descendants (my children and the descendants of my children) who survive me.

   AUTOGRAPH

   b) Choice Two: Nothing to my spouse or domestic partner, registered with the California Secretary of State; all to my descendants (my children and the descendants of my children) who survive me.

   AUTOGRAPH

   c) Choice Three: All to the following person if he or she survives me: (Insert the name of the person):

   _____

   AUTOGRAPH

   d) Choice Four: Equally among the following persons who survive me: (Insert the names of two or more persons):

   _____
   _____
   _____
   _____

   AUTOGRAPH

6. **Guardian of the Child's Person.** If I have a child under age 18 and the child does not have a living parent at my death, I nominate the individual named below as First Choice as guardian of the person of such child (to raise the child). If the First Choice does not serve, then I nominate the Second Choice, and then the Third Choice, to serve. Only an individual (not a bank or trust company) may serve.

| Name of First Choice for Guardian of the Person | Name of Second Choice for Guardian of the Person |

| Name of Third Choice for Guardian of the Person |

7. **Special Provision of Property of Persons Under Age 25.** (Optional - Unless you use this paragraph, assets that go to a child or other person who is under age years of 18 may be given to the parent of the person, or to the Guardian named in paragraph 6 above as guardian of the person until the person is 18 years of age, and the court will require a bond; and assets that go to a child or other person who is age 18 or older will be given outright to the person. By using this paragraph you may provide that a custodian will hold the assets for the person until the person reaches any age between 18 and 25 as indicated by your choice below).

   If a beneficiary of this Will is between age 18 and 25, I nominate the individual or bank or trust company named below as First Choice as custodian of the property. If the First Choice does not serve, then I nominate the Second Choice, and then the Third Choice, to serve.

| Name of First Choice for Custodian of Assets | Name of Second Choice for Custodian of Assets |

| Name of Third Choice for Custodian of Assets |

Insert any age between 18 and 25 as the age for the person to receive the property: (If you do not choose an age, age 18 will apply.)

(continued)

EXHIBIT 5.7   (Continued)

8. Executor. I nominate the individual or bank or trust company named below as First Choice as executor. If the First Choice does not serve, then I nominate the Second Choice, and then the Third Choice, to serve.

Name of First Choice for Executor	Name of Second Choice for Executor

Name of Third Choice for Executor

9. Bond. My signature in this box means a bond is <u>not</u> required for any person named as executor. A bond may be required if I do not sign in this box:

No bond shall be required.

Autograph

**Notice: You must sign this Will in the presence of two (2) adult witnesses.
The witnesses must sign their names in your presence and in each other's presence.
You must first read to them the text below.**

"This is my Will. I ask the persons who sign below to be my witnesses."

I herewith affix my autograph to this Statutory Will on this, the _____ day of _____, _____

At _____, in the presence of the Witnesses identified below; who both witnessed and subscribed this Will at my request and in my presence.

_____
AUTOGRAPH OF PERSON EXECUTING WILL

**Notice to Witnesses: Two (2) adults must sign as witnesses. Each witness must read the following clause before signing.
The witnesses should not receive assets under this Will.**

<u>Each of us declares under penalty of perjury under the laws of the State of California that the following is true and correct:</u>

a) On the date written below the maker of this Will declared to us that this instrument was the maker's Will and requested us to act as witnesses to it;

b) We understand this is the maker's Will;

c) The maker signed this Will in our presence, all of us being present at the same time;

d) We now, at the maker's request, and in the maker's and in each other's presence, sign below as witnesses;

e) We believe the maker is of sound mind and memory;

f) We believe that this Will was not procured by duress, menace, fraud or undue influence;

g) The maker is age 18 or older; and

h) Each of us is now age 18 or older, is a competent witness, and resides at the address set forth after his or her name.

Autograph of Witness	Autograph of Witness

_____   _____
Print Name   Print Name

Dated: _____   Dated: _____

_____   _____
Home Address   Home Address

_____   _____

_____   _____

the original will before it is signed. Give one to the personal representative and another to the spouse, if he or she is not the personal representative, and explain where the original will is located.

ASSIGNMENT 5.8

Jessica's original will cannot be found. A photocopy with Jessica's signature has been located, however. According to the laws of your state, would the copy be a valid testament? See *Matter of Wheadon's Estate*, 579 P. 2d 930 (Utah 1978).

Guideline 7: Include a Residuary Clause

The testator's entire estate must be transferred. This requires the use of a residuary (or residue) clause such as the following:

> I give all the rest, residue, and remainder of my estate, consisting of all property, real, personal, or mixed, of whatever kind and wherever located, that I can dispose of by will and not effectively disposed of by the preceding articles of this will, as follows:

Guideline 8: Choose Witnesses Carefully

To improve the probability the witnesses will be available when the will is probated, it is good practice to have the will witnessed by individuals who live in the same county and who know and are younger than the testator. Also, the witnesses should not be beneficiaries or devisees of the will. If the testator's testamentary capacity might be questioned, the testator's physician should be one of the witnesses (see the previous discussion and examples of who may be a competent witness in Chapter 6). Some states now provide for attestation clauses that result in "self-proved" wills (see Chapter 6).

Guideline 9: Tell Witnesses What Might Be Expected of Them

The witnesses should be informed that they are witnessing the testator's signature on a will and that they may be called on to testify to this fact in court. They need not read the will, however, nor be informed of its contents before they sign as witnesses.

Guideline 10: Do Not Make Additions after Execution

Generally, if words are added to the will after execution, they do not revoke or affect the will's validity. However, additions to the will are not legally enforceable unless the testator and two witnesses sign the will a second time. If the testator wants to make valid major or minor additions to the existing will, the proper and best way to accomplish this result is by the creation of a new will.

ASSIGNMENT 5.9

After executing and signing her will, Macy writes the following beneath her signature: "All of the provisions of my will previously mentioned shall take effect after my death unless my son, Trevon, predeceases me." What effect, if any, would such an alteration have on Macy's will in your state?

Guideline 11: Use Computer Technology for All Changes

With the use of computer technology, a new will should be drafted for all will modifications, including minor changes. This is faster and more efficient than the use of an obsolete codicil.

Guideline 12: Avoid Erasures and Corrections

Great care should be taken to avoid all erasures and corrections in the final draft of a will. When a page is found to contain an error, the entire page should be retyped. Where, because of time and unusual circumstances, it is necessary to use an altered page, the testator should approve it by dating, signing, or initialing the alteration in the margin of the page. The witnesses should also sign in the margin to indicate that the alteration was made prior to execution of the will. It is also a good idea to identify the corrections made in the attestation clause.

Guideline 13: Word Conditions to Avoid Ambiguity

condition precedent
A condition or specific event that must occur before an agreement or obligation becomes binding.

condition subsequent
A condition that will continue or terminate an existing agreement or duty if the condition does or does not occur.

If a condition is added to a devise, it can change the effect of the gift and possibly negate the testator's wishes. The drafter must recognize the importance of using correct words. A conditional devise is one that takes effect, or continues in effect, with the occurrence of some future event. A **condition precedent** is one in which a specified event must occur before the estate or interest vests in (passes to) the named devisee. A **condition subsequent** is one in which an estate that is already vested in a named devisee will not continue to be vested unless a specified event occurs. If it does not occur, the devisee will be divested of the estate and will not continue to receive the interest.

Courts generally refuse probating a will "if it is clear that the will is no longer operative due to the failure of occurrence of a specified event upon which the effectiveness of the will is conditioned," *Johnson v. Hewitt*, 539 S.W. 2d 239 (1976).

Condition Precedent

When a decedent devises property with a condition precedent attached, title (ownership) in the property does not vest until the stated event (condition) occurs. The devisee must perform some act *before* (precedent to) ownership of the devise will vest in the devisee.

> **EXAMPLE:** Andrew devises Blackacre "to Ralph when he marries Florence." Ownership of Blackacre will vest in Ralph only if and when Ralph marries Florence. If the marriage never occurs, the ownership of property will not pass to Ralph but will pass to another person named in the will or, if no one is named, will revert to the testator or his heirs by operation of law.

> **EXAMPLE:** Andrew makes a gift of $20,000 "to Renee when she receives her college degree."

> **EXAMPLE:** Andrew devises Blackacre "to Saul at such time as he comes back to Texas to live and takes possession of Blackacre." (Saul is living in California at the time the will is drafted.)

The will may provide that the condition precedent be an act performed by the testator or by another person.

EXAMPLE: Andrew gives "the automobile owned by me at the time of my death to my son, Chris." Andrew might buy and sell many cars prior to his death. However, only the car owned by Andrew at his death will go to Chris. If Andrew does not own a car at his death, Chris is out of luck; he will get no car.

EXAMPLE: Andrew makes a gift of $30,000 "to the person who is taking care of me at death." The person taking care of Andrew at his death may be different from the one taking care of him at the time he drafts the will. The fact that Andrew may not now know the identity of his devisee does not invalidate the devise. The identity of the "person who is taking care of me at death" is ascertainable. Whoever that person is would be entitled to the $30,000 gift.

Caution must be taken to prevent vague conditions from being inserted into a will. The last example illustrates a potential problem. At his death, Andrew may have several people caring for him, e.g., his niece, with whom he lives; a nephew who helps dress and feed him; his doctor, who visits him routinely; and a physical therapist who helps him exercise daily.

When a decedent-testator places a condition precedent on a gift, the condition may fail because it is regarded as socially unacceptable.

EXAMPLE: Andrew makes a gift of $1,000,000 "to my daughter Rachael, if she divorces the man to whom she is now married."

ASSIGNMENT 5.10

Emma is planning a trip abroad and wants to have all her records in order before she leaves. She replaces her existing will with a new one changing the beneficiary of her home to her favorite grandson, Peter. She states in her will that she "gives her home to Peter in case she dies while traveling in Europe." Emma returns from Europe in good health. She dies two years later. Her daughter Josie, the beneficiary of the former will, challenges the devise to Peter saying it was only valid if Emma died while traveling in Europe, a condition precedent. Will the court decide in Josie's favor or will it find that Emma was simply expressing a reason to make a will? How does the ruling in *Martin v. Young*, 55 Md. App. 401, 462 A 2d 77 (1983), which stated, "if provable, valid, and lawful, the primary motive and intent of the testator controls the enforcement of the condition," affect Josie's challenge? Check your state's statutes and case law.

Condition Subsequent

A condition subsequent is one in which the nonhappening of the event or a violation (breach) of a condition will terminate an estate that has already vested. If an estate vests in (passes to) the devisee when the will becomes operative but is subject to being divested on the future happening or nonhappening of an event or on a breach, the condition is subsequent. If the event occurs or fails to occur, or if a specified condition is breached, the devisee will be divested of ownership of the devise (property) by "operation of law." This is also called **defeasance**.

defeasance
The termination of a vested estate by the happening or nonhappening of an event (condition subsequent).

EXAMPLE: Ralph devises Blackacre "to my wife, Tina, to hold while she remains a widow." The estate vests in Tina on the death of her husband, Ralph, and will be divested on Tina's remarriage.

EXAMPLE: Sara devises her summer home "to my daughter, Rose, but if Rose fails to return to the family home within five years, then to my son, Waldo." The devise vests in Rose on her mother's death. If Rose does not return to the family home within five years from the date of Sara's death, Rose will then be divested of the estate, and it will vest in Waldo. Waldo's potential future estate is not subject to divestment (i.e., not subject to any condition) but is a *fee simple absolute*.

In theory, the defeasance occurs by operation of law; in practice it occurs after a court action has been brought. If the devisee who has been divested of ownership in the property is in actual physical possession of the property, it will nearly always be necessary for the grantor, the grantor's heirs, or another person named by the grantor to retake or recover ownership of the property after the defeasance to (1) exercise a right of reentry (this must be a positive physical act of reentering the land) and (2) bring an action in **ejectment** in court to regain possession of the property.

ejectment
An action (a lawsuit brought in a court) for the recovery of the possession of land.

Generally, the determination of whether a condition is precedent or subsequent will depend on the intention of the testator as interpreted from the language of the will in light of the circumstances. The particular expression used is not conclusive. Since the law prefers a vested estate, the presumption of courts favors a condition subsequent rather than a condition precedent. Therefore, the courts will construe ambiguous testamentary language as a condition subsequent rather than a condition precedent. The reason for this is that a vested estate is more marketable, i.e., it can be sold or conveyed more easily.

ASSIGNMENT 5.11

Emma died testate. In her will she devised her home to Peter with the provision that he obtain his college degree. She stated in her will: "If he does not obtain his degree, the property is to go to the State University Foundation to be used for their scholarship program." Peter takes possession of the house, enrolls in college, but dies intestate in a traffic accident one month before receiving his degree. Did Peter satisfy the condition subsequent? Is Emma's home part of his estate or does it belong to the State University Foundation? See *Teasdale v. Harrison*, 16 N.J. Super. 335, 84 A 2d 563 (1951), which states that unless performance of a condition is waived or nonperformance excused, depending on the testator's provable intent and motive, failure of the occurrence of a valid, lawful, and enforceable condition will trigger losing an interest. Check your state's statutes and case law.

Guideline 14: Include Full Data on Beneficiaries and Devisees

The full names, addresses, and relationship to the testator of the beneficiaries and devisees in the will must be accurately written. This avoids uncertainty as to whom the assets are to be transferred. When the beneficiary or devisee is a charitable corporation, the corporate name and address should be given.

Guideline 15: Give the Client a Rough Draft

Check and verify that all client information transferred from checklists and attorney or client notes has been accurately incorporated into the will. A rough draft of the will should be presented to the client to be scrutinized so the client can make corrections, deletions, or additions. Also, clearly mark the document as a rough draft so the client does not sign it.

Key Terms

advancement	condition subsequent	ejectment
condition precedent	defeasance	

Review Questions

1. What procedures would you recommend to put a new client at ease and overcome his or her reluctance when you need to elicit confidential family and financial information for the preparation of legal documents such as wills?

2. Are there additional checklists you recommend to obtain the necessary information for drafting wills?

3. What would you add to the checklists in the text to make them more comprehensive and useful?

4. Diagram your family tree beginning with your grandparents and including all their descendants.

5. What are some of the tax issues and rights of the surviving spouse and children that the attorney and paralegal must discuss at the family conference?

6. Which states have statutory wills? What are statutory wills?

7. What is the distinction between a condition precedent and a condition subsequent?

8. What are the guidelines recommended for the preparation of wills?

9. Are there any other guidelines for preparing wills you would add to those in the text?

10. What are the advantages of a typewritten or computer-printed will versus a holographic will?

Case Problems

Problem 1

Based on the guidelines for drafting a will, point out as many errors in the following sample will as you can.

LAST WILL AND TESTAMENT OF Colin Furthmiller

1. I, Colin Furthmiller, declare this my last will and testament.

2. I direct that my debts be paid out of my estate.

3. I give my son, Curtis, my ~~two~~ *three* rings, ~~10~~ *8* guns, clothing, and all my other personal property.

4. I give my beloved wife, Althea, my interest in our home that we own jointly; all the money (cash) I have in savings and checking at our local bank; and if she does not remarry, my interest in the summer cottage I own with my brother.

5. I request that no bond be required of my executor.

6. If my wife does not survive me, I request that ~~Robert Brown~~ *Jerry Clark* be executor of this will, and he be appointed guardian of any minor children of mine.

IN WITNESS WHEREOF, I set my hand to this my last will and testament.

Colin Furthmiller

Date: _____

Practical Assignments

1. Using the Family Data Checklist contained in Exhibit 5.1, complete the Checklist as it relates to you and your family.

2. Using the Assets Checklist contained in Exhibit 5.3, complete the Checklist of your assets, including the value and form of ownership.

3. Using the Liabilities Checklist contained in Exhibit 5.4, complete the Checklist as it pertains to your personal liabilities.

FINAL DRAFT AND EXECUTION OF A VALID WILL

Outline

Objectives

After completing this chapter, you should be able to:

- Analyze the collected data and make sure that the information conforms to the client's objectives when preparing a draft of the will.

- Identify and include the appropriate clauses for the client's will.

- Verify that the will's construction and execution have followed the relevant state statutes.

- Draft a preliminary will, for the supervising attorney's review, that is free from errors of construction that might invalidate the will or lead to a will contest.

- Explain the purpose and function of a self-proving affidavit, living will, health care proxy, and durable power of attorney.

SCOPE OF THE CHAPTER

This chapter covers the procedures involved in drafting a client's will under an attorney's supervision, an important task of the paralegal. Exhibit 6.1 outlines these procedures. The contents of a standard will are discussed, and a formal will is provided. Sample clauses used in drafting a will and statutes that pertain to such clauses are examined, as are other documents that are not part of a standard will but are related to it. These include a self-proving affidavit, letter of instructions, right-to-die advance directives such as a living will, health care proxy, and a durable power of attorney.

CONTENTS OF A STANDARD WILL

A standard will has the following clauses or provisions.

1. Introductory or exordium and publication clause

2. General revocation clause

3. Provision for payment of debts and funeral expenses

4. Instructions for funeral and burial (*Note: It is preferable to express these plans in a letter of instructions.*)

5. Specific testamentary gifts

6. Provision for residue of estate

7. Appointment of personal representative (and digital executor, if appropriate)

8. Appointment of personal and/or property guardian

9. Simultaneous death clause

EXHIBIT 6.1   Events in Drafting a Will under an Attorney's Supervision

Understand the client's objectives
(initial interview)
↓
Gather data from client
(via checklists)
↓
Analyze the information
(coordinate it with objectives)
↓
Develop and present
preliminary drafts
↓
Review the selected draft with client
(additions, modifications)
↓
Draft final will
↓
Supervise execution of will by client and witnesses
(testator)   (testatrix)

10. Testamentary trust clause

11. Testimonium clause

12. Testator's signature

13. Attestation clause of witnesses

14. Witnesses' signatures and addresses

The next sections discuss each of these clauses and provisions in detail, along with relevant statutes and sample clauses.

In addition, the following documents, which are not part of a standard will but are related to it, are identified and discussed.

1. Self-proving affidavit clause

2. Letter of instructions

3. Power of attorney

4. Living will

5. Medical power of attorney

6. Memorandum of digital assets

Introductory or Exordium and Publication Clause

exordium clause
The beginning or introductory clause of a will.

The **exordium clause** identifies the maker of the will and states or declares the maker's intention that the provisions in this written document be followed after death. To be valid and enforceable, the document must appear to be a will or testamentary in nature. The introductory clause should also include the address (optional), city, county, and state of its maker, which help to determine domicile for probate proceedings; any alias or other name by which the maker is known (often written "a/k/a"—also known as) so all property owned by the maker can be identified, located, and properly transferred or eventually distributed; and a statement of the maker's capacity and freedom from undue influence.

The purpose of the exordium clause is to declare to the public the following: (1) the identity of the testator; (2) the testator has the intent and capacity to create a will; (3) the document is the testator's last will; and (4) the location of the

POINT OF INTEREST

A variety of do-it-yourself (DIY) books, software programs, and online forms encourage the layperson to draft his or her own will. However, the outcome can be very different from what was expected. Although most require the testator to provide a listing of their assets, the lists may not be comprehensive. If there is no residuary clause included and assets are excluded, property may pass to unintended beneficiaries. Many of these options are incapable of competently advising the drafter regarding tax consequences, establishing trusts, including future children, or properly executing a will pursuant to state law. What many don't realize is that if the DIY will is improperly drafted or executed, property passes according to the decedent's state intestacy laws.

testator's principal residence (city, county, and state) or domicile, which enables the personal representative to determine which state has the proper authority to tax the testator's property and which court has jurisdiction over the administration of the decedent-testator's estate.

Sample Exordium Clause

I, Rowley D. Morse, also known as R. David Morse, of 4607 Elmors Drive, City of Knoxville, County of Marion, State of Iowa, being of sound mind and not acting under undue influence of any person whomsoever, do make, publish, and declare this document to be my last will and testament. I do hereby cancel, revoke, and annul all former wills and testaments or codicils made by me.

ASSIGNMENT 6.1

1. Examine the following exordium clause. "Being of sound mind and body, I, D. E. Pearson, of 2914 Columba Street, Bloomington, dispose of the following property by will: . . . ."

   a. Is this adequate for the purposes of an exordium clause? Why or why not?

   b. Could any word or phrase be misinterpreted so as to prevent the document's admission to probate?

   c. Redraft the parts of the clause likely to cause difficulty. If necessary, include information not found in the original clause and explain the reasons for including it.

2. Tom Hardy lives in Yuma, Arizona. He owns a cottage in Wisconsin and has a savings and checking account in Yuma. The deed to the cottage is recorded as to "Thomas William Hardy," and both bank accounts are in the name, Tom W. Hardy. Draft an appropriate exordium clause for Tom and explain your reasons for the draft.

General Revocation Clause

A decedent's new will generally revokes an earlier will. State statutes vary on the requirements necessary for a new will to revoke a prior will. Some require a specific statement saying the new will revokes the prior will; in most states, however, a prior will is automatically revoked when the maker writes, dates, and signs a new will. The testamentary document last in time also supersedes existing codicils attached to previous wills. The safest way to ensure revocation by a new will is to include a **revocation clause** as part of the exordium clause. For example, "I hereby revoke all prior wills and codicils made by me, and declare this to be my last will and testament." Review Chapter 4 on the revocation of wills.

revocation clause
A clause or statement in a will that revokes all prior wills and codicils.

Provision for Payment of Debts and Funeral Expenses

The maker of a will often directs the named personal representative or executor to pay all debts, administration expenses, and expenses of the last illness, funeral, and burial out of estate funds before the decedent's property is distributed. These duties are automatic responsibilities of the personal representative of the estate, however, and need not be embodied in a formal clause. The phrasing of the debt payment clause can also present a problem. For example, if the clause reads "I direct my personal representative or executor to pay all of my valid debts and administration expenses out of the residue of my estate," and the decedent-testator was personally liable for a debt such as a mortgage on the decedent's home, the specific devisee of the home in the will, who would normally be responsible for the mortgage payment, could require that the mortgage be paid out of the residue (according to the rules of abatement). Many states avoid this problem by statute, unless the decedent's will specifically states otherwise; see Cal. Prob. Code § 21131; N.Y. EPTL § 3-3.6; and UPC § 2–607. A more appropriate clause is the following:

Sample Debt Payment Clause

I direct my personal representative hereinafter named, to pay all my just debts, estate administration expenses and taxes, and expenses of my last illness, funeral, and burial out of my estate as soon as possible after my death.

The inclusion of a clause in the testator's will that requires payment of debts and administration expense from the estate can lead to a deduction on federal estate or fiduciary income tax returns for those payments (see IRC §§ 2053, 642 [g], and 212).

The cost of funeral and burial expenses continues to escalate. When the burden of making the necessary arrangements falls on the bereaved family, emotions often play a part in their financial decisions concerning, for example, the casket, flowers, headstone, reception, and religious service. *To alleviate this unpleasant burden, many people prearrange and pay for their funeral and burial prior to death. You should discuss this sensitive but responsible option with the client and suggest possible methods to accomplish it; e.g., the client could open a bank savings account covering the estimated cost of a client-selected casket, headstone, reception, and so on, or execute a simple trust agreement with a funeral home in which the money for these expenses would be held in trust by the funeral director until the client's death.* However, this prepayment plan could result in the loss of the tax deduction for funeral expenses for death tax purposes. Some state statutes establish monetary limits for the funeral and burial expenses. If the decedent has many creditors and the personal representative overspends the reasonable limit, the personal representative is liable for this breach of fiduciary duty, and the court can order the personal representative to pay damages to the estate.

ASSIGNMENT 6.2

1. Check your state statutes and determine the priority of payment of decedent's debts in your state (compare UPC §§ 3–805 and 3–807).

2. In writing his will, Quincy Rudd included a clause directing his executor to pay the debts owed by him at the time of his death from the residue of the estate. Draft a clause for Quincy's will to this effect. Explain the hardship that your draft may cause if the residuary clause is the sole provision in a testator's will that provides for the surviving spouse and children.

3. Draft a clause for Quincy Rudd's will that identifies how any taxes owed by his estate will be paid.

Instructions for Funeral and Burial

As previously mentioned, a letter of instructions rather than a will is the more appropriate and preferred written document used to contain the plans for a testator's funeral and burial arrangements. Since copies of the letter are given to the family and personal representative, a primary advantage of the letter is it ensures the funeral plans are known at the time of the testator's death, whereas a will may not be found in time. Having stated the above preference, it is a fact many testators continue to place, or already have, funeral instructions in their wills or codicils. Therefore, the discussion that follows has been retained in the text.

A simple clause such as the following may be included in a will to inform the decedent's family of the previous plans or instructions the deceased has made for the funeral.

Sample Clause

I direct that my funeral is to be conducted according to my letter of instructions, a copy of which is on file at the Benson Funeral Home, 1404 Second Avenue, City of Cedar Falls, County of Black Hawk, State of Iowa. The said written instructions are hereby incorporated into and made part of this will.

Including funeral and burial instructions in a will may be futile, since the will may not be found in time or, in many states, the desires of the decedent's surviving spouse or next of kin legally supersede any such instructions by the decedent. A conflict between the wishes of the family and the testator may also arise when the testator desires to be cremated. Concerning cremation, a testator can simply add a clause in the will that states:

Sample Clause

At my death, I direct that my body be taken to the Nielson Chapel and Cromatory, my remains cremated, and my ashes buried in our family plot.

Another challenge to burial instructions may occur when the testator desires to donate his or her body for educational or medical purposes (e.g., to an organ transplant bank), but the nearest relatives object. *To resolve questions associated with anatomical gifts, the Uniform Anatomical Gift Act, which has been adopted in all 50 states, provides the maker may legally determine in a will the disposition of all or any part of the body for organ transplant, medical research, or educational purposes.* Although the words have been modified in some states, the act substantively regulates who may be a donor and a donee, the manner of executing, delivering, and amending the gift, and the rights and duties of the parties. A sample clause follows.

Sample Clause

I hereby direct my personal representative on my death to see that my body be delivered to the State University Medical School to be used for educational purposes.

In addition to a provision in a will, under the act, any person, 18 or older, may donate organs by a donor card or other document that becomes legally enforceable once signed and dated by the donor and witnesses as determined by individual states. The act permits medical schools, universities, physicians, hospitals, and organ banks to receive the body or organ donations. Whenever the testator intends to donate his or her body or organs for transplants or medical research, he or she should carry a written expression of those wishes, such as a donor card or driver's license with organ donor designation, on his or her person at all times. It is *important* the testator inform the family to ensure that his or her wishes are carried out (see comments in Chapter 2). Otherwise, by the time the will is located and read, his or her body may have been cremated or buried, or the organs to be donated may not be useful for transplants.

If a potential organ donor has taken no action during lifetime to make a gift of body organs, only specific relatives have the ability to make a gift of the decedent's organs (absent any evidence of a contrary decision by the decedent). The following are excerpts of typical state statutes concerning anatomical gifts and the relatives of the decedent who are allowed to make the gifts.

Fla. Stat. Ann. § 765.512 Persons Who May Make an Anatomical Gift

(1) Any person who may make a will may give all or part of his or her body for any purpose specified in § 765.510, the gift to take effect upon death ...

(2) ...

(3) ... a member of one of the classes of persons listed below, in the order of priority stated and in the absence of actual notice of contrary indications by the decedent or actual notice of opposition by a member of the same or a prior class, may give all or any part of the decedent's body for any purpose specified in § 765.513:

(a) The spouse of the decedent;

(b) An adult son or daughter of the decedent;

(c) Either parent of the decedent;

(d) An adult brother or sister of the decedent;

(e) An adult grandchild;

(f) A grandparent of the decedent;

(g) A close personal friend as defined in § 765.101;

(h) A guardian of the person of the decedent at the time of his or her death; or

(i) A representative ad litem....

(4) A donee may not accept an anatomical gift if the donee has actual notice of contrary indications by the donor or actual notice that an anatomical gift by a member of a class is opposed by a member of a priority class.

(5) The person authorized by subsection (3) may make the gift after the decedent's death or immediately before the decedent's death.

(6) A gift of all or part of a body authorizes:

(a). Any examination necessary to assure medical acceptability of the gift for the purposes intended.

(b). ...

(7) Once the gift has been made, the rights of the donee are paramount to the rights of others, except as provided by § 765.517.

Fla. Stat. Ann. § 765.513 Persons and Entities That May Become Donees; Purposes for Which Anatomical Gifts May Be Made

(1) The following persons or entities may become donees of anatomical gifts of bodies or parts of them for the purposes stated:

(a) Any procurement organization or accredited medical or dental school, college, or university for education, research, therapy, or transplantation.

(b) Any individual specified by name for therapy or transplantation needed by him or her.

(2) If multiple purposes are set forth in the document of gift but are not set forth in any priority order, the anatomical gift shall be used first for transplantation or therapy if suitable. If the gift cannot be used for transplantation or therapy, the gift may be used for research or education.

ASSIGNMENT 6.3

1. Iris is dying. She is unconscious and in a coma from which her doctors do not expect her to recover. Iris's family is aware another patient is seeking a kidney transplant, and the doctors have informed the family Iris could be a successful donor. Iris's husband and children are in favor of donating Iris's kidneys after her death; Iris's parents are opposed. How would this conflict be resolved in Florida? In your state?

2. Deasia's will does not contain an anatomical gift clause. She thinks it would be a good idea to leave her eyes to the State Society for the Prevention of Blindness eye bank. Draft such a provision for the revised will she is writing.

3. Deasia realizes her family may hold the funeral and burial before reading her will and the provision mentioned above. What should she do to prevent this potential problem?

Specific Testamentary Gifts

It is important to remember that under the orthodox system of terminology, *legacies* are gifts of money, *bequests* are gifts of personal property, and *devises* are gifts of real property. Nevertheless, these terms are often used interchangeably. Under UPC terminology, the disposition of both real and personal property under a will is called a devise. Both sets of terminology are used in this section of the text.

One of the most important functions of a will is the determination of "what goes to whom." To prevent family arguments over specific items of a decedent's estate, the will should provide for the disposition of property as its maker chooses. The maker may have many reasons for leaving specific property to certain individuals. These gifts must be made before the maker transfers the remaining assets in a residuary clause. Marital deduction provisions (discussed in Chapters 11 and 14) must also be stated before the residue is transferred. For example, Shen Jin has three sons. His will provides:

Sample Clause

I give the sum of Two Thousand Dollars ($2,000) to my son, Li Jin; my diamond ring to my son, Myo Jin; and my collection of guns and rifles to my son, Alex P. Jin. If any of my three sons predeceases me, the gift designated for that son shall pass into the residue of my estate. All my sons' addresses are currently the same as my own.

I give the land that I own in the County of Adams, State of Iowa, legally described as follows: Lot 17, Block 8, consisting of 20 acres, known as Stonybroke, according to the plat filed with the Registrar of Titles in and for the County of Adams, State of Iowa, to my wife, Ashika Jin, as fee owner in severalty, if she survives me. If not, I give the aforementioned land, legally described above, known as Stonybroke, to my three sons equally as tenants in common. Also, I give my automobiles and other items of personal property to my wife, Ashika Jin, to do with as she sees fit, if she survives me. If not, I give the aforementioned property to my three sons equally.

An important point to recall is that a will is *ambulatory* (not yet operative), so regardless of a clause like the above, its maker is free before death to destroy the will, give away, or sell any property constituting a specific gift in the will. Any intentional act of the testator can cancel a gift in the will, such as the destruction, sale, or gift of the property to another person. In such cases, the testamentary gift is *adeemed*, and the beneficiary or devisee is not entitled to receive the property unless a substitute for the gift is mentioned in the will.

> **EXAMPLE:** In the clause above, if the diamond ring and gun collection are not in Shen Jin's estate at his death, the two sons do not receive their specific bequests or devises.

ASSIGNMENT 6.4

1. Tomas's will provides, in part, "To my daughter, Gabriela, I give 100 shares of common stock in the Hopewell Corporation, if she survives me." What kind of gift is this? If Tomas owns 75 shares of common stock in the Hopewell Corporation at the time of his death, would Gabriela be entitled to them plus the fair market value of 25 shares? Why or why not?

2. Lillian wishes to leave her antique rosewood furniture to her daughters, Lilly and Daisy. Draft a provision in Lillian's will for this gift (bequest or devise).

3. At Lillian's death, Lilly and Daisy are living in separate houses. They cannot agree on the division of the furniture. Could Lillian's will have been written to avoid the dispute? If necessary, redraft your provision to illustrate.

4. "To my son, Julian, I leave 30 acres of land in Marsh County." What kind of devise is this? Is it **defeasible**? Why or why not?

defeasible
Capable of being defeated, annulled, revoked, or undone upon the happening of a future event or the performance of a condition subsequent, or by a conditional limitation, as a defeasible title to property.

memorandum
A written list of the testator's personal property and the name of the beneficiary who receives each item. It is signed by the testator but is not a legally enforceable document.

In most states, statutes have established procedures for the disposition of the tangible personal property, other than money, that remains after the testator has made specific testamentary gifts (see UPC § 2–513). The testator is allowed to write a separate **memorandum** (list of property) in the handwriting of the testator and signed by the testator. The memorandum describes the property, item by item, and the beneficiary or devisee who is to receive it with "reasonable certainty." The following sample will clause identifies the separate memorandum that lists the decedent's tangible personal property and names the beneficiary who is to receive each item listed.

Sample Clause

I give my tangible personal property to the beneficiaries and devisees named herein, in accordance with any written list or memorandum which is signed and dated by me and is incorporated by reference in this will, and which is prepared in accordance with the provisions of [add appropriate state statute]. The most recent memorandum shall control if there are inconsistent dispositions. I give all tangible personal property not disposed of by the provisions of any such memorandum to my wife, if she survives me, or if she does not survive me, I give such property in equal shares to my children who survive me.

Such statutes allow the testator who owns numerous items of tangible personal property, such as antiques, jewelry, art objects, stamp or coin collections, and the like, to identify and list the property and the beneficiaries and devisees to whom it is to be given on a separate memorandum from the will. The testator can easily add to or modify this memorandum without having to revoke the will and draft a new one.

Family complications make it necessary to draft the will carefully to satisfy the purposes and intentions of the client. These complications may occur when the testator has been married more than once and two or more sets of children are potential beneficiaries or devisees. The rule that the testator may favor or exclude family and others in the will still applies, and so does the rule that a spouse cannot be disinherited. Children, however, can be disinherited according to the wishes of the testator. The following illustrates a typical family problem that could affect the validity of a will.

> **EXAMPLE:** A man divorces his first wife, with whom he had two children, remarries, and has a child by his second wife. His will, written during the first marriage, leaves half his estate to the wife and children of the first marriage and, obviously, says nothing of the second wife or their child. If he dies without revising his will, his estate may be distributed as though he had died intestate, since the will may be revoked by "operation of law" by some state statutes. For example, in states that have adopted the Uniform Probate Code, his divorce revokes the provisions of the will that benefit his first wife (UPC §§ 2–802 and 2–804); in others, remarriage or remarriage and the birth of issue may revoke a will. The result of such revocation is the same as if the testator died without a will, i.e., intestate. In such a case, the second wife and all his children from both marriages will take under the state intestate succession statute; the first wife will be entitled to nothing.

During will construction, problems may arise concerning the client's children, e.g., natural, adopted, nonmarital, and stepchildren, when the client attempts to identify the persons to be included or excluded in the will. Words such as *issue, heirs, descendants*, and, of course, *child* or *children*, are often ambiguous or misleading. In the statutes of most states, the terms just mentioned include natural and adopted children of the testator, exclude stepchildren, and may vary concerning nonmarital children. To resolve these problems, the following clause should be used if it matches the client's wishes:

> **Sample Clause**
>
> As used in this will, words such as *issue, child,* and *children*, describing a person or class of persons by relationship to another, shall refer to persons who are related by blood and also to persons who are related by adoption.

If the testator wishes to make a provision for stepchildren, that intention must be expressly stated in the will. Understanding the law of wills and careful drafting are necessary to resolve such problems.

Provision for Residue of Estate

The **residuary clause** allows the maker to transfer the remaining property of an estate that has not been specifically given to beneficiaries or devisees. This includes any additional property that may come into the estate after the will has been executed or after the maker's death. Generally, the bulk of an estate falls within the residue, which is usually the source for paying all federal and state death taxes, debts, and expenses of the decedent. *Remember:* Always name an alternate or successor residuary beneficiary. The following is an example of a residuary clause.

residuary clause
A clause in a will that disposes of the remaining assets (residue) of the decedent's estate after all debts and gifts in the will are satisfied.

ASSIGNMENT 6.5

Harold Wilson is currently married to his second wife, Edwina. They have two teenage children, Veronica and Dennis. Previously, Harold was married to and later divorced from Thelma Wilson. Harold and Thelma were married for 10 years and also had two children, Wilbur and Maude. The following is an excerpt from a will written by Harold when he was married to Margaret.

Article IV

I give all my personal effects, including books, art objects, jewelry, furnishings, and other tangible items, to my wife, Thelma, and children, Wilbur and Maude, to be divided equally, as determined by my executrix.

Article V

I give the sum of two thousand dollars ($2,000) to my secretary, Jerome Davis, if he is employed by me at the time of my death.

Article VI

I give the sum of ten thousand dollars ($10,000) to be divided equally to my children, if they survive me, or if they do not survive me, then to my issue who survive me, per stirpes.

Article VII

I give the sum of five thousand dollars ($5,000) and all stocks, bonds, and debentures which I shall hold at the time of my death to my wife, if she survives me, or if she does not survive me, to my children who survive me in equal shares.

Answer the following questions and draft appropriate clauses to change or modify Harold's will as requested.

1. If Harold and his first wife, Thelma, as part of their divorce agreement, had a fair and complete property settlement between themselves and for the benefit of their two children, Wilbur and Maude, could Harold exclude these three members of his first family from the benefits of his current will according to your state laws? Draft the necessary provisions in Harold's will that would exclude all three members of his first family.

2. Suppose in the example above that Maude is now married and has a son, Kirby, who is Harold's grandson. Kirby is physically handicapped. According to your state's laws, could Harold exclude Kirby from his will? Could Harold include Kirby but exclude Maude? Draft sample will provisions that accomplish these purposes if allowed by your state statutes.

3. Suppose that, while married, Harold and Thelma had adopted a daughter, Marjory. At the time of the divorce, Marjory had requested that she be allowed to live with her father, Harold. The request was granted. In your state, what are the rights of an adopted child to inherit from either of the adoptive parents? Due to his affection for Marjory, Harold wants half of his entire estate to go to her with the remaining half to be split equally by his current wife, Edwina, and his two minor children, Veronica and Dennis. Would such a provision be legal in your state? If so, draft the appropriate provision(s).

4. While married to his first wife, Thelma, Harold fathered a nonmarital son, Jeb. Although their relationship is known by all, Harold has never acknowledged in writing that he is Jeb's father.

   a. According to your state's laws, what rights would a nonmarital child (Jeb) have in his father's (Harold's) estate?

   b. Must a provision be included in Harold's will in order to exclude Jeb?

  c. If Harold had acknowledged Jeb as his son in writing or in any requisite statutory manner, could Jeb claim a share in Harold's estate even though he (Jeb) was not mentioned in the will?

  d. Can any children, natural, adopted, or nonmarital, demand or claim a share of their parent's estate when they are not mentioned in their parent's will? What are the rights of stepchildren?

  e. Can property from an estate be willed to some of the testator's children while other children are disinherited? If so, draft such a provision in Harold's will including Veronica, Dennis, and Marjory but excluding Wilbur and Maude.

5. A different complication would result if the facts in the Harold Wilson case were changed as follows: Instead of Harold and his second wife, Edwina, having two children, they are childless. If Harold were to die testate and leave his entire estate to Edwina, on Edwina's subsequent death her relatives may receive the entire estate to the exclusion of Harold's children by his first wife. Harold wants to leave his estate to Edwina if she survives him, but he also wants to provide for his two children, Wilbur and Maude. How could this be accomplished? Draft at least two clauses, one of which includes a life estate that would allow Harold to ensure that all or part of his estate would be received by his children on the death of either Harold or Edwina.

6. Suppose that Harold Wilson was injured in an automobile accident, crippling him for life. He decided to leave his entire estate to his faithful nurse, Agnes, who had cared for him continuously since the year of the accident. According to your state laws, can Harold leave his estate to his nurse, excluding his wife and children?

Sample Clause

I give all the rest, residue, and remainder of my estate, of whatever kind, real, personal, or mixed, and wherever located, not effectively disposed of by the preceding articles of this will, to my surviving spouse, [add name], if she survives me, but if she does not survive me, to my children in equal shares.

When the residue is insufficient to meet priority obligations of the estate, e.g., debts, taxes, and expenses, payment must come from legacies or devises made in the will. *Remember:* The *abatement* process will determine the order in which property in the estate will be applied to the payment of such obligations causing some gifts to be diminished or totally abolished. Consequently, state statutes that control the abatement process must be checked (see UPC § 3–902).

Some residuary clauses are simple, leaving everything to one person. Others are complex, with lengthy provisions concerning the establishment of testamentary trusts and the powers and duties of the named trustee. In either case, the will's maker must remember that if the named residuary beneficiaries or devisees should predecease the maker, there would be no one to receive the residue, so all or part of it will be distributed according to appropriate state intestate succession statutes. Thus, the residuary clause must be carefully drafted to cover potential problems caused by the sequence of deaths of named devisees and must list alternative or successor beneficiaries or devisees.

Finally, it is important to keep in mind that without a residuary clause or in any circumstances in which some or all of the decedent's estate passes by intestacy, there are no specific or general legacies or devises. Therefore, the estate's net assets or income are divided among the heirs on a pro rata basis. An example of a case in which the decedent died testate but the will contained an invalid residuary clause, thereby causing the property not disposed of to pass by the state's intestate succession statute, is *Estate of Cancik,* 121 Ill.App.3d 113, 76 Ill.Dec. 659, 459 N.E.2d 296 (1984).

ASSIGNMENT 6.6

1. Suppose in the Shen Jin example above in which Li Jin received $2,000, Myo Jin the diamond ring, and Alex P. Jin the gun collection, the testator, Shen Jin, added the following provision, "all the rest, residue, and remainder of my estate I leave to my wife, Ashika Jin." The residue is valued at $10,000. If Shen Jin died and left debts and expenses amounting to $11,000, how would his testamentary gifts abate according to your state's laws?

2. In the Jin case, if Ashika Jin, the residual beneficiary, predeceases Shen, the testator, and has not named a successor residual beneficiary, all the assets included in the residue will pass according to the intestate succession statute. Check to see how this problem is handled in your state.

3. Draft a residuary clause for Shen Jin containing a successor residual beneficiary.

fiduciary
A person, such as a personal representative, guardian, conservator, or trustee, who is appointed to serve in a position of trust and confidence and controls and manages property exclusively for the benefit of others. By law the fiduciary's conduct is held to the highest ethical standard.

 *Ethical Issue*

Appointment of Personal Representative

To acquire the powers and authority of a personal representative, a person must be appointed by a court (e.g., the probate judge or, for informal proceedings, a registrar). Generally, unless the person is unqualified, the court approves and appoints the personal representative named in the will. Since personal representatives are **fiduciaries** who are entrusted with the assets and property of others (the decedent), they must be intelligent, organized, honest, and loyal to the beneficiaries or devisees of the estate while performing all estate administration tasks. They must also be capable of engaging in business transactions or making contracts such as selling assets. Therefore, they should not be minors, incompetent persons, felons, or persons who have or *may have a conflict of interest, e.g., an attorney or paralegal who drafts a will and who influences a client to name him as the personal representative* (see UPC § 3–203 and Tex. Prob. Code Ann. § 78).

State statutes often enumerate the powers granted a personal representative or trustee. The testator, however, may want to list certain specific powers and duties to help the personal representative facilitate the administration of the estate. Giving the personal representative the power to sell one's property, for instance, saves time and perhaps money; otherwise, the personal representative would have to obtain permission from the probate court for such a sale. Such permission is called a *license to sell.* When the estate requires detailed handling, it is best the testator direct the personal representative's course of action. For example, promissory notes payable to the testator should be collected by the personal representative. Unless the testator mentions collection on such notes in the letter of instructions, the personal representative might overlook this detail, with the result that the probate court might hold the personal representative liable (for an example of a statute on executor's and administrator's powers and duties, see Wash. Rev. Code Ann. § 11.48.010 and compare UPC §§ 3–701 and 3–703). In addition, just as a contingent devisee should always be named in the event the original devisee predeceases the maker, a contingent or alternate personal representative should be selected in case the original one is unable or unwilling to serve in that capacity.

Sample Clause

If the testator opts to appoint a digital executor, a specific provision granting those rights should be included.

Sample Clause

I nominate and appoint my son, Marvin Jameson, as personal representative of this my last will and my estate and authorize him to (among other powers) sell at public or private sale any real or personal property of my estate. If Marvin Jameson predeceases me, fails to qualify, or ceases to act as my personal representative for any reason, I nominate and appoint my daughter, Myrtle B. Jameson, as successor personal representative with all powers hereinbefore mentioned, and I request that my personal representative be permitted to serve without bond or surety thereon. [See detailed discussion of bond and surety in Chapter 8.]

A typical statute on the time for commencing the personal representative's duties is the following North Dakota law.

N.D. Cent. Code § 30.1-18-01 Time of Accrual of Duties and Powers
The duties and powers of a personal representative commence upon appointment. The powers of a personal representative relate back in time to give acts by the person appointed which are beneficial to the estate occurring prior to appointment the same effect as those occurring thereafter. Prior to appointment, a person named executor in a will may carry out written instructions of the decedent relating to the decedent's body, funeral, and burial arrangements. A personal representative may ratify and accept acts on behalf of the estate done by others where the acts would have been proper for a personal representative.

The personal representative appointed is responsible for collecting and preserving the estate assets, paying all allowed debts of the decedent, as well as estate expenses and taxes, and distributing the balance to devisees named in the will (see UPC § 3–703). The procedures for appointing the personal representative are discussed in Chapters 8 and 9.

It is important that you be able to interpret statutory language correctly. A phrase in the North Dakota statute above, "The powers of a personal representative relate back in time," refers to the fact that although personal representatives do not have authority to handle the administration of the estate until appointed, they do possess limited authority (e.g., to preserve the assets of the estate before the personal representatives can be duly appointed), universal though unwritten rule that several states, including UPC states, have incorporated into their probate codes. Formal qualification of the personal representative requires a hearing before a probate judge, registrar, or clerk of the court, an order signed by the judge, and issuance of documents called Letters Testamentary or Letters of Administration (see Chapter 8), which officially authorize the named personal representative to commence the administration.

The cost of selecting and utilizing fiduciaries such as personal representatives, trustees, or attorneys handling an estate is governed by state law. In some states, such as New York, California, and Iowa, personal representatives are paid commissions (fees) according to a sliding scale based on the monetary value of the estate or trust. Typically, the statutory fee percentage of the estate's value decreases as the value of the estate increases. The statutory fees paid to personal representatives in the above states follow next.

- California: 4 percent of first $100,000; 3 percent on next $100,000; 2 percent on next $800,000; 1 percent on next $9,000,000; 0.5 percent on next $15,000,000; and a "reasonable amount" for anything over $25,000,000 (see Cal. Prob. Code § 10800).

- Iowa: Up to 6 percent of first $1,000; 4 percent on next $4,000; and 2 percent on anything over $5,000 (see Iowa Code Ann. § 633.197).

- New York: 5 percent of first $100,000; 4 percent on next $200,000; 3 percent on next $700,000; 2.5 percent of next $4,000,000; and 2 percent on anything over $5,000,000 (see N.Y. SCPA § 2307).

New York also uses such scales to compensate trustees, while California uses them for personal representatives and attorneys but not for trustees. Formerly, state bar associations established minimum attorney fee schedules based on the size of the estate. However, the U.S. Supreme Court in *Goldfarb v. Virginia State Bar,* 421 U.S. 773, 95 S.Ct. 2004, 44 L.Ed.2d 572 (1975), ruled that such minimum fee schedules were prohibited by antitrust laws as a method of price fixing. Currently, the trend is to use "reasonable compensation" commensurate with the value of personal representative and attorney services rather than the value of the estate to determine fees. Today, many states and the UPC use the "reasonable compensation" method; see UPC § 3–719. Custom and local practice play a major part in determining what constitutes "reasonable compensation," but the court makes the final decision and must also approve the payment of fees to the personal representative and estate attorney. *Check your state's current status on "reasonable compensation" to ensure that you do not overcharge an estate.*

⚖️ *Ethical Issue*

In addition to a personal representative for the estate, there may be a need to appoint a representative for the disposition of the digital data estate. They can be appointed in the will or designated by the personal representative to follow the instructions established in the digital estate plan.

Some contend that the personal representative and digital fiduciary should not necessarily be the same person since the digital fiduciary requires technical skills that a personal representative may not possess. Others believe that the named personal representative, who should have been granted powers to handle the digital estate, and the appointment of a digital representative, could potentially result in a conflict. If there is no appointment of a personal representative for the digital estate, the personal representative who lacks technological expertise should

Sample Clause

My executor shall have the power to access, handle, distribute and dispose of my digital assets. "Digital assets" includes files stored on my digital devices, including but not limited to, desktops, laptops, tablets, peripherals, storage devices, mobile telephones, smartphones, and any similar digital device that currently exists or may exist as technology develops or such comparable items as technology develops for the purpose of accessing, modifying, deleting, controlling, or transferring my digital assets. The term "digital assets" also includes but is not limited to emails received, email accounts, digital music, digital photographs, digital videos, software licenses, social network accounts, file sharing accounts, financial accounts, domain registrations, DNS service accounts, web hosting accounts, tax preparation service accounts, online stores, affiliate programs, other online accounts, and similar digital items which currently exist or may exist as technology develops or such comparable items as technology develops, regardless of the ownership of the physical device upon which the digital item is stored.

engage the services of a third party. Clearly, the personal representative would then retain control and responsibility over the management of the digital estate, thereby avoiding a potential conflict.

Appointment of Personal and/or Property Guardian

A parent has a statutory obligation to support children until they reach majority. The law establishes two types of guardianships: a personal guardian and a property guardian. Whenever the testator has minor children who are physically or mentally handicapped and the other parent is deceased or unable to care for them, a personal guardian should be named in the will to ensure proper care of the children after the testator's death. Otherwise, if there is no will, the court is required to determine who shall have custody and/or *guardianship of the person* (i.e., the child or the incompetent).

> **EXAMPLE:** Walker dies testate. He had sole custody of his minor daughter, Eliza. Walker's wife had died several years earlier. Walker's brother, Houston, with whom Walker and Eliza had lived for a number of years, and Eliza's maternal grandmother both claim to be the better choice for guardian of the child. The probate court must choose between the two if Walker's will fails to name a guardian.

The testator should also appoint a *guardian of the property* or *conservator to* manage property left to minor or incompetent children. If such an appointment is not made, the probate court must do so. The testator should empower the property guardian or conservator to hold, accumulate, and manage the funds and property for incapacitated or minor devisees or beneficiaries under a trust for the duration of their minority or incapacity (compare UPC §§ 5–207 to 5–209, 5–314 to 5–316, and 5–401). The personal guardian and the property guardian may or may not be the same person. *Remember:* Godparents are not legal guardians. However, the testator may name one or both godparents in the will as his or her choice to be the personal and/or property guardian. The following is an example of a clause that appoints a personal and property guardian.

A statute that grants testamentary appointment of a guardian is *Tex. Prob. Code Ann. § 676(d)*, Guardians of Minors.

> The surviving parent of a minor may by will or written declaration appoint any eligible person to be guardian of the person of the parent's minor children after the death of the parent. Unless the court finds that the person designated in the will or declaration to serve as guardian of the person of the parent's minor children is disqualified, is dead, refuses to serve, or would not serve the best interests of the minor children, the court shall appoint the person as guardian in preference to those otherwise entitled to serve as guardian under this chapter. On compliance with this code, an eligible person is also entitled to be appointed guardian of the children's estates after the death of the parent.

A statute that treats the order of preference for the appointment of a guardian is *Ind. Code Ann. § 29-3-5-5*, Consideration for Appointment of Guardian; Order of Consideration; Priorities.

> **Sec. 5 (a) The following are entitled to consideration for appointment as a guardian under section 4 of this chapter in the order listed:**
> (1) A person designated in a durable power of attorney.
> (2) The spouse of an incapacitated person.
> (3) An adult child of an incapacitated person.
> (4) A parent of an incapacitated person, or a person nominated by will of a deceased parent of an incapacitated person or by any writing signed by a parent of an incapacitated person and attested to by at least two (2) witnesses.
> (5) Any person related to an incapacitated person by blood or marriage with whom the incapacitated person has resided for more than six (6) months before the filing of the petition.
> (6) A person nominated by the incapacitated person who is caring for or paying for the care of the incapacitated person.
> > (b) With respect to persons having equal priority, the court shall select the person it considers best qualified to serve as guardian. The court, acting in the best interest of the incapacitated person or minor, may pass over a person having priority and appoint a person having a lower priority or no priority under this section.

A controversial and often stressful situation arises whenever a single parent attempts to appoint a guardian for a child in a will and specifically excludes from the appointment the other natural parent. The surviving natural parent, without regard to marital status, has the right to custody of the child and to be the guardian unless the parent is found to be unfit. The custodial parent cannot change the rights of the surviving parent (see Minn. Stat. Ann. § 524.5-202 [g]).

EXAMPLE: In her will, Delilah, the custodial parent, selects her sister, Cora, to be the personal guardian of Delilah's minor son, Wyatt. Delilah also states she does not want her former husband, Zeke, who is the father of Wyatt, to obtain custody of Wyatt. Upon Delilah's death, the court would appoint Zeke as the personal guardian unless he was unwilling or unfit.

ASSIGNMENT 6.7

Rhoda's husband, Steven Clark, has a will, leaving his estate equally to Rhoda and their three-year-old adopted daughter, Karen, who has muscular dystrophy.

1. Draft a provision to be added to Steven's will that adequately protects Karen's interest in her father's estate.

2. If Rhoda remarries and dies intestate five years after Steven's death, would her new husband or Karen's maternal grandparents have a statutory preference to the appointment of guardian for Karen in the state of Indiana? In your state?

Simultaneous Death Clause

Most states have enacted statutes that govern the distribution of a decedent-testator's property when there is insufficient evidence to determine if a beneficiary survived the testator. Due to the frequent occurrence of these inheritance and distribution problems whenever two people, such as a married couple or a parent and adult child, die at the same time in a common disaster, nearly all states have adopted the Uniform Simultaneous Death Act. The act provides where the inheritance of property depends on the priority of death of the decedents, and there is no sufficient evidence that the decedents have died other than simultaneously, the property of each decedent involved shall be distributed as if he or she had survived the other (see UPC § 2–702). This provision can be added to the decedent's will. A typical state statute is *Conn. Gen. Stat. Ann. § 45a-440,* Simultaneous Death; Disposition of Property.

(a) When no sufficient evidence of survivorship. When the title to property or the devolution thereof depends upon priority of death and there is no sufficient evidence that the persons have died otherwise than simultaneously, the property of each person shall be disposed of as if he had survived, except as provided otherwise in this section.

EXAMPLE: Margaret and her daughter, Mirabella, are at home asleep. Gas leaks into the house, causing an explosion that destroys the house and kills Margaret and Mirabella. Margaret's will named Mirabella as her sole beneficiary, but in the event of Mirabella's death before Margaret, the property was to pass to Margaret's brother, Oliver. The will contained a **simultaneous death clause** that allowed the property to go to Oliver instead of possibly passing into Mirabella's estate.

simultaneous death clause A clause in a will that determines the distribution of property in the event there is no evidence as to the priority of time of death of the testator and another, usually the testator's spouse.

The Uniform Simultaneous Death Act has also resolved the following problem. If two individuals owning property in joint tenancy die simultaneously under circumstances in which it cannot be determined who died first, the property is divided equally and distributed to the beneficiaries named in the residuary clause of their respective wills. In the previous example, if Margaret and Mirabella owned a house in joint tenancy and they died simultaneously in a plane crash, half of the value of the house would pass to Margaret's brother, and the other half would pass to Mirabella's beneficiaries or heirs depending on whether she died testate or intestate.

Unfortunately, the act may result in a significant financial loss to surviving beneficiaries and devisees, because the act implies that if there is adequate proof of the sequence of deaths, the surviving beneficiary, no matter how long the person survives, will be entitled to the property passed by will from the first decedent's estate. For example, suppose a daughter, who died a few days after her father in a common disaster was the sole beneficiary of her father's will; after his estate is taxed and debts are paid, the residue would be added to the daughter's estate, where it would be taxed again. Most states, including those that have adopted the UPC, have eliminated this problem by adding a "delay clause" to the simultaneous death provision, which requires that a person must survive the first decedent by at least 120 hours to qualify as a surviving beneficiary. If the beneficiary does not survive the decedent-testator by 120 hours, the beneficiary does not receive the property through the will. *Caution:* A delay clause that exceeds 180 days will disqualify a bequest to the spouse for the marital deduction (see U.S.C.A. § 2056[b][3]; Federal Tax Regulations, § 20.2056). The following is a sample clause, taken from West's McKinney's Forms, ESP, § 7:235, that can be used to resolve the "delay" problem.

Sample Clause

I nominate and appoint Francine E. Richter as personal and property guardian of my minor child, Nancy G. Thorsby, and empower her with the right to have care, custody, and control of said minor child, and to collect, invest, and manage, without court approval, any property passing to said minor child by this will. The guardian may use the income from the property for the support, education, and well-being of said child and distribute the principal balance to her on her 25th birthday or her marriage, whichever occurs first. In the event Francine E. Richter fails to qualify or is unable, or unwilling, or ceases to act as guardian, I nominate and appoint William B. Kruger to serve in her place as successor personal and property guardian with all the hereinbefore mentioned powers. I direct that the appointed guardian in this will shall not be required to give any bond or other surety in connection with qualifying or acting in this capacity.

In cases involving intestacy and simultaneous deaths, Section 47 of the Texas Probate Code establishes a "delay" period of 120 hours (5 days) that must pass in order for an heir to "survive" and inherit from the intestate. If the heir does not survive the intestate by the 5 days, the beneficiary is considered to have predeceased the intestate, and none of the intestate's property will be passed to the beneficiary. The UPC § 2–104 has the same provision.

ASSIGNMENT 6.8

Claire and Edmund Barnet, husband and wife, live in Connecticut. Edmund's will gives his country house to Claire, if she should survive him, but if she does not, to his sister, Estelle. Claire's will gives her collection of antiques to Edmund, if he should survive her, but if he does not, to her brother, Spenser. Claire and Edmund die simultaneously in an automobile collision. Answer these questions according to your state laws:

1. Who inherits which property?

2. Would your answer differ if Claire had died one day later than Edmund? Is there "sufficient evidence" to prevent the Connecticut statute above from operating?

3. If Claire receives injuries in the accident and dies 90 days afterward, would she be entitled to receive Edmund's gift? Would Estelle?

Although the Uniform Simultaneous Death Act is the most common provision for directing how a testator's property will be distributed, i.e., that the beneficiary in the will predeceased the testator, a different presumption of death can be established in the will by an appropriate provision. For example, when estate planning for spouses is an important consideration, it is common to provide that the spouse with the smaller estate is determined to survive in the event of simultaneous death.

Testamentary Trust Clause

Often, a person wishes to transfer ownership of property to another without giving the recipient full power over the designated property. In a will, a method frequently used for the benefit of minor children is a *testamentary trust*. The will, and therefore the trust, takes effect when the testator dies and the probate court assumes the management and administration of the trust.

Sample Clause

In the event that my said wife shall die within a period of [six] months after the date of my death, my said wife shall be deemed to have predeceased me, and all provisions contained herein for her benefit shall be cancelled and my estate shall be administered and the assets of my estate distributed as though I had died immediately after the death of my said wife. (Source: Thomson/West from West's McKinney's Forms.)

The probate court requires annual accounting by the trustee throughout the life of the trust.

Testimonium Clause

The **testimonium clause** contains a statement by the maker of the will that it has been freely signed and a request has been made of the proper number of witnesses to do the same.

Since the testimonium clause does not contain any new information and in most instances only repeats what the testator has stated in the opening paragraphs, it would appear to be expendable. Although each state demands the will conform to standards that require wills be written, signed by the testator, and witnessed, state statutes do not prescribe a form for the testimonium clause.

The following is an example of a testimonium clause.

testimonium clause
A clause in a will in which the maker states that he or she has freely signed and dated the will and requests the proper number of witnesses to do the same.

Sample Clause

In the event any of my children are under the age of 18 at the time of my death, I give the remainder of my estate to the trustee, hereinafter named, in trust for the benefit of said child or children until they reach the age of 21. I direct said trustee to pay or apply the net income of this trust for the support, maintenance, and education of said children. When all my surviving children reach the age of 21, I direct the trustee to give the remainder of the trust to said children equally.

A typical statute on this matter is *N. J. Stat. Ann § 3B:3-2,* Execution; Witnessed Wills; Writings Intended as Wills:

(a) Except as provided in subsection b. and in N.J.S.3B:3-3, a will shall be:
    (1) in writing;
    (2) signed by the testator or in the testator's name by some other individual in the testator's conscious presence and at the testator's direction; and
    (3) signed by at least two individuals, each of whom signed within a reasonable time after each witnessed either the signing of the will as described in paragraph (2) or the testator's acknowledgment of that signature or acknowledgment of the will.

(b) A will that does not comply with subsection a. is valid as a writing intended as a will, whether or not witnessed, if the signature and material portions of the document are in the testator's handwriting.

(c) Intent that a document constitutes the testator's will can be established by extrinsic evidence, including writings intended as wills, portions of the document that are not in the testator's handwriting.

ASSIGNMENT 6.9

After reading a copy of a will prepared for him by an attorney, Owen decides that he does not like the antiquated language of the testimonium clause. He crosses it out and writes the following clause in its place.

    At the time this will was executed, the testator knew of and fully complied with the statutes of this state relating to the execution of wills.

          /S/_____
                    (Testator)

Witnessed this same day, April 13, 2015.

          /S/_____
                    (Witness)

          /S/_____
                    (Witness)

1. Would this clause serve in lieu of the traditionally worded testimonium clause? Why or why not?

2. Point out potential difficulties caused by this testimonium clause when the will's executor offers the document for probate. Are there any words or omissions likely to be challenged in a will contest? Why?

3. If necessary, add to or modify the clause to make it conform both to the requirements of the law and to Owen's desire to modernize its language.

Testator's Signature

For a will to be valid, its maker must sign, make a mark, or direct another to sign. In most states, the signature must be witnessed by two or more persons acting as attesting witnesses. The date, either in the beginning, within, or at the end of the will, is essential. Without it, it may be impossible to prove the will is the last (in time) made by the testator.

A typical statute on the execution of a will is Ill. *Compiled Stat. Ann. Ch. 755 § 5/4-3*, Signing and Attestation.

(a) Every will shall be in writing, signed by the testator or some person in his presence and by his direction and attested in the presence of the testator by 2 or more credible witnesses. [Compare UPC § 2–502.]

EXAMPLE: Walter typewrites his will. He puts his signature at the beginning of it, but types his name at the end. In some states, e.g., New York, the will may not be valid for lack of a proper signature in the proper place.

EXAMPLE: Ahmad writes a second will but neglects to date it. Previously, he made a will but decided to discard it. He did not destroy the former will. Both documents are found after his death. The latter will may not supersede the former or prevail over it for lack of evidence that it was written at a later time.

ASSIGNMENT 6.10

Edith wishes to make a will, but she is partially paralyzed and cannot write her name. Her nephew, Arthur, agrees to draw up the will and to witness the X she will make in place of her name. The clause preceding the signature follows.

_____

I, the testatrix, Edith B. Pendergast, on this 19th day of March, 2015, subscribe my mark to this will.

_____

I, Arthur G. Pendergast, have witnessed this mark made by Edith B. Pendergast, who affixed it in lieu of her signature.

_____

_____

1. Do these clauses fulfill your state's statutory requirements for a signature by the testator? Why or why not?

2. If necessary, add to or modify the clauses to make them conform to your answer in question 1 (compare UPC § 2–502). Is Arthur's signature sufficient to validate the will?

Attestation Clause of Witnesses

The **attestation clause** identifies the individuals who are witnesses to the will. Witnesses must state they have attested the maker's signature on the will and sign the clause. As in the case of the testimonium clause, each state has legislation requiring subscription by witnesses, although none prescribes the words or form to be used to accomplish this. The traditional form of the attestation clause, like the familiarly worded testimonium clause, is illustrated in the following example.

attestation clause
Witnesses to a will state that they have attested the maker's signature and that they have subscribed (signed) a clause in the will to this effect.

Sample Clause

In Witness Whereof, I, the undersigned testator (trix), do hereby declare that I willingly sign and execute this instrument as my last will consisting of _____ pages, including this page, on this _____ day of _____, _____, at City of _____, County of _____, State of _____, in the presence of the witnesses whose names appear hereafter. _____Testator (trix)]

Note: Some states have enacted statutes that substitute a self-proving affidavit clause for the traditional attestation clause (see discussion below).

ASSIGNMENT 6.11

"We, the undersigned, declare that Lyman Jarrett validly signed and executed this will. We sign at his request, all of us signing in each other's presence."

1. Does such a clause comply with statutory requirements? Why or why not?

2. If necessary, add to or modify the clause to make it conform to the statutory requirements.

Witnesses' Signatures and Addresses

Only the original copy of the will is signed. Copies should be made before the original is signed. All states require at least two witnesses sign the will. Witnesses should sign using the same pen as the testator.

EXAMPLE:

	Address
Pamela C. Hunter	*111 Wheelock Drive*
Fredrick G. Burns	*2307 Ayleshire Avenue*

ASSIGNMENT 6.12

You are a paralegal and also a notary public. At the execution of a will, while you are discussing the procedures with the attorney, the testator inadvertently signs the will, and now wants you to notarize it. What would you have the testator do to resolve this problem?

SAMPLE PRELIMINARY WILL

Exhibit 6.2 is a worksheet used to prepare a draft of a client's will. The will drawn from the information on the worksheet follows in Exhibit 6.3.

In a hypothetical situation, Leona Bayn Farrell wishes to make a will. She is married and has a husband, Oren, and four children, Randolph, Jonathan, Daria, and Thomas. Her estate consists of both real and personal property, all of which she acquired prior to the marriage or as gifts to her individually as separate property during the marriage. Leona lives in Arizona, a community property state, which allows her to convey by will her separate property and half of the community property acquired by Leona and her husband while they are married.

EXHIBIT 6.2	**Sample Worksheet for Drafting a Will Without Digital Assets**

Client's Name: <u>Leona Bayn Farrell (also known as Leona Alice Bayn)</u>
Address: <u>913 Garth Avenue</u>, City <u>Sierra Vista</u> , County <u>Cochise</u>, State <u>Arizona</u>
(if more than one) <u>17 Mesa Grande, Carlsbad, New Mexico.</u>

Permanent Residence (Domicile): <u>913 Garth Avenue, Cochise County, Sierra Vista.</u>

Funeral and Burial Directions: <u>I direct that my kidneys be delivered, immediately upon my death, without autopsy having been performed, to the Carlsbad State School of Medicine, 403 Alamoreal Street, Carlsbad, New Mexico, to be used for educational purposes.</u>

Method (source of payments of debts and all taxes): I direct that my executor pay all my expenses, debts, and taxes from the residue of my estate.

Specific Gifts

Personal Property (community property)

Beneficiary: <u>Oren Johnstone Farrell</u>	Contingent beneficiary: <u>Children</u>
Relationship: Husband	Relationship: Sons and daughters

Item: Share of community property consisting of household furnishings, clothing, jewelry, books, and other personal effects.
Method: Legacy

Personal property

Beneficiary: <u>Randolph Bayn Farrell</u>	Contingent beneficiary: <u>Ella Gamble Dean</u>
Relationship: Son	Relationship: Niece

Item: The Buick automobile that I own, serial number 70–5015–9229
Present location: <u>At my permanent residence, 913 Garth Avenue</u>
Method: Legacy

Personal Property

Beneficiary: <u>Oren Johnstone Farrell</u>	Contingent beneficiary: <u>Jonathan Bayn Farrell</u>
Relationship: Husband	Relationship: Son

Item: All the farm equipment located at Siete Rios
Method: Legacy

Personal Property

Beneficiary: <u>Jonathan Bayn Farrell</u>	Contingent beneficiary: <u>Angela Bayn Rodgers</u>
Relationship: Son	Relationship: Niece

Item: All the horses and riding equipment located at Vallejo Grande
Method: Legacy

Real Property: Ranch—"Vallejo Grande"

Beneficiary: <u>Jonathan Bayn Farrell</u>	Contingent beneficiary: <u>Angela Bayn Rodgers</u>
Relationship: Son	Relationship: Niece
Location: County: Eddy	State: New Mexico

Legal description of "Vallejo Grande": <u>"The West half of Section 12, being 320 acres more or less, Township 4 North, Range 28 West of the 4th Principal Meridian, according to the United States Government survey."</u>

(continued)

Exhibit 6.2   (Continued)

Amount of interest: Fee simple
Method: Fee simple devise
Real Property: Farm—"Siete Rios"
Beneficiary: Oren Johnstone Farrell   Contingent beneficiary: Daria Eileen
                                             Farrell

Relationship: Husband   Relationship: Daughter
Location: County: Eddy   State: New Mexico
Legal description of "Siete Rios": "The Southwest Quarter of Section 13, being 160
acres more or less, Township 4 North, Range 28 West of the 4th Principal Meridian,
according to the United States Government survey."

Amount of Interest: Fee simple
Method: Fee simple devise
Residue
Beneficiary: Daria Eileen Farrell   Contingent beneficiary: Randolph
                                             Bayn Farrell

Relationship: Daughter   Relationship: Son
Interest given: Legacy or devise; if any residue remains after payment of debts,
expenses, and taxes
Name and Address of Executor: Randolph Bayn Farrell
                                             119 Golden Valley Road
                                             Sierra Vista, Arizona
Contingent (Successor) Executor: Farmers National Bank, Sierra Vista, Arizona
Powers of Executor: To sell publicly or privately all or part of my residual property
                      to carry on the operations of "Vallejo Grande" and "Siete
                      Rios" until the dispositions thereof are complete
Trusts
Trustee: Carl A. Woodward, Farmers National Bank, Sierra Vista, Arizona
Property: $75,000 (cash)
Location: Farmers National Bank, Account #922160
Duration of trust (life, years, etc.): For the life of my son, Thomas Earl Farrell
Remainder: First United Methodist Church of Waco, Texas
Trustee's powers
Investment: To invest and reinvest the corpus
Management: To distribute the earned income for the benefit of Thomas Earl
                Farrell
Payment of income: Quarterly if possible; at least semiannually
Payment of principal: At the trustee's discretion or at the request of Thomas Earl
Farrell's natural or legal personal guardian
Power of sale: N/A
Special Provisions: Both principal and interest may be used for education, training,
and maintenance of Thomas Earl Farrell. If guardian and trustee disagree,
guardian's opinion is to prevail.
Guardians
Guardian of person: Oren Johnstone Farrell, my husband
Name and address: 913 Garth Avenue, County of Cochise, City of Sierra Vista,
Arizona

EXHIBIT 6.2	(Continued)

Ward: Thomas Earl Farrell   Successor Guardian: Randolph
                                                        Bayn Farrell

Bond: None required

Guardian of property: Randolph Bayn Farrell, my son

Name and address: 119 Golden Valley Road, County of Cochise, City of Sierra
                  Vista, Arizona

Ward: Thomas Earl Farrell   Successor Guardian: Oren
                                                        Johnstone Farrell

Bond: None required

Common Disaster Provision: If my husband and I should die under circumstances
that make it impossible to determine the order of deaths, he shall be deemed to
have predeceased me.

Witnesses

Name and Addresses: Raymond Meador, Route 34, Bisbee, Arizona
                    Mildred Wagoner, Route 7, Benson, Arizona

General Notes

Location—safe deposit box: Leona and Oren Farrell, joint tenants, Farmers
                           National Bank

Location where will shall be placed: In the custody of Frank R. Goad,
                                     Attorney-at-law

Will prepared by: Joyce Bell, paralegal assistant under supervision of attorney
                  Judith K. Larson

Date: July 6, 2015

ASSIGNMENT 6.13

Peter Rice Cochran wishes to make a will. He is currently unmarried. He divorced Viola Leigh after a five-year marriage during which two children, Maria and Casey, were born. His estate consists of both real and personal property, namely, a townhouse; household goods; automobile; checking account of $587; certificate of deposit of $7,000; insurance policy on his life, payable to his brother, Desmond Cochran, $10,000; 100 shares of Xerox Corporation stock; and a savings account of $10,525.

1. Make a preliminary outline of a will for Peter Cochran using the form suggested by the Leona Farrell example. Make up facts in the testator's life (e.g., devisees who are not named above, testamentary trusts to be created) if you wish.

2. Using the will of Leona Farrell, which follows as a guide, write a will for Peter Cochran. (Assume the testator lives in your state. Be sure to consult the probate laws of your state before drafting the will.)

EXHIBIT 6.3 Last Will and Testament of Leona Bayn Farrell

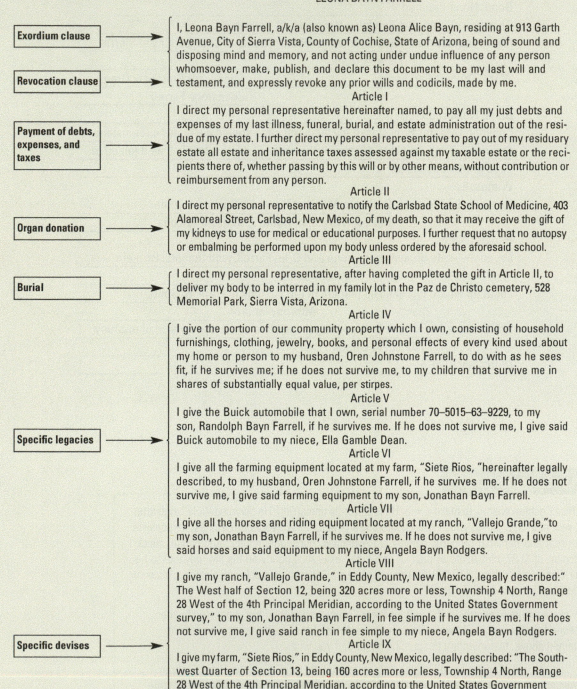

LAST WILL AND TESTAMENT
OF
LEONA BAYN FARRELL

Exordium clause

Revocation clause

I, Leona Bayn Farrell, a/k/a (also known as) Leona Alice Bayn, residing at 913 Garth Avenue, City of Sierra Vista, County of Cochise, State of Arizona, being of sound and disposing mind and memory, and not acting under undue influence of any person whomsoever, make, publish, and declare this document to be my last will and testament, and expressly revoke any prior wills and codicils, made by me.

Article I

Payment of debts, expenses, and taxes

I direct my personal representative hereinafter named, to pay all my just debts and expenses of my last illness, funeral, burial, and estate administration out of the residue of my estate. I further direct my personal representative to pay out of my residuary estate all estate and inheritance taxes assessed against my taxable estate or the recipients there of, whether passing by this will or by other means, without contribution or reimbursement from any person.

Article II

Organ donation

I direct my personal representative to notify the Carlsbad State School of Medicine, 403 Alamoreal Street, Carlsbad, New Mexico, of my death, so that it may receive the gift of my kidneys to use for medical or educational purposes. I further request that no autopsy or embalming be performed upon my body unless ordered by the aforesaid school.

Article III

Burial

I direct my personal representative, after having completed the gift in Article II, to deliver my body to be interred in my family lot in the Paz de Christo cemetery, 528 Memorial Park, Sierra Vista, Arizona.

Article IV

I give the portion of our community property which I own, consisting of household furnishings, clothing, jewelry, books, and personal effects of every kind used about my home or person to my husband, Oren Johnstone Farrell, to do with as he sees fit, if he survives me; if he does not survive me, to my children that survive me in shares of substantially equal value, per stirpes.

Article V

Specific legacies

I give the Buick automobile that I own, serial number 70–5015–63–9229, to my son, Randolph Bayn Farrell, if he survives me. If he does not survive me, I give said Buick automobile to my niece, Ella Gamble Dean.

Article VI

I give all the farming equipment located at my farm, "Siete Rios, "hereinafter legally described, to my husband, Oren Johnstone Farrell, if he survives me. If he does not survive me, I give said farming equipment to my son, Jonathan Bayn Farrell.

Article VII

I give all the horses and riding equipment located at my ranch, "Vallejo Grande,"to my son, Jonathan Bayn Farrell, if he survives me. If he does not survive me, I give said horses and said equipment to my niece, Angela Bayn Rodgers.

Article VIII

I give my ranch, "Vallejo Grande," in Eddy County, New Mexico, legally described:" The West half of Section 12, being 320 acres more or less, Township 4 North, Range 28 West of the 4th Principal Meridian, according to the United States Government survey," to my son, Jonathan Bayn Farrell, in fee simple if he survives me. If he does not survive me, I give said ranch in fee simple to my niece, Angela Bayn Rodgers.

Article IX

Specific devises

I give my farm, "Siete Rios," in Eddy County, New Mexico, legally described: "The Southwest Quarter of Section 13, being 160 acres more or less, Township 4 North, Range 28 West of the 4th Principal Meridian, according to the United States Government survey," to my husband, Oren Johnstone Farrell, in fee simple if he survives me. If he does not survive me, I give said farm in fee simple to my daughter, Daria Eileen Farrell.

Exhibit 6.3   (Continued)

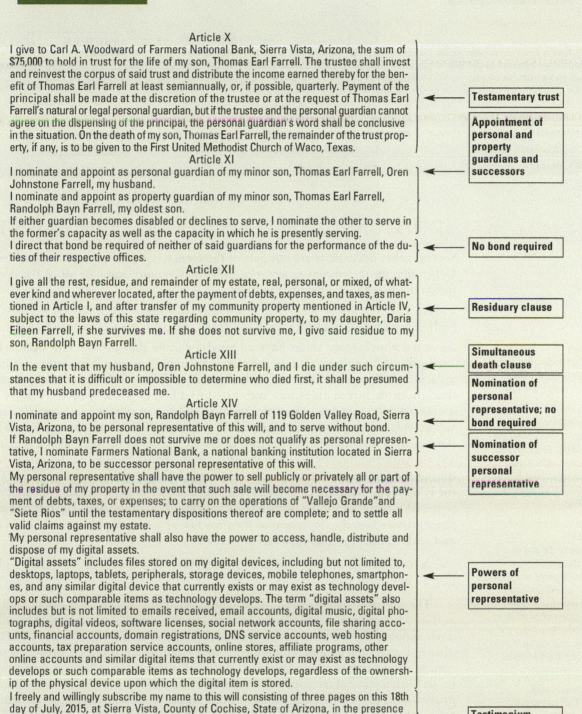

Article X

I give to Carl A. Woodward of Farmers National Bank, Sierra Vista, Arizona, the sum of $75,000 to hold in trust for the life of my son, Thomas Earl Farrell. The trustee shall invest and reinvest the corpus of said trust and distribute the income earned thereby for the benefit of Thomas Earl Farrell at least semiannually, or, if possible, quarterly. Payment of the principal shall be made at the discretion of the trustee or at the request of Thomas Earl Farrell's natural or legal personal guardian, but if the trustee and the personal guardian cannot agree on the dispensing of the principal, the personal guardian's word shall be conclusive in the situation. On the death of my son, Thomas Earl Farrell, the remainder of the trust property, if any, is to be given to the First United Methodist Church of Waco, Texas.   [Testamentary trust]

Article XI

I nominate and appoint as personal guardian of my minor son, Thomas Earl Farrell, Oren Johnstone Farrell, my husband.

I nominate and appoint as property guardian of my minor son, Thomas Earl Farrell, Randolph Bayn Farrell, my oldest son.

If either guardian becomes disabled or declines to serve, I nominate the other to serve in the former's capacity as well as the capacity in which he is presently serving.   [Appointment of personal and property guardians and successors]

I direct that bond be required of neither of said guardians for the performance of the duties of their respective offices.   [No bond required]

Article XII

I give all the rest, residue, and remainder of my estate, real, personal, or mixed, of whatever kind and wherever located, after the payment of debts, expenses, and taxes, as mentioned in Article I, and after transfer of my community property mentioned in Article IV, subject to the laws of this state regarding community property, to my daughter, Daria Eileen Farrell, if she survives me. If she does not survive me, I give said residue to my son, Randolph Bayn Farrell.   [Residuary clause]

Article XIII

In the event that my husband, Oren Johnstone Farrell, and I die under such circumstances that it is difficult or impossible to determine who died first, it shall be presumed that my husband predeceased me.   [Simultaneous death clause]

Article XIV

I nominate and appoint my son, Randolph Bayn Farrell of 119 Golden Valley Road, Sierra Vista, Arizona, to be personal representative of this will, and to serve without bond.   [Nomination of personal representative; no bond required]

If Randolph Bayn Farrell does not survive me or does not qualify as personal representative, I nominate Farmers National Bank, a national banking institution located in Sierra Vista, Arizona, to be successor personal representative of this will.   [Nomination of successor personal representative]

My personal representative shall have the power to sell publicly or privately all or part of the residue of my property in the event that such sale will become necessary for the payment of debts, taxes, or expenses; to carry on the operations of "Vallejo Grande" and "Siete Rios" until the testamentary dispositions thereof are complete; and to settle all valid claims against my estate.

My personal representative shall also have the power to access, handle, distribute and dispose of my digital assets.

"Digital assets" includes files stored on my digital devices, including but not limited to, desktops, laptops, tablets, peripherals, storage devices, mobile telephones, smartphones, and any similar digital device that currently exists or may exist as technology develops or such comparable items as technology develops. The term "digital assets" also includes but is not limited to emails received, email accounts, digital music, digital photographs, digital videos, software licenses, social network accounts, file sharing accounts, financial accounts, domain registrations, DNS service accounts, web hosting accounts, tax preparation service accounts, online stores, affiliate programs, other online accounts and similar digital items that currently exist or may exist as technology develops or such comparable items as technology develops, regardless of the ownership of the physical device upon which the digital item is stored.   [Powers of personal representative]

I freely and willingly subscribe my name to this will consisting of three pages on this 18th day of July, 2015, at Sierra Vista, County of Cochise, State of Arizona, in the presence of these witnesses; Raymond Meador and Mildred Wagoner, each of whom I have requested to subscribe their names in my presence and in the presence of all the others.   [Testimonium clause]

(continued)

EXHIBIT 6.3	(Continued)

> /S/ Leona Bayn Farrell → **Signature of testatrix**
>
> On the last date shown above, Leona Bayn Farrell, known to us to be the person whose signature appears at the end of this will, declared to us, the undersigned, that the foregoing instrument was her will. She then signed the will in our presence; at her request, we now sign our names in her presence and the presence of each other. → **Attestation clause**
>
> Names   Addresses
> /S/ Raymond Meador   Route 34, Bisbee, Arizona
> (Witness)
> /S/ Mildred Wagoner   Route 7, Benson, Arizona → **Signatures of witnesses**
> (Witness)

ADDITIONAL NONTESTAMENTARY DOCUMENTS

Several other documents are not part of the formal will itself, but are related to it. Depending on the circumstances, the client may require some or all of the documents discussed in the next paragraphs.

Self-Proving Affidavit Clause That Creates a Self-Proved Will

affidavit
A printed declaration made voluntarily under oath or affirmed before a notary public.

notary public
A person authorized by the state whose function is to administer oaths, certify documents and deeds, and attest to the authenticity of signatures.

self-proving affidavit (clause)
A clause at the end of a will that contains an acknowledgment or affidavit of the testator and affidavits of witnesses signed by them in the presence of a notary public who also signs and seals it. This clause is used to replace the traditional attestation clause.

self-proved will
A will that replaces the traditional attestation clause with another state statute clause that contains a self-proving affidavit signed by the testator and witnesses in the presence of a notary public who also signs and seals it, thereby creating the self-proved will.

As noted above, some states have adopted a statute that provides an option for "self-proving" a will without the witnesses' testimony in court. The statute requires an acknowledgment or **affidavit** of the testator and the affidavits of the witnesses that are made before an officer authorized to administer oaths by the state, e.g., a **notary public**. In a few states, the testator and the two witnesses sign the same **self-proving affidavit (clause)** as shown in Exhibit 6.4. The acknowledgment or affidavits can be signed either at the time of the execution of the will, which is generally the case and thereby replaces the attestation clause, or at any subsequent date during the lifetime of the testator and witnesses. The document recites the testator is of sound mind and the testator and the subscribing witnesses followed the required formalities for the proper and legal execution of the will. The testator and the witnesses sign the document in the presence of a notary public who also signs and seals it, thereby creating a **self-proved will**.

A form for the acknowledgment and affidavit of self-proved wills is provided in § 2–504 of the UPC.

The self-proving provision or affidavit signed and sealed by a notary public at the end of the will is *not* required to validate the will. The execution of the affidavit supplies the requisite evidence to admit the will to probate, but the affidavit does not waive the formal requirements for a valid will, nor does it prevent a will contest on legitimate grounds such as duress, fraud, undue influence, revocation, or lack of testamentary capacity of the testator. *Remember:* To be a valid *self-proved will*, the self-proving affidavit must strictly follow the statutory language required by the state where the testator lives.

Letter of Instructions

The letter of instructions is not part of the will and has no legal effect. It may be incorporated by reference into the will. It is a letter to the personal representative and family that explains where the will and important assets and records are located, including all bank accounts, safe deposit boxes, and other legal documents; lists current market values of assets or recommends appraisers; and makes management suggestions and investment recommendations to the personal representative. A letter of instruction may also be used for the disposition of the digital estate. Like their tangible assets, clients should list their digital assets, whether the asset has financial or sentimental value, and the services along with instructions on how to access them. Included in the letter should be instructions on how to handle these assets, i.e., closed, deleted, or passed to a named beneficiary. These letters should be updated yearly. A letter of instruction for a digital estate comes with risk as the decedent is recording sensitive information. Precautions should be taken to properly secure this information through an encrypted electronic list, an inventory secured in a safe-deposit box, or a fireproof safe with instructions that only the fiduciary should be granted access.

Power of Attorney

Another nontestamentary document to consider for estate planning purposes is a **power of attorney**. In this legal instrument, one person, the **principal**, designates another, the **agent** or **attorney in fact**, to have the authority to make legal decisions for and otherwise act on behalf of the principal. Any type of decision-making authority a principal can undertake is transferable to another. However, in today's world, it should also include specific powers regarding digital assets. The extent of authority delegated to the agent can be either broad, covering a variety of situations, i.e., a **general power of attorney**, or limited and narrow in scope, covering a few specific situations, i.e., a **limited power of attorney**.

Sample Clause

Digital Assets. My attorney-in-fact shall have (i) the power to access, use and control my digital devices, including, but not limited to, desktops, laptops, tablets, peripherals, storage devices, mobile telephones, smartphones, and any similar digital device that currently exists or may exist as technology develops or such comparable items as technology develops for the purpose of accessing, modifying, deleting, controlling or transferring my digital assets; and (ii) the power to access, modify, delete, control and transfer my digital assets, including but not limited to, my emails received, email accounts, digital music, digital photographs, digital videos, software licenses, social network accounts, file sharing accounts, financial accounts, domain registrations, DNS service accounts, web hosting accounts, tax preparation service accounts, online stores, affiliate programs, other online accounts, and similar digital items that currently exist or may exist as technology develops or such comparable items as technology develop.

A power of attorney can be an especially useful advance-planning tool. It can provide for crucial property, financial, insurance, business, tax, health care, investment, inheritance, digital data, or other legal matters to be handled in a straightforward, simplified manner under circumstances where the principal is incapable of making such decisions himself due to mental or physical disability, illness, catastrophic accident, or other debilitating emergency or condition. This can save family and friends the emotional and financial costs and the time-consuming effort necessary to make crucial life decisions for an incapacitated loved one during times of crisis-triggered stress.

Executing a Power of Attorney

Anyone who has the capacity to enter a valid contract can execute a power of attorney. Similarly, anyone who has such contractual capacity can be named the attorney in fact. The person authorized to act does not need to be an attorney. Care must be

power of attorney
A document, witnessed and acknowledged, authorizing another to act as one's agent or attorney in fact.

principal
A person who authorizes another (agent) to act on the person's behalf.

agent
A person authorized by another person (principal) to act in place of the principal.

attorney in fact
An agent, not necessarily an attorney, who is given authority by the principal in a written document called a power of attorney to perform certain specific acts on behalf of the principal.

general power of attorney
A written document in which a principal appoints and authorizes an agent or attorney in fact to perform a variety of acts on behalf of the principal.

limited power of attorney
A written document in which a principal appoints and authorizes an agent or attorney in fact to perform a few specific acts on behalf of the principal.

EXHIBIT 6.4   Kentucky Self-Proving Affidavit Clause

I, _____, the testator, sign my name to this instrument this _____ day of _____, 20____, and being first duly sworn, do hereby declare to the undersigned authority that I sign and execute this instrument as my last will and that I sign it willingly (or willingly direct another to sign for me), that I execute it as my free and voluntary act for the purposes therein expressed, and that I am eighteen (18) years of age or older, of sound mind, and under no constraint or undue influence.

_____
TESTATOR

We, _____ and _____, the witnesses, sign our names to this instrument, being first duly sworn, and do hereby declare to the undersigned authority that the testator signs and executes this instrument as his last will and that he signs it willingly (or willingly directs another to sign for him), and that each of us, in the presence and hearing of the testator, and in the presence of the other subscribing witness, hereby sign this will as witness to the testator's signing, and that to the best of our knowledge the testator is eighteen (18) years of age or older, of sound mind, and under no constraint or undue influence.

WITNESSES   ADDRESSES

_____   _____

_____   _____

THE STATE OF _____)
COUNTY OF _____)
Subscribed, sworn and acknowledged before me by _____, the testator, and subscribed and sworn before me by _____ and _____, witnesses, this _____ day of _____, 20___.

_____
OFFICIAL CAPACITY OF OFFICER

_____

_____

My Commission Expires:
This form is used when it is executed at the same time the will is executed.

Source: Ky. Rev. State. Ann. § 394.225(1).

Sample Clause

The above and foregoing instrument, consisting of three (3) typewritten pages, including this page, was on the date hereof, signed by _____, the testator herein named and published and declared by him to be his last will and testament, in our presence, and we at his request and in his presence and in the presence of each other, have hereunto signed our names as witnesses and believe the testator to be 18 years of age or older, of sound mind, and under no constraint or undue influence.

_____ address _____
(Witness)

_____ address _____
(Witness)

taken in selecting the individual(s) who will assume the responsibility. Trusted, competent, and experienced family members or close personal friends, as well as professionals, with unquestioned reputations for honesty and integrity, are likely candidates. If there is an extensive digital estate, consideration should be given to someone who possesses technological knowledge to appropriately handle these assets. The testator should include a clause authorizing the personal representative to hire a designated third party who possesses the technical skills to administer the digital estate.

A variety of responsibilities may be granted under a power of attorney. They include the authority to buy, sell, and manage property, investments, or businesses; conduct financial transactions (banking, retirement, tax, insurance, etc.); assert legal claims and commence lawsuits; make gift and inheritance decisions; make assisted living and convalescent care decisions; access, use, and control digital assets and modify, delete, and/or transfer them; and the like. Some states require that a health or *medical power of attorney* be specifically identified for that purpose, sometimes called a *health care proxy*. See N.Y. Stat. Pub. Hlth. Law § 2981.5(d) as an example. This type of instrument is discussed in greater detail below.

One or several agents may be designated to act for the principal. When multiple agents are appointed, the principal should state in the document whether the co-agents can act separately and independently or must act jointly to avoid the emotional and financial costs as well as time lost to resolve possible conflicts and misunderstandings over how the principal intended the co-agents to exercise their power. When co-agents must act jointly, the soundness of their decisions is more protected, but at the cost of delays and inaction encountered when disagreements arise over the best action to take. To avoid delays and facilitate quick decision making, the document may be drafted to allow co-agents to act separately, possibly at the expense of thoughtful, effective action. An alternative approach to consider, in an effort to eliminate the potential problems stemming from appointing multiple agents, is to grant authority to one individual and provide for others as substitutes to replace the first choice when the necessity arises, e.g., in the event that he or she is unwilling or incapable to assume such responsibility. Another way to avoid the possible pitfalls of co-agency is to grant independent decision-making power to separate individuals for specific, different tasks.

Unless a power of attorney is used for a real property transaction, it is not necessary that the document be filed in a country clerk's office. The signature of the maker of the document, the *principal,* must be notarized. Several original copies of the instrument should be made to avoid confusion resulting from misplaced documents or businesses requiring original copies to complete a transaction requested by the agent.

Although not required, it is advisable to consult a lawyer about drafting a power of attorney. This can avoid costly problems, conflicts, and ambiguities that may arise in situations where high financial stakes are involved or where concerned, directly interested parties are in disagreement over the terms, conditions, or necessity of the document. Some states (Arkansas, California, Colorado, Idaho, Montana, New Mexico, Oklahoma, and Wisconsin) and the District of Columbia have adopted the Uniform Statutory Form Power of Attorney, which provides model forms to follow. Other states have enacted their own laws providing statutory "short forms" that may be used for drafting instruments for various purposes. These laws list the types of powers that may be granted, the scope of an agent's authority in various types of transactions, and other information and guidance to facilitate the execution of the document. See Minn. Stat. Ann. § 523.23(1) as an example.

Types of Powers of Attorney

Various types of powers of attorney are recognized. They differ depending on the time span covered and the breadth of authority granted in the instrument. A *non-durable* (conventional) power of attorney *starts when signed by the principal and lasts until a specified event occurs,* e.g., the principal becomes mentally incapacitated, dies, or revokes the document. This type of instrument is normally used to achieve a specific, limited purpose such as buying or selling a particular item of property or managing certain financial or business-related matters for a specified period of time.

A *durable* power of attorney *commences when signed by the principal and continues even if he or she becomes mentally incapacitated. It lasts until the principal dies or cancels the instrument.* To validly create this type of authority, the document must specifically state that the agent's power remains intact beyond the mental incapacitation of the principal. Most states have enacted the Uniform Durable Power of Attorney Act, which outlines procedures and provides forms for persons wishing to utilize this type of instrument (see Exhibit 6.7).

A third type of instrument, the *"springing"* power of attorney, is tied to specified situations (usually the principal's incapacitation) that might arise at some future date. *When the anticipated event occurs, the authority of the attorney in fact to act is triggered* and lasts until the principal dies, cancels the instrument, or the power expires upon the occurrence of a stated event or specified date being reached. A typical use of this document occurs in situations where certain financial or business transactions must be carried out at a time when the primary interested parties are not available to conduct them.

> **EXAMPLE:** Cletus and Wilma have listed their home for sale. If they are called out of town for an indefinite period, their absence may complicate and delay a potential sale. To avoid this, they could execute a springing limited power of attorney to be effective when they leave town and name a trusted friend, Beau, to handle the specific matters related to the sale of the home if the sale occurs while they are gone. The authority given to Beau would terminate when Cletus and Wilma return.

Possible Risks Surrounding a Power of Attorney

The risks a principal faces by a transfer of certain decision-making authority to another are not generally significant. Since the agent does not acquire ownership of the principal's property under the instrument, the principal remains in control of his or her own property. Also, the agent must follow the reasonable, competent instructions of the principal and the stated terms of the instrument. If the principal loses confidence in the effectiveness, competence, or trustworthiness of the agent, or decides the document no longer serves a useful or desired purpose, he or she can cancel (revoke) the instrument at any time.

As the designated representative of the principal, the agent must act in the principal's "best interest" and not take actions that benefit himself at the principal's expense. Since the agent is *a fiduciary,* he or she must adhere to strict standards of loyalty, honesty, and competence. An agent must protect the principal's property and not *commingle* his or her own assets with those of the principal. Another hedge against possible misconduct by an agent is the latter's obligation to maintain accurate, complete records of his or her activities and to supply periodic accountings of those actions to the principal. Possible risks of poor decision making by the agent can be reduced by a carefully planned and drafted instrument, i.e., a clear, comprehensive declaration of the terms and conditions of the delegation of authority, as well as thoughtful selection of a competent and trustworthy agent.

Inherent in the execution of this type of document is the possible risk the agent might abuse his or her authority if he or she acts dishonestly and engages in *self-dealing,* i.e., makes decisions that serve his or her own self-interest and not the interest of the principal. To protect against this possibility, in addition to the agent's duty to supply records and accountings to the principal, the document may provide for this information to be transmitted to a trusted third party (family member, friend, or professional) who would oversee the agent's activities and have the authority to intervene if suspicions of mismanagement or dishonesty arise.

Right-to-Die Laws and Related Advance Medical Directive Documents

State statutes and case law have established and recognized the right of a dying person to refuse extraordinary medical treatment to prolong life or the right of a person's guardian or proxy to make such a request. The development of **right-to-die laws** began with the landmark case of *Matter of Quinlan,* 70 N.J. 10, 355 A.2d 647 (1976), which involved a young woman, Karen Ann Quinlan, who had lapsed into a coma. When it became clear their daughter would not recover, her parents went to court to request that the respirator supporting Karen's breathing be removed. After a long court battle, the New Jersey Supreme Court ordered the respirator removed. The case caused the legal and medical professions to resolve their differences concerning the legal and medical positions on a person's right to die and to acknowledge and eventually to agree to grant that all persons have the right to determine their quality of life, including the right to die.

In a later case, *Cruzan v. Director, Missouri Dept. of Health,* 497 U.S. 261, 110 S.Ct. 2841, 111 L.Ed.2d 224 (1990), the U.S. Supreme Court confirmed the constitutional **right to die**. In this case the patient, Nancy Cruzan, was critically injured in a car accident, leaving her in a coma with no hope of recovery. Her family knew she would not want to live in this condition and asked the hospital to stop her tube feeding. Since Nancy had not made her wishes known in writing such as a living will, the Missouri Supreme Court rejected the family's request. The family appealed to the U.S. Supreme Court. The Court ruled that the tube could not be removed (thereby allowing the tube feeding to continue) but said it assumed the right to die existed and a competent person could refuse medical treatment as long as the wishes of the person are known and "clear and convincing evidence" of those wishes is established. The Court acknowledged that competent and incompetent persons have the same rights, except that a surrogate or agent must be named to exercise the rights for the incapacitated person, e.g., a patient such as Nancy Cruzan.

A court-appointed surrogate seeking to exercise privacy and self-determination rights of an incapacitated person was also the issue in the Terri Schiavo *right-to-die* case in Florida; see *In re Guardianship of Theresa Marie Schiavo,* Cir. Ct., Pinellas Cnty., Prob. Div., File No. 90-2908GD-003 (2000) and *In re Guardianship of Theresa Marie Schiavo,* Fla. App.Ct. 2d Dist., No. 2D00-1269 (2001). While most of us plan in advance for job, education, or family-related major life decisions, few make similar advance plans for death. Not planning for the type and extent of desired medical care as death nears leaves these wrenching, emotionally charged, end-of-life decisions to family and loved ones, already burdened with grief. The emotional trauma that can accompany failure to make advance end-of-life medical care plans is demonstrated in the Schiavo case. This tragedy started in February 1990 when Ms. Schiavo, seemingly healthy, suffered cardiac arrest that left her severely brain-damaged. Never regaining consciousness, she was cared for in nursing homes over the next eight years, fed and hydrated by tubes. Over that time, although well cared for by her husband, parents,

right-to-die laws
Cases and statutes that recognize the right to die and the right of a dying person's guardian to ask the court to substitute its judgment for that of the dying person who no longer has the mental capacity to make such a judgment.

right to die
The right of a dying person to refuse extraordinary medical treatment to prolong life.

and attending medical professionals, her condition deteriorated to a persistent, totally reflexive, vegetative state, with no cognition or awareness of her surroundings. Totally dependent on others and machines to sustain her life, medical experts concluded that no realistic expectations existed for a medical cure for her condition. Ms. Schiavo's court-appointed guardian husband petitioned the Florida court in 1998 to have the life-prolonging medical attention and procedures ended, asserting this is what she would have wanted for herself. Ms. Schiavo's parents opposed the petition. The husband, as the court-recognized surrogate decision-maker (similar to his having her *power of attorney* had she executed such a document), acting on behalf of his wife, based his request on the "substituted judgment" concept recognized under Florida law, asserting the rights of privacy and self-determination that Ms. Schiavo's medical condition precluded her from making herself. In February 2000, the trial judge, ruling in favor of the husband, found that "clear and convincing" evidence was presented to support the contention that Ms. Schiavo, in conversations and discussions with family and friends prior to being stricken, had expressed the intent and desire not to live under artificially maintained and supported life conditions, as was her state for some time, and that she would have wanted to be allowed to die naturally. The trial judge ordered these wishes be followed and the feeding tubes sustaining her life withdrawn. Ms. Schiavo's parents disagreed with the court's decision and appealed. A five-year battle between the husband and the parents ensued, involving the Florida courts, legislature and governor, federal courts, Congress, the President, and eventually the U.S. Supreme Court. The agonizing ordeal ended on March 18, 2005, when the trial court's initial ruling was finally carried out. Ms. Schiavo died 13 days after the feeding tubes were removed. Although the Schiavo case is not typical of most end-of-life medical care decision-making situations, health care and legal professionals agree the message this case carries is to take steps in advance to not only make one's intentions and desires known to others but to ensure they are actually carried out, avoiding the traumatic conflict that engulfed Terri Schiavo's family for so long.

To alleviate an individual's concern and anxiety about becoming incompetent due to aging, illness, or accident, several forms of right-to-die **advance medical directives** have been established by state legislatures. These directives allow a competent person to determine, in advance and in writing, the kind of future medical care and treatment he or she wishes to have in case he or she becomes incapacitated or terminally ill, or to appoint a surrogate, agent, or proxy to exercise his or her wishes to continue or discontinue future medical treatment. The two forms of advance directives used to make medical decisions for disabled or terminally ill persons are (1) a living will and (2) a medical power of attorney. Each state has various forms of one or both of these documents. See definitions in Exhibit 6.5. Health care and legal experts also recommend that, in addition to these formal legal documents, individuals should make their wishes known through recordable (letters, e-mail messages, diary entries, and the like) conversations and discussions with friends and family.

In an effort to provide greater consistency, stability, and certainty in making end-of-life medical decisions, the Uniform Law Commissioners promulgated an Act that addresses the problems of health care decision making and who decides when to withdraw treatment, allowing a patient to die. This Act, known as the **Uniform Health Care Decisions Act (UHCDA)**, applies to both adults and emancipated minors. An important provision of UHCDA is that it assures the validity of any advance health care directive that complies with it, regardless of when or where executed or communicated. Every state now has legislation authorizing the use of some sort of advance health care directive.

advance medical directives
Various legal documents individuals execute and use to ensure their wishes for medical care and treatment are followed after they become terminally ill and can no longer make their own decisions.

Uniform Health Care Decisions Act (UHCDA)
Uniform law issued by National Conference of Commissioners on Uniform State Laws intended to give increased consistency and stability for individuals making end-of-life medical decisions.

The Patient Self-Determination Act enacted by Congress in 1991 was created to bring the existence of the directives to the attention of the public and promote their use. The law requires health care providers who work with the Medicaid and Medicare programs to provide each patient or the patient's authorized surrogate, usually a family member, with written information about the patient's right to (1) make health care and medical treatment decisions including the use of life-support systems, (2) be informed on admission by the health care facility, e.g., the

---

EXHIBIT 6.5   Legal Terminology of Titles and Sources of Authority

Titles:

Principal
A person who permits or directs an agent to act for the principal's benefit subject to the principal's direction and control; such acts of the agent become binding on the principal.

Agent
A person authorized to act for the principal. Also called surrogate or proxy.

Attorney in fact
An agent, not necessarily an attorney, who is given authority by the principal in a written document called a power of attorney to perform certain specific acts on behalf of the principal.

Sources of Authority:

Power of attorney
A written document in which a principal appoints and authorizes an agent or attorney in fact to perform specific acts or kinds of acts on behalf of the principal and grants either a general (full) power of attorney or special (limited) power of attorney.

Durable power of attorney
A written document whereby a principal grants a power of attorney which continues to be or becomes effective in the event the principal later becomes disabled, e.g., mentally incapacitated. If the power does not take effect until the principal becomes disabled (incapacitated), the power is called a springing durable power of attorney. All states have statutes that establish the exact words required for this document (see UPC § 5-501).

Advance Medical Directives—Sources of Authority:

Living will
A written document that expresses a terminally ill person's wish to be allowed to die a natural death and not be kept alive by life-sustaining treatment. Also called advance health care directive.

Medical power of attorney
A written document that enables the principal (patient) to appoint an agent, proxy, or surrogate to make decisions for medical care when the principal becomes incapacitated and is unable to make such decisions. It may be called a durable power of attorney for health care, health care proxy, or appointment of a health care agent.

Durable power of attorney for health care
A written document signed by the principal that gives an agent the power and authority to make all medical and health care decisions which become or remain effective when the principal is disabled and unable to make the decisions.

Health care proxy
A written document in which a patient designates and authorizes a proxy, surrogate, or agent to make future medical and health care decisions if the patient becomes incapacitated. The proxy receives full information of the patient's medical condition before a decision is made.

hospital, hospice, or nursing home in which the patient resides or is being treated, of its policies concerning patient's rights, and (3) sign any of the above-mentioned advance directives for health and medical care decisions. Information on advance directives and state-specific forms is available on the Internet.

ASSIGNMENT 6.14

Does the organ donor registry in your state act as an advance directive? Does it require next-of-kin consent?

Living Will: Death with Dignity

Although it has been a long and hard-fought battle, it is apparent that constitutional and common law assure any adult person the right to refuse medical treatment, including life-sustaining treatment; however, an incompetent person, e.g., a terminally ill patient, may be unable to communicate these wishes to exercise that right. The controversial decision to withhold or withdraw medical care and treatment must be made on the patient's behalf by someone else, e.g., a family member, doctor, or other medical care provider. Legislation has been passed and the U.S. Supreme Court has issued decisions that have established guidelines for the execution and implementation of a terminally ill patient's advance written health care directives, including what is commonly known as a *living will*. Such a will states that in the event a person becomes incompetent due to a physical or mental disability with no reasonable expectation or hope for recovery, and because of the disability is unable to take part in decisions, the person can request not to be kept alive by artificial means, e.g., life-support treatment. Examples of famous public persons who have elected to make this request in their living wills are former first lady Jacqueline Kennedy Onassis and former president Richard Nixon. The purpose of the request is to relieve family members from the responsibility of making the decision, to alleviate guilt feelings on their part, and to protect the physician and health care institution from personal liability if they refrain, as requested, from using certain medical treatment. The patient can revoke the living will at any time by spoken or written directions in the presence of witnesses. Due to a preference for the appointment of a health care agent, Michigan incorporates the language of a living will into its *medical power of attorney* in the form of a health care proxy or agent. Massachusetts and New York title their advance health care directives a "health care proxy."

The living will is not part of the will a testator makes to transfer property after death. It is a separate and distinct document. To be valid in most states, the living will must either be signed by the testator and two witnesses in the presence of one another or signed by the testator and notarized. Generally, neither of the witnesses may be related to the testator; beneficiaries or heirs of the testator's estate; the attending physician; or employees of the physician, hospital, or care facility. Copies of the living will should be placed in the testator's medical record file and given to family members and the testator's personal representative. A copy should be placed with the testator's will and a notation of the will's location should be made in the letter of instructions. See Wyoming's living will in Exhibit 6.6.

Another, relatively new, type of advance medical directive is the Physician Orders for Life-Sustaining Treatment **POLST**. This document spells out precisely the kind of care an individual wants at end-of-life situations and directs family and medical professionals to follow the dying person's wishes.

POLST
A dying individual's statement specifying the type of care wanted in end-of-life situations, directing family and medical professionals to follow the stated wishes.

EXHIBIT 6.6	Wyoming Living Will

LIVING WILL DECLARATION OF WESLEY BIGSTONE

I state that this is my State of Ohio Living Will Declaration. I am of sound mind and not under or subject to duress, fraud or undue influence. I am a competent adult who understands and accepts the consequences of this action. I voluntarily declare my wish that my dying not be artificially prolonged. If I am unable to give directions regarding the use of life-sustaining treatment when I am in a terminal condition or a permanently unconscious state, I intend that this Living Will Declaration be honored by my family and physicians as the final expression of my legal right to refuse health care.

DEFINITIONS OF LEGAL & MEDICAL TERMS

Several legal and medical terms are used in this document. For convenience they are explained below.

Anatomical gift means a donation of all or part of a human body to take effect upon or after death.

Artificially or technologically supplied nutrition or hydration means the providing of food and fluids through intravenous or tube "feedings."

Cardiopulmonary resuscitation or CPR means treatment to try to restart breathing or heartbeat. CPR may be done by breathing into the mouth, pushing on the chest, putting a tube through the mouth or nose into the throat, administering medication, giving electric shock to the chest, or by other means.

Declarant means the person signing this document.

Donor Registry Enrollment Form means a form that has been designed to allow individuals to specifically register their wishes regarding organ, tissue and eye donation with the Ohio Bureau of Motor Vehicles Donor Registry.

Do Not Resuscitate or DNR Order means a medical order given by my physician and written in my medical records that cardiopulmonary resuscitation or CPR is not to be administered to me.

Health care means any medical (including dental, nursing, psychological, and surgical) procedure, treatment, intervention or other measure used to maintain, diagnose or treat any physical or mental condition.

Health Care Power of Attorney means another document that allows me to name an adult person to act as my agent to make health care decisions for me if I become unable to do so.

Life-sustaining treatment means any health care, including artificially or technologically supplied nutrition and hydration, that will serve mainly to prolong the process of dying.

Living Will Declaration or Living Will means this document that lets me specify the health care I want to receive if I become terminally ill or permanently unconscious and cannot make my wishes known.

Permanently unconscious state means an irreversible condition in which I am permanently unaware of myself and my surroundings. My physician and one other physician must examine me and agree that the total loss of higher brain function has left me unable to feel pain or suffering.

(continued)

Exhibit 6.6   (Continued)

Terminal condition or terminal illness means an irreversible, incurable and untreatable condition caused by disease, illness or injury. My physician and one other physician will have examined me and believe that I cannot recover and that death is likely to occur within a relatively short time if I do not receive life-sustaining treatment.

Health Care if I Am in a Terminal Condition. If I am in a terminal condition and unable to make my own health care decisions, I direct that my physician shall:

1. Administer no life-sustaining treatment, including CPR and artificially or technologically supplied nutrition or hydration; and

2. Withdraw such treatment, including CPR, if such treatment has started; and

3. Issue a DNR Order; and

4. Permit me to die naturally and take no action to postpone my death, providing me with only that care necessary to make me comfortable and to relieve my pain.

Health Care if I Am in a Permanently Unconscious State. If I am in a permanently unconscious state, I direct that my physician shall:

1. Administer no life-sustaining treatment, including CPR, except for the provision of artificially or technologically supplied nutrition or hydration unless, in the following paragraph, I have authorized its withholding or withdrawal; and

2. Withdraw such treatment, including CPR, if such treatment has started; and

3. Issue a DNR Order; and

4. Permit me to die naturally and take no action to postpone my death, providing me with only that care necessary to make me comfortable and to relieve my pain.

Special Instructions. By placing my initials at number 3 below, I want to

specifically authorize my physician to withhold or to withdraw artificially or technologically supplied nutrition or hydration if:

1. I am in a permanently unconscious state; and

2. My physician and at least one other physician who has examined me have determined, to a reasonable degree of medical certainty, that artificially or technologically supplied nutrition and hydration will not provide comfort to me or relieve my pain; and

3. I have placed my initials on this line: _____

Notifications. In the event my attending physician determines that life-sustaining treatment should be withheld or withdrawn, my physician shall make a reasonable effort to notify one of the persons named below, in the following order of priority:

First Contact:
Name: <u>Wesley Bigstone, Jr. (son)</u>
Address: <u>1809 Pinemeadow Drive</u>
<u>Cincinnati, Ohio 45231</u>
Telephone: <u>(513) 444-4448</u>

Second Contact:
Name: <u>Sylvia Snapp (daughter)</u>
Address: <u>8255 Hanford Lane</u>
<u>Cincinnati, Ohio 45231</u>
Telephone: <u>(513) 888-5555</u>

EXHIBIT 6.6   (Continued)

ANATOMICAL GIFT OF WESLEY BIGSTONE

In the hope that I may help others upon my death, I hereby give the following body parts:

_____   _____

for any purpose authorized by law: transplantation, therapy, research, or education.

Signed by Wesley Bigstone, donor and the following two witnesses in the presence of each other:

_____   _____
WESLEY BIGSTONE, Donor   Date Signed
DOB:

_____
WITNESS

_____
WITNESS

This is a legal document under the Uniform Anatomical Gift Act or similar laws.

NOTARY ACKNOWLEDGMENT

State of Ohio
County of Hamilton ss.

On the ___ day of _____, 20__, before me, the undersigned Notary Public, personally appeared WESLEY BIGSTONE, known to me or satisfactorily proven to be the person whose name is subscribed to the above Living Will Declaration as the Declarant, and who has acknowledged that he executed the same for the purposes expressed therein. I attest that the Declarant appears to be of sound mind and not under or subject to duress, fraud or undue influence.

My Commission Expires:

_____   _____
                                                      NOTARY PUBLIC

Medical Power of Attorney

The *medical power of attorney* is a second type of right-to-die advance directive used in place of a living will. It may be called a *durable power of attorney for health care, health care proxy,* or appointment of a health care agent. It is a written document that gives another person (agent), as a substitute for the

Exhibit 6.7   Idaho Durable Power of Attorney for Health Care

DURABLE POWER OF ATTORNEY FOR HEALTH CARE

I, [Principal], am of sound mind, and I voluntarily make this designation.

I designate [Designee], my [relationship to principal], living at [address] as my patient advocate to make care, custody, and medical treatment decisions for me in the event I become unable to participate in medical treatment decisions. If my first choice cannot serve, I designate [full name], [relationship] living at [address] to serve as patient advocate.

The determination of when I am unable to participate in medical treatment decisions shall be made by my attending physician and another physician or licensed psychologist.

In making decisions for me, my patient advocate shall follow my wishes of which he or she is aware, whether expressed orally, in a living will, or in this designation.

My patient advocate has authority to consent to or refuse treatment on my behalf, to arrange medical services for me, including admission to a hospital or nursing care facility, and to pay for such services with my funds. My patient advocate shall have access to any of my medical records to which I have a right.

OPTIONAL
I expressly authorize my patient advocate to make decisions to withhold or withdraw treatment that would allow me to die and I acknowledge such decisions could or would allow my death.

_____

(Sign your name here if you wish to give your patient advocate this authority.)

My specific wishes concerning health care are the following: (if none, write "none")
I may change my mind at any time by communicating in any manner that this designation does not reflect my wishes.

It is my intent that my family, the medical facility, and any doctors, nurses and other medical personnel involved in my care shall have no civil or criminal liability for honoring my wishes as expressed in this designation or for implementing the decisions of my patient advocate.

Photostatic copies of this document, after it is signed and witnessed, shall have the same legal force as the original document.

I sign this document after careful consideration. I understand its meaning and I accept its consequences.

Signed: _____ Date: _____
Address:

Exhibit 6.7 (Continued)

NOTICE REGARDING WITNESSES

You must have two adult witnesses who will not receive your assets when you die (whether you die with or without a will), and who are not your spouse, child, grandchild, brother or sister, an employee of a company through which you have life or health insurance, or an employee at the health care facility where you are a patient.

STATEMENT OF WITNESSES

We sign below as witnesses. This declaration was signed in our presence. The declarant appears to be of sound mind, and to be making this designation voluntarily, without duress, fraud or undue influence.

Signature of witness: _____

_____
(Print or type full name of witness)

Address: _____

_____

Signature of witness:_____

_____
(Print or type full name of witness)

Address: _____

_____

ACCEPTANCE BY PATIENT ADVOCATE

(A) This designation shall not become effective unless the patient is unable to participate in treatment decisions.

(B) A patient advocate shall not exercise powers concerning the patient's care, custody and medical treatment that the patient, if the patient were able to participate in the decision, could not have exercised in his or her own behalf.

(C) This designation cannot be used to make a medical treatment decision to withhold or withdraw treatment from a patient who is pregnant that would result in the pregnant patient's death.

(D) A patient advocate may make a decision to withhold or withdraw treatment that would allow a patient to die only if the patient has expressed in a clear and convincing manner that the patient advocate is authorized to make such a decision, and that the patient acknowledges that such a decision could or would allow the patient's death.

(E) A patient advocate shall not receive compensation for the performance of his or her authority, rights, and responsibilities, but a patient advocate may be reimbursed for actual and necessary expenses incurred in the performance of his or her authority, rights, and responsibilities.

(F) A patient advocate shall act in accordance with the standards of care applicable to fiduciaries when acting for the patient and shall act consistent with the patient's best interests. The known desires of the patient expressed or evidenced while the patient is able to participate in medical treatment decisions are presumed to be in the patient's best interests.

(continued)

EXHIBIT 6.7   (Continued)

(G) A patient may revoke his or her designation at any time or in any manner sufficient to communicate an intent to revoke.

(H) A patient advocate may revoke his or her acceptance to the designation at any time and in any manner sufficient to communicate an intent to revoke.

(I) A patient admitted to a health facility or agency has the rights enumerated in Section 20201 of the Public Health Code, Act No. 368 of the Public Acts of 1978, being section 333.20201 of the Michigan Compiled Laws.

I understand the above conditions and I accept the designation as patient advocate for [Principals' Name].

Dated: _____ Signed: _____
                                              PATIENT ADVOCATE

patient (principal), the power and authority to make all decisions relating to the performance of medical and health care treatment by health care providers such as doctors, surgeons, and nurses. Some states use the term *durable power of attorney for health care* for their medical power of attorney. A person granted a *durable power of attorney* does more than simply act as an agent for another. Instead, the durable power of attorney for health care allows the authorized designated agent not only to make health care and medical decisions in place of the patient (principal) when the patient is disabled and unable to make such decisions but also to direct the withholding or withdrawal of such care and life-sustaining treatment. These decisions are based on current medically known facts and the wishes of the patient, even though he or she is incompetent. The durable power of attorney for health care document also gives the designated agent the right to (1) employ and discharge health care personnel (doctors, nurses, etc.); (2) obtain and disclose the principal's medical records; and (3) select the health care facility, e.g., elder care, nursing home, or hospital, as the appropriate residence for the principal based on the level of need for medical care and assistance. Unlike the living will, which is limited to situations where the principal (patient) has a terminal condition due to illness or injury and death is imminent, the durable power of attorney for health care has no such limitation, has a broader grant of authority, and gives the patient a wider range to exercise self-determination.

All states, except Alaska, have statutes that authorize an agent, also called a proxy or surrogate. Alaska does have a durable power of attorney, but it does not cover end-of-life decisions; therefore, a living will is required. Idaho's durable power of attorney for health care appears in Exhibit 6.7.

ASSIGNMENT 6.15

Does an advance directive containing end-of-life instructions, e.g., do not resuscitate, and an election for organ donation cause a conflict? Does one invalidate the other?

WHERE TO KEEP THE WILL

The will should be kept in a safe and accessible location. It is good practice to include the location of the will in the letter of instructions. The will itself is often kept in one of four places: (1) in the lawyer's office vault, which was the traditional practice but not commonly done today; (2) with the client, the most frequent location today since it is readily available for review (good choices would be a fireproof metal box or family safe at the client's home or office); (3) in a personal safe deposit box in a bank; or (4) filed with the clerk of the appropriate probate court, which is allowed in a few states. If the choice for safekeeping a will is the latter, anyone holding the receipt issued for the filed will and signed by the testator may obtain the original will while the testator is living. After the testator's death, the probate court retains the original will and gives copies to the personal representative (see UPC § 2–515).

A will kept in a personal safe deposit box is less desirable because it makes the will less accessible. This is also the case if the will is filed. If the will is in a safe deposit box, probate proceedings may be delayed. Ordinarily, a person must have permission from the state tax commission representative or a county treasurer to open the safe deposit box belonging to another. Generally, when the safe deposit box is rented in the decedent's name only, bank representatives will seal the box when they are notified of the person's death after first removing the will if it is known that the box contains the will. However, once the box is sealed, a court order is often required to open the box to remove the will (see the Petition and Order to Open Safe Deposit Box in Exhibit 6.8). After the will is removed, the box is resealed. Depending on the state in which the testator resides, one of the following procedures is advisable.

1. If the testator lives in a state in which the county treasurer or the state tax representative does not have to be present when the safe deposit box is opened, the box should be rented in the names of the testator and the testator's spouse or another person as joint tenants. Whenever either spouse dies, the other may open the box. Widows, widowers, or single parents may want to name themselves and an adult child as the joint tenants for the same reason.

2. If the testator lives in a state in which the county treasurer or the state tax representative must be present, the testator should put the will in a safe deposit box rented in the name of the testator's spouse. Upon the testator's death, the testator's will is readily accessible.

If the safe deposit box is placed in joint tenancy between spouses or others, the joint owners must remember to state in detail on the bank account cards whether or not the joint tenants also share ownership of all the contents in the box and not just access to it. For further discussion on opening a safe deposit box, see Item 19 in Chapter 9.

Leaving the will with the testator's lawyer with whom the testator is familiar and has had a long time working relationship based on confidence and trust makes for easy access and convenient periodic review of the will whenever the testator wishes. A request for the review should be initiated by the testator and *not solicited by the attorney or paralegal.*

⚖ *Ethical Issue*

EXHIBIT 6.8   Petition and Order to Open a Safe Deposit Box

Approved, SCAO   JIS CODE: DBP, DBO

STATE OF MICHIGAN PROBATE COURT COUNTY OF _____	PETITION AND ORDER TO OPEN SAFE-DEPOSIT BOX TO LOCATE WILL OR BURIAL DEED	FILE NO.

USE NOTE: File this petition in the county where the safe-deposit box is located.

Estate of _____

PETITION

1. I, _____, am interested in the decedent's estate and make this
   Name

   petition as _____.
   Relationship to decedent, i.e. heir, devisee, etc.

2. Decedent died _____, domiciled in _____.
   Date   County and state or other jurisdiction

3. _____, as lessor, leased to decedent, alone or jointly, safe
   Name of bank, trust company, or safe-deposit company

   deposit box number _____ , located at _____ in _____ in this
   Branch   City or township

   county, and the safe-deposit box may contain decedent's will and/or a deed to a burial plot in which the decedent is to be interred.

4. **I REQUEST** that this court issue an order directing the lessor to permit _____
   Name

   to examine the contents of the safe-deposit box in the presence of an officer or other authorized employee of lessor for the purpose of locating and removing a will and/or a deed to a burial plot only.

I declare under the penalties of perjury that this petition has been examined by me and that its contents are true to the best of my information, knowledge, and belief.

_____
Date

_____	_____
Attorney signature	Petitioner signature
_____	_____
Name (type or print) Bar no.	Name (type or print)
_____	_____
Address	Address
_____	_____
City, state, zip Telephone no.	City, state, zip Telephone no.

ORDER

IT IS ORDERED:

5. The above petition is granted and the lessor is ordered to permit _____ to examine the safe-deposit box described above in the presence of an officer or other authorized employee of the lessor. Only a will of the decedent and/or a deed to a burial plot shall be removed from the box and shall be delivered by the person named above to the probate register or deputy register of this court.

6. At the time of the opening of the safe-deposit box, all persons in attendance shall execute a written statement certifying whether a will and/or a deed to a burial plot was found and that no other items were removed from the safe-deposit box. The person named above shall file that written statement with the probate register or deputy register of this court within 7 days of opening the box. If no safe-deposit box is located, the person named above shall filvve a written statement indicating that no box was found.

_____   _____
Date   Judge   Bar no.

Do not write below this line - For court use only

PC 551 (9/11)   **PETITION AND ORDER TO OPEN SAFE-DEPOSIT BOX TO LOCATE WILL OR BURIAL DEED**   MCL 700.2517

ASSIGNMENT 6.16

1. Explain your position on a living will, health care proxy, and a durable power of attorney for health care. Are you in favor of any of them or not? Has your state passed any of these directives?

2. In your state, must a doctor or hospital follow the patient's requests that are written in a living will? If they are required to honor the requests, are there any exceptions? Discuss these questions with your family physician.

3. Are patients who execute a living will in your state allowed to designate a proxy? Who would you select as your proxy? Why?

4. Must a patient hire a lawyer to make a valid living will, a health care proxy, or a durable power of attorney? If not, why might the patient choose to have a lawyer draft these directives?

5. If you execute a valid living will in your home state and then move your domicile (home) to another state that has no living will statute, will your wishes in the living will be honored in your new domicile? Explain.

6. Draft a living will. Obtain your state's living will form and compare it to your draft. How do they differ? How are they similar? Also draft and execute forms for a health care proxy and a durable power of attorney for health care and compare them to your state's forms, if any.

Key Terms

exordium clause

revocation clause

memorandum

residuary clause

fiduciary

simultaneous death clause

testimonium clause

attestation clause

affidavit

notary public

self-proving affidavit [clause]

self-proved will

power of attorney

principal

agent

attorney in fact

general power of attorney

limited power of attorney

right-to-die laws

right to die

advance medical directives

Uniform Health Care Decisions Act (UHCDA)

Physician Orders for Life-Sustaining Treatment (POLST)

defeasible

Review Questions

1. What is the purpose of the following clauses of a will? Exordium, Revocation, Residuary, Simultaneous death, Testimonium, and Attestation.

2. If a testator uses more than one name or alias when signing written statements or documents, is it necessary to include all such names in the will? Explain.

3. How does any person who wishes to donate body organs accomplish that purpose both within a will and using other nontestamentary documents?

4. According to your state statute, if any, who may make an anatomical gift in addition to the testator-decedent?

5. When a testator has numerous items of tangible personal property to leave to an equal number of beneficiaries, how can this be accomplished and ensured that they are distributed to the desired recipients without writing them directly into the will?

6. Confusion exists in the law of wills concerning the use of the words *issue, child, heirs, descendants,*

and adopted, natural, nonmarital, and stepchildren. How would you avoid this confusion when drafting a client's will?

7. If there is no residuary clause in a will and not all the testator's estate is distributed to named beneficiaries, how and to whom would such property be distributed?

8. How are personal representatives appointed (authorized to act)? In general, what are the powers granted to them?

9. What is the difference between a property guardian and a conservator?

10. Does your state have any requirements for the placement of the testator's signature on the will? Are initials, a nickname, electronic signature, or simply an "X" valid signatures in your state?

11. Which of the statutory requirements of a will is eliminated by the self-proving affidavit or the self-proved will?

12. What are the purposes of the two kinds of advance medical directives, i.e., the living will and the medical power of attorney? How do these directives differ?

13. Where is the best place to keep your will?

Case Problems

Problem 1

Hans Heidelberger died testate. He owned a considerable amount of property and made many specific legacies and devises to numerous relatives and friends. However, his will had no residue clause. In the will, Hans specifically disinherited by name his only two children. A number of very valuable stock certificates and bonds that Hans owned were not included as gifts in the will. Answer and explain the following:

A. Through what process and to whom will the valuable stocks and bonds be distributed?

B. Since Hans specifically stated that his two children were not to receive any of his estate, does that provision of the will bar them from receiving an interest in the stocks and bonds? See *Ferguson v. Croom, 73 N.C.App. 316, 326 S.E.2d 373 (1985).*

Problem 2

While on a weekend trip, Stewart and Patricia Kincaid and their two minor children die simultaneously in a plane crash.

Two adult children, Frank and Ruth, living at home, are the surviving family members. The major asset Stewart owned was a life insurance policy worth over $500,000 payable to Patricia as the primary beneficiary and to all four children as the secondary beneficiaries. The Kincaids live in a state that has adopted the Uniform Simultaneous Death Act. Under the act, when the insured policyholder (Stewart) and the beneficiary (Patricia) die simultaneously, the life insurance proceeds are distributed as if the insured has survived the beneficiary.

A. To whom would the life insurance proceeds be paid? How is this decision determined?

B. If all six members of the Kincaid family had died in the crash, to whom would the life insurance proceeds be paid? Explain. See *Keegan v. Keegan's Estate, 157 N.J.Super.279, 384 A.2d 913 (1978).*

C. If Stewart and Patricia had owned property in joint tenancy, how does the Uniform Simultaneous Death Act resolve the problem of dividing the jointly owned property?

Practical Assignments

1. Draft a clause to be included in your power of attorney that provides authorization to use, access, control, and manage digital assets.

2. Find a free will template on the Internet. Compare this to the will contained in Exhibit 6.3, Last Will and Testament of Leona Bayn Farrell. Does the free template cover all of the provisions that Leona Farrell requested? Why or why not?

3. Assume that a member of your family has passed away without providing any instructions on the disposition of their body. Determine, according to your state law, who has authority to make the decision regarding the disposition of the body.

THE PARTICIPANTS AND THE PROPER COURT

7

Outline

Objectives

After completing this chapter, you should be able to:

- Identify the participants who are essential for drafting wills and trusts and for administering the estate of a decedent and explain their basic functions.

- Identify the proper court that supervises the administration and distribution of a decedent's estate.

- Explain what is meant by probate and jurisdiction.

- Identify the various elements of jurisdiction required by a specific court, such as the probate court.

- Determine the proper place (county/state) to commence probate proceedings of a decedent's estate.

- Recognize the necessity for establishing a second or ancillary administration of a decedent's estate when property of the decedent is located in another state.

SCOPE OF THE CHAPTER

Many different participants are involved in the creation of wills and trusts and the administration of estates. This chapter reviews the basic functions of these participants and describes the role of the proper court in the administration of an estate. Important terms associated with the selection and function of the court, such as probate, jurisdiction, domicile, venue, and ancillary administration, are defined and explained in the second half of the chapter.

THE PARTICIPANTS

The following people are involved in the preparation of wills and trusts and the administration of a decedent's estate: the personal representative of the estate, an attorney, a paralegal, the probate court (judge), the registrar, and the clerk. We begin our discussion by examining the functions of each of these participants.

The Personal Representative

The personal representative is a person or corporate institution, such as a bank or trust department, appointed by a proper court, often called the probate court, to administer the estate of a decedent who died with or without a will. As a fiduciary, a person who serves in a position of trust and loyalty, a personal representative has obligations called "fiduciary duties" to act in good faith solely for the benefit of another person. Trustees, guardians, and conservators are three other types of fiduciaries commonly appointed by will. Personal representatives act for the beneficiaries or heirs of the estate; trustees act for beneficiaries of trusts; guardians act for minors; and conservators act for incompetent persons.

In most cases, before executing the final draft of the will, the testator asks the prospective personal representative if he or she is willing to serve. Even if the person agrees, he or she has a right to change his or her mind and reject the position before being appointed or resign the position after appointment by the probate court. *Note*: The personal representative can also be a beneficiary or heir of the decedent's estate.

Most personal representatives are family members or friends who accept their appointments. The knowledge that the court and professional assistance (an attorney and you, the paralegal) are available to help complete the necessary tasks can help reluctant personal representatives overcome their anxiety about dealing with matters that are unfamiliar to them.

digital executor
The representative of an estate who is responsible to manage the digital assets of the estate.

Some propose that it may be beneficial for the testator to appoint a separate personal representative, known as the **digital executor**, to serve over the digital estate. This is especially true if the named primary executor has limited technology skills. In most states, a digital executor is not a legally binding or enforceable designation. Unless the personal representative has not been granted authority over the digital assets in the will, a conflict could arise between the personal representative and the digital executor. To avoid any potential conflicts, the personal representative could select and hire a third party to deal with the digital assets. This enables the personal representative to maintain control and responsibility over the management of the digital assets.

Appropriate Terminology

If the personal representative named in the will is a man, he is traditionally called the executor; if a woman, she is the executrix.

> **EXAMPLE:** Howard dies with a will. He names his sister, Nanette, as his personal representative to administer his estate and distribute his property according to the terms of his will. Nanette is Howard's personal representative or executrix. If Howard had named the First National Bank's trust department as his personal representative to administer his estate, the bank would be his personal representative or executor.

If there is no will, the court appoints the personal representative, traditionally called an administrator (man) or administratrix (woman).

> **EXAMPLE:** Howard dies without a will. The probate court appoints his sister, Nanette, to oversee the distribution of his estate to his heirs as determined by state law. Nanette is Howard's personal representative or administratrix.

Generally, executors and administrators perform similar duties, face similar liabilities, and hold similar powers. Many states now use the term *personal representative* instead of executor or administrator, and this practice will be followed here. Throughout this book, any person (man or woman) who administers the estate of a decedent will be referred to as a personal representative, whether the decedent died with or without a will. The various types of personal representatives and the fiduciary duties they perform are discussed in detail in Chapter 8.

The Role of the Personal Representative

Although state statutes often grant numerous fiduciary powers to personal representatives, usually the powers are limited to those stated explicitly in the will or incorporated into the will by reference to a statute authorizing them. As an example, see Section 3-715 of the Uniform Probate Code, which lists 27 transactions the personal representative can perform. You should review these functions carefully.

Generally, the role of the personal representative is

- to probate the will or petition for estate administration when there is no will. To collect, protect, preserve, and manage the probate estate of the decedent. To publish notice to creditors to submit their claims by a specific date.

- to pay all federal and state taxes and approved creditor claims.

- to distribute the remaining assets to the beneficiaries named in the will or to the decedent's heirs if no will exists.

- to refrain from engaging in acts of self-dealing, often referred to as the duty of loyalty; e.g., *the personal representative cannot borrow, sell, or buy estate property. It may be appropriate for you to remind the personal representative of this duty.*

 *Ethical Issue*

- to commence a civil lawsuit for claims on behalf of the estate or to defend the estate against claims brought by creditors or disgruntled family members.

- *to keep all collected estate assets separate from the personal representative's own assets,* i.e., to not commingle these assets.

 *Ethical Issue*

⚖ *Ethical Issue*

- *to not delegate the management of the probate estate or these fiduciary duties to others.* Obviously, this does not prevent the personal representative from selecting and hiring professional advisers (an attorney, a paralegal, or one with technical knowledge, such as a digital executor) to help perform these duties.

Circumstances may arise that make the personal representative's task more difficult. Some problems that may occur include the following:

- A beneficiary or heir cannot be found.
- A beneficiary or heir challenges the personal representative's appointment or authority to act and proposes an alternate candidate.
- Someone contests the will.
- Someone challenges the personal representative's payment to creditors or distributions to beneficiaries or heirs.
- Passwords to digital assets are not known.

The court will ultimately resolve these problems, but they may cause lengthy delays in the estate administration and add considerable expense that depletes the assets of the estate.

The personal representative distributes only the probate property of the decedent's estate, i.e., the assets that are disposed of by will or that descend as intestate property. The personal representative does not have administrative power to distribute nonprobate property such as jointly owned property, the proceeds from an insurance policy payable to a named beneficiary other than the decedent's estate, and the like. Statutes generally require that the personal representative report all the property (probate and nonprobate) in the estate for tax purposes. These tax requirements will be discussed in Chapter 11.

Pre-Probate Duties of the Personal Representative

Neither this list of the personal representative's duties nor the lists in the following sections are intended to be all-inclusive. Not only do these duties vary from state to state, many aspects of estate administration depend on the provisions of the will, if one exists, and the amount and nature of the assets the decedent owned. The personal representative will generally perform these tasks with the advice of an attorney and your assistance, which will be discussed in more detail in Chapters 8 and 9. The following are the main tasks of the personal representative prior to probate.

1. Upon request, assist with anatomical gifts and funeral arrangements. Obtain copies of the death certificate from the funeral director.

2. Although not mandatory, the personal representative generally hires an attorney to *represent the estate* and to help with its administration.

3. Help find and review any existing will.

4. Contact all of the decedent's financial advisers to obtain information about business records, papers, a safe deposit box, and the like.

⚖ *Ethical Issue*

5. Convene a conference of family members and other interested persons to discuss the provisions of the will or intestate laws, election rights, immediate financial needs, maintenance, and similar matters. Advise a surviving spouse

of *the right to obtain his or her own attorney and elect against the will.* Determine whether fiduciaries (guardians or conservators) are needed for minors and incompetent persons.

6. Locate and notify witnesses of the testator's death.

7. Discontinue the telephone and other utilities if advantageous and notify the post office to forward mail to the address of the personal representative. Stop newspaper and other deliveries.

8. Determine the appropriate probate proceedings—solemn (formal) or common (informal). See the discussion in Chapters 9 and 10.

Probate Duties Prior to Appointment as Personal Representative

The personal representative is expected to file all required legal documents, petitions, and accounts, as discussed in detail in Chapters 8 and 9. Before being formally appointed, the personal representative should attend to the following:

1. Petition for probate of the will or for general administration if there is no will and, in either case, for appointment of the personal representative (out-of-state property may require ancillary administration, see later discussion in this chapter).

2. Give notice of the decedent's death and notice of the date for the hearing to probate the will and for appointment of the personal representative to beneficiaries, heirs, creditors, and other interested persons.

3. Notify the surviving spouse and minor children of their rights.

Estate Administration Duties from Appointment to Closing of the Estate

The personal representative will perform the following tasks in administering the estate.

1. Obtain from the court the **Letters Testamentary** or **Letters of Administration** that establish the authority of the personal representative and file an oath of office as personal representative. Letters are one-page certificates of appointment authorizing the personal representative to act on behalf of the decedent's estate in performing the tasks of estate administration.

2. Arrange for a **bond** with **surety,** if necessary. Unless a state statute requires a bond, it may be waived in the will.

3. Apply for an Employer Identification Number (Form SS-4).

4. Open an estate checking account.

5. Open the decedent's safe deposit box.

6. Defend the estate against will contests.

7. Discuss the need for survivors to draft or rewrite their own wills and review their health and life insurance.

8. Protect, collect, and preserve assets.

   a. Find and review all documents, records, digital assets and papers (e.g., business records, checkbooks, tax returns, pension plans, insurance policies, domain names) concerning the decedent's financial affairs. Notify local banks of the decedent's

letters testamentary
The formal document of authority and appointment given to a personal representative (executor) by the proper court to carry out the administration of the decedent's estate according to the terms of a will.

letters of administration
The formal document of authority and appointment given to a personal representative (administrator) by the proper court to carry out the administration of the decedent's estate according to the proper state intestate succession statute.

bond
A certificate whereby a surety company promises to pay money if the personal representative of a deceased fails to faithfully perform the duties of administering the decedent's estate. The bond is the contract that binds the surety.

surety
An individual or insurance company that, at the request of a personal representative, agrees to pay money up to the amount of a bond in the event that the personal representative fails to faithfully perform his or her duties.

death and request information on accounts or an unknown safe deposit box. Determine whether a digital inventory was prepared.

b. Take possession of all personal property not set aside for the spouse and/or minor children and transfer all cash from such sources as savings and checking accounts, life insurance payable to the estate, and dividends from securities into the new estate checking account.

c. Inspect the condition of all real estate and review all written documents, including promissory notes, leases, mortgages, and deeds. Arrange for security, management, and collection of rents and pay insurance premiums, rent, and other obligations.

d. Determine the form of ownership of all real and personal property.

e. Protect both real and personal property with adequate and appropriate kinds of insurance coverage (obtain confirmation in writing) and keep all property in reasonable repair. Place valuable personal property in a new estate safe deposit box or vault.

f. Collect information on all nonprobate assets to be used later in preparing tax returns, e.g., property in joint tenancy or trusts and other assets designated for a named beneficiary (e.g., life insurance, IRA, and pension plans).

g. Collect all debts, including family debts owed to the decedent, and place the funds in the estate account. Contact the decedent's employer and collect any amounts owed to the decedent, such as unpaid salary, bonus, and vacation pay. Make sure the decedent was not involved in any pending litigation. If the decedent or the estate is entitled to sue others, e.g., debtors and the like, then the personal representative must perform these tasks.

h. File claims for any Social Security, veterans' pension benefits, and the like to which the decedent's estate is entitled.

i. Determine whether the decedent made any gifts for which a gift tax return must be filed.

j. Determine whether ancillary administration of out-of-state assets is necessary and make appropriate arrangements for such administration when required (see the discussion under Ancillary Administration later in the chapter).

9. Ascertain whether the decedent owned any business (sole proprietorship or partnership) and determine whether the business should be liquidated, sold, or continued. Arrange proper management for the business as needed.

10. Review all securities (stocks and bonds) and collect all interest and dividends, make decisions on proper investments, and determine whether any of these assets will have to be liquidated to pay administration expenses, taxes, or creditors' claims.

11. Once the assets are determined and collected, inventory and make arrangements to have all assets appraised according to their value at the date of the decedent's death or the alternate valuation date.

12. Distribute family allowances, including support and maintenance to the surviving spouse and/or minor children, as determined by statute.

13. Examine all claims made against the estate; determine their reasonableness, timeliness, validity, and priority; defend the estate against any improper claims.

14. Defend the estate against any litigation filed against it.

15. Pay all allowed claims against the estate according to their statutory priority.

16. Prepare and file all necessary federal and state tax returns and pay all taxes due.

17. Terminate the ancillary administration, if one exists, and pay any debts or taxes due.

18. Obtain and keep detailed records of all receipts (income) and vouchers for all disbursements (expenses and debt payments) and prepare all necessary data for the final accounting, listing assets, receipts, disbursements, and sales (if any), noting any gains or losses, and providing a reconciliation of beginning and ending balances.

19. Obtain court approval of attorney's and personal representative's fees.

20. Distribute proper title to remaining assets of the estate to beneficiaries according to the will or to heirs according to the intestate statute.

21. After the final accounting, obtain approval of the settlement of the estate and a discharge of the personal representative by order of the court.

22. Cancel the personal representative's bond, if one was necessary, with the surety (bonding) company, claim any refund, and close the estate.

The Attorney

In many cases the personal representative appointed by the decedent will lack the knowledge, experience, or expertise to handle the complexities of estate administration. For this reason, the personal representative generally requests the assistance of an attorney. Once the attorney is hired, you also will begin your tasks.

Potential ethical problems, of which you, too, must be aware, arise for the supervising attorney who is hired to draft the will *whenever the following occur.*

⚖️ *Ethical Issue*

1. The attorney or attorney's family is named a beneficiary in the will. The case of *In re Peterson's Estate*, 283 Minn. 446, 168 N.W.2d 502 (1969), illustrates this problem.

    Grace Peterson, a 74-year-old spinster asked her attorney, Chester Gustafson, to draft her will. Over several years, the attorney prepared seven wills and a codicil for Peterson, with the last will leaving her entire estate to Gustafson's children. Peterson died, and Gustafson sought to have the last will probated.

    • Issue: Is a will valid when the entire estate is left to the family of the attorney who drew the will?

    • Decision: No, said the Minnesota Supreme Court. The will was a product of the attorney's undue influence and cannot be probated.

    Rule 1.8(c) of the Model Rules of Professional Conduct provides that an attorney cannot seek a significant gift from a client, including a testamentary one, or draft a document for a client or a relative in which the attorney is given a significant gift unless the attorney or other recipient of the gift is a relative of the client. Such relatives include a spouse, child, grandchild, parent, grandparent, or other person who has a close, familial relationship with the attorney or client.

In Comment (6) clarifying the interpretation and application of Rule 1.8(c), attorneys are allowed to accept a gift from a client if the transaction is fair, e.g., a holiday or "thank you" gift. More substantial gifts are allowable but can be avoided by the client under the doctrine of undue influence, which views these types of client gifts as presumptively fraudulent. Acknowledging issues concerning overreaching and imposition on clients, an attorney receiving a gift under the above circumstances should be careful to ensure that the transaction complies with the provisions of Rule 1.8 (c).

> **EXAMPLE:** Attorney John Edwards drafts a will for Elizabeth Thompson, the mother of John's wife, Sarah Edwards. In the will, Elizabeth leaves her lake cottage in Maine to her daughter, Sarah Edwards. This gift would be ethically acceptable.

2. The attorney is named in the will to be the personal representative.

3. The attorney is named in the will as the testator's choice to assist the personal representative.

⚖️ *Ethical Issue*

Both situations 2 and 3 raise a serious ethical issue. In each case, the appointment would be financially rewarding to the attorney, especially when the compensation is a percentage of the estate. For this reason, *the attorney or paralegal must not solicit or suggest either appointment to the client.*

A leading case on these issues is *State v. Gulbankian*, 54 Wis.2d 605, 196 N.W.2d 733 (1972), in which the Wisconsin Supreme Court stated

> It is clear an attorney cannot solicit either directly or by any indirect means a request or direction of a testator that he or a member of his firm be named executor or be employed as an attorney to probate the estate . . . . An attorney, merely because he drafts a will, has no preferential claim to probate it.
> A lawyer must not only avoid solicitation but also the appearance of solicitation so as not to damage the confidence the public has in the legal profession.

The Wisconsin court added that a lawyer may draft a will that names him or her as executor *if that* is the *unprompted* intent of the client. The court also observed that testators rarely name the attorney who drafts the will to be their personal representative or to assist the personal representative.

Furthermore, even when the will recommends an attorney to assist in probating the estate, that attorney may not be the one to do so. The personal representative of the estate has the sole discretion to select the attorney and is under no obligation to choose the one named in the will.

⚖️ *Ethical Issue*

Having been retained to help the personal representative settle an estate, the attorney has a duty to inform the beneficiaries or heirs of the estate that the attorney represents and works for the estate while advising the personal representative and not individually for them. In case of conflict, such as when named beneficiaries to the will want to sue the estate, they must hire their own attorney. *They cannot retain the attorney who is representing the estate because that would create a conflict of interest for the attorney.* The attorney, like the personal representative, has a fiduciary responsibility, a basic duty of loyalty to the client (the estate), and cannot become involved in a situation where a conflict may develop or where the attorney has a personal interest in the outcome of the proceedings.

ASSIGNMENT 7.1

Sharon, the personal representative of her father's estate, hires Tamara Colby, an attorney, to help administer the estate. The will names all of Sharon's brothers and sisters beneficiaries except Charles. Charles intends to contest the will. Answer the following questions with yes or no and explain your position according to your state's statutory code for wills *and* the Model Rules of Professional Conduct.

1. Can Charles hire Tamara to represent him in the will contest?

2. If Tamara and Sharon's father were business partners, can Tamara accept the position offered by Sharon?

3. Can the attorney who drafted the will act as the attorney for the estate?

4. Charles owns his own business. On occasion, he has retained Tamara to handle various legal problems for the business. The business has no legal actions pending at this time. Can Tamara accept the position offered by Sharon?

POINT OF INTEREST

The Public Is Using the Internet to Locate an Attorney

The marketing of legal services on the Internet has exploded. Many attorneys and law firms have a Web page advertising their services. The firm's address, telephone number, and other vital information are often listed. Photographs and profiles of firm employees are a popular feature. A creative page will allow the prospective client to communicate with the firm, request information, or e-mail a question.

Two sites that assist clients in locating attorneys are *http://www.findlaw.com* and http://www.martindale.com. Find Law advertises its directory as the Web's most useful. The lawyer locator directory information published by Martindale Hubbell is extensive. Most online directories allow a user to search for an attorney by name, city, state, or area of practice.

The Paralegal or Legal Assistant

As the legal assistant, you must act under the direction and supervision of an attorney and cannot give legal advice. Many tasks must be performed when drafting wills and trusts and administering decedents' estates, but not all of them must be handled personally by an attorney. The specific duties you will perform when assisting the attorney and the personal representative in estate administration will be discussed in later chapters. The next paragraphs provide a brief overview of your tasks in wills, trusts, and estate administration.

Wills

Your tasks concerning wills include the following:

1. Collect all data and information necessary for making a client's will, including helping the client complete questionnaires and handling all communication (phone calls, letter writing, and interviews) to obtain the required information.

2. After reviewing the client's financial information, discuss with the attorney the contents of the will. You should be prepared to discuss such topics as the need to incorporate trusts; tax considerations, including methods of reducing taxes; the identification and clarification of all assets; and the beneficiaries to whom the property is to be distributed according to the client's wishes.

3. Prepare a preliminary draft of the will.

4. Review the draft with your attorney and the client and make any corrections, additions, deletions, or modifications necessary to avoid inconsistencies and ensure that the will reflects the wishes of the client.

5. Assist in the execution of the final draft of the will.

Trusts

The following are your main tasks in relation to trusts.

1. Obtain from the client data and information needed for the creation of a trust (e.g., the purpose of the trust, parties, property to be transferred, powers of the trustee, distributions of income and principal, and tax considerations).

2. Draft a preliminary trust.

3. Review the preliminary draft with your supervising attorney and the client and make corrections, additions, deletions, or modifications as necessary.

4. Assist in the final execution of the trust.

Estate Administration

Your *pre-probate tasks* in estate administration generally include the following:

1. If requested, help locate the will, if one exists.

2. Set up a family conference and notify all family members and beneficiaries or heirs.

3. Assist in reviewing the will or intestacy procedures with the family and beneficiaries of the will or the heirs of the intestate.

4. Explain the **"tickler" system** and probate procedures to the client.

5. Set up the "tickler" system with the personal representative and prepare for the maintenance and monitoring of the procedures (e.g., dates for filing, correspondence, and filing of documents).

Probate tasks include the following:

1. Help locate, collect, preserve, and maintain assets and ensure that *estate assets are not commingled with other assets of the law firm.*

2. Handle communication (phone calls, letter writing, and personal interviews) with parties holding assets (e.g., insurance companies, banks), creditors, beneficiaries, and heirs. *None of your communications may contain legal advice, and any information you receive must remain confidential.*

3. Assist in preparing preliminary drafts of legal documents (forms) associated with estate administration.

"tickler" system
A chronological list of all the important steps and dates in the stages of the administration of the decedent's estate.

 *Ethical Issue*

 *Ethical Issue*

4. Maintain records of all collected assets (filing of documents, creditors' claims, and the like).

5. Prepare an inventory and appraisal of all probate assets and also list all nonprobate property and its value for federal and state death tax purposes.

6. Prepare preliminary drafts of final estate accounts and necessary tax returns.

7. Record the payment of debts and taxes due.

8. File legal documents (from the original petition to the final account).

9. File tax returns after review with the attorney.

Your handling of such tasks frees the attorney from the time-consuming but important details of estate administration, thus decreasing the cost of legal services. You are responsible for seeing that these matters move smoothly and chronologically. By doing so, you can handle queries that do not involve the dispensing of legal advice and can indirectly improve attorney–client rapport by allowing the attorney more time to advise the client. The ethical conduct required of paralegals when performing these tasks under the supervision of an attorney is discussed throughout the text. Exhibit 7.1 summarizes the duties a paralegal can and cannot perform.

The Probate Court

Another participant with an essential role in the administration of a decedent's estate is the judge. The words *court* and *judge* are frequently used synonymously in statutes and in legal writings. As a courtesy, the judge who presides over a court is referred to as "the court." Throughout the remaining chapters of this text, the words will be used interchangeably. Chapters 8 and 9 discuss the role of the court in greater detail. In some states, the court that handles estate administration is called the probate court, but in other states, this court is called a surrogate, orphans', or chancery court. In many states, the court is part of the state's regular judicial system, e.g., a district, circuit, county, or superior court. The designation, probate court, will be used throughout this text. Exhibit 7.2 identifies the name of the appropriate court in each state.

In general, once the probate court has jurisdiction, its function is to ensure that the personal representative properly administers the estate so that (1) the homestead exemption, exempt property, family allowances, and maintenance are granted; (2) creditors who have valid claims are paid; (3) taxes owed are paid; (4) the remaining property is distributed to the rightful beneficiaries according to the testator's wishes as expressed in the provisions of the will if a will exists or, in the alternative, according to the controlling state intestate succession statute; and (5) disputes that may arise in the course of the administration of the estate are settled. By approving the will or identifying the decedent's rightful heirs according to statute, the probate court establishes clear title to the property distributed to the beneficiaries of the will or to the heirs. Terminology relating to the functions of the probate court will be covered in a later section of this chapter.

The Registrar or Magistrate

The **registrar**, also known as magistrate, **surrogate** or Register of Wills, is an officer of the probate court who is in charge of keeping records and at times acts on behalf and in place of the court. The registrar may be a judge but more often is a

registrar (aka surrogate)
A person designated by the judge to perform the functions of the court in informal proceedings.

EXHIBIT 7.1	Duties and Functions a Paralegal with Proper Supervision Can or Cannot Perform

Duties/Functions	Paralegal Can Perform	Paralegal Cannot Perform
Accept an employment (client) contract.		X
Establish legal fees with a client when working for a firm.		X
Interview a client to gather relevant data needed for drafting wills, trusts, and estate administration forms.	X	
Prepare questionnaires for estate planning and checklists for wills and trusts.	X	
Give legal advice on estate planning, e.g., gifts, taxes.		X
Perform legal research.	X	
Draft preliminary wills, trusts, and estate documents.	X	
Verify that the creation and execution of all documents and estate administration procedures comply with state statutes.	X	
Assist in the final execution of the will or trust.	X	
Set up and explain to appropriate parties the "tickler" system used in probate.	X	
Handle communication (phone calls, correspondence, interviews, etc.) with the decedent's family, beneficiaries, heirs, and creditors.	X	
Perform legal advocacy (represent a client before a court in a will contest).*		X
Identify and keep records of all probate and nonprobate property for preparing the estate inventory.	X	
File legal documents for probate and estate administration.	X	
Determine if federal and state death taxes are due and execute tax returns.	X	

*Exceptions currently allow paralegals or other nonlawyers to act on behalf of a client in a few situations, e.g., appeals at Social Security hearings.

person designated by the judge to perform functions of the court in certain probate proceedings, e.g., common, independent, or informal proceedings in Uniform Probate Code states. Although registrars cannot, by statute, give legal advice, they can answer questions about forms and procedures that are common concerns for paralegals working in estate administration.

The Clerk or Court Administrator

clerk
An administrative assistant to the court who receives and files documents and keeps records of court proceedings.

The **clerk** (of the probate court) is an administrative assistant to the court (judge). The clerk administers oaths and authenticates and certifies copies of instruments, documents, and records of the court. Like the registrar, the court clerk in the county

EXHIBIT 7.2   State Courts Having Jurisdiction over Wills, Probate, and Distribution of Decedents' Estates

Probate court:	Alabama, Arkansas, Connecticut, Georgia, Maine, Michigan, New Hampshire, Rhode Island, South Carolina, Vermont
Probate and family court:	Massachusetts
Probate court or district court:	New Mexico
Surrogate court:	New Jersey, New York
Orphans' court or circuit court in Hartford and Montgomery counties:	Maryland
Court of common pleas or orphans' court division of court of common pleas:	Pennsylvania
Probate division of court of common pleas:	Ohio
Court of chancery:	Delaware, Mississippi
Court of chancery, court of general sessions, or probate court in Davidson and Shelby counties:	Tennessee
District court:	Idaho, Iowa, Kansas, Kentucky, Louisiana, Montana, Nevada, North Dakota, Oklahoma, Utah, Wyoming
District court or Denver probate court:	Colorado
Probate division of district court:	Minnesota
Circuit court:	Florida, Hawaii, South Dakota, Virginia, Wisconsin
Probate division of circuit court:	Illinois, Missouri
Circuit court, superior court, or probate court in St. Joseph county:	Indiana
Superior court:	Alaska, Arizona, California, North Carolina, Washington
Circuit court or county court:	Oregon
County court:	Nebraska
County court or probate court:	Texas
County commission or circuit court:	West Virginia

of the decedent's domiciliary state cannot give legal advice, but both are essential and extremely helpful sources of information about probate procedures and the execution of the required forms. Since your county may follow "local customs" in administering decedents' estates, you should contact the registrar or clerk and become familiar with their procedures. Frequently, these officers of the court have written a pamphlet or outline of "Guidelines for Probate Procedures" customarily followed in your county. The pamphlet usually identifies the rules, procedures, and required state forms you will use. Since you will file all forms and other documents with these officers of the court, you will find their help invaluable in ensuring that your forms are complete and accurate.

ASSIGNMENT 7.2

1. If Anna Brown was appointed executrix of her mother's estate, did her mother die intestate or testate?

2. Does either an executor(trix) or administrator(trix) have the duty to collect money from insurance policies naming a specific person as the beneficiary? Do they have this duty if the beneficiary predeceased the decedent?

3. To whom is a personal representative responsible?

4. Look up the sections in your state's statutes describing the appointment and duties of the personal representative. Cite the sections.

TERMINOLOGY RELATED TO PROBATE COURT PROCEEDINGS

Since probate court proceedings are an essential part of estate administration, you need to become familiar with the basic terminology related to probate. Jurisdiction, domicile, venue, and ancillary administration are all important aspects of probate proceedings.

Probate

probate [of a will]
The procedure by which a document is presented to the court to confirm it is a valid will.

Originally, the term **probate [of a will]** referred to a proceeding in the appropriate court to prove that a certain document was a will. To prove a will means to acknowledge its existence and validity as the properly executed last will of a decedent. A will that is proved is said to be admitted to probate. Initially an adjective, *probate* today is commonly used as a noun meaning **probate proceedings**, which expands the definition and use of the term *probate* to include the process of distributing the estate assets of a person who died testate in accordance with the will or according to state intestate statutes if there is no will. The probate process passes title to the decedent's property to the beneficiaries or heirs. The term *probate* is also used to include all other matters over which probate courts have jurisdiction during the completion of the entire administration of the decedent's estate, including such matters as the settlement of a dispute concerning a will. Such suits, known as **will contests**—for example, a contest between two beneficiaries who claim that the same item of property was given to each of them—may arise after the will is admitted to probate. Further discussion concerning the actual procedures of probate versus estate administration is included in Chapter 9.

probate proceedings
The process of distributing the estate of a person who died testate or intestate; includes all other matters over which probate courts have jurisdiction.

will contests
Litigation to overturn a decedent's will.

Jurisdiction

jurisdiction
The authority by which a particular court is empowered by statute to decide a certain kind of case and to have its decision enforced.

Jurisdiction is the authority by which a particular court is empowered by statute to hear and decide a certain kind of case and to have its decision enforced. As mentioned previously, the court that has authority (jurisdiction) over wills and the administration of decedents' estates is often called the probate court.

In general, the jurisdiction of a probate court extends to the administration and distribution of a decedent's estate, including the primary function of proving that a certain legal document is a valid will. The powers and duties of the probate court are set out in the statutes or constitution of each state. See the following Missouri statute.

> *Mo. Rev. Stat. § 472.020* Jurisdiction of Probate Division of Circuit Court
> The probate division of the circuit court may hear and determine all matters pertaining to probate business, to granting letters testamentary and of administration, the appointment of guardians and conservators of minors and incapacitated and disabled persons, settling the accounts of personal representatives and conservators, and the sale or leasing of lands by personal representatives and conservators, including jurisdiction of the construction of wills as an incident to the administration of estates, of the determination of heirship, of the administration of testamentary and *inter vivos* trusts, of disability and incapacity proceedings as provided by law and of such other probate business as may be prescribed by law.

Note that in this statute the probate court operates as a division of the circuit court instead of a separate court. In other states, the probate court may be a division of another system of courts (e.g., of the court of common pleas, as in Ohio) or a special court (as in New York, where it is called the Surrogate Court, or in Maryland, where it is called the Orphans' Court).

Note also that the Missouri statute enumerates the powers of the probate court. It may make orders or decrees (decisions) in respect to wills and estate administration. No other state court has jurisdiction over the construction of a decedent's will or to decide matters concerning the estate. Although the probate court's jurisdiction is limited to powers given to it by statutory law, it has "superior" jurisdiction in the matters on which it rules; that is, its decisions can be overruled only by the highest state court, often called the state supreme court.

Domicile

Domicile (legal home) has been defined as the place a person has adopted as a permanent home, and to which the person intends to return when absent. A probate court has jurisdiction over decedents who were domiciles, i.e., legal residents within its authority (county). Determination of a person's **domiciliary state** is essential when the person dies and owns real and personal property located in more than one state. The domiciliary state has jurisdiction over the decedent and all of the decedent's property except real property located in the other state(s). The administration of the decedent's estate is referred to as the primary or **domiciliary administration**. Real property located in other states is probated through secondary court proceedings called ancillary administration (see further discussion in this chapter). The terms *domicile* and *residence* are often confused and frequently used interchangeably, but they are distinguishable. **Domicile** is the legal home, the fixed permanent place of dwelling, whereas **residence** is a temporary place of dwelling. Therefore, a temporary residence, such as a summer home, is not a domicile. A person may have more than one residence but only one domicile.

> **EXAMPLE:** Shaquille's permanent home is in Dayton, Ohio. He spends every winter at his condominium in Miami and two weeks each summer at a friend's cottage on Cape Cod. All three places are Shaquille's residences, but only the home in Dayton is his domicile.

domiciliary state
The state in which the decedent's domicile (legal home) is located.

domiciliary administration
The administration of an estate in the state where the decedent was domiciled at the time of death.

domicile
The legal home where a person has a true, fixed, and permanent place of dwelling and to which the person intends to return when absent.

residence
The dwelling in which one temporarily lives or resides.

Domicile, not residence, determines venue (see the next section). A permanent legal address is determined by where one lives, banks, goes to church, buys license plates, pays state taxes, and votes. If an uncertainty does arise, e.g., if a person abandons his or her domicile in one place and has not yet taken up another before dying, probate proceedings are usually conducted in the county where the assets of the decedent's estate are located. Some cases and examples will illustrate how a court determines a person's domicile.

In the case of *Application of Winkler*, 171 A.D.2d 474, 567 N.Y.S.2d 53 (1991), the court held that a person's domicile is "determined by the conduct of the person and all the surrounding circumstances which may be proven by acts and declarations." Documentation, such as a person's voting records, passport, marriage certificate, and driver's license, as well as witnesses' testimony can also be used to verify a person's true intention as to domicile. In the case of *In re Estate of Elson*, 120 Ill.App.3d 649, 76 Ill. Dec. 237, 458 N.E.2d 637 (1983), the court was asked to decide whether Illinois or Pennsylvania was the true and intended domicile of the decedent. The court stated

1. "Domicile" has been defined as the place where a person has her true, permanent home to which she intends to return whenever she is absent.

2. "Domicile" is a continuing thing, and from the moment a person is born she must, at all times, have a domicile.

3. A person can have only one "domicile," and once a domicile is established, it continues until a new one is actually acquired.

4. To effect a "change of domicile," there must be actual abandonment of the first domicile, coupled with intent not to return to it, and physical presence must be established in another place with intention of making the last-acquired residence a permanent home.

5. "Domicile" is largely a matter of intention and, hence, is primarily a question of fact.

6. Once a "domicile" is established, it is presumed to continue, and the burden of proof in such cases rests on the party who attempts to establish that change in domicile occurred.

7. "Very slight circumstances" often decide questions of "domicile," and the determination is made based on the preponderance of evidence in favor of some particular place as a domicile and depends upon facts and circumstances of the particular case.

In reaching a decision, the court considered various actions of the decedent: in particular, when the decedent left Illinois five or six days prior to her death, she took most of her personal possessions with her, closed her bank accounts in Illinois, and established new accounts in Delaware near her new home in Pennsylvania. In addition, in an unmailed letter she penned the day before her death, she wrote that she had "moved to Pennsylvania." The court found that this evidence was sufficient to support a finding that the decedent intended to abandon her Illinois domicile permanently and acquire a permanent domicile in Pennsylvania, despite other evidence that she intended to stay in Pennsylvania for only one year and planned to return to Illinois.

EXAMPLE: Aiyanna legally resides, i.e., is domiciled, in Kennebec County, Augusta, Maine. The probate court of Kennebec County in Maine would be the proper court to probate her will. Aiyanna moves her household goods from Augusta to Hartford, Connecticut, but dies before establishing legal residence there. If she still owned land in Augusta, the probate court of Kennebec County would remain the proper court to probate her will.

EXAMPLE: Adina owns real estate in more than one state, i.e., a house in Ohio, a farm in Kentucky, and a cottage in Minnesota, but only one residence is her domicile. Since the house in Ohio is Adina's permanent address and Ohio is the state where she pays taxes, votes, and has a driver's license, Ohio would be Adina's domiciliary state.

Venue

Venue is the particular place (either city or county) where a court that has jurisdiction may hear and decide a case. Venue and jurisdiction are not interchangeable, although they are closely related. "Jurisdiction" is abstract, denoting the power or authority of a court to act; "venue" is concrete, denoting the physical place of a trial. "Venue" approximates the definition of territorial jurisdiction and will be used throughout this text to signify the location of the proper court, usually the county within a specific state.

In determining which probate court is the proper one to handle the decedent's estate, the question of the court's jurisdiction is primary. After that has been resolved, the question of venue arises. Usually, venue corresponds to the decedent's place of domicile (legal home) or to the decedent's residence at death. In other words, the proper venue (place) for the probate administration of the estate of a deceased state resident is usually the county in which the decedent was domiciled at his or her death. The venue for out-of-state residents is generally the county in which the nonresident left real property.

venue
The particular place, city, or county, where a court having jurisdiction may hear and decide a case.

EXAMPLE: Avraham Abrams was living in Cook County, Chicago, Illinois, at the time of his death. The administration of his estate will be supervised by the probate (circuit) court of Cook County. Thus, the venue in this instance is Cook County. "Change of venue" means to transfer the location of the court proceedings; a change of venue may be granted if a devisee of the will shows a good reason for the transfer to another location. If Avraham's will gave a farm located in Gogebic County, Michigan, to his cousin, and the cousin could prove that Avraham's actual domicile was Gogebic County, the venue of the probate proceedings would be changed to that county in Michigan.

EXAMPLE: Hans Schollander wrote a will three years ago identifying himself as a resident "of the . . . County of Marion, State of Indiana." Last year he moved to St. Joseph County (Indiana) to live with his sister. If Hans dies in St. Joseph County, venue for the probate of his will would be a question for the probate court of Marion County to decide. The court would have to consider, among other things, whether Hans intended to give up permanent legal residence in Marion County and establish it in St. Joseph County (i.e., to remain there indefinitely).

The following are examples of statutory regulation of jurisdiction and venue.

Cal. Prob. Code § 7050 **Jurisdiction over Estate Administration**
The superior court has jurisdiction of proceedings under this code concerning the administration of the decedent's estate.

Cal. Prob. Code § 7051 Venue; County of Domicile

If *the* decedent was domiciled in this state at the time of death, the proper county for proceedings concerning administration of the decedent's estate is the county in which the decedent was domiciled, regardless of where the decedent died. [Compare Uniform Probate Code § 1–303.]

In addition to its value in determining the venue of a probate proceeding, the fact of the decedent's domicile aids the court in establishing ***in rem* jurisdiction** over the estate's probate assets. Similarly, when two or more states are involved in the probate of a single will, the state that can claim the testator as its citizen will collect the greater share of the state inheritance or estate taxes. The fact of domicile controls not only the state's power to levy taxes but also its right to collect taxes on the decedent's property passed by will. Therefore, the tax liability of an estate may vary noticeably, depending on the inheritance tax demands, if any, of the state in which the estate assets are located.

Ancillary Administration or Ancillary Probate Administration

As mentioned above, if at death the decedent-testator owns any real property (e.g., cottage, condominium, timeshare, or vacation home) in a state other than his or her domiciliary state and, in some cases, any tangible personal property in another state, his or her will must be admitted to probate in each state where the property is located. These separate or secondary court proceedings are known as ancillary probate administration or simply **ancillary administration**. Ancillary administration is necessary because the court in the county of the decedent's domicile has no jurisdiction over real property located in another state, often referred to as the **"foreign state"**. Furthermore, by admitting the will to probate in each state and holding ancillary administration there, any local creditors of the decedent are protected. The court in the case of *Wisenmantle v. Hull Enterprises Inc.*, 103 I11. App.3rd. 878, 432 N.E. 2d 613 (1981), provided a good explanation of ancillary administration.

> Decedent may have an estate in each jurisdiction in which he or she left property. The estate established by jurisdiction where decedent was last domiciled is the domiciliary estate [and] any estate created by any other jurisdiction is the ancillary estate.

Thus, when a person dies leaving real property in more than one state, not only are separate domiciliary and ancillary administrations required but the property is administered under the laws of the state where it is located.

Usually, the testator or the court of the state of domicile appoints a person, called an **ancillary administrator(trix)**, to handle the administration in each state where the decedent's assets are located. Some states allow the personal representative of the domiciliary state to administer the ancillary proceedings. In such cases, the personal representative is also the ancillary administrator. However, state law often requires the ancillary administrator to be a resident of that state, thereby increasing the expense of ancillary administration. Exceptions are sometimes made to allow nonresident family members (e.g., the spouse of the testator) to serve as ancillary administrators, but at the same time, the court must take care to safeguard the rights of the creditors of the decedent who live in the foreign state. Section 3–203(g) of the Uniform Probate Code gives the domiciliary personal representative priority in being appointed the ancillary administrator. See Exhibit 7.3 for the various state requirements for personal representatives who want to be appointed the ancillary administrator in the foreign state. Consider the following examples.

in rem jurisdiction
The authority of the court over the decedent's property.

ancillary administration
Additional administration used to dispose of and distribute that portion of the decedent's estate located in a state other than the decedent's domiciliary state.

"foreign state"
Any state other than the decedent's domiciliary state.

ancillary administrator(trix)
The personal representative appointed by the court to distribute that part of a decedent's estate located in a state other than the decedent's domiciliary state.

EXAMPLE: Toby resides in Virginia and owns a summer cottage in North Carolina. Several years ago she mortgaged the cottage to a bank in Raleigh. If she dies without having paid the mortgage, the bank would have no notice of her death even though it is an **interested party [person]** by virtue of being her creditor. For this reason, an ancillary administration of her North Carolina property is necessary. In North Carolina the ancillary administrator must be 18 or older; must not be declared incompetent or convicted of a felony; and, if a nonresident, must designate a resident agent for service of process.

interested party [person]
A person including heirs, devisees, beneficiaries, personal representatives, creditors, and any others having a property right to or claim against the estate of a decedent.

Exhibit 7.3	State Eligibility Requirements for Personal Representatives

Age Requirements

21 or older: Arkansas, Colorado, Utah
19 or older: Alabama, Alaska, Nebraska
18 or older: All other states not listed

Unsuitability Disqualifications

Legal disqualifications:
- Felony or infamous crime conviction:
  Alabama, Arkansas, Delaware, Florida, Illinois, Indiana, Louisiana, Maryland, Mississippi, Missouri, Nevada, New York, North Carolina, Oklahoma, Oregon, South Dakota, Texas, Washington
- Disbarred from practice of law: Oregon
- Misdemeanor involving "moral turpitude": Washington

Capacity disqualifications:
- Mentally incapacitated: Delaware
- Adjudged disabled: Illinois
- Incapacitated: Indiana
- Habitual drunkard: Missouri
- An alcoholic, or a spendthrift: Iowa
- Bad moral character: Louisiana
- Mentally incompetent: Maryland
- Not having proper capacity: Massachusetts
- Mentally or physically unable to perform: Florida
- Unsound mind or not of sound mind:
  Arkansas, Illinois, Mississippi, Missouri, Washington, Wisconsin
- Incompetent, adjudged incompetent, or decreed incompetent:
  Alabama, Iowa, Nevada, New York, North Carolina, Oklahoma, Oregon, South Dakota, Texas, Wisconsin, Wyoming

Nonresident Requirements

Many states allow appointment of nonresidents to serve as personal representatives without any restrictions. Others have restrictions on the appointment of nonresident personal representatives, which include the following: judicial consent or approval; appointing a specific person/agent to receive service of process or act as co-administrator; or prohibiting nonresidents from serving in specified situations. Other states ban nonresidents entirely from serving as personal representatives.

EXAMPLE: North Dakota is Ahmet's domicile. Most of his assets are in North Dakota, but he has a winter home in Georgia. In his will Ahmet appoints his wife, Elma, his personal representative. Under Georgia law, Elma could also be appointed ancillary administratrix to administer the assets in Georgia, including the winter home.

The ancillary administration in the foreign state generally includes the following procedures.

1. Acceptance by the foreign state court of the will admitted to probate in the decedent-testator's domiciliary state.

2. Issuance of letters of authority, e.g., Letters Ancillary Testamentary, to the ancillary administrator that permit the real property to be transferred to the designated devisee named in the will if all creditors of the testator in the foreign state have been paid.

3. If any inheritance or estate taxes are imposed by the foreign state, these taxes must be paid to that state and not to the testator's domiciliary state.

If the decedent died intestate, then the persons entitled to the decedent's real property in the foreign state will be determined by that state's intestate succession statute. However, generally, all of the decedent's personal property, wherever located, will pass to the persons entitled to it according to the decedent's domiciliary state's intestate succession statute. Specific tasks of paralegals concerning ancillary administration are discussed in Chapter 9.

Key Terms

Letters Testamentary	probate proceedings	venue
Letters of Administration	will contest	*in rem* jurisdiction
bond	jurisdiction	ancillary administration
surety	digital executor	foreign state
tickler system	domiciliary state	ancillary administrator (trix)
registrar (aka surrogate)	domiciliary administration	interested party [person]
clerk	domicile	
probate [of a will]	residence	

Review Questions

1. A personal representative is a fiduciary. What does that mean?

2. Who may act as a personal representative?

3. Why is a personal representative sometimes called an executor or an administrator?

4. What are Letters Testamentary and Letters of Administration and how do they differ?

5. Summarize the duties of a personal representative.

6. What are three ethical problems an attorney and paralegal face when drafting a client's will?

7. What are the general duties a paralegal may perform concerning wills, trusts, and estate administration?

8. What other titles besides probate court do states use to identify the court that supervises the administration of the decedent's estate?

9. How do the functions of a registrar and a court clerk differ?

10. Why are the terms *probate* and *probate proceedings* often confused? Explain.

11. Are domicile and venue the same thing? Explain.

12. When is an ancillary administration necessary and what is its purpose?

13. Who is authorized to act as an ancillary administrator in your state?

Case Problems

Problem 1

Alberto Gomez owns real and personal property in three states, California, New Mexico, and New York. Alberto is 102 years old and has outlived his only spouse and their three children. When he dies intestate, Alberto has no surviving family, i.e., blood relatives. Answer the following:

A. What facts would be required for you to determine Alberto's domiciliary state?

B. What is the difference between Alberto's domicile and his residence?

C. Where would the proper venue be for Alberto's estate administration?

D. If a conflict arises over which of two or three states is the decedent's domicile, how does the Uniform Probate Code resolve the problem? See UPC § 3–202 and *Riley v. New York Trust Co.*, 315 U.S. 343, 62 S.Ct. 608, 86 L.Ed. 885 (1942).

E. Which state would determine how Alberto's property would be inherited? *Caveat:* Discuss both real and personal property. For personal property, see *Howard v. Reynolds*, 30 Ohio St.2d 214, 283 N.E.2d 629 (1972).

Problem 2

Maura Hanlon, legally a resident of Amarillo, Texas, dies while traveling in Waterford, Ireland. Maura owns a house in Amarillo and an apartment building in Tulsa, Oklahoma. Answer and explain each of the following:

A. In which state should Maura's will be probated?

B. Is an ancillary administration necessary in this case?

C. Whether Maura dies testate or intestate, is an ancillary administration still necessary?

D. What are the eligibility requirements for appointment of an ancillary administrator in the foreign state in this case?

E. Find and cite the section of the Uniform Probate Code or your state's statute, if any, that gives the domiciliary personal representative priority to be appointed the ancillary administrator.

Practical Assignments

1. Determine which court has subject matter jurisdiction over the administration of estates in your state.

2. Using the online version of the Martindale Hubbell directory, find an attorney in your area who handles probate administration cases.

3. Assume that you are the executor for an estate. Prepare the required form (IRS SS-4) to obtain an employer identification number, using your personal information to complete the form.

8

PERSONAL REPRESENTATIVES: TYPES, PRE-PROBATE DUTIES, AND APPOINTMENT

Outline

Objectives

After completing this chapter, you should be able to:

- Identify and define the various types of personal representatives involved in the administration of decedents' estates.

- From the dialogue, identify and appreciate your role in the practice of the law of wills and probate.

- Understand the procedures for appointment of the personal representative in formal probate proceedings.

- Explain the basic functions and duties performed by the personal representative in the preparation of probate and estate administration.

- Recognize your role as an assistant to the personal representative in the performance of the required duties of estate administration.

SCOPE OF THE CHAPTER

This chapter provides a more in-depth review of the law governing personal representatives. It identifies and defines them and reviews their duties in preparation for the administration of a decedent's estate. The chapter discusses only those functions that must be performed soon after the decedent's death, i.e., duties the personal representative should be ready to perform even before the probate court confirms his or her appointment. Since you will often be asked to assist the personal representative, knowledge of these duties is essential.

The chapter begins by defining additional types of personal representatives not previously discussed, describing their powers and functions, and citing sample statutes that establish their authority. Next, the basic powers and duties of the personal representative in preparation for formal proceedings are explained, along with your role in assisting with these duties. For an overview of the duties of the personal representative, see Chapter 7.

Types of Personal Representatives

The UPC term *personal representative* refers to anyone empowered or authorized to administer the estate of the deceased, whether the deceased died testate or intestate. Minors, incompetent persons, convicted felons, and judges of a court are prohibited from being personal representatives. Personal representatives need not be U.S. citizens but noncitizenship is a factor to consider for the suitability of the appointment of a personal representative.

The role of the personal representative may be performed by a private individual (usually a family member), an attorney, or a trust officer of a corporate business such as a bank or trust company. If the personal representative is also in charge of the digital estate, he or she should have the requisite technical knowledge. In intestacy cases, the personal representative is selected according to the order of preference for appointment set by statute. An example of a state statute illustrating the order of preference is 20 Pa. Stat. Ann. § 3155 Persons Entitled.

  (a) *Letters testamentary*—Letters testamentary shall be granted by the register to the executor designated in the will, whether or not he has declined a trust under the will.
  (b) *Letters of administration*—Letters of administration shall be granted by the register, in such form as the case shall require, to one or more of those hereinafter mentioned and, except for good cause, in the following order:
  (1) Those entitled to the residuary estate under the will.
  (2) The surviving spouse.
  (3) Those entitled under the intestate law as the register, in his discretion, shall judge will best administer the estate, giving preference, however, according to the sizes of the shares of those in this class.
  (4) The principal creditors of the decedent at the time of his death.
  (5) Other fit persons.
  (6) If anyone of the foregoing shall renounce his right to letters of administration, the register, in his discretion, may appoint a nominee of the person so renouncing in preference to the persons set forth in any succeeding paragraph.
  (7) A guardianship support agency serving as guardian of an incapacitated person who dies during the guardianship administered pursuant to Sub-chapter F of Chapter 55 (relating to guardianship support).

(c) *Time limitation*—Except with the consent of those enumerated in clauses (1), (2), and (3), no letters shall be issued to those enumerated in clauses (4) and (5) … of subsection (b) until 30 days after the decedent's death.

(d) *Death charges*—Notwithstanding the provisions of subsections (a) and (b), the register shall not grant letters testamentary or letters of administration to any person charged, whether by indictment, information or otherwise, by the United States, the Commonwealth or any of the several states, with voluntary manslaughter or homicide, except homicide by vehicle, in connection with a decedent's death unless and until the charge is withdrawn, dismissed or a verdict of not guilty is returned. [For comparison see UPC § 3–203.]

POINT OF INTEREST

Information for the Personal Representative

Estate law firms need to provide information to the personal representative about the duties of the job. Creative brochures or handouts containing the information can be created on the office computer. A good brochure will include a summary of the required duties and the law office's contact information. Web articles exist that discuss the personal representative's duties. The court's probate office or Web site may also provide such information. By providing this vital information, it will help ensure that the personal representative will act within his or her boundaries and eliminate possibilities that he or she will be held personally liable for undue mistakes made in the administration of the decedent's estate.

In some states, if no one appears who is entitled to act as administrator, the court or registrar may appoint an official, called the public administrator, to administer the estate of an intestate decedent. This and other terms relating to personal representatives not previously discussed are defined below.

- *Special administrator or administratrix.* The special administrator or administratrix is the personal representative, either man or woman, appointed temporarily by a probate court to handle certain immediate needs of an estate, such as managing a business in place of the decedent, until a general administrator or executor can be appointed. This representative usually handles Summary Administration proceedings when the amount of the decedent's property qualifies as a "small estate" (see Chapter 9).

- *Administrator or administratrix* cum testamento annexo. The administrator or administratrix *cum testamento annexo*, also called administrator C.T.A. (means administrator with the will annexed), is the personal representative appointed by the court in two situations: (1) where the maker of the will does not name an executor or executrix or (2) where the maker of the will does name an executor or executrix but the latter cannot serve because of a deficiency in qualifications or competency. The following state statutes identify the position of administrator C.T.A.

20 Pa. Stat. Ann. § 3325 Administrator C.T.A.
An administrator with the will annexed shall have all the powers given by the will to the executor, unless otherwise provided by the will. When he has been required to give bond, no proceeds of real estate shall be paid to him until the court has made an order excusing him from entering additional security or requiring additional security, and in the latter event, only after he has entered the additional security.

Cal. Prob. Code § 8441 Priority for Appointment
(a) Except as provided in subdivision (b), persons and their nominees are entitled to appointment as administrator with the will annexed in the same order of priority as for appointment of an administrator.

Cal. Prob. Code § 8442 Authority over Estate
(a) Subject to subdivision (b), an administrator with the will annexed has the same authority over the decedent's estate as an executor named in the will would have, (b) If the will confers a discretionary power or authority on an executor that is not conferred by law and the will does not extend the power or authority to other personal representatives, the power or authority shall not be deemed to be conferred on an administrator with the will annexed, but the court in its discretion may authorize the exercise of the power or authority.

EXAMPLE: Geraldine writes and executes a will, but she neglects to name an executor. On her death, the probate court will decide if the document is admissible to probate and, if so, will appoint an administrator C.T.A. for Geraldine's estate.

- *Administrator or administratrix* de bonis non. The administrator or administratrix *de bonis non*, also called administrator D.B.N. (means administrator of goods not administered), is a court-appointed personal representative who replaces a previous personal representative who has begun but failed to complete the administration of a decedent's estate for any reason, including death. The following is a sample statute that creates the administrator D.B.N. position.

20 Pa. Stat. Ann. § 3326 Administrator D.B.N. and D.B.N.C.T.A.
An administrator *de bonis non*, with or without a will annexed, shall have the power to recover the assets of the estate from his predecessor in administration or from the personal representative of such predecessor and, except as the will shall provide otherwise, shall stand in his predecessor's stead for all purposes, except that he shall not be personally liable for the acts of his predecessor. When he has been required to give bond, no proceeds of real estate shall be paid to him until the court has made an order excusing him from entering additional security or requiring additional security, and in the latter event, only after he has entered the additional security.

EXAMPLE: Frazier is named executor in Eleanor's will. While in the process of settling her estate, he dies. The probate court will appoint a replacement, who will have the title of administrator D.B.N.C.T.A.

- *Public administrator.* The public administrator is a public official appointed by the court to administer the property of an intestate who has left no kindred (blood relative) entitled to apply for appointment and Letters of Administration.

EXAMPLE: Arnold dies intestate. He never married and has no blood relatives (kindred). Some states would appoint a public administrator to handle Arnold's estate.

Exhibit 8.1 summarizes the different types of personal representatives.

EXHIBIT 8.1   Types of Personal Representatives: Summary Chart

- The personal representative of a testate decedent is called executor (if a man) or executrix (if a woman).
- The personal representative of an intestate decedent is called general administrator or simply the administrator (if a man) or administratrix (if a woman).
- A special administrator (-trix) is appointed by the probate court to handle problems and immediate needs of the estate administration that arise before the court appoints a personal representative.
- A public administrator is appointed by the probate court to administer the property of an intestate who has left no person entitled to appointment.
- In special cases the personal representative for either a testate decedent or an intestate decedent may be called:
  1. An administrator (-trix) C.T.A. is the person appointed by the court when the maker of the will either does not name an executor or does name one, but that person cannot serve.
  2. An administrator (-trix) D.B.N. is the person appointed by the court to replace a previous personal representative who has failed to complete the administration of a decedent's estate.
  3. An ancillary administrator (-trix) is the person appointed by the court to oversee the administration of a decedent's estate located in a foreign state.

ASSIGNMENT 8.1

Joshua Foley's will named his son, Ethan, to be executor, but Ethan refused to serve after Joshua's death and no contingent (successor) executor was named in the will.
1. If Joshua's wife, Ethel, was appointed as personal representative by the probate court, what title would she have?
2. If instead Ethan had commenced probate proceedings but was unable to complete them due to illness, and Ethel was then appointed by the court as his replacement, what would her title be?
3. If Ethel was appointed by a probate court to handle the administration of the estate of her brother, George Clark, who lived and died in another state, what would her title be?
4. If Joshua had forgotten to name an executor, what would the court most likely do?
5. If Joshua had been in the process of completing a transfer of the majority interest in a corporation when he died and the court named a person to continue the transfer before a regular probate proceeding could be held, what would the title of the person be?

INTRODUCTION TO ESTATE ADMINISTRATION: A DIALOGUE

The following discussion describes the probate procedures involved in a typical case. The participants include the decedent's named personal representative (the executor), the attorney for the estate, and the paralegal. It is essential the participants maintain continuous communication between and among themselves so the administration of the decedent's estate will be timely and efficient. The participants and facts of the case are as follows.

Participants
- Decedent—John T. Smith
- Executor—William R. Smith

- Attorney—Ms. Brown
- Paralegal—Ms. Jones

Facts. John T. Smith, the decedent, died August 15, 2014, owning property in two states, State A and State B. He was domiciled at 1024 Pleasure Lane, Heavenly City, in Cotton County, State A, owning a house there. In addition to the homestead held in joint tenancy with his wife, John owned the following property: a car, licensed in State A and owned in his name only; stocks and bonds owned jointly with his wife; a savings account jointly owned; a checking account in his name only; a life insurance policy with his wife named beneficiary; some valuable paintings given to him by his grandfather; and a summer cottage in his name only, located in State B. John had only a few debts at the time of his death, and no one owed him any money. He was survived by his wife, Mary, and only child, William, age 22.

An attorney, Ms. Brown, had previously been retained to draft John Smith's will. Ms. Jones, the paralegal, had collected all the pertinent information from John Smith and had written a preliminary draft of the will, which had been finalized in a meeting between John Smith, Ms. Brown, and Ms. Jones on January 10, 2011 (see Exhibit 8.2). The final draft of the executed will had been placed in a vault in Ms. Brown's office at Mr. Smith's request.

The provisions of John's will left his wife all property not already transferred to her by joint ownership, gift, or other means. William R. Smith, son of the decedent, had been named executor of the will. He had made all the necessary funeral arrangements for his father's burial according to the directions in his father's letter of instructions, and, knowing he had been named executor, went to the office of Ms. Brown to discuss the procedures for the administration of his father's estate.

In the presence of the paralegal (Ms. Jones), the attorney (Ms. Brown), and the executor (William Smith), the following dialogue takes place.

Attorney: Come in and sit down, William. Here is your father's will. As you know, you have been asked to be his executor.

Executor: (Reads the will) Before his death, my father and I discussed his will and estate. I knew he had named me executor, and I agreed to serve. We also decided, and my mother agreed, to ask you, Ms. Brown, to act as the estate's attorney and help me carry out the duties of the executor since I have no experience in these matters and feel I should learn and understand my responsibilities.

Attorney: I will be happy to serve as the attorney for the estate. It has been the practice of this law firm when advising clients named as executors to work with our paralegal in the field of estate administration. As you know, William, Ms. Jones helped collect the necessary data and prepare the preliminary draft of your father's will. Now, under my supervision, she will handle many of the details necessary to help settle your father's estate. She will participate in our conferences on administration and will keep you informed of all meetings, hearings, correspondence, and the current status of the administration of your father's estate. She will be available to answer some of the questions you might have about your executor's duties. Others she will discuss with me, and then we shall communicate the information to you. As we have previously informed you, Ms. Jones is a paralegal. As such, she cannot provide you with legal advice, so I will respond to those questions. Please feel free to ask any questions or contact us any time you have matters you want to discuss.

Executor: Yes, I have met Ms. Jones. My father told me how pleased he was with the help she had given him in drafting his will. I am very happy Ms. Jones will be working with us.

EXHIBIT 8.2   John T. Smith's Will

LAST WILL AND TESTAMENT
OF
JOHN T. SMITH

I, John T. Smith, residing at 1024 Pleasure Lane, Heavenly City, Cotton County, State A, declare this instrument to be my Last Will and Testament, hereby revoking all former Wills and Codicils made by me.

Article I
I direct that all my just debts, expenses of my last illness, funeral expenses, expenses of the administration of my estate, and estate taxes be paid as soon as possible after my death.

Article II
I give all of my property, now owned or hereafter acquired by me, to my wife, Mary K. Smith, if she survives me.

Article III
In the event my said wife, Mary K. Smith, shall predecease me, or if we should die in a common disaster, then I give all of my said property, now owned or hereafter acquired by me, to my son, William R. Smith, now residing at 1024 Pleasure Lane.

Article IV
I hereby nominate and appoint my son, William R. Smith, Executor of this, my Last Will and Testament. In the event he should predecease me or should be unwilling or unable to serve in that capacity, then I hereby nominate and appoint my brother, Joseph B. Smith, Executor of this, my Last Will and Testament. I hereby give and grant unto my said Executor full power to sell and convey, lease or mortgage any and all real estate that I may own at the time of my death or which may be acquired by my estate, without license or leave of court. I further give and grant unto my said Executor the power to access, handle, distribute and dispose of my digital assets. "Digital assets" includes files stored on my digital devices, including, but not limited to, desktops, laptops, tablets, peripherals, storage devices, mobile telephones, smartphones, and any similar digital device that currently exists or may exist as technology develops or such comparable items as technology develops. The term "digital assets" also includes but is not limited to emails received, email accounts, digital music, digital photographs, digital videos, software licenses, social network accounts, file sharing accounts, financial accounts, domain registrations, DNS service accounts, Web hosting accounts, tax preparation service accounts, online stores, affiliate programs, other online accounts and similar digital items that currently exist or may exist as technology develops or such comparable items as technology develops, regardless of the ownership of the physical device upon which the digital item is stored.

EXHIBIT 8.2   **(continued)**

Article V

No bond shall be required of any individual named above as Executor of this Will.

IN WITNESS WHEREOF, I have hereunto signed this my last Will and Testament this 10th day of January, 2011.

_____ *John T. Smith*

John T. Smith—Testator

THIS INSTRUMENT, consisting of one (1) typewritten page, bearing the signature of the above named Testator, was on the date hereof signed, published and declared by him to be his Last Will and Testament in our presence, who, at his request and in his presence, and in the presence of each other, we believing him to be over 18 years of age, of sound mind and disposing memory, and under no constraint or undue influence hereunder do sign our names as attesting witnesses.

Francis R. Miller   residing at   *1712 Flute Street*

Witness

Janet F. Strom   residing at   *34 F. Tenth Street*

Witness

Paralegal: Thank you. Before we begin our discussion about your father's will and the administration of his estate, let me review for you the things that have been done to this point. As you know, our firm assisted your father in planning for the distribution of his estate after his death. Ms. Brown discussed with him the purpose of and need for a will. I compiled checklists of all the property your father owned or in which he had any interest. After discussing the estate plan with Ms. Brown, I drew up a preliminary draft of the will. Ms. Brown, utilizing methods that took advantage of all possible tax considerations, prepared the final draft of your father's will in its present form. The will ensures the estate will be distributed according to your father's wishes.

Attorney: Let's get started. What we try to accomplish, William, when we assist executors, is to explain the basic procedure that must be followed in administering an estate from beginning to end.

> Estate administration procedures

Executor: A few years ago my uncle died without a will. I recall my aunt talking about it. Are the same procedures followed whether a person dies with or without a will?

Attorney: I intend to discuss with you procedures that occur whether a decedent dies *testate*, meaning with a will, as in your father's case, or *intestate*, which means without a will, as in your uncle's case. In either case, a *personal representative* must be appointed to administer the decedent's estate. In the situation such as your father's, where someone has died leaving a will, the personal representative named in the will is generally called an *executor*, if a man, or an *executrix*, if a woman. When a person has died without a will, the personal representative is referred to as an *administrator*, if a man, or an *administratrix*, if a woman. An executor is named in the will and confirmed by the court to handle the estate. An administrator, however, must be appointed by the court when there is no will. You, William, will perform the duties of an executor.

Executor: Well, how do we begin? What must I do?

Attorney: Any personal representative must perform three basic duties.

1. All your father's assets must be collected.

2. His debts, claims against the estate, and taxes due must be paid.

3. The remainder of his estate or property must be distributed according to his will within guidelines set by the *statutes* or laws of this state.

When a person dies, the state that is the decedent's *domicile* (legal home) and the county that is the proper *venue* become the location for the *domiciliary administration* of the decedent's estate. In this state, as in many states, the court that handles the decedent's estate is called the *probate court*. Each county has its own probate court. The right, power, and authority a probate court has to hear and decide these matters are referred to as the court's *jurisdiction*. Jurisdiction of the probate court over the administration of a decedent's estate continues until the proceeding is finished. Since your father also owned *real property*, your summer cottage in State B, a second or *ancillary administration* must be commenced in that state. The county in which the property is located is the proper venue for the ancillary proceeding. Ms. Jones will give you additional information and assistance in handling such matters.

Executor: So far I believe I understand the basic functions that must be performed and how the probate court fits into the picture. Since my father named me executor, do I give the money and property to the people mentioned in his will?

Attorney: Not right away. Although you have been named executor, you have no authority to act as personal representative until you file a petition and are appointed by the probate court. This will be done once your father's will has been admitted, which means the will is validated and accepted by the probate court. Now that we are ready to discuss procedural steps and the checklists of information necessary to accomplish them, I am turning you over to Ms. Jones to have her go through the steps with you. As we previously mentioned, if you have any questions about your responsibilities, please call. We shall see that any problems are resolved.

Executor: Thank you for the information, Ms. Brown. If I have any problems, I'll be sure to ask you. Good-bye, and thanks again.

Paralegal: As Ms. Brown mentioned, in order for you to become authorized as executor, you must petition the court to admit and accept your father's will. This is done by filling out one of the numerous forms required for estate administration. We have in our law office all the necessary forms you must complete as part of this administration. In addition, we will set up what is called a "tickler" system, which lists chronologically all the important steps and dates in the stages of the administration of the estate.

Here is an example of a "tickler" form (see Exhibit 8.3). Using both this system and a list of procedural steps will help reduce the possibility that some important

---

Personal representative's duties

Domicile and venue identified

Probate court's jurisdiction

Petition to probate will

Tickler system

EXHIBIT 8.3	Sample "Tickler" Form

ESTATE OF JOHN T. SMITH
"Tickler"

ESTATE OF _____ deceased, _____, 20 _____
Date of Death _____ Date of Birth _____ Domicile _____
Probate Court _____ County, File No._____
Name, Mailing Address, and Telephone of Personal Representative and Date of Appointment: _____
_____
Ancillary Administration Necessary _____
Date of Last Will _____ Tax Identification No. _____

Proceeding	Person Who Performed	Due or Dated	Filed or Paid
Original will filed with probate court	_____	_____	_____
Petition for probate, administration, etc.	_____	_____	_____
Mailing of notice of hearing	_____	_____	_____
Hearing on petition for probate or appointment with registrar	_____	_____	_____
Affidavit of mailing (family allowances, etc.)	_____	_____	_____
Bond	_____	_____	_____
Letters issued	_____	_____	_____
Notice to creditors and affidavit of mailing	_____	_____	_____
Inventory and appraisement	_____	_____	_____
Personal property tax		Feb.	_____
Real estate taxes: (first half; second half) if necessary		May 15 Oct. 15	_____
Last date for spouse's election	_____	_____	_____
Property set apart for surviving spouse and/or minor children	_____	_____	_____
Maintenance ordered	_____	_____	_____
State and other inheritance tax waivers obtained	_____	_____	_____
Last date for filing claims	_____	_____	_____
Claims hearing	_____	_____	_____
Decedent's final income and gift tax returns due			
Federal	_____	_____	_____
State	_____	_____	_____
Fiduciary's final income tax returns due			
Federal	_____	_____	_____
State	_____	_____	_____
Last date for filing claims with leave of court	_____	_____	_____
Optional alternative valuation date	_____	_____	_____
Federal estate tax return due	_____	_____	_____
State inheritance and/or estate tax due	_____	_____	_____
Closing letter (federal estate tax)	_____	_____	_____
Date maintenance ends	_____	_____	_____
Final account	_____	_____	_____
Closing statement	_____	_____	_____
Hearing on final account	_____	_____	_____
Decree or order of distribution issued	_____	_____	_____
Discharge of personal representative	_____	_____	_____
Bond refund	_____	_____	_____

detail or significant date might be forgotten, with resulting damage to the beneficiary's *(successor's)* interest and with potential liability to you, the executor.

Executor: In that case, let's set up this "tickler" system right away. If we each have a copy, we can remind one another of the essential steps and important dates. Right?

Paralegal: Yes. This is exactly what we will do. But remember, you must first get your position as executor authorized as well as establish the necessary ancillary administration in State B where the summer cottage is located. You recall that administration in your father's county of residence is called the "domiciliary" administration. Administration necessary in any other state is "ancillary." Although your father left a will naming you as executor of his estate, a person must also be appointed in State B to handle the ancillary administration. Even though there is a will, that person, who is usually a resident of State B, is called the *ancillary administrator.*

Executor: Now I understand the term. How is the ancillary administrator authorized, and what does he or she do?

Paralegal: You and your mother are given the opportunity to select the person from State B to act in this *fiduciary* capacity. As a representative of the estate, the ancillary administrator must submit a copy of your father's will, a certified copy of his death certificate, and a petition for appointment to the probate court of the county in which the *real property*, the cottage, is located, using a form similar to the one you will use for authorization in our state. Once authorized by the local county probate court in State B, the ancillary administrator will

1. collect the local assets.

2. pay the local creditors and taxes, if any.

3. transfer the balance of the estate to you, the domiciliary representative.

Some states allow the domiciliary representative to apply for appointment as ancillary administrator if there is no law to the contrary. We shall check this out because, if it is allowed, your acting as ancillary as well as domiciliary representative might be desirable. If there are creditors of your father in State B, you will be faced with the choice of paying their claims out of ancillary assets or the domiciliary estate funds. If you want to protect the summer cottage against being sold to satisfy such debts, you must discuss this with Ms. Brown.

Executor: By all means, I will consult with Ms. Brown. We would not want to sell the summer cottage unless necessary, since both my mother and I enjoy it so much.

Paralegal: Once you petition the court for probating the will, and the court has proved and accepted it, you will be the authorized personal representative—the executor. The probate court signs an order admitting the will as valid and issuing to you *Letters Testamentary.* This particular legal form is the authorization given to executors to handle the administration of a decedent's estate. If your father had died intestate, without a will like your uncle, either your mother or you as *next of kin* would petition the probate court for general administration of your father's estate, and request the probate court appoint one or both of you as administrators. The form used to authorize an administrator is called *Letters of Administration.*

Letters Testamentary

Letters of Administration

Executor: Letters Testamentary authorize an executor named in a will to handle the decedent's estate, and Letters of Administration authorize a general administrator to do the work when the decedent dies leaving no will. Are the duties of the executor and administrator the same?

Paralegal: Basically, yes. Administrators do much the same thing as executors, but they must rely on the state laws to guide their actions, whereas executors follow the provisions of the will within statutory limitations, of course.

Executor: I've heard in some cases an estate can be probated in a simpler manner—informally, I believe it is called. Is this possible?

Paralegal: That is a good question. Many states, including our own, have adopted the *Uniform Probate Code's* recommendations for administration of decedents' estates. Two forms of probate procedures are included in the Code: *formal*, or *solemn*, and *informal*, or *common*. Some states use only the formal procedures; some follow the Uniform Probate Code and use both formal and informal procedures; others use a variation of these forms.

Estate administration

Basically, formal probate refers to proceedings or a hearing conducted before a *judge* with the requirement that *notice* be given to all *interested persons*, such as beneficiaries, devisees, or heirs, so they might be present to contest the will or, in *intestacy* cases, to contest the appointment of a general administrator. Informal probate, on the other hand, is also known as unsupervised probate since it is necessary only to present a will or petition for administration to an appropriate court representative, who may be a judge but more likely will be a *registrar* or *clerk*. After the will has been admitted or the administrator appointed, no notice to interested parties is necessary. The administration of the decedent's estate can therefore be completed faster. Another advantage of informal probate is that it may reduce the expenses of administration, including the elimination of the need for an attorney to assist in the procedures. Every personal representative should consider informal administration.

After hearing of the person's death, interested parties such as beneficiaries, heirs, or devisees of the decedent who want to contest the validity of the will or the appointment of the administrator must request a formal hearing. An original informal proceeding then becomes a formal one, with all associated procedures. Due to the size of your father's estate and the real property involved, you will have to discuss with Ms. Brown the type of proceeding to be followed.

Executor: So what are the advantages of formal as opposed to informal probate for an estate like my father's?

Paralegal: Basically, the choice of formal or informal probate depends on a number of variables, such as the nature of estate assets and the preferences of the personal representative. The probate court must supervise formal probate, whereas it does not have to supervise informal probate unless someone who has an interest in the estate requests it. The personal representative might feel that it would be better for the court rather than the registrar to oversee administration of the estate because of problems presented by certain assets. Since your father's estate hasn't been inventoried or valued yet, I can't give you facts or figures. However, Ms. Brown will advise you of the method that would better suit your case. One word of caution—informal probate sounds effortless, but I assure you it isn't. It allows the personal representative to administer the estate with the help of the registrar. The court will step in only when requested, but knowing when to request the court's help isn't all that easy.

Executor: I can see the procedures can be complicated. What information is needed to commence the formal probate?

Paralegal: First we need a *petition to prove the will* (see Form 1*). It requests the following information.

- The name, age, and usually the Social Security number of the decedent
- His domicile
- The place and date of his death
- The name and address of the executor (personal representative) named in the will
- The date and original copy of the will being probated
- The estimated value of the decedent's estate, including both real and personal property
- The names, ages, relationships, and addresses of the decedent's known beneficiaries, heirs, and devisees
- The will be admitted to probate, and the petitioner be appointed executor and Letters Testamentary issued

The petition, like many of the forms we use, may be verified; that is, signed and sealed by a notary public. A certified copy of the decedent's death certificate usually accompanies the petition.

Executor: What happens after the petition is completed?

Paralegal: We file the petition with the probate court, which establishes the court's jurisdiction over the estate, and the probate judge sets a date and time for the hearing on the petition. This order also limits the time for any of your father's creditors to file their claims and sets the date for hearing any disputed claim. Notice of the hearing is given to all interested parties either by direct mail to each beneficiary, heir, or devisee, or by publication once a week for three weeks in a legal newspaper within the county for the benefit of creditors. Copies of this notice are also given to the state's tax department.

Executor: What happens at the hearing?

Paralegal: Before the actual hearing, we will correspond with the witnesses to your father's will and make arrangements to have them meet you and Ms. Brown at the judge's chambers on the hearing day. Ms. Brown will have with her at that time the necessary forms for presentation to the court. You and I shall prepare these forms with Ms. Brown's supervision and review. The forms include the following:

- *A proof of publication* of notice of the hearing (Form 3*)
- An *affidavit* stating when and where publication was made, obtained from the newspaper publishing the notice (Form 4*)
- An *order admitting the will to probate* (Form 6*), which states that this is the last will of the decedent, grants *Letters Testamentary* (Form 7*), and specifies the amount of *bond*, if required
- The personal representative's *oath of office*

---

* See Appendix A.

We shall also prepare Letters Testamentary for the signature of the probate judge. These authorize you to act as the executor of your father's estate. Remember, had your father died intestate like your uncle, we would prepare Letters of Administration instead.

Executor: Yes, now I understand.

Paralegal: The final forms we prepare and present to the court are the following:

- The *order appointing the appraisers*, which names the persons who will appraise or value the estate.
- The *notice to the surviving spouse*, your mother, of her *right to renounce* or waive what your father left to her in the will and take, instead, a percentage of his total probate estate, as she is allowed by statute (Form 5*). Widows or widowers who receive little under their spouse's will find this *statutory election*, also known as the "forced or elective share," advantageous, but since your father left your mother everything, she will obviously not pursue this right.

Executor: All right. We have the forms and the witnesses to my father's will at the courtroom. Are we ready for the hearing?

Paralegal: Yes. As petitioner, you will take the stand and be sworn in. Ms. Brown will elicit from you the information contained in the petition. Under oath, you will verify that it is correct and request appointment as executor of your father's estate. Then Ms. Brown will ask the witnesses who *attested* and *subscribed* your father's will to take the stand and under oath testify that your father *acknowledged* the document as his last will and signed it in their presence and that they each signed in each other's presence as attesting witnesses. They will also testify that your father was of sound mind at the time he signed the will. Ms. Brown then asks the court to admit the will to probate and that you be authorized as executor.

> Hearing on petition to probate will

Executor: What happens if my father's brother, Uncle Joe, objects to the will?

Paralegal: Good question. That's called a contest of the will. The probate court would have to set up a separate hearing date for the will contest. Do you expect this to happen?

Executor: No, I was just wondering about the procedure.

Paralegal: In that case, I assume the probate judge will agree to the requests made by Ms. Brown. The execution of the will is thereby proved, and probate of the estate can begin.

Executor: What happens at the hearing?

Paralegal: The probate judge asks you to take the required oath and sign the executor's *bond* if the judge deems it necessary. Since your father's will specifically requested that his representative be exempted from this, the judge will try to comply with the request, unless our statute requires the personal representative to be bonded in estates like your father's. A bond guarantees to the court and to those parties with an interest in the decedent's estate (beneficiaries, devisees, creditors, and the like) that you, the executor, will act in a fiduciary manner and perform your duties faithfully. The amount of the bond is determined by the court, and if it is needed, we will seek the lowest amount possible to lessen the bond premium expense.

> Bond

* See Appendix A.

After you have signed the bond and it is approved by the court, Ms. Brown asks the court to appoint two persons, previously agreed on, as appraisers for your father's estate. Not all states require appraisers, but ours does. Before the hearing, we will contact and receive the consent of these persons to act as appraisers. They are paid for their work out of the assets of the estate by you, the executor.

Letters testamentary issued

Finally, Ms. Brown requests the clerk to issue *Letters Testamentary* to you. These become your official authorization from the court to act as executor of your father's will and estate. You will use the Letters to obtain the assets of your father's estate that are currently in the possession of others such as banks and corporations. A few of the forms I have mentioned are provided by the court, but it will be necessary for us to prepare and execute most of the forms we previously discussed.

Executor: The procedures are just as complex as I imagined. What next?

Paralegal: Well, remember we discussed ancillary administration?

Executor: Yes, in connection with the summer cottage.

Paralegal: That's right. We petition the county probate court in State B, where the cottage is located, asking that you be appointed ancillary administrator. I shall check to make sure you qualify. If I remember correctly, State B does not require the personal representative to be a resident of that state. I will research this and check on all similar matters under instructions from Ms. Brown before we act. If you are appointed, you will follow procedures similar to those we have discussed. You should notify creditors, if any, collect other assets, and pay taxes and debts. Doing these things will prevent creditors from attaching the cottage to satisfy debts, so you will be able to transfer it to your mother according to your father's wishes.

Executor: I am sure my father had no debts in State B where the cottage is located.

Paralegal: We must still go through these procedures, but the ancillary administration should create no problems.

Executor: Good. Let's get back to our state procedures.

Inventory and appraisal

Paralegal: The next step is to prepare a complete inventory of your father's property with an estimate of the value of each asset. I prepare an *inventory and appraisal form* (Form 8*), which Ms. Brown reviews. The two appointed appraisers will value the inventory according to one of the methods allowed by the Internal Revenue Code—assigning to each asset either the value it had at the time your father died (§ 2031) or the value it had six months after his death (§ 2032). We will discuss the tax advantages of both methods and choose the one we think best once we have completed the inventory. The inventory and appraisal serve as a basis for the federal and state tax returns, if the state return is necessary, that must be filed and provide information to all interested parties concerning the value of the estate. You will also find them helpful when filing your *final account* (Form 9*) after completing all required procedures.

Executor: I was wondering about the taxes. What taxes must be paid and when are they due?

Paralegal: This area, resolving tax problems, is probably one of the most important functions Ms. Brown and I will help you perform in administering the estate. Death tax laws, both state and federal, are very complex. Ms. Brown

---

* See Appendix A.

determines whether any of the following tax returns must be filed and paid: *federal estate tax* (Form 29*), *State A and B inheritance tax* (Form 33*) *and/or estate tax* (Form 32*), *federal and state individual income tax* (Forms 21* and 22*), *federal and state fiduciary income tax* (Forms 25* and 26*), *federal and state gift tax* (Forms 27* and 28*). As I previously said, some states have eliminated estate taxes so will check State B to determine their status.

Federal and state tax forms

Now you see why the "tickler" system and the checklists we previously discussed are so valuable. They help us stay on top of any important steps or dates in the administration of the estate. They are especially useful and timely when dealing with potential tax problems.

I prepare all the necessary tax returns, and we review them thoroughly with Ms. Brown. She files them, along with your check as executor for any tax payments due, with the appropriate federal or state tax department as well as the probate court.

Executor: I am glad we have the opportunity to review the tax consequences together. I know very little about this area, even though I have been interested in it.

Paralegal: Now, let's discuss the major items of property included in your father's estate. As you know, your duties as executor are basically to collect the estate assets, to pay your father's creditors and necessary taxes, and to distribute the remaining assets according to the provisions of his will.

Probate and nonprobate assets

Some of your father's property was owned by him and your mother in *joint tenancy* and will automatically pass to her by *operation of law*. This results from the *right of survivorship*, which means that the surviving joint tenant (your mother) gets the property without having to wait for a court order. The home, the stocks and bonds, and the savings account automatically belong to your mother because she is a joint tenant owner. These property items, along with the benefits from your father's life insurance policy, are called *nonprobate assets* since they do not have to be disposed of by will nor do they *descend* to an heir as intestate property. Other items, which he owned, were in his name alone, such as the car, the checking account, the paintings, and the summer cottage. These are *probate assets*, and, I might add, anything he may have owned as a tenant in common with someone else would be a probate asset also. Tenancy in common is a form of ownership between two or more persons. It differs from joint tenancy in that each co-owner can transfer his or her property interest not only while alive as in joint tenancy but also, unlike joint tenancy, after death, for example, through a will.

As executor, you must collect and preserve only *probate assets* such as the car, paintings, and checking account. All probate and generally all nonprobate assets are included, however, in the decedent's estate for computing death taxes. There are additional procedural steps we will follow to clear the passage of the nonprobate property to your mother.

Executor: What do we need to do now?

Paralegal: At this time, you must open a checking account at your father's bank in your name as executor of his estate. In order to do this, we must file for an employer identification number using Form SS-4 from the Internal Revenue Service and a Notice Concerning Fiduciary Relationship (Forms 23* and 24*). These

---

* See Appendix A.

forms must be executed and the employer identification number obtained before we can open the account. Here is an example of what the check imprint on your father's account should look like (see Exhibit 8.4). You can then submit to the bank Letters Testamentary authorizing you to withdraw your father's checking account and have it transferred to the estate account. All the estate funds you collect must be deposited into this account, and receipts for such funds and any disbursements you make must be retained. You will need the canceled checks and other receipts or vouchers you receive during the administration of the estate when you present your *final account* to the probate court. It is essential that you keep complete and accurate records of all transactions affecting the estate because the court will hold you personally responsible for any discrepancies or negligence.

Executor: What about some of the other property that I can't deposit—the probate assets I believe you called them—like the car, the paintings, the digital assets, and Dad's life insurance?

Paralegal: Let's back up one moment and discuss again which are probate assets and which are nonprobate assets. Probate assets are those that can be passed by will or by intestate succession statutes. They include property owned solely in the decedent's name or, as previously mentioned, owned as a tenant in common. No other person takes them automatically when the owner dies. The car, the digital assets, and the paintings that belonged to your father are probate assets because he alone owned them. Some of the digital assets may have only sentimental value, while others may have monetary value. Those with monetary value are probate assets. The life insurance benefits are different. When the owner dies, the named beneficiary more-or-less automatically becomes the owner of the benefits—because life insurance benefits are derived from a contract between an insured person and an insurer (the insurance company) to pay a certain sum of money to a third person, the beneficiary, after the insured dies. When your father died, your mother, whom he named beneficiary, became entitled to the insurance benefits directly, without having to wait for the probate court's approval.

Exhibit 8.4	Sample Check Imprint for Deceased's Estate

ESTATE OF JOHN T. SMITH   1001
1024 Pleasure Lane
Heavenly City, State A 12345   _____
                                                                    Date
Pay to
the order of _____ $ _____

_____ Dollars

FIRST NATIONAL BANK

For _____   _____

                                                              Executor*

_____

*Or other titles for the personal representative may be used.

_____

* See Appendix A.

Executor: I see. The insurance benefits are nonprobate assets like the property my parents owned as joint tenants?

Paralegal: That's right. You must notify the insurance agent of your father's death and verify the agent receives the policy so your mother can be given its proceeds without their passing through probate. Remember, however, we still must report this insurance as part of your father's *gross (total) estate* for federal estate tax purposes, unless he had relinquished the *"incidents of ownership"* on the policy. If your father contacted his insurance agent three years before his death and gave up the incidents of ownership, which are certain contractual rights under the policy, such as the right to cancel the policy or change the beneficiary and the right to borrow on or assign the policy, then the amount of the policy will not be part of his gross estate for federal estate tax purposes. We must check this out.

Life insurance and incidents of ownership

Executor: It's getting complicated.

Paralegal: Right now I'm sure it seems complicated. Let me assure you that if we work on this together in a systematic manner, everything will go smoothly. Let's see. We were discussing the car, the digital assets, and the paintings. The title to the car must be transferred to your mother. This cannot be accomplished until you receive Letters Testamentary. The following, however, will be necessary.

- The *title registration card* (Exhibit 8.5) or certificate of title must be executed (filled in with any required information and signed by you as executor).

- A transfer fee must accompany the executed registration card or certificate and be mailed within a prescribed time, e.g., 14 days of the date of transfer, to the state motor vehicle office to avoid penalties.

- A certified copy of Letters Testamentary—your authorization from the court to act as executor.

- A certified copy of the *Order Setting Apart Personal Property*. (We will discuss this in greater detail later.)

The paintings and digital assets, like the car, are part of the inventory, and title will be transferred to your mother after creditors' claims and taxes due are paid. Determination of your father's debts and payment of those claims are other topics we must discuss.

Creditors' claims

Executor: Suppose my mother wanted to obtain and use some of the probate property now. Could she?

Paralegal: Yes. Some states, including ours, allow a surviving spouse and/or minor child to petition the probate court for a *family maintenance allowance* and the receipt of certain *exempt personal property* reserved for them by law. Your mother can petition for these things as the surviving spouse. Since your father was solvent and left his entire estate to your mother, I do not believe this will be necessary. If some unknown creditors of your father with considerable claims appear, we will then review the situation.

Executor: If the creditors do appear and there isn't enough property in my father's estate to pay all of them, would my mother still receive these things?

Paralegal: Yes. This is true in our state. Such claims of the spouse are given priority even over funeral expenses as well as various other debts within statutory limitations. Now, concerning creditors' claims, do you remember what was said

EXHIBIT 8.5   Registration Card or Certificate of Title

STATE OF MINNESOTA
CERTIFICATE OF TITLE
TO A MOTOR VEHICLE
THIS TITLE IS PRIMA FACIE PROOF OF OWNERSHIP
KEEP IN A SAFE PLACE — ANY ALTERATION OR ERASURE VOIDS THIS TITLE

VEHICLE IDENTIFICATION NUMBER   MAKE   YEAR   TYPE

TITLE NUMBER   DATE ISSUED   NEW OR USED   IF NEW, DATE OF FIRST SALE   FOR CENTRAL OFFICE USE ONLY

FIRST SECURED PARTY'S INTEREST RELEASED BY.   SECOND SECURED PARTY'S INTEREST RELEASED BY

AUTHORIZED SIGNATURE X   AUTHORIZED SIGNATURE

ASSIGNMENT BY RECORDED OWNER(S): I (WE), CERTIFY THIS VEHICLE IS FREE FROM ALL SECURITY INTERESTS, WARRANT TITLE, AND ASSIGN THE VEHICLE TO:
PRINT BUYER'S NAME(S)   OWNER'S SIGNATURE(S) ALL OWNERS MUST SIGN   DATE OF SALE
X

APPLICATION FOR TITLE BY BUYER(S)   COMPLETE FRONT AND BACK   PLEASE PRINT (DARK INK)

PRINT BUYER'S NAME(S) LAST, FIRST, AND MIDDLE   DATE OF BIRTH

STREET ADDRESS   CITY   COUNTY   STATE   ZIP CODE

IS THIS VEHICLE SUBJECT TO SECURITY AGREEMENT(S)?   YES ☐   NO ☐   IF YES, COMPLETE SECTION BELOW

FIRST SECURED PARTY (PRINT NAME)   DATE OF SECURITY AGREEMENT

STREET ADDRESS   CITY   STATE   ZIP CODE

SECOND SECURED PARTY (PRINT NAME)   DATE OF SECURITY AGREEMENT

STREET ADDRESS   CITY   STATE   ZIP CODE

IF THERE IS AN ADDITIONAL SECURITY AGREEMENT(S) COMPLETE AND ATTACH DPS2017.   NAME OF INSURANCE COMPANY   POLICY NUMBER

BUYER SUBSCRIBED AND SWORN TO BEFORE ME:
X

I (we), certify I (we) am (are) of legal age, have bought this vehicle subject to liens shown and no others, this vehicle is and will continue to be insured while operating upon the public streets and highways, and all of my (our) declarations are true and correct.
X

NOTARY SIGNATURE   DATE

COUNTY   DATE MY COMMISSION EXPIRES   BUYER'S SIGNATURE(S) ALL BUYERS SIGN.

DETACH THIS PORTION   DO NOT SEPARATE UNTIL SOLD

MINNESOTA MOTOR VEHICLE REGISTRATION CARD   RECORDED OWNER(S) RECORD OF SALE

PLATE NUMBER   TITLE NUMBER   PLATE NUMBER
PLATES EXPIRE   TAX   TAX BASE   TITLE NUMBER
MAKE   MODEL YEAR   TYPE   V.I.N.
V.I.N.   STICKER NUMBER
RECORDED OWNER(S)   BUYER'S SIGNATURE(S)   SALE DATE
    STREET ADDRESS
    CITY   STATE   ZIP CODE

Courtesy: State of Minnesota.

during our earlier discussion about creditors and the hearing on the petition to approve the will?

Executor: Yes. You mentioned that time limits are set for filing creditors' claims against my father's estate.

Paralegal: Right. When that time expires, we shall check to determine whether any filed claims should be contested. If you reasonably believe a particular claim is not legitimate, you will file an *Objections to Claim* form with the probate court and serve a copy on the alleged creditor. Contested claims are not heard on the same date as uncontested claims. A separate hearing date is set, at which time the court will decide which contested claims are to be allowed. Since it appears that your father had only a few debts and you have already acknowledged their validity, a hearing for contested claims may not be necessary. If one is necessary, however, you must pay the claims the court allows.

Executor: How do I pay the claims?

Paralegal: By writing checks on the estate account. Remember to ask for receipts from each creditor so the receipts and the canceled checks can be filed with the court as evidence of payment. Be cautioned that overpayment to a creditor, or payment of an invalid claim, makes you, the executor, personally liable. This means you must be very careful not to pay any doubtful claim until the hearing is over.

Executor: What if debts occur during our handling of the estate?

Paralegal: These expenses, including the fee our law firm will charge for its assistance in handling the estate, are priority debts according to statute and are paid just before you make the final distribution of the assets of the estate. As executor, you also are entitled to reasonable compensation as the personal representative of the estate, which is another priority debt.

Executor: My father mentioned that to me, but I do not intend to charge a fee.

Paralegal: That, of course, is entirely up to you. After claims are paid and receipts filed, the *final account* can be prepared. Each state generally sets a time limit for settlement of an estate, which the court may extend for proper reasons. This state allows the personal representative, you as executor, one year from the date of the appointment to settle the estate. Again, a hearing is held for final settlement, and forms must be prepared.

Final account

Executor: What forms are required, and what is the procedure?

Paralegal: To close the estate after having distributed its assets

- you must submit a *final account* that contains a list of all the assets you have collected, such as personal property and monies from sales, rents, and other sources.
- you must list the liabilities you claim as credits against the estate, including payments for expenses of administration, creditors' claims allowed by the court, funeral expenses, taxes due, and other necessary and proper expenses. Your account must show in detail these receipts and disbursements.
- you must sign and file a *petition for settlement and distribution*.
- you must prove you have distributed the *remaining assets* of the estate, and this figure must correspond to the actual inventory.

The court will then issue an *order* setting a hearing on the final account so parties interested in the estate can have the opportunity to be present and make any objections to the accounting.

As with the hearing to prove the will, *notice* must be published within a prescribed time, e.g., once a week for three consecutive weeks, in a local newspaper for the probate court. Copies of the notice must be sent to all beneficiaries, heirs, or devisees as well as the state Department of Taxation within a specified statutory time period before the hearing. In our state, it is 14 days. *Proof* of this publication and mailing must be filed with the court (Form 4*).

Executor: Then is the hearing held?

Paralegal: Yes. At the hearing, if satisfied the final account is correct and all taxes due have been paid, the probate judge will sign an order allowing the final account. Proof of payment of necessary taxes is provided by a certificate of release of tax lien. All the tax returns I have previously mentioned must be filed and any tax due must be paid before the court will determine the persons entitled to the remaining assets of the estate. The court will then issue the Decree of Distribution (Form 10*) assigning these assets. The Decree of Distribution states that notice of the final account and settlement was given; the decedent died testate; the final account was approved and allowed; all allowed claims were paid; all other expenses, such as funeral and administration expenses, have been paid; and all beneficiaries or heirs are named and the share of the decedent's property to which each is entitled is listed.

Executor: Is that it? Are my duties finished?

Paralegal: No. You must record a certified copy of the Decree of Distribution with the county recorder's office, specifically the register of deeds, for the real estate your father willed to your mother. Other documents might also have to be recorded in State B, depending on its laws.

Finally, you can distribute the estate in compliance with the Decree of Distribution. Each distributee or recipient must sign a receipt for the property passed to him or her, and you must file the receipts with the court. The last act is *petitioning* the court for your discharge as personal representative (Form 11*). In this case, the court will sign an *order* discharging you, as executor (Form 12*). If there was a bond, a certified copy of the order should be sent to the surety company, and you should request any refund. With that, you have completed your responsibilities.

Executor: And there are quite a few! I very much appreciate your taking the time to explain the probate procedures to me. It gives me a much clearer picture of what happens in an administration and what duties I have to perform.

Paralegal: Well, I enjoy being able to assist you in these matters. I am sure we will work well together. I have some questionnaires and checklists for you to complete, and I will give you some written materials on the duties of a personal representative and procedures for probating a will that our office has prepared. I would like you to take these home and read them. Also, our local county probate court in the county courthouse has a website accessible to the public that includes answers to many of your questions on probate and estate administration. It explains the tasks you will perform and may clear up any confusion

---

Decree of
distribution

---

* See Appendix A.

you may have about the things we have discussed today. We may need to cover some matters more fully, such as what happens if you decide to sell any of your father's real property; however, we can wait to discuss those matters with Ms. Brown when they arise. Now let's set up our "tickler" system.

PREPARATION FOR PROBATE AND ESTATE ADMINISTRATION—GENERAL OVERVIEW

The personal representative has a fiduciary obligation with respect to the assets of the estate, that is, a duty to utilize the highest degree of care and integrity in handling the decedent's property for the benefit of the estate beneficiaries and devisees. Once appointed by the court, the personal representative has the following general responsibilities.

1. To discover, collect, and preserve all probate assets of any value and manage the probate estate of the decedent if it includes real estate, securities, or an ongoing business until the estate is settled

2. To notify the deceased's creditors of the death, give them the opportunity to present their claims, settle all just claims against the estate, and verify the creditors are paid (money for this will come out of the estate assets)

3. To file all required federal and state income, gift, estate, or inheritance tax returns and pay all taxes due

4. To distribute the remainder of the estate as required by the terms of the will or by law (the intestate succession statutes when there is no valid will)

The mechanics of administering an estate are complex and varied. The authority of the personal representative to administer the decedent's property is governed by the will or state statute. Statutes vary from state to state. Therefore, the list of duties presented here is intended only to provide a basis for understanding the major duties in any given administration; it is not meant to be all-inclusive or exhaustive.

Pre-Probate Duties of the Personal Representative and Paralegal

Both you and the personal representative will have numerous duties to perform in the days immediately after the decedent's death. If the decedent left a letter of instructions concerning funeral and burial or had entered into a prepaid contract with a funeral director, the personal representative will help the family make the necessary arrangements according to the decedent's wishes or will defer to those of the surviving spouse and family members. Generally, your supervising attorney will be hired by the personal representative at this time, and your work as the paralegal in this case will begin.

Preparations for probate should begin immediately after the death of the testator. The needs of the family take priority on the death of one of its members, especially when the decedent was the family breadwinner. As the paralegal acting for the law firm selected by the personal representative to assist in administering the estate, you must see that the family's needs are satisfied. The duties you may be asked to perform include the following: (1) search for and obtain the will and other personal and business records; (2) notify appropriate parties of the decedent's death; (3) obtain certified copies of the death certificate from the funeral director; and (4) after contacting the appropriate persons, set a date for the family conference.

Search for and Obtain the Will and Other Personal and Business Records

One of your first responsibilities while assisting the client, i.e., the personal representative, in testate proceedings is to obtain, review, and make copies of the will. As you perform this investigative function, you should check the letter of instructions for the will's location or your law firm's files. If your firm did not draft the will, you should contact the office of the decedent's attorney who drafted the will. At this point, if you have not discovered the will, check other locations such as the decedent's safe deposit box and places in the decedent's home considered secure. You should also determine if the will was filed with the court.

> **EXAMPLE:** Maxine has a will. Her husband, Malcolm, has seen the will and knows he has been named executor. Maxine dies and her will cannot be found. Malcolm believes the will is located in Maxine's safe deposit box. Although a bank must seal the safe deposit box on learning of the owner's death, generally an officer of the bank will be allowed to determine whether the owner's (decedent's) will is in the box. If it is, the bank may forward the will directly to the probate court before sealing the safe deposit box, thereby avoiding unnecessary delays in locating the will and enabling the decedent's estate administration to begin.

You must interview family, friends, business advisers, and associates (such as partners, accountants, brokers, agents, and the employer of the decedent), or contact them by phone or mail and request information about the will's existence and location and about other personal or business records that may help you locate all assets belonging to the decedent. If the search is successful and the will is found, copies of the will are prepared for the beneficiaries, devisees, and the court, and a summary of the contents of the will is made. The original will must be given to the probate court in the county of the state that is the decedent's legal home (domicile) within a specific period, usually 30 days after death. Any person in possession of a will who neglects or refuses to deliver the will to the court may, by law, be civilly liable for damages caused by such neglect or possibly criminally prosecuted. Some states have established a "procedure to compel production of a will" when there is reason to believe that a will or codicil exists but the written document cannot be located. The petition requests the judge issue an order that requires the person who allegedly has knowledge of the location or existence of the document to appear and be examined in court. A case that illustrates the use of this procedure to compel production to determine the existence of a will is *In re Coffman's Estate*, 170 Ok. 171, 474 P.2d 942 (1970).

ASSIGNMENT 8.2

To test your investigatory abilities, make a list of as many places as possible where a will might be kept. Select members of your family, e.g., spouse, parents, brothers, or sisters, who have made wills and determine if your list would help you find their wills. If your list does not locate their wills, what additional steps would you follow to discover whether a will exists and its location?

Notify Appropriate Parties of the Decedent's Death

After finding the will, you may be asked to summarize it and send copies to persons named in the will. You also must locate and notify by phone or mail the witnesses and other appropriate parties, such as banks or depositories, e.g., savings and loan associations or credit unions, of the decedent's death so these financial institutions may meet certain legal obligations including the following:

- Prevent persons (holders of accounts with the decedent) from withdrawing money from the decedent's accounts in an attempt to avoid death taxes levied on the transfer of assets at the time of death.

- Provide for the safekeeping of any safe deposit box contents. Close all demand accounts (checking accounts) of the decedent.

- Cancel all credit cards.

Obtain Certified Copies of the Death Certificate

Your attorney will seldom be contacted to assist in sorting out a decedent's estate before the funeral arrangements are complete. The funeral director obtains the necessary burial permits and the death certificate, which is the document executed by a physician listing the name of the decedent and the place, time, date, and cause of death. Once your attorney is employed, you will obtain certified copies of the death certificate from the funeral director. You should work with your attorney to determine the number of certified copies required to complete all the necessary transactions. If additional copies are needed, you may obtain them from the state health department, the Bureau of Vital Statistics, the clerk of district court, or a state registrar. A certified copy of the death certificate is usually filed with the Petition for Probate. Also, you must include a certified copy when you file claims, obtain life insurance or accidental death benefits, open a decedent's safe deposit box, collect money from POD accounts, end a joint tenancy, transfer stocks, collect benefits from Social Security or the Veterans Administration, and file deeds transferring title to real estate with the county recorder's office or the Registrar of Deeds office (see the sample death certificate in Exhibit 8.6).

Set a Date for the Family Conference

Shortly after the decedent's death, you will schedule a family conference. All persons named in the will should be asked to attend this conference. In addition, whether the decedent died testate or intestate, you must give notice of the death to all heirs (blood relatives of the decedent) and request that they—and, of course, the surviving spouse—attend the family conference. In some states, a convenient time for this meeting may be on the day of the opening of the safe deposit box, if the decedent had one.

The Family Conference

At the family conference, you must obtain information pertinent to future administrative duties. While assisting the personal representative, you or your supervising attorney should openly discuss the following points with the family.

1. *Explain the provisions of the will* if it is available. If no will exists, you must explain in detail how the intestate-decedent's property will be inherited, by whom, and which state statute will apply to specific property of the deceased. Only a paralegal who has mastered the intestate succession statutes and is experienced in responding accurately to any questions should perform this function, *but remember legal advice about family concerns must come from the attorney.* If property such as real property is located in another state, you must explain the need for an ancillary administrator. The attorney and you should also explain the general nature of probate administration, including the appointment of the

⚖️ *Ethical Issue*

EXHIBIT 8.6　Certificate of Death

Type/Print
in Permanent
Black Ink

MINNESOTA DEPARTMENT OF HEALTH.
Section of Vital Statistics
CERTIFICATE OF DEATH

Local File Number　　　　　　　　　　　　　　　　　　　　　　　State File Number

Signature of Sub-Registrar / Date

1a Name of Deceased - First	Middle	Last	Suffix

1b Alias	2 Social Security No.	3 Sex	4 Date of Death

5 Date of Birth	6a Age (in years)	Under 1 Yr. 6b months / 6c days	Under 1 Day 6d hours / 6e minutes	7 Place of Birth (city and state/foreign country)

8a Father's Name (first, middle)	8b Father's Last Name	9 Mother's Name (first, middle, maiden surname)

10 Race	11a Hispanic Origin ___No ___Yes →	11b If Yes, Specify Cuban, Mexican, etc...	12 Decedent's Education 12a Primary/Secondary (0-12) / 12b College (1-4, 5+)

13a Marital Status ___Mar. ___Div. ___Wid. ___Never Mar.	13b Name of Spouse (If wife, specify maiden name)	14 Decedent's Usual Occupation

15 Kind of Business or Industry	16 U.S. Veteran ___No ___Yes	17a State of Residence	17b County of Residence

17c City or Township of Residence	17d Address of Decedent (number, street, zip)

17e Residence in City or Township ___City Limits ___Township Limits	18a City or Township of Death	18b County of Death

19a Place of Death (specify one) ___Hosp. ___N.H. ___Res. ___Other →	Specify	19b If Hospital (specify one) ___Inpatient ___ER ___DOA ___Other

19c Name of Facility Where Death Occurred (If not institution, specify address)

~~COPY~~

20a Name of Informant	20b Informant is _____ of the deceased (spouse, child, parent, sibling, etc.)

21 Method of Disposition (check all that apply) ___Burial ___Cremation ___Donation ___Entombment ___Other →	Specify	22 Date of Disposition

23 Name of Cemetery	City	State

24 If Cremation, Specify Name of Crematory	25 If Cremation, Specify Name of M.E. / Coroner Authorizing Cremation

26a Name of Funeral Establishment	26b License No.	27a Signature of Funeral Service Licensee	27b License No.	28 Date Signed

29a Name of Person Certifying Cause of Death (please type)	29b Title (check one) ___M.D. ___Coroner / M.E. ___D.O.	29c License No. of Certifier #

29d Address of Certifier (street & number)	29e City	29f State	29g Zip Code

30 Signature of M.D. / M.E. / Coroner / D.O.	31 Date Signed	32 Signature of Registrar	33 Date Filed

PLEASE TYPE

34 PART I
IMMEDIATE cause of death (final disease or condition resulting in death)

Enter the diseases, injuries, or complications that caused death. Do not enter the mode of dying, such as cardiac or respiratory shock or heart failure. List only one cause per line.

Interval between onset and death.

a. _____

Sequentially list conditions, if any, leading to immediate cause. Enter UNDERLYING cause last, (disease or injury that initiated events resulting in death).

b. _____

c. _____

35 I attended the deceased from ___ MO ___ DAY ___ YEAR to ___ MO ___ DAY ___ YEAR and last saw him/her on ___ MO ___ DAY ___ YEAR . I viewed the body after death ___Yes ___No

36 PART II Other significant conditions contributing to death but not resulting in the underlying cause given in Part I.

38 Time of Death

37 Was Female Pregnant: At Death? ___Yes ___No ___Unknown　In Last 12 Months? ___Yes ___No ___Unknown

39 MANNER OF DEATH ___Natural	40 M.E./Coroner Notified ___Yes ___No	41 Autopsy ___Yes ___No	42 Were autopsy results available when filling in cause of death ___Yes ___No	43 Diagnosis Deferred ___Yes

MUST BE REFERRED TO M.E. or CORONER { ___Accident ___Homicide ___Suicide ___Pending Inves. ___Cannot be Det. ___Not Classifiable

44a Place of Injury (street & number, city / township, state)

44b Describe How Injury Occurred

44c Type of Place Where Injury Occurred	44d Date of Injury	44e Time of Injury	44f Injury at Work? ___Yes ___No

personal representative, the preparation of the inventory and appraisal, the various tax returns, and the final account and decree of distribution. You should point out the dates by which these steps must be taken and explain how a "tickler" system can prevent important deadlines from being overlooked (see No. 16 below). If possible, provide an estimate of how long the administration will take.

2. *Discuss with the family the need for appointing fiduciaries*, e.g., guardians for minors or conservators for incompetent persons, if the decedent died intestate. If there is a will, and the persons selected to act in these capacities, including a trustee named in a testamentary trust, are present at the conference, find out whether they are willing to serve.

If the fiduciary does not feel qualified to handle the digital estate, discuss the possibility of hiring a competent third party who will report to the fiduciary.

3. *Obtain information from the family about the general size and nature of the decedent's estate* using checklists similar to those in Chapter 5. You will need to explain that only probate assets will be subject to probate and that nonprobate property passes directly to the beneficiary or joint owners. The total value of probate and nonprobate assets is included in the decedent's estate for federal and state death tax purposes but only probate assets are subject to creditors' claims. Nonprobate assets include property in joint tenancy, property in living trusts, and assets where a named beneficiary is to receive the property, as in life insurance policies, annuities, pension, profit-sharing, 401(k), and self-employed retirement plans, or IRAs (traditional and Roth). Based on the information obtained in the checklists, determine the type of probate proceeding to be used, or for UPC states, determine whether formal or informal probate proceedings should be followed or whether it is possible to settle the estate by a method other than probate proceedings. (See the discussion on administering "small estates" by affidavit or by Summary Administration in Chapter 9.)

4. *Verify that the personal representative protects and sufficiently insures* all real and personal property and any premiums due are paid. Written verification of coverage must be obtained from insurance agents. You should also advise the personal representative to safeguard expensive personal property such as jewelry, coin collections, and other valuables by placing them in a newly opened safe deposit box.

5. *Identify and obtain a list of personal debts and those relating to any business interest* of the decedent known to family members so you can give these creditors actual notice of the death and the need to file their claims. Other creditors will be given notice by publication, which is discussed in detail in Chapter 9.

6. *Obtain the facts necessary to prepare the Petition to Prove the Will*, if the decedent died testate, or Petition for General Administration, if the decedent died intestate. Be sure you use the appropriate state or county forms for these and subsequent petitions.

7. *If the deceased owed any members of the family a debt*, explain to that creditor the need to file a claim. The time limits for procedures to approve such claims will be discussed in other chapters.

8. *To alleviate the family's anxiety and concern about immediate financial matters*, you must discuss the various forms of protection given a surviving spouse and children by some state statutes, such as the homestead exemption or allowance;

exempt property; family allowances or maintenance; dower, curtesy, or election rights of a surviving spouse; and children's rights, including rights of pretermitted children, adopted children, and nonmarital children. You should determine the wishes of these family members and prepare the necessary documents and forms to implement their requests.

9. *Explain what a disclaimer is*, its procedures, and effects. Some states allow a beneficiary or devisee to disclaim in whole or in part any interest received from the will by filing a disclaimer in probate court (see Exhibit 14.3). If a beneficiary or devisee determines a disclaimer is in the best interests of both the family and himself, you may be asked to obtain and execute the disclaimer form and file it with the probate court. Disclaimers can also be executed and filed by an executor or administrator on behalf of the estate of a deceased devisee or beneficiary or by a guardian on behalf of a minor. The interest disclaimed will be distributed according to the directives of the will or by intestate succession, and it will be disposed of just as if the disclaimant had died immediately before the decedent (compare UPC § 2–801).

10. *Determine whether assets will need to be sold during probate administration* to pay debts, taxes, and expenses of the decedent's estate. If assets must be sold, ask the family whether they wish to retain any particular items. Otherwise, if the personal representative has been given the power of sale by the will, he might sell an item of property, e.g., a painting, that the family would prefer to keep for sentimental reasons. If property must be sold to pay debts, you will have to explain the abatement process to the family and heirs.

11. *If authorized by state statute or the decedent's will*, you must discuss the arrangements that will be necessary for the continuation or sale of the decedent's business, e.g., a sole proprietorship, partnership, or limited partnership.

⚖ *Ethical Issue*

12. *Check the estate plans of the surviving spouse and*, if requested, make arrangements to amend his or her will. *Be careful about improper solicitation for this will.* If there is no surviving spouse and the decedent was the last occupant in a home, you may be asked to notify the post office to forward mail to the personal representative of the estate and stop newspapers and all other deliveries.

13. *In all cases, you must determine if the decedent made any advancements* to any of the beneficiaries or heirs.

14. *Discuss or inquire about any other documents that may have a direct or indirect bearing on the status or transfer of the decedent's estate*, such as marital agreements, a legal separation or divorce, or transactions such as living trust agreements.

15. *Obtain names and addresses of the decedent's financial advisers*, including tax advisers, accountant, banker, trust officer, insurance agent or broker, and stockbroker.

16. *In preparation for the probate procedure*, you must create a checklist of probate procedures and prepare a calendar checklist (tickler) of important tax dates and deadlines (see Exhibit 8.3). After you obtain the necessary information, explain the probate process, and answer the questions of the family members, the conference is concluded. Your duties and the duties of the personal representative, however, are just beginning.

Appointment Procedure—The Beginning

To begin the probate process and obtain appointment, the personal representative must complete the following steps. You will assist the personal representative in performing some of these tasks.

- File the original will and codicil if there is one.
- File a petition either for (1) probate of the will and appointment of the personal representative (executor) or for (2) administration and appointment of the personal representative (administrator). These petitions are usually two separate forms that request, basically, the same information.
- Contact the witnesses to the will who, if needed, must be present to testify at the hearing for probate of the will and appointment of the personal representative (executor). Witnesses are not needed if the will is self-proved.
- File a death certificate, if required.
- Pay filing fees, which you will verify.
- Arrange for bond, if necessary (see the discussions of bond and surety in the next sections).

In some states, e.g., Minnesota, the mechanics for beginning the probate procedures when a decedent dies testate or intestate require the use of one of two legal forms. When the decedent dies with a will, the form that commences probate is called the Petition for Probate of Will and for Appointment of Personal Representative (Executor). If the decedent dies without a will, the form is called the Petition for Appointment of Administrator. Both petitions contain facts that establish that a specific probate court has jurisdiction. *Note*: Whether the decedent died testate or intestate, these petitions must list all heirs, i.e., persons who would have inherited under the laws of intestate succession. For their protection, these heirs must be given notice of the court hearing on the petition and also the opportunity to be present to contest the will or challenge the personal representative's appointment. In most states, the petitions include the name and domicile (address) of the decedent; the date and place of death; the names, ages, relationship to the decedent, and addresses of heirs; the value and the nature of the decedent's real and personal property; the decedent's debts; and the name and address of the petitioner. As you would expect, the forms used for this petition vary from state to state. Other states, e.g., Michigan, use the same form for commencing probate for all decedents, whether they die with or without a will, by simply having the petitioner check the appropriate box on the form. The following state forms reflect this diversity.

- Exhibit 8.7 Michigan Petition for Probate and/or Appointment of Personal Representative (Testate/Intestate)
- Exhibit 8.8 Delaware Petition for Authority to Act as Personal Representative

In both testate and intestate cases, the probate court sets a time and place for a hearing on the petition. At the hearing, after the witnesses testify, if the probate court allows the will or grants administration, the court appoints the personal representative (executor or administrator), who must file an oath of office and in some cases post a bond, which constitutes an expense of the estate and may be deducted on the death tax forms. These procedural matters will be discussed in greater detail in subsequent chapters.

EXHIBIT 8.7   Michigan Petition for Probate

Approved, SCAO   OSM CODE: PFA

STATE OF MICHIGAN PROBATE COURT COUNTY OF	PETITION FOR PROBATE AND/OR APPOINTMENT OF PERSONAL REPRESENTATIVE (TESTATE/INTESTATE)	FILE NO.

Estate of _____

1. I,_____ , am interested in the estate and make this petition as
      Name of petitioner

   _____ as defined by MCL 700.1105(c).
      Relationship to decedent, i.e., heir, devisee, child, spouse, creditor, beneficiary, etc.

2. Decedent information: _____ m. _____ _____
                              Date of death   Time (if known)   Age   Social Security Number

   Domicile (at date of death): _____ _____ _____
                                     City/Township/Village   County   State

   Estimated value of estate assets: Real estate: $_____   Personal estate: $_____

3. So far as I know or could ascertain with reasonable diligence, the names and addresses of the heirs and/or devisees of the decedent, the relationship to the decedent, and the ages of any who are minors are as follows:

NAME	ADDRESS	RELATIONSHIP	AGE (if minor)

Of the above interested persons, the following are under legal disability or otherwise represented and presently have or will require representation:

NAME	LEGAL DISABILITY	REPRESENTED BY Name, address, and capacity

4. ☐ a. Venue is proper in this county because the decedent was domiciled in this county on the date of death.
   ☐ b. The decedent was not domiciled in Michigan, but venue is proper in this county because property of the decedent was located in this county at the date of death.

5. ☐ An application was previously filed and a personal representative was appointed informally.

PLEASE SEE OTHER SIDE

Do not write below this line - For court use only

PC 559 (3/00) PETITION FOR PROBATE AND/OR APPOINTMENT OF PERSONAL REPRESENTATIVE (TESTATE/ INTESTATE)   MCL 700.3402; MSA 27.13402, MCL 700.3502; MSA 27.13502, MCR 5.302(A), MCR 5.308, MCR 5.310(B)

EXHIBIT 8.7   (continued)

6. ☐ A personal representative has been previously appointed in _____ County, _____
   and the appointment has not been terminated. The personal representative's name and address are: State

   _____   _____
   Name   Address

   _____
   City, state, zip

7. ☐ The decedent's will, dated _____ , with codicil(s) dated _____
      is offered for probate and is   ☐ attached to this petition.   ☐ already in the court's possession.
   ☐ An authenticated copy of the will and codicil(s), if any, probated in _____ County, _____
      is offered for probate, and documents establishing its probate accompany this petition.   State
   ☐ Neither the original will nor an authenticated copy of a will probated in another jurisdiction accompanies the petition. The
      will is lost, destroyed, or otherwise unavailable, but its contents are: (attach additional sheets as necessary)

   _____

8. ☐ The decedent's will was ☐ formally ☐ informally   probated on _____ in _____ County.
9. To the best of my knowledge, I believe that the instrument(s) subject to this petition, if any, was validly executed and is the
   decedent's last will.   After exercising reasonable diligence, I am unaware of an instrument revoking the will or codicil(s).
10. ☐ After exercising reasonable diligence, I am unaware of any unrevoked testamentary instrument relating to property located
   in this state as defined under MCL 700.1301.

11. ☐ I nominate _____ , as personal representative, who is qualified and has priority
               Name
   as: _____ . His/her address is: _____
                                                               Address

   _____
   City, state, zip

   Other persons having prior or equal right to appointment are:

   _____   _____
   Name   Name

   _____   _____
   Name   Name

12. ☐ The will expressly requests the personal representative serve with bond.
13. ☐ a. The decedent left a will that directs supervised administration.
    ☐ b. The decedent left a will that directs unsupervised administration, but supervised administration is necessary for the
         protection of persons interested in the estate because: (complete on line below)
    ☐ c. The decedent died intestate or left a will that does not direct supervised administration, but supervised administration is
         necessary because: (complete on line below)

   _____

14. ☐ A special personal representative is necessary because _____ .

I REQUEST:
15. ☐ An order determining heirs and that the decedent died   ☐ testate.   ☐ intestate.
16. ☐ Formal appointment of the nominated personal representative   ☐ with   ☐ without   bond.
17. ☐ Supervised administration.
18. ☐ Appointment of a special personal representative pending the appointment of the nominated personal representative.

   I declare under the penalties of perjury that this petition has been examined by me and that its contents are true to the best of my
   information, knowledge, and belief.

                                                _____
                                                Date

   _____   _____
   Attorney signature   Petitioner signature

   _____   _____
   Attorney name (type or print)   Bar no.   Petitioner name (type or print)

   _____   _____
   Address   Address

   _____   _____
   City, state, zip   Telephone no.   City, state, zip   Telephone no.

Exhibit 8.8   Delaware Petition for Authority to Act as Personal Representative

Form No. 1 – Petition for Authority to Act as Personal Representative

Petition For Authority To Act As Personal Representative

TO: The Register of Wills for the County of New Castle in the State of Delaware

in the matter of the estate of: _____ }

Decedent   }

_____ {   **PETITION**

                                                   }

I. _____, the (Petitioner(s)) states under oath that:

(1) The decedent died on _____ a resident of _____

                                                                              Street Address

_____   _____   _____
            City   State   Zip Code

(2) The decedent had (a / no) will (dated _____)

(3) After the Will was signed, the decedent (a) did / did not marry [did / did not enter into a civil union or other legal relationship under the laws of another jurisdiction recognized as a civil union under Delaware law] and (b) no / _____ child(ren), was / were born to the decedent. _____

(4) The qualification to act as Personal Representative is _____

_____

_____

(5) Each Petitioner swears that (he / she) has never been convicted of a felony in this or any other jurisdiction.

II. Petitioner/Petitioners Requests the grant of: (check one)

○ Letters Testamentary   ○ Letters of Ancillary Administration with Will Annexed

○ Letters of Administration   ○ Letters of a Successor Administrator/rix

○ Letters of Administration with Will Annexed   ◉ Letters of a Successor Administrator/rix with Will Annexed

○ Letters of Ancillary Administration

III. The decedent solely owned personal property valued at $_____ and/or solely owned real estate to the value

$_____ located in New Castle County, State of Delaware, as follows: (street address or parcel number)

_____

Revised 2-23-12   Petition Page 1   Folio No. _____

EXHIBIT 8.8   (continued)

Form No. 1 – Petition for Authority to Act as Personal Representative

IV. The decedent was survived by the following persons:

NAME	RELATIONSHIP	ADDRESS
SPOUSE OR [CIVIL UNION PARTNER]:		
NEXT OF KIN:		
(Nearest relative of decedent, by blood relationship or legal adoption.)		

V. A Bond is / is not required.

> **STATE OF DELAWARE**
>
> **NEW CASTLE COUNTY** } **ss.**

_____ the Petitioner(s) named in the application, being duly sworn according to law say (s) that the matters alleged in this petition are true and correct to the best of (his, her, their) knowledge and belief.

Attorney of Record _____   **X** _____

Firm _____   Address _____

Address _____   _____

Phone _____   Phone _____

SWORN TO AND SUBSCRIBED before me, at Wilmington, Delaware this _____ day of _____,
_____.

_____
REGISTER OF WILLS

Revised 2-23-12   Petition Page 2   Folio No. _____

Bond

A bond or surety bond is a certificate in which a "surety," an individual or insurance company, promises to pay up to the amount of the bond to the probate court if the personal representative fails to faithfully perform the duties of administering the decedent's estate. A "surety," or "bonding," company is licensed to offer bonds to fiduciaries, such as personal representatives. The purpose of the bond is to protect beneficiaries, heirs, creditors, and government tax collectors from losses due to the personal representative's improper, negligent, or fraudulent administration of the decedent's estate. If required, a bond must be filed at the time of the personal representative's appointment or shortly thereafter. Often an employee of a bonding company will be present at court on hearing days with the appropriate bond forms, and arrangements can be made to complete and file the bond with the court immediately after the hearing.

The requirement that a personal representative file a bond is generally set by state statute. Typical statutes are Sections 8480(a) and 8481(a)(1) of the California Probate Code.

Cal. Prob. Code § 8480
(a) Except as otherwise provided by statute, every person appointed as personal representative shall, before letters are issued, give a bond approved by the court. If two or more persons are appointed, the court may require either a separate bond from each or a joint and several bond.

Cal. Prob. Code § 8481
(a) A bond is not required in either of the following cases: (1) The will waives the requirement of a bond.
Another example of a statute requiring a bond is

20 Pa. Stat. Ann. § 3175 Requiring or Changing Amount of Bond
The court, upon cause shown and after such notice, if any, as it shall direct, may require a surety bond, or increase or decrease the amount of an existing bond, or require more or less security therefor. (See also UPC §§ 3–603 and 3–604 for examples of when a bond is required and the amount of the bond.)

The requirements for a bond and surety vary from state to state.

- In some states, a bond may be required of all personal representatives.

- A bond is generally required if the testator requests it in the will, but the court can decide it is "unnecessary."

- In most states, a bond is not required if the testator states in the will that the personal representative may serve without bond. A sample clause reads:

  I direct that no bond or other indemnity shall be required of any personal representative including successor personal representatives nominated or appointed pursuant to this will. The term personal representative shall include any person appointed to administer this will.

- Even if the will waives the bond, a probate court may agree to require one at the request (sometimes a demand) and for the protection of interested parties, e.g., beneficiaries and creditors (see Md. Estates and Trusts Code Ann. § 6-102[b]); Ohio Rev. Code Ann. § 2109.04; and Cal. Prob. Code § 8481 (b). However, compare the comment in UPC § 3–603 rejecting the idea that a bond always be required, or required unless the will waives the bond.)

- If a will does not mention the bond, and the personal representative is a family member or close friend and a resident of the state in which the estate is administered, the court can agree to exclude a bond if all the beneficiaries agree and waive the filing of a bond.

- *No bond* is required if a corporation, e.g., a bank or trust company, is appointed personal representative.

- If there is no will, generally the personal representative must post a bond, especially if one or more minor children survive the intestate.

Today the majority of financial planners believe a bond is unnecessary. When a bond is required, the amount of the bond is based on the value of the estate, the type of assets, the relationship of the personal representative to the decedent, and other relevant facts including the demands of beneficiaries and creditors. The amount varies from state to state and ranges from the same as the estimated value of the decedent's personal property to twice that amount. Generally, the value of real property, unless sold at the direction of the testator's will to pay for estate debts, is not included in determining the value of the bond. If a bond is required, you must remind the personal representative to purchase the bond and file it promptly. Since the bond premium is payable annually and is automatically renewed, you must cancel the bond as soon as the estate is closed, deliver a copy of the Order Discharging the Personal Representative to the surety company, and request a refund of the unearned premium (see Form 12*). Since the testator can waive the requirement of a bond in the will, this expense can be avoided. In any event, the cost of the personal representative's bond is charged to the estate and paid with estate funds.

Surety

The surety is an insurance company or individual who guarantees payment of a specified sum of money to the court if the personal representative fails to properly perform his or her fiduciary duties.

ASSIGNMENT 8.3

Determine whether your state has bond requirements. If so, state briefly what they are. Cite all relevant statutes.

Probating (Proving) the Will or Granting Administration

Depending on the state, a will is proved in a variety of ways. The court may require the subscribing witnesses to testify to the following in court.

- That the testator, his attorney, and the two witnesses were present in the lawyer's office.

- That the testator declared to the witnesses the document held in his or her hand was his or her will and requested them to act as witnesses to the execution of his or her will. *Note:* The witnesses are not asked to read the will.

- That the witnesses watched the testator sign the will and also sign his or her initials in the margin on each page of the will.

- That the testator handed the will to one witness who, at the request of the testator, read aloud the attestation clause that precedes the place for the witnesses' signatures.

---

* See Appendix A.

- That both witnesses knew the testator and that he or she was over the age of majority (18), of sound mind, and not acting under any constraint or undue influence.
- That each witness then signed the will and added his address while the testator and the other witness watched.

Note: If a notary public is present at the execution of the will, hears the oaths and observes the acknowledgments and signatures, and officially notarizes the will, the will is "self-proved," and the witnesses' testimony in court is not necessary.

Another method used to prove a will is to have an affidavit signed by one or more of the witnesses who attest to the facts and the proper execution of the will (see Exhibit 8.9).

Once the probate court has approved the will or, in intestate cases, has granted administration, the court issues **Letters of Authority**. These are certificates of appointment that are often called Letters Testamentary or Letters of Administration.

Letters of Authority

Certificates of appointment called either Letters Testamentary, when there is a will, or Letters of Administration, when there is no will.

Letters Testamentary and Letters of Administration

When the probate court grants Letters Testamentary, an executor or executrix is appointed; when it grants Letters of Administration, an administrator or administratrix is appointed (see Forms 7* and 20*). Both Letters Testamentary and Letters of Administration are conclusive proof and evidence that the person named therein is the duly appointed, qualified, and acting personal representative of the decedent's estate with the powers, rights, duties, and obligations conferred by law. Certified copies of the letters issued to the personal representative by the probate court or registrar will be required for specific estate administration procedures including the following:

EXHIBIT 8.9   Affidavit of Attesting Witnesses

The undersigned, being severally duly sworn on their respective oaths, depose and say that on the _____ day of _____, 20___, _____, the Testator of the attached Will, in their presence, subscribed said Will at the end thereof and at the time of making such subscription declared the instrument so subscribed by him [her] to be his [her] Last Will and Testament; that they, at the request of said Testator and in his [her] presence and in the presence of each other, thereupon witnessed the execution of said Will by said Testator by subscribing their names as witnesses thereto; that in their opinion said Testator at the time of the execution of said Will was in all respects competent to make a Will and not under any restraint; and that they make this affidavit at the request of said Testator.

Witness
_____

Witness
_____

[Notary]

Reprinted with permission of Thomson/West from West McKinney's Forms. ESP. §7-79.

---

* See Appendix A.

- Open the decedent's safe deposit box, remove contents, and cancel the box.

- Open an estate safe deposit box to safeguard certain valuable assets, such as expensive jewelry, coins, and other valuables, and documents, such as deeds, birth and marriage certificates, divorce decrees, passports, insurance policies, stock certificates, record of military service, automobile and boat titles and registrations, mortgages, savings certificates, promissory notes, bills of sale, and other contracts.

- Withdraw money from existing savings and checking accounts of the decedent.

- Open a bank account for the estate to hold all cash from the decedent's accounts and from all property sold by the personal representative, debts collected, dividends from securities, salary checks, and other funds or benefits owed to the decedent.

- Transfer all assets (e.g., sale of real estate, sale or gift of stock, life insurance proceeds when the estate is the beneficiary, and so on).

- Forward the decedent's mail to the personal representative.

The person who applies for either Letters Testamentary or Letters of Administration must be competent, i.e., suitable in the opinion of the court, to discharge the personal representative's obligations. A person who has a felony record, is not a resident of the domicile state, or has a history of mental illness may be rejected as "unsuitable." The decision on competency is an exercise in discretion by the court. An executor is named by the will, so the court cannot arbitrarily appoint someone else to fill the position. This does not mean, however, that the court is compelled to appoint the named executor or that the appointee must be the most suitable and competent of all possibilities. For example, the court will not name a minor as executor even though he was selected by the testator. The minor lacks competency since a minor cannot make binding contracts for the estate. If the minor, however, had attained majority age at the time of the testator's death or subsequently at the time for admission or proof of the will, he can be competent to act as personal representative and may be appointed by the court.

The appointment of an administrator calls for greater discretion on the part of the court. Where the decedent has not designated a person to distribute the estate, the court will decide which applicant is appropriate. In many states the order of preference is set by statute. Again, the court cannot overrule a preference with or without cause unless the state statutes grant the court this power, but the court may use its discretion to appoint someone who occupies a lower position in the statutory order.

EXAMPLE: Ridgely names his wife, Yvonne, personal representative in his will. Following his death, she will be appointed executrix unless the court finds her incompetent or otherwise subject to disqualification. Ridgely's sister, Loretta, is an accountant and more experienced in business than Yvonne, but the court will not replace Yvonne with Loretta or anyone else unless it finds Yvonne unqualified. Similarly, if Ridgely had died intestate, Yvonne, his wife, would be the first choice in most states to be appointed personal representative.

If, in intestacy, an administrator has been appointed, but later a will is discovered and admitted to probate, the court will terminate the powers of the administrator and appoint the named executor, who will continue the probate of the estate. The following statute illustrates the basis for the termination of an intestate or testate appointment.

20 Pa. Stat. Ann. § 3181 Revocation of Letters

(a) When no will—The register may revoke letters of administration granted by him whenever it appears that the person to whom the letters were granted is not entitled thereto.

(b) When a will—The register may amend or revoke letters testamentary or of administration granted by him not in conformity with the provisions of a will admitted to probate. [Compare UPC § 3–612.]

(c) Death charges—Whether or not a will has been submitted or admitted, the register may revoke letters testamentary or of administration when it appears that the person to whom the letters were granted has been charged with voluntary manslaughter or homicide, except homicide by vehicle, as set forth in sections 3155 (relating to persons entitled) and 3156 (relating to persons not qualified), provided that the revocation shall not occur on these grounds if and when the charge has been dismissed, withdrawn or terminated by a verdict of not guilty.

EXAMPLE: Chin-Sun Bridges dies intestate. After her husband, Paul, is appointed administrator and Letters of Administration are issued, he discovers a will drawn by Chin-Sun in an old shoebox in the family home. Chin-Sun named her father, Kang-Dae Kim, executor of the will. On the basis of this discovery, if the court decides it is appropriate, Paul's administration terminates, and Kang-Dae will be appointed personal representative in order to continue the probate administration.

The specific procedures of administration and the personal representative's duties after appointment are discussed in succeeding chapters.

ASSIGNMENT 8.4

Juliana was in the final stages of a terminal illness when she made a will naming her brother, Roland, executor. Unknown to her, Roland had been declared legally insane the previous year. A month after Juliana's death, Roland is declared sane and applies for Letters Testamentary. Juliana's sister, Clarissa, contests Roland's application, and states that his insanity disqualifies him from acting as executor. In your state, is she correct?

Key Term

Letters of Authority

Review Questions

1. Who is prohibited from being a personal representative?

2. What is the difference between the following: an executor v. an executrix; a general administrator v. a special administrator; an administratrix *cum testamento annexo* v. an administratrix *de bonis non;* and a public administrator v. an ancillary administrator?

3. The personal representative is one type of a fiduciary. What does that mean? List other fiduciaries.

4. What are the primary or general duties of a personal representative when administering a decedent's estate?

5. How is a "tickler" system used for an estate administration?

6. Is there a time limit for commencing probate in your state? How long does your state allow for the completion of an estate administration? Cite your state statute for each period.

7. In general, what are a paralegal's duties in organizing, preparing, and conducting a family conference after a testator's death?

8. When does the probate court require a personal representative to post a bond? What is a surety bond? Draft a bond using your state's form.

9. How do Letters Testamentary and Letters of Administration differ?

10. Using the attesting and subscribing witnesses, what procedures are required to prove a will's validity?

Case Problems

Problem 1

Assume that some married member of your family has died. Perform the following tasks. (To preserve confidentiality, you should change the names of all parties concerned.)

A. Determine whether the decedent left a will.

B. If a will exists, locate it.

C. Using the sample from this text, prepare a "tickler" system.

D. Using the text's checklists or your own, determine the assets and liabilities of the "decedent's" estate. Fill in the checklists.

E. Obtain the facts necessary for the Petition to Prove the Will or, if no will exists, the Petition for General Administration. Then fill out the appropriate form.

F. Assume the decedent owed you a $5,000 debt based on a promissory note and you are willing to cancel the debt. How might this be done?

G. Determine whether your state grants an election right to a surviving spouse. Cite the statute and determine whether the decedent's spouse would receive a greater share under the will or under the statute.

H. Assume you are named as a beneficiary or devisee in the will. Fill out the disclaimer form. Can you assign your interest to your best friend?

I. Cite your state statute, if any, on maintenance, family allowance, and exempt property. Fill out the forms that pass these property items to family members.

J. Check to see if the "decedent's" spouse has a will. Ethically, could your supervising attorney be hired by the spouse to prepare the will? Explain.

Problem 2

Carmella Lamas is a wealthy widow. She has prepared a preliminary draft of her will but has not decided who she will name as her personal representative. Answer and explain the following questions according to your state's statutes.

A. Carmella's favorite relative is her nephew, Ferdinand, age 19. If she names him to be her personal representative, is he qualified to serve in your state? See and compare UPC 3–203(f).

B. Would Ferdinand be eligible to serve if he had been convicted of the felony of possessing and using drugs? See *Smith v. Christley*, 684 S.W.2d 158 (Tex.App. 1984).

Unless the person is unsuitable, courts routinely appoint the personal representative the testator names in her will.

C. If Carmella appoints her brother, Carlos, personal representative, can Carlos be removed after his appointment because he is insolvent? See *In re Quinlan's Estate*, 441 Pa. 266, 273 A.2d 340 (1971).

D. Once appointed, can Carlos be removed for any of the following acts of misconduct?

1. Carlos fails to file a final account.

2. Carlos omits items from the inventory he files with the court. See *Matter of Aaberg's Estates*, 25 Wash. App. 336, 607 P.2d 1227 (1980).

3. Carlos makes payments to himself for work he performs while administering Carmella's estate.

Since all states provide for the choice of a personal representative for an intestate's estate, answer the following if Carmella dies intestate.

E. Since Carmella is a widow and never remarried, who has priority in your state to be appointed her personal representative?

F. Some states do not allow persons who live in another state to become personal representatives. If Carlos lived in a different state than Carmella's domicile (your state), could he be appointed her personal representative?

Practical Assignments

1. Prepare a clause to be included in your will naming your executor and an alternate executor. Make sure you waive the necessity of a bond for the named executor.

2. Prepare a letter to the appropriate agency in your state requesting a certified copy of the death certificate for Dimitri Kostas, DOB: 2-19-1923, DOD: 3-1-2015; Place of Death: Your city, county, state; Father's Name: Anatole Kostas; Mother's Name: Althea Kostas (Maiden Name: Pappas). Make sure you reference the correct fee to obtain one copy of the death certificate.

3. Research your state laws to determine what authority, if any, an executor has over digital assets of the estate.

PROBATE AND ESTATE ADMINISTRATION

9

Outline

Objectives

After completing this chapter, you should be able to:

- Explain the distinction between probate proceedings and estate administration.

- Identify and explain state alternative procedures to probate and estate administration when administering "small estates."

- Recognize and define the traditional forms of probate and estate administration and compare the Uniform Probate Code alternative.

- List the circumstances under which solemn or formal probate proceedings are appropriate.

- Identify and explain the use of formal probate procedures and forms for administering a decedent's estate whether death occurred testate or intestate.

- Explain the potential liability of the personal representative.

- Apply the procedures and prepare the legal forms used in formal probate and estate administration for a set of facts involving a decedent's estate.

SCOPE OF THE CHAPTER

The probate and estate administration procedures involved in administering a testator's or an intestate's estate are the concerns of this and the next chapter. The distinction between probate and estate administration is explained, and alternative methods for administering "small estates" are listed and discussed. The two traditional methods of probate and estate administration, solemn and common, are explained, and the Uniform Probate Code alternatives, formal and informal probate, are introduced. The chapter then discusses the procedures and forms used in administering a typical estate using the formal probate method. The chapter ends with illustrated case problems, one with accompanying executed forms (found in Appendix A), and one with an assignment asking you to complete a similar case problem.

PROBATE OR ESTATE ADMINISTRATION

In previous chapters of the text, you have learned the identity, role, and duties of the participants (e.g., personal representative, attorney, paralegal, probate judge, registrar, clerk) in preparation for the administration of a decedent's estate. You have traveled through the procedures that begin soon after death, whether the decedent died testate or intestate. For example, you possibly helped to arrange for the funeral and burial; find the will, if one exists; hold the family conference; locate witnesses, if necessary; and obtain the information to begin the probate process.

The remaining steps of the probate procedures involved in the administration of an intestate's or testator's estate are the concerns of this and the following chapter. The word *estate*, also called the gross estate, includes the interest in every type of property, real and personal, owned by the decedent at the time of death. When death occurs, everything the decedent owns becomes part of the estate. The decedent's personal representative holds and manages only the probate assets of the estate until those who are entitled to them (beneficiaries and devisees, if the decedent left a will; heirs, if the decedent died without a will) can assume ownership. In either instance, the personal representative's work is termed *estate administration* or *the probating of the estate of the deceased*. The decedent's estate, or gross estate, includes probate as well as nonprobate property and is subject to federal and state taxes when the owner dies. Only the probate property, however, is subject to the payment of creditors' claims. These assets are the ones handled by the probate court whether or not a will exists. A decedent's will gives the court specific instructions as to what is to be done with the decedent's probate property, i.e., the solely owned property and any property owned in tenancy in common. It has no effect on nonprobate assets. Estate administration is not an issue and is not needed if the decedent's entire estate consists of nonprobate property. If there is no will, the court follows the probate procedures under the laws of intestate succession.

This chapter deals with the required probate procedures for the administration of an estate when the decedent dies either testate or intestate. Included in the discussion are samples of the various forms that must be completed. It is the personal representative's duty to see that these procedures and forms are properly and timely executed. With your assistance, the attorney will help the personal representative perform this duty. The "tickler system" (see Exhibit 8.3) will play an important role in keeping the estate administration on schedule.

The term *probate* initially meant "the act or process of proving the validity of a will." Over the years, the term has evolved so that, in many states, probate generally refers to all matters over which the court, often called the probate court, has jurisdiction. Thus the probate court has the power and authority to

- establish the validity of a will and appoint the personal representative (executor) or appoint the personal representative (administrator) of an estate when there is no will.
- determine and verify the statutory rights of a spouse and children.
- supervise the guardianship of minors or incompetent persons.
- supervise and approve the personal representative's payment of creditors' claims, administration expenses, taxes due, and distribution of the decedent's estate.
- supervise all other matters pertaining to these subjects.

Sometimes the terms *probate administration* (or probate proceedings) and *estate administration* are used synonymously to refer to the actual administration of the decedent's estate from appointment of the personal representative to the final distribution of the property and the personal representative's discharge. Therefore, to avoid confusion, this chapter and Chapter 10 use the term *probate* to refer to the process and procedures that establish the validity of a will and the appointment of the personal representative in testate or intestate cases. The term *estate administration* is used for the remaining procedures and duties of the personal representative, which include the collection and inventory of assets, the payment of approved claims against the estate, the payment of all state or federal taxes due, and the final distribution of the remaining assets to the beneficiaries, devisees, or heirs entitled to them.

Before we discuss the various methods and procedures individual states use to administer a decedent's estate, it is important to identify those cases in which estate administration may not be needed. In some states, such cases may avoid estate administration if the decedent

1. has no property in registered form, e.g., recorded deeds for real property and certificates for securities (stocks and bonds).

2. has no individually owned property in the possession of third parties, e.g., savings and checking accounts, employee benefit plans, and the like, that cannot be transferred to a personal representative without the authorization of Letters Testamentary or Letters of Administration.

3. has no outstanding creditors' claims, e.g., the decedent has no debts or all creditors have been paid.

4. has an estate that is classified as a "small estate," where all assets consist entirely of exempt property with a limited monetary value such as family allowances or a homestead and no other real property (see Tex. Prob. Code Ann. §§ 137 and 138; Cal. Prob. Code § 13100; and compare UPC §§ 3-1203 and 3-1204).

As an alternative to probate and estate administration, some states allow the heirs and devisees to collect, divide, and distribute the decedent's assets in "small estates" subject to their personal liability for paying all valid creditors' claims and all taxes (see Cal. Prob. Code §§ 13650–13655; and compare UPC §§ 3-312 to 3-322). In addition, as previously discussed, there is no need for estate administration if all of the decedent's assets consist of nonprobate property.

Small Estate Settlement and Administration

All states allow decedents with "small estates" to avoid the more common, but also more expensive, methods of probate or estate administration. Most states set a certain monetary limit for the total value of an estate's assets that can qualify as a **small estate**. The amount varies from state to state. If the value of a decedent's estate is below the statutory amount, the estate can be administered as a "small estate." Lengthier, more expensive probate procedures are unnecessary. Small estate procedures are simple: for example, collection of assets is quick and easy; court fees are greatly reduced; debts are generally minimal and promptly paid; death taxes are usually not owed; and assets can be distributed almost immediately, typically to a spouse and children. State statutes also commonly identify **qualified small estates** as those in which estate assets are within a certain limited monetary amount and/or consist entirely of exempt property, homestead allowance or exemption, family allowances, and where the estate debts are limited to funeral and burial expenses, and hospital and medical costs of the decedent's last illness (see UPC § 3–1203).

The procedures adopted by state legislatures for expediting the distribution of small estates vary widely. You must review your state statutes and these procedures and familiarize yourself with the required forms, some of which will be available from your local county probate court. *Note*: The county clerks or registrars will give you the forms they can distribute or make them available online. In addition, they often have developed an outline, pamphlet, or booklet for personal representatives that lists the required forms and procedures for handling small estates. Other necessary forms will generally be available from local or state publishers of legal documents and on the Internet from the appropriate agencies.

Although specific procedures for small estate administration vary from state to state, in general four traditional methods are used: Collection by Affidavit, Summary Administration, Universal Succession, and Family Settlement Agreements.

Collection by Affidavit

Many states allow an affidavit procedure to collect and transfer personal property to a beneficiary, devisee, or heir; to collect debts owed to the decedent; or to take possession of the decedent's property held by third parties, e.g., banks and credit unions (see UPC § 3–1201 and Exhibit 9.1). Title and possession of personal property are transferred without involvement of others, e.g., this collection method eliminates the need for the appointment of a personal representative, for supervision by the probate court, or for notice to creditors. To collect the property, the beneficiary, devisee, or heir must present a certified copy of the decedent's death certificate to the debtor or possessor of the property with an affidavit stating the following:

- That the value of the entire estate, less liens and encumbrances, does not exceed the state's maximum limit (up to $275,000 depending on the state)
- That a minimum number of days, usually 30 to 45, have elapsed since the death of the decedent to allow creditors to present their claims
- That no application or petition for the appointment of a personal representative (executor) is pending or has been granted in any state court
- That the claiming beneficiary or heir is legally entitled to inherit the decedent's estate including the right to the payment or delivery of the property

small estate
A decedent's estate with few assets and a limited monetary value.

qualified small estate
A decedent's estate that consists entirely of statutory exempt property or allowances and funeral and administration expenses, and is within a certain limited monetary value.

EXHIBIT 9.1 Affidavit for Collection of Personal Property

AFFIDAVIT FOR COLLECTION OF PERSONAL PROPERTY
Minnesota Statutes § 524.3-1201

Estate of:

_____, **Decedent**.

_____

I, state that:

1. My name is: _____.
2. My address is: _____.
3. Decedent died on _____. A certified copy of Decedent's death certificate is attached to this Affidavit.
4. I am the successor of the Decedent and I have legal standing to complete this form because: _____
_____.
5. The value of the probate estate, determined as of the date of death, wherever located, involving any contents of a safe deposit box, less liens and encumbrances, does not exceed $50,000.
6. Thirty days have elapsed since the death of the Decedent, or in the event the property to be delivered is the contents of a safe deposit box, 30 days have elapsed since the filing of an inventory of the contents of said box.
7. No application or petition for the appointment of a personal representative is pending or has been granted in any jurisdiction.
8. I, as claiming successor, am entitled to payment or delivery of the following described property: _____
_____
_____.

Dated: _____   _____
                                      (Signature of person who filled out this form)

Notarial stamp or seal (or other title rank)	Signed and sworn to (or affirmed) before me on _____(date)
	by:_____.
	(Print name of the person that signed this form)
	_____
	SIGNATURE OF NOTARY PUBLIC OR OTHER OFFICIAL

| PRO202 | State | ENG | Rev | 8/09 | www.mncourts.gov/forms | Page 1 of 1 |

The affidavit procedure can be used to transfer insurance proceeds, accounts in banks or credit unions, promissory notes, and the property kept in a safe deposit box so long as their combined value does not exceed the maximum limit set by statute. Generally, real property cannot be transferred by affidavit. If the decedent died with a will, some possessors, e.g., banks, may require a copy of the will plus an affidavit and death certificate before they will transfer the property. In Illinois, the affidavit method allows the holder of the property, e.g., a debtor who pays the beneficiary or heir, to be discharged of the debt (see Ill. Compiled Stat. Ann. Ch. 755 § 5/25-1). After the property is transferred, the affiant-recipient is personally liable for the decedent's debts if, subsequently, they become known. For example, if the **affiant** was not legally entitled to the collected property, the affiant is responsible to the person who had the legal right to possession of the property, and the former possessor (such as the debtor above) who acted in good faith on the affidavit is released from any further liability based on the transfer.

affiant
The person who makes, subscribes, and files an affidavit.

> **EXAMPLE:** Akela's will left his entire estate to his daughter, Melia, his only heir. When he died, Akela had $10,500 in a savings account; a fishing boat in joint tenancy with his best friend, Keanu; a $75,000 life insurance policy naming Melia the beneficiary; and an unpaid debt of $15,000 owed to Akela by Luka for a car Akela sold to Luka. The boat and the proceeds of the life insurance are nonprobate assets and do not apply toward the state maximum for collection by affidavit, which is $100,000 in Illinois, Akela's domiciliary state. After 30 days, Melia can execute an affidavit stating that she is Akela's only heir and entitled to his estate under his will and the total value of Akela's probate assets (i.e., $25,500) is below the state's limit. With an affidavit and death certificate, Melia would be entitled to collect the $25,500 (the savings account plus the debt) from the bank and from Luka. Melia may also have to present a copy of Akela's will with the affidavit.

Other individual state restrictions on the use of an affidavit for collection include the following: allowing only spouses and children to collect by affidavit; allowing only certain personal property (e.g., bank accounts) to be collected by affidavit; and requiring some minimal court involvement such as filing the affidavit with the probate court.

Summary Administration

After appointment, a personal representative may apply for a special form of administration called Summary Administration for certain small estates. This form of administration, which is shorter and simpler than the regular estate administration, can be utilized when the sum of the decedent's probate assets does not exceed the maximum limit set by state statute. Many states have both a Collection by Affidavit and a Summary Administration procedure for administering small estates. Exhibit 9.2 lists the maximum amounts allowed for settling small estates by Affidavit or Summary Administration in each state that has these procedures. Summary Administration is generally limited to small estates that have survivors, which include a spouse and minor children and insufficient assets to pay all creditors. In other words, if the value of the entire estate, less liens and encumbrances, does not surpass the amount payable for exempt property, family allowances, administration expenses, reasonable funeral and burial costs, the homestead exemption or allowance, and reasonable and necessary hospital and medical expenses of the last illness of the decedent, then Summary Administration may be permitted (see UPC § 3–1203). When this method is allowed, the personal representative immediately distributes the estate assets according to the will or in the order of priority set by an intestate statute and files a sworn closing statement with the probate court (see UPC § 3–1204 and Exhibit 9.3). Accordingly, the intermediate procedures required under the solemn or formal probate process may be eliminated including notice to creditors,

	Monetary Limits That Allow the Transfer of Small Estates by Affidavit or Summary Administration by State
EXHIBIT 9.2	

State	Amount ($)	State	Amount ($)
Alabama	25,000	Montana	50,000
Alaska	150,000 (1)	Nebraska	25,000
Arizona	50,000	Nevada	20,000/100,000 (3)
Arkansas	100,000	New Hampshire	No ceiling
California	100,000	New Jersey	10,000/120,000 (4)
Colorado	50,000	New Mexico	30,000
Connecticut	40,000	New York	30,000
Delaware	30,000	North Carolina	20,000/30,000 (5)
Florida	75,000	North Dakota	50,000
Georgia	10,000	Ohio	35,000 (6)
Hawaii	100,000	Oklahoma	150,000
Idaho	100,000	Oregon	275,000 (7)
Illinois	100,000	Pennsylvania	25,000
Indiana	50,000	Rhode Island	15,000
Iowa	100,000	South Carolina	10,000
Kansas	20,000	South Dakota	50,000
Kentucky	20,000	Tennessee	25,000
Louisiana	75,000	Texas	50,000
Maine	20,000	Utah	100,000
Maryland	30,000 (2)	Vermont	10,000
Massachusetts	15,000	Virginia	50,000
Michigan	15,000	Washington	100,000
Minnesota	50,000	West Virginia	100,000
Mississippi	30,000	Wisconsin	50,000
Missouri	40,000	Wyoming	150,000

(1) Vehicles up to $100,000; all other personal property up to $50,000.
(2) $50,000 (surviving spouse is only heir).
(3) Affidavit: $20,000. Summary Administration: $100,000.
(4) $20,000 (surviving spouse or domestic partner; $10,000 other heirs).
(5) $30,000 surviving spouse sole heir; $20,000 other heirs.
(6) $100,000 (surviving spouse is only heir).
(7) $75,000 (personal property); $200,000 (real property).

presentation of their claims, the formal inventory and appraisal, and the court's decree of distribution.

EXAMPLE: Arnel dies intestate and is survived by his spouse, Jocelyn, and a minor child. Jocelyn is appointed his personal representative. A preliminary inventory of the estate's probate property shows that the estate assets are not sufficient to pay Arnel's unsecured creditors' claims. Arnel's estate qualifies for Summary Administration as a "small estate." Jocelyn immediately distributes Arnel's assets according to the order of priority set by his state's statute and files a sworn closing statement with the court. Copies are sent to all distributees (recipients) of the estate and known creditors (see UPC § 3–1204).

Exhibit 9.3	Closing Small Estate by Sworn Statement of Personal Representative

---

ND PROBATE CODE FORM 16   10/01/03

SWORN STATEMENT OF PERSONAL REPRESENTATIVE CLOSING A SMALL ESTATE. (N.D.C.C. 30.1-23-04).

Name, Address, and Telephone No. of Attorney

_____

_____

_____

Attorney _____ for:

Space below for use of District Court only

Probate No. _____

IN THE DISTRICT COURT OF _____ COUNTY, STATE OF NORTH DAKOTA

In the Matter of the Estate of _____, Deceased.

SWORN STATEMENT OF PERSONAL REPRESENTATIVE
CLOSING A SMALL ESTATE

STATE OF NORTH DAKOTA   }
                               }   ss.
County of _____   }

_____, being duly sworn, states the following under oath:

1. I am the duly appointed, qualified and acting personal representative of the above estate, appointed on _____
    _____, _____, in the above Court.

2. To the best of my knowledge, the value of the entire estate, less liens and encumbrances, did not exceed the homestead allowance, exempt property, family allowance, costs and expenses of administration, reasonable funeral expenses, and the reasonable, necessary medical and hospital expenses of the last illness of the decedent.

3. I have fully administered the estate by disbursing and distributing it to the persons entitled thereto.

4. I have sent a copy of the closing statement to all distributees of the estate and to all creditors or other claimants of whom I am aware whose claims are neither paid nor barred and have furnished a full account in writing of personal representative's administration to the distributees whose interests are affected.

5. No order of the Court prohibits closing of the estate and the estate is not being administered by a supervised personal representative.

    This statement is filed for the purpose of closing the above estate and terminating my appointment as personal representative pursuant to N.D.C.C. 30.1-23-04.

                                                        _____

Subscribed and sworn to before me this _____ day of _____, _____.

                                                        _____
                                                                                    Notary Public

                                                        _____ County, North Dakota

(Seal)   My commission expires:_____

In some states, e.g., Massachusetts and New York, the person who performs duties similar to those involved in Summary Administration is called a "voluntary administrator."

Universal Succession

The Uniform Probate Code has established another method of transfer of a decedent's estate that requires an application to a registrar and no further court involvement. It is called Universal Succession and is included in UPC §§ 3–312 through 3–322. The recipients of the estate are designated the universal successors, and there is no limit on the value of an estate that can be distributed to them. Universal succession allows heirs of an intestate or beneficiaries and devisees under a will, except minors and incapacitated, protected, or unascertained persons, to take possession, control, and title to a decedent's property. The universal successors assume personal liability to pay taxes, debts, claims against the decedent, and distributions to others legally entitled to share in the decedent's estate. At least 120 hours must elapse after the decedent's death before an application can be made. If it is granted, the registrar issues a written statement that identifies and describes the assets of the estate and states that the applicants are the universal successors who have title to the assets and assume liability for the obligations of the decedent.

Family Settlement Agreements

A Family Settlement Agreement is a private written agreement among heirs of an intestate or beneficiaries of a will by which these parties unanimously agree on the distribution of the decedent's estate without supervision by the court having jurisdiction over the estate. In either testate or intestate cases, the settlement must be agreed to by all interested parties, and once it is executed, the settlement agreement supersedes and replaces the intestate succession statute or the will (see UPC § 3–912). The Uniform Probate Code requires the settlement agreement to be in writing. Although the Family Settlement Agreement speeds the distribution of estate assets, a court order is still required to protect the estate from creditors and to clear title to the assets involved (see UPC §§ 3–1101 and 3–1102).

FORMS OF PROBATE OR ESTATE ADMINISTRATION

Before the creation and subsequent adoption of the Uniform Probate Code, traditionally two forms of probate or estate administration, *solemn* and *common* probate, were used. Many states continue to use these two methods today. With **solemn probate**, also called probate in solemn form, formal court supervision is required throughout the administration of the estate, and notice must be given to all *interested parties*, e.g., beneficiaries, heirs, and creditors of the decedent, so they may be present at an initial hearing to contest the validity of the will or the appointment of a personal representative. Solemn probate procedures are followed in intestate as well as testate estates. Solemn probate is established by an order of the court that recognizes the existence and validity of a will and may be used to set aside an earlier common probate proceeding or prevent a pending petition for common probate.

solemn probate
Formal probate proceedings that require court supervision throughout the administration of the decedent's estate.

Common probate
Informal probate proceedings that involve limited court supervision, if any, and are primarily used for smaller estates.

Common probate, which is primarily used for smaller estates and is usually uncontested, is less formal, and involves less supervision or none. It is a simpler procedure that does not require notice to all interested parties. In company with the witnesses to the will, the nominated personal representative delivers the will to an officer of the court, usually a registrar or surrogate. This officer has the power and authority to do what the probate judge would normally do, i.e., appoint the personal representative, either the executor or administrator, and make findings of fact in relation to the will or the intestate succession statutes when there is no will. Under oath, the witnesses attest that the testator asked them to sign the will; they saw the testator sign it; and their signatures are also on the will. Once this is done, the will is considered proven (admitted to probate). If others contest the will, they must petition the clerk, registrar, magistrate, or surrogate to hold a formal hearing to determine the will's validity. The burden of proof is on the contestant. As mentioned above, common probate may be superseded and set aside by a request of an interested party for implementation of solemn probate. Common probate provides a faster and less expensive statutory method of administering an estate than solemn probate (see and compare Cal. Prob. Code §§ 10500 and 10501; Tex. Prob. Code Ann. §§ 145 et seq.; and Wash. Rev. Code Ann. § 11.68.011).

The Uniform Probate Code has added another method for administering an estate. The options are similar to the traditional forms of probate except they are called *formal* and *informal* probate rather than *solemn* and *common* probate. Under the Code, formal probate (proceedings) is conducted under the supervision of the judge with notice to interested persons; informal probate (proceedings) is conducted, without notice to interested persons, by an officer of the court acting as a registrar for probate of a will or appointment of a personal representative; see UPC §§ 1–201(17) and (22). "Interested person" includes heirs, devisees, children, spouses, creditors, beneficiaries, and any others having a property right in or claim against… the estate of a decedent; see UPC § 1–201(23). Formal probate can be either supervised or unsupervised. With formal (supervised) probate, the probate court has supervision over the entire duration of the estate administration. With formal (unsupervised) probate, the estate administration commences formally, but it becomes less supervised by the court after the appointment of the personal representative unless an interested party requests that formal (supervised) probate continue.

The purpose of the Uniform Probate Code is primarily to

- simplify and clarify the law, terms, and procedures in estate administration.
- lessen the expense and time for the administration.
- provide an alternative system, which, if adopted by the states, establishes uniform law.

Uniform International Wills Act
A section of the UPC intended to streamline probating wills in American courts that were drafted in a foreign country and vice versa.

Several states (see Exhibit 9.4) have adopted the **Uniform International Wills Act**, a section of the Uniform Probate Code intended to facilitate using American courts to validate and implement wills executed in another country and vice versa.

The states are not required to adopt the Code, although they are free to adopt it individually through their legislatures. As noted earlier, many states have continued to use the more traditional methods of estate administration, sometimes in revised form. Exhibit 9.4 identifies the states that use the traditional forms of estate administration, those that have adopted the Uniform Probate Code. As the exhibit shows, 18 states have adopted, at least in part,

EXHIBIT 9.4	**Method of Estate Administration by State**

States that have followed the English system of common and solemn form probate are the following:

Delaware	Mississippi
Georgia	New Hampshire
Indiana	Tennessee
Kentucky	Virginia
Louisiana	West Virginia

States that have adopted the Uniform Probate Code with some modifications are the following:

Alaska	Maine	New Jersey
Arizona	Massachusetts	New Mexico
Colorado	Michigan	North Dakota
Florida	Minnesota	South Carolina
Hawaii	Montana	South Dakota
Idaho	Nebraska	Utah

States that have adopted the Uniform International Wills Act with some modifications are the following:

Alaska	Illinois	New Mexico
California	Michigan	North Dakota
Colorado	Minnesota	Oregon
Connecticut	Montana	Virginia
Delaware	New Hampshire	

States that require some form of notice prior to the admission of a will to probate and afford an opportunity to interested persons to object to the probate of the will are the following:

Alabama	Massachusetts	Oregon
Arkansas	Missouri	Rhode Island
California	Nevada	Texas
Connecticut	New York	Vermont
Illinois	North Carolina	Washington
Iowa	Ohio	Wyoming
Kansas	Oklahoma	
Maryland		

the Uniform Probate Code, and 10 have followed the solemn-common form. The remainder either follow a hybrid mixture that possibly combines some features of the Code with their own statutes or have adopted an independent method. *Note*: A few states have established a type of estate administration called *independent administration* that is essentially free of court supervision or intervention. The person appointed to administer the estate is sometimes called the *independent administrator* (see Ill. Compiled Stat. Ann. Ch. 755 § 5/28-1, Mo. Ann. Stat. § 473.780, Tex. Prob. Code Ann. § 145, and Wash. Rev. Code Ann. § 11.68.011). Whatever the method, all states require some form of notice prior to the admission of a will to probate and afford an opportunity to interested parties to object to the probate of the will or to the appointment of the personal representative or executor.

In the majority of cases, formal or solemn probate is used for the administration of decedents' estates. Formal probate is unnecessary, however, when the value of the estate is minimal (see the earlier discussion of small estates), when the estate is not complex, or when the estate assets consist solely of nonprobate property. In such cases, the services of an attorney are generally not required. Formal probate would normally be the choice in any of the following situations: some beneficiaries are minors whose rights must be protected; real estate problems exist; a beneficiary or creditor intends to challenge the proceedings; the estate presents tax law difficulties; in an intestate case, the number of the decedent's heirs is uncertain; in a testate case, the beneficiaries cannot be located; or family members disagree about their respective inheritances or the continuation or sale of a family business.

COMMENCING PROBATE AND ESTATE ADMINISTRATION PROCEEDINGS

Assuming all the preliminary work and correspondence have been completed by the personal representative with the attorney's assistance and your help, probate and estate administration can begin.

You will assist the personal representative with the following procedures and prepare the necessary probate forms.

1. Petition for probate of will or petition to prove a will.

2. Petition for administration when no will exists.

3. Obtain an Order for Hearing the Petition to Prove a Will or for Administration.

4. Arrange for publication of the Notice of Order for Hearing and Affidavit of Publication.

5. Mail the Notice of Order for Hearing and Affidavit of Mailing Notice to all interested persons, including creditors.

6. Mail notice of rights to the spouse and minor children and prepare an Affidavit of Mailing.

POINT OF INTEREST

Electronic Forms

In many states the process of estate administration involves filing many documents with the proper court official. Many jurisdictions will allow those forms to be filed electronically, while others will accept only hard copies. See Nev. Rev. Stat. Ann. § 133.085, which recognizes electronic wills. Trips to the courthouse to obtain the proper forms or to file them are being eliminated. The necessary forms can be accessed through the Internet, the local court system, or the appropriate state agency that creates and supplies the documents. Exceptions to electronic filing are generally granted if the individual is proceeding pro bono or can prove undue hardship or significant prejudice.

7. Pay funeral bills and obtain a receipt for the records.

8. Identify and review objections and arrange for the appearance of witnesses.

9. Perform miscellaneous duties before the hearing.

Probate forms and procedures vary from state to state. You must become familiar with your state forms and the time limits for filing them.

The following discussion includes a series of **"What You Do"** lists or **"You Must"** notations, which identify tasks you may be asked to perform. Although not mentioned in each "What You Do" list, you should always be in contact with the clerk or registrar of the probate court to verify that you have completed the required forms and procedures accurately and to obtain helpful advice and guidance. However, the clerk or registrar is forbidden by law to give you legal advice.

1. *Petition for probate of will or petition to prove a will.* The form used to commence probate proceedings with a will is the Petition for Probate of Will or Petition to Prove a Will (Form 1*). The petitioner may be any person who has an interest in the estate, such as a spouse, adult child, beneficiary, heir, devisee, successor, the named executor, or creditor of the decedent, and may file the will and a petition with the court to have the will proved (admitted to probate). Most states have a statute of limitations that limits the time allowed to file the petition, e.g., Arizona and Montana (see *Matter of Estate of Taylor*, 207 Mont. 400, 675 P.2d 944 [1984], which allowed a limit of three years after the decedent's death, and compare UPC § 3–108). Other states have no limits on the time for allowing probate, e.g., Oklahoma.

A petition is a written document addressed to a court or judicial official that requests the court order certain legal actions. The petition and subsequent order establishes the court's jurisdiction over the decedent's estate. The original will is filed with the petition. To establish jurisdiction, the petition to prove a will generally must include the following:

- The name and aliases, date of death, age, place of death of the decedent, and, if required, the Social Security number.

- The domicile of the decedent.

- The existence and date of the will and, in some cases, the names of its witnesses. Unless it has previously been forwarded to the court, the original will usually accompanies and is filed with the petition.

- The name and address of the petitioner named in the will who seeks appointment as personal representative (executor or executrix) and requests Letters Testamentary. Verification that the petitioner is legally qualified for the appointment is often required.

- Names, addresses, ages, relationship to the decedent, and identity of those persons under legal disability (e.g., incompetents), of all devisees, and also of those heirs who would be entitled to distribution of the decedent's estate in the absence of the will. *Caveat*: For all estates, whether testate or intestate, the heirs must be listed in the court petition for probate of a will or for administration of an intestate's estate.

- The estimated value of the real and personal property that are probate assets.

- The amount and general character of the decedent's debts, if known.

---

* See Appendix A.

- In some states, if the decedent was survived by children and a spouse, a statement that "the children of the decedent are/are not also children or issue of the decedent's surviving spouse." *Note*: This statement and the affidavit of Medical Assistance that follows are also included in the petition for administration when no will exists.

- In some states, if the decedent was over 65 years of age, an affidavit of Medical Assistance must be filed and sent to the Department of Welfare with a copy of the Petition for Probate of Will if the decedent received any health benefits from the state's Medical Assistance program.

What You Do

- Contact the county clerk or registrar, or go online, and obtain the forms and information they provide for commencing probate. Obtain all other required forms from local (state) legal form publishers. Your law office will have most of these forms utilizing computer software to produce and prepare them.

- Collect all necessary information needed to complete and execute the Petition for Probate of Will.

- Make sure that you or the personal representative files the will, petition, and death certificate, if required.

- Obtain and file an affidavit of Medical Assistance, if needed.

- Whenever any document is filed, see that the personal representative pays the filing fee. *Note*: Filing fees will be required on many occasions, so this statement will not be repeated on the ensuing pages.

2. *Petition for administration when no will exists.* When there is no will, a form called the Petition for Administration sets forth facts similar to the Petition for Probate of Will. It should contain the following:

- The name and aliases, date of death, age, place of death of the decedent, and, if required, the Social Security number

- The domicile of the decedent

- The name and address of the petitioner requesting appointment as personal representative (administrator or administratrix) and Letters of Administration

- The name and address of the surviving spouse of the decedent, if any

- The names, ages, relationship to the decedent, and addresses of all heirs or heirs at law of the decedent so far as they are known to the petitioner

- The estimated value of the real and personal property that are probate assets

- The amount and general character of the decedent's debts, if known

As a general rule, the surviving spouse has first priority to be appointed as general administrator, then the next of kin, or both, at the discretion of the court. If the surviving spouse or next of kin so choose, they may nominate another person to serve as administrator. If all of the possible administrators are incompetent, unsuitable, or unwilling to serve, or if no petition has been filed within a statutory number of days, e.g., 45 days after the decedent's death, administration may be granted to one or more creditors of the decedent or to the creditors' nominee. In that case, the petition must be accompanied by an itemized and verified statement of the creditor's claim. Generally, minors, mentally incompetent persons (as determined by a court), and often nonresidents of the state cannot act as personal representatives. Additional probate proceedings, called ancillary administrations, are necessary whenever a decedent-intestate owns real property or, in some cases, tangible personal property in more than one state.

What You Do

- Obtain the information needed to execute the required forms and obtain the forms from the county clerk, local publishers of legal forms, or online through your Probate Court if your firm does not have them.
- Check your state statutes on priority of appointment of a personal representative (administrator) and ask the person who has first priority, i.e., the surviving spouse, whether he or she is willing to serve (see UPC § 3–203 [a]).
- Make sure you or the personal representative files the petition and death certificate, if required.

3. *Obtain an Order for Hearing the Petition to Prove a Will or for Administration.* As soon as possible after the filing of the petition either to have the will admitted to probate or for administration of the intestate estate, the court will make and enter its order (also called a **citation**) fixing a date, time, and place for hearing the petition. In some states the date of the order generally signals the beginning of the statutory period for creditors of the estate to file their claims against the estate (see the discussion of claims below). A court officer, such as the clerk, may prepare the order, but you should check to make sure this is done (Form 2*).

4. *Arrange for publication of the Notice of Order for Hearing and Affidavit of Publication.* The next task you must perform for the attorney and client is to contact a legal newspaper (one that specializes in printing legal notices), or at least a newspaper that is generally circulated in the county in which the proceedings are pending, and arrange for publication of the Notice of the Order for Hearing (Form 3*).

citation
The legal form, used in some states, that is the court's order fixing a date, time, and place for hearing the petition to prove a will or for administration; the petitioner is required to give notice of the hearing to all interested persons.

What You Do

- Call the county clerk for information about procedures for publication. The clerk may tell you which newspapers are available for this purpose. Then contact a local "legal notice" newspaper publisher and arrange for publication of the executed Notice of the Order for Hearing. Make sure that the order is published within the statutory time required *before* the hearing is held.
- File the Affidavit (Proof) of Publication. This affidavit will include an attached cutout copy of the notice as it appeared in the newspaper. For an example of such a publication, see Form 4*.

Publication requirements vary from state to state. In some states, the order must be published once a week for two or three consecutive weeks. The first newspaper publication must occur within a statutory period, e.g., two weeks after the date of the court order fixing the time and place for the hearing. In addition, the Affidavit (Proof) of Publication must be filed with the probate court within a statutory number of days (usually 15 days) prior to the hearing. Sometimes the county clerk of the probate court makes the arrangements for publication, but

* See Appendix A.

you must check to be sure it is done within the time allotted by court rules. In some counties, the newspaper publisher sends the Affidavit of Publication directly to the court; in others the publisher fills out the affidavit, which is filed with the probate court by the personal representative, the attorney, or you. Discuss the procedure with the publisher.

5. Mail the Notice of Order for Hearing and Affidavit of Mailing Notice to all interested persons, including creditors. The Order for Hearing requires the petitioner to serve the order personally or, after the order is published in a local legal newspaper, to mail the publication attached to the Notice of Order for Hearing the Petition to all interested persons named in the petition and to creditors whose names and addresses are known, informing them that the petition has been filed and the order given listing the date, time, and place for the hearing (Form 5*). In states like New York that use the *citation*, the form contains notice and the affidavit of service which all interested persons must receive.

"Interested persons" who must receive formal legal notice include all those who have a property right or claim against the decedent's estate; they include creditors as well as all heirs, devisees, beneficiaries, spouses, and children (see UPC § 1–201 [23]). Therefore, **you must** identify all known individuals or businesses to whom the decedent owed money (e.g., family, friends, business associates, credit card companies, loans from banks, utilities, hospitals, doctors, financial advisers) and see that they receive actual notice, i.e., you will deliver notice to them personally or mail a copy of the notice to their homes and place of business. Other unknown creditors will be given notice by publication, as mentioned above, in a local newspaper as required by state statutes. Notice is required to set the starting date for the statutory period, usually two to six months from the date of the order *or* the appointment of the personal representative and issuance of the Letters of Authority, that creditors have to file their claims with the court stating the amount and basis of their claim. Once a creditor files a claim, the creditor is known as the **claimant**. Notice also serves the purpose of allowing the interested person to file an objection to the appointment of the personal representative and propose another candidate or to contest the will. In addition, notice allows the surviving spouse to choose the elective share rather than the will's provisions and enables the family to claim the statutory family allowance available in many states (see Item 6).

claimant
A creditor who files a claim against the decedent's estate.

Notice is necessary to establish the court's jurisdiction over the decedent's estate, and the proceedings will be invalid if it is not delivered and/or mailed. If there are no heirs, beneficiaries, or devisees, the property will escheat (pass) to the state, and notice should be sent to the state attorney general. If an heir does not receive notice, the heir may later contest the will (see the *Tobin* case in Chapter 4). If the decedent was born in a foreign country, notice must also be mailed to the consul or other representative of that country if a consul resides in the state and has filed a copy of the appointment with the state's secretary of state. The personal representative must submit the affidavit, attesting to the mailing of the notices, to be filed with the court.

What You Do

- Mail a copy of the Notice of Order for Hearing to all interested persons listed in the petition, e.g., heirs, beneficiaries, devisees, and all known creditors. Actual notice to known creditors informs them of the deadline they have to file a claim against the decedent's estate.

---

* See Appendix A.

- Make sure personal (actual) service or service through the local paper is accomplished. Prepare the Affidavit of Mailing notice and verify the personal representative sends the Affidavit of Mailing of these notices, and that it is filed with the court.

Any person (called the **demandant**) having financial or property interests in the decedent's estate may file with the court a demand for notice of any order of filing pertaining to the estate. The **demand** must state the person's name, address, and the nature of the interest in the estate. The clerk mails a copy of the demand to the personal representative who must, in turn, mail the Notice of the Order for Hearing the Petition to the demandant (see also Chapter 10).

6. *Mail notice of rights to the spouse and minor children and prepare an Affidavit of Mailing.* In most states, if a decedent has left a spouse or minor children, a notice of right to the *homestead exemption* (unless it is in joint tenancy between spouses), *exempt property*, and *family allowances* must be mailed to each such person within a period set by statute, e.g., 14 days prior to the date set for hearing on the petition (Form 5*). Also, if the spouse has not already contested the will, notice of rights dealing with renunciation and *election* must be mailed to the spouse. **You must** prepare these notices and the affidavit the personal representative must file with the court showing the mailing of the notices. *Note*: An explanatory letter accompanying these notices can help avoid confusion. A child of the testator does not have the right to elect against the will. Only the surviving spouse has the *right of election.*

7. *Pay funeral bills and obtain a receipt for the records.* The funeral bill is a debt for which a claim can be filed by the funeral director. The personal representative cannot pay the bill until appointed and need not pay it until the claim period expires; however, it may be possible to obtain a discount by paying the bill promptly. Sometimes, by statute, there is a limit on the amount that can be spent for funerals. In addition, the *funeral bill* is generally a *preferred claim* (see the discussion of priority of debts later in the chapter). Timely payment is important when an estate has few assets since failure to pay this bill and other priority debts before distributing the assets can lead to individual liability for the personal representative.

What You Do

- You must contact the decedent's spouse and family or the funeral director to determine how payment is to be made. Sometimes the decedent prepaid the expenses by arrangement with the funeral director. In other cases, the spouse and family make separate arrangements for the funeral, burial, and reception with the funeral director and pay the bill themselves with the understanding that the decedent's estate will reimburse them. You must remind the personal representative that funeral expenses must be "reasonable" considering the amount of assets and liabilities of the estate and these expenses must be discussed with the family. You must also obtain copies of the receipts for all funeral and related expenses from family members or the funeral director.

demandant
Any person who has a financial or property interest in a decedent's estate and who files with the court a demand for notice of any order or filing pertaining to the estate.

demand
To assert and file a claim for payment based on a legal right.

---

* See Appendix A.

8. *Identify and review objections and arrange for the appearance of witnesses*. If anyone with an interest in the estate raises objections to the will, he must file them with the court before the hearing and the witnesses to the will must be contacted. Objections are most commonly filed by the following:

- A spouse dissatisfied with the amount received in the will
- A child who has been omitted or disinherited
- A devisee who claims the will is a forgery or was signed under fraud or undue influence
- A devisee who claims the testator was incompetent

What You Do

If there are any objections to the will, you must arrange for the witnesses to the will to appear in court to testify the testator knew and declared the document to be a will and freely signed it in accordance with state statutes. If a witness lives more than a hundred miles away from the place of the hearing, a written statement the witness affirms to be true (a **deposition**) may serve in lieu of testimony in open court. Usually, the testimony of one witness is sufficient to establish the will's validity. If neither witness can be found, then others familiar with the testator's signature, such as a banker or business associate, may acknowledge the validity of the signature. Many states provide for the self-proved will, which makes the testimony of subscribing witnesses in court unnecessary (see UPC § 2–504). Also, holographic wills do not have to be witnessed, but they are not legal in all states.

9. *Perform miscellaneous duties before the hearing*. Before the hearing, you may be asked to perform various other tasks under the supervision of an attorney.

What You Do

- Send copies of the will and a preliminary estimate of the estate to the appropriate beneficiaries, devisees, and/or heirs.
- Collect all available pertinent information for final income tax returns and prepare a "tickler" form (see Exhibit 8.3), a list of the probate and estate administration procedures with all deadline dates and the person who performs the tasks.
- Assemble data on nonprobate property (see the discussion later in the chapter).
- If the decedent owned real property in joint tenancy with another, contact the state department of taxation and determine whether an affidavit of survivorship will be necessary to resolve tax concerns (Exhibit 9.5).
- Since the title to the property will now be in the name of the survivor, check the state public records division to verify the documents required to transfer the title are accurate. Frequently, the survivorship affidavit must be cleared with the proper county tax official and filed with the county real estate recorder along with a certified copy of the decedent's death certificate, if required. Your state procedure must be followed.
- Inquire into all substantial gifts made by the decedent and all transfers made in trust. Such items have special tax considerations and are discussed further in Chapter 11.

deposition
A written statement signed under oath by a witness that may serve to validate a will in place of testimony given in open court.

EXHIBIT 9.5   Affidavit of Survivorship

(Top 3 inches reserved for recording data)

AFFIDAVIT OF IDENTITY AND SURVIVORSHIP   Minnesota Uniform Convoyancing Blanks
                                                               Form 50.2.2 (2011)

State of Minnesota, County of _____   Name of Decedent: _____

I, _____
                                (insert name and address of affiant)
_____ ,

being first duly sworn, on oath state from personal knowledge:
  1. That Decedent is the person named in the certified copy of the Certificate of Death attached hereto and made a part hereof.
  2. That the name(s) of the survivor(s) is/are: _____
_____ .

  3. That on the date of death, Decedent was an owner as a joint tenant/life tenant of the land legally described as follows:

Check here if all or part of the described real property is Registered (Torrens) ☐

as shown by instrument recorded on _____ , as Document Number _____ (or in Book _____
                                          (month/day/year)
of _____ Page _____), in the Office of the ☐ County Recorder ☐ Registrar of Titles of _____
                                                           (check the applicable boxes)
County, Minnesota. (If filed with the Registrar of Titles, insert the Certificate of Title number _____ .)

                                                           Affiant

                                                           _____
                                                           (signature)

Signed and sworn to before me on _____ , by _____
                                        (month/day/year)

_____
                                  (insert name of person making statement)

_____ .

(Stamp)

                                                           _____
                                                           (signature of notarial officer)

                                                           Title (and Rank): _____

                                                           My commission expires: _____
                                                                                       (month/day/year)

THIS INSTRUMENT WAS DRAFTED BY: TAX STATEMENTS FOR THE REAL PROPERTY DESCRIBED IN THIS
(insert name and address)   INSTRUMENT SHOULD BE SENT TO:
                                                          (insert name and address of person to whom tax statements should be sent)

PROBATE COURT PROCEDURE

The next steps in probate and estate administration include the following:

10. Hearing on petition to prove the will or petition for administration

11. Selection of the personal representative

12. Order admitting the will or granting administration

13. Issuance of Letters Testamentary or Letters of Administration

14. File for a federal employer identification number

15. Open a checking account for the estate

16. Notice to creditors

17. Appointment of trustees and guardians

18. Order admitting a foreign will to probate

10. *Hearing on petition to prove the will or petition for administration. Note*: This discussion covers both testacy and intestacy cases. On the date set for the hearing to prove the will or, if there is no will, for general administration, the petitioner seeking appointment as personal representative and at least one subscribing witness, if a testate case, should accompany the attorney to court. **You must** make arrangements to see that the witness(es) are notified and appear in court on time on the appropriate day. No testimony from a subscribing witness is necessary if the will is self-proved. Any person who has an interest in the estate and who wishes to contest the validity of the will or the appointment of the petitioner as administrator must file the objection with the court and should appear at the hearing. *Remember*: Creditors can challenge the appointment of the personal representative, but they cannot contest the will. For a will contest, the court will set a different hearing date and time. If no interested person raises an objection, the petitioner, i.e., either the person who petitions to have the will admitted to probate or the person seeking appointment as administrator, testifies to the facts of the will or intestacy. Usually, this testimony will suffice to prove the will or to appoint the administrator (but compare UPC § 3–405). If the petitioner is unable to testify to the facts, another person who can give such evidence must be present at the hearing. This person testifies under oath and answers questions that elicit such information as the date of the decedent's birth, death, and will, the domicile of the decedent, the probable value of the decedent's estate and debts, and the names of devisees, heirs, and other interested parties (any person entitled to receive a share of the decedent's assets). If necessary when the hearing is to prove a will, one or both of the subscribing witnesses are also sworn and testify as to the execution of the will and the capacity (age and sanity) of the testator. In addition, they verify the testimony of the first witness, the petitioner, insofar as possible. Exhibit 9.6 is an example of a typical transcript at a hearing to prove a will. Note that the questions are asked by the attorney from the information requested on the petition itself in a manner that requires a simple yes or no answer (Form 1*). Proof of publication and mailing of notice of the hearing to all interested parties should also be offered in evidence at this hearing. Finally, after the hearing, the testimony of the subscribing witness(es) should be signed and delivered to the judge unless the signature(s) may be waived.

---

* See Appendix A.

EXHIBIT 9.6	Transcript of Hearing to Prove a Will

1. Are you the petitioner _____ as named in the petition for the probate of the estate of _____, the deceased?
2. And you reside at _____?
3. And have an interest in the proceeding as _____?
4. And to your knowledge decedent was born _____ at _____?
5. And that the decedent died on _____ at _____?
6. And the decedent at the time of his death resided at _____ in the city of _____, county of _____, state of _____?
7. And that the names and addresses of decedent's spouse, children, heirs, and devisees and other persons interested in this proceeding and the ages of any who are minors so far known or ascertainable with reasonable diligence by you are _____? Is that correct?
8. And that no personal representative of the decedent has been appointed in this state or elsewhere whose appointment has not been terminated?
9. And that the original of decedent's last will duly executed on _____, _____, is in the possession of the court including codicil or codicils to the will?
10. And that to the best of your knowledge, you believe the will has been validly executed. Is that correct?
11. And that you are unaware of any instrument revoking the will?
12. And that you are entitled to priority and appointment as personal representative because you are nominated in the last will of the decedent as personal representative with no bond required. Correct?

Finally, that you request the court enter a judicial order formally
1. finding that the testator is dead
2. finding that venue is proper
3. finding that the proceeding was commenced within the time limitations prescribed by the laws of this state
4. determining decedent's domicile at death
5. determining decedent's heirs
6. determining decedent's state of testacy
7. probating the valid and unrevoked last will of decedent including any valid and unrevoked codicil thereto
8. determining that petitioner is entitled to appointment as personal representative under the laws of this state
9. appointing petitioner as the executor of the estate of decedent with no bond in a(n) (formal) (informal) administration
10. authorizing issuance of letters testamentary to petitioner upon qualification and acceptance
11. granting such other and further relief as may be proper

If the will is contested and a date is set for the contest hearing, all witnesses to the will's execution should be present to testify at the hearing. A witness living more than a hundred miles away or an ill or disabled witness may testify by deposition, as mentioned above. If the party contesting the will is successful, the probate court may set aside part or all of the will and declare it invalid. The decedent's estate will then pass by the state's intestate succession statute.

11. *Selection of the personal representative.* As discussed in Chapter 8, the kind of personal representative the court appoints at the hearing depends on the action, or lack of action, taken by the decedent. If the decedent names a personal representative in the will, the court usually confirms and appoints that individual

executor (or executrix) to carry out the directions and requests of the testator. The decedent may also have named a personal representative over his or her digital assets. As we previously discussed, this may be the same representative or two different representatives. If the decedent dies intestate, the court appoints an administrator to handle the estate. Review the priority of appointment of the administrator in Chapter 8 and compare UPC § 3–203(a).

12. *Order admitting the will or granting administration.* At testate proceedings, after the witness(es) testify and the will has been proved, the court makes its order admitting the will to probate (Form 6*). In intestate proceedings, the court issues an order granting administration of the estate. In both cases, the court appoints a personal representative (i.e., executor or administrator) and fixes the amount of the personal representative's bond, if one is needed, based on the value of the estate, the type of assets, the relationship of the personal representative to the decedent, and other relevant facts.

Before a bond is purchased from a surety (bonding) company, **you must** shop around for the best price and make arrangements with the bonding agent. Although the bond may be prepared by a surety (bonding) company or others, the personal representative or the attorney is responsible for it. Therefore, it may become your task to prepare the form(s) of both bond and oath. To facilitate this process, an employee of a bonding company may be present in court on hearing days with appropriate bond forms. In that case, the bond and oath can be completed and you can file them with the court immediately after the hearing. The order will require the filing of an acceptance of the position of personal representative of the estate. No bond is required in the case of a corporate representative, and bond may not be required of a personal representative. The court will consider, and usually grants, a request for a minimum bond or no bond when the request is made in a decedent's will or is signed by all persons interested in the estate and submitted at or before the time of the hearing. The personal representative will normally make this request for the benefit of interested parties.

13. *Issuance of Letters Testamentary or Letters of Administration.* After the court has signed an order appointing the personal representative and approved the bond, if one is required, the personal representative will file an oath of office, and the court issues the appropriate documents conferring authority on the personal representative. In most states, these documents, for an executor or executrix, are called Letters Testamentary; for an administrator or administratrix, they are called Letters of Administration.

The authority conferred by these letters is the same. The letters are certified (accompanied by a certificate from the clerk of the probate court stating they are in full force). The personal representative is then authorized and qualified to act for the decedent's estate (Forms 7*, 20*, and Exhibit 9.7).

14. *File for a federal employer identification number (EIN).* After the appointment, one of the first duties of the personal representative is to file Form SS-4 to obtain a federal employer identification number, which is required on fiduciary income tax returns and is needed before a Notice Concerning Fiduciary Relationship can be filed as required by the IRC § 6903 (Forms 23* and 24*). This process can be done online to obtain the EIN immediately. Since the decedent's estate is an

* See Appendix A.

EXHIBIT 9.7	Domiciliary Letters

STATE OF WISCONSIN, CIRCUIT COURT,_____ COUNTY   -PROBATE-

IN THE MATTER OF THE ESTATE OF

_____   **DOMICILIARY**
_____   **LETTERS**

File No. _____

To:_____
                        Name(s)

The above named person died, domiciled in _____ County, Wisconsin, on
_____.
            Date
You are appointed personal representative and have fully qualified.

THEREFORE, these Letters are issued to you, and you are ordered to administer this estate according to law.

                                    BY THE COURT:

    Seal

                                    _____
                                              Circuit Judge
                                    _____
                                              Date

PR-1403, 6/85 - (16A) DOMICILIARY LETTERS   Wisconsin Legal Blank Co., Inc.
s.856.21, Wisconsin Statutes   Milwaukee, WI

entity in itself and will be taxed as such on income produced by the estate after the decedent's death, **you must** prepare and file these forms to establish that a fiduciary relationship exists. The employer number identifies the fiduciary responsible for preparing the fiduciary income tax return and for paying any tax due. This filing enables the Internal Revenue Service to mail the notices and tax forms to the new fiduciary (personal representative) who is now responsible for the tax liability of the decedent's estate.

15. *Open a checking account for the estate.* To help the personal representative keep complete and accurate records of all financial transactions throughout the administration of the decedent's estate, a bank checking account for the estate must be opened. Once the federal employer identification number is obtained, the account is opened in the name of the estate of the decedent with the personal representative authorized to make deposits or withdrawals. The estate checking account allows the personal representative to consolidate and deposit into this one account all current and future liquid probate assets, e.g., all existing cash and funds obtained from the sale of estate assets; payments of debts owed to the decedent; dividends from stock; checking and savings deposits located in other banks, credit unions, or savings and loan associations; proceeds from life insurance, pension or profit-sharing plans, and other retirement plans *if the* estate was named the

beneficiary; and all other funds that belong to the decedent's estate as they mature during the estate administration.

All cash transactions of the estate will be handled through the estate checking account. Therefore, using the estate checks, the personal representative pays the decedent's debts, taxes due, and all of the expenses throughout the estate administration, including funeral expenses, court costs and filing fees, costs of insuring and maintaining estate property, and fees of the personal representative and attorney. The remaining property is distributed to the estate beneficiaries or heirs.

The estate checking account allows the personal representative and you to keep an accurate and complete accounting of all receipts and disbursements. The final account that is filed with the probate court to settle and close the estate and the death tax returns that must be prepared are absolutely dependent upon the accuracy and completeness of the checkbook records. The checks accomplish three essential record-keeping functions.

- They establish a record of all payments and disbursements.
- Once the check is endorsed, they act as creditors' admissions of the payment of their debts.
- When canceled, they serve as evidence and verification of payment of taxes and the personal representative's final account.

The personal representative should select a competitive interest-bearing checking account that is insured by the Federal Deposit Insurance Corporation (FDIC). See Exhibit 8.4 for a sample check imprint for a deceased's estate.

What You Do

- If the personal representative asks you to open a checking account for the estate and cannot come with you to the bank, you should bring to the bank a signature card signed by the personal representative, a check for the initial deposit, a certified copy of the Letters Testamentary or Letters of Administration, and the death certificate, if required.

16. *Notice to creditors.* Many states give notice to creditors either by formal (actual) notice or by publication *after* the Notice of Order for Hearing or the "Letters" have been issued. The procedure covered previously in Item 5 would be performed at this time. The United States Supreme Court has held that actual notice, i.e., delivery of notice directly to a creditor or by mail, must be given to all known or readily identified creditors of the deadline to file a claim against a decedent's estate.

17. *Appointment of trustees and guardians.* Other fiduciaries besides the personal representative can be selected and appointed by the testator. While alive, the testator can establish testamentary trusts in the will to take effect upon death. This allows the testator to appoint a trustee who will administer the trust created in the will. Since the will and therefore the trust become effective only on the death of the testator, technically, the trustee is appointed at that time. The trustee's powers must conform to statutory guidelines whether or not the testator incorporated them into the testamentary trust. A better choice and another possibility would be for the parent to create a living trust for the benefit and care of the child(ren) since it would be in operation while the parent was alive and could be modified to meet the child's needs as determined by the parent.

Other fiduciaries appointed by the probate court include guardians for minor children of the deceased. The guardian *of the person* of a minor is responsible for the custody and care, specifically, the education, health, and welfare of the minor. The guardian or conservator *of the property* is responsible for managing and safeguarding the minor's property, prudently investing the assets when appropriate, and making disbursements in accordance with the will or living trust and the laws of the state until the minor reaches adulthood. Both guardians should be named in the will and may be the same person, but like the personal representative, they must be approved and appointed by the probate court. Once appointed, the guardians are accountable to the court. The guardian's duties and powers are set by statute or the will's provisions. When acting in the name of the minor, the guardian should always sign legal documents listing the minor's name followed by the words "by_____, guardian."

If the decedent-testator has included a clause that names and appoints a surviving spouse as guardian of the person and property of minor children, the court generally appoints the spouse. If the decedent fails to name either type of guardian or dies intestate, the court will appoint a suitable guardian(s) for the benefit of the minor children. Guardians or conservators may also be appointed for persons who may or may not be minors but are physically or mentally handicapped. In choosing a person to administer a will or trust or a guardian of a minor's property, the testator or settlor should select a person who is responsible, competent, experienced in the management of property and investments, and capable of maintaining well-organized checkbooks and records.

What You Do

- Contact the local county clerk or the clerk's website and identify and/ or obtain the proper forms used by the county for the appointment of fiduciaries and review the procedures with the clerk.

- If the deceased died intestate, your work will be more complex and time-consuming since substantial legal research may be necessary to convince the probate judge your client's nominee for guardian is "in the best interests of the minor (or incapacitated) children," the criterion used by the court when considering the application for guardianship. For example, your research would discover that in cases involving a minor child aged 14 or older, some states allow the child to request a person other than the natural parent be appointed guardian (see UPC § 5–203).

Parents are considered, by law, to be the natural guardians of their children but are not necessarily considered natural guardians over the children's property. Usually, a parent will act as guardian of both the child's person and the child's property, but in all states, the court has the final word in the appointment of guardians. State laws that allow a parent to act as guardian of the child's property or to act as guardian of both the child's person and property are permissive rather than mandatory. The following example illustrates a typical problem of guardianship.

EXAMPLE: In his will, Alastair Kyte leaves his estate to his wife, Beatrix, and their two minor children, Hilda, age 16, and Duncan, age 13, equally as tenants in common. Alastair dies. Beatrix is appointed guardian of the children. If Beatrix wants or needs to use inherited family funds, sell family property, or move to another state, she must get permission from the court. This is both time-consuming and expensive. Using similar facts, except Alastair dies intestate, the state intestate succession statute also passes Alastair's estate to Beatrix and the two children. Beatrix is again appointed guardian, and once again, she will need court approval for decisions involving the property. Alastair could have avoided these problems if he had left all his estate to Beatrix and relied on her to care properly for their children or if he had established a living or testamentary trust, naming Beatrix the trustee or co-trustee with another responsible and suitable person. Unlike a testamentary trust, the assets in the living trust are nonprobate property, and the court has no control over them.

18. *Order admitting a foreign will to probate*. The decedent may die leaving real property, or, in some cases, tangible personal property, in another state (foreign state) as well as in the state of domicile. All of the decedent's property, wherever located, must be distributed to interested parties, e.g., beneficiaries, devisees, heirs, or creditors. As previously discussed, the disposition of property in the state of residence is the domiciliary administration, and the disposition of property located in a different state, the foreign state, requires a separate procedure called ancillary administration. If a will has been admitted to probate by a proper court in the state where the decedent was domiciled, this will may thereafter be admitted to probate as a foreign will in the other state. In many states, the personal representative appointed to administer this property in the other (foreign) state is called the ancillary administrator, and the form used is the Petition for Probate of Foreign Will discussed below.

If the decedent was born in or has left heirs in another country and no petition has been filed within a statutory number of days, e.g., 30 days after the decedent's death, administration may be granted to the consul or other representative of that country or his nominee, but only if the person appointed ancillary administrator resides in the state and files a copy of the appointment with the state's secretary of state. Finally, administration may be granted to any suitable and competent person, whether the person has an interest in the estate or not, provided the court considers the appointment to be in the best interest of the estate and heirs.

According to provisions in the will or the statutes, the ancillary administrator collects assets and pays debts and taxes due in the state where the property is located and remits the residue and final documents to the personal representative of the principal (domiciliary) state for final settlement. The estate cannot be closed until the ancillary administration is completed since the determination of estate tax cannot be settled until the property, debts, and claims in all states are known.

The ancillary procedures in the foreign state generally include the following:

- The Petition for Probate of a Foreign Will must be filed. Along with the petition, the personal representative may be asked to send the following documents: an authenticated copy of the will; a certified copy of the death certificate, if required; a certificate from the clerk of the court in the domiciliary state affirming the will's correctness; a certificate from the probate judge reinforcing the clerk's certificate; a certificate affirming the court's authority to admit the will; and a copy of the order admitting the will to probate in the domiciliary state. Note, however, the requirements vary from state to state.

- The Order for Hearing on the Petition must be published, and notice of the Order for Hearing must be sent to all interested persons, including creditors.

- After the hearing on the petition, the court will execute an order accepting and admitting the will admitted to probate in the testator's domiciliary state and appointing the ancillary administrator. In a few states, a person appointed ancillary administrator must meet the same qualifications as a domiciliary administrator. Most states, however, do have specific qualifications for a person to be appointed an ancillary administrator (see Exhibit 7.3).

- The court will issue Letters of Authority, e.g., Letters Ancillary Testamentary, to the ancillary administrator. The Letters permit the real property located in the foreign state to be transferred to the designated devisee named in the will if all creditors of the testator in the foreign state have been paid.

- If the foreign state imposes any inheritance or estate tax, these taxes must be paid to that state before the property can be transferred back to the domiciliary state.

What You Do

- Identify the property that must be administered and its location (county) in the foreign state.

- Check the foreign state's statutes to determine the qualifications and residency requirements for the ancillary administrator, and see if your client, the domiciliary personal representative, qualifies. If so, you will continue to do the remaining tasks.

- Contact the county court personnel in the foreign state and obtain the forms and written procedures they make available for ancillary administration and solicit their advice and guidance regarding any local requirements.

- Execute all required forms and documents (see the listed examples above) and file them with the foreign state's court.

- Verify that all foreign state creditors and death taxes, if any, are paid and retain receipts.

- Verify that legal title to property in the foreign state has been cleared and is submitted to the domiciliary state court for distribution to the beneficiaries or devisees of the decedent's will or to the heirs of the decedent according to the foreign state's intestate succession statute for appropriate assets, e.g., real property located in the foreign state.

What You Do (if the ancillary administrator is a resident of the foreign state rather than the domiciliary personal representative)

- Obtain the name and address of the person selected by the testator's will or by the personal representative to be the ancillary administrator in the other state.

- Obtain all required documents listed above, or others required by the local county court, execute them with appropriate signatures, and mail them to the ancillary administrator for filing.

- Keep in contact to help with any other data or documents the ancillary administrator may need.

- Once the foreign state's court accepts the approved will from the domiciliary state, the court issues the Letters Ancillary Testamentary to the ancillary administrator to authorize that person to administer the property of the decedent located in the foreign state. If there is no will, Letters of Ancillary Administration are issued.

• After the court in the foreign state completes its responsibilities, obtain the final documents and personal property from the foreign state and add it to the inventory. If the property consists of real estate, the personal representative generally does not include it in the inventory but may elect to include it in a memorandum at the end of the inventory.

Exhibit 9.8 is a summary comparison of the procedures to follow in formal probate administration for testate and intestate cases. Note there are some differences between the two procedures (testate and intestate) up to the point of appointment and acceptance. Thereafter, for all practical purposes, the testate

---

EXHIBIT 9.8   Comparison of Formal Testate and Intestate Procedures

Testate Procedures

1. File will (and codicils if any) and petition to prove (admit) will and for appointment of the personal representative (executor) and, if required, file death certificate.
2. Order for hearing on petition.
3. See to publication of order for hearing (in some counties the clerk does this).
4. File affidavit of publication (in some counties the publisher does this).*
5. Mail notices to interested parties entitled to them.
6. Mail notice of rights of spouse and minor children, if required.
7. File affidavit of mailing notices.
8. Ensure appearance of petitioner and witness(es) to will at hearing.
9. File request for reduced bond, if appropriate. Will can waive bond.
10. Hearing to prove will.
11. Order admitting will to probate and appointing personal representative (in some counties this is prepared by the clerk).
12. Prepare and file bond and oath (if personal representative is an individual).
13. Prepare and file acceptance (if personal representative is a corporation).
14. Issuance of Letters Testamentary.
15. Apply for federal employer identification number.
16. Send notice of fiduciary relationship to IRS.
17. Establish checking account for estate.
18. Notice to creditors.
19. Appointment of guardians or trustees, if any.
20. Review ancillary administration matters, file petition for probate of foreign will, and obtain order admitting foreign will.

Intestate Procedures

1. File petition for administration and appointment of the personal representative (administrator) and, if required, file death certificate.
2. Order for hearing on petition.
3. See to publication of order for hearing (in some counties the clerk does this).
4. File affidavit of publication (in some counties the publisher does this).*
5. Mail notices to interested parties entitled to them.
6. Mail notice of rights of spouse and minor children, if required.
7. File affidavit of mailing notices.
8. Ensure appearance of petitioner at hearing.
9. File request for reduced bond, if appropriate.
10. Hearing for administration.
11. Order granting administration and appointing administrator (in some counties this is prepared by the clerk).
12. Prepare and file bond and oath (if personal representative is an individual).
13. Prepare and file acceptance (if personal representative is a corporation).
14. Issuance of Letters of Administration.
15. Apply for federal employer identification number.
16. Send notice of fiduciary relationship to IRS.
17. Establish checking account for estate.
18. Notice to creditors.
19. Appointment of guardians or trustees, if any.
20. Review ancillary administration matters.

*Some publishers send the affidavit directly to the probate court; others fill out the affidavit form, but the personal representative must file it with the court.

and intestate procedures are similar until it is time to distribute the assets of the estate. Then, either the will directs the personal representative, or the intestate succession statute does.

PROCEDURES BEFORE ESTATE DISTRIBUTION

We have covered probate procedures up to and including the order appointing the personal representative and the establishment of the personal representative's authority by issuance of Letters. In both testacy and intestacy, before the estate is distributed, the personal representative must be concerned with the following:

19. Open the safe deposit box.

20. Collect and preserve the decedent's assets.

21. Prepare the inventory.

22. Prepare an appraisal (can be same form as for inventory).

23. Prepare a schedule of nonprobate assets.

24. File the inventory and appraisal.

It is essential that the personal representative, with the attorney's and your assistance, accomplishes these tasks accurately and expeditiously since complete information as to the value of the decedent's gross estate, including the probate and nonprobate assets, is necessary for the determination of death taxes. Thus the personal representative must not only take possession of all property when required to do so, but must also inventory (list) all probate assets accurately and report all nonprobate assets, making certain these assets are properly valued in preparation for executing and filing the necessary federal and state tax returns.

19. *Open the safe deposit box.* Most states require that once a bank learns of a decedent's death, it must freeze all savings and checking accounts and seal any safe deposit box leased by the decedent (whenever the decedent held the box solely) until the contents of the box have been examined by the county treasurer's office or a representative thereof. Bank requirements to open a safe deposit box frequently vary, but most banks require, at minimum, a certified copy of the decedent's death certificate (see Exhibit 8.6). In some states the statutory requirements for opening the box may cause serious problems because of the delay in obtaining the will. In many states, if the decedent's will is in the safe deposit box, the bank usually is allowed to take it out and forward it to the probate court before sealing the box. It is the responsibility of the bank to prevent anyone from removing any other contents of the box. The box should be unsealed only when the personal representative, the county treasurer or deputy, a representative of the bank, and you or the estate's attorney are present. After the box is unsealed, the bank's representative is permitted to distribute the contents to the personal representative. **You must** make a complete inventory of the contents of the box.

Proper disposition of the contents may present problems. In some states, if the box had been owned jointly, the surviving owner could be entitled to its contents. If the contents were not also jointly owned, however, the survivor is not entitled to them and may have to relinquish possession if the will or intestacy statute gives them to others.

Often life insurance policies are kept in safe deposit boxes. When the named beneficiary is someone other than the estate of the decedent, the policies may be handed over to the appropriate beneficiary, but **you must** make and retain photocopies so they can be used in the calculation of possible state and/or federal death taxes.

20. *Collect and preserve the decedent's assets.* One of your vital duties and major responsibilities is to help the personal representative find, collect, preserve, value, and either liquidate or distribute all of the decedent's probate personal property. This can be especially challenging with the digital estate, as personal contractual rights of the decedent may not pass to the fiduciary unless specifically provided for in the contract or allowed by state law. The personal representative does not take title to the decedent's real property unless it must be used to satisfy creditor claims. Your job concerning the real property is to locate it and keep records for future tax concerns or distribution. Apart from personal property set aside as family allowances or exempt property for the surviving spouse and minor children, all personal property owned solely by the decedent comes under the care of the personal representative. The court holds the personal representative personally responsible for collecting and preserving existing probate assets. On request, you will help the personal representative perform the following duties.

a. To locate the decedent's real and personal property. It will be necessary for the personal representative and you, by phone, by letter, or in person, to contact many people: relatives, friends, business associates, tax adviser, banking officials, stockbrokers, accountant, attorneys, trust officers, insurance agent or broker, employers, and persons handling the decedent's claims within the Social Security Administration and the Veterans Administration. With the help of the family or these advisers, examine financial records to find all bank accounts, stock and bond holdings, insurance policies (including credit life insurance on any credit cards, loans, or savings accounts), outstanding loans or other debts owed to the decedent, and any stock options or deferred compensation.

Digital assets may require more assistance in locating. If the decedent has prepared a list containing a description of the asset, web address, user identification, password, account number, and special notes, the digital assets will be easy to find. However, the identification of the assets is just the beginning. Depending on your particular jurisdiction, issues relating to accessing and transferring digital assets may be barred by federal and state law and the ISP's terms of service.

b. To take possession of all the decedent's probate personal property. Nonprobate assets, including jointly owned property, life insurance benefits, and the like, are not subject to the marshaling (collection) authority of the personal representative. You will prepare a separate list of nonprobate assets that must be maintained (see the later discussion). Title to the decedent's personal property passes to (vests in) the personal representative when appointed by the probate court. This passage of title is retroactive to the decedent's death. In other words, title vests in the personal representative as if the personal representative had assumed title as soon as the decedent died.

What You Do

At the direction and with the consent of the personal representative

- you must identify all nonprobate assets and list them for future required documents, e.g., a schedule of nonprobate assets required for filing death tax returns.

- you will contact in person or by phone all persons listed above and prepare all correspondence, e.g., letters to banks (for checking and savings accounts), insurance companies (for policies and named beneficiaries), stockbrokers (for all investments), and business associates, for the personal representative's signature to identify, locate, and collect, when appropriate, all personal property of the decedent to which the personal representative is entitled and required to possess. With the use of Letters of Authority and certified copies of the death certificate, if needed, you will obtain the assets mentioned below. You will verify all checking and savings accounts wherever located are closed and the cash and money obtained from the sale of all personal property is transferred into the estate account. You will also verify proceeds collected from life insurance and retirement plans naming the estate the beneficiary are deposited in the account. If the will specifically states that securities (stocks and bonds), certificates of deposits, and mutual funds are to be given to named persons, these will pass through the will; otherwise the personal representative may have to sell them. The money from this sale must also be transferred to the estate account. The collected assets, wherever located, are to be used to pay all valid creditors' claims and death taxes due. After payment of all debts and taxes, the personal representative will distribute the remaining personal property to those who are entitled to it.

Title to the decedent's real property, however, vests immediately, upon the decedent's death, in the beneficiaries or devisees of a testate estate or the heirs of an intestate estate, but it is subject to divestiture (to be taken away) to pay creditors of the estate. In appropriate instances, therefore, the personal representative may obtain possession of real property (by entering onto the land with a court order) and convey (sell) it in order to satisfy creditors' claims. A typical state statute on this matter is Pennsylvania's.

> *20 Pa. Stat. Ann. § 3311* Possession of Real and Personal Estate; Exception
> A personal representative shall have the right to and shall take possession of, maintain and administer all the real and personal estate of the decedent, except real estate occupied at the time of death by an heir or devisee with the consent of the decedent. He shall collect the rents and income from each asset in his possession until it is sold or distributed, and, during the administration of the estate, shall have the right to maintain any action with respect to it and shall make all reasonable expenditures necessary to preserve it. The court may direct the personal representative to take possession of, administer and maintain real estate so occupied by an heir or a devisee if this is necessary to protect the rights of claimants or other parties. Nothing in this section shall affect the personal representative's power to sell real estate occupied by an heir or devisee. [Compare UPC § 3–709.]

   c. keep all real property (e.g., houses and other buildings) protected and in reasonably good repair.

What You Do

You must contact an insurance company and obtain information so the personal representative can maintain reasonable coverage for all real property. This must include both property and liability insurance usually in the form of a "homeowner's policy." If such a policy already exists, you will determine the expiration date. If necessary, a policy must be purchased until the home is sold or transferred to the devisee. If the property needs repair, you must inform the personal representative so the property is properly maintained until it is distributed or sold. You must also make sure that no property taxes or mortgage payments become delinquent. The transfer or distribution of real estate is discussed in detail later in this chapter. You must immediately notify all tenants in possession of any real property owned by the decedent that rent is to be paid to the personal representative and give them the name and address. You must verify that all such rent payments are included in the estate account.

d. search for important documents, records, and papers that might contain information on the location of unknown assets.

What You Do

You may be asked to help in finding checkbooks, savings account statements, insurance policies, charge account cards, credit cards, canceled or uncashed checks, income tax returns for the last seven years and any gift tax returns, deeds, contracts for deed, trust documents, bills of sale for personal property, title cards or certificates for automobile, boat, and mobile home ownership transfer, and cards for membership in various agencies and fraternal organizations. You must review records filed with various county and city departments for additional clues to unknown or missing property.

e. protect certain items of value in the estate, once they are collected, including stocks, bonds, insurance policies, promissory notes, mortgages, jewelry, and stamp or coin collections. **You must** contact a bank and, with the personal representative, rent a safe deposit box for their safekeeping.

f. check other insurance policies (life, hospitalization, disability, and automobile liability) for coverage and expiration dates. Although the personal representative decides these matters, **you must** prepare all the correspondence to terminate, continue, or transfer the benefits under the policies to the appropriate parties or to transfer ownership to the "Estate of John Doe" account. You also verify these transfers.

g. check for miscellaneous items. Inheritance due to the decedent from others (predeceased family and friends not yet collected). **You must** discover, collect, and add this property to the assets of the estate.

Procedures for Collecting Specific Estate Assets

Collecting estate assets can be complex work, depending on the number and diversity of the assets. The personal representative of a typical estate will be dealing with such assets as bank accounts, securities, debts owed to the decedent, causes of action, jointly owned property, insurance benefits, sale of a business, death benefits, digital assets, and automobiles. Complete, accurate, and detailed records of each asset must be kept, including a record of all cash receipts and expenditures on a check register (see the previous discussion of opening a checking account).

- *Bank accounts.* Accounts solely in the name of the decedent will be released only to the personal representative of the estate. After determining the location of the decedent's bank accounts (savings, checking, and credit union), the personal representative must withdraw the funds using the decedent's bank statement and certified copies of the Letters Testamentary or Letters of Administration and the death certificate. The personal representative may wait to withdraw these funds until after the interest earning period, e.g., monthly or quarterly. The withdrawn funds are to be placed in the "Estate of John Doe" account.

What You Do

If asked by the personal representative

- you must prepare a letter for the signature of the personal representative with an order directing that the account be closed and a check for the balance including interest payable to the estate of the decedent be sent to the personal representative's address. Other required documents, e.g., Letters Testamentary or Letters of Administration and the death certificate, must accompany your letter.

Joint accounts must also be located, although these accounts go to the surviving joint tenant, e.g., a spouse. The date on which the joint account was established, the source from which the account was created, and the amounts must be obtained and reported on the death tax forms. For further discussion on tax consequences of joint ownership, see Chapter 11.

"Totten trusts" (savings account trusts in the decedent's name in trust for another) and payable-on-death (POD) accounts are payable directly to the named beneficiary in many but not all states. For tax purposes, you must obtain information on these accounts and the date they were opened.

- *Securities*. Securities are often found either among the decedent's possessions or in a safe deposit box.

What You Do

- You must search for all the decedent's securities (stocks, bonds), including accounts with brokers or stocks held in the broker's name. Generally, securities remain registered in the decedent's name and are transferred to the proper beneficiaries or devisees named in the will or to heirs through intestate succession after administration of the estate is completed. Determination must be made as to whether the decedent, before death, effectively transferred ownership of the stock to another. Transfer of securities is discussed in detail later in the chapter. In other situations, the personal representative must decide whether to liquidate (sell) the securities immediately or wait until a later time when their value may increase. When the securities are sold, you must verify the proceeds are placed in the estate checking account.
- *Debts owed the decedent*. Inquiries should be made into all outstanding debts owed to the decedent.

What You Do

- You must review county and city records and files to determine whether the decedent held any mortgages, contracts for deed, promissory notes, or similar evidences of indebtedness to the decedent.

- You must interview family to determine if such debtors may include friends, relatives, devisees, or heirs. Since they must repay the estate, their debts might cancel out the benefits they receive from it unless their debts are forgiven in the will.

- You must arrange by letter, phone, or personally for the continued collection of loans, rents from tenants, interest from financial institutions, alimony (maintenance) from a divorced spouse, dividends, royalties from publishers, unemployment compensation, worker's compensation, and federal or state income tax refunds and attempt to collect delinquent obligations. These monies must be transferred into the estate account. At the request of the personal representative, you may have to contact and hire a collection agency to collect delinquent debts. The probate court will approve a reasonable compromise settlement of a disputed debt owed to the decedent so long as it appears to be in the best interest of the estate. *Since legal advice may be involved in the settlement, this must be done by the attorney and personal representative.*

Ethical Issue

damages
The monetary remedy from a court of law that can be recovered by the person who has suffered loss or injury to person, property, or rights by the unlawful act, omission, or negligence of another.

cause of action
The right of a person to commence a lawsuit.

- *Causes of action.* A legal wrong for which a civil lawsuit for **damages** can be brought creates for the wronged or injured party a **cause of action**, i.e., a right to sue. If the person suing dies while in the process of litigation, the claim or "cause of action" may also die (end). When by statute, the personal representative is allowed to pursue the "cause of action" for the benefit of the decedent's estate or heirs, any recovery in damages becomes an asset of the estate. State statutes on the subject of "causes of action" as assets of the estate allow or bar such lawsuits depending on the circumstances surrounding death, the nature of the action, and many other factors.

What You Do

Ethical Issue

- You must carefully read the state statutes and commentaries on them and perform any necessary legal research to determine if a particular decedent's "cause of action" survives the decedent's death and should be continued. *The findings must be discussed with the supervising attorney for final resolution.*

EXAMPLE: Elsa Larsson negligently backs her car into her neighbor's yard, striking a supporting beam of the neighbor's porch that causes the porch roof to collapse. Considerable property damage results. Inge Lundgren, the neighbor, sues Elsa in civil court, but after commencing the lawsuit, Inge dies. The personal representative of Inge's estate must continue the suit if no settlement is reached. Any recovery becomes an asset of Inge's estate and is paid into the estate's checking account.

EXAMPLE: Sven Jensen is struck by a car driven negligently by Yan Gast. Although Sven is seriously injured, causing him to be hospitalized, his doctors assure him he will completely recover over time. While convalescing two months after the accident and after commencing a lawsuit against Yan, Sven has a heart attack and dies. Medical experts establish that the heart attack is totally unrelated to the previous accident. Under these circumstances in some states, Sven's "cause of action" dies with him. The personal representative of Sven's estate would not be allowed to continue Sven's lawsuit except to recover "special damages," i.e., the medical and hospital expenses and loss of wages incurred by Sven because of the automobile accident. "Pain and suffering" damages are not recoverable.

- *Jointly owned property.* Property of any kind, real or personal, held in the form of ownership known as joint tenancy does not become a probate asset of the decedent's estate. If the decedent held such property with another person as joint tenants, the property would automatically become the surviving joint tenant's upon the decedent's death.

What You Do

To clear title to real property held in joint tenancy by the decedent, you must help the personal representative to take the following steps:

- Execute in duplicate an Affidavit of Survivorship if the property is the homestead and the surviving joint tenant is the decedent's spouse (see Exhibit 9.5). *Remember*: Due to the *homestead exemption*, in some states, a surviving spouse and family are protected from eviction from their home by creditors whether the homestead was owned in joint tenancy or in severalty.

- File a certified copy of the death certificate of the decedent (see Exhibit 8.6) and one copy of the Affidavit of Survivorship with the proper section of the county land office, i.e., the county recorder or registrar.

- Send one copy of the Affidavit of Survivorship to the office of the commissioner of taxation or the appropriate state tax officer.

- If the real property is Torrens (registered) property, the surviving joint tenant must also file an Affidavit of Purchaser of Registered Land and the owner's duplicate Certificate of Title.

- A Decree of Distribution will also be recorded (see Item 35 below).

In some states, when the value of the homestead does not exceed a statutory amount and the homestead goes to the surviving joint tenant, i.e., the spouse, the above procedures may cancel the state inheritance tax lien (claim) on the homestead that would otherwise exist. To cancel an inheritance tax lien on all other jointly held real property, the surviving joint tenant must file the following with the county land office.

- An Affidavit of Survivorship on which the appropriate state tax official, e.g., commissioner of taxation, has certified that no inheritance tax is due or that the tax has been paid.

- A certified copy of the decedent's death certificate.

- *Insurance benefits*. A life insurance policy is a written contract between the buyer (our decedent) and an insurance company in which the buyer pays annually a specified amount of money called a premium to the company and it, in turn, agrees to pay a designated beneficiary named by the buyer an agreed-on amount of money, usually at the time of the buyer's death. If the decedent held life insurance policies payable to named beneficiaries (e.g., a spouse or children) and did not retain any incidents of ownership (see below), then the proceeds of the policy are paid directly to the beneficiaries, are not part of the estate, and, therefore, are not subject to federal estate tax. They are also exempt from federal income tax. For each policy to be listed on the federal estate tax return, the personal representative should obtain United States Treasury Form 712 Life Insurance Statement (Form 30*). These forms must be filed with the return and contain information (names of the beneficiary, decedent, insurance company, face amount of the policy, premium cost, and the like) needed in order to prepare the death tax returns (see Chapter 11).

---

* See Appendix A.

If the decedent retained any of the incidents of ownership (e.g., the right to change the beneficiary, to assign ownership of the policy to another person, or to cancel it altogether), the Internal Revenue Service considers the decedent held enough control over the policy for it to be considered an asset of the estate. As such, it is subject to both state and federal death taxes. Death benefits will go directly to the named beneficiary without being subject to death taxes, *only if the* insurance company was informed in writing that the insured person was giving up these rights (incidents of ownership) at least three years before death (see IRC §§ 2035 and 2042 and Chapter 11). *Caveat*: No death taxes are due on an insurance policy if the policy is taken out on the decedent's life *by another person* (owner) who pays the premiums, unless the beneficiary is the decedent's estate.

What You Do

- At the request of the personal representative, obtain and partially complete IRS Form 712 for every insurance policy on the life of the decedent. Mail the forms to each insurance company for final completion and signature.

- When the decedent's estate is the beneficiary of the policy, help the personal representative execute the proper forms for filing the claim to receive the proceeds from the policy. Notice of the date of the decedent's death should be given to the insurance company, and all other documents required by the company should be prepared. These generally include a certified copy of the death certificate, the return of the original life insurance policy, and, if required, a certified copy of the Letters Testamentary or Letters of Administration. Make sure you keep a copy of the life insurance policy.

- Hospitalization, medical (doctor), and disability insurance companies must be notified, especially where the decedent was hospitalized for any length of time due to a last illness before death. Payments from these policies may be made directly to those who provided care during the last illness; otherwise, they are paid directly into the decedent's estate. Receipts must be obtained for these payments. Any uncollected claims owed and unpaid by an insurance company due to incidents prior to the decedent's death must be paid into the estate checking account. Cancellation of life, disability, auto, home, and other types of insurance premiums, when appropriate, must be made, and refunds received should be paid into the estate checking account. As needed, you will perform the above tasks.

- *Sale of or continuation of a business—sole proprietorship, partnership, or limited partnership.* If the decedent was the sole owner and manager of a business, the personal representative may have to run the business until it can be liquidated. This is further complicated if the business is online and the representative has no technological skills. A personal representative has no authority to continue a decedent's business, and most states hold that the business must be liquidated. However, if the testator-decedent named a devisee to inherit the business and/or manage it, or a state statute authorizes it, the personal representative may select a long-time employee willing to continue to manage the business until the devisee or heir takes over or the business is liquidated. Complete and accurate records of all business activities must be kept and reviewed by the personal representative during this transition.

If the decedent was a partner in a partnership or limited partnership, the personal representative must obtain a copy of the partnership or limited partnership agreement to determine the procedures and partner's rights when a partner dies. If the agreement contains a clause that allows a buyout of the decedent partner's interest, the personal representative must see that a fair price is obtained for the estate.

Sample Clause [Will]: (West's McKinney's Forms ESP, § 7:379)

I authorize my Personal Representative(s) for the time being to carry on the whole or any part of the [name of business] now operated and managed by me at [address] until such time as they shall deem it expedient to sell the same or to wind up the said business, as the case may be. (Source: Thomson/West from West's McKinney's Forms.)

- *Death benefits.* Other death benefits, payable to the decedent's estate, must be collected.

What You Do

- You must contact federal and state government benefit plans, such as Medicare, Medicaid, Social Security, and, if appropriate, farm subsidy benefits, Railroad Retirement Fund benefits, and the Veterans Administration for benefits.

- You must contact the decedent's employer to determine if the decedent was entitled to accrued earned pay, accrued vacation pay, commissions, sick leave, terminal pay, pension or profit-sharing plans, 401(k) plans, deferred compensation plans, employee stock-ownership plans, group insurance plans, stock options, year-end bonus, or back pay uncollected, and labor union benefit plans. Such compensation should go into the estate checking account.

If the benefits are a form of employee compensation such as pension or profiting-sharing plans, the personal representative must identify them and determine to whom these benefits are to be paid.

If the decedent was a veteran of any war, including WWII to the present conflicts, the decedent's beneficiaries or heirs may be entitled to benefits such as insurance, pensions, and burial expenses, according to the rules of the Veterans Administration or state law. Death benefits under Social Security and veterans benefits are generally either paid directly to the surviving spouse or applied to the payment of funeral and burial expenses. The Social Security death benefit is a maximum of $255.

A union or fraternal lodge to which the decedent may have belonged should be checked to see if any benefits are due to the decedent or the successors. In addition, the surviving spouse and minor children of a decedent covered under Social Security benefits may have the right to a claim for monthly income benefits given to survivors of the decedent. The local Social Security office must be contacted.

Automobiles. As owner of the decedent's automobile(s), the estate or the personal representative could become legally liable for injuries or damage caused by improper and negligent use. Therefore, the automobile(s) should be transferred to the persons entitled to them as soon as possible after the death of the decedent or, if a state statute demands, within a certain number of days. The ways of transferring title to the decedent's car to the appropriate person vary from state to state. State statutes or regulations control the transfer of title to the car. The appropriate person to whom title is transferred could be a surviving spouse who elects to take the car (see Minn. Stat. Ann. § 524.2-403 for a typical state statute), a surviving joint tenant owner, a devisee in the decedent's will, or a purchaser who pays the market value to the personal representative. The statutory requirements or regulations for title transfer must be checked.

Digital assets. Determine whether digital assets are transferable. Businesses controlling a decedent's digital assets often deny the fiduciary authority over such assets and, thus, deny the fiduciary access. A recently approved law, the Uniform Fiduciary Access to Digital Assets Act, should allow fiduciaries access and control over these assets without threat of criminal prosecution or civil liability.

inventory
A detailed list of property and other assets containing a description or designation of each specific item and its value at the time of the decedent's death.

21. *Prepare the inventory.* An **inventory** is a complete physical check of all the probate assets owned by the decedent and a detailed listing of these assets and their estimated fair market value at the time of the decedent's death on the forms provided for the inventory (Form 8* and Exhibit 9.9). The inventory should be made jointly by the personal representative and either the attorney or you. In practice, this becomes one of your more important paralegal tasks. Nonprobate assets are not included in the inventory but are listed separately for death tax purposes. The organization of the inventory and the degree of particularity with which items should be listed are matters of judgment, but the inventory should include serial numbers of certificates for stocks, automobiles, or deposits; account numbers for savings or checking; and legal descriptions of real property. Real property must be included in the inventory and the final account of the personal representative. The inventory should be well organized, complete, and accurate. The appraisers hired by the personal representative and appointed by the court (if required by state law or on demand by an interested party) can then expeditiously appraise and value the assets. **You must** complete this inventory so all data will be available as necessary for the preparation of the federal estate tax return. As previously mentioned, the value of securities for purposes of the inventory is generally computed as of the date of the decedent's death or the alternate valuation date, as are all the other assets, and must include the following often forgotten items: (1) interest and rent accrued at the date of death and (2) any dividends declared before death. A preliminary or partial inventory can be made if it is necessary to sell assets before the inventory and appraisal can be completed; if additional property is found, an amended inventory may be required.

appraisal (appraisement)
A market-based valuation of the decedent's real or personal property by a recognized expert (appraiser).

22. *Prepare an appraisal.* An **appraisal** or **appraisement** is a market-based valuation of the decedent's real or personal property by a recognized expert called an appraiser. The inventory and appraisal are often combined on the same form and, therefore, are filed together. All estate property must be appraised, but if the value of the property can be easily estimated, the personal representative is allowed to do it. When the estate property is real estate or expensive personal property such as art, jewelry, antiques, collections of coins or stamps, furs, digital assets, boats, or aircraft, **you must** employ professional appraisers, or the court will appoint them (usually two are selected). Once the inventory is completed and the personal representative has signed an oath stating that all known property of the decedent has been inventoried, ask the clerk which type of appraisers you will need and, if court-appointed appraisers are necessary, how to contact them. Generally, if real

---

* See Appendix A.

EXHIBIT 9.9   Inventory

STATE OF WISCONSIN, CIRCUIT COURT, _____ **COUNTY**   **-PROBATE-**

IN THE MATTER OF THE ESTATE OF

_____

_____   }   **INVENTORY**

File No. _____

I, the undersigned personal representative, certify that to the best of my knowledge this Inventory (with attached schedules) includes all property, encumbrances, liens or charges of the decedent required to be shown and identifies marital property, if any.

Subscribed and sworn to before me

on _____

_____
      Notary Public, Wisconsin

_____
                     Signature

My commission expires: _____

_____
                     Signature

SUMMARY OF PROPERTY (Value of Decedent's Interest at Date of Death)	Date of Death	TOTAL VALUES
1. PROPERTY SUBJECT TO ADMINISTRATION		
(a) Net Value of Property Other Than Marital Property (Individual and Predetermination Date Property)	$_____*	
(b) Net Value of Decedent's Interest in Marital Property	$_____*	
NET VALUE OF PROPERTY SUBJECT TO ADMINISTRATION		$_____
2. PROPERTY NOT SUBJECT TO ADMINISTRATION		
(a) Net Value of Decedent's Interest in Joint Property	$_____*	
(b) Net Value of Decedent's Interest in Survivorship Marital Property	$_____*	
(c) Other (s. 814.66, Wis. Stats.)	$_____*	
NET VALUE OF PROPERTY NOT SUBJECT TO ADMINISTRATION		$_____
TOTAL VALUE OF PROPERTY		$_____

*ATTACH SCHEDULES SHOWING DETAILS.

PR-1422, 3/86-(19A) INVENTORY
s. 858.01 and 858.07, Wisconsin Statutes

Wisconsin Legal Blank Co., Inc.
Milwaukee, WI

property is involved, the appraisers are real estate agents or brokers selected from the local real estate association. An appraiser must not have any interest in the estate or property.

In states that require appointment of appraisers, the probate judge generally appoints qualified persons to determine the value of the particular type of property of the estate. Often the appointment is made at the original hearing without the necessity of filing a petition. Even in those states in which appointment of appraisers is not required, the personal representative, the court, or any interested party may request a professional appraisal.

Before the appraisers begin their work, they should sign the oath of appraisers. Then, accompanied by the attorney or more often by you, they should complete their work. Appraisers are often used to resolve disagreements between heirs or devisees about the value of the decedent's property. They are also used when the beneficiaries are uncertain about the property's true market value.

After a written appraisal is obtained, you will assign the appraised fair market value to each property item as of the date of the decedent's death or the alternate

---

Exhibit 9.10   Nonprobate and Probate Assets

Nonprobate Assets
Not Subject to Creditors' Claims
but Are Subject to Federal Estate Tax

1. Real property owned in joint tenancy, tenancy by the entirety, or, in certain states, community property with right of survivorship.
2. Personal property owned in joint tenancy, tenancy by the entirety, or, in certain states, community property with right of survivorship (automobile, stocks and bonds, jewelry, art, savings and checking accounts, etc.).
3. Real property subject to transfer under a transfer-on-death deed or beneficiary deed.
4. Life insurance proceeds with a named beneficiary and not payable to the estate as long as the policyholder retained incidents of ownership.
5. Annuity contracts with named beneficiary (not the estate).
6. Employment contract benefits that contain named beneficiary (pension, profit-sharing, 401[k], group life insurance, etc.) and not payable to the estate.
7. Individual retirement accounts (IRAs) with named beneficiary (not the estate).
8. Living (*inter vivos*) trusts, Totten trusts, and POD accounts.
9. Securities, including brokerage accounts, registered in transfer-on-death (TOD) form.
10. United States savings bonds payable on death to a named beneficiary (not the estate).

Probate Assets
Subject to Creditors' Claims
and Federal Estate Tax

1. Real property owned in severalty (single) ownership or tenancy in common.
2. Personal property owned in severalty or as tenants in common (jewelry, art, automobile, boat, coin collection, stocks and bonds, bank accounts, digital assets, etc.).
3. Life insurance proceeds payable to the estate.
4. Monies owed the decedent (mortgage, promissory notes, contracts for deed, loans, rents, dividends, income tax refunds, interest, royalties, copyrights, etc.).
5. Sale of business.
6. Social Security, Railroad Retirement, and Veterans Administration benefits.
7. Civil lawsuit for money damages.
8. Testamentary trusts.

valuation date and ensure that the personal representative files this inventory and appraisal with the probate court and pays the appraisers' fees. The normal fee for each appraiser is generally set by statute (either a percentage of the estate or whatever the court determines to be fair and reasonable). Some states set minimum and/or maximum appraisal fees depending on the size of the estate. Other states no longer permit percentage fees. Fees charged by the appraisers can be deducted as a proper administration expense on both federal and state estate tax returns.

23. *Prepare a schedule of nonprobate assets.* Previously, we have discussed probate and nonprobate assets (property). In summary, property that passes by will is probate property and is the only property subject to estate administration. After the decedent's assets have been collected and the inventory and appraisal have been completed, assets that are not part of the probate estate but are included in the decedent's gross estate for estate tax purposes must be identified. All such assets are exempt from creditors' claims since only probate assets are subject to the debts of the decedent. Exhibit 9.10 contains examples of nonprobate and probate assets.

24. *File the inventory and appraisal.* When completed, the original Inventory and Appraisal form with attached appraisal reports from any independent or court-appointed appraisers is filed with the probate court. **You must** also mail copies to the surviving spouse and interested persons, i.e., heirs, beneficiaries, devisees, and creditors who have requested it. Some states do not require an inventory to be filed and use their state death tax return instead. Often both of these documents are filed at the same time for those states that use an inventory. The time limit for filing the inventory is determined by state statute, but is usually between 60 and 90 days.

DISTRIBUTION OF THE ESTATE AND PAYMENT OF CLAIMS

The following procedures are essential for the distribution of a decedent's estate.

25. Distribute family allowances (including maintenance) and/or exempt property to surviving spouse and/or minor children.

26. Attend hearing on creditors' claims and pay allowed or approved claims.

27. Transfer of assets—real estate and securities (corporate stock). See 27A and 27B.

25. *Distribute family allowances (including maintenance) and/or exempt property to surviving spouse and/or minor children.* After the property is appraised, and the Inventory and Appraisal form is filed, the surviving spouse or minor children, or the guardian of minor children, may submit a petition to set apart the exempt personal property of the decedent allowed by statute whether the decedent died testate or intestate. **You must** prepare the petition. Most states grant the family allowance and/or exempt property to a surviving spouse and/or minor children, and some states also grant a homestead allowance or exemption prior to the payment of any creditor claims, but care must be taken to avoid premature or improper distributions. Some states, e.g., Pennsylvania, include the family allowance or exemption in their priority of payment of debts (see the later discussion). After approving the petition, the court will issue an order "setting apart"

said property. In some states, separate petitions and orders are used, one for the homestead, another for the personal property.

We have already discussed the types and value of the property that can be set aside according to one state's law (see Chapter 3). If the homestead passes directly by state statute to the surviving spouse and/or the minor children, you also determine if the state exempts the homestead from inheritance taxation. If a fee simple ownership in the homestead passes directly to a surviving spouse, federal tax law will allow the homestead to qualify as part of the marital deduction for federal estate tax purposes. It would not qualify for the marital deduction if the spouse receives only a life estate in the homestead (IRC § 2056). *Note*: State statutes should be consulted to determine if any family allowance or exemption is allowed for inheritance tax purposes. No federal estate tax deduction is granted for such property (see IRC §§ 2056 and, generally, 2053-2057). Until final settlement of the estate, the surviving spouse and/or minor children may receive reasonable maintenance from the assets of the estate. The amount is determined by the value of the estate and the socioeconomic status of the decedent, but compare Tex. Prob. Code Ann. § 288, where no family allowance is granted if the surviving spouse has adequate separate property. State statutes determine the length of time the family may receive maintenance (e.g., usually 12 to 18 months). The court, at its discretion, may lengthen this period. In most states, the statutory family allowances, including maintenance, are exempt from the claims of all creditors, including claims for administration of the estate and funeral expenses, but compare 20 Pa. Stat. Ann. § 3392, where a family allowance (exemption) is granted after administration expenses.

26. *Attend hearing on creditors' claims and pay allowed or approved claims.* After the family allowances (including maintenance) and exempt property have been set apart (granted), the decedent's valid and approved debts must be paid before any of the decedent's assets can be distributed to the beneficiaries, devisees, or heirs of the estate. Those to whom the decedent owed money are given actual notice or notice through publication (see Items 5 and 16) that their debtor has died and they must file their claims with the probate court or with the decedent's personal representative within the period set by each state.

What You Do

- You collect and keep complete records of all claims sent to the personal representative and those filed with the probate court.
- You determine and verify all claims have been filed within the required period.
- You refer the personal representative to the attorney for legal advice to contest any claim. If appropriate, the clerk of court should be contacted to help explain the procedures to deny claims.

Statutes have established a definite time and procedure to file and hear creditors' claims. In most states, the time limits for creditors to file their claims are established by either (1) the court's order setting the date for the hearing of the Petition to Prove the Will or the Petition for Administration or (2) the official appointment of the personal representative and the issuance of Letters. For this purpose, creditors should use the Proof of Claim form containing the claimant's address and signature and the affirmation of a notary public (Exhibit 9.11). Section 3–804 of the

Exhibit 9.11 Claim against Estate

STATE OF WISCONSIN, CIRCUIT COURT, _____ COUNTY   -PROBATE-

IN THE MATTER OF THE ESTATE OF

_____ } **CLAIM AGAINST ESTATE**

_____

File No. _____

Name of claimant: _____

STATEMENT OF CLAIM: *(If a claim is founded on a written instrument, a copy with all endorsements must be attached.)*

If the decedent was survived by a spouse, the classification of the obligation is as follows:

☐ Support obligation owed spouse or child [s. 766.55(2)(a), Wis. Stats.].
☐ Obligation incurred in the interest of the marriage [s. 766.55(2)(b), Wis. Stats.].
☐ Obligation incurred prior to marriage or prior to January 1, 1986 [s. 766.55(2)(c), Wis. Stats.].
☐ Tort [s. 766.55(2)(cm), Wis. Stats.].
☐ Other [s. 766.55(2)(d), Wis. Stats.].

I swear that this statement is correct and there is due to claimant from this estate

$ _____

No payments have been made which are not credited, and there are no offsets except as stated above.

Subscribed and sworn to before me

on _____   _____
                                                          Signature of Claimant

_____   _____
Notary Public, Wisconsin   Address

My commission expires: _____   _____

_____   _____
Attorney for Claimant

_____
Address

NOTE: A statutory filing fee of $3.00 shall accompany each claim.

PR-1421, 3/86-(25A) CLAIM AGAINST ESTATE   s. 859.13, Wisconsin Statutes   Wisconsin Legal Blank Co., Inc.
                                                                                  Milwaukee, WI

Uniform Probate Code allows a claimant to file the claim with the probate court or "deliver or mail to the personal representative a written statement of claim." If the claim is based on any written instrument, such as a contract, promissory note, or bank draft, the claimant must attach a copy of the instrument to the Proof of Claim. Records must be kept of all claims.

In many states, creditors have from two to six months from the date of the first publication of notice to creditors to file their claims; alternatively, the time commences after the "Letters" are issued by the court and the personal representative is officially appointed. An estate cannot be closed before this time has expired. If the claimant does not act within the time allowed, the right to present the claim, even if valid, is lost. **You must** remind the personal representative that payment of late claims will create personal liability. If, however, the claimant can demonstrate a good reason for requesting an extension, the court may extend the period by giving notice to the personal representative.

During and after the time for filing claims, **you must** check with the personal representative to determine whether any of the claims should be contested. If the decision is made to contest a claim, the personal representative must, before or on the date of the hearing, file all objections to the claim or file a claim against the claimant (a counterclaim) asserting that the decedent was actually entitled to the property. The document you prepare to file an objection or counterclaim is called the Objection to Claim and is served on the claimant and filed with the probate court. Contested claims are not heard on the date set for hearing allowed claims, but on another hearing date, for which arrangements must be made. Notice of this second date for contested claims must be given to the creditors.

The personal representative of the estate can admit, in writing, the claims that are valid and proper debts of the decedent. All contested claims must be proven legitimate at this second hearing in order to be allowed (approved) by the court. Also, claims of the personal representative or claims in which the personal representative has an interest are allowed only if proven by evidence satisfactory to the court. Once the claims are allowed, it is the duty of the personal representative to pay them and to file receipts or vouchers (canceled checks). **You must** keep records of all payments for the Final Account (Form 9* and Exhibit 9.12) when it is presented to the probate court. Payments to creditors should be made from the estate checking account. *Note*: Creditors' debts are generally payable only from probate assets, but taxes due are payable from *both* probate and nonprobate assets.

The laws that regulate probate procedures have given certain kinds of debts priority. In the event assets of the decedent's estate are insufficient to pay all valid creditors' claims in full, all states have statutes that set the priority of payment of debts. In most states, any or all of the following may be paid before the debts: maintenance and family allowances, homestead allowance or exemption, and the exempt property. The priority of debts in the following Pennsylvania statute is typical.

> *20 Pa. Stat. Ann. § 3392* **Classification and Order of Payment**
> If the applicable assets of the estate are insufficient to pay all proper charges and claims in full, the personal representative, subject to any preference given by law to claims due the United States, shall pay them in the following order, without priority as between claims of the same class.

---

* See Appendix A.

EXHIBIT 9.12 Final Account and Petition

STATE OF WISCONSIN, CIRCUIT COURT, _____ COUNTY   -PROBATE-

IN THE MATTER OF THE ESTATE OF

_____

_____   } FINAL ACCOUNT
                                                    AND PETITION

_____

                            File No. _____

I, the personal representative of this estate, certify that this Final Account is true and correct, and this estate is ready for final settlement.

The following is my account of the administration of this estate from

_____ to _____

ATTACH SCHEDULES SHOWING DETAILS AND A LIST OF INTERESTED PERSONS (Include Addresses).

RECEIPTS	ITEMS	DISBURSEMENTS		ITEMS
Inventoried Assets	$	Funeral Expenses (Schedule F)		$
Added Property (Schedule A)		Debts (G)		
Dividends (B)		Claims by Judgment (H)		
Interest (C)		Taxes Paid (I)		
Capital Gains (Losses) (D)		Interest Paid (J)		
Other Receipts (E)		Administration Expenses		
		Other Than Fees (K)		
		Other Payments (L)		
		Distributions Paid to Date (M)		
		TOTAL DISBURSEMENTS		$
		Assets on Hand (N)		$
BALANCING TOTALS	$			$

Assets on Hand (Schedule N) $ _____

Less Requested Fees:

    Attorney $ _____

    Personal Representative   _____

    Guardian Ad Litem   _____   - $ _____

BALANCE AVAILABLE FOR DISTRIBUTION $ _____

Schedule O, showing the proposed distribution of the balance is attached.

The personal representative requests that the Court schedule a hearing to approve this account, the classification of assets, and the allocation of expenses; to certify that the decedent's interest in life estates and joint tenancies has terminated and that survivorship marital property has vested in the surviving spouse; and to assign the assets of the estate.

Subscribed and sworn to before me   _____
                                                      Signature of Personal Representative

on _____   _____
                                                      Name (Typed)

_____   _____
Notary Public, Wisconsin   Address

My commission expires: _____

PR-1423, 3/86-(27A) FINAL ACCOUNT AND PETITION   s. 862.07, Wisconsin Statutes

(1)   The costs of administration
(2)   The family exemption
(3)   The costs of the decedent's funeral and burial, and the costs of medicines furnished to him within six months of his death, of medical or nursing services performed for him within that time, of hospital services including maintenance provided him within that time, of services provided under the medical assistance program provided within that time; and of services performed for him by any of his employees within that time
(4)   The cost of a gravemarker
(5.1)   Claims by the Commonwealth and the political subdivisions of the Commonwealth
(5.2)   Rents for the occupancy of the decedent's residence for six months immediately prior to his death
(6)   All other claims

Notice that, unlike many states, the Pennsylvania statute lists the costs of administration before the amount of the family exemption granted in Pennsylvania.

EXAMPLE: In Pennsylvania, Rashanna's estate has assets worth $40,500. The approved claims against her estate are as follows.

a. $2,500 in administration expense

b. $6,000 for family exemption

c. $4,000 for funeral and burial

d. $50,000 for medical, hospital, and nursing expenses

e. $2,000 in credit card expenses

The $2,500 in administration expenses is paid first; then the $6,000 family exemption is granted; next, since the funeral/burial expenses ($4,000) and the expenses for medical, hospital, and nursing services ($50,000) are on the same priority level (3) and their sum exceeds the remaining assets of the estate, each creditor on that level gets a prorated share of the remaining assets calculated as follows.

Total estate assets	$40,500
Less administration expenses and family exemption	8,500
Remaining estate assets	$32,000
Combined level 3 claims	$54,000
Percentage of remaining assets to level 3 claims	59.259%

There are 10 creditors in priority level 3 with claims of varying amounts for a total of $54,000. Each creditor will receive 59.259 percent of his total claim, using up the remaining $32,000 of estate assets. The credit card company would receive nothing for its $2,000 claim.

For the priority of creditors' claims as set out in Section 3–805 of the Uniform Probate Code, see Exhibit 9.13.

One of the personal representative's primary functions is to pay all approved creditors' claims from the estate assets according to the domiciliary state's statutory list of priorities. **You must** identify, locate, and give notice to all creditors and then review their claims. Your next tasks will be to classify the approved claims and categorize them by priority. All creditors must be paid according to their priority rights before the personal representative can distribute the balance of the estate assets according to the decedent's will or by intestacy when the decedent died without a will. *The accuracy of your classification must, of course, be confirmed by your supervising attorney.*

Remember: Only probate assets of the decedent's estate are subject to creditors' claims. Nonprobate assets and statutory allowances or exemptions are not.

Since creditors have a prior claim to the assets of the decedent's estate, the named devisees of the testator or the heirs may receive nothing from the estate through the will or the intestate statute. It is quite possible that no assets will be left after all the creditors have been paid. An estate that has more debts than assets is called an **insolvent estate**. Unless they are co-signers with the decedent on any of the debts, the spouse and family have no personal liability to pay all or any part of the debts. The decedent's probate estate is solely responsible.

⚖️ *Ethical Issue*

insolvent estate
An estate where the debts are greater than the assets.

ASSIGNMENT 9.1

Erma Gledig dies and leaves the bills listed below. According to your state law, in what order are the following to be paid, if at all, by her executor, Sherwin Gledig, her husband?

1. Salary payable to Erma's nurse-companion for a week prior to Erma's death.

2. State inheritance tax due on a devise to Erma from her brother, who predeceased her.

3. Attorney's fee payable to a lawyer who advised Erma during a real estate transaction.

4. Claim for services rendered by the Cahill Funeral Home.

5. Claim from the United States Commissioner of Internal Revenue for income tax unpaid in the previous year.

6. Sherwin's executor's bond.

7. Unpaid installment on an automobile owned jointly by Erma and Sherwin.

27A. *Transfer of assets—real estate.* If the decedent's personal property is sufficient to pay the allowances, expenses, taxes, and the rest of the debts, all real estate will pass free and clear to the named devisees in the will or to heirs by intestate succession. Since title to real property vests in the devisees or heirs on the death of the owner, the personal representative is usually not authorized or obliged to take possession of the real estate but, if required, must manage it or verify that monthly mortgage payments, insurance premiums, real property taxes, utility bills, and maintenance expenses are paid until it is distributed to the devisees or heirs or sold. In addition, if the decedent's personal property assets are insufficient to pay the debts, the personal representative is obligated to divest possession of the real estate (excluding the homestead, if exempt) from the person with vested title and sell it to satisfy these obligations. Also, the court may decide the sale of the real estate is in the best interest of the persons with an interest in the realty and order such a sale. The homestead, however, may not be sold without written consent of the surviving spouse, which must be filed with the court.

EXHIBIT 9.13   Priority of Debts According to Section 3–805 of the Uniform Probate Code

1. **Costs and expenses of administration.** Expenses of the estate administration such as mailing and filing fees; court costs; publication and advertising expenses; renting an estate safe deposit box; opening an estate checking account; bond fees; costs for protecting, preserving, and selling estate property, including a computer expert for the digital estate; appraisers' and auctioneers' costs; and attorney and personal representative fees are examples of debts within this priority.

2. **Reasonable funeral expenses.** As determined by the probate court, reasonable expenses include transporting the body to the funeral home; the funeral director's fees; burial or cremation costs; and payment for religious services, reception expenses, and other necessary funeral costs.

3. **Debts and taxes with preference under federal law.** Any financial obligations the decedent owed the federal government while alive, including debts and taxes, are the next priority. The federal estate tax is not included in this priority category, however, because it is a death tax, i.e., payable after death. The following are examples of federal debts and federal taxes included in this priority category:

   Federal Debts
   - Student loans
   - Tax court judgments
   - Fines for criminal convictions
   - Overpayments for:
     - Medicare
     - Welfare benefits
     - Social Security benefits or disability
     - Veterans' benefits

   Federal Taxes
   - Individual income tax
   - Gift tax
   - Tax lien levied against the decedent for prior years

4. **Expenses of the last illness.** This category includes unpaid debts that were incurred during the decedent's last illness such as the following:
   - Reasonable and necessary medical (doctor), nurse, and hospital services
   - Hospice care
   - Outpatient and home health care by professional personnel
   - All prescription drugs
   - Physical, occupational, and speech therapy
   - Necessary medical equipment, e.g., walker, wheelchair, hospital beds, and the like
   - Drug and alcohol treatment
   - Personal live-in attendant, e.g., nurse or companion who cared for the decedent in the last months before death and may qualify for this category

5. **Debts and taxes with preference under state law.** Included are debts due to the individual state government and state agencies and those due to local, county, and city government agencies, which may be a state specific priority, e.g., a creditor priority for only the domiciliary state, not for other states where the decedent had debts or taxes that were due. State taxes are also part of this priority; however, state death taxes such as the inheritance tax, estate tax, and credit estate tax are excluded. The following are examples of items in this category:

   State Debts
   - Waste disposal
   - Water and sewer charges
   - Overpayments for:
     - Medicaid
     - Unemployment compensation
     - Worker's compensation

   State Taxes
   - Individual income tax
   - Property tax
   - Sales tax
   - Gift tax
   - Tax lien

   Some states combine federal and state debts and taxes into one priority category.

6. **All other claims.** The remaining creditors of the decedent constitute the last category of priority creditors. Although a contract for personal services, e.g., a singer to perform a concert, a tailor to make a suit of clothes, a surgeon to perform an organ transplant, or a professional athlete to play a game, may obviously be terminated by injury or death, most other creditor claims are binding and can be collected from the decedent's estate.

Example: If Anthony negligently causes bodily harm to Leonard or damages Leonard's property, or if Leonard sells a car to Anthony or lends Anthony money, and Anthony dies before paying Leonard in each of these cases, Leonard is the creditor, and Anthony's estate is responsible for these creditor's claims.

The assistance of a real estate broker is usually obtained when real estate is to be sold. The sale can be accomplished in two ways: (1) if the decedent's will gives the personal representative the power to sell the estate's real estate, the personal representative needs no court order to proceed, or (2) if the decedent had no will or failed to include in the will a power of sale, the personal representative may not proceed without a court order, which may authorize either a private or public sale of the real property. In either instance, the personal representative must execute numerous legal forms. **You must** prepare all the necessary documents for execution by the personal representative and the purchasers including a certified copy of the will, a certified copy of the Order Admitting Will to Probate, a certified copy of the Letters Testamentary, and a Probate Deed. *Caution*: The personal representative may *not* sell, encumber, lease, or distribute real estate for 30 days from the date the Letters are issued.

If the decedent's will does not contain a power of sale or if the decedent dies intestate and the personal representative determines it is necessary to sell the real estate owned by the decedent, the probate court may authorize a *private sale* as requested. Note: The procedures that follow present the sale of real estate in the estate administration process in its most formal format. Most judges conduct these procedures less formally. **You must** learn your local customs. The county clerk and staff will be an immense help and valuable advisers. They cannot give legal advice, such as how to fill out forms, but they will identify the required documents and review your executed forms to determine if they are complete and accurate.

What You Do

- You must assist the personal representative to prepare and file a Petition to Sell-Mortgage-Lease Real Estate to be presented to the court after the Inventory and Appraisal has been filed.

- The probate judge signs the Order for Hearing Petition to Sell-Mortgage-Lease Real Estate requested by the personal representative. The order sets the date, place, and time for the hearing and must be published and printed in the same manner as the hearing to prove the will. You send notice of this hearing in the form of the publication or a copy of the Order for Hearing to the devisees or heirs in order to comply with the general probate notice requirements.

- At the Hearing on the Petition to Sell-Mortgage-Lease, the personal representative presents certified copies of the will, the Order Admitting Will to Probate, the Letters Testamentary, and a Probate Deed, along with the probate judge's order and testifies to the facts set forth in the petition. If satisfied the need to sell the real estate exists, the judge signs the Order for Sale-Mortgage-Lease of Real Estate at Private Sale.

- When a considerable time has elapsed since the earlier order was issued, the court may require the real estate to be reappraised because of the possible substantial increase or decrease in the property's value. The form used is the Warrant to Appraisers at Private Sale. Therefore, you contact the appraisers who are usually the same persons who made the original appraisal. Once the market value of the realty has been determined, the property cannot be sold at private sale for less than that price. The appraisers sign the Oath of Appraisers and Appraisal of Lands Under Order for Sale.

- At its discretion, the court may require the personal representative to post an additional bond.

- Once the private sale is completed, you prepare and you or the personal representative files the Report of Sale of Land at Private Sale Under Order for Sale with the court.

- After the personal representative files the report and complies with the Order for Sale, the court approves the sale and enters its Order Confirming Private Sale of Real Estate. Next, the court authorizes the personal representative to execute and deliver the Probate Deed.

- To complete the sale and to ensure the buyer will have clear and marketable title to the land, you must verify that the personal representative has filed the following in the county real estate recorder's office: certified copies of the Letters of Administration or Letters Testamentary, the Order for Sale of Real Estate at Private Sale, the Order Confirming Private Sale of Real Estate, and the Probate Deed issued by the personal representative, often called either the administrator's deed or the executor's deed.

Public sale of real estate may also be authorized by the court. The personal representative executes the same documents as those used in a private sale, including the Petition and Order for Hearing to Sell Real Estate; the Order for Sale of Real Estate at Public Auction; the Report of Sale of Land at Public Auction; and the Order Confirming Sale of Real Estate at Public Auction. **You must** obtain these documents, file an additional bond, if necessary, and prepare and file certified copies of the same instruments used in the private sale previously mentioned. The only additional requirement for the public auction is if such a sale is authorized by the court, published notice of the time and place of the sale are often required for a specific statutory notice period. Proof of such publication must be filed with the court before the court will formally confirm the sale. You perform these tasks (see the procedures previously discussed).

27B. *Transfer of assets—securities (corporate stock).* As a general rule, stocks need not be transferred to the name of the personal representative of the estate. They may be left in the name of the decedent and sold or transferred to the persons entitled to them at the conclusion of the administration of the estate. *If the securities are sold, the proceeds must be placed in the estate checking account and not, even temporarily, in the personal representative's account.* Whenever stock is transferred from one person to another, whether by sale, gift, devise, or inheritance, the transfer is handled by a transfer agent or corporation. A transfer agent (often a bank) is the party designated by the corporation as the one to be contacted whenever a stock transfer, e.g., a sale or gift of stock, is performed. When the decedent's stock is to be transferred to a devisee under the will or an heir under intestacy proceedings, **you must** give the transfer agent the following:

⚖ *Ethical Issue*

- The stock certificate that represents the number of shares to be transferred, endorsed (signed) by the personal representative, whose signature is guaranteed by a bank or a member firm of the New York Stock Exchange

- A certified copy of the Letters Testamentary or Letters of Administration

- A certified copy of the Decree of Distribution (Form 10*)

- The name, address, and Social Security number of the devisee or heir receiving the stock

If the securities are registered in the name of the decedent and another person as joint tenants, a transfer from joint tenancy to sole ownership requires, in addition to the documents and data mentioned above, that you send to the transfer

---

* See Appendix A.

agent a certified copy of the decedent's death certificate and a state inheritance tax waiver for those states that require a stock transfer tax to be paid. After these required documents are received, the transfer agent changes the registry on the corporate books by writing in the new owner's name and address and issues new stock certificates to the new owner. Questions about transferring corporate stock can best be answered by contacting the appropriate stock transfer agent.

If the decedent lived in a rural area, you should make inquiries concerning the decedent's ownership of stock in a grain elevator, creamery, or other farmer cooperatives. It is possible the decedent kept no records of such stock ownership in obvious locations such as the safe deposit box or at home; consequently, a thorough check of outside sources (e.g., the associations themselves) is necessary.

If the decedent owned any U.S. savings bonds that were not redeemed before death, they should be presented immediately for payment if they have matured and no longer bear interest. Most banks are able to assist the personal representative to reissue bonds in the name of the distributee, if that is the person's preference. The personal representative will be required to endorse the existing bonds in the presence of the appropriate bank official.

THE FINAL ACCOUNT AND CLOSING THE ESTATE

Before the probate court can discharge the personal representative, the following final procedures must be completed.

28. File the Final Account and Petition for Settlement and Distribution.

29. Request Order for Hearing on Final Account and Petition for Distribution.

30. Give notice of the hearing to interested parties.

31. Prepare and file copies of federal and state estate and income tax returns with the Final Account.

32. Explain and defend the Final Account and Petition for Distribution.

33. Request Order Allowing Final Account.

34. Compute and file state inheritance tax return or waiver.

35. Receive Order for Settlement and Decree of Distribution.

36. Collect receipts for assets by distributee.

37. File Petition for Discharge of Personal Representative.

38. Request Order Discharging Personal Representative.

39. Cancel personal representative's bond.

28. *File the Final Account and Petition for Settlement and Distribution.* Once all just claims have been paid and receipts for such payments collected, **you must** prepare and the personal representative must file a verified (notarized) final account (see Form 9* and Exhibit 9.12) and petition the court for settlement of the estate. Beginning with the original inventory, the personal representative's final account must show all changes in the assets of the estate, including debits and credits of cash and any interest that may have accrued during administration of

---

* See Appendix A.

the estate. This final account should fully disclose the balance of property available for distribution to named devisees under the will or to heirs by inheritance after the payment of creditors.

You must identify property remaining on hand for distribution in such a way that the personal representative may readily determine the persons entitled to receive such property. The personal representative should keep vouchers in the form of canceled checks or receipts to substantiate the payments for any and all disbursements or for assets distributed during administration of the estate including the personal representative's own fees and claims against the estate, and you must keep records of all these matters.

You must verify the final account is filed within the time allotted by statute for settlement of the estate, which in some states is one year from the date of the personal representative's appointment. For good cause, the probate court may grant an extended time for settlement.

The form for the final account lists the steps and information that must be included for the court's review. Incidental expenses (for miscellaneous items such as copies of the final decree and filing fees) necessarily occur after the final decree has been granted and can only be estimated.

29. *Request Order for Hearing on Final Account and Petition for Distribution.* The probate court issues an order for a hearing on the final account, setting the time and place for the hearing. Notice of the hearing must be published in conformity with the state's statutory requirements, e.g., publication of the notice once a week for two or three weeks in a legal newspaper in the county of the court's jurisdiction. As before, **you must** handle this notice requirement. Either the newspaper is required to file an affidavit with the probate court to prove the notice was published and to send a copy of this proof to the personal representative or you must file the affidavit (Form 4*).

30. *Give notice of the hearing to interested parties.* On request of the personal representative, **you must** give notice of the hearing to interested parties by mailing a copy of the court's order for a hearing to each devisee or heir within a statutory period, e.g., at least 14 days before the hearing. You also prepare an affidavit, which the personal representative submits to the court, verifying that notice has been mailed to these persons and also the state's tax official, e.g., the state officer of taxation.

31. *Prepare and file copies of federal and state estate and income tax returns with the Final Account.* Before the Final Account is allowed and the Decree of Distribution is issued, **you must** complete all federal and state death and income tax returns and file them with the final account (see Chapter 11).

32. *Explain and defend the Final Account and Petition for Distribution.* The hearing on the Final Account and Petition for Distribution gives all parties with an interest in the estate of the decedent the opportunity to appear and examine the personal representative's accounting. Explanations and corrections of the account and the intended distribution are discussed and resolved at this time. Then the personal representative requests the court accept the final account.

33. *Request Order Allowing Final Account.* After all taxes have been paid and the final account has been accepted, the court signs an Order Allowing Final Account.

---

* See Appendix A.

34. *Compute and file state inheritance tax return or waiver.* In states that have an inheritance tax, **you must** file a copy of the Order Allowing the Final Account with the state's official tax collector. You also prepare a tax return if an inheritance tax is due and is an obligation of the estate, in which case, the personal representative pays the tax after the final account has been allowed. If no tax is due, the personal representative prepares the tax waiver. Within a specified time after filing the tax return, objections to the amount of tax may be made. After this period expires, the state inheritance tax return becomes final.

35. *Receive Order for Settlement and Decree of Distribution.* After the final account has been allowed, the court enters an Order of Complete Settlement of the Estate and Decree of Distribution (Form 10*). In its decree, the court determines the persons entitled to the estate, names the heirs, beneficiaries, or devisees, states their relationship to the decedent, describes the property, and determines the property to which each person is entitled. This decree also states (1) that notice for the final hearing was duly given; (2) that the deceased died testate or intestate, including the date of death and the residency of the decedent; (3) that the estate has been fully administered, including the payment of all allowed claims, and administration, funeral, and last illness expenses; (4) that the final account has been approved and settled; and (5) that all inheritance, gift, estate, and income taxes have been paid.

Once the final decree is entered, the assets of the decedent's estate can be transferred. The personal representative distributes and passes legal title to personal property to the appropriate heirs, beneficiaries, or devisees. In some states, real property passes differently. Excluding the homestead, the right to possess the decedent's real property passes to the heirs or devisees after the Decree of Distribution is executed, but legal title may remain with the personal representative until a certified copy of the decree has been filed with the county real estate recorder or other official in the county where the land is located. The statutes of the individual state must be checked to determine the exact procedure.

Remember: To transfer legal title to real property held in joint tenancy by the decedent to the surviving joint tenant or tenants, the following must be filed with the county recorder: an Affidavit of Survivorship that has been certified by the state department of taxation, a certified copy of the death certificate, and a certified copy of the Decree of Distribution.

36. *Collect receipts for assets by distributee.* After all distributions have been made, the personal representative must collect receipts for all property distributed, real or personal, from each person to whom property has been distributed. You must add these receipts to your records. The personal representative must file these receipts in order to account for all the assets transferred.

37. *File Petition for Discharge of Personal Representative.* When the distributions have been made and the receipts obtained from the heirs, beneficiaries, or devisees, the personal representative (executor or administrator) files a form **you must** prepare called the Petition for Discharge of Personal Representative (Form 11*).

38. *Request Order Discharging Personal Representative.* After presenting the Petition for Discharge, the personal representative will request an Order for Discharge from the probate court. This order or, in some states, the form called

---

* See Appendix A.

the Order for Final Distribution terminates the potential personal liability of the personal representative. Local custom determines whether the attorney for the estate or the probate court prepares this order allowing the personal representative to close the estate (Form 12*). You may have to prepare this form.

39. *Cancel personal representative's bond.* **You must** send a copy of the Order Discharging Personal Representative to the bonding company (surety) to cancel the personal representative's bond and request the return of any unused premium for the bond. This act terminates the administration of a decedent's estate.

SPECIAL PROBATE PROCEEDINGS

In certain circumstances, special probate proceedings may be required. They include special administration, administration of omitted property, and decree of descent.

Special Administration

In some states, special administration is a procedure used by the probate court to administer the estate of a decedent under specific circumstances. It has limited purposes and is commenced only when a good reason for it exists. Reasons for appointing a special administrator include the following: (1) to preserve the decedent's estate until an executor or administrator is appointed, e.g., in cases where a will or the appointment of an executor or administrator is being contested, and (2) to give immediate attention, when necessary, to the management of a business left by the decedent.

Special administration is accomplished in the following manner.

1. A person having an interest in the estate files a Petition for Appointment of a Special Administrator. The petition includes an itemized listing of the estate's real and personal property and a valid reason why it is necessary and expedient to have a special administrator appointed.

2. The judge signs the Order Granting Special Administration and appoints the special administrator.

3. The special administrator files the *bond*. The amount of the bond is fixed by the court. You must check individual state statutes to see if a bond is required.

4. The court issues Letters of Special Administration conferring appropriate powers on the special administrator.

5. The special administrator files an Inventory and Appraisal of the personal property of the decedent (Form 8*). As a rule, if another person is to act as general administrator, the special administrator does not take possession or control of real property. If there is to be a summary distribution without general administration, then the special administrator must include real estate in the inventory and may take possession of it.

6. The powers of the special administrator officially cease when the personal representative is appointed and the Letters Testamentary or Letters of Administration are issued. Before being discharged, the special administrator must file a Final Account and Report of the Special Administrator, including

* See Appendix A.

vouchers and receipts for all disbursements. This final account will also provide for all remaining assets of the estate to be delivered into the hands of the new personal representative.

7. The probate judge signs the Order Approving the Final Account and Report of the Special Administrator. The order allows the final account and discharges the special administrator and the sureties. When the special administrator and the personal representative are the same person, only one inventory and one final account need be filed.

Administration of Omitted Property

After the estate has been closed and the personal representative discharged, someone may discover additional property belonging to the decedent that has not been administered (e.g., rare books, to which the will referred but which could not be located during administration). Proper disposition of the assets will necessitate reopening the estate. A petition may be filed by any person claiming an interest in the omitted property. The court that has jurisdiction of the recently discovered assets will, on petition by the interested person, appoint a personal representative, the same person as previously appointed, if possible (see UPC § 3–1008). Reopening the estate and subsequent administration are both court-supervised proceedings. At the hearing on the petition, the court will determine to whom the omitted property will be distributed. The court can then, without notice, summarily decree the distribution of the property once all tax liability has been paid.

Decree of Descent

When more than three years have passed since the date of the decedent's death and no probate proceedings have been commenced, an interested party may petition the court to determine the descent of the decedent's property. The petition requires that a formal proceeding be held with notice and a hearing.

LIMITATIONS ON AND LIABILITY OF THE PERSONAL REPRESENTATIVE

Throughout the collection and management of the assets of an estate, the personal representative cannot personally profit because profit taking would violate the fiduciary duty to the estate. Therefore, the personal representative is not allowed to purchase property or encumbrances against the estate or to sell property to the estate while retaining a personal interest in the estate (compare UPC § 3–713).

EXAMPLE: Paulina Neven, the administratrix of Charlotte Neven's estate, obtained an order from the probate court allowing her to rent out land belonging to Charlotte while the estate was being settled. Paulina rents it to herself. If one of Charlotte's heirs objects to this apparent self-dealing, Paulina would have to prove that she had paid as much or more rent than anyone else would have been charged.

The personal representative who acts reasonably and in good faith faces no personal liability for decreases in the value of estate assets during administration. If decreases occur because of a breach of fiduciary duties due to negligence or delay, however, the court will impose damages on the personal representative

surcharge
An overcharge beyond what is just and right, e.g., an amount the fiduciary is required by court order to make good because of negligence or other failure of duty.

to compensate the estate for the loss. The compensation, often called a **surcharge**, is paid by the personal representative out of personal funds (compare UPC § 3–808).

> **EXAMPLE:** If in the above example the court had found Paulina guilty of self-dealing with the estate's assets, it would require her to compensate the estate, e.g., by paying, from her own funds, the amount of loss she had caused the estate.

When total assets of an estate are not sufficient to pay all approved debts and other charges against it, the law provides an order of priority for payments, as described earlier. The personal representative is individually liable for placing a less preferred creditor in a more favorable position than is appropriate and thus causing improper payment.

> **EXAMPLE:** Charlotte died with unpaid bills for her last illness, federal taxes payable for the previous year, and a bill from a local grocery. Paulina pays the grocer's bill before the federal tax lien. Since the grocer is a "less preferred creditor," Paulina must pay the amount due to the federal government from her own funds if the estate cannot pay it.

If the decedent's estate owes any federal taxes, the personal representative is held personally liable for any taxes that are not paid; see IRC § 2002.

Key Terms

small estate	claimant	insolvent estate
qualified small estate	demandant	inventory
affiant	demand	appraisal (appraisement)
solemn probate	deposition	surcharge
common probate	damages	Uniform International Wills Act
citation	cause of action	

Review Questions

1. What are the steps in the probate or estate administration of a decedent's estate? List each step and explain your function in the performance of each procedure.

2. What is the distinction, if any, in your state between the words *probate* and *estate administration?*

3. How are "small estates" administered in your state? What is the monetary limit in your state that allows an estate to be classified as a "small estate"?

4. How do the following differ: solemn v. common probate; formal v. informal probate; and solemn v. formal probate (under the UPC)?

5. When would you choose to follow formal (solemn) probate instead of informal (common) probate when administering a decedent's estate?

6. In what ways can a county clerk or registrar assist you in your estate administration tasks? What are some things they cannot do?

7. What information must you obtain to complete the form used to petition to probate a will? Is this information and the form the same when a person dies intestate?

8. In your state, what are the statutory requirements for giving notice to creditors? When and how is the notice given in your state, and what is the time limit creditors have to file their claims?

9. How is a personal representative appointed? What document authorizes a personal representative to manage a decedent's estate? How is a fiduciary employer identification number obtained, and for what purposes does a personal representative use it?

10. What are the various assets you will help the personal representative collect and preserve in an estate administration, and what procedures do you use for the collection? List 10 assets.

11. What are the inventory and appraisal, and how are they prepared?

12. How does a creditor present a claim against the decedent's estate, and how does the personal representative contest a claim?

13. What is your state's priority for payment of creditors' claims? Cite the statute and give examples of items within each category.

14. How is the final account prepared, and what does it contain?

15. At what point can the personal representative transfer the decedent's assets (both real and personal property) to the appropriate parties? When does legal title pass to them?

16. Can a decedent have more than one domicile? How would you resolve this problem so that ancillary proceedings can be finalized?

17. What happens to property of the decedent that is discovered after the estate administration has been completed?

18. Who is responsible for paying a surcharge, and under what circumstances would this occur?

19. Should all states adopt the Uniform Probate Code? Explain.

Case Problems

Problem 1

Shelley Mertens of 1005 Elm Street, St. Paul, Minnesota, died testate (with a will) on September 20, 2014. She was married to Christopher Mertens, age 83, and had one child, Lindsay Mertens, age 55. Mrs. Mertens was born on November 6, 1930, in the state of Michigan. Her parents moved to Minnesota that year. On September 4, 1951, she married Christopher Mertens in St. Paul, Minnesota. Mrs. Mertens was a retired real estate broker, and her legal residence (domicile) at the time of her death was St. Paul, Minnesota. Mrs. Mertens died in the Porta Veta Hospital in St. Paul after suffering from cancer for approximately nine months. Her attending physician was Dr. Norma J. Dennison, 2067 Doctor's Exchange Building, St. Paul, Minnesota. Her attorneys were Jaycox and Jackson, First State Bank Building, Minneapolis, Minnesota.

Beneficiaries under Mrs. Mertens's will are her husband, Christopher Mertens, who is also the personal representative of the estate; daughter Lindsay R. Mertens; and the American Cancer Society. Beneficiaries under insurance contracts are her brother, Jayson A. Daw; husband, Christopher Mertens; and the estate.

Exhibit 9.14 shows the assets that Mrs. Mertens individually owned or in which she owned an interest as specified at her death. Exhibit 9.15 shows liabilities and debts owed by Mrs. Mertens at her death. Exhibit 9.16 shows costs incurred after Mrs. Mertens's death. Exhibit 9.17 shows the beneficiaries

of Mrs. Mertens's estate and the maintenance of the family during administration.

Forms must be completed (executed) for the formal probate of the Shelley Mertens's estate. From the following list, selected sample forms (found in Appendix A) have been executed.

1. Petition for Formal Probate of Will and for Formal Appointment of Personal Representative (Form 1*)

2. Order and Notice of Hearing on Petition for Formal Probate of Will and Appointment of Personal Representative and Notice to Creditors (Form 2*)

3. Proof of Placing Order for Publication (Form 3*)

4. Affidavit of Publication (Form 4*)

5. Affidavit of Mailing Order or Notice of Hearing (Form 5*)

6. Notice to Spouse and Children and Affidavit of Mailing (Form 5*)

7. Testimony of Witness to Will (not executed)

8. Order of Formal Probate of Will and Formal Appointment of Personal Representative (Form 6*)

9. Acceptance of Appointment as Personal Representative and Oath by Individual (not executed)

10. Bond, if required, or Request for Waiver of Bond (not executed)

---

* See Appendix A.

EXHIBIT 9.14   Assets of Shelley Mertens

Cash*
Traveler's checks (not cashed)	$ 1,000
Checking account—First National City Bank of St. Paul No. 55–5555	50,000
Savings deposit—American National Bank of St. Paul No. 44–4444	15,000

Stocks and Bonds
Innovative Software, 500 shares (six months after Mrs. Mertens's death decreased in value to $17,000)	$ 20,000
Minnesota Co-op, 1,000 shares	10,000
American National Oil Company, 1,000 shares (joint tenancy with husband)	75,000
Minnesota Company, 100 shares (joint tenancy with daughter)	5,000

U.S. Government Bonds
Bond No. R4502363	$ 1,500
Bond No. R4502364	1,500

Personal Property
Clothing—personal effects	$ 4,500
Furs—mink coat	11,500
Automobile—2009 Mazda	12,000
Furniture and household goods	50,000

Real Property
Residential (homestead)	$500,000

1005 Elm Street
St. Paul, MN
Legal description: Lot 615, Block 42, Reiser's Addition to St. Paul

Rental Property
Duplex	$ 75,000

776 Cliff Road
St. Paul, MN
Legal description: Lots 16 & 17, Block 20, Lovey's Addition to St. Paul
$300,000: ¼ interest = $75,000

Receivables
Johnson Furriers—Promissory Note (accrued interest = $350)	$ 10,350

Interests in Trusts and Other Estates
St. Paul Trust Co.—Annual income to Mrs. Mertens until her death, then to her daughter, Lindsay R. Mertens until her death. Established by Mrs. Mertens's uncle.	$ 6,000	annual
Power of Appointment (general; unexercised)—To distribute income or corpus (500 shares Green Giant). Established by Mrs. Mertens's father.	50,000	

Insurance and Annuities
Prudential Life Insurance Company—No dividends. Beneficiary: Jayson A. Daw (brother).	$200,000	
Minnesota Life Insurance Company—Dividends. Beneficiary: Estate.	600,000	
Accumulated dividends.	1,000	
Ecko Life Insurance Company (premiums of $50 per month paid by Order of the Doves). $100 per month to Mrs. Mertens for life; then $100 per month to her husband for his life.	100	per month
Life expectancy of 4 years.	4,800	($100 per month times 48 months)

*Note: Five months prior to her death, Mrs. Mertens transferred funds from her checking account to her husband ($30,000) and to her daughter ($20,000). Mrs. Mertens obtained this cash by selling Airco Corporation stock that she owned, and she then placed the cash in her checking account.

EXHIBIT 9.15	Debts of Shelley Mertens

Debts
Approved claims against the estate
Ace's Plumbing Co. (company claims *$500* is owed; Mrs. Mertens's personal
    representative claims *$300* is owed) (contested claim) $ 500

EXHIBIT 9.16	Costs Incurred after Shelley Mertens's Death

Funeral Expenses

Newark and Newark Funeral Home	$ 9,500
Morningside Florists	200
Riverside Cemetery	1,000
Brown Monument Company—gravestone	1,000
Total	$11,700

Administration Expenses

Philip Masterson Co., Inc., appraisals	$ 500
Smith & Smith, Inc., preparation of tax returns	1,500
Attorney's fees	15,000
Compensation of personal representative	10,000
Publication of orders	50
Certified copies	30
Bond premiums (none)	0
Miscellaneous expenses	470
Expenses of last illness unpaid at death (Porta Veta Hospital)	850
Total (Additional charges for medical attendance of $1250 were approved by the personal representative)	$28,400

11. Letters Testamentary (Form 7*)

12. Application for Employer Identification Number (Form 23*)

13. Notice Concerning Fiduciary Relationship (Form 24*)

14. Inventory and Appraisement (Form 8*)

15. Petition to Allow Selection of Personal Property (not executed)

16. Order Allowing Selection of Personal Property (not executed)

17. Petition for Family Maintenance (not executed)

18. Order for Family Maintenance (not executed)

19. Final Account (Form 9*)

20. Petition to Allow Final Account, Settle and Distribute Estate (not executed)

21. Notice and Order for Hearing on Petition for Formal Settlement of Estate (not executed)

22. Affidavit of Mailing Order or Notice of Hearing on Final Account (not executed)

23. Federal and state income and death tax returns (see Chapter 15)

24. Order Allowing Final Account (not executed)

25. Order of Complete Settlement of the Estate and Decree of Distribution (Form 10*)

26. Receipt for Assets by Distributee (not executed)

---

* See Appendix A.

EXHIBIT 9.17	**Those Who Receive Benefits from the Estate of Shelley Mertens**

Individuals
Christopher Mertens (husband)
   Under will—Any interest in real property, and residue after
      specific gifts (bequests) $1,367,290
     Joint tenancy—   75,000
     Stock Gift—Cash   30,000
Lindsay R. Mertens (daughter)
     Joint tenancy— $ 5,000
     Stock Gift—Cash   20,000
Jayson A. Daw (brother)
   Life insurance policy $ 200,000
Charitable Devises
American Cancer Society
   Under will $ 10,000
Estate
Life insurance policy (part of residue, see above) $ 601,000
Family Maintenance during Administration
$400 per month for 12 months $ 4,800

27. Petition for Discharge of Personal Representative (Form 11*)

28. Order Discharging Personal Representative (Form 12*)

A. Review the checklists shown in Exhibits 9.14 through 9.17 and the executed forms in Appendix A in the Shelley Mertens case. Develop checklists and add to your checklists the data necessary to fill in the required forms for formal (solemn) probate of a testator's estate in your state. Use and follow the probate procedures in your state to execute (complete) the necessary forms.

B. Using the facts and information you have added to complete the forms in the Shelley Mertens case above, identify and complete the forms for formal probate if Shelley Mertens had died intestate in your state.

Practical Assignments

1. Prepare IRS Form SS-4 to obtain a federal employer identification number for your own estate with a family member identified as the named personal representative. A hard copy of the form can be found online.

2. Prepare a letter on behalf of the named personal representative in Assignment 1 to a local bank of your choice requesting the following:

  a. that your bank account be closed (Account #1960310970)

  b. that a check for the balance including interest payable to your estate be sent to the personal representative's address

  c. reference enclosures including the Letters Testamentary (or Letters of Administration) and the death certificate

3. Prepare a clause to be included in your will that allows your personal representative to continue your online business pending the final transfer in probate court. You must supply the name and address of your business.

---

* See Appendix A.

INFORMAL PROBATE ADMINISTRATION

10

Outline

Objectives

After completing this chapter, you should be able to:

- Identify and explain the informal probate method of administering decedents' estates under the Uniform Probate Code.

- Recognize the circumstances under which informal probate procedures are appropriate.

- Explain the steps in informal probate administration of a decedent's estate.

- Apply the procedures and prepare the legal forms used in informal probate administration for a set of facts involving a decedent's estate.

SCOPE OF THE CHAPTER

This chapter outlines the method of selection and the proceedings involved in informal probate according to the Uniform Probate Code (UPC). The procedures are listed, the relevant UPC sections are cited, and sample forms that are available in Appendix A are identified. Next, a case study of an estate that would appropriately be administered by informal probate procedures is presented. You are taken step by step through the informal proceedings so you can become familiar with the procedures. Case problems involving both testate and intestate situations illustrate estate administrations that use informal probate procedures. Selected forms required for informal probate administration are executed and available in Appendix A for your review.

THE CHOICE OF FORMAL OR INFORMAL PROBATE

The administration of a decedent's estate may be initiated by any of several procedures under the UPC.

- Formal appointment of the personal representative and formal proceedings thereafter, in testacy and intestacy (UPC §§ 3–401 through 3–414) (see the discussion in Chapter 9)
- Informal appointment of the personal representative and informal proceedings thereafter, in testacy and intestacy (UPC §§ 3–301 through 3–311)
- Collection of the decedent's personal property by Affidavit and Summary Administration proceedings thereafter for small or moderate-sized estates (UPC §§ 3–1201 through 3–1204) (see the discussion in Chapter 9)

Some states require the personal representative to follow a formal, also called solemn or probate in solemn form, procedure in the course of administration. Others combine the UPC procedures, noted above, with local practices such as elimination or lowering of the requirement for a personal representative's bond. The states that have adopted all or part of the UPC are able to offer the above-mentioned procedures. Noteworthy contributions of the UPC include the introduction of (1) procedures that are unsupervised or only partially supervised by the court and are called informal, common, or probate in common form and (2) simplified affidavit or summary administration procedures that reduce the expenses of administration and make the transfer of small estates to the heirs or devisees easier. In view of the great diversity among state practices, even among those that have enacted the UPC, your wisest course is to become familiar with the laws and estate administration procedures of the state in which you live and work.

When one applies for the position of personal representative of an estate that exceeds the limits for summary administration proceedings (see Exhibit 9.2), the applicant may select a formal or informal method of settling the estate. The UPC defines formal proceedings as those "conducted before a judge with notice to interested persons" (UPC § 1–201 [17]) and informal proceedings as "those conducted without notice to interested persons by an officer of the court acting as a registrar for probate of a will or appointment of a personal representative" (UPC § 1–201 [22]). In informal probate, a court-appointed officer (registrar, surrogate, or

Register of Wills) skilled in overseeing decedents' estates takes the place of the judge. That officer has the power to do whatever the judge normally would do (e.g., appoint the personal representative and make findings of fact in relation to the will).

The UPC allows a unique *in and out* method of settling estates—partly "in" the probate court (formally) even though most of the administration takes place "out" of it (informally). In informal proceedings, the personal representative or any person interested in the estate, as defined by UPC § 1–201(23), may petition the court to adjudicate a disputed issue (e.g., the amount of a creditor's claim). After settlement of the dispute, the personal representative may resume informal procedures. This flexible *in and out* use of formal proceedings within informal probate proves advantageous to the personal representative who prefers the freedom of informal probate but who may encounter a complexity the court is better suited or may be required to handle.

> **EXAMPLE:** Reginald Canby died testate, leaving all his property to his son, Damon. Reginald's wife predeceased him. Vanessa, Reginald's daughter, contends that Damon unduly influenced their father during his last illness to persuade him to write the will. Although the executor of Reginald's estate had elected to follow informal probate procedures, Vanessa may petition the probate court to settle this question using formal probate procedures. After the court has made its decision, it may allow the estate to resume informal probate or order it to continue formal, supervised probate (UPC §§ 3–501, 3–502).

Informal probate generally reduces the time required to complete the administration of a decedent's estate. It involves fewer steps and less complicated procedures (e.g., the filing of fewer papers) than formal probate. The estate can be more easily distributed since the personal representative does not have to give notice of hearings, or obtain court approval for every item distributed, and may not be required to obtain a bond or submit an account at the end, depending on the circumstances.

The personal representative may request formal court supervision at any time; however, informal probate does not demand the court supervise even the personal representative's closing of the estate after administering it. Since the purpose of informal probate is in part to help relieve congestion in the probate court, the greater part of informal probate transactions are carried out without the court's direct involvement. Not infrequently a hearing to prove the will and to appoint a personal representative is the only in-court proceeding. Of course, this is not always the case because any person interested in the estate (e.g., a creditor, heir, or devisee) may petition the court to determine a matter using formal proceedings.

> **EXAMPLE:** Fred McManus dies intestate, survived by a son, Bruce, and a brother, Paul. The registrar, who is empowered to conduct informal probate proceedings, appoints Paul personal representative of Fred's estate. Bruce successfully challenges the informal appointment of his uncle, Paul. Therefore, the court will appoint a personal representative in a formal proceeding, according to the order of priority (see the next section).

Although informal probate eliminates the required appraisal of estate assets unless demanded by the personal representative, another interested party, or the court, the value of real estate and closely held businesses should be appraised by an independent expert. The personal representative is entitled to hire and pay the appraiser(s) out of estate assets (UPC § 3–707).

EXAMPLE: According to her will, Tillie's estate is to be divided equally among her two sisters, Sherie and Noreen, and one brother, Waldo. Included in her estate are valuable paintings. Waldo, who is informally appointed to administer the estate, sets the value of the paintings at $50,000. The remaining property in the estate is sold at public auction for $100,000 cash. Waldo decides to keep the paintings for himself and give Sherie and Noreen each $50,000 in cash. The two sisters, who believe the art collection is worth much more, can demand that it be appraised by an art expert.

The availability of informal proceedings to probate a will and settle the estate is one of the chief advantages of the UPC.

PRIORITY OF PERSONS SEEKING APPOINTMENT AS PERSONAL REPRESENTATIVES

In both formal and informal proceedings, persons who qualify as personal representatives of the estate are considered in the following order of priority.

1. The person named as personal representative in the will, if there is one.

2. The surviving spouse of the decedent who is a devisee of the decedent.

3. Other devisees of the decedent.

4. The surviving spouse of the decedent.

5. Other heirs of the decedent.

6. Any creditor of the decedent, provided no one with a higher priority standing has applied for appointment within 45 days of the death of the decedent (UPC § 3–203[a]). Compare a non-UPC state statute, Okl. St. Ann. § 58-122.

The person who has the highest standing in this order and who is willing to serve does not always become the personal representative. The court or the registrar must appoint the personal representative but will not appoint a person who is under the age of 18, a felon, or otherwise unsuitable for the position. This decision must be made by the court on the petition of an interested person.

In some instances, persons having priority fail to apply or are in some way disqualified. If that happens, the court, in a formal proceeding, will consider the nominees or persons having priority and try to arrive at a solution beneficial to the estate and satisfactory to those interested in it (UPC § 3–203[b]). Any objection to the appointment of a personal representative must be made in a formal proceeding.

APPLICATION FOR INFORMAL PROBATE AND APPOINTMENT OF PERSONAL REPRESENTATIVE

Informal probate commences when an applicant who seeks to be appointed personal representative submits a completed application for informal probate and informal appointment to the registrar for screening and acceptance. If your firm has been hired to assist the personal representative, you will be asked to perform the following tasks to help with these procedures.

• Gather the information necessary to complete the forms.

• Prepare the forms and file them or verify the filing.

- Communicate with the personal representative and registrar to ensure that all procedures and forms are properly executed.

The applicant must verify (i.e., swear under oath) that the application is accurate and complete to the best of the applicant's knowledge. It is filed with the registrar or clerk of the probate court (UPC § 3–301 and Form 13*).

1. The following general information is required on all applications for informal probate of a will or for informal appointment.

   - The interest of the applicant in the decedent's estate (e.g., named personal representative—executor)

   - Name, age, date of death of decedent, county and state of decedent's domicile at time of death; names and addresses of spouse, children, heirs, devisees, and ages of those who are minors

   - A statement indicating the county or city where the proceedings are to take place, if decedent was not domiciled at the date of death in the state where the application for informal probate has been filed

   - The name and address of any personal representative of the decedent who has been appointed in this state or elsewhere whose appointment has not been terminated

   - A statement that the applicant has not received nor is aware of any "demand for notice of any probate or appointment proceeding concerning the decedent that may have been filed in this state or elsewhere"

   - A statement that the time limit for informal probate or appointment has not expired either because three years or less have passed since the decedent's death or, if more than three years from death have passed, circumstances as described by UPC § 3–108 authorizing late probate or appointment have occurred

2. If the application is for informal probate of a will, it must, in addition to the information and statements listed under 1 above, affirm the following:

   - That the court has possession of the original last will, or that the original will or an authenticated copy probated in another jurisdiction is included with the application

   - That the applicant believes the will to have been validly executed

   - That the applicant is unaware of any instrument that revokes the will and believes the submitted instrument is the decedent's last will

3. An application for informal appointment of a personal representative to administer an estate under a will sets forth the following in addition to the general information referred to in 1 above.

   - A description of the will by date of execution

   - The time and place of probate or the pending application or petition for probate

   - An adaptation of the statements in the application or petition for probate and the name, address, and standing of the applicant among those who are entitled to be personal representative under UPC § 3–203

---

* See Appendix A.

4. In addition to the statements listed in 1 above, an application for informal appointment of an administrator when the decedent died intestate states the following:

- That the applicant is not aware of any unrevoked testamentary instrument relating to property located in the state, or if the applicant is aware of any such instrument, the reason for its not being probated (UPC § 3–301 [4])
- The priority of the applicant, and the names of any other persons who have a prior or equal right to the appointment under UPC § 3–203

EXAMPLE: Martha Engle's father died testate and named Martha executrix of his will. Martha desires to be appointed informally and to have the will probated informally. She must complete the data listed in 1, 2, and 3 above.

EXAMPLE: Corey Davis desires to be named personal representative of the estate of his father, who died intestate. Corey's mother predeceased his father. Corey must complete the data listed in 1 and 4 above.

In the example of Martha Engle, after her father died, no will could be found, and Maria Engle, Martha's sister, was informally appointed personal representative in intestacy. Subsequently, the will was discovered and Martha sought the appointment. In addition to the data listed in 1, 2, and 3, Martha would have to complete a "change of testacy status" form, requesting that she replace Maria (UPC § 3–301 [5]).

In the example of Corey Davis, after his father died, Corey's brother, Alton, produced an instrument that resembled a will in which Alton was named executor. Therefore, he was appointed personal representative by the court. Subsequently, the instrument was proved not valid, and Corey sought appointment as personal representative. Corey would also have to complete a "change of testacy status" form because the decedent, formerly considered testate, is now intestate.

By definition, informal probate of a will and informal appointment are proceedings conducted "without notice to interested persons" (UPC § 1–201 [22]). A person applying for informal appointment and/or informal probate of a will does not have to notify persons interested in the estate unless those persons have filed a written demand to be notified in accordance with UPC § 3–204 (see also UPC § 3–306). The applicant must, however, notify anyone who has a superior right to be personal representative, e.g., a person who has been previously appointed personal representative or a person who stands higher in the order of priority for appointment.

EXAMPLE: Ernest Falcott wants to be informally appointed personal representative to his father's estate and have the will informally probated. No personal representative has been previously appointed. His cousin, Julia, files a demand to be notified. Ernest must, therefore, notify Julia of his applications for informal probate of a will and informal appointment. He must also notify his mother, Letitia, who has a superior right to be personal representative.

Persons applying for informal proceedings must verify under oath the statements on their applications. The registrar is required to make "proofs and findings" for informal probate and informal appointment applications to check the truth and accuracy of statements therein and has the power to disqualify or decline applications if not satisfied (UPC §§ 3–303, 3–305, 3–308, 3–309). Unintentional mistakes made by the applicant are correctable, but deliberate falsification that injures someone interested in the estate will give the injured person a cause of action against the applicant (UPC §§ 1–106 and 3–301[b]).

ACCEPTANCE BY THE REGISTRAR

After the forms necessary for informal proceedings are executed, the applicant submits them to the registrar, who scrutinizes them for errors or omissions that might invalidate the application. The registrar must be satisfied with the following:

- That the applicant has carried out the requirements of the UPC
- That the applicant has solemnly affirmed the statements made in the application to be true to the best of the applicant's knowledge
- That the applicant is an interested person as defined by UPC § 1–201(23)
- That the applicant has chosen the proper venue (county) for the will to be probated or for the appointment of the personal representative
- That persons who have demanded notice of proceedings (UPC § 3–204) have been notified
- That 120 hours have elapsed since the decedent's death—UPC § 2–104 requires that a person must survive the decedent for 120 hours to be an heir

In addition, the registrar will check each application for particular requirements. For example, for informal probate, the registrar must possess the original of a properly executed will that has not been revoked, the statutory time limit for probate must not have expired, and the will must be the kind that may be probated informally. Informal probate of certain wills may not be advisable. The registrar has a duty to decline informal probate of alleged copies of lost or destroyed wills, wills consisting of a series of testamentary instruments (rather than a single one), and other irregular instruments. For informal appointment, the priority of the person who is entitled to appointment is determined by statute (UPC § 3–203).

The registrar may not be satisfied with the contents of the application for any of several reasons. Some examples are illustrated below.

EXAMPLE: The registrar denies Joceyln Galbreth's application for informal probate of her brother's will because another sister, Elin Galbreth, had applied for probate earlier.

EXAMPLE: The registrar denies Gilbert Havlicek's application for informal probate of his mother's will because the will is written on two apparently unconnected papers and it is not clear if one revokes the other.

EXAMPLE: The registrar denies Conrad Marquart's application for informal appointment as personal representative of his sister's estate because another person with a higher priority had been appointed and has not died or resigned.

EXAMPLE: The registrar denies Marina Yladak's application for informal appointment as personal representative of her father's estate because she indicated on her application that her father might have had another will that is still in existence (UPC §§ 3–305, 3–309).

Informal probate is available only for uncomplicated wills or estates. The registrar's denial of an application usually results in the commencement of formal probate proceedings. When the registrar accepts an application, it does not constitute a recommendation of informal over formal probate for a particular estate. The responsibility for that choice belongs to the applicant. The acceptance of an application by the registrar means only that the application meets the statutory requirements for filing.

If satisfied with the information contained in the application for informal proceedings, and if 120 hours have elapsed since the decedent's death, the registrar signifies acceptance of the application by issuing a written Statement of Informal Probate (Form 14*) and/or appoints the applicant the personal representative of the estate by issuing Letters Testamentary or Letters of Administration (Forms 7* and 20*). The Letters empower the applicant to assume the powers and duties of the office of personal representative but do not take effect until the applicant has filed a statement of acceptance of these powers and duties and has paid the necessary fees. At this time, the personal representative's bond, if required, must be filed with the court. Any person who has an interest in the estate worth more than $1,000, including creditors with claims greater than $1,000, may demand the personal representative be required to post a bond, or the court may require it (UPC §§ 3–603 and 3–605).

ASSIGNMENT 10.1

Laurel Shepard, the granddaughter of Maryanna Means, who died intestate, intends to apply to be informally appointed personal representative (administratrix) of her grandmother's estate. Before she submits the application, she brings it to be checked by you, the paralegal of the attorney who represents the estate. Comment on the following concerns you must bring to the attention of the attorney.

1. Laurel is not sure she qualifies as an "interested person" because she had seen her grandmother only two or three times before her death.

2. Laurel believes her priority may be inferior to that of Florence Kingsley, Maryanna's nurse for 17 years, who had lived with and cared for Maryanna.

3. Laurel has not given notice to Georgina Means, Maryanna's daughter, because she does not know Georgina's address and has not been in contact with her for a long time.

4. Maryanna resided and died in Lewis County, Idaho, but left a farm and a bank account in Orange County, California. Laurel does not know if Lewis County, where she intends to submit her application, is the proper place for administration.

5. Laurel thinks her uncle, Jason Means, who lives in Orange County, may have been appointed personal representative. If so, this might present a challenge to her own application.

6. Laurel does not believe she can affirm the truth of her statements in the application because of the uncertainties stated above.

NOTICE REQUIREMENTS

Informal probate is not supervised by the probate court and does not require notice be given to interested parties. However, persons who have an interest in the estate may file a demand to be notified of the petitioner's application for informal probate or informal appointment (UPC § 3–204). (See the discussion of notice requirements and methods below.) An interested person might be one who has a financial interest in the estate, a previously appointed personal representative who is still acting in that capacity, or someone who occupies a place in the order of priority for appointment (UPC §§ 1–201 [23] and 3–203).

* See Appendix A.

Once a demand has been filed, the registrar will notify the personal representative to keep the demandant informed of proceedings related to the estate. If the demandant believes that the applicant is not qualified to be the personal representative, is using a revoked will, or otherwise objects to informal proceedings, the demand for notice ensures an opportunity to request formal or supervised administration when necessary. If the demandant is not given notice of a subsequent order or proceeding, it remains effective. However, the personal representative will be liable for any damages the demandant suffers as a result of the absence of notice (UPC § 3–204).

Notice of Application for Informal Probate

After the registrar accepts the application and grants informal probate and appointment of the personal representative, the petitioner who seeks informal probate must give notice as required by UPC § 1–401 of the application for informal probate to any person who demands it pursuant to UPC § 3–204 and Form 15*. No other notice of informal probate is required.

Notice of Application for Informal Appointment

The petitioner seeking informal appointment as personal representative must give notice as required by UPC § 1–401 of the intention to seek an informal appointment to any person who has a financial or property interest and who demands notice pursuant to UPC § 3–204 and to any person who has a prior or equal right to appointment not waived in writing and filed with the court (UPC § 3–310 and Form 15*). No other notice of an informal appointment proceeding is required.

Demand for Notice of Order or Filing

At any time after the death of the decedent, any person who has a financial or property interest in a decedent's estate may file a demand with the court for notice of any order or filing relating to the estate (see UPC §§ 3–204, 3–306). The demand for notice must state the name of the decedent, the nature of the demandant's interest in the estate, and the person's address or that of the attorney who represents the person. The clerk will mail a copy of such demand to the personal representative, if any. After such a demand is filed, no order or filing to which the demand relates can be made or accepted without notice to the demandant or attorney, as required in UPC § 1–401. If such notice is not given, the order or filing is still valid, but the person who receives the order or makes the filing may be liable for any damage caused by the absence of notice.

The notice requirement arising from a demand may be waived in writing by the demandant and will cease when the demandant's interest in the estate terminates. Interested persons are protected by their right to demand prior notice of informal proceedings (see UPC § 3–204) or to contest a requested appointment by use of a formal testacy proceeding, or by use of a formal proceeding seeking the appointment of another person. Interested persons also have available to them the remedies provided in UPC § 3–605 (demand for bond by interested persons) and § 3–607 (order restraining personal representative).

---

* See Appendix A.

Although not obligated to do so unless a demand has been filed, since publication under UPC § 3–801 is sufficient, the personal representative should give personal notice to creditors. The UPC allows creditors four months from the date of the first publication of notice to file claims (see UPC §§ 3–801, 3–802, and 3–803). If the estate is still open, the court has the discretion to allow late claims but can refuse them unless good cause is shown. Once the account of the personal representative is settled, the court cannot allow the claim (Form 15*).

Method and Time for Giving Notice

If notice of a hearing on any petition, application, order, or filing is required (except for specific notice requirements as otherwise provided in the UPC), the petitioner or applicant must give notice of the time and place of hearing of any petition, application, order, or filing to any interested person or the attorney (UPC § 1–401). Again, if requested, the petitioner must give notice in one of three ways.

- By mailing a copy of the notice at least 14 days *before the time set* for the hearing by certified, registered, or ordinary first-class mail addressed to the person being notified at the post office address given in the demand for notice, or at the person's office or place of residence

- By delivering a copy of the notice to the person being notified personally at least 14 days before the time set for the hearing

- If the address or identity of any person is not known and cannot be ascertained with reasonable diligence, by publishing at least once a week for three consecutive weeks a copy of the notice in a newspaper having general circulation in the county where the hearing is to be held, the last publication of which is to be at least 10 days before the time set for the hearing

For good cause, the court may provide a different method or time of giving notice for any hearing. Prior to or at the hearing, proof of giving the notice and the Affidavit of Mailing Notice must be made and filed (see UPC § 1–401 and Form 16*). Any person, including a *guardian ad litem*, conservator, or other fiduciary (see Glossary), may waive notice by a writing signed by the person or the attorney and filed in the proceeding in court (see UPC § 1–402).

Notice must be given to every interested person or to one who can bind an interested person, as described in UPC § 1–403, which also describes pleading and notice requirements when parties are bound by others.

DUTIES AND POWERS OF THE PERSONAL REPRESENTATIVE IN INFORMAL PROBATE

The primary responsibility of the personal representative is the proper distribution of the decedent's estate. In a testate administration, the personal representative distributes the estate assets according to the will and within the bounds of the law (e.g., the personal representative pays priority family allowances and debts first). In an intestate administration, the personal representative distributes the estate

---

* See Appendix A.

assets according to state statutes of descent and distribution (intestate succession statutes).

The duties and powers of the personal representative in informal probate are outlined generally in UPC §§ 3–701 to 3–721.

As a fiduciary, the personal representative must observe the standards of care applicable to fiduciaries. Since it is necessary for the personal representative to hold temporary title to personal property assets that belong and are distributed to others (devisees or heirs), the personal representative is liable to successors for damage resulting from improper use of power or mishandling estate assets, e.g., selling an asset when there was no need to do so (UPC §§ 3–703, 3–712).

An informally appointed personal representative who possesses Letters Testamentary or Letters of Administration needs no further approval before beginning distribution (Forms 7* and 20*). Only when the personal representative or another interested person requests court supervision of heretofore unsupervised proceedings (the "in and out" feature) does the personal representative have to obtain the court's order to proceed (UPC § 3–704).

Notification to Devisees or Heirs and Creditors

No later than 30 days following appointment, the personal representative must notify the decedent's devisees or heirs of the appointment (UPC § 3–705). The notice is sent by ordinary mail and must include the name and address of the personal representative, indicate that it is sent to all persons who have or may have some interest in the estate, indicate whether bond has been filed, and describe the court where all estate documents are on file. This notice is part of the fiduciary obligation, but the personal representative's neglect to give notice will not invalidate the appointment or powers of the office. If it causes loss or damage to a devisee or heir, however, that person has a cause of action for damages against the personal representative for breach of the fiduciary duty (UPC §§ 3–204 and 3–712).

> **EXAMPLE:** Eula Gribben died intestate in Colorado, leaving a small estate. All of her heirs live in Colorado except her son, Lewis, who lives in Delaware. Her brother, Lloyd Adcock, was informally appointed personal representative (administrator) and gave notice to all of the heirs except Lewis. If Lloyd omits Lewis in the distribution of the estate, Lewis would have a cause of action against Lloyd for the omitted share and possibly for damages (e.g., needless expense of court fees).

The personal representative must also notify creditors of the estate of the appointment by publishing in a general-circulation county newspaper the announcement of the personal representative's appointment. The notice must appear once a week for three successive weeks. Creditors have four months after the date of the first publication to present their claims; otherwise the claims are barred (UPC § 3–801).

Payment of Creditors' Claims

After the four-month period, the personal representative must pay creditors' claims that are determined to be valid (i.e., are approved or allowed). The order in which valid claims are to be paid is found in UPC §§ 3–805 to 3–807. The personal

---

* See Appendix A.

representative has the power to disallow or disqualify claims creditors have made fraudulently or otherwise unjustly against the estate (UPC § 3–803). The creditors can appeal the personal representative's decision in court.

> **EXAMPLE:** Bertrand Dorn had a credit account with the National Oil Company. Before his death, the company sent him a bill for $148.79. Bertrand disputed it and claimed that he owed only $48.79 according to service station receipts. His personal representative may refuse to pay the additional $100 claim by following UPC procedures for "allowance of claims" (UPC § 3–806).

Inventory Property

Within the time set by state statute, e.g., three to six months after appointment or nine months after the date of the decedent's death, the personal representative must prepare an inventory of all real or personal property owned by the decedent at the time of death and mail it to the surviving spouse and all other interested persons who request it. The personal representative may also file the original copy of the inventory with the court (UPC § 3–706). The inventory must list the assets of the estate with sufficient description for accurate identification, value the assets at fair market value, and include the kind of mortgage or other encumbrance on each item and the amount of the encumbrance (Form 17*).

Two typical inventory problems may arise: the nature and kind of estate assets may be so unique the personal representative is unable to adequately estimate their fair market value; or the court may order an independent person who has no interest in the estate to appraise these difficult-to-value estate assets. In either case, the personal representative usually has permission to hire independent appraisers to assist in valuation, and if they do perform appraisals, the personal representative must list on the inventory their names, addresses, and the items they valued (UPC § 3–707).

Hold and Manage the Estate

Until discharged or released from the appointment, the personal representative has the same power over the title to the decedent's property as the decedent (UPC § 3–711). Both a trustee and the personal representative hold title in a similar manner and are given powers and duties that require the exercise of prudence and restraint expected of a fiduciary for the benefit of others: the trustee for beneficiaries; the personal representative for devisees, heirs, or creditors. The personal representative is liable for loss or damage caused to such persons by improper exercise of these powers (UPC § 3–712).

> **EXAMPLE:** Merle Hendricks, the informally appointed personal representative for his father's estate, was given the power of sale by the will. He sells an antique lamp from the estate to his wife at a lower price than he would have asked of a stranger. Merle has violated his fiduciary duty by self-dealing with estate assets (UPC§ 3–713).

The various transactions authorized and performed by a personal representative, e.g., acquire or dispose of assets; sell, mortgage, or lease real or personal property; and vote shares of stock are listed in UPC § 3–715.

---

* See Appendix A.

Final Account and Closing the Estate

After the minimum period for closing an estate has passed and all approved creditor claims have been paid, the personal representative must prepare and file the final account. It consists of a list of the decedent's probate assets; any increases or decreases in the assets; the payment of creditors' claims; administration expenses; funeral and last illness expenses; taxes; and the balance of assets on hand for distribution. Only after a copy of the final account has been given to every distributee of the estate can the personal representative distribute the remaining assets to the persons entitled to receive them and seek a discharge (termination) from office.

An informally appointed personal representative may choose to close the estate informally and be discharged by signing a sworn **closing statement** (affidavit) to the effect that he or she believes the estate's assets have been distributed correctly and its business transacted. The personal representative may use this method if the administration has not been continuously supervised by the court. In the case of continuous supervision, the UPC demands a final account and formal closing, as described in detail in Chapter 9, by either of the methods described in UPC §§ 3–1001, 3–1003, and 3–505 or 3–1002 (Forms 9* and 12*).

closing statement
An affidavit signed by the personal representative at the end of informal probate proceedings to close the estate and to be discharged.

The personal representative's sworn closing statement informally closing the estate must verify the following:

- That a notice to creditors was published more than six months before the date of the present statement.

- That the personal representative has fully administered the estate, paid all federal and state taxes and valid claims (including creditors' and successors' claims), and that the assets of the estate have been distributed to the persons entitled. If the personal representative has not completed distribution, the reasons for partial distribution must be explained in the closing statement.

- That the personal representative has mailed a copy of this closing statement to all of the claimants (creditors) who have made themselves known and to all distributees of the estate (see UPC § 3–1003). Once copies have been mailed, the original "Statement to Close" is filed with the probate court.

The periods creditors have to assert and present claims include the following:

- Under UPC § 3–803, all claims against a decedent's estate that arose before the decedent's death are barred against the estate, the personal representative, and the heirs and devisees of the decedent unless presented within four months after the date of the first publication of notice to creditors if notice is given in compliance with UPC § 3–801, or within one year after the decedent's death, if notice to creditors has not been published.

- Under UPC § 3–1005, the rights of all creditors whose claims have not been previously barred against the personal representative for breach of fiduciary duty (see UPC § 3–803 above) are barred unless a proceeding to assert the claim is commenced within six months after the filing of the personal representative's *closing statement*. Creditors do, however, have the right to recover from a personal representative for fraud or inadequate disclosure related to the settlement of the decedent's estate.

---

* See Appendix A.

If a personal representative has distributed the assets of the estate to other claimants, e.g., devisees, heirs, or other creditors, a creditor with a valid but undischarged claim must press the claim in a judicial proceeding against one or more of those who received the assets (UPC § 3–1004).

EXAMPLE: Annelise Frechette closes her mother's estate informally by filing a sworn statement with the probate court. Two months afterward, the owner of a gift shop who had not been given notice presents a bill for some items that Annelise's mother had bought on credit. Annelise is personally liable to the creditor for not having given him notice as she had given the other creditors. The creditor can obtain payment of the bill by initiating a judicial proceeding against Annelise or any distributee, but the creditor cannot collect from both. If the creditor obtains a judgment and payment from Corinee Mays, one of the five distributees, then Corinee may demand of the other four distributees, who were given notice of the creditor's claim and pending litigation, four-fifths of the amount she had to pay so all will bear the burden equally.

If no proceedings involving the personal representative are pending in the court one year after the closing statement is filed, the personal representative's appointment is terminated (UPC § 3–1003). Termination does not automatically accompany closing. The authority of the personal representative remains active for one year. Once the authority is terminated, the personal representative has no power to conduct affairs in the name of the estate. The UPC provides the one-year grace period between closing and termination for the resolution of unforeseen business, such as in the preceding example.

It is important that the personal representative obtain receipts or evidence of payment for everything distributed from the estate whether or not he has decided to close the estate under one of the methods described in UPC § 3–1001 through § 3–1003. *(Note:* It is legitimate but impractical not to close the estate at all but simply to rely on the receipts collected to show the estate has been fully distributed. Relying on receipts affords no protection to the personal representative should complications arise.) Collecting and retaining receipts enables the personal representative to support the closing statement and the request that the court formally close the estate. Alternatively, the personal representative may obtain an affidavit from each distributee that states he or she received the correct amount.

After the estate has been closed and the personal representative discharged, someone may discover additional omitted property that belonged to the decedent and obviously has not been administered, e.g., rare books referred to in the will but not located during administration. Proper disposition of the assets will necessitate reopening the estate (UPC § 3–1008).

STEP-BY-STEP PROCEDURES IN INFORMAL PROBATE

The following case study describes an estate that could conveniently be administered through the use of the UPC informal probate procedures by an informally appointed personal representative. Follow the personal representative step by step through the informal procedures. As a further review of informal probate procedures, three Case Problems, with appropriate forms and/or questions, are included.

Case Study

Elvira Krueger died testate on February 4, 2015, in a state that has adopted the UPC. Elvira left a son, Ralph, and two daughters, Sara and Christa, none of whom are minors. Elvira's husband predeceased her. Elvira owned property valued at $16,500 at the time of her death: household furniture and goods valued at $12,500, antique furniture valued at $2,000, an automobile valued at $1,400, and a tent trailer for camping valued at $600. In her will, Elvira appointed her daughter, Sara, personal representative (executrix) of her estate and directed the estate assets be distributed as follows: "the automobile and tent trailer to my son, Ralph; the antique furniture to my daughter, Sara; and the household furniture and goods to be sold and the proceeds to be distributed to my three children, Ralph, Sara, and Christa, so each of them will receive an equal amount of my property." Sara later sells the household furniture and goods for $12,500.

Under the terms of the will, Sara must distribute the antique furniture (valued at $2,000) and $3,500 cash to herself (total—$5,500), $5,500 cash to Christa, and the automobile (valued at $1,400), the tent trailer (valued at $600), and $3,500 cash to Ralph. These devises, however, will be reduced by expenses and debts that must be paid first out of the estate assets.

Informal Procedures

Sara files an application with the registrar that requests both informal probate of her mother's will and her informal appointment as personal representative (executrix). She verifies that the application is accurate and complete to the best of her knowledge and belief. The application must include Sara's interest in the estate and identify the required information about the decedent, e.g., name, age, domicile, date of death, and the names and addresses of her children (UPC § 3–301). Since Elvira resided in the state in which Sara is applying for informal appointment, Sara must wait 120 hours (five days) after Elvira's death before the registrar will finalize her appointment (UPC § 2–104).

> File Application

Sara must give notice of the application for informal probate and appointment by one of the methods specified by UPC § 1–401 to (1) any interested person who has filed a written demand with the clerk pursuant to UPC § 3–204; (2) any personal representative of the decedent whose appointment has not been terminated; and (3) any interested person who has a prior or equal right to appointment that has not been waived in writing and filed with the court (UPC §§ 3–306 and 3–310).

> Notice

Both Ralph and Christa have filed demands for notice with the court. Therefore, Sara gives notice of the application to her sister and brother. The validity of an order that is issued or a filing that is accepted without notice to Ralph or Christa will not be affected by the lack of notice, but Sara may be liable for any damage caused to either of them by the absence of notice (UPC § 3–204).

EXAMPLE: In her demand, Christa stated her interest as a devisee in Elvira's estate and signed her name and address. Sara discovered that it was necessary to use all the money from the sale of Elvira's household goods to pay creditors and obtained a court order permitting her to do this. Christa's share in the proceeds of the sale is therefore reduced, but in anticipation of the share of cash she was to receive originally, she had negotiated a bank loan. If Sara fails to notify her of the order that permitted payment to creditors and Christa is subsequently unable to repay the loan, Christa may have a cause of action against Sara.

Application for
appointment

Appointment of personal
representative

Bond

Acceptance of application

After a review of Sara's application, the registrar makes the findings required by UPC § 3–303 and issues a written Statement of Informal Probate. The informal probate is conclusive on all persons unless the probate court, upon petition of an interested party, issues a superseding order that changes the estate administration to a formal testacy proceeding. Defects in Sara's application or in procedures followed in informally probating her mother's will do not by themselves render the probate void (UPC § 3–302).

When the registrar approves Sara's application for informal probate and appointment as personal representative, she must qualify and file her acceptance pursuant to UPC §§ 3–307, 3–601, and 3–602. Once the registrar issues the Letters of Authority (Letters Testamentary or Letters of Administration) (UPC § 1–305), Sara will have all the powers and be entitled to perform all the duties pertaining to her office pursuant to UPC Article III, Part 7.

As an informally appointed personal representative, Sara will not have to file a bond. She would be required to post a bond if it is demanded by any interested party, e.g., a creditor or devisee, who has an interest in the estate exceeding $1,000, or if the will had required her to file a bond, or if she had been appointed special administratrix (see Chapter 8) (UPC §§ 3–603, 3–605). The person who demands a bond must file a written request with the court (UPC §§ 3–603 through 3–606). For example, if Ralph files a written demand for a bond with the court, the registrar will mail a copy of the demand for a bond to Sara. Sara must then obtain a bond and file it with the court unless the court determines in formal proceedings that a bond is unnecessary or that Sara had deposited cash or collateral with an agency of the state to secure performance of her duties (UPC §§ 3–603, 3–605).

If the registrar is satisfied that Elvira had complied with the requirements for executing a will pursuant to UPC § 2–502, e.g., that the will contains the required signatures of two witnesses and attestation clause, the registrar will allow the proceedings to continue without further proof. The registrar may assume execution if the will appears to have been properly executed or may accept an affidavit (sworn statement) of any person who has knowledge of the circumstances of execution, whether or not that person actually witnessed the will (UPC § 3–303[c]).

Elvira's will contained signatures of two competent witnesses (her brother and aunt) and a proper attestation clause. The registrar approved Sara's application for informal probate and appointment. If for any reason the registrar had decided the will should not be admitted to probate or the informal appointment should be denied, the application would have been denied. In that case, if the estate were to be administered, Sara would be required to initiate formal probate proceedings (UPC §§ 3–305 and 3–309).

Sara is now officially Elvira's personal representative. She possesses the powers (e.g., to distribute the assets according to the will) and duties (e.g., to pay creditors before devisees) of a personal representative (UPC § 3–307[b]). Her appointment can be terminated, either voluntarily or by court order, at any time during administration of the estate. Sara's death, disability (such as being declared legally insane), or resignation would terminate her office. She might be removed by court order after a hearing initiated by a person interested in the estate (UPC §§ 3–608 through 3–612).

EXAMPLE: Marston Keefe, a creditor of Elvira, believes that Sara should be removed from office for failing to pay his claim against the estate. Pursuant to UPC § 3–611, he files a petition with the court for a hearing seeking her removal. The court arranges a hearing at which Sara must appear to defend her action. If the court decides she has abused the power of a personal representative, it may direct that Sara be removed and someone else appointed to the position. Also, the court may regulate the disposition of assets remaining in the estate until a successor is appointed.

Sara must inform the heirs and devisees, Ralph and Christa, of her appointment by personal delivery or ordinary mail not later than 30 days after the appointment. Her failure to do this constitutes a breach of her fiduciary duty but does not render invalid her acts as personal representative (UPC § 3–705).

Within three months after her appointment, Sara must prepare and file with the court, either by mail or in person, an inventory of all property owned by Elvira at the time of her death. The inventory must list all assets with reasonable detail and indicate, for each listed item, its fair market value at the date of her mother's death and the type and amount of all encumbrances against any item (UPC § 3–706). Sara is allowed to appoint appraisers without the approval of the court, but the appointment may be challenged by an interested party as provided by UPC § 3–607. Sara must send a copy of the inventory to interested persons who have requested it (UPC § 3–706). She may also file the original with the court.

Inventory

A personal representative owes a fiduciary duty to the devisees comparable to that of a trustee and is not permitted to engage in "self-dealing," i.e., dealing for one's own benefit (UPC § 3–713).

EXAMPLE: Sara appraises the fair market value of a grand piano at $1,500 and decides she will purchase it from the estate. Ralph and Christa object, and assert that the fair market value of the piano is at least $5,000. Ralph petitions the probate court to issue an order to restrain Sara from purchasing the piano and orders an independent appraisal, pursuant to UPC § 3–607. The court issues an order that temporarily prohibits Sara from proceeding with the purchase and notifies both of them of a hearing on the matter to take place within 10 days. At the hearing, the court decides that Sara's course of action is improper and issues an order permanently restraining Sara's action.

Sara would be liable to Ralph and Christa for any damage or loss resulting from any breach of her fiduciary duty to the same extent as a trustee of an express trust.

If Sara had bought the piano from the estate for $1,500 instead of its fair market value, i.e., $5,000, the estate would suffer since less money would be available to pay Elvira's creditors or to be distributed to her devisees. According to law, creditors are the first to be paid from nonspecific or general devises, e.g., in this example, the sale proceeds (money). If Elvira left many debts and expenses, these obligations might consume much of the general devise and diminish the distribution to Ralph or Christa (UPC § 3–712).

EXAMPLE: Suppose the sale of household goods brings $7,500 to the estate. If Elvira's bills total $7,600, all of which must be paid from the estate's assets, the $7,500 will have to be apportioned among the creditors. They will receive a percentage of what Elvira had owed them. Any of the creditors would have a cause of action against Sara, who undervalued the piano.

Elvira specified in her will that Sara would not receive any compensation for her services as personal representative, but nothing was mentioned about payment of creditors' claims, funeral expenses, and the like. Elvira had hospitalization and medical insurance that paid all the expenses of her last illness except for $300 to her doctor and $735 to the hospital. She also owed $90 to a local department store for clothing she had purchased. There was no provision in the will for payment of these obligations or for payment of funeral expenses ($1,800) or expenses of administration, such as filing fees ($75). Since the funeral and administration expenses have priority, Sara must pay these bills before the other debts (UPC § 3–805).

Since none of Elvira's three children are minors or dependent children, UPC § 2–402 (homestead allowance) and UPC § 2–404 (family allowance) are not applicable to her estate. The three children, however, are entitled to share the $10,000 exempt property allowance (UPC § 2–403). Together they are entitled to a sum not exceeding $10,000 in the form of household furniture, automobiles, furnishings, appliances, and personal effects, except for the portion of these chattels owned by creditors with security interests, e.g., an unpaid car dealer who sold the decedent a car on an installment payment plan.

EXAMPLE: Two months prior to her death, Elvira had bought a $900 stove from an appliance dealer. She agreed to make a down payment and pay $25 per month plus interest. The dealer was to retain title to the stove as a security interest until Elvira had finished paying for it. At the time of her death, she had paid $150 toward the purchase price. Under the terms of the contract, the dealer could repossess the stove if Elvira died before completing the payments. Therefore, the stove is not available as part of the exempt property. The children's rights to the exempt property have priority over all claims against the estate. Homestead and family allowances, however, are not applicable in this case because there is no surviving spouse or minor children. Elvira's estate has sufficient assets, after distributing the exempt property ($10,000) to Sara, Ralph, and Christa, to pay debts, expenses of a last illness, and expenses of administration. Therefore, Sara will distribute the assets of her mother's estate as follows.

Exempt property (to be shared by Sara, Ralph, and Christa)	$10,000
Funeral expenses	1,800
Administration expenses	75
Doctor	300
Hospital	735
Department store	90
Total prior obligations	$13,000
Value of all estate assets	16,500
Less prior obligations	13,000
	$ 3,500

After prior obligations are accounted for, $3,500 in estate assets remain. Sara will add that amount to the $10,000 exempt property to determine the shares of the three children.

$$\begin{array}{r} \$10,000 \\ +3,500 \\ \hline \$13,500 \div 3 = \$4,500 \end{array}$$

Each child is entitled to estate assets valued at $4,500. The children will receive less than Sara had determined prior to consideration of debts and expenses. Originally, each child would have received estate assets and/or cash valued at $5,500. After payment of debts and expenses, each child is entitled to receive estate assets and/or cash valued at $4,500.

Therefore, Sara may distribute the assets of Elvira's estate to Ralph, Christa, and herself as follows.

Asset distribution

Sara		Ralph		Christa	
Antique furniture	$2,000	Automobile	$1,400	Cash	$4,500
Cash	2,500	Tent trailer	600		
Total	$4,500	Cash	2,500	*Total*	$4,500
		Total	$4,500		

Sara must make the distribution expeditiously and may do so without order by the court (UPC § 3–704). Ralph, Christa, Sara (the distributees of the estate), and Elvira's creditors take the property subject to the proviso they return it to the personal representative should some unexpected event occur (UPC § 3–909). This section of the UPC protects the personal representative from unjustified litigation by distributees. The personal representative is liable, however, for improper distribution or payment of claims (UPC §§ 3–703, 3–712, and 3–808).

> **EXAMPLE:** If Sara had overlooked the hospital bill ($735) and therefore paid $245 more to each devisee, each devisee (including herself) would be responsible for returning his or her share of the money improperly paid plus one-third of the interest that would have accrued on $735 from the date of distribution to the present date. The reason for the payment of interest is the creditor does not have the use of the money until later, so interest is added.

Persons who purchase from the distributees are also protected (UPC § 3–910). Sara will execute instruments or deeds of distribution that transfer or release the antique furniture, automobile, and the tent trailer to Ralph and herself as evidence of their respective titles to these assets (UPC § 3–907).

Once she completes the distribution of estate assets, Sara's last duty is to close the estate (wind up its affairs) in one of two ways.

Closing the estate

- Formally, by petitioning the court to declare that the estate has been settled fully in regard to all persons interested in it. This method protects the estate against potential danger from details overlooked by the personal representative, e.g., the payment of inheritance taxes, because it avails the estate of the court's experience (UPC § 3–1001).
- Informally, by filing a sworn closing statement with the court in which Sara verifies she has completed every detail of the administration.

If Sara chooses to close her administration by filing a closing statement with the court, she need not file a formal accounting with the court. She must, however, furnish Ralph and Christa and other interested parties with a full account in writing, together with a copy of the verified closing statement filed with the court (UPC §§ 3–1001, 3–1002, and 3–1003).

Sara elects to close the estate by filing a sworn closing statement with the court pursuant to UPC § 3–1003. No earlier than six months after the date of her original appointment, she files a verified statement that asserts she has (1) published notice to creditors and the first publication occurred more than six months prior to the date of the present statement; (2) fully administered her mother's estate by making payment, settlement, or other disposition of all claims presented, paying expenses of administration and estate, inheritance, and other death taxes, except as specified in the statement, and distributing the assets of the estate to the persons entitled; and (3) sent a copy of the closing statement to all the distributees of the estate and to all creditors or other claimants of whom she is aware whose claims are neither paid nor barred and has furnished a full account in writing of her administration to the distributees (UPC § 3–1003).

Closing statement sent to
creditors and distributees

If no proceedings that involve Sara are pending in court one year after the closing statement is filed, her authority (appointment) terminates. An order closing an estate under UPC § 3–1001 or 3–1002 would terminate Sara's appointment. Her closing statement under UPC § 3–1003 would not terminate the appointment since the statement is an affirmation by Sara that she believes the affairs of the estate are completed. Any creditor not paid whose claim has not been barred by the time limit can assert the claim against the distributees, i.e., Sara, Ralph, and Christa (UPC § 3–1004).

EXAMPLE: When Sara was appointed, she published a notice to creditors in accordance with UPC § 3–801. Several creditors presented claims within the period allowed for presentation, and Sara paid all except the $90 clothing bill from a local store. The store may obtain payment, even though Sara has filed a closing statement, by demanding $90 from one of the three distributees. The distributee is then entitled to demand $30 from each of the other distributees so they will have contributed an equal amount. Sara can also be sued pursuant to UPC § 3–608 for actions she performed before the termination of her appointment. Under UPC § 3–610(a), her authority ends one year after she has filed the closing statement. Even after termination, Sara remains subject to a lawsuit unless the applicable statute of limitations has run or her administration has been terminated by an adjudication that settles her accounts (UPC § 3–1005).

EXAMPLE: Before giving the automobile to Ralph, as Elvira had directed in her will, Sara used it for her personal convenience. She was involved in a collision resulting in $1,000 damage to the automobile. Since this occurred while Sara was the personal representative of the estate, Ralph may sue her for having failed to exercise due care with respect to one of the estate's assets during or within six months after the termination of her administration.

Suits against Sara by successors of the will and creditors for breach of her fiduciary duty are barred unless begun within six months after Sara filed the closing statement. Rights of successors and creditors to recover for fraud, misrepresentation, or inadequate disclosure are not barred by the six-month limitation (UPC §§ 3–1005, 3–807, and 3–808).

Termination of
administration

Using a closing statement offers Sara more protection than if she had relied merely on the receipts collected to show the estate has been fully distributed.

Sections 3–1001, 3–1002, and 3–1003 of the UPC provide for judicial proceedings for closing by which Sara could gain protection from all interested persons or from Ralph and Christa, the other devisees (successors), only. Section 3–703 of the UPC provides very limited protection for a personal representative who relies only on receipts. These sections afford protection to the personal representative for acts or distributions that were authorized when performed but became doubtful due to a later change in testacy status. There is no protection against later claims of breach of fiduciary obligation except for those arising from consent or waiver of individual distributees who may have bound themselves by receipts given to the personal representative.

In addition, the closing statement method provides notice to third persons that Sara's authority has terminated, whereas reliance on receipts alone does not. The closing statement method provides a useful means of closing small, uncomplicated estates where the distributees are all members of the family and disputes are unlikely.

ASSIGNMENT 10.2

1. Make a list of and obtain all the forms Sara would use to administer her mother's estate according to the Uniform Probate Code. Fill in the forms after reviewing Case Problem 2 below.

2. Suppose six months before Sara filed the closing statement, Christa found a will that devised all Elvira's property to Christa. The will was executed by Elvira at a date later than the probated will. What should Christa do?

3. If Christa had been a minor at the time of her mother's death, would distribution of the assets of Elvira's estate be different? If so, how? Suppose Elvira in her will had appointed neither a personal guardian nor a property guardian for Christa. How would the guardianship be determined?

4. Ralph claims he, not Sara, should be appointed personal representative since he is the oldest of the children and thus has a higher priority. Should he petition the court to remove Sara and appoint himself on these grounds?

5. In her inventory, Sara omits a living room chair valued at $50. If she discovers the error but neglects to file an amended inventory, what is the consequence?

6. Before her death, Elvira began negotiations for the sale of her automobile to Moira Byrne, but they had not agreed on a purchase price. Sara completes the sale at a price of $1,350. She intends to give the money, instead of the automobile, to Ralph. Has Sara breached her fiduciary duty?

7. Sara discovers a policy of insurance on Elvira's life that Elvira had taken out 25 years ago and was not mentioned in the will. The beneficiary of the policy is Elvira's estate. Should Sara record the value of this policy in her inventory of estate assets? May she use the proceeds to pay Elvira's creditors?

8. Elvira had opened a charge account at a local department store. Prior to her death she had charged but had not yet paid for $50 worth of merchandise. The credit manager of the store wants to be sure Sara will not overlook or disallow the claim. Could he demand Sara be bonded to ensure against loss to the store?

9. The registrar declines to issue an order of informal probate because the registrar doubts Elvira's signature on the will is genuine. One of the witnesses to the will is deceased, and the other cannot be located. How could Sara have the will admitted to probate? Could she still follow informal procedures as planned?

Key Term

closing statement

Review Questions

1. According to your state statute, who has top priority to be appointed the personal representative of a testator's estate? Of an intestate's estate?

2. What function does a registrar or surrogate perform in an informal or common probate administration?

3. How do informal probate procedures differ in testate versus intestate cases?

4. Under what circumstances can a registrar reject an application for informal probate proceedings? If the registrar denies an application, what results?

5. Since informal probate procedures are not supervised by the court and do not require that notice be given, what rights and procedural steps are available to creditors?

6. Explain what is meant by the Uniform Probate Code's *in and out* feature available for those using informal probate proceedings.

7. Must an inventory be prepared in informal probate? If required, to whom must the inventory be given?

8. Using informal probate, how is an estate administration closed?

9. In informal probate, what time limits are placed on creditors for claims against the decedent's estate and the personal representative for breach of fiduciary duty?

10. In informal probate, when does the personal representative's authority officially terminate?

Case Problems

Problem 1

Carl Bergmeister dies intestate on September 19, 2014, leaving outstanding assets valued at $322,800.

Homestead	$ 88,000
Furniture and household items	16,000
Shares of stock in Alcoa Aluminum	62,000
One-half interest in an apartment building held in tenancy in common (building valued at $250,000)	125,000
Two Miro paintings	28,000
2000 automobile	3,800
Total	$322,800

Several relatives survive Carl: Jenneille Bergmeister, wife; Naomi Bergmeister, daughter; Scott Bergmeister, son, who is a minor; David Bergmeister, son from a previous marriage; Carolyn Bergmeister, mother; Gustaf Bergmeister, father; Nora Stark, sister; Robin Stark, niece (daughter of Nora); Jarod Harrison, brother-in-law (wife's brother); and Verlayne Sather, first cousin.

Naomi Bergmeister, Carl's daughter, makes an application for informal appointment of herself in intestacy pursuant to UPC § 3–301.

A. Who has priority for such an appointment?

B. If someone else who has priority over Naomi is an invalid and does not feel capable of assuming the duties of administering Carl's estate, could the person decline the appointment? How can the priority be waived?

C. What steps must Naomi take to ensure her informal appointment? What forms would she use?

Assume that Naomi is appointed personal representative.

D. Describe the steps she will take to administer, distribute, and close her father's estate. Use the informal methods you think most appropriate.

E. Make a list of and fill in all forms Naomi will use. Assume prior to his death on September 19, 2014, Carl earned $30,000 from his employment, $8,000 from dividends on his stock, and accrued but unpaid dividends amounted to $1,000. Assume, also, a $10,000 mortgage exists on the homestead; funeral expenses were $3,500; expenses for Carl's last illness were $270 to his doctor and $420 to the hospital; and Carl owed $4,200 to a contractor for repairs on the homestead.

F. It must also be determined whether federal or state estate and/or inheritance taxes must be paid. Read Chapter 11 and obtain and complete the necessary tax forms for the Bergmeister estate, including the decedent's final income tax return and the fiduciary income tax return for income earned by the estate.

With regard to the administration of the real property owned by Carl at his death, Naomi should consider UPC § 3–715, especially subparagraphs 3, 6, 7, 8, 9, 10, 11, 15, 18, and 23, which discuss the transactions authorized for a personal representative that relate to land transactions. She must also consult the probate court of the county where Carl's land is located (if different from the county of his domicile) to see if there are local laws pertaining to real estate transactions (e.g., the personal representative must obtain the court's permission to sell, mortgage, or lease real estate, and wait a certain number of days before finalizing such transactions).

How will Naomi convey real property to heirs entitled to it—by deed or otherwise?

Assume that David Bergmeister, Carl's son by a previous marriage, files a petition with the probate court for formal appointment of a personal representative because he is dissatisfied with Naomi's appointment. What is the result? Could Naomi still exercise her powers while the formal proceeding is pending (see UPC § 3–401)?

What documents, if any, should Naomi file in order to convey a clear marketable title to the successors?

Problem 2

Cheryl Ann Kennedy died testate on August 1, 2015, at 1010 Willow Street in Ramsey County, St. Paul, Minnesota 55409. She was born January 13, 1971, in Minneapolis, Minnesota.

Cheryl's successors include her husband, Charles; one daughter Cindy; two sons, Carl and Corey; her mother, Catherine Kelly; and one sister, Karen Kelly. The ages of the family members are Charles, 44; Cindy, 3; Carl, 5; Corey, 9; Catherine Kelly, 64; and Karen Kelly, 38. All members of the family live at 1010 Willow Street.

Cheryl's estate included the following assets.

- A home, the family residence, owned by Cheryl before her marriage and still recorded in her name only, valued at $195,000

- A summer cottage in joint tenancy with Charles, given to Cheryl and Charles by Cheryl's father, valued at $50,000

- A savings and a checking account in joint tenancy with Charles with a total value of $10,000

- A checking account at Allied First Bank of Minneapolis in her name only with a total value of $2,000.

- One thousand shares of Execo stock in joint tenancy with Charles worth $12,000

- One hundred shares of Users, Inc., stock left to Cheryl by her father, worth $4,000 in her name only

- A car (2004 Ford) worth $5,500 in her name

- A life insurance burial policy payable to Charles with a face value of $5,000

- A diamond ring worth $1,500

- Clothing worth $3,000

- A mink coat worth $4,000

- Household goods worth $15,000

- Other personal property worth $300

The only debt Cheryl owed was $110 for two wigs from Beauty Products, Inc.

Except for the diamond ring, which was left to her sister, Karen, Cheryl's will stated that all of her estate should go to her husband, Charles, if he survived her, and if not, to her children in equal shares. The will names Charles personal representative (executor) and was executed on November 21, 2010. Charles hires an attorney, Susan Brown, 1400 Main Street, Minneapolis, Minnesota 55455, to help with the estate administration.

For the informal, unsupervised probate administration of Cheryl's will, the following forms may be executed. Review sample forms selected for execution in Appendix A.

1. Application for Informal Probate of Will and for Informal Appointment of Personal Representative (Form 13*)

2. Testimony of Witness to Will (not executed)

3. Statement of Informal Probate of Will and Order of Informal Appointment of Personal Representative (Form 14*)

4. Notice of Informal Probate of Will and Appointment of Personal Representative and Notice to Creditors (Form 15*)

5. Proof of Placing Order for Publication (Form 16*)

6. Affidavit of Publication, often provided to registrar by publisher (not executed; see Form 4*)

7. Affidavit of Mailing Notice of Informal Probate of Will (not executed; see Form 5*)

8. Notice to Spouse and Children and Affidavit of Mailing (not executed; see Form 5*)

9. Acceptance of Appointment as Personal Representative and Oath by Individual (not executed)

10. Bond, if required (not executed)

11. Letters Testamentary (not executed; see Form 7*)

12. Inventory and Appraisement (Form 17*)

13. Written Statement of Claim (not executed)

14. Final Account (not executed; see Form 9*)

* See Appendix A.

15. Receipt for Assets by Distributee (not executed)

16. Unsupervised Personal Representative's Statement to Close Estate (not executed)

   A. After reviewing the forms that may be executed in the Cheryl Ann Kennedy case, create a new set of facts necessary to fill in the required forms for informal, unsupervised probate administration of a testator's estate in your state. Use and follow the probate procedures in your state to execute (complete) the necessary forms.

Problem 3

All the facts in the Cheryl Kennedy case, including the assets and liabilities listed, are the same, except in this instance Cheryl died intestate. The forms that may be executed for the informal probate administration of Cheryl's estate in Minnesota are the following:

1. Application for Informal Appointment of Personal Representative (Intestate) (not executed)

2. Notice of Informal Appointment of Personal Representative and Notice to Creditors (Intestate) (Form 18*)

3. Proof of Placing Order for Publication (Form 19*)

4. Affidavit of Publication, often provided to registrar by publisher (not executed; see Form 4*)

5. Affidavit of Mailing Notice of Informal Appointment (not executed; see Form 5*)

6. Notice to Spouse and Children and Affidavit of Mailing (not executed; see Form 5*)

7. Acceptance of Appointment as Personal Representative and Oath by Individual (not executed)

8. Bond, if required (not executed)

9. Letters of General Administration (Form 20*)

10. Inventory and Appraisement (Form 17*)

11. Written Statement of Claim (not executed)

12. Final Account (not executed; see Form 9*)

13. Deed of Distribution by Personal Representative (not executed)

14. Receipt for Assets by Distributee (not executed)

15. Unsupervised Personal Representative's Statement to Close Estate (not executed)

16. Application for Certificate from Registrar—Application for Release of Bond (not executed)

17. Certificate of Registrar—Release of Bond (not executed)

   A. Review the forms that may be executed in Case Problem 3, the Cheryl Ann Kennedy intestate case. Identify and complete the forms required for the informal probate administration of her estate if Cheryl had died intestate in your state. Compare your executed forms with those in Appendix A.

Practical Assignments

1. Most states require a paid copy of the decedent's funeral bill to be presented to the court. Prepare a letter to a local funeral home of your choosing requesting a copy of the paid funeral bill for your client, Elvira Krueger, who died on February 4, 2015.

2. Using the assets contained in Elvira Krueger's estate discussed in this chapter under the original facts of the Case Study, prepare an excel spreadsheet that lists the beneficiaries of the estate, the property each will receive, the value of each piece of property and the total value each beneficiary will receive. For this assignment, assume there are no expenses of the estate and that all appraisals of property are accurate.

3. Under the facts of the Elvira Krueger Case Study, two of the beneficiaries challenged the fair market value of $1,500 for the grand piano as determined by the personal representative. Assume that you are representing the contesting beneficiaries, locate two appraisers in your local area who would be competent to appraise a grand piano.

_____

* See Appendix A.

TAX CONSIDERATIONS IN THE ADMINISTRATION OF ESTATES

11

Outline

Objectives

After completing this chapter, you should be able to:

- Distinguish and identify the income, gift, and death taxes that must be paid.

- Understand and explain various ways to transfer assets while alive in order to lessen the amount of taxes owed to the state and federal governments by a decedent's estate.

- Understand the current tax consequences for gifts and estates created by changes in the tax laws.

- Prepare the tax returns of a decedent's estate.

SCOPE OF THE CHAPTER

There are numerous tax considerations that may impact the administration of an estate. There may be federal and state income taxes that must be paid and filed for the decedent. In some cases, the estate must also pay federal and state estate or inheritance taxes. Additionally, the estate may be responsible for gift taxes that relate back to previous tax years. The management of these tax issues is often complex. Although the personal representative and the attorney have the ultimate responsibility for probating an estate properly and promptly, as the paralegal assisting the attorney, you must also be knowledgeable about legal and procedural matters applicable to estate administration, including the tax consequences to the estate of the decedent. If you intend to specialize in estate administration, you will need to acquire an extensive knowledge of tax laws and procedures. Federal and state statutes must be checked to see if they have been repealed or amended, or if new statutes have been enacted. A good source for updated federal tax laws is the CCH tax service as well as the Internal Revenue Service (IRS) *(http://www.irs.gov)* and state publications. *You will need to consult with other professionals, i.e., the attorney and an accountant, who are familiar with current tax laws and the preparation of tax returns.*

⚖️ *Ethical Issue*

This chapter provides a foundation for understanding tax considerations in the administration of estates. For purposes of illustration, it incorporates the basic materials used in the preparation of federal tax returns and some state death tax returns. State tax forms vary substantially. You must familiarize yourself with your state's forms and tax law.

The first part of this chapter provides an introduction to tax concerns and a discussion of such tax considerations as the applicable credit amount (unified credit) and applicable exclusion amount; the unified transfer gift and estate tax rates; the marital deduction; trusts; lifetime gifts; and generation-skipping transfers. Next, the tax returns themselves are discussed, including the decedent's final federal and state income tax returns; the fiduciary's federal and state income tax returns; the federal and state gift tax returns; the federal and state estate tax returns; and the state inheritance tax return.

INTRODUCTION TO TAX CONCERNS

Income Tax

The federal government and all but seven state governments (Alaska, Florida, Nevada, South Dakota, Texas, Washington, and Wyoming) levy and collect taxes on income. The income subject to such tax includes personal income, corporate income, and trust income, which is a form of personal income. In two states, New Hampshire and Tennessee, an income tax is levied on interest and dividend income only. It is the duty of the personal representative of the decedent's estate to file the decedent's personal income tax returns for the decedent's year of death and to see that any income tax owed to the federal and state governments is paid out of estate assets. In addition, the personal representative must file federal and state income tax returns for any income that accrues or is earned after the decedent's death until the close of the taxable year or until the date of final distribution of the estate. These tax returns are called United States or state fiduciary income tax returns.

Death Tax

Death taxes are measured by the amount of property transferred at death. There are two kinds of death taxes: federal and state *estate taxes* and state *inheritance taxes*.

The estate tax is a tax levied on the transfer of property at death. This tax is levied on the estate itself, not on the **successors**. The rate and amount of the estate tax are determined by the size of the estate; like the income tax, the estate tax is progressive, i.e., the larger the estate, the higher the tax rate. At the present time, the *federal gift and estate tax rate* ranges from 18 percent to 40 percent. The tax rate is applied only to that taxable amount that exceeds the unified credit exemption. For example, in 2015, the unified credit exemption is $5,430,000, so only the value of the estate that exceeds that amount would be taxable.

successor
An all-inclusive UPC term meaning any person, other than a creditor, who is entitled to real or personal property of a decedent either under the will or through intestate succession.

A state inheritance or succession tax is levied on the transfer of property from a decedent at death. The rate or amount of this tax is determined by state law and depends on the amount of the share of the decedent's estate received by a particular successor and on the relationship of the successor to the decedent. Several states impose an inheritance tax on successors. Individual state statutes must be checked. A number of states have repealed or revised their estate and inheritance taxes in recent years.

Gift Tax

A gift tax is a tax levied on the transfer of property during life. This is a tax on the donor, not on the donee. The federal gift tax rate generally follows the same schedule used for the federal estate tax. As of 2015, Connecticut stands as the only state with a gift tax.

The federal government imposes an estate tax and gift tax but no inheritance tax. States may have an estate tax, an inheritance tax, a gift tax, or some combination of the three. The federal and state estate, gift, and inheritance tax statutes require the personal representative to file the appropriate tax returns by a prescribed time, unless an Application for Extension of Time to File has been filed with the appropriate agencies. These statutes also require the personal representative to pay the tax due within the prescribed time. Generally, extensions of time to file do not extend the time to pay taxes, which are due by the regular due date. Extensions may be allowed in certain cases where reasonable cause can be shown. *A personal representative who fails to make timely payment is personally liable for any interest charged or penalties resulting from this neglect. The attorney should apprise the personal representative of this responsibility.*

⚖ *Ethical Issue*

The personal representative is responsible for paying all taxes out of the estate assets. These include income, fiduciary, gift, estate, and inheritance taxes, unless the will specifies that the devisees pay the inheritance tax out of their legacies or devises. If prior to distribution of the estate the personal representative proves that the estate does not have enough cash (or assets to be sold) to pay the taxes and this shortfall is not due to any fault on his part, the personal representative is free from individual liability to pay the taxes. If, however, he distributes the estate and does not have enough assets left to pay the taxes, the personal representative must pay the taxes out of his own pocket (IRC § 2002). Therefore, it is imperative that the personal representative makes sure sufficient assets remain for the payment of all taxes and debts before distributing any of the estate assets. Certain preferred claims have priority for payment before taxes are paid, e.g., administrative expenses, funeral expenses, and expenses of the last illness (see Chapter 9 for an example of Pennsylvania's priority of debts statute and compare UPC § 3-805 in Exhibit 9.13)

GENERAL TAX CONSIDERATIONS

Congress continually considers and revises the tax laws of the United States. State legislatures do the same with their individual state tax structures. These revisions typically result from economic and political considerations. Regardless of the motives for such changes, they often have a tremendous impact on estate planning and administration as well as on income tax considerations for grantors, testators, and beneficiaries. Many of the provisions are complex and require numerous qualifying regulations and rulings. Attorneys, paralegals, and others who specialize in estate planning and administration must be well versed on these comprehensive changes and their effects. Under these laws, death tax payments are assessed only against the wealthy and the moderately wealthy. Smaller estates have benefited from the changes; the vast majority of estates that were previously required to file federal estate tax returns and pay estate taxes are now required to do neither. For example, a 2015 estate valued at less than $5,430,000 would owe no taxes. When the exclusion was much lower, it created a problem for estates that owned valuable real estate. Large family farms were actually required to sell all or a portion of the real estate in order to pay the estate taxes when the farm passed to the children of the deceased.

Before turning to the various tax returns that usually must be completed as part of the administration of a decedent's estate, certain general tax considerations need to be mentioned. One should remember that after the decedent's death, the estate is a new legal being; the legal existence of the decedent has terminated. The estate has rights and obligations, and it is a taxpayer.

Everybody wants to reduce the death taxes owed to the government or to avoid them entirely whenever legally possible. There are numerous ways to accomplish tax savings on a decedent's estate. The most frequently used methods include (1) making use of the applicable credit amount (unified credit) and applicable exclusion amount and the Unified Rate Schedule for federal gift and estate taxes; (2) making use of the marital deduction; (3) creating trusts; and (4) making gifts during the decedent's lifetime.

Applicable Credit Amount (Unified Credit) and Unified Transfer Gift and Estate Tax Rates

The 1976 Tax Reform Act (TRA) not only created a unified transfer tax credit for gifts and estates, but also unified federal gift and estate tax rates into a single schedule. The unified rate is applied to all transfers of assets subject to tax, whether the transfers occur during life by *inter vivos* gift or after death by will or intestate succession.

Applicable Credit Amount (Unified Credit)

The 1997 Taxpayer Relief Act (TRA), which took effect on January 1, 1998, replaced the **unified credit** with an **applicable credit amount**, which is subtracted from the tentative tax due.

Unified Transfer Gift and Estate Tax Rates

In the 1976 TRA, the tax rates for estate and gift taxes were unified into a single schedule. The rates are progressive and based on cumulative lifetime and death-time transfers.

With the Economic Growth and Tax Relief Reconciliation Act (EGTRRA) of 2001, the top applicable tax rate was 45 percent for 2009 and the estate **applicable exclusion amount** was $3,500,000. Under the 2010 Tax Relief Act, the top applicable rate was 35 percent and the exclusion amount $5,000,000 for the years 2010–2012. The gift tax applicable exclusion amount remained $1,000,000 for 2010 and increased to $5,000,000 for 2011 and 2012 with a top tax rate of 35 percent. *Caveat:* Under legislation covering years 2010–2012, the generation-skipping transfer taxes had applicable exclusion and lifetime exemption amounts of $5,000,000 and a top rate of 35 percent. As discussed previously, the exclusion currently increases annually and the rates are adjusted by the U.S. Congress.

The Tax Relief Act of 2010 created a new concept—portability—that applies to surviving spouses. **Portability** allows the unused portion of a predeceased spouse's estate or gift tax exclusion amount to be combined with the surviving spouse's applicable exclusion amount at their death. Thus, if at the death of Frank Jensen's wife, Clarissa, on April 16, 2014, her estate uses only $2,000,000 of her applicable $5,340,000 estate tax exclusion for 2014, Frank's estate, if he were to die in 2015 and had not remarried prior to his death, could "carry over" the $3,340,000 estate tax exclusion balance from Clarissa's estate to his own applicable exclusion of $5,340,000 for a combined exclusion total of $8,770,000. This "carryover" right held by a surviving spouse for estate or gift tax exemptions may be used only if the predeceased spouse's estate elected in a timely filed estate tax return to permit the surviving spouse to apply the unused exemption to their own estate or gift tax return.

Under the law, gift taxes are computed by applying the Unified Rate Schedule to cumulative lifetime taxable transfers and subtracting the taxes paid for prior taxable periods. Federal estate taxes are computed by applying the Unified Rate Schedule to cumulative lifetime and deathtime taxable transfers and then subtracting the gift taxes payable. In some circumstances, adjustments must be made for taxes on lifetime transfers in the decedent's estate (see the discussion under Lifetime Gifts below). The amount of the applicable credit amount (unified credit) allowed cannot be greater than the amount of the computed transfer tax.

The Role of Credits in the Calculation of Federal Estate Tax

The amount of the federal estate tax is computed by applying the unified rates to the decedent's cumulative taxable lifetime transfers and taxable transfers made at death and then subtracting any applicable credits. Credits may include taxes already paid on any lifetime transfers such as gifts, credit for state death taxes, credit for

applicable credit amount (unified credit)
A credit against the federal unified transfer tax on gifts (prior to death) and estates (after death).

applicable exclusion amount
The maximum value of property that can be transferred to others without incurring any federal gift or estate tax because of the application of the applicable credit amount (unified credit).

portability
Surviving spouse's right to carry over the unused portion of a predeceased spouse's estate or gift tax exemption and combine it with his or her own exemptions at death.

foreign death taxes, and estate taxes paid by the estates of other decedents for assets included in the current decedent's estate. Exhibit 11.1 provides an outline of the process involved in computing federal estate taxes.

The Marital Deduction

The marital deduction can be a substantial tax-saving device for an estate (see the discussion under Determining the Taxable Estate below). The 1981 Economic Recovery Tax Act (ERTA) provided for an unlimited federal estate tax marital deduction for transfers between spouses, which continue today. A testator's estate is entitled to the marital deduction if there is a surviving spouse and if the decedent leaves all or a portion of his or her estate to the surviving spouse. If the decedent spouse dies intestate, the surviving spouse is entitled to a statutory share of the decedent's estate. The amount of the surviving spouse's statutory share is the amount of the marital deduction in such cases.

The 1981 ERTA also added language to IRC § 2056, pertaining to the estate tax marital deduction, and to IRC § 2523, pertaining to the gift tax marital deduction (see Gifts and the Marital Deduction below). The 1981 law contains a "terminable interest rule," which allows certain property to qualify for the estate and gift tax marital deduction that previously did not qualify. The eligible property is called "qualified terminable interest property" (QTIP), i.e., property that passes from the decedent spouse in which the surviving spouse has a qualified income interest for life. Examples of QTIP property that qualify for marital deduction treatment are (1) trusts with a life interest to the surviving spouse, the remainder to the children, and (2) a legal life estate to the surviving spouse and the remainder to others, e.g., their children.

As Chapter 14 observes, the qualifying of QTIP property for the marital deduction can be an important estate-planning tool that also permits the testator to direct the disposition of the trust principal at the death of the surviving spouse (e.g., providing for children of a previous marriage and the like).

In order for property to qualify as QTIP property for marital deduction treatment, the following are necessary.

- The surviving spouse life tenant must have a "qualifying income interest for life" in the property. The surviving spouse has a qualified income interest for life if (1) the surviving spouse is entitled to all the income for life from the property, payable at least annually or at more frequent intervals, and (2) no person during the surviving spouse's lifetime has the power to appoint any part of the property to any person other than the surviving spouse.
- The personal representative or executor of the decedent spouse's estate must *elect* to treat the property as QTIP property on the decedent's federal estate tax return (IRS Form 706). If the executor makes the election, the property will qualify for the marital deduction. In the case of a lifetime transfer, however, the donor-spouse makes the QTIP election (see definition in the Glossary).

Gifts and the Marital Deduction

The marital deduction can also be used when there is a transfer by gift of any property between spouses. The annual gift tax exclusion for 2015 is $14,000 per donee per year (indexed annually for inflation), and the marital deduction on gift taxes for lifetime transfers (gifts) of any property between spouses is unlimited. Therefore, whether Miguel gives his spouse, Camila, $14,000, $100,000, or $1,000,000,

EXHIBIT 11.1 Method for Computing Federal Estate Tax

Gross estate (all property owned at decedent's death) $_____

Less:
Qualified conservation easement exclusion _____

Equals:
Total gross estate less exclusion _____

Less:
Funeral and administration expenses _____
Debts, including taxes accrued prior to death _____
Mortgages and liens _____
Losses during administration _____
Total equals: _____

Adjusted gross estate _____

Less:
Marital deduction _____
Charitable deduction _____
State death tax deduction _____
Total equals: _____

Taxable Estate (gross estate less deductions) _____

Plus:
Adjusted taxable gifts (post-1976 lifetime taxable
transfers not included in gross estate) _____

Equals:
Tentative tax base (taxable amount) _____

Compute:
Tentative tax

Less:
Gift taxes payable on post-1976 taxable gifts _____

Equals:
Gross estate tax before credits _____

Less:
Unified credit (applicable credit amount) _____
Credit for foreign death taxes _____
Credit for estate taxes on prior transfers _____
Total tax credits _____

Equals:
Federal estate tax due _____

Plus:
Generation-skipping transfer taxes _____

Equals:
Total transfer taxes due $_____

_____

Note: When a decedent leaves everything to his or her surviving spouse, there would be no estate tax because of the unlimited marital deduction.

none of the property or cash is subject to gift tax. There is no upper limit on how much Miguel can give his spouse. Regardless of the amount of the gift transferred between spouses that is offset by the unlimited marital deduction, such gifts do not require the filing of the IRS gift tax return Form 709. Computation of the federal gift tax is outlined in Exhibit 11.2.

EXHIBIT 11.2   Method for Computing Federal Gift Tax

Total gifts made during current calendar year (IRC §§ 2511–2519)	$_____
Less:	
Political organization exclusion (IRC § 2501[a][4]) _____	
Educational exclusion (IRC § 2503[e]) _____	
Medical exclusion (IRC § 2503[e]) _____	
Annual exclusion (IRC § 2503[b]) _____	
($14,000 per donee indexed for inflation)	
Unlimited marital deduction (IRC § 2523) _____	
Charitable deduction (IRC § 2522) _____	
Total exclusions and deductions _____	_____
Equals:	
Taxable gifts for calendar year (IRC § 2503[a])	_____
Plus:	
Taxable gifts for prior years (IRC § 2504)	_____
Equals:	
Total taxable gifts (current and prior years)	_____
Compute:	
Tentative tax	_____
Less:	
Tentative tax on prior taxable gifts	_____
Equals:	
Gift tax before unified credit	_____
Less:	
Allowable unified credit (IRC § 2505)	_____
Equals:	
Federal gift tax due (for current period)	_____
Plus:	
Generation-skipping transfer taxes (for current period)	_____
Equals:	
Total transfer taxes due	$_____

Creation of Trusts

Another method used to diminish death taxes is the creation of trusts (see Chapters 12 and 13). It is possible to leave property in a testamentary trust for beneficiaries named by the testator-settlor so that additional estate taxes are not due at the death of the beneficiary. If properly planned and executed, one such trust, combined with the marital deduction, can result in substantial savings to the estate of a decedent over the course of two generations (see the discussion under Determining the Taxable Estate). An example of such a trust is included in Appendix B. Taxes can also be diminished using *inter vivos* or lifetime trusts.

Lifetime Gifts

A person who makes a gift is called a *donor,* and a person who receives a gift is called a *donee.* A federal gift tax is levied on the transfer of property from a donor to a donee for less than full or adequate consideration. The donor is responsible for the payment of the tax. Gifts made during the lifetime *(inter vivos)* of the decedent can, in some cases, result in tax advantages. Tax laws have unified the gift and estate tax rates into a single rate schedule with progressive rates that are computed on the basis of cumulative transfers made both during lifetime and at death. All taxable gifts made after December 31, 1976 (called adjusted taxable gifts), are added to the decedent's taxable estate and are subject to the federal estate tax. A credit against the estate tax for gift taxes previously payable is then deducted.

However, some incentives for *inter vivos* gift giving remain under the laws. The annual exclusion has increased to $14,000 per donee to allow larger gifts to be exempt from the federal gift tax. The increase reflects the economy's inflationary trend and encourages compliance with the tax law by taxpayers. Congress will likely increase the exclusion amount in future years to accommodate inflation. Any appreciation in value of a lifetime gift that may accrue between the date the gift is made and the date of the donor's death is not subject to a transfer tax. *Note:* When the donee sells the property, any appreciation will be subject to income tax. Income taxes may be reduced when the gift property produces income and the property is transferred during life to a donee who is in a lower income tax bracket than the donor. Finally, lifetime gifts can reduce the value of the decedent's estate and thereby also reduce the federal estate tax.

The laws governing gifts and taxes on such gifts provide as follows.

- A gift must be intended and delivered by the donor.
- Any person can give a gift of up to $14,000 per year (indexed annually for inflation) tax-free to each donee, and, if the donor's spouse joins in the gift, the exclusions of both spouses may be used, resulting in an exclusion of $28,000 or more when adjusted for inflation. This is called *gift splitting.* These joint gifts are tax-free to both the donor and the donee.
- Some gifts made within three years of the donor's death are automatically included in the donor-decedent's gross estate and are subject to federal estate tax (IRC § 2035).
- The federal unified gift and estate tax rate is a progressive and cumulative tax.
- When the gift is to the donor's spouse, there is an unlimited gift tax marital deduction (IRC § 2523).
- When a gift is made to a charitable organization, some limits are placed on the amount of the charitable deduction from the gift tax, depending on the type of gift and the charity to which it is given (IRC § 2522).
- Transfers to a political organization (IRC § 2501 [a] [4]) or amounts paid on behalf of a donee to an educational organization as tuition or a care provider for medical care (IRC § 2503[e]) are not subject to the gift tax.

Before becoming too enthusiastic about transferring property by gift, it is well to remember that, once transferred, the property can no longer be controlled by the donor. The property passes to the new owner, the donee, and that person alone has title to it. Also, one must guard against giving gifts with strings attached. In most cases, when the donor retains control over the gift, income from the gift property will be taxed to the donor, and the property will be included in the donor's gross estate for federal estate tax purposes on the donor's death (IRC §§ 2036–2038).

Gift making, gift splitting between spouses, and the applicable credit amount (unified credit) are all means of reducing tax liability. However, remember, the applicable credit amount is allowed against lifetime gift taxes or estate taxes, or both. Unlike the $14,000 per donee annual exclusion (indexed for inflation) that is available to the donor each year, once the applicable credit amount is used, it is terminated. It can be used to diminish or eliminate the tax on lifetime gifts or to diminish or eliminate the estate tax.

The Gift-Splitting Provision

Gift splitting by spouses has been retained under the current law. When married, the donor, with the other spouse's consent, may split the lifetime gift to the donee. The gift will then be treated as though half were given by the donor and the other half by the spouse, even though the entire gift comes from only one spouse's assets. Thus, the spouses may give $28,000 or more annually, when adjusted for inflation, to each donee tax-free if each spouse consents to having the gift treated as each spouse having given half. As a result, a married donor can put more property into a trust while paying less gift tax than a single person would pay (IRC § 2513).

> **EXAMPLE:** Using the $14,000 annual exclusion, a gift may be given free of gift tax as in the following examples.
>
> | If You Are | Married | Single |
> | --- | --- | --- |
> | and giving to one person | two $14,000 annual exclusions = $28,000 | one $14,000 annual exclusion = $14,000 |
> | and giving to two persons | four $14,000 annual exclusions = $56,000 | two $14,000 annual exclusions = $28,000 |
> | and giving to three persons | six $14,000 annual exclusions = $84,000 | three $14,000 annual exclusions = $42,000 |

ASSIGNMENT 11.1

Michele and Bruce, husband and wife, decided to give $1,100,000 to their niece, Trudy, in December 2015. Assuming the couple has not used either of their $14,000 exclusions for Trudy for 2015, determine what portion of their joint gift to Trudy would be subject to the federal gift tax.

Do the same computations, except the amount of the gift is $2,100,000.

Uniform Transfers to Minors Act

Today, all states, except South Carolina and Vermont, have adopted the Uniform Transfers to Minors Act (UTMA), which revised and replaced the Uniform Gifts to Minors Act (IRC § 2503 [c]). The UTMA allows *any kind* of real or personal property, wherever located, to be transferred to a custodianship as a gift to a minor. Money and securities are common gifts to minors; others include annuities, life insurance policies, and real estate. In addition to lifetime gifts, transfers from trusts and wills can be added to the custodianship. A person or generation-skipping transfer financial institution, called the custodian, is selected by the donor of the gift to manage and invest the property for the support, education, and welfare of the minor who, as the donee, has legal title to the property (assets). The custodian can be a parent or other family member, a guardian, a bank, or a trust company. However, a parent-donor should not be named custodian because, if the parent-donor dies before the minor-donee receives the final distribution of the assets (gifts) at age 18, 21, or 25 (depending on the state), the assets will be taxed as part of the parent-donor's estate.

A custodianship is a less expensive alternative to the appointment of a guardian in a will because a will must be probated and the probate court has strict rules on how funds can be invested. Court approval or supervision of a custodian's investment decisions is not required.

Although a will or living trust can be used to establish a custodianship, a faster and easier method is to use a written instrument that transfers the property to the name of the custodian followed by the words "as custodian for the donee, [name of the minor], under the State of [name of state] Uniform Transfers to Minors Act" for the appropriate state, which can be the residence of the custodian, donor, minor, or the location of the property. This procedure incorporates by reference all provisions of the state's act and requires that each gift must be made to just one minor with only one person acting as the custodian. For their services, custodians may be paid "reasonable compensation" from the transferred property.

Any gift transferred under the act is irrevocable. It belongs to the minor, and both the property and its income must be used solely for the benefit of the minor. Accurate records must be kept for all investments, and annual tax returns must be filed by the custodian for the minor since income earned on the property is taxable to the minor. When the minor reaches age 18, 21, or 25 (depending on the state), the custodianship terminates, and the custodian must transfer all assets and any undisposed income to the minor. If the minor dies before age 18, 21, or 25, the property passes to the minor's estate or to whomever the minor may appoint under a general power of appointment. Generally, an UTMA custodianship terminates upon the child reaching the age of majority according to the law of the state of residency. Many states, however, have enacted legislation that calls for the termination at the age of 21 rather than 18. A few states allow the donor parent to extend the termination to age 25. It is imperative to determine the age of termination for the individual state.

For the donor, the creation of a custodianship under the UTMA is a gift of a present interest, and as such it qualifies for the $14,000 annual gift tax exclusion, which is indexed annually for inflation.

Generation-Skipping Transfers and Their Tax Consequences

The stated purpose of the federal estate and gift taxes is not only to raise revenue but also to tax death transfers consistently generation by generation. Congress realized that a tax loophole existed by which family members could create a **generation-skipping transfer** using a **generation-skipping transfer trust** to partially avoid federal gift and estate taxes on large transfers of money or other valuable assets between generations of family members. Therefore, Congress closed the tax loophole by creating the **generation-skipping transfer tax** so that every

generation-skipping transfer
A transfer of assets to a person two or more generations below the transferor, e.g., from a grandparent to a grandchild.

generation-skipping transfer trust
A trust that partially avoids federal gift and estate taxes on transfers of large sums of money or other valuable assets established to transfer these assets to a beneficiary two or more generations below the transferor.

generation-skipping transfer tax
A federal tax on the transfer of property when its value exceeds the lifetime exemption to a person two or more generations below the generation of the transferor (donor or decedent), e.g., a grandparent who transfers property to a grandchild, thereby skipping a child.

generation-skipping transfer is subject to the generation-skipping transfer tax (IRC § 2601). Most states imposed a generation-skipping transfer tax to absorb the federal transfer tax credit, which was eliminated in 2005. A few states separated the generation-skipping transfer tax from federal law or fixed that tax to a credit allowable prior to the EGTRRA. *Caveat:* The definitions and rules concerning generation-skipping transfers and their tax computations are complicated. You must review the Code provisions carefully and work closely with your supervising attorney or tax professional when preparing the appropriate tax returns.

The generation-skipping transfer tax is levied on transfers of property that exceed the current lifetime exemption under trusts that have beneficiaries who are two or more generations below that of the **transferor,** and by direct transfers to persons who are two or more generations below that of the transferor. The generation-skipping transfer tax applies to lifetime transfers by gift or transfers by will or trust.

The generation-skipping transfer tax is imposed on the following generation-skipping transfers whenever any one of these three taxable events occurs.

A **direct skip**. A generation-skipping transfer of assets made to a **skip person** that is also subject to federal gift or estate tax. A skip person is the person who receives the property in a generation-skipping transfer and who is two or more generations younger than the transferor (IRC § 2612[c][1]). The transferor is subject to federal gift or estate tax, and the **transferee** is a skip person. The phrase "subject to federal gift or estate tax" means that the asset transfer must be a gift or included in the transferor's gross estate, but it does not require that actual gift or estate tax liability must occur. Direct skips are of two types: (1) an outright transfer to persons two or more generations lower than the transferor's generation or (2) a transfer in trust for the exclusive benefit of persons two or more generations lower than the transferor's generation. When a direct skip is made, the taxable amount is based on the value of the property received by the transferee. If a lifetime direct skip is made to an individual, the tax return is filed and the generation-skipping transfer tax is paid by the transferor while living or by the transferor's personal representative for direct skips occurring at death (IRC § 2603[a][3]). However, when the direct skip is made from a trust, the tax is paid by the trustee.

EXAMPLE: The most common example of a direct skip is a gift made by a grandparent to a grandchild whose parent is living. Harrison Montgomery makes a gift of $1,500,000 to his granddaughter, Natalie, while Harrison's son, Dylan Montgomery (Natalie's father), is alive. Harrison is the transferor, Natalie is the transferee and skip person, Dylan is a non-skip person, the taxable amount is the $1,500,000, which is subject to federal gift tax, and the generation-skipping transfer tax is paid by the transferor (Harrison). *Note:* If Dylan Montgomery is not living at the time of Harrison's transfer (gift), the transfer of the gift to the grandchild is not a direct skip (IRC § 2612[c][2]). In this case, Natalie has "moved up" to her father's generation and has become a non-skip person; therefore, this is not a generation-skipping transfer.

EXAMPLE: Harrison makes the same $1,500,000 gift as above, but this time he transfers the money to a trust in which the trustee is to pay the income and, eventually, the principal exclusively for the benefit of Harrison's granddaughter, Natalie. In this case, the trust itself is the skip person because no non-skip person (e.g., Harrison's child, Dylan) has any "interest" in the property. The taxable amount is still $1,500,000, which is subject to federal gift tax, but the generation-skipping transfer tax is now paid by the trustee.

---

transferor
The decedent or donor who creates a generation-skipping transfer trust.

direct skip
A generation-skipping transfer of an interest in property to a skip person; a direct skip is subject to the federal generation-skipping transfer tax and also the federal gift or estate tax.

skip person
An individual (such as a grandchild) who receives the property in a generation-skipping transfer and is two or more generations below the generation of the transferor.

transferee
The beneficiary who receives the benefits of a generation-skipping transfer trust.

- A **taxable termination**. An interest in property held in trust terminates and trust property is held for or distributed to a skip person (IRC § 2612[a]). The trustee of the trust is responsible for filing the generation-skipping transfer tax return and for payment of the generation-skipping transfer tax (IRC § 2603 [a] [2]). The trustee must obtain a taxpayer identification number once a trust is created.

- A **taxable distribution**. Any distribution from a trust (income or principal) that is not a taxable termination or direct skip (IRC § 2612 [b]). The transferee of a taxable distribution is responsible for the filing of the return and the payment of the generation-skipping transfer tax (IRC § 2603[a][1]). Transfers that are not subject to gift tax because of the annual exclusion (indexed annually for inflation) and the unlimited exclusion for direct payment of medical and tuition expenses are not subject to generation-skipping transfer tax (IRC § 2642[c][1]).

taxable termination
Any termination of an interest in property held in trust.

taxable distribution
Any distribution of income or principal from a trust to a skip person that is not a taxable termination or direct skip.

Lifetime Exemption

Every transferor, including, after death, the transferor's personal representative, is allowed a lifetime exemption from the generation-skipping transfer tax, which can be applied to any generation-skipping transfer (IRC § 2631). If spouses elect to split their gifts, the total amount of the exemption is combined (IRC § 2652[a][2]). The tax is calculated by multiplying the taxable amount of the generation-skipping transfer by the applicable rate (IRC § 2602) and can be reduced or eliminated using this exemption. The exemption applies at the time of transfer as selected by the transferor, and any appreciation of the asset or property transferred is not subject to the generation-skipping transfer tax.

TAX RETURNS

It is the responsibility of the personal representative (the fiduciary) of the decedent's estate to file tax returns for the estate and to pay any taxes owed out of the estate assets. Depending on the situation, the personal representative may have to file some or all of the following returns.

- Federal Individual Income Tax Return
- State Individual Income Tax Return
- Federal Fiduciary Income Tax Return
- State Fiduciary Income Tax Return

POINT OF INTEREST

Contacting the IRS Is Easy

Some estates will require the filing of tax forms with the IRS. Access the IRS at *http:/www.irs.gov*. You can request online that up to 10 forms be sent through the mail, or forms can be downloaded. Information about estate taxes, gift taxes, returns, and electronic filing is included at this site.

- Federal Gift (and Generation-Skipping Transfer) Tax Return
- State Gift Tax Return
- Federal Estate (and Generation-Skipping Transfer) Tax Return
- State Estate Tax Return
- State Inheritance Tax Return

Decedent's Final Income Tax Returns, Federal and State

The personal representative of the decedent's estate, who is also known as the fiduciary, has the obligation to file the required federal and state income tax returns for the decedent. The filing and payment of the income tax due must be completed within the period determined by law, e.g., on or before the 15th day of the fourth month following the close of the taxable year in which the decedent died. Failure to do this may make the personal representative personally liable for any interest and penalties assessed. The deadline may be extended by the Internal Revenue Service upon written request by the personal representative. States generally allow for extensions concurrent to the federal extension.

Internal Revenue Code § 6109 requires an identification number on tax returns and other documents. On the decedent's final federal income tax return, this number is the decedent's Social Security number.

Federal Individual Income Tax Return

A final Form 1040, United States Individual Income Tax Return, must be filed for persons having a specified minimum of gross income (IRC § 6012).

Examples of income that must be reported include income from wages, salaries, tips, self-employment, rents, pensions, annuities, royalties, alimony, dividends, profits from partnerships, income from trusts or estates, bartering income, and interest on deposits, bonds, or notes. Examples of income that need not be reported are gifts and inheritances, compensation for injuries or sickness, child support, life insurance proceeds received due to a person's death, interest on most state or local bonds, and the $250,000 (single) or $500,000 (joint return) exclusion of gain from the sale of a home.

If a refund is due for income withheld for taxes during the year of the decedent's death, the personal representative can file a Statement of Person Claiming Refund Due a Deceased Taxpayer along with the federal income tax return. Alternatively, the personal representative can attach to the return a copy of the court certificate showing the appointment as personal representative.

When preparing the decedent's final federal income tax return, there are a number of special tax considerations. First, if the decedent is survived by a spouse, a joint return can be filed if the surviving spouse agrees and if the surviving spouse has not remarried before the close of the taxable year (IRC § 6013). A joint federal return includes the income of the decedent to the date of death and the income of the surviving spouse for the entire year. For the client's benefit, both federal and state tax returns should be computed separately and jointly to determine which method results in the lesser tax and whether prompt filing or requesting an extension would be more advantageous. If the decedent's final federal income tax return is filed as a separate return, it may be advantageous to file the return as soon as possible and to request early audits by the IRS. This prevents the discovery of a large unplanned tax deficiency at some later date. With a joint federal return, the proportion of the total tax due to be paid by each spouse is determined by the percentage of the total income each earned during the year.

Second, IRC § 213(a) permits the personal representative to treat the decedent's medical expenses (including prescription drug expenses) that are paid from the estate within one year after death as deductions on the income tax return for the year. If the personal representative makes this election, a Medical Expenses Deduction Waiver must be filed, waiving the right to claim the medical expenses as an estate tax deduction (IRC § 2053). The personal representative has the option of using the medical expenses either as a deduction for the final income tax return or as an expense of the decedent's last illness on the estate tax return. Generally, the choice should be made on the basis of which offers the greater tax saving. For example, if the decedent's income was small for that year but he dies leaving a large estate, it would be more advantageous to use medical costs as an expense for estate tax purposes, if an estate tax is due after the applicable credit amount (unified credit) and marital deduction, because this deduction will reduce the taxable estate. This election may not be available on a state return. *Note:* Only medical and dental expenses that exceed 7.5 percent of the taxpayer's adjusted gross income may be deducted on the income tax return.

Third, on the decedent's final federal income tax return, a personal exemption is allowed for each taxpayer. An additional exemption is allowed for a spouse and for each dependent who qualifies under the tax law.

Finally, income "in respect of the decedent" is the gross income the decedent had a right to receive or could have received had he continued to live. This income should properly be included in the decedent's final return. The interest on stocks, bonds, income from sales of assets on an installment basis, and the like are examples of continuing income that should be included in the decedent's final return. For various reasons, certain income may be omitted from the decedent's final return, e.g., where the decedent's final return is filed before such income is received by the executor. Income "in respect of the decedent" that has been omitted from the decedent's final income tax return would then be included in the fiduciary's income tax return for the year in which the income is received. For example, if the decedent died in December 2014, interest on bonds received in May 2015 (which would have been omitted from the decedent's final income tax return filed by April 15, 2015) would be included in the fiduciary's income tax return. Tax may be saved on certain bonds, e.g., United States savings bonds, by electing not to pay the tax on the interest earned until the earlier of the year they are cashed or the year they mature (IRC § 454).

State Individual Income Tax Return

On the state level, a final individual income tax return is also required if the state has an income tax. As with any state income tax return, the personal representative must be conscious of the deadlines and the specific tax requirements of that individual state. For example, some income that is included as taxable income on the federal form may not be taxable under the state return.

Extensions for Federal and State Returns

An Application for Automatic Extension of Time to File United States Individual Income Tax Return (IRS 4868) may be filed, *except* in cases where the IRS is requested to compute the tax, there is a court order to file the return by the original due date, or a six-month extension while traveling abroad had previously been given. This application must be filed on or before April 15 or the normal due date of the return.

The extension of time for filing usually does *not* extend the time for payment of the tax due. If the tax is not paid at this time, interest accrues from the regular due date of the return until the tax is paid. In addition, for each month the return is late, the law provides a 5 percent penalty of the tax due, not to exceed a maximum of 25 percent. If the taxpayer intends to request an extension to file both federal and state income tax returns, a copy of the federal automatic extension form must accompany the state return when that return is filed.

States may or may not require that the taxpayer file a form requesting an extension to file, but as with the federal extension, all tax must be paid on or before the original due date, i.e., April 15, even if the return is not filed. Interest and penalties apply to any unpaid tax.

Assignment 11.2

Find out how a taxpayer in your state obtains an extension of time to file the state income tax return. Is there a form? If so, what is it called and what is its number? Check your state statutory code and/or your state tax regulations on this. If an extension is permitted in your state, for how long and under what conditions can it be obtained? Is there an interest assessment? Any penalty?

Fiduciary's Income Tax Returns, Federal and State

Federal Fiduciary Income Tax Return

In addition to filing the decedent's final federal individual income tax return, the personal representative of the estate must also file the federal fiduciary income tax return (IRC § 6012). This return includes accrued income and income earned after the decedent's death that is not included on the decedent's final individual income tax return. The personal representative is obligated to prepare and file such an income tax return for the estate for the period from the date of the decedent's death to the date of final distribution. Any tax due to the federal government for that period must be paid by the personal representative out of estate assets.

Within a statutory number of days of appointment (e.g., 30 days), the personal representative must file a Notice Concerning Fiduciary Relationship with the IRS (see IRC § 6903 and IRS Form 56). Accompanying the form must be satisfactory evidence that the personal representative has the authority to act as a fiduciary, such as a certified copy of the Letters appointing the personal representative.

The identification number used on the fiduciary income tax return is not the decedent's Social Security number. Instead, the personal representative or trustee uses the Employer Identification Number obtained from the IRS Center for the district where the decedent lived (see IRS Form SS-4).

IRS Form 1041, United States Income Tax Return for Estates and Trusts, must be filed for all domestic decedent estates with gross income for the taxable year of $600 or more; for estates or trusts that have a beneficiary who is a nonresident alien; and for some domestic trusts (IRC § 6012). The return must be filed on or before the 15th day of the fourth month following the close of the taxable year of the estate or trust. When filing the first return, a personal representative may choose the same accounting period as the decedent, e.g., a calendar year or any fiscal year. If the decedent's accounting year (most likely a calendar year) is chosen, the first return will cover that part of the year from the decedent's date of death to the end of the tax year. For consistency in filing returns, the personal representative should choose a taxable year that coincides with the state estate filing requirements. The return is sent to the IRS Center for the state where the fiduciary resides.

If an extension of time is needed, the personal representative can file an Application for Extension of Time to File (IRS Form 7004). Once the tax payment is due, interest and penalties will accrue on the tax due from the due date until total payment is made. Prior to distribution of the estate assets, the fiduciary pays the tax on income earned; after distribution, the successors (heirs or devisees) pay tax on income earned from assets that were distributed to them.

> **EXAMPLE:** Sophie Waterson died on February 3, 2015. Stocks that Sophie owned earned dividends of $5,000 between the date of Sophie's death and October 19, 2015, the date of distribution of estate assets to heirs and devisees. The $5,000 will be included in the federal fiduciary income tax return. All dividends earned by the stock after October 19, 2015, will be income of the heirs or devisees to whom the stocks were distributed. For instance, if the stock was distributed to Kari Wirtz and earned $2,000 in dividends from October 19, 2015, through December 31, 2015, Kari would report the $2,000 on her own individual income tax return for the year 2015, which she will file on or before April 15, 2016.

When the federal fiduciary return is filed, a copy of the will, if any, must be filed with it only if the IRS requests it. When a copy of the will is required, the personal representative must attach to the copy a written declaration that it is a true and complete copy; the personal representative should also include a statement that the will, in his opinion, determines the extent to which the income of the estate is taxable to the estate and the beneficiaries, respectively (Reg. § 1.6012-3[a][2]).

State Fiduciary Income Tax Return

As with the individual decedent's income, an estate may also have to file a state fiduciary income tax return if there is any income earned by the estate that has not been included on the decedent's income tax return. The personal representative is responsible for the filing of such a state return and complying with all documentation and deadline requirements.

ASSIGNMENT 11.3

1. Whose obligation is it to complete and file income tax returns for a decedent's estate in your state?

2. How much interest, if any, is charged in your state for filing a late income tax return? Are there any penalties? Who is liable for interest and penalties in your state?

3. What constitutes sufficient income to require the filing of a decedent's final income tax and fiduciary income tax returns—state and federal?

4. What are the conditions under which a joint tax return can be filed by the surviving spouse?

5. Describe the content and purposes of the federal fiduciary income tax return. Where is this explained in the Internal Revenue Code?

ASSIGNMENT 11.4

Abe Meredith died in June. Following his death, his personal representative received checks from the A & M Mining Co. ($350), Bester Power & Light ($50), and Pronot Can Co. ($500). Will the personal representative have to file a federal fiduciary income tax return? Assume that the estate earned no other income after Abe's death.

Decedent's Gift Tax Returns, Federal and State

Federal Gift (and Generation-Skipping Transfer) Tax Return

Internal Revenue Service Form 709, the United States Gift (and Generation-Skipping Transfer) Tax Return, must be executed and filed whenever a donor makes an *inter vivos* gift in excess of $14,000 (indexed annually for inflation) in any calendar year to any person (donee). The method of calculating the gift tax was discussed previously under Lifetime Gifts. The return is due on or before the 15th day of April following the close of the calendar year the donor made the gifts. If the donor dies, the personal representative must file the return no later than the earlier of the due dates for the donor's estate tax return or April 15. The identification number used on this return is the donor's Social Security number. Payment of the tax is due when the tax return is filed. United States Treasury Form 709 is also used to report generation-skipping tax due to the federal government on *inter vivos* direct skips. An extension of time for filing the return can be accomplished by extending the time to file the federal income tax return, which will also extend the time to file the gift tax return, or by filing United States Treasury Form 8892, Application for Extension of Time to File Form 709 and/or Payment of Gift/GST Tax. A separate request must be made for an extension of time to *pay* the gift or generation-skipping transfer taxes. Penalties apply for the late filing of returns, late payment of tax, and valuation understatements that cause an underpayment of tax. A married couple may not file a joint gift tax return. If, however, the couple agrees to split the gifts (see discussion in Chapter 14), both individual tax returns should be filed together. If a donor elects gift-splitting for his or her gifts and no tax is due, Form 709 can be filed by the donor spouse, and the consenting spouse signifies consent to the gift-splitting on that form. The instructions that accompany Form 709 (the United States Gift Tax Return) should be reviewed carefully. As mentioned previously, only one state currently provides for a gift tax, and in that case, a state return must be filed.

Decedent's Estate Tax Returns, Federal and State

Federal Estate (and Generation-Skipping Transfer) Tax Return

Internal Revenue Service Form 706, United States Estate (and Generation-Skipping Transfer) Tax Return, must be filed within nine months of the decedent's death for the estate of every citizen or resident of the United States whose gross estate on the date of the person's death is greater than the lifetime exclusion. The same Form 706 is also used to report any generation-skipping transfer tax owed to the federal government on direct skips occurring at death. The identification number used on this return is the decedent's Social Security number. An extension of time to file Form 706 and to pay the tax may be obtained by completing the application on Form 4768, Application for Extension of Time to File a Return and/or Pay United States Estate (and Generation-Skipping Transfer) Taxes. Like the gift tax, penalties apply for late filing and late payment as well as underpayment of tax due to valuation understatements.

The federal government imposes a tax on the total value of a decedent's estate, i.e., the value of all property, real or personal, tangible or intangible, wherever situated, to the extent of the decedent's interest therein at the time of death (IRC §§ 2031, 2033). However, any personalty (household furnishings, stocks and bonds, an automobile, and the like) that a surviving spouse claims belongs to said spouse is not included in the deceased person's total estate for estate tax purposes if such a claim can be reasonably supported. The value of the decedent's property transferred under circumstances subject to the tax is called the gross estate (IRC § 2033).

Determining the Gross Estate

The gross estate includes all assets owned by the decedent at death and the value of any interest the decedent held in any property, e.g., the entire interest in a home less the mortgage balance. The gross estate will also include lifetime gifts of property in which the decedent retained "incidents of ownership."

For estate tax purposes, the property owned by a decedent that is included in the gross estate is valued in one of two ways. The assets may be valued on the basis of their fair market value on the date of the decedent's death. This date-of-death rule is established by statute (IRC § 2031). Or, the personal representative of the decedent's estate may elect an *alternate valuation date* for determining the fair market value of the decedent's property (IRC § 2032). (However, if the election is to be allowed, the alternate valuation date must decrease both the value of the gross estate and the federal estate tax liability.) The purpose of the alternate valuation date is to prevent an unreasonable tax liability on the decedent's estate whenever the value of this property takes a drastic plunge shortly after the decedent's death. For example, if the decedent owned a large number of shares of stock and the stock's value on the market decreased substantially shortly after death, the estate could have an enormous tax burden if the property was valued at the date of death for estate tax purposes. Therefore, the IRC provides that property included in the gross estate that has not been distributed, disposed of, sold, or exchanged as of the alternate valuation date, a date six months after the decedent's death, may be valued as of that date if the personal representative so elects instead of assigning the value that prevailed at the date of death (IRC § 2032). The personal representative must elect the alternate valuation date on the decedent's estate tax return during the statutory period allotted for filing such a return, e.g., nine months after the date of the decedent's death unless an extension of time has been properly requested and granted; otherwise the right to the election is lost. Once the alternate date is elected, it cannot be changed, and all property included in the gross estate is valued at the alternate valuation date. Property that is sold, exchanged, distributed, or otherwise disposed of during the six-month period is valued on the date of disposition rather than the alternate valuation date.

EXAMPLE: Benito died on July 2, 2015. On that date, 5,000 shares of stock that he owned in Benitoville Mining Company were valued at $500,000. Six months later, the value of the stock had dropped to $250,000 (a $250,000 loss). In determining the value of Benito's gross estate, the personal representative has the option of assigning the value to the stock (and all other estate assets) that prevailed on July 2, 2015, i.e., the stock would be valued at $500,000, or assigning the value to the stock (and all other estate assets) that prevailed on January 2, 2015, six months after Benito's death, i.e., the stock would be valued at $250,000.

In the example above, assuming that the value of other estate assets had not increased sufficiently to offset the $250,000 loss on the stock, it would be advantageous to the estate to choose the alternate valuation date. Since the gross estate would therefore be reduced by $250,000, no estate tax would be paid on that amount. *Note:* Any taxpayer who dies leaving a taxable estate of the value of the applicable exclusion amount or less would not be liable for any federal estate tax; thus, using the alternate valuation date would apply to larger estates.

The problem of taxing the proceeds from life insurance policies is also resolved by the IRC. Obviously, if the decedent's estate or personal representative (executor) is the named beneficiary of the life insurance policy, the proceeds of the policy are part of the decedent's gross estate for tax purposes. Under IRC §2042, the gross estate will also include the proceeds of all life insurance policies payable to all other beneficiaries in which the decedent at death possessed any of the "incidents of ownership," or, within three years of death, had assigned all the "incidents of ownership," as defined by the IRC. "Incidents of ownership" refer to the right of the insured (decedent) or the estate to the economic benefits of the policy. Therefore, they include the right to change the beneficiary or to cancel the policy. Proceeds from a life insurance policy that passes to a specific beneficiary other than the estate is not included in the gross estate as long as the decedent did not have the "incidents of ownership."

The assets comprising the decedent's gross estate must be listed in separate sections, called schedules, and identified as Schedules A through I in the United States Estate Tax Return. Exhibit 11.3 describes some of the basic data to be included on each schedule. For more complete information on the individual schedules, see the updated instructions for Form 706, United States Estate Tax Return, published by the IRS.

Exhibit 11.4 shows a gross estate as an example of some of the kinds of property found in Schedules A through I.

Determining the Taxable Estate

After all the decedent's property subject to the federal estate tax, i.e., the gross estate, has been determined, the various exemptions, deductions, and claims allowed by statute are subtracted from the gross estate to determine the *taxable estate,* which is the estate on which the tax is imposed (IRC § 2051).

In determining the taxable estate and computing the tax, the deductions, claims, and credits allowed by statute include the following:

- Specific deductible items (expenses, liens, encumbrances, debts, and taxes)
- Losses during the handling of the estate
- Marital deduction

EXHIBIT 11.3	Basic Data for Schedules A–I of the United States Estate Tax Return

Schedule A—Real Estate

Regardless of the property's location, all interests in real property (except joint tenancy and tenancy by the entirety) owned by the decedent in severalty and the decedent's share of property owned with others as tenants in common at the time of death must be listed in Schedule A at their fair market value. This includes all land, buildings, fixtures attached to the real estate, growing crops, and mineral rights. The value of the real property includes all mortgages for which the decedent is personally liable. The mortgage will be listed as a debt of the decedent on Schedule K. Property owned in joint tenancy and tenancy by the entirety is not included in Schedule A, but is listed in Schedule E.

Schedule A—1—Section 2032A Valuation

The personal representative may elect to value certain real property in the decedent's estate that is devoted to farming or used in a closely held business on the basis of the property's actual use for these purposes, as opposed to its fair market value based on its potential or best use. Property passing in trust and property owned indirectly through a corporation or partnership qualify for this valuation. *This is a complex schedule that will require the expertise of other professionals (i.e., an attorney and tax accountant) to prepare.*

Schedule B—Stocks and Bonds

All stocks and bonds owned by the decedent are listed in Schedule B at their fair market value. The exact name of the corporation, the number of shares, the class of shares (common or preferred), the price per share, the CUSIP (Committee on Uniform Securities Identification Procedure) number, and the par value, if any, are some of the data listed for stocks. The principal stock exchange on which the stock is listed and traded should be given. For unlisted stock, the state and date of incorporation and the location of the principal place of business must be given.

The data on bonds must include the number held, the principal amount, the name of the obligor, the date of maturity, the rate of interest, the dates on which interest is payable, the series number if there is more than one issue, and the principal exchange on which the bonds are listed. Also, interest accrued on bonds to the date of the decedent's death must be shown. For unlisted bonds, the business office of the obligor must be given.

Schedule C—Mortgages, Notes, and Cash

Information on Schedule C should include the following:

- Mortgages owned by the decedent (original face value and unpaid balance of principal, date of mortgage, date of maturity, name of maker, property mortgaged, interest dates, and rate of interest)
- Promissory notes owned by the decedent (principal amount and unpaid principal and interest, date given, date of maturity, name of maker, interest dates, and rate of interest)
- Contracts to sell land (description of interest owned by the decedent, name of buyer, date of contract, description of property, sale price, initial payment, amounts of installment payments, unpaid balance of principal and accrued interest, interest rate, last date to which interest has been paid, and termination date of the contract)
- Cash and its location, whether in possession of the decedent, other person, or safe deposit box
- All bank accounts except accounts in joint tenancy (name and address of bank, amount on deposit, account or serial number, whether checking, savings, or time deposit account, rate of interest, and amount of interest accrued and payable as of date of death)

Schedule D—Insurance on the Decedent's Life

Included in Schedule D are proceeds of insurance on the decedent's life received or receivable by or for the benefit of the decedent's estate or personal representative; insurance on the decedent's life receivable by any other beneficiary if the decedent at death possessed any incidents of ownership in the policy or within three years of death had assigned all the incidents of ownership; benefits received from fraternal benefit societies operating under a lodge system, group insurance, accidental death benefits, double indemnity, and accumulated dividends on life insurance, but not annuities (annuities are included in Schedule I).

| EXHIBIT 11.3 | continued |

Schedule E—Jointly Owned Property

Schedule E includes the value of any interest in property held by the decedent and any other person in joint tenancy or tenancy by the entirety. The full value of jointly owned property must be included in the decedent's gross estate, except where a surviving joint tenant can prove he provided all or a portion of the consideration for the property or that the property or a fractional share therein was acquired by gift, bequest, devise, or inheritance. However, if the property is owned in a joint tenancy by a spouses, regardless of who paid for the property, only one-half of the value of the property is included in the estate of the first spouse to die.

Schedule F—Other Miscellaneous Property Not Reportable Under Any Other Schedule

Schedule F is a catchall schedule for probate assets owned by the decedent but not reportable in other schedules. It includes debts due to the decedent; interest in business (sole proprietorship or partnership); patents, copyrights, and royalties; leaseholds; judgments; insurance on the life of another; household goods, clothing, and personal effects; automobiles; farm machinery; livestock; farm products and growing crops that have been severed from the land; reversionary or remainder interests; interests in other trusts and estates; uncashed checks payable to the decedent; and numerous other items.

Schedule G—Transfers During Decedent's Life

Transfers made by the decedent during life where the decedent retained the benefits of the property (except life insurance included in Schedule D) or transferred the benefits within three years of death, by trustor otherwise, except for bona fide sales for an adequate and full consideration in money or money's worth, are subject to tax and are included in Schedule G.

Schedule H—Powers of Appointment

Included in the gross estate under Schedule H is the value of certain property with respect to which the decedent possessed a general power of appointment at the time of death or once possessed a general power of appointment and exercised or released that power prior to death, unless the decedent released the power completely and held no interest in or control over the property.

Schedule I—Annuities

Annuities (periodic payments for a specified period of time) are included in Schedule I. These include annuities or other payments receivable by any beneficiary by reason of surviving the decedent under any form of contract or agreement (other than life insurance) entered into after March 3, 1931. The amount to be included is only that portion of the value of the annuity receivable by the surviving beneficiary that the decedent's contribution to the purchase price of the annuity or agreement bears to the total purchase price. Such benefits as pension, retirement, and profit-sharing plans and IRAs are included in this schedule.

- Charitable deductions
- State death tax deduction
- Applicable credit amount (unified credit) and other allowable credits, e.g., foreign death taxes and tax on prior transfers

Deductions, credits, and special taxes are reported on Schedules J through U of the United States Estate Tax Return. Exhibit 11.5 shows the basic data to be included in Schedules J through U.

Deductible Items

IRC § 2053 identifies deductible expenses and liabilities. The expenses that are deductible from the gross estate include funeral and estate administration expenses, e.g., the fees for the personal representative and the attorney (if used) for

EXHIBIT 11.4 Sample Gross Estate

1. Home	$140,000
Household furniture	$ 20,000
IT&T Stocks	$ 50,000
2. Joint tenancy with spouse in an apartment building, which, when established, was not subject to a gift tax. One-half of the value is included in decedent's gross estate.	$150,000
3. 100 shares of Nelson Manufacturing Co. stock. Decedent devised the income (dividends) from the stock to his son for life, the stock itself to be transferred to the decedent's daughter upon his son's death.	$ 25,000
4. *Office building* Decedent had placed the building in a trust for his niece—the income to be paid to himself for 10 years, then the building to be transferred to the niece. The decedent, however, had retained the right to change the beneficiary of the trust to revoke it.	$100,000
5. *Annuity* Decedent made deductible payments of $1,500 each for five years to an Individual Retirement Account. In addition, nondeductible payments of $1,000 each were made for five years. The surviving spouse is eligible to receive the benefits of this account as an annuity having a value of $18,000. The amount of the annuity to be included is arrived at as follows	$ 7,200

$$\frac{\text{Nondeductible payments}}{\text{Total payments}} \quad \frac{1,000 \times 5}{2,500 \times 5} = \frac{5,000}{12,500} = 40\% \text{ of } 18,000 = 7,200$$

6. The decedent's uncle established a trust in which he placed $100,000 worth of various stocks. The trust named the decedent the trustee and gave the decedent a general power of appointment over the trust income and the trust property.	$100,000
7. Accumulated, undistributed income from trust.	$ 10,000
8. Life insurance policy naming the executor as beneficiary.	$ 10,000
9. Life insurance policy naming the estate as beneficiary.	$ 5,000
TOTAL ASSETS (gross estate)	$617,200

the estate. As such, these fees are deductible either for federal estate tax purposes (IRC § 2053) or for purposes of figuring the federal fiduciary income tax of the estate (IRC § 642). If administration expenses are taken as a deduction on the federal estate tax return, they cannot be used again as a deduction on the federal fiduciary income tax return. The same is true of medical expenses for the last illness, which cannot be used again on the decedent's final individual income tax return. Proper administration expenses besides the personal representative's compensation and attorney's fees include such miscellaneous items as court costs, surrogate's (judge's) fees, accountant's fees, appraiser's fees, storing costs, and other expenses necessary for preserving and distributing the assets of the estate. The rule regarding funeral expenses is that "a reasonable amount may be spent." What is reasonable must be considered in light of the size of the estate and the amount of indebtedness. Objections usually come from other successors, not from the IRS. If one successor spends too much out of the residuary estate for funeral or other expenses, other successors can object. If the court determines that such expenditure was unreasonable, it may order the spender to reimburse the estate. When the estate is small after obligations are paid, the court is concerned that enough will be left to support the family and will not allow excessive funeral expenses.

EXHIBIT 11.5	Basic Data for Schedules J–U of the United States Estate Tax Return

Schedule J—Funeral Expenses and Expenses Incurred in Administering Property Subject to Claims

All deductible funeral expenses, including burial, headstone, mausoleum, cost of transporting the body to the funeral home, and payment of clergy, are included in Schedule J. Funeral expenses must be reasonable, as judged by the size of the decedent's estate. Other deductible expenses are the administration expenses, including the personal representative's commission, attorney's fees, court filing fees, accountant's fees, expenses of selling assets if the sale is necessary to pay decedent's debts, and so on.

Schedule L—Net Losses During Administration and Expenses Incurred in Administering Property Not Subject to Claims

Only valid debts owed by the decedent at the time of death can be included on Schedule K. Any debt that is disputed or the subject of litigation cannot be deducted unless the estate concedes it is a valid claim. Property tax deductions are limited to taxes that accrued prior to the date of the decedent's death. Federal taxes on income during the decedent's lifetime are deductible, but taxes on income received after death are not deductible. Notes unsecured by a mortgage or another lien are also included in this schedule. "Mortgages and liens" are those obligations secured on property that are included in the gross estate at the full values and are deductible only to the extent that the liability was contracted for an adequate and full consideration in money or money's worth.

Schedule M—Bequests, etc., to Surviving Spouse (Marital Deduction)

Included in Schedule L are losses limited strictly to those that occur during the settlement of the estate from fire, storm, shipwreck, or other casualty, or from theft to the extent that such losses are not compensated for by insurance or otherwise. Expenses incurred in administering property not subject to claims are usually expenses resulting from the administration of trusts established by the decedent before death or the collection of other assets or the clearance of title to other property included in the decedent's gross estate for estate tax purposes but not included in the decedent's probate estate.

Schedule O—Charitable, Public, and Similar Gifts and Bequests

Schedule M lists any property that passes to the surviving spouse. The marital deduction is authorized for certain property interests passing from the decedent to the surviving spouse. It includes property interests that are part of the decedent's gross estate. The QTIP marital deduction election is made on this schedule.

Schedule P—Credit for Foreign Death Taxes

Included in Schedule O are charitable gifts or transfers made during life or by will or other written instruments. A gift is charitable if it is for a public purpose, such as the furtherance of religion, science, literature, education, art, or to foster national or international amateur sports competition, and the prevention of cruelty to children and animals.

Schedule K—Debts of the Decedent, and Mortgages and Liens

Schedule P includes credit for foreign death taxes, which is allowable only when the decedent was a citizen or resident of the United States. In some cases, noncitizens who are residents may claim credit if the president has issued a proclamation granting the credit to citizens of a foreign country of which the resident was a citizen and if that country allows a similar credit to decedents who were citizens of the United States residing in that country.

Schedule Q—Credit for Tax on Prior Transfers

Included in Schedule Q is property received by the transferee (the decedent) from a transferor who died within 10 years before or 2 years after the decedent (see the earlier discussion). Credit is allowable for all or a part of the federal estate tax paid by the transferor's estate with respect to the transfer as long as the specified period of time has not elapsed. Where the transferee was the transferor's surviving spouse, no credit is given to the extent that a marital deduction was allowed the transferor's estate. Also, no credit is authorized for federal gift taxes paid in connection with the transfer of the property to the transferee.

EXHIBIT 11.5   **continued**

Schedules R and R-1—Generation-Skipping Transfer Tax

Included in Schedules R and R-1 are the reporting and computation of the generation-skipping transfer tax imposed only on "direct skips occurring at death."

Schedule U—Qualified Conservation Easement Exclusion

Schedule U is for the election and exclusion of a portion of the value of land included in the gross estate that is subject to a qualified conservation easement.

The lifetime debts of the decedent are proper deductions. Debts incurred after death as part of the administration of the estate are not deductible as debts of the decedent, but they may be deductible as administration expenses. All allowed debts, including unpaid mortgages, are proper deductions.

The deduction for taxes is limited to taxes that accrued against the decedent while alive. It does not extend to taxes accruing after death. Thus, the final federal income tax paid by the personal representative for the decedent's own income is deductible, but the income tax on the estate's income is not. Federal estate tax is not deductible. However, a deduction is allowed for state death taxes and a credit for foreign death taxes that must be paid (see below).

Note: Although double deductions (Form 706 and 1041) are disallowed, deductions for taxes, interest, and business expenses accrued at the date of the decedent's death are allowed both as (1) claims against the estate (Schedule K, Form 706), see IRC § 2053(a), and (2) deductions in respect of the decedent (Form 1041), see IRC § 691(b).

Losses

The next deduction subtracted from the gross estate is for losses sustained during the administration of the decedent's estate (IRC § 2054). Such losses do not include the lessening of the value of assets of the estate, e.g., a drop in the value of stock or the loss in the sale of some property. Losses that are deductible are theft and casualty losses that occur during the administration of the estate. Casualty losses include losses due to fires, storms, shipwrecks, and the like. When such losses are recovered from insurance policies or from a suit for damages, they are not deductible. In addition, if the casualty or theft loss has already been deducted from the decedent's or the estate's income tax, such losses cannot be deducted from the gross estate for tax purposes.

When the above expenses, losses, and debts have been subtracted from the gross estate, what remains is called the adjusted gross estate. After the adjusted gross estate has been computed, the marital deduction, charitable deduction, and state death tax deduction are subtracted to arrive at the taxable estate.

Marital Deduction

The next and potentially most valuable deduction, the marital deduction, is then calculated (IRC § 2056). The current statute gives each spouse the right to leave to the surviving spouse an unlimited amount of the decedent spouse's estate free from estate tax.

For example, suppose a decedent's gross estate is $1,000,000. The total amount of deductions allowed for expenses, liens, debts, taxes, and losses is $300,000. The decedent has left $100,000 to various charitable organizations, with the balance of the estate going to the decedent's surviving spouse. The *adjusted gross estate* is the gross estate minus the deductions for expenses, encumbrances, indebtedness, taxes, and losses previously mentioned. Therefore, the adjusted gross estate in our example is $1,000,000 less the $300,000—or $700,000. Note that the charitable deduction is not involved in determining the adjusted gross estate. It is a proper deduction in determining the *taxable estate,* but it is deducted only after the amount of the marital deduction has been determined and deducted.

The marital deduction allowed in this illustration would then be $600,000 because the decedent has left the entire estate (less the $100,000 to various charities) to his spouse. If a decedent had left the surviving spouse less than $600,000, i.e., had given the spouse $400,000, the amount of the marital deduction would be limited to the amount passing to the spouse outright, the $400,000.

Note that in every state, a surviving spouse is entitled to common law dower or curtesy rights, or statutory rights in lieu thereof. If a decedent devises less to the surviving spouse than the amount to which he or she is entitled under applicable state law, the spouse may elect to receive the amount to which he or she is entitled under the above rights. The amount received by the spouse pursuant to such election then becomes the amount of the marital deduction up to the statutory maximum.

The marital deduction applies to either the husband's estate or the wife's estate when one dies and the other spouse survives. Due to its tax-saving advantages, the marital deduction is an important tax consideration in estate planning. However, indiscriminate use of the marital deduction without regard for other methods of disposition, such as successive estates to avoid a second tax on the death of the surviving spouse, may actually increase rather than decrease the tax liability of the two estates. Such overuse of the marital deduction may needlessly subject too much property to taxation when the surviving spouse dies.

Many spouses were reluctant to take advantage of the marital deduction because they did not want to give their spouses the general power of appointment that allowed the surviving spouse to determine to whom the trust property would be given on that spouse's death. They wanted to be sure, for example, that the assets acquired during a first marriage eventually went to the children of that marriage. Granting a general power of appointment made property eligible for the marital deduction tax advantages, but it also created the problem of the children's inheritance if, for example, the surviving spouse remarried or chose to leave the property to someone other than the children. This problem was resolved with the creation of the "qualified terminable interest property" (QTIP) and its QTIP trust. This trust allows property to qualify for the marital deduction *and* ensures the right of the children to receive the assets when the second spouse dies. The requirements for property with its "qualifying income interest" to be used in a QTIP trust were discussed previously and must be reviewed (see Chapter 14). The essential difference between the standard marital deduction trust with the general power of appointment and the QTIP trust is the executor's election on the decedent spouse's estate tax return to specifically elect QTIP status for that trust. In other words, the QTIP trust, would give income to the wife for life, then the remainder to the children, but the wife has no power to dispose of the principal at her death. The executor would elect to have this trust become a QTIP trust, and the property would then be transferred to the children when the husband dies. The one disadvantage is that the executor's election causes the QTIP trust property to be taxed in the second spouse's (the wife's in our case) estate when she dies even though she does not get the property or have the right to determine to whom it will go. The IRC provides that any additional taxes generated by the QTIP trust will be paid from assets of the QTIP trust unless the surviving spouse (the wife in our example) directs otherwise. In other words, those who inherit the QTIP property must pay these additional taxes.

Charitable Deductions

Another federal estate tax deduction allowed by statute is the **charitable deduction** (IRC § 2055). The charitable deduction includes any transfer of estate assets for public, charitable, educational, and religious purposes. The amount of the charitable deduction allowed is the value of property in the decedent's gross estate that was transferred by the decedent during life or by will to a charitable institution. The deduction is limited to the amount actually available for charitable uses. Therefore, if under the terms of a will the federal estate tax, the federal generation-skipping transfer tax, or any other state estate or inheritance tax is payable in whole or in part out of any bequest, legacy, or devise that would otherwise be allowed as a charitable deduction, the amount that can be deducted is the amount of the bequest, legacy, or devise reduced by the total amount of these taxes. The kinds of transfers that qualify for the charitable deduction are described in IRC § 2055 and include the following:

charitable deduction
Under tax law, a contribution to a qualified charity or other tax exempt institution for which a taxpayer may claim an income tax deduction (IRC § 170[c]). Also applicable to trusts (IRC § 512[b][11]).

(a) *In general*—For purposes of the tax imposed by section 2001, the value of the taxable estate shall be determined by deducting from the value of the gross estate the amount of all bequests, legacies, devises, or transfers.

(1) to or for the use of the United States, any State, any political subdivision thereof, or the District of Columbia, for exclusively public purposes;

(2) to or for the use of any corporation organized and operated exclusively for religious, charitable, scientific, literary, or educational purposes, including the encouragement of art, or to foster national or international amateur sports competition (but only if no part of its activities involve the provision of athletic facilities or equipment), and the prevention of cruelty to children or animals, no part of the net earnings of which inures to the benefit of any private stockholder or individual, which is not disqualified for tax exemption under section 501(c)(3) by reason of attempting to influence legislation, and which does not participate in, or intervene in (including the publishing or distributing of statements), any political campaign on behalf of (or in opposition to) any candidate for public office;

(3) to a trustee or trustees, or a fraternal society, order, or association operating under the lodge system, but only if such contributions or gifts are to be used by such trustee or trustees, or by such fraternal society, order, or association, exclusively for religious, charitable, scientific, literary, or educational purposes, or for the prevention of cruelty to children or animals, such trust, fraternal society, order, or association would not be disqualified for tax exemption under section 501(c)(3) by reason of attempting to influence legislation, and such trustee or trustees, or such fraternal society, order, or association, does not participate in, or intervene in (including the publishing or distributing of statements), any political campaign on behalf of (or in opposition to) any candidate for public office;

(4) to or for the use of any veterans' organization incorporated by Act of Congress, or of its departments or local chapters or posts, no part of the net earnings of which inures to the benefit of any private shareholder or individual; or

(5) to an employee stock ownership plan if such transfer qualifies as a qualified gratuitous transfer of qualified employer securities within the meaning of section 664 (g).

Since charities may have similar names, it is important that the charity be designated in the will or trust by its full and correct name. It is also possible that another charity may have the same name. It is wise to consider this possibility and make sure the charity is properly identified to prevent later conflicts. The testator may limit the use of the gift if he wishes. Gifts made to individuals are not deductible under the charitable deduction provision. Two tax advantages may be obtained by making charitable gifts: (1) by decreasing the value of the donor's estate and (2) by claiming an income tax deduction for the amount of the gift on the donor's federal income tax return.

State Death Tax Deduction

Prior to 2005, a credit was allowed for state death taxes paid on property included in the gross estate. The credit has been repealed and replaced with a deduction for state estate, inheritance, legacy, or succession taxes paid as the result of the decedent's death. The deduction may be taken as an anticipated amount before the taxes have been paid; however, the deduction will not be finally allowed unless the state death taxes are paid and the deduction claimed within four years after the return is filed.

Gross Estate Tax

After the taxable estate (total gross estate less allowable deductions) is determined, the *adjusted taxable gifts* made by the decedent after 1976 (lifetime taxable gifts from all the decedent's gift tax returns, IRS Form 709, not included in the gross estate [see Schedule G]) are added to the taxable estate. A tentative estate tax is calculated on this sum using the Unified Rate Schedule. The *gift* tax payable on the post-1976 adjusted taxable gifts is then subtracted from the tentative tax to arrive at the gross estate tax, which is subject to the allowable credits.

Credits

A credit is deducted directly from the gross estate tax.

The following credits against the gross estate tax are included under IRC §§ 2010–2015.

- The applicable credit amount (unified credit) (IRC § 2010).
- The credit for state death taxes that have actually been paid to the decedent's state for years 2010 to 2012 if this credit has not been repealed and changed to a deduction depending on IRS application of the 2010 Tax Relief Act.
- The credit for federal gift taxes on certain transfers the decedent made before January 1, 1977, that are included in the gross estate (IRC § 2012). Obtain Form 4808, Computation of Credit for Gift Tax, to calculate this credit.

- The credit for foreign death taxes (to help alleviate the burden of double taxation on the decedent's estate from two or more nations) (IRC § 2014).

- The credit for tax on prior transfers, e.g., a credit for estate taxes paid on the estate of the spouse of the decedent when the spouse died 10 years or less prior to or two years after the decedent (IRC § 2013).

Net Estate Tax

Once the allowable credits are determined and subtracted from the gross estate tax, the remaining figure, called the net estate tax, is the tax due to the federal government.

Additional Taxes

The generation-skipping transfer tax imposed on direct skips is added to the net estate tax to arrive at the total transfer taxes to be paid when the federal estate tax return is filed.

Federal estate, state estate, and state inheritance taxes must be paid either out of the estate assets or by the persons to whom the estate assets are distributed. The will may contain a provision that requires such persons to pay estate and/or inheritance taxes due on a devise; otherwise, these taxes are generally paid out of the residue of the estate. Sometime after the personal representative files the estate tax return, the IRS sends an "estate tax closing letter" or notifies the personal representative that the return is not acceptable. If it is not acceptable, the IRS will determine the proper tax and request prompt payment. Since an estate tax return is routinely audited, the personal representative should file IRS Form 2848, Power of Attorney and Declaration of Representative, with the federal estate tax return, authorizing the attorney for the personal representative to represent the estate. The timing of the final approval of the federal estate tax return may have an impact on the administration of the estate in the probate court since the case cannot be closed until a final accounting of the distribution of assets has been determined. Most probate courts provide for an extension of their time frames in the event the final estate tax issues have not yet been determined.

ASSIGNMENT 11.5

1. List examples of property subject to federal estate tax. Give imaginary figures for your examples (e.g., $10,000 to Mary Doe as provided in paragraph 3 of decedent's will). Using the examples, create a fact situation from which a sample federal estate tax return can be completed.

2. Explain the marital deduction and its use. Review the section of the Internal Revenue Code where it is discussed.

3. List the expenses, claims (debts), deductions, and credits allowed by the federal government when computing the federal estate tax.

4. List examples of charitable deductions.

State Estate Tax Return

State estate taxes are imposed on the decedent's transfer of property and are measured by the value of the property transferred. Only the state of the decedent's domicile has power to impose an estate tax on the decedent's estate. The exception to this general rule is that property located in a state other than the decedent's domicile is taxable in that state.

After the enactment of the EGTRRA, which provided for the phaseout of the state tax credit, several states amended their estate tax laws to fix their tax to a credit allowable under the federal estate tax law in effect prior to the EGTRRA or have a stand-alone estate tax that will continue without regard to federal law. Individual state statutes must be checked for any estate taxes imposed and for applicable deductions, exemptions, and credits.

The due date for the state estate tax return is usually the same as for the federal return, and any extension of time granted for the federal return automatically extends the filing deadline for the state return. State statutes vary, however, and should be reviewed.

State Inheritance Tax Return

A number of states impose an inheritance tax on the recipients of both real and personal property transferred to them from the estate of a decedent resident of the state. It is a tax on inherited property, i.e., a tax on the beneficiaries who receive the decedent's property, and the rate of tax (usually graduated) varies with the relationship of the heir or devisee to the decedent and the value of the property received. As with the estate tax, state statutes must be checked for deductions, exemptions, and credits that apply to the inheritance tax as well as due dates and extensions of time to file and pay the tax.

Key Terms

successor	generation-skipping transfer	skip person
unified credit	generation-skipping transfer trust	transferee
applicable credit amount	generation-skipping transfer tax	taxable termination
applicable exclusion amount	transferor	taxable distribution
portability	direct skip	charitable deduction

Review Questions

1. What is the difference between estate and inheritance taxes? Are they levied by both the state and federal governments?

2. What types of taxes, e.g., income, gift, or death taxes, are imposed or levied by your state?

3. Who is responsible for paying taxes of the estate, and what funds are used to pay them?

4. What is the alternate valuation election? Under what circumstances is it used?

5. What is meant by the "applicable exclusion amount"?

6. How does the use of the marital deduction save estate taxes?

7. What is QTIP property and how does it qualify for the marital deduction?

8. How are gifts made between spouses taxed before and after death? Also, explain gift splitting.

9. Briefly explain the Uniform Transfers to Minors Act.

10. Who is responsible for filing the decedent's tax returns? What liability exists? How is a tax refund obtained?

11. Does your state have an income tax?

12. When preparing the federal estate tax return, how are the decedent's gross estate and taxable estate determined?

13. Briefly explain the generation-skipping transfer tax.

Case Problems

Problem 1

As a paralegal, you have been asked to interview a gentleman whose wife recently passed away. Your task is to gather information regarding the decedent and her estate's tax liability. Develop an appropriate checklist for the interview. Assume that the client would have sufficient assets that would require the filing of a federal estate tax return.

Problem 2

Determine the estate and inheritance laws in the state in which you reside.

Practical Assignments

1. Identify on which schedule of the United States Estate Tax Return the following assets would be included:

    a. 150 shares of stock for the Roberts Leasing Corporation;

    b. the cost of decedent's headstone for his grave;

    c. checking account;

    d. land contract.

2. Select a corporation whose stock is traded on the New York Stock Exchange *(https://www.nyse.com /index)*. Determine the value of the stock at close for yesterday's date. Now determine the value of the stock six months earlier from yesterday's date using the historical price section available on the website. Assume that your client died six months ago from today's date. Considering just the value of the stock, which date would be most advantageous for tax purposes?

3. Select an immediate member of your family. Complete IRS Form 2848, Power of Attorney and Declaration of Representative, authorizing you to serve as the personal representative to represent your immediate family member's estate. There are no limitations placed upon your representation.

12

INTRODUCTION TO TRUSTS

Outline

Objectives

After completing this chapter, you should be able to:

- Understand the basic terminology of trusts.
- Identify and define the essential elements of trusts.
- Identify the participants in the creation and operation of a trust and be able to explain their functions and roles.
- Explain the ways in which a trust terminates.

SCOPE OF THE CHAPTER

To practice successfully in the field of trusts, you must learn the terminology of trust law. Once you acquire a basic vocabulary, you will be able to identify the various kinds of trusts, understand their functions, and draft trust agreements that meet your client's objectives. After you gain work experience under the supervision of a trust attorney, you will be able to handle these matters with confidence. The purpose of this and the following chapter on trusts is to help you obtain that confidence.

Although all states have adopted or enacted some form of probate code by statute, very few states have comprehensive trust codes. A major authority on trusts, often cited by legal scholars, is the Restatement of Trusts published by the American Law Institute (ALI). In 2000, the National Conference of Commissioners on Uniform State Laws (NCCUSL) approved the Uniform Trust Code (UTC), an endeavor to codify the law of trusts. Updated in 2010, the UTC has been adopted in 28 states plus the District of Columbia. Six other states are considering adopting it. For the most part, the law of trusts is found in a combination of state statutes, judicial decisions, the Restatement, and the UTC.

This chapter begins with the terminology associated with trusts and presents an example of how a trust works. You will be asked to identify the terms in an actual trust instrument. The remaining units of the chapter discuss the elements of a trust, including the participants, their interests, selection, duties, and liabilities; the trust property; and the ways in which a trust terminates.

TERMINOLOGY RELATED TO TRUSTS

Before you can prepare a preliminary draft of a trust agreement, you must master the terminology of trusts. The major terms are defined as follows.

- *Trust*. A trust is a property arrangement in which real or personal property is transferred from the settlor to one or more trustees who hold the legal title to the property for the benefit of one or more beneficiaries who hold the equitable title.

  EXAMPLE: Hazem gives Amel $30,000 to hold and invest in trust for the benefit of Aiden.

POINT OF INTEREST

ALI and NCCUSL Information Online

Learn more about the Restatement of Trusts and the American Law Institute at http://www.ali.org. The Institute, which was created in 1923, has published restatements in many areas of the law. The National Conference of Commissioners on Uniform State Laws can be accessed at http://www.uniformlawcommission.com/. Organized in 1892, the association of state commissioners on uniform laws has drafted over 300 uniform laws including the Uniform Probate Code and the Uniform Trust Code.

- *Settlor*. The person who creates a trust is the settlor, also called the creator, donor, grantor, or trustor. In the above example, Hazem is the settlor.

- *Trustee*. The trustee (or co-trustees) is the person who holds the legal title to property in trust for the benefit of one or more beneficiaries. A trustee is a fiduciary and, as such, is required to perform all trustee duties according to the terms of the trust instrument with loyalty, honesty, and in good faith for the sole benefit of the beneficiary. In the above example, Amel is the trustee; he holds legal title to the property and must invest it for the benefit of Aiden, the beneficiary.

legal title (of a trust)
The form of ownership of trust property held by the trustee giving the trustee the right to control and manage the property for another's benefit, i.e., the holder of the equitable title.

- *Legal title*. **Legal title** is a title, enforceable in a court of law, that is the complete and absolute right of ownership and possession. However, in the law of trusts, the trustee, who manages and administers the trust, holds the legal title but without the benefits of the trust, i.e., without the right to receive financial profit from it. The benefits of the trust go to the beneficiary who holds this beneficial interest, called the equitable title.

  EXAMPLE: By deed, Colt transfers a farm to Addison to hold in trust for the benefit of Vanna. Addison is the trustee and has legal title. Vanna is the beneficiary and holds the equitable title.

- *Beneficiary or "cestui que trust."* The beneficiary (also called the *cestui que trust*) is the person (or persons) who has the enjoyment and benefit of the property. The beneficiary is said to hold equitable title; i.e., the beneficiary has the right to the benefits (profits) of the trust.

equitable title (of a trust)
The right of the party who holds the equitable title or beneficial interest to the benefits of the trust.

- *Equitable title*. In the law of trusts, **equitable title**, or beneficial title, refers to the right of the beneficiary to receive the benefits of the trust. Another way to view equitable title is that the beneficiary of the trust is regarded as the real "owner"; i.e., the beneficiary is entitled to the beneficial interest (the right to profit or benefit from the trust property), although the legal title to the property is held by another, the trustee (see Exhibit 12.1).

- *Trust property*. The trust property is the real or personal property that the trustee holds subject to the rights of one or more beneficiaries. The trust property in the example above is the farm transferred by Colt. Other names for trust property are the trust corpus, trust res, trust fund, trust estate, or subject matter of the trust.

- *Trust instrument*. A written instrument that creates a trust, i.e., a will, trust agreement, or declaration of trust. These terms are defined next.

  - *Will*. A trust included in a will is called a testamentary trust.

  - *Trust agreement*. A written agreement (contract) between the settlor and trustee(s) that creates the trust and is signed by them (see Exhibit 12.2). In a trust agreement, the settlor transfers the legal title to the trustee and either retains the equitable title or transfers it to another person but not to the trustee.

- *Declaration of trust*. A document that creates a trust in which the settlor is also the trustee. The document declares the creation of a trust in which the settlor names himself as trustee and retains the legal title but transfers the equitable title to the trust property to another person, the beneficiary.

- *Revocable living trust*. A revocable living trust is a trust that the settlor has a right or power to revoke or change at any time prior to death. Such a power must be expressly stated or reserved by the settlor in the trust instrument; otherwise trusts are generally irrevocable. Property placed in revocable living

EXHIBIT 12.1   Creation of a Trust

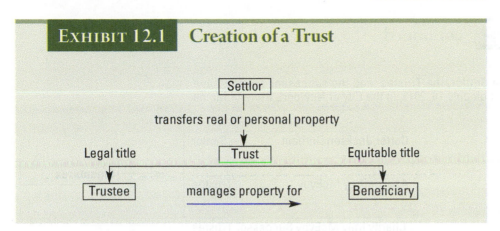

EXHIBIT 12.2   The Durham Trust

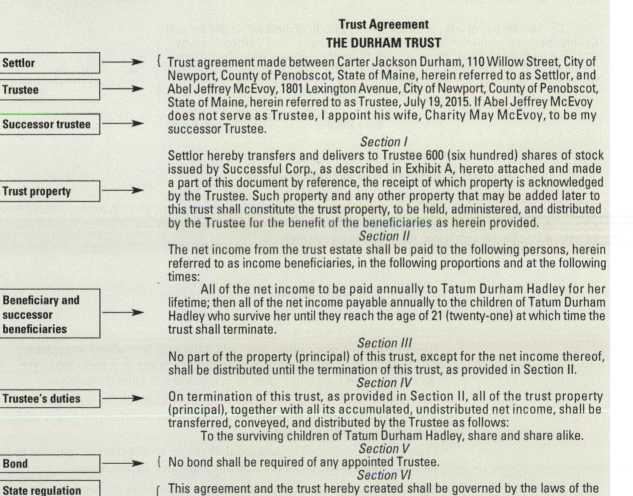

Trust Agreement

THE DURHAM TRUST

Settlor → { Trust agreement made between Carter Jackson Durham, 110 Willow Street, City of Newport, County of Penobscot, State of Maine, herein referred to as Settlor, and

Trustee → Abel Jeffrey McEvoy, 1801 Lexington Avenue, City of Newport, County of Penobscot, State of Maine, herein referred to as Trustee, July 19, 2015. If Abel Jeffrey McEvoy does not serve as Trustee, I appoint his wife, Charity May McEvoy, to be my

Successor trustee → successor Trustee.

Section I

Settlor hereby transfers and delivers to Trustee 600 (six hundred) shares of stock issued by Successful Corp., as described in Exhibit A, hereto attached and made a part of this document by reference, the receipt of which property is acknowledged by the Trustee. Such property and any other property that may be added later to this trust shall constitute the trust property, to be held, administered, and distributed by the Trustee for the benefit of the beneficiaries as herein provided.

Trust property →

Section II

The net income from the trust estate shall be paid to the following persons, herein referred to as income beneficiaries, in the following proportions and at the following times:

All of the net income to be paid annually to Tatum Durham Hadley for her lifetime; then all of the net income payable annually to the children of Tatum Durham Hadley who survive her until they reach the age of 21 (twenty-one) at which time the trust shall terminate.

Beneficiary and successor beneficiaries →

Section III

No part of the property (principal) of this trust, except for the net income thereof, shall be distributed until the termination of this trust, as provided in Section II.

Section IV

On termination of this trust, as provided in Section II, all of the trust property (principal), together with all its accumulated, undistributed net income, shall be transferred, conveyed, and distributed by the Trustee as follows:

Trustee's duties → To the surviving children of Tatum Durham Hadley, share and share alike.

Section V

Bond → { No bond shall be required of any appointed Trustee.

Section VI

State regulation and irrevocable trust → { This agreement and the trust hereby created shall be governed by the laws of the State of Maine, and this trust shall be irrevocable and it shall not be terminated, amended, or altered by the Settlor or any other person.

EXHIBIT 12.2   continued

In witness whereof, the Settlor, the Trustee, and the successor Trustee have executed this agreement on July 19, 2015, in the City of Newport, State of Maine.

Carter Jackson Durham   Settlor

Abel Jeffrey McEvoy   Trustee   ◄— **Signatures**

Charity May McEvoy Successor Trustee

[Exhibit A omitted here]

STATE OF MAINE
                                    } SS.
COUNTY OF PENOBSCOT

On this 19th day of July, 2015, before me, a Notary Public within and for said County, personally appeared Carter Jackson Durham, Abel Jeffrey McEvoy, and Charity May McEvoy, to me known to be the persons described in and who executed the foregoing instrument, and acknowledged that they executed the same as their free act and deed.   ◄— **Notary**

Sally Dolle   Notary Public

My commission expires June 1, 2016

Acceptance of the said Trust and Trust Property

I, Abel Jeffrey McEvoy, do hereby, as evidenced by my signature hereto, acknowledge the receipt of the trust property in said trust, to be held by me in escrow until the operation of the said trust as set forth, and I do accept said trust to be administered in my own name, for purposes therein set forth.
Dated this 19th day of July, 2015.

Abel Jeffrey McEvoy   Trustee

---

trusts becomes a nonprobate asset and, although not subject to probate proceedings, may still be subject to creditors' claims. It is included in the decedent's gross estate and, therefore, is subject to federal estate tax.

- *Irrevocable living trust.* Once created, an irrevocable living trust cannot be revoked or changed by the settlor. Property placed in the trust is not subject to probate or federal estate tax.

- *Principal.* The principal is the capital or property of a trust as opposed to the income, which is the product or profits generated by the capital.

  EXAMPLE: The farm Colt transferred to Addison would be the principal, and the profits generated by the farm would be the income.

- *Income*. Income is the financial gain measured in money that is generated from the principal.

- *Income beneficiary*. The income beneficiary is the person or charity that is entitled to receive the income produced from trust property (principal).

- *Restatement of Trusts*. In 1935, recognizing the need to simplify and clarify the American law of trusts, a group of trust experts working for the American Law Institute set forth the existing rules of law affecting trust creation and administration and included illustrations and comments. The completed work was called the Restatement of the American Law of Trusts, which is considered to be the authority on trust law in most states. In 1959, the original Restatement was revised, and the revisions were incorporated into the Restatement (Second) of Trusts. In 1992, another revision was completed. In 2003, the Restatement of Trusts [Third] was issued. Throughout the trust chapters of this book, relevant sections of the Restatement (Second) or (Third) of Trusts are referenced.

- *Uniform Trust Code*. In response to the expanding interest in trusts, the National Conference of Commissioners on Uniform State Laws determined that there was a need to develop a code of trust law to govern the creation, administration, and termination of trusts. The **Uniform Trust Code (UTC)** was approved in 2000 and updated in 2010. The Code is based on existing state statutes, judicial decisions, and the Restatement. It has been adopted in 28 states and the District of Columbia.

Uniform Trust Code (UTC)
A uniform law available for adoption by the states to provide a uniform codified law on trusts.

- *Parol evidence*. Parol evidence is oral or written evidence.

- *Statute of Frauds*. State laws that provide that no lawsuit or civil action shall be maintained on certain classes of oral contracts unless the agreement is put in writing in a note or memorandum and signed by the party to be charged, i.e., the person being sued, or an authorized agent of the person. The statute's objective was to avoid numerous frauds and perjuries. In the law of trusts, the majority of states require trust agreements that transfer title of real property to the trust to be written and signed by the parties to the contract. The Statute of Frauds makes oral trusts of real property invalid.

Use of Trust Terminology

To better understand the meaning and use of trust terms, consider the following situation.

The Facts

Carter Jackson Durham gives 600 shares of Successful Corp. stock to his financial adviser and best friend, Abel Jeffrey McEvoy, to hold in trust and to invest for the benefit of Carter's only child, Tatum, and Tatum's children, Rhea and Ryder. Named as successor trustee is Abel's wife, Charity May McEvoy, who is also an accountant. This instrument (written agreement) provides that Abel will pay Tatum the income from the stock annually for the rest of her life, and after Tatum's death, the stock will be given to Tatum's children (Carter Durham's grandchildren). Exhibit 12.2 presents the trust agreement establishing the Durham Trust.

Review of Terminology

Carter Durham, the person who creates the trust, is the *settlor*, a word that comes from traditional legal language of "settling the property in trust." He may also be called the *trustor, donor, grantor*, or *creator*. The *trustee*, the person to whom the property is transferred in trust for the benefit of another and who manages and administers the trust, is Abel McEvoy. The *legal title* to the property is held by Abel, the trustee, while the right to the use and benefit of the income from the property, i.e., the *equitable title*, is enjoyed (held) by the beneficiaries, Tatum and Tatum's children. Another name for the *beneficiary* is *cestui que trust*, which means "he for whom certain property in trust is held." Property held in trust (in this case the 600 shares of stock) is called the *trust property, trust fund, trust corpus, trust estate, trust res*, or the *subject matter of the trust*. The *trust instrument* that created this contract or agreement between the settlor, Carter, and the trustee, Abel, is the Durham Trust. The objectives of the Durham Trust are to vest in (transfer to) the trustee and the beneficiaries the property interests it describes and to establish the parties' respective rights and duties. If the trustee fails to perform the terms of the trust or to act within the laws of the state (Maine), the beneficiaries are entitled to seek remedies from a *court of equity*.

A distinction is made between the *principal*, the property held in trust, and the *income*, which is earned by the principal and distributed by the trustee to the beneficiaries. In this case, the principal would be the shares of stock, and the income would be the profits in the form of dividends paid by the corporation to the shareholders. According to the trust instrument's provisions, Tatum is entitled to the income (dividends) from the trust property (stock) for the duration of her life. Tatum's children are entitled to a future interest called the *remainder* in the trust property, i.e., the principal (the stock) remaining after their mother dies. The children are called *remaindermen*. A trustee may also be given the power to distribute part of the *trust property* (the stock) to the beneficiaries on the basis of financial need or simply the wishes of the beneficiary. In this *trust agreement*, however, the trustee was not given this power. *Powers* are granted by the settlor when the trust is created (see Restatement [Third] of Trusts §§ 2, 3 for definitions and §§ 25, 64 for reservation and creation of powers).

ASSIGNMENT 12.1

Cece Schrader gives a four-unit apartment building to her nephew, Garrett Patrick, to hold in trust for the benefit of his children (Cece's grandnieces and grandnephews). The trust agreement provides the monthly rents, less maintenance, insurance, taxes, and other expenses, are to be given to the children until Garrett's death, when ownership of the property will pass to them.

1. Who is the cestui que trust in the above case? What other terms are used to identify such persons?

2. Explain the difference between income and principal in reference to this case.

3. Who is the settlor? What other terms are used to identify the settlor?

4. Who is the trustee? What is the trustee's function?

THE ESSENTIAL ELEMENTS OF A TRUST

Each trust has the following elements: (1) a settlor who creates the trust; (2) one or more trustees who administer and manage the trust; (3) one or more beneficiaries who receive the benefits (income and/or principal) and enforce the trust; and (4) real or personal property that must be transferred to the trust. Since a trust differs from other legal property transactions, such as a sale or gift of property, it is essential that all participants' interest in a trust be understood. After a sale or gift of property, the entire legal title passes from seller to buyer (sale) or from donor to donee (gift). However, after the creation of a trust, title to property placed in the trust passes to at least two persons. The title is "split" into legal title and equitable title. The trustee receives the legal title, and the beneficiary receives the equitable title. For this reason, the trustee and the beneficiary are indispensable to the existence of a trust. In fact, a trust does not begin until legal and equitable interests (title) in specific property are vested in different individuals or sets of individuals, i.e., co-trustees or co-beneficiaries. The trust relationship commences when the separation of legal and equitable title takes place; see *Friedrich v. BancOhio National Bank*, 14 Ohio App. 3rd 247, 470 N. E. 2d 467 (1984). Once a trust is created, the settlor's involvement often ends (see discussion below).

Another feature that distinguishes a trust from a sale is that consideration, i.e., payment to the settlor based on the trust property's reasonable value, is not a requirement for the creation of a trust. In other words, when property is placed in trust for the beneficiary, the settlor does not require the beneficiary to pay for the transfer. A trust is a gratuitous transfer of property; consideration is not necessary (Restatement [Third] of Trusts § 15).

The Settlor: The Creator of the Trust

When a trust is created by the settlor, it is common practice to execute a written document called a **trust agreement** or **declaration of trust**. Provided the settlor manifests a clear intent to establish a trust, i.e., the settlor expressly imposes a duty on the trustee with respect to specific property, no particular words are necessary to create the trust as long as the trust purpose, property, and beneficiaries are designated (Restatement [Third] of Trusts § 13). A common trust provision is "to X, as trustee, to have and hold under the trust's provisions hereinafter set forth," but the settlor could also establish a valid trust by giving property "to X for the benefit of Y." Use of the word *trust* or *trustee* is helpful but not mandatory, as illustrated by the case of *Mahoney v. Leddy*, 126 Vt. 98, 223 A.2d 456 (1966), in which Teresa Egan signed a paper stating that "in the event of my death" certain stock held in her name "belongs to Miss Peck." This was held to be a trust. Also, as noted above, the settlor's creation of the trust is not invalidated by its gratuitous nature; i.e., the beneficiary is not required to give the settlor money, service, or any other consideration in return for the settlor's act of establishing the trust.

trust agreement
A written agreement (contract) between the settlor and trustee(s) that creates the trust and is signed by them.

declaration of trust
A document that creates a trust in which the settlor is also the trustee.

ASSIGNMENT 12.2

Ruby gives Candy $30,000 cash to hold and invest for the benefit of Kirby. A trust is created even though the words *trust* and *trustee* are not used in its creation. The trust property is transferred as a gift. Neither Candy nor Kirby has purchased the property, so neither of them pays for receiving it.

1. Name the settlor, beneficiary, trustee, and trust corpus.

2. How does this trust differ from a sale or a gift?

Who may be a settlor? What qualifications or limitations exist that allow courts to enforce the trust the settlor creates? To be a settlor, a person must own a transferable interest in property, have the right or power of disposing of a property interest, and have the ability to make a valid contract. Only those who have contractual capacity, i.e., who are not insane, intoxicated, or minors, can make an outright transfer of property into a trust (Restatement [Third] of Trusts § 11 (1–5)). Thus, the limitations placed on persons to make contracts, wills, and other legal transactions are also limitations on settlors of trusts. Unless a person meets the qualifications, he cannot create a trust, and any attempt to do so is voidable. In addition, even though a person is qualified to make a trust, if the property transfer is accomplished through duress, fraud, or undue influence, the settlor may avoid or cancel the trust.

Once the settlor intentionally creates a trust, assuming he does not appoint himself trustee or beneficiary, the settlor's functions terminate, i.e., he has no further rights, duties, or liabilities with respect to the trust administration.

EXAMPLE: Harding owns a farm, Blackacre, which he conveys by deed to Barrett in trust for the benefit of Stewart. Harding is the settlor and retains no interest. He has no further powers, duties, rights, or liabilities concerning the trust administration. Barrett is the trustee and has legal title. Stewart is the beneficiary and has equitable title. Blackacre is the trust property.

At the termination of the trust, the settlor may have the right to the return of the trust property, i.e., the settlor's (grantor's) reversionary interest (see Chapter 1).

While alive, the settlor may expressly retain the power to revoke or cancel the trust and recover the trust property. When the settlor has such a power, the trust is called a **revocable trust** (Restatement [Third] of Trusts § 63). When the settlor does not expressly reserve this power, the trust is **irrevocable**.

At first, the settlor may want the trust to be revocable in order to have the opportunity to see how well it works and what changes, if any, are necessary before the trust is made irrevocable. Eventually, the settlor may wish to make the trust irrevocable, since the retention of control over the trust arrangement, including the power to revoke, exposes the settlor to tax liability for the trust income. Generally, the settlor must make the trust irrevocable and retain only limited powers over the trust before death; if these requirements are not met, the trust income and principal will be included in the settlor's gross estate and will be subject to estate and inheritance taxes.

The Settlor as Trustee or Beneficiary

Although three parties usually participate in the creation of a trust, the law demands the involvement of at least two. The same person cannot be the settlor, trustee, and beneficiary, but the same person could be the settlor and trustee, or the settlor and beneficiary. Thus, a settlor may appoint himself sole trustee and legally transfer the trust property from himself personally to himself as trustee using a declaration of trust document.

revocable trust
A trust that the settlor has a right or power to cancel or revoke.

irrevocable trust
A trust that may not be revoked by the settlor after its creation.

EXAMPLE: Harding owns 1,000 shares of IBC, Inc. stock and declares himself trustee of the stock for the benefit of Stewart. Harding is the settlor and trustee who retains legal title. Stewart is the beneficiary and has equitable title. The IBC, Inc. stock is the trust property.

A settlor may also convey property in trust to another for his own benefit, i.e., the settlor is the beneficiary.

EXAMPLE: Harding owns a farm that he conveys by deed to Barrett in trust for the benefit of himself (Harding). Harding is the settlor and beneficiary with an equitable interest in the farm. Barrett is the trustee and has legal title. The farm is the trust property.

Notice, however, the same person cannot be both the sole trustee and the sole beneficiary. A trust exists when the trustee has a fiduciary obligation to administer the trust property for the benefit of another, i.e., the beneficiary, who can enforce the obligation. Therefore, a sole trustee cannot also be a sole beneficiary because there would be no one to enforce the trust. If the trustee, who holds legal title to the trust property, acquires the equitable title of the beneficiary, the legal and equitable titles merge, and the trust ends. However, when the sole trustee is also one of several beneficiaries, or the sole beneficiary is also one of several trustees, the legal and equitable titles do not merge, and the trust is valid (Restatement [Third] of Trusts § 32). Thus, the settlor can name himself sole trustee and co-beneficiary or co-trustee and sole beneficiary, but not sole trustee and sole beneficiary (see Exhibit 12.3).

EXAMPLE: A settlor, Ray Norton, signs a declaration of trust naming himself trustee of stock certificates for the benefit of himself and his wife, Vera. Since he holds complete legal title but only partial equitable title to the trust property, Ray is allowed to fill all three of these roles (settlor, trustee, and co-beneficiary) while Vera is alive. When Vera dies, however, Ray holds the entire equitable as well as legal title. This merger of title in one person ends the trust.

EXHIBIT 12.3	Creation of Valid or Invalid Trusts

Valid Trust Combinations

Settlor	Trustee or Co-Trustees	Beneficiary or Co-Beneficiaries
Peter	Rachel	Christopher
Peter	Peter and Rachel	Christopher
Peter	Rachel	Peter and Christopher
Peter	Peter and Rachel	Peter and Christopher
Peter	Peter	Christopher
Peter	Rachel	Peter
Peter	Peter and Rachel	Peter
Peter	Peter	Peter and Christopher

Invalid Trust Combinations

Settlor	Trustee or Co-Trustees	Beneficiary or Co-Beneficiaries
Peter	Peter	Peter
Peter	Rachel	Rachel

The last two examples do not create a valid trust since the same individual cannot be the sole trustee and the sole beneficiary; that would cause the legal and equitable titles to be merged and would automatically terminate the trust.

The Trustee: The Fiduciary and Administrator of the Trust

The trustee is the participant in a trust who holds legal title to the trust property for the benefit of the beneficiary. The trustee is a *fiduciary* and, as such, owes fiduciary duties to act honestly and loyally for the sole benefit of the beneficiary. This fiduciary relationship between the trustee and the beneficiary is identified and defined in the case of *Scotti's Drive In Restaurants, Inc. v. Mile High-Dart In Corp.*, 526 P.2d 1193 (Wyo. 1974). Normally, the settlor has the right or power to select the trustee, but this right may be given to the beneficiary or to another; *failure of the settlor to name a trustee is not fatal to the trust*, however, because in such cases the court will appoint a trustee.

Natural or Legal Person as Trustee

Generally, the trustee selected is a person, either natural (e.g., settlor, family member, attorney, or financial adviser) or legal (e.g., a private corporation authorized to act as a trustee by its charter and state statute, such as a trust company or bank). If a trust is created to last a considerable length of time, it may be best to select a corporate trustee (bank) to assure continued reliable management. As a matter of practicality, settlors often choose a bank as the trustee or co-trustee because of the experience and expertise of bank trust officers. The cost of using such trustees is always an important consideration. Corporate trustees make their published fee schedules available to attract prospective clients. Close family members may not charge any fee, but their management advice may not be as productive.

Any natural person who has the legal capacity to hold, own, and administer property may receive trust property as a trustee. However, even though minors, intoxicated individuals, and mentally incompetent persons can take and own property, they lack the capacity to make a valid contract; therefore, they cannot properly administer a trust since their contracts are voidable (revocable). In other words, if such persons make contracts as part of their duties while administering a trust, they can avoid, disaffirm, or cancel their contracts because their contracts are voidable. Therefore, such trustees will ordinarily be removed and a new trustee appointed by the equity court on request of the beneficiary.

In most cases, the settlor selects the trustee on the basis of the person's proven integrity, ability, experience, and, of course, capacity. If there is a question about the selected person's fitness or capacity, the equity court either ratifies (confirms) or denies the selection. Therefore, in some instances, the settlor is considered to have only nominated a trustee; selection is within the court's prerogative (see Cal. Prob. Code § 17200). The *most important rule* of trust law concerning the selection of a trustee is that the court will not allow a trust to fail for lack of a trustee. Thus, the court has the power and authority to appoint or replace a trustee if any of the following events occurs.

1. No one is nominated as trustee.

2. The trustee dies.

3. The trustee is incompetent.

4. The named trustee declines the position.

5. No successor is named as a replacement in the provisions of the trust.

EXAMPLE: The trust department of the Lincoln National Bank, a private corporation, has experienced financial advisers who offer their services to the public as professional trustees. Since the bank's charter enables it to act as a trustee, it does so through these employees. Rosalind Vernon transfers her Microsoft stock to the bank to hold and manage for the benefit of her son, Willard. The bank's trust advisers perform this service for an agreed-on fee.

EXAMPLE: Ella Cunningham, age 80, transfers part of the assets of her estate in trust to her favorite niece, Madison, age 17. Ella is the beneficiary. Madison signs a contract as trustee, but, as a minor, she decides not to honor her obligation. Minors make voidable contracts and may choose to avoid or cancel them. Since Madison avoided the trust agreement, Ella may appoint a successor trustee.

EXAMPLE: Darnella Swanson, a single parent, appoints Newton Marshall, a close friend, trustee of a trust for the benefit of her son, Roy. Newton sells some of his property to the trust, buys other trust property for his family, and adds the money to his account instead of the trust account. Darnella can have Newton replaced as trustee because of these serious breaches of his fiduciary duties.

Co-Trustees

The following rules generally apply when co-trustees have been appointed and decisions concerning the administration of the trust must be made.

- If there are two trustees, both must agree on any action concerning trust property.
- If there are more than two trustees, the general rule is that all must agree, but the trust document determines whether action can be taken only by unanimous vote, majority vote, or even by one trustee (usually the settlor-trustee) acting alone (Restatement [Third] of Trusts § 39). Some states allow a majority vote when more than two people are co-trustees.

Acceptance or Disclaimer of Trusteeship

Normally, the settlor will name a trustee, but if the settlor does not, a trustee will be appointed by a court (Restatement [Third] of Trusts §§ 34, 31). Since the trust imposes fiduciary duties on the trustee, the trustee has the right to renounce or reject (disclaim) the trust. The person named as trustee is free to choose whether to accept or reject the appointment by words or conduct.

In the absence of a definite rejection or **disclaimer**, acceptance will be presumed, and any positive act such as taking possession of the trust property will confirm the trustee's acceptance. Likewise, the failure of a trustee to do or say anything to indicate acceptance within a reasonable length of time will be considered a disclaimer.

disclaimer
The right a person has to refuse or reject appointment as trustee of a trust.

EXAMPLE: Lydia Metaxis creates a testamentary trust for her grandchildren and names her friend, Isabel Leclerc, trustee. Isabel is unable to carry out the tasks of administration. Therefore, she executes a disclaimer of responsibility as trustee and files it with the probate court that has jurisdiction over Lydia's will. The court will appoint a different trustee. Isabel's disclaimer is shown in Exhibit 12.4.

Once disclaimed, a trusteeship cannot thereafter be accepted. The disclaimer does not affect the validity of the trust, however, because a court will appoint a successor trustee if the settlor did not provide for one. The best way to eliminate any doubt of the trustee's acceptance or rejection is for the trustee

EXHIBIT 12.4   Sample Disclaimer

I, Isabel Andrewes Leclerc, named as trustee under the will of Lydia Metaxis, deceased, respectfully decline to act as said trustee.
In witness whereof, I have executed this instrument at the City of Punta Gorda, Charlotte County, Florida.

_____
Isabel Andrewes Leclerc

January 16, 2015

to deliver to the proper person, e.g., the settlor, a signed document of the decision to accept or disclaim.

Removal or Resignation of Trustee

Trusteeship is a solemn undertaking. After accepting the duties outlined in a trust, a trustee can be relieved of the duties and office by the settlor, by death, by removal by the equity or probate court, or by resignation (Restatement [Third] of Trusts §§ 34, 31, 36). Resignation is an exercise of the trustee's discretion and must be accepted by the proper court (a court of equity or probate court). Removal of the trustee is an exercise of the court's discretion when it believes the continuation of acts by the trustee would be detrimental to the beneficiary's interests (Restatement [Third] of Trusts § 37). Grounds for the removal of a trustee include the following:

- Lack of capacity
- Commission of a serious breach of trust
- Refusal to give bond when bond is required
- Refusal to account for expenditures, investments, and the like
- Commission of a crime, particularly one involving dishonesty
- Long or permanent absence from the state
- Showing of favoritism to one or more beneficiaries
- Unreasonable failure to cooperate with the co-trustee if one exists (Restatement [Third] of Trusts § 37)

If the trustee selected is a corporation, the beneficiaries are given the right to remove the trustee and name a successor corporate trustee. However, mere friction between the trustee and the beneficiary is not sufficient grounds for removal. Remember, if a trustee resigns or is appropriately removed, the court will appoint a new (successor) trustee as a replacement unless the trust document provides for a successor.

Unless required by a state statute, by terms of the trust, or by an order of a court of equity, a trustee is not required to take an oath that he will faithfully discharge the duties or to secure a certificate of authority from a court. Whether or not an oath is required, the trustee still has a fiduciary duty to the beneficiary. In some jurisdictions, becoming a trustee depends on performance of one or more of these acts, and failure to perform the act prevents the person from assuming the office. In other jurisdictions, failure of the trustee to perform a required qualifying act does not prevent assumption of the office but is considered a breach of trust that will allow the court to remove the trustee at the request of a beneficiary and to appoint another trustee (Restatement [Third] of Trusts § 37).

Powers of the Trustee

The powers of the trustee are determined by the following:

- The express authority granted by the terms of the trust instrument
- The statutes in the state in which the trust is established (for an example of the powers granted by a typical state statute, see N.Y. EPTL § 11–1.1)

The powers granted to the trustee by the trust document are often purposely broad to give the trustee the flexibility, like that of the owner-settlor, to manage and administer the trust property. It is common, in modern trusts, to give the trustee wide discretionary powers to determine and resolve problems that the settlor could not have foreseen.

EXAMPLE: By the terms of the trust, Hannah, the trustee, is given discretionary power to "use and disburse principal as well as income if, in the opinion of the trustee, it is necessary for the education or medical care of the beneficiary."

A trustee in the trust instrument is granted the power to

1. sell assets, including real estate, and reinvest the proceeds.
2. lease or rent trust property.
3. carry on a business.
4. vote stock and give proxies.
5. lend or borrow money, including pledging or mortgaging trust property.
6. hire attorneys, stockbrokers, accountants, and insurance agents.
7. compromise, settle, contest, or arbitrate claims and disputes.
8. subdivide, exchange, develop, or improve real property.
9. do anything necessary to carry out any of the above.
10. do whatever a legal owner of property can do subject to the required performance of the trustee to act as a fiduciary.

Duties of the Trustee

In general, a trust does not exist unless specific actions and enforceable duties are performed by the trustee, such as a duty to manage the property in some manner or to exercise discretion or judgment (Restatement [Third] of Trusts § 3). The settlor's mere order to the trustee to hold the property in trust without any direction as to its use or distribution does not suffice to create a valid trust; it creates, instead, a passive trust that the law declares void (see Chapter 13).

EXAMPLE: In his will, Drew, the decedent, gives $100,000 to Howard and expresses the hope that Howard will use the money "for religious and family purposes." Such phraseology does not clearly indicate Drew is "settling" or creating a trust. He has not identified the duties Howard must perform as the trustee of an active trust. Drew might well have intended the $100,000 as a gift to Howard with "advice" on its use.

When a trust is created, it establishes a fiduciary relationship of trust and confidence between the trustee and beneficiary, in which the trustee, as the fiduciary, must faithfully follow the directions of the trust and be loyal to the beneficiary throughout its duration. Acting as a fiduciary, the trustee has the following duties.

1. *Duty of performance and due care (Restatement [Third] of Trusts §§ 76, 77)*

   - The trustee's main duty is to carry out the terms and purpose of the trust. The trustee is personally liable, i.e., must pay out of personal funds, for any loss sustained by failure to perform the duties of the trust unless the failure can be justified. There is no personal liability for loss sustained if the trustee has exercised the degree of care a reasonable person would exercise under the circumstances.

   - The trustee can delegate the performance of some personal duties to others (Restatement [Third] of Trusts § 80). The case of *U.A. of Joliet v. First National Bank of Joliet*, 93 Ill.App.3d 890, 49 Ill. Dec. 250, 417 N.E.2d 1077 (1981), illustrates a trustee's inability to delegate duties.

   - The trustee has a fiduciary duty to use ordinary, reasonable skill, prudence, and diligence in the administration of the trust and in the performance of trust duties (Restatement [Third] of Trusts § 77). In other words, the trustee must use the care a reasonable, prudent person would exercise under the circumstances. In the case of *Law v. Law*, 753 A.2d 443 (2000), the court defined a trustee's responsibility as follows: "… trustees are held to a prudent investment standard in the management and investment of a trust's assets … and must act with the skill, care, diligence and prudence that a man of ordinary prudence would exercise in dealing with his own property…." The law does not hold a trustee who acts in accord with such a rule responsible for errors in judgment.

   EXAMPLE: Maxwell Daniels transfers 100 shares of stock to Stacy Robertson in trust to hold and invest for the benefit of Maxwell's invalid mother, Beatrice.

Whether a trustee, such as Stacy Robertson in the example above, receives compensation for his services or not, he must use at least ordinary care, skill, prudence, and diligence in the execution (performance) of the trust. The degree of ability required may be increased if Stacy actually has greater than normal abilities or if he, as trustee, represented to the settlor that he possessed unusual capabilities before the trust was created. Therefore, professional fiduciaries, such as banks and trust companies with specialists in various areas of trust work, may be held to a higher standard since they give a sense of security to a trust, because of their claims of special expertise and because of the rule that more is expected of a trustee who has a special skill or knowledge of the subject. At the very least, professional fiduciaries must measure up to the standard of skill and prudence of the average, ordinary professional corporate trustee located in the community where the trust is created.

The law would not hold Stacy, as trustee, responsible for every error in judgment he might make, but he is obliged to use the care and skill of an ordinary capable person who is charged with conserving a trust. If Stacy disregards this obligation, he cannot defend himself against liability on the grounds he acted in good faith or did not intentionally misuse the trust property. In addition, Stacy, as trustee, cannot disclaim any personal liability on the grounds he was simply following the practices the settlor had previously followed when ordinary skill and prudence would dictate another course.

ASSIGNMENT 12.3

In performing the following acts, is Stacy Robertson violating his duty of reasonable care of the trust property? Why or why not?

1. Stacy receives a dividend on one of the shares of stock in the amount of $90. He uses it to buy a birthday present for Beatrice.

2. One of the stocks Stacy holds is performing poorly. On the advice of another executive in the corporation where Stacy works, he sells the stock and invests in Goldbrick, Inc., which subsequently falls in value below the level of the stock formerly owned.

2. *Duty of loyalty (Restatement [Third] of Trusts § 78)*

- The trustee is not permitted to profit personally from his position as trustee, other than to receive the compensation allowed by contract or by law. The loyalty duty applies to all persons in a fiduciary capacity.

EXAMPLE: The will of Colin Wilcox appoints Judith Ames trustee of a business, the Wilcox Bakery, for the benefit of Colin's minor sons, Reynold and Richard.

Loyalty to the beneficiaries of the trust is one of the most important duties of a trustee. The duty of loyalty means that the trustee is obliged to act solely in the best interests of the beneficiary. A disloyal act would include any transaction by Judith as trustee that creates a **conflict of interest** between herself and the beneficiaries of the trust, or between the beneficiaries and third persons. A conflict of interest is the creation of circumstances by the fiduciary (trustee) in the administration of the trust that benefits someone other than the beneficiary, thereby establishing the conflict. The other party benefited is most often the trustee, but it could be any person. In the case above, a disloyal act by Judith is not automatically void. The beneficiaries may elect to disaffirm and avoid such transactions or to treat them as legal and binding. As trustee, Judith must avoid placing herself in a position where her personal interest or that of a third person might conflict with the interest of the beneficiaries.

conflict of interest
Divided loyalties (it would be a conflict of interest for an attorney to represent both sides in a dispute).

The trustee must act in the sole and exclusive interests of the beneficiaries. In the above example, *if Judith buys or leases trust property for herself or profits from the sale of her own property to the trust, she commits acts of disloyalty.* It does not matter that Judith acted in good faith or with honest intentions, or that the beneficiaries suffered no loss because of her disloyal acts. It is also immaterial that the trustee has made no profit for herself from her disloyal transaction, even though in most cases she does benefit in some manner. When responsible for such disloyal acts, the trustee (Judith) may be held liable for the amount of gain to herself or a third person, and the court may even remove her from the trusteeship. These strict standards are designed not only to prevent actual unfair dealing but also to help trustees avoid a conflict of interest.

⚖ *Ethical Issue*

ASSIGNMENT 12.4

Judith Ames performs the following acts in the course of trusteeship. Are they disloyal? Are they voidable? What additional facts, if any, would you need in order to answer these questions?

1. In the example above, Judith buys a display case from the bakery. She pays fair market value for it. Reynold is fully aware of the purchase.

2. Colin Wilcox dies and his executor prepares to sell some real estate as instructed by the will. Judith withholds one piece of property from the sale so a friend may buy it. Her friend pays the amount of the property's appraised value.

3. As trustee, Judith persuades the bakery manager to sign a contract to buy flour from the Hanrahan Co. for the next year. Hanrahan does not offer the lowest contract price for flour, nor is there any evidence that its product is better than that of other companies; however, the Ameses and the Hanrahans have been friends for many years.

3. *Duty to take possession of and preserve trust property (Restatement [Third] of Trusts § 76)*

- The trustee has a duty to take possession of and preserve the trust property from possible loss or damage, and if the property includes outstanding debts, the trustee has the duty to collect them, *but the trustee must not add the money collected to his own bank account.*

EXAMPLE: Chao Wang creates a living trust that consists of an apartment building, stocks, bonds, and promissory notes for the benefit of his son, Jiang. He names as trustee his sister, Lin, who is an attorney.

In accordance with the terms of the trust instrument, Lin has the duty to take possession of the property. If the trust property consists of money or goods and chattels, she should take immediate possession of the chattels and open a separate fiduciary bank account for the cash. Such an account should be identified as a trust account, i.e., "Lin Wang, Trustee for Jiang Wang." Since Lin handles funds for the benefit of Jiang, she has a duty to keep the trust property separate from her own individual property and from property held for other trusts. Since the trust property includes promissory notes, bonds, shares of stock, and a deed to the apartment, Lin should take possession of the documents representing title (ownership) to such property and place them in a safe deposit box registered in the name of the trust. If you are a paralegal who works for Lin, you should remind her that *all trust property should be clearly distinguished from Lin's own property.* If it is not, Lin will have the burden of proving which commingled property belongs to whom and might even lose her own property in the process if a court rules that the mixture of trust and personal property belongs to the trust. Possession is usually obtained from the settlor, or, if the trust was created in a will (a testamentary trust), from the named executor or personal representative. The failure to act promptly and reasonably to secure possession of the trust property makes the trustee personally liable for any loss caused by such negligence.

⚖️ *Ethical Issue*

In brief, Lin has the duty to perform whatever acts a reasonably prudent businesswoman would deem necessary in order to preserve and protect the trust property. Such acts would include placing cash in a trust account; filing legal documents such as deeds and mortgages; depositing important legal papers, documents, and valuable personal property in an appropriate place such as a safe deposit box; paying taxes on realty and maintaining the property in reasonable condition to avoid deterioration; transferring shares of stock to the appropriate person's name; maintaining adequate insurance coverage on all appropriate trust property; and the like.

ASSIGNMENT 12.5

Are the following acts examples of a violation of the trustee's duty to preserve and protect the trust property? What additional facts would you want to know to assist you in answering the questions?

1. Lin withdraws a substantial part of the trust fund from its bank account and gives it to a friend to invest. Her friend is not a professional investor, and the advice proves shortsighted financially. All the investments depreciate.

2. Same facts as in question 1 above except the friend's advice is very lucky. The earnings on the investments suggested by Lin's friend triple the trust account.

3. The apartment that Lin holds in trust for Jiang has a defective staircase. While on a visit to the apartment, Flora Atkinson falls down the stairs and is injured. Was Lin's failure to repair the staircase a breach of her fiduciary duty?

4. *Duty to invest the trust property (Restatement [Third] of Trusts §§ 79, 80)*

   • The trustee is required to invest the money or property in enterprises or transactions that will yield an income to the trust.

   EXAMPLE: Carmine diGrazia, a widower living in Maryland, created a testamentary trust of $100,000 and his interest in a building construction business for the benefit of his two sons, Paola and Carlo. He appoints as trustee his cousin, Katarina, who is his accountant. Carmine dies and Katarina assumes trusteeship.

Katarina must make the trust property productive by investing it in income-producing investments as soon as possible. Delay could constitute negligence and make her liable for any loss. Generally, Katarina's investment policies are controlled by the authority granted her by Carmine, by the court, and by statute. Today some states establish by statute a list of specific types of investments that may or must be made by the trustee. The law of the state of Maryland lists examples of the statutory investments fiduciaries may make.

Md. Estates and Trusts Code Ann. § 15–106 Lawful Investments
(a) List of lawful investments—The following investments shall be lawful investments for any person:
   (1) Debentures issued by federal intermediate credit banks or by banks for cooperatives;
   (2) Bonds issued by federal land banks or by the Federal Home Loan Bank Board;
   (3) Mortgages, bonds, or notes secured by a mortgage or deed of trust, or debentures issued by the Federal Housing Administration;
   (4) Obligations of national mortgage associations;
   (5) Shares, free-share accounts, certificates of deposit, or investment certificates of any insured financial institution, as defined in § 13–301 (h) of this article;
   (6) Bonds or other obligations issued by a housing authority pursuant to the provisions of Article 44A of the Code, or issued by any public housing authority or agency in the United States, when such bonds or other obligations are secured by a pledge of annual contributions to be paid by the United States or any agency of the United States;
   (7) Obligations issued or guaranteed by the International Bank for Reconstruction and Development.

* * *

(e) *Liability for lack of reasonable care*—This section shall not be construed as relieving any person from the duty of exercising reasonable care in selecting securities.

* * *

(g) *Other investments*—This section shall not be construed to make unlawful any investment not listed in this section.

Katarina must periodically review her investment methods and policies. If she fails to examine or review at regular intervals the investments that she has made, she can be liable for the loss or decrease in the value of the trust property.

The case of *Witmer v. Blair*, 588 S.W.2d 222 (Mo.App. 1979), involved this duty. Since the trustee of the testamentary trust had kept no records and had not invested the money of the trust, the court ruled the trustee had violated the fiduciary duty to "make the trust property productive" by properly investing the trust funds.

Unless the trust property consists solely of real estate or a family business, corporate trustees, with their experience and expertise, are sometimes selected over family members when trust property is to be invested. A comparison of average annual rates of return of the management and investment performance of professional corporate trustees over a number of years can be evaluated and ranked. This comparison is useful for two reasons. It allows the settlor to

1. choose a comfort level on the degree of risk he or she is willing to take in the investment, e.g., *safe* versus *high risk*.

2. select a leading corporate trustee who has a history of successful, dependable, and acceptable investment strategies.

ASSIGNMENT 12.6

Katarina makes the following investments. Do they violate her duty to make the trust property productive? What additional facts must you know to assist you in answering the following?

1. Carmine had recently complained that his building construction business was unprofitable. At the time of his death, he was preparing to sell it to a business associate. Katarina, who was also named executrix of Carmine's estate, executes the sale in the name of the estate and adds the money to the trust fund.

2. Katarina buys bonds issued by the Vittore Emanuele Lodge, to which Carmine had belonged. The bonds pay 4 percent annual interest. Several of Katarina's neighbors and friends hold similar bonds. Other kinds of debentures that cost the same price yield higher rates of interest.

3. After Carmine's death, Katarina is preoccupied with details of his funeral and putting his affairs in order. She neglects to deposit part of the cash portion of the trust, i.e., $8,000, in a bank until it is too late to earn interest on the money for the quarter. Carmine kept the $8,000 in a small safe at home.

5. *Duty to make payments of income and principal to the named beneficiaries (Restatement [Third] of Trusts § 49)*

- Most trusts establish two kinds of beneficiaries: income beneficiaries, who receive the net income from the trust property for a determined number of years or for the beneficiaries' lives, and remainder beneficiaries, who receive the principal of the trust after the rights of the income beneficiaries in the trust are terminated. A person who receives the property after an income beneficiary is called the remainderman.

EXAMPLE: Fionna Brosniak, the oldest child in her family, is named trustee of a large sum of money in the will of her aunt. The trust is for the benefit of Fionna's brothers and sisters, who are to receive investment income from the money until the youngest attains majority. At that time, according to the will, Fionna is to receive the balance (principal) of the trust fund. Fionna's brothers and sisters are the income beneficiaries, and Fionna is the remainder beneficiary and remainderman.

If the settlor provides for separate disposition of the trust income and trust principal, and if the trust property is cash, it is advisable that the trustee open two accounts, one for the principal and one for the interest. In the example above, this would be necessary. The aunt not only designated income-receiving beneficiaries but also chose Fionna to receive the principal as a lump sum. Fionna should open a separate principal account so that she may readily take her gift when the time comes. Also, when there are two or more beneficiaries, as in this case, the trustee, Fionna, must deal with them impartially, i.e., treat them equally.

It may happen that during the course of the trust administration, Fionna will obtain money or property other than what she was given in the trust. In such cases she must decide whether to credit the receipt of such property to the income or principal account of the trust. If a trust agreement does not specify how to allocate the trust funds, a statute, the Uniform (or Revised Uniform) Principal and Income Act adopted in most states, provides for the method of allocation. These acts define in detail the duties of the trustee in regard to the receipt of property and its disbursement into the income or principal account. Trustees are personally liable for any loss if they fail to comply with the trust agreement or the statute.

The general rule for disbursement is that money paid for the use of the trust property and any benefit received from the employment of that property are to be treated as trust income, while substitutes for the original trust property, such as the proceeds from the sale of the property, are to be considered trust principal. When allocating receipts or expenses between the income beneficiaries and remaindermen, the general rule is that ordinary or current receipts and expenses are allocated or assigned to the income beneficiary, whereas extraordinary receipts and expenses are allocated to the remaindermen (see Exhibit 12.5).

EXAMPLE: Elijah wills his property to a trust. The trustees are to pay the income from the property to his wife, Olivia, during her life and to distribute the property to their children when Olivia dies. Elijah can direct the trustees to allocate receipts and charge expenses between the income beneficiary (Olivia) and the remaindermen (children).

ASSIGNMENT 12.7

If the trust agreement in the Fionna example authorized her to distribute income "at best, quarterly, and at least, annually," would she be acting within her fiduciary obligations if she withheld certain amounts from the quarterly distributions for possible emergency expenses and thereby created a separate fund?

6. *Duty to account (Restatement [Third] of Trusts § 83).*

- The trustee must keep accurate records so that it can be determined whether the trust has been properly administered.

EXHIBIT 12.5	**Allocation of Ordinary and Extraordinary Receipts and Expenses between Beneficiaries and Remaindermen**

Ordinary—Income Beneficiary	**Extraordinary—Remaindermen**
Receipts	Receipts
Rents	Proceeds from sale or exchange of
Royalties	trust principal
Cash dividends	**Stock Dividends**
Interest	**Stock Splits***
	Settlement of claims for injury to
	principal
Expenses	Expenses
Insurance	Extraordinary repairs
Ordinary taxes	Principal amortization
Ordinary repairs	Costs incurred in the sale or
Depreciation	purchase of principal
Interest payments	Long-term improvements

*A stock split is the issuance by a corporation of a number of new shares in exchange for each old share held by a stockholder; the result is a proportional change in the number of shares owned by each stockholder. A common purpose of a stock split is to reduce the per share market price to encourage wider trading and ownership and eventually a higher per share value (i.e., price).

stock dividend
A dividend of shares of stock distributed to stockholders.

stock split
One share of stock is split into a larger number of shares resulting in a proportional change in the number of shares owned by each stockholder.

EXAMPLE: Nicholas Walheimer creates a living trust for the benefit of his mentally handicapped son, David. He names Felix Basch trustee of the fund, which consists of $65,000 worth of stock. Felix is given the power to sell and invest the stock. Nicholas dies. Frederika Wolfram is appointed David's personal and property guardian.

Felix has the duty to render an account (complete and accurate information) of his administrative activities at reasonable intervals to those who are "interested" in the trust, namely, the settlor, Nicholas, while alive, and the beneficiary, David, acting through his personal and property guardian, Frederika. The trustee, Felix, alone has the right to manage and control the trust property. He must retain trust documents and records, secure and file vouchers for all expenditures and disbursements, and keep an accurate and complete set of books. He is obliged to show these to Nicholas and Frederika on request. Felix has a fiduciary duty to account voluntarily (e.g., quarterly) for changes in the trust property. If the trustee fails to perform these duties, the trustee may be removed by the court, denied compensation, or even charged with the cost to the beneficiary of an accounting proceeding.

ASSIGNMENT 12.8

Felix has been a trustee for two years. He tries to make periodic reports on the trust, but this is not always feasible because he frequently travels while conducting business. In performing the following acts, did Felix violate his duty to account? (These are opinion questions, but you must give reasons for your answers).

1. Felix sells some stock from the trust and buys land in the Santo Affonso Valley. Frederika asks him to account for this, so he sends her copies of the contract of sale and the deed of title.

2. At the end of the calendar year, Felix sends a balance sheet indicating the financial status of the trust property but neglects to include a dividend paid one week before the issue date of the balance sheet. Later he discovers his error. He sends Frederika a receipt for payment of the dividend, informing her that he will rectify the error on the next annual statement.

3. Felix has the second annual statement prepared by an accountant. After reading it, Frederika complains that it is too technical for her to understand. Felix replies that the statement is correct to the best of his knowledge and that he has fulfilled the duty to account required of a trustee.

ASSIGNMENT 12.9

1. Alexei Burov, a customer's representative in a stock brokerage firm, is appointed sole trustee of the Durham Trust. If Alexei uses the firm to buy and sell stock for the trust, is this a violation of Alexei's fiduciary duty? If so, which duty?

2. Continuing with the Alexei Burov case in question 1, if Alexei temporarily put the money obtained from the sale of trust property, e.g., shares of stock owned by the trust, into his own bank account, would this violate his fiduciary duty? If so, which duty?

3. Lena Balicki is an attorney and sole trustee of a trust. An unhappy beneficiary of the trust demands that Lena transfer the trust property to an investment company, which will manage and invest the property. Must Lena make the transfer? Would this violate her fiduciary duty? If so, which duty?

Liability of Trustee to Beneficiary

A breach of trust by the trustee may occur in a variety of ways, which in turn determine the remedies available and the party who is entitled to bring suit. To restore the damage committed by a trustee, the beneficiary has the right to judicial remedies at law or a suit in equity. An action at law is a civil lawsuit commenced by the person, called the plaintiff, who seeks the remedy at law called damages, i.e., to be compensated monetarily.

- The beneficiary can maintain a civil lawsuit to compel the trustee to reimburse the trust for any loss or depreciation in value of the trust property caused by the trustee's breach of the trust instrument (Restatement [Second] of Trusts §§ 199, 205).

  EXAMPLE: Sharona has agreed to act as trustee for Sandy's benefit. The trust property is a lake cottage. Sharona has obtained the deed but has not insured the property. Lightning strikes the cottage, and it is destroyed. Sharona would be personally responsible and liable for this loss.

- The beneficiary can obtain an injunction, i.e., a court order, to compel the trustee to do, or refrain from doing, an act that would constitute a breach of trust.

  EXAMPLE: Reuben Washington holds shares of stock in trust for Evelyn Sandberg. According to the terms of the trust agreement, he is not authorized to sell the stock. The value of the stock has recently increased substantially. Reuben intends to sell the stock. Evelyn, on learning of the pending sale, could obtain an injunction from the equity court forbidding the sale by Reuben.

- The beneficiary can trace and recover the trust property that the trustee has wrongfully taken, unless the property has been acquired by a purchaser who, believing the trustee has a right to sell, pays an adequate price and purchases the property without having been informed of the breach of trust (Restatement [Second] of Trusts §§ 202, 284).

EXAMPLE: In the preceding example, Reuben sells the stock to Deidre Harrington, who pays full market value for the stock unaware that Reuben has no right to sell the stock or that the stock is trust property. Deidre becomes the owner of the stock. Evelyn would not have a right to sue Deidre, a good-faith purchaser, but she would have a right to sue Reuben for damages because of his fraud.

- The beneficiary can request the court of equity to remove the trustee for misconduct and to appoint a successor trustee (Restatement [Third] of Trusts §§ 34, 37). The *Witmer v. Blair* case previously discussed illustrates the removal of a trustee for misconduct, i.e., failure to invest the trust property.

EXAMPLE: Ronald Caster is the trustee, and Vincent Prima is the beneficiary of a trust. The trust agreement gives Ronald the discretion of determining the amount of income from the trust property that Vincent shall receive each year. The amount actually given to Vincent by Ronald causes a great deal of friction between them. Vincent can petition the court to remove Ronald as trustee, but the court will not do so unless Vincent can prove that the hostility causes Ronald to mismanage his trusteeship. By itself, hostility between the trustee and beneficiary is not enough reason for the court to remove the trustee.

- The beneficiary can sue for specific performance to compel the trustee to perform the duties created by the terms of a private trust (Restatement [Second] of Trusts §§ 198, 199).

EXAMPLE: According to the trust agreement, the trustee, Monet Murphy, is to give the trust property to the beneficiary, Julia Anders, when she reaches age 21. Six months have passed since Julia's 21st birthday, and Monet has not transferred the property. Julia sues Monet in the court of equity for specific performance of the agreement. If Julia proves Monet has violated her duty, Monet must complete the transfer.

- The beneficiary can sue for breach of the trustee's loyalty (Restatement [Second] of Trusts § 206). Breach of loyalty by the trustee includes many things. In general, breach of loyalty is any action by the trustee that upsets the trustee–beneficiary relationship. It results from the trustee's failure to administer the trust solely in the interest of the beneficiary.

EXAMPLE: By will, Hollis Stately leaves his ranch, Bluelake, to Lavinia Turner in trust for his son, Francis, directing her to sell or exchange Bluelake for investment securities. Lavinia sells Bluelake for $200,000 and uses the money to buy bonds that she owns. Lavinia has breached the duty of loyalty by "self-dealing" with trust money (the proceeds of the sale).

Cost of a Trustee

Trustees perform work for the trust when they buy, sell, invest, and receive income, on behalf of the beneficiary, and they must be paid, although trustees who are family members may decline compensation. The settlor may provide a reasonable fee for the trustee in the trust instrument; if the settlor does not, state statutes fix the amount, or in the absence of such statutes, the courts will fix a reasonable annual compensation. There is an opinion (originating in common law) that the trustee should not make an unreasonable profit from the trust; therefore the actual amount of compensation is usually a small percentage of the trust's annual income and principal set by statute (see N.J. Stat. Ann. § 3B: 18–24, 18–25). In a testamentary trust, the probate court may set the annual fee for a corporate trustee, such as a bank, at an appropriate percentage of the fair market value of the trust estate. In determining whether the fee charged is reasonable, the court considers the size of the estate, the services performed, the time spent, and the results achieved. In a living trust, fees are generally negotiated. State statutes may also set fees in some cases.

THE BENEFICIARY: THE RECIPIENT OF THE TRUST PROPERTY OR BENEFITS

Every trust must have a beneficiary. In a private trust, the beneficiaries must either be identified by name, description, designation of the class to which the beneficiaries belong, or if no beneficiary is in existence at the time the trust is created (such as a trust for the benefit of unborn children), the trustee must be able to ascertain the identity of the beneficiary within the period of the Rule Against Perpetuities (Restatement [Third] of Trusts § 44). In a charitable trust, however, it is sufficient that the beneficiaries be members of the public at large or a general class of the public (Restatement [Third] of Trusts §§ 46, 47, 28).

To create a private trust, the settlor must name or sufficiently describe a beneficiary or co-beneficiaries, of whom the settlor may himself be one, to receive the equitable interest in the trust property. If the trust instrument describes the beneficiary too vaguely, a court of equity cannot validate the trust. There must be someone to enforce the trust and to ensure that the trustee will faithfully perform the previously mentioned duties. That was the position in the case of *Scotti's Drive In Restaurants, Inc. v. Mile High—Dart In Corp.*, cited earlier, where the court stated, "A trust is an obligation imposed, either expressly or by implication of law, whereby the obligor [trustee] is bound to deal with property over which he has control for the benefit of certain persons [beneficiaries], of whom he may himself be one, and any one of whom may enforce the obligation." Consequently, the beneficiaries of a trust must be specifically identified.

> **EXAMPLE:** Elijah establishes a trust and directs Olivia, the trustee, to pay the trust income to "whomever Olivia selects" without adequately describing the persons or class of persons from which the selection is to be made. Such a trust is too vague and is invalid.

Any person who is capable of owning property, including infants, insane persons in some states, and public or private corporations, may be a beneficiary in a trust, but incompetents and minors generally require guardians to act as "beneficiaries" for them. Trusts in which aliens, the United States, a state, a municipality, and a foreign country are beneficiaries have been upheld. In sum, the beneficiary may be any entity capable of taking title to property in the manner as a person, whether natural or created by law, e.g., a corporation, state, or nation. It is important to note that the beneficiary of the trust, however, need not have capacity to hold property or to make a contract, since the trustee has legal title to and control of the trust property. Many trusts are created specifically because the beneficiary lacks legal or actual capacity to manage property without assistance.

> **EXAMPLE:** Martha Kilpatrick places $20,000 in trust for the benefit of the Red Cross. The Red Cross is a "corporate person." It is a definite beneficiary. This trust is as valid as if Martha had created it for the benefit of a natural person.

> **EXAMPLE:** Giovanna Bonetto belongs to a card club. The members meet once a month to play cards and perform works of charity. She dies and leaves a trust fund to enable the members of the club to continue to carry on their activities. This trust will fail because the card club, as such, is not a "person." The individual members are. If Giovanna's trust had named them individually as beneficiaries, the trust would have been valid.

Although it is required that the beneficiaries be definite, they need not be, and frequently are not, described by name but rather by class designation. Examples of such designation are "my grandchildren" or "my issue," in which cases the identification of the beneficiaries is ascertainable, i.e., capable of being determined (Restatement [Third] of Trusts § 45). Words such as *friends, family*, and *relatives* used to designate beneficiaries, have sometimes caused trusts to fail for lack of definite beneficiaries because such terms have broad and varied application. A trust to benefit "relatives," however, occasionally proves an exception to the rule. A court, construing "relatives" to mean those who would inherit the settlor's property according to the statutes of descent and distribution rather than those who are related to the settlor either closely or remotely by either blood or marriage, would in all likelihood uphold the trust (Restatement [Third] of Trusts § 45). Similarly, interpretation of the word *family* to mean "the settlor's spouse and issue" leads to the same result (Restatement [Third] of Trusts § 45). Note that this requirement of definiteness of beneficiary for a private trust directly opposes the requirement of indefiniteness of beneficiary for a public (charitable) trust.

Beneficiaries need not always be persons or institutions. As the case *In re Searight's Estate*, 87 Ohio App. 417, 95 N.E.2d 779 (1950), illustrates, placing property "in trust for" the care and benefit of pets, such as dogs or cats, or for the maintenance of pet cemeteries has been declared valid and enforceable because of the social interests that are involved. Compare *In re Estate of Russell*, 69 Cal.2d 200, 70 Cal.Rptr. 561, 444 P.2d 353 (1968).

ASSIGNMENT 12.10

1. Harding Mulholland lived at the home of his niece, Cecelia, and her husband, Edwin. He provided in his will that a trust be set up for the benefit of his nieces and nephews, Cecelia being the only one of that class at the time. Subsequently, another niece, Teresa, was born, and Cecelia died in the same year. When Harding died, Edwin petitioned the court to set aside the trust, claiming that Harding neither knew nor could have known of the current beneficiary, Teresa. Should the trust fail for lack of a definite beneficiary?

2. Willis Rokeby lives in Bangor, Maine. For five months each year, he visits his daughter in Texarkana. He hires Jacques Santin, a citizen of Canada, to take care of his house in Maine. He pays Jacques a small salary and creates a testamentary trust of the house and surrounding land for Jacques's benefit. After Willis's death, his sister, named trustee in the trust instrument, claims that Jacques cannot be the beneficiary because he is not subject to the laws of either Maine or the United States. Is she correct?

Nature of the Beneficiary's Interest

The length of time the beneficiary holds the equitable interest in the trust property may be limited to a period of years, to the life of the beneficiary or that of someone else, to a condition precedent, to a condition subsequent, or to the nonoccurrence of a specified event.

> **EXAMPLE:** Patrice Avery sets aside stocks and bonds for living trusts for each of her three children: The first is created for her son, Vinton, on the condition that he return to the family home in West Virginia. This trust is based on a condition precedent. The second is for her daughter, Susanna, on the condition that she continue to support Patrice as she had been doing. This trust is created on a condition subsequent. The third is for her daughter, Alberta, as long as she continues to study medicine at State University. This trust is created on the nonhappening of a specific event, e.g., Alberta's switching to another course of study or another school.

Note that both Susanna's and Alberta's trusts begin immediately but the possibility of the premature termination of the trusts exists, whereas Vinton's does not begin until he has complied with the condition precedent.

The beneficiary's equitable interest in realty (real property) usually passes on his or her death to the beneficiary's heirs or devisees; personal property passes to the beneficiary's personal representative, e.g., the administrator or executor. Another possible result is that the trust instrument itself may provide that the beneficiary's interest terminates on death, as in the case in which the beneficiary receives a life estate.

A single trust may have more than one beneficiary. Multiple beneficiaries usually hold the property as tenants in common unless the settlor expressly makes the beneficiaries joint tenants or tenants by the entireties. The doctrine of survivorship applies if the co-beneficiaries are joint tenants or tenants by the entireties (Restatement [Third] of Trusts §§ 43, 44, 48). For example, if Cody and Beckett are co-beneficiaries as joint tenants, and Cody dies, Beckett will then be the sole beneficiary and will own the entire equitable interest in the trust property, just as any joint owner with the right of survivorship succeeds to full ownership upon the death of the other joint owner.

The beneficiary of a trust is free to transfer the interest in trust property by mortgage or devise, in the absence of any restriction imposed by statute or by the terms of the trust, to the same extent that a person who holds both equitable and legal titles is free to do so (Restatement [Third] of Trusts § 51). In some states, all transfers of beneficial interests must be in writing and signed by the beneficiary; in other states, this requirement applies only to the transfer of real property (Restatement [Third] of Trusts § 53).

Unless prohibited by statute or the trust agreement, beneficiaries may ordinarily transfer their interest in a trust by an assignment. This legal transaction allows the beneficiary to transfer to another the benefits of the trust. This may be done to make a gift of the trust benefits or to pay the beneficiary's debts.

> **EXAMPLE:** Owen receives an income as a beneficiary of a trust. He assigns his interest (transfers his right to receive income) to Carissa. Thereafter, Carissa receives the income from the trust.

Creditors may attach the beneficiary's equitable interest in trust property unless statutes or trust provisions exempt the interest from creditors' claims (Restatement

[Third] of Trusts § 56). If statutes exempt a legal interest from creditors' claims, a corresponding equitable interest of a beneficiary in trust property is also exempt, e.g., homestead exemptions (which apply to both legal and equitable interests). The method by which a creditor reaches an equitable interest varies from state to state. The only remedy in some states is a creditor's bill in chancery (equity) in which the creditor commences the lawsuit in an equity court. In other states, the equitable interest is subject to execution, attachment, and garnishment by the beneficiary's creditors just as if it were a legal interest. An exception occurs when the settlor has restricted the trust so that the beneficiary cannot assign nor creditors reach the equitable interest of the beneficiary; such a trust is commonly called a spendthrift trust (see the discussion in Chapter 13).

Trust Property

The trust property is the property interest that is transferred to the trustee to hold for the benefit of another. It is sometimes called the *res, corpus, principal*, or *subject matter* of the trust. Any transferable interest in an object of ownership may become trust property. This includes ownership of real or personal property. Thus, a fee simple estate in land, a co-owner's interest (joint tenants, tenants in common, and the like), a mortgage, a life estate in land, a right to remove coal, a business interest, promissory notes, bonds or shares of stock (securities), a trade secret, copyright, patent, or cash could serve as trust property. Examples of nontransferable property are government pensions, existing spendthrift trusts, or tort claims for wrongful injury, i.e., the victim's right to sue a negligent party for personal injury. Nontransferable property interests may not be the subject matter of a trust.

A trust involving the transfer of personal property only may be created orally, but a settlor transferring title to real property to a trust must comply with the state statute, i.e., the Statute of Frauds, requiring a written agreement establishing the details of the trust. The latter requirement is designed to prevent fraud and perjury (see further discussion below). Two cases illustrating this rule are *In re Estate of Gates*, 876 So. 2d 1059 (Miss. 2004), and *Matter of Catanio*, 306 N. J. Super. 439, 703 A.2d 988 (1971). In the former, the Mississippi Supreme Court said, "An express trust may be oral but only if real property is not involved." In the latter case, the New Jersey Supreme Court held "When real property is involved, the trust must be in writing." See also the *Mahoney* case, cited earlier, where the court stated that a "trust involving only personal property may be instituted [commenced] without being reduced to writing." The terms of the written trust agreement as designated by the settlor must include the purpose of the trust, the length of time the trust will last, and a description and conveyance of the trust property. It must also include the names of the trustee and beneficiary, and the powers, duties, and rights of such parties, including how much the beneficiaries are to receive, and when they will receive it. It is not necessary to use a particular form or particular language to frame the trust as long as the settlor makes these elements clear.

ASSIGNMENT 12.11

Read the Durham trust (see Exhibit 12.2) and determine whether the requirements in the preceding two paragraphs have been met.

The English **Statute of Frauds** was enacted in 1677 to prevent fraud and perjury between sellers and buyers by requiring certain kinds of contracts to be written. Its American counterparts, drawn chiefly from sections 4 and 17 of the original statute, demand that a written contract, signed by the parties, be used in certain transactions. If the trust property transferred into an *inter vivos* (living) trust is an interest in land, the Statute of Frauds requires that, if it is to be enforced, it must be written, signed, and include the essential elements of a trust (Restatement [Third] of Trusts, § 22). Many states have enacted statutes that require certain trusts to be written to be valid. South Dakota is an example.

> **So. Dak. Cod. Laws Ann. § 43–10–4**
> Requisites of Trust Relating to Real Property
> No trust in relation to real property is valid unless created or declared:
> 1. By a written instrument, subscribed by the trustee or by the trustee's agent thereto authorized in writing;
> 2. By the instrument under which the trustee claims the estate affected; or
> 3. By operation of law.

In addition to requiring a written agreement whenever land is transferred in trust, the method of transfer is also strictly regulated. Land must be transferred by specific legal documents, e.g., either a deed or a will. Personal property, on the other hand, may be simply delivered to the trustee.

EXAMPLE: Liz signed a trust agreement transferring title to Greenvale, a country home, to Gabriela in trust for the benefit of Harry. Liz executed and delivered the deed to Greenvale to Gabriela. Liz and Gabriela are parties to a trust agreement. Liz is the grantor. Gabriela is the trustee and holds the legal title that she received from Liz. Harry is the beneficiary *(cestui que trust)* of the agreement and holds equitable title.

The agreement satisfies the state Statute of Frauds because it is written. It also complies with requirements for trusts of this nature, i.e., trusts to which real property is transferred, and is therefore enforceable.

ASSIGNMENT 12.12

Simon Rothstein executes a trust instrument with the Third National Bank, placing his lakeshore property in trust for the benefit of his nephew, Norman. However, Norman is unaware of the trust. Simon dies one year later. His widow, Helen, contends that the trust is not valid because it was not signed by Norman. Norman contends that it is valid. Who is right?

As noted above, the trust instrument must either specifically describe the trust property or clearly define the manner to be followed in identifying it. The validity of a trust depends on its enforceability. If a court is to enforce a trust, the trust property must be *in existence* (i.e., definite and certain on the *date* the trust is created, or definitely ascertainable) and *owned* by the settlor.

EXAMPLE: Nadia Bailey is an investor and collector of art. If Nadia attempts to create a trust by declaring herself trustee of the next work of art she buys, no trust is created, because the trust property is neither specifically identifiable nor owned and in existence at the time of the trust creation.

However, a testamentary trust created in the "residue of the decedent's estate" *is* valid, even though the exact amount of the residue cannot be determined until the decedent's assets and liabilities are known. In this case, the facts needed to

Statute of Frauds
State laws that provide that no lawsuit or civil action shall be maintained on certain classes of oral contracts unless the agreement is put in writing in a note or memorandum and signed by the party to be charged, i.e., the person being sued, or an authorized agent of the person.

specifically identify the amount of the residue do exist on the date the trust is created, i.e., the date of the testator's death.

EXAMPLE: In a living trust instrument, Alicia Schell states, "I give to Joanna Warfield, to hold and to manage, the amount of my savings and checking accounts for the benefit of Roberta Polenek." This instrument creates a valid trust. The trust corpus is not stated, but it is ascertainable. It is the amount of money in Alicia's checking and savings accounts on the date of the trust instrument's execution.

The fact that trust property may change from time to time during the trust period does not make the trust void.

EXAMPLE: Alexa Knight, trustee of real estate for the benefit of Letita Kruse, has the power of sale and reinvestment. She sells part of the land for cash and deposits this cash in Citizens Bank. She buys bonds for the trust and pays for them by drawing a check on Citizens Bank. She has effected three changes in the trust property—real estate into cash, cash into a claim on the bank (i.e., a right to withdraw the amount deposited), and the claim on the bank into bonds. The trust property has changed, but the trust is still valid.

TERMINATION OF TRUSTS

A trust may be terminated in the following ways.

- In accordance with the trust's terms (Restatement [Third] of Trusts §§ 63, 61)

   EXAMPLE: Stephanie gives Nina $100,000 to hold and invest in trust for Katherine and to pay the income produced to Katherine annually for 10 years. At the end of the 10 years, the trust terminates.

- By the completion of the trust's valid purpose (Restatement [Third] of Trusts § 65)

   EXAMPLE: Stephanie gives Nina $100,000 to hold and invest and to pay the income produced to Stephanie's mother annually for her lifetime and then return the trust property to Stephanie. When Stephanie's mother dies and the property is returned, the trust purpose is accomplished.

- By revocation by the settlor when allowed by the terms of the trust (Restatement [Third] of Trusts § 63)

   EXAMPLE: Stephanie creates a trust that includes a provision that states "This trust is revocable and the settlor reserves the right to amend or revoke the trust in whole or in part at any time." The trust will terminate if Stephanie chooses to revoke it.

- By merger of all interests (legal and equitable) in the same person (Restatement [Third] of Trusts §§ 65, 69)

   EXAMPLE: Stephanie creates a trust in which she names herself trustee and names Nina and herself the beneficiaries. Nina dies, and Stephanie now holds both the legal and equitable titles to the trust property by herself. Since the titles have merged in one person, the trust terminates.

- On the request of all the beneficiaries when there is no express purpose that requires continuation of the trust (Restatement [Second] of Trusts § 337)

The majority of United States courts holds that if one or more of the settlor's purposes for creating the trust can still be achieved by the continuance of the trust, the court will not allow termination unless all beneficiaries join in the request for termination with the settlor. When a trust does terminate, the trustee must also account for all assets and obtain a receipt and release from the recipients. Remember, a trust does not terminate for want of a trustee.

Key Terms

legal title [of a trust]	declaration of trust	conflict of interest
equitable title [of a trust]	revocable trust	stock dividend
Uniform Trust Code (UTC)	irrevocable trust	stock split
trust agreement	disclaimer	Statute of Frauds

Review Questions

1. What is meant by the statement "The most unique feature of a trust is that a trust splits title to property"? Explain.

2. In trust law, what is the difference between legal and equitable title?

3. In what ways can a trust be created?

4. What are the essential elements of a valid trust?

5. What are the qualifications required for a person to become a settlor, the creator of a trust?

6. Why would a settlor create a revocable trust, and what are the advantages of making the trust irrevocable?

7. What are the standard powers and duties of a trustee who, like a personal representative, is a fiduciary?

8. What are the beneficiary's rights for breach of trust by a trustee? Explain.

9. Must a person have contractual capacity to be a beneficiary of a trust? Explain.

10. May a settlor be the sole trustee and sole beneficiary of a trust? Explain.

11. Does a trust always have to be in writing? Explain.

12. Are there any limits on the kind of property that can be placed in trust? Explain.

13. How are trusts terminated?

Case Problems

Problem 1

Suki Nakajima, a widow in failing health, intends to leave her estate equally to her adult children, a daughter, Tomoko, and a son, Hito. Suki has two concerns. With good reason, she lacks confidence that Hito can manage property because of his irresponsible spending habits, and she does not want any property she gives to Tomoko to pass to Tomoko's husband. Suki writes, but does not sign, a letter to her best friend, Tomura, requesting that he manage money for the benefit of her two children, and asking him, if he agrees, to sign and return the letter. After receiving the letter back from Tomura with his signature and acceptance, Suki mails a cashier's check for $200,000 to Tomura. Answer and explain the following:

A. Is Suki's letter a valid holographic will?

B. Is the use of the words *trust* or *trustee* in a formal written document necessary to create a valid trust?

C. Does Suki's letter create an *inter vivos* (living) trust? See *In re Barker's Estate*, 82 Misc.2d 974, 370 N.Y.S.2d 404 (1975).

D. *If* a trust exists, must it be written and signed to be valid?

Problem 2

In a testamentary trust, Alanzo Lopez names his friend, Ricardo LaPalma, trustee of substantial property placed in trust for the benefit of Alanzo's wife, Maria, and his sister, Yolanda. Hostility existed between Ricardo and Maria long before the trust was created, and it became worse soon after Alanzo's death when the trust became active. Alanzo gave Ricardo broad discretion in distributing trust income, and when Ricardo distributed a much greater percentage of the trust's annual income to Yolanda than to Maria, Maria became outraged. She demanded that Ricardo be removed as an unsuitable trustee because of his act of disloyalty by favoring one beneficiary over another.

A. Is hostility between a trustee and beneficiary a valid reason for the removal of a trustee?

B. If there were five beneficiaries in the trust and three were pleased with the trustee's actions and two were incensed and wanted the trustee removed, should the "majority rule" apply to this decision?

C. Read and compare the cases *Matter of Brecklein's Estate*, 6 Kan.App.2d 1001, 637 P.2d 444 (1981), and *Edinburg v. Cavers*, 22 Mass. App. Ct. 212, 492 N.E.2d 1171 (1986). What are the circumstances a court should consider before deciding a request for removal of a trustee based on hostility between the trustee and a beneficiary?

Practical Assignments

1. Complete Form SS-4, which can be found on the IRS website, for the Durham Trust established in Exhibit 12.2. The grantor's Social Security number is 554-08-9841.

2. Prepare a sample clause to be included in a trust that terminates the trust when the child identified as the sole beneficiary of the trust reaches the age of 25 years.

3. Find three local banks that provide services as a trustee. Determine what they charge for their services as a trustee.

CLASSIFICATION OF TRUSTS, THE LIVING TRUST, AND OTHER SPECIAL TRUSTS

13

Outline

Objectives

After completing this chapter, you should be able to:

- Identify and define the classes of trusts.

- Explain the uses and functions of the various kinds of trusts.

- Explain the formation, use, advantages, and disadvantages of revocable and irrevocable living trusts.

- Identify and explain the function of Totten, spendthrift, and sprinkling trusts and a pour-over will.

- Prepare preliminary drafts of private express trusts, including living trusts.

- Avoid common errors in the initial drafts of living trusts.

- Explain the pre-death and post-death administration of the revocable living trust.

SCOPE OF THE CHAPTER

This chapter identifies and discusses the various kinds of trusts, including the increasingly popular living *(inter vivos)* trust. The chapter begins with the classification of trusts, followed by an examination of a private express trust, including various examples that eventually lead to a detailed discussion of the living trust. The chapter outlines the steps necessary for drafting trusts, including the accumulation of data through appropriate checklists. Actual drafts of these trusts and a pour-over will are also contained in the chapter, followed by a discussion of pre-death and post-death administration of the revocable living trust.

CLASSIFICATION OF TRUSTS

express trust
A trust created or declared in explicit terms for specific purposes by a written document (deed or will) or an oral declaration.

All trusts may be divided into two major categories, express and implied. An **express trust** is created or declared in explicit terms for specific purposes and is represented by a written document (deed or will) or an oral declaration. A simple statement that a settlor intends to hold property in trust for another creates a trust by declaration. No special words, such as *trust* or *trustee*, are required to create an express trust, provided the intent of the settlor to establish the trust is clear. In most jurisdictions, as previously mentioned, an express trust of real property *must be in writing* to meet the requirements of the Statute of Frauds.

Depending on the purpose for which they are created, express trusts fall into the following subcategories: (1) private or public (charitable) trusts; (2) active or passive trusts; or (3) *inter vivos* (living) or testamentary trusts. The most common types of express trusts are the testamentary and living trusts. The living trust is one of the major topics of this chapter.

implied trust
A trust created by operation of law or the equity court based on the implied or presumed intent of the person who holds legal title and, generally, to prevent fraud.

Implied trust are created not by the settlor's expressed terms but by the implied or presumed intent of the person holding legal title or by a decree (order) of the equity court generally to prevent fraud. Implied trusts are either resulting trusts or constructive trusts (see Exhibit 13.1).

Express Trusts—Private versus Public (Charitable)

Private Trust

A *private trust* is created expressly (orally or in writing) between a person who has the power to be a settlor and one or more trustees who hold legal title to trust property for the financial benefit of a certain named beneficiary or beneficiaries. The following are essential elements of an express private trust.

- The settlor must intend to create a private trust.
- A trustee must be named to administer the trust.
- A beneficiary must be named to enforce the trust.
- The settlor must transfer sufficiently identified property to the trust.

The court *in Jennings v. Jennings*, 211 Kan. 515, 507 P.2d 241 (1973), upheld these elements as being essential for a private trust.

EXAMPLE: Ester Katz owns a one-third interest in a boutique. In her will she gives the interest to her nephew, Avram, to hold and manage in trust for the benefit of

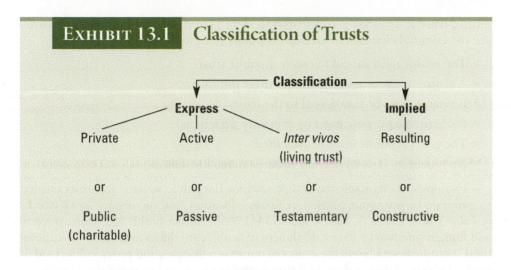

EXHIBIT 13.1   Classification of Trusts

Classification

Express — Implied

Private — Active — *Inter vivos* (living trust) — Resulting

or — or — or — or

Public (charitable) — Passive — Testamentary — Constructive

her niece, Mariam. Ester, the owner of the interest, is the settlor. Avram, to whom she conveys the legal title to the one-third interest, is the trustee. Mariam, who is to receive the benefit of the interest (i.e., one-third of the profits of the boutique), is the beneficiary. This is a private (for benefit of a person), express (written), and testamentary (established by will) trust.

ASSIGNMENT 13.1

Sebastian Bianchi transfers (assigns) the royalties from his book, to which he holds the copyright, to his business adviser, Randall Martinez, to hold and invest for the benefit of Martha Giesler.

1. Does the settlor intend to create a trust?

2. Is there a trustee to administer the trust?

3. Is trust property included in the instrument?

4. Is there a beneficiary or cestui que trust?

Public Trust

A *public* or *charitable trust* is an express trust established for the purpose of accomplishing social benefit for the public or the community (Restatement [Third] of Trusts § 28). Although charitable trusts are public trusts, the beneficiary of the trust does not have to be the *general* public. The trust fund, however, must be designated either for the benefit of the general public, e.g., a charitable trust that benefits a hospital, *or* a reasonably large, **indefinite class** of persons within the public who may be personally unknown to the settlor, e.g., a charitable trust that benefits the deaf in a certain city (Restatement [Third] of Trusts § 28). If the terms of the trust limit the distribution of its fund to named individuals rather than to an indefinite class of persons, the trust will not be classified as public. Instead, it would be a private trust. In the majority of states, the true test for creation of a valid public trust is not the indefiniteness of the persons aided by the trust but rather the amount of social benefit given to the public (Restatement [Third] of Trusts § 28). Also, the purpose of the charitable trust must not include profit-making by the

indefinite class
A group of persons within the public whose number is not specified and are unknown to the settlor of the trust.

settlor, trustee, or other persons (Restatement [Third] of Trusts § 28). Following are the essential elements of an express public (charitable) trust.

- The settlor must intend to create a public trust.
- A trustee must be named to administer the trust.
- Property must be transferred to the trust.
- A charitable purpose must be expressly designated.
- The general public must be benefited.
- An indefinite class of persons must be named beneficiaries.

Examples of charitable trusts that advance the public welfare are trusts created to maintain or propagate religion, religious education, and missionary work (see *In re Faber's Will*, 259 Ia. 1, 141 N.W.2d 554 [1966]); further health and relieve poverty and human suffering by the establishment of health care clinics and other institutions, fund scientific research into the causes of numerous diseases, and provide direct aid of food, clothing, shelter, and medical care to the needy; found or maintain educational institutions, art galleries, museums, or libraries (see *Alden v. Lewis*, 254 Miss. 704, 182 So.2d 600 [1966]); aid students or teachers; care for and maintain public cemeteries; erect monuments to public figures or national heroes; construct and maintain public buildings or improvements, such as an irrigation system or a playground; further patriotism; conserve natural resources and scenery; and prevent cruelty to animals.

EXAMPLE: Florence Winter died testate, providing in her will, "I give State University $100,000 to provide scholarships for single mothers who major in the field of nurse's training." In the absence of other evidence, an express, testamentary, charitable trust is created.

Florence is the settlor, State University is the trustee, and "single mothers who major in nurse's training" are the beneficiaries. The $100,000 is the trust property. Florence intended to create a public or charitable trust, which she expressed in her will. The class of persons to be benefited is smaller than "the general public" but sufficiently large and indefinite enough to enable the trust to be classified as public. For example, Betsy Nelson, a single mother, decides to major in nurse's training a year after Florence dies; therefore, Florence could not have named Betsy as a beneficiary. Betsy was not a member of the class to be benefited when Florence made her will, but now she qualifies. She and others in the same situation are indefinite beneficiaries.

The mere fact that the purpose of a trust is to give money to others does not make it a charitable trust. The settlor of a charitable trust must describe a purpose that is of substantial public benefit.

ASSIGNMENT 13.2

Stone Michaelson gives $100,000 to Luke Marra to be distributed as Luke feels is appropriate for the support of orphans living in South Dakota.

1. Did the settlor intend to create a trust?
2. Is there a trustee to administer the trust?
3. Is trust res (property) included?
4. Is a charitable purpose expressly designated?

5. Will the general public be benefited?

6. Are there indefinite beneficiaries within a definite class who are the persons who actually receive the benefit?

Public Trust—*Cy-Pres* Doctrine

Where it is clear the donor intended a private trust to be performed exactly as indicated or not at all, the trust fails (terminates) when it is not possible to follow such direction. However, in the absence of this clear intent by the donor in the trust agreement, the law will *not* permit a *public charitable* trust to end (fail) even though the beneficiary no longer exists or the original purpose has been accomplished or can no longer be achieved. Instead, the courts will apply the doctrine of **cy-pres** (an abbreviation of the French words *cy pres comme possible* or "as near as possible") (Restatement [Third] of Trusts § 67), which is applicable only to public (charitable) trusts. In practice, the **cy-pres doctrine** means that where a settlor makes a gift to charity or for a charitable purpose and it subsequently becomes impossible or impractical to apply the gift to that particular charity, the equity court may order the gift applied to another charity "as near as possible" to the one designated by the settlor.

> **EXAMPLE:** Etta Barranger establishes a trust fund to provide relief to victims who suffer from a particular kidney disease. Later, an inventor creates a kidney machine that alleviates the problem. In order to continue the trust, it is necessary for the court to apply the *cy-pres* doctrine by the substitution of another charity whose purpose corresponds "as near as possible" to Etta's original motives for the trust. For example, the court might apply the trust principal to a charity that aids the victims of a liver ailment.

The rationale behind the application of *cy-pres* is that the law desires to continue the operation of charitable trusts in order to avoid the termination of public benefits. If a charitable trust fails for lack of foresight on the part of its settlor or simply due to modern-day advances in medical science and technology, a court will review the settlor's intended use of the trust and, if possible, transfer the trust fund to a charity with a more viable use that approximates the intent. The courts are anxious for the public to receive the benefits. For the doctrine to be applied to a charitable trust, however, the settlor's intent must be broad and general and not restricted to one specific objective or to one particular method of accomplishing the purpose of the trust.

> **EXAMPLE:** Through his will, Dean Kirkpatrick gives the National Polio Foundation $500,000. Dr. Salk discovers a vaccine that prevents polio. Dean's heirs ask the court to distribute the money to them now that the disease is preventable. Instead, the court of equity would apply the *cy-pres* doctrine and transfer the balance of the funds to a charity as near as possible to the testator's (Dean's) wishes, e.g., the court may give the money to the National Crippled Children's Foundation.

The case *of In re Bletsch's Estate*, 25 Wis.2d 40, 130 N.W.2d 275 (1964), illustrates the use of the *cy-pres* doctrine. The testator, Jack Bletsch, left his entire estate to his wife and daughter if they survived him; if they did not, he left his estate to the Masonic Home for Crippled Children in Illinois. Both his wife and daughter predeceased Jack, but there was no Masonic Home for Crippled Children in Illinois. However, there was a Shriner's Hospital for Crippled Children in Illinois. The Wisconsin court ruled the hospital was "… an identifiable beneficiary whose charitable or public program and goals are reasonably close to those expressed by the testator." The estate passed to the Shriner's Hospital, because the *cy-pres* doctrine was applied and upheld by the court.

cy-pres
As near as possible.

cy-pres doctrine
The equity court may order a gift intended for a charity, or for a charitable purpose, that is now nonexistent be given or applied to another charity whose purpose is as near as possible to the one originally chosen by the settlor.

Express Trusts—Active versus Passive

The features that distinguish *active trusts* from *passive trusts* are the obligations of management and administration that active trusts impose on the trustee.

An **active trust** is an express trust that can be either private or public (charitable). A settlor who desires to create an express private active trust must give oral or written affirmative powers and duties to a trustee to perform discretionary acts of management or administration for the benefit of named beneficiaries.

In contrast, in a **passive trust,** the trustee does not have responsibilities or discretionary duties to perform; in fact, a passive trust often involves no administrative duties at all. The trustee of a passive trust merely holds the trust property for the beneficiary with no obligations or administrative powers. Implied trusts, such as resulting and constructive trusts, are passive trusts. Modern-day passive trusts stem from the failure of the settlor to create an active trust, either accidentally, e.g., through a poor choice of words in the trust instrument, or deliberately, e.g., an attempt to evade the law for the settlor's own fraudulent purposes. To avoid accidentally creating a passive trust, the drafter must properly designate the active functions or duties of the trustee. The following example illustrates a trust declared passive by the equity court.

> **EXAMPLE:** Silvia appoints Arnold trustee of securities for the benefit of Harriet but neglects to give him duties to perform. Silvia dies. Legal title to the securities would normally pass to Arnold, but instead, under these circumstances, it passes directly to Harriet, who holds equitable title as well. Since the legal and equitable titles are held by one person, no trust is created.

Additional examples involving resulting and constructive trusts are discussed below.

ASSIGNMENT 13.3

Neal Sanderson owns a farm, Springlake, which he conveys by deed to Rudolf Meyerling for the benefit of Sarah Beth Jacoby. Neal directs Rudolf to rent the land to tenants and to use part of the income produced thereby to pay taxes and to apply the remainder for Sarah Beth's benefit at his own discretion. Answer the following and compare your answers with the statements in the next paragraph.

1. Is the trust express or implied?

2. Is the trust private or public?

3. Are there administrative duties that the trustee must perform?

4. Is the trust active or passive?

This trust is a private express trust. Neal Sanderson, the settlor, conveyed his farm, the trust property, to Rudolf Meyerling, the trustee. Sarah Beth Jacoby is the beneficiary. The trust is active since Rudolf has the duties of renting the farm, collecting income (rent), paying taxes, and giving the remainder of the income to Sarah Beth.

Express Trusts—*Inter Vivos* (Living) versus Testamentary

The most common types of express trusts are living trusts and testamentary trusts. Both *inter vivos (living) trusts* (Restatement [Third] of Trusts §§ 10, 16) and *testamentary trusts* (Restatement [Third] of Trusts §§ 10, 16, 17, 19) refer to express trusts either private or public in nature. As the generic names of these trusts imply, they are created at different times in the settlor's life: *inter vivos* (pertaining to a gift in trust made "between living persons" and hereafter called living trusts) and testamentary (pertaining to a gift in trust made after death as a testament, i.e., as part of a last will). In the event of a question of whether a trust is living or testamentary, the criterion will be the time at which the trust became effective. If a settlor wishes to see how well the trust operates while alive, a living trust should be established. Otherwise the living trust differs little from the testamentary trust. Both types of trusts are widely employed as a means of conserving property for the benefit of a surviving spouse and children or for the child or children of a single parent. *Note:* The testamentary trust is probated; the living trust is not.

Sample Testamentary Clause for Minor Children of a Single Parent

I give the residue of my estate to [name of trustee] of [address, city, county, state] as trustee of a trust, which shall be held, administered, and distributed by my trustee as follows.

(a).   Until my youngest living child reaches the age of twenty-five (25) years, my trustee may pay to or apply directly for the benefit of my children and other issue sums from the net income and principal of this trust as my trustee determines necessary to provide for their proper support, health, maintenance, and education. It is not required that such payments be for the equal benefit of my children and other issue. In making any payment or application, my trustee shall take into consideration other resources and income of my children and other issue. Any undistributed net income of the trust property shall be accumulated and added to the principal.

(b).   When my youngest living child has reached the age of twenty-five (25) years, my trustee shall divide this trust into equal shares and shall provide one share for each of my then living children, and one share to be divided equally among the living issue, collectively, of each deceased child of mine. In making such division, my trustee shall take into account all advances of principal to a child made after such child reached the age of twenty-five (25) years. It shall be within the discretion of my trustee to take into account some, none, or all advances of principal to a child made before such child had reached the age of twenty-five (25) years. After such division has been made, said shares shall be distributed outright to such children and to the issue of deceased children by right of representation.

ASSIGNMENT 13.4

Norman gives Janet $40,000 to be distributed as she sees fit for the benefit of poor Amish children in Kentucky between the ages of 6 and 12. Determine whether the essential elements of an express, active, living, public trust are present.

1. Does the settlor intend to create a trust?

2. Is there a trustee to administer the trust?

3. Is trust res included?

4. Is a charitable purpose expressly designated?

5. Is the general public benefited?

6. Are there indefinite beneficiaries within a definite class who are the persons who actually receive the benefit?

Rule Against Perpetuities
The principle that no interest in property is good (valid) unless it must vest (take effect), if at all, not later than 21 years, plus the period of gestation, after some life or lives in being at the time of the creation of the interest. The rule fixes the time within which a future interest must vest. The period of gestation is included to cover cases of posthumous birth.

The **Rule Against Perpetuities**, a common law rule that originated in England, affects the validity and duration of *all private noncharitable trusts*. The rule places a term (time limitation) on how long a private noncharitable trust may exist. The rule regulates the creation of future interests in trusts and holds that to be valid, an interest in property must vest (take effect); that is, some future beneficiary must get full and unrestricted possession and control over the property, no later than 21 years, plus the period of gestation, after some life or lives in being (a living person or persons) at the time of the creation of the interest. The word *vest* referred to above creates an immediate interest, not an immediate possession. A future interest may vest in interest long before it vests in possession.

The Rule Against Perpetuities has an important bearing on testamentary trusts that prevents testator-settlors from controlling property long after they are dead. Since public policy, as enunciated in the rule, opposes the accumulation and monopolization of property and income over many generations, the maker of a will may not create a trust that lasts longer than 21 years together with the period of gestation after the life of a named living person. The life of such a person is referred to as a "life in being" when the trust is created. To illustrate: A settlor of property currently without children cannot create a testamentary trust for grandchildren (children's children, neither of which class is yet born), since there is no "life in being" at the time of the creation of the trust. The trust is void because of the rule. However, if the settlor were to create a trust leaving property at death in trust to a daughter now living—the "life in being"—and on her death to the daughter's children, the trust would be legal since the duration of the trust would be measured by the life of the daughter. The trust terminates no later than 21 years after her death, at which time her child or children would receive the trust property. If the daughter were to die childless, the trust property would revert (return) immediately to the settlor or the settlor's beneficiaries or heirs.

> **EXAMPLE:** In her will, Lashandra creates a trust to pay the income to her husband, Rashad, for life, and then to pay the income to her two children, Kendra and Kirby, for their lives, and on the death of the last child, to pay the principal to her grandchildren. Lashandra dies survived by her husband and children. This trust does not violate the rule and is valid.

Most states have enacted the rule into statutory law, but some states have modified it to inquire whether the gift did in fact vest within the time period. If it did vest, the gift is upheld (valid).

The following Iowa law exemplifies state statutes on the Rule Against Perpetuities.

Iowa Code Ann. § 558.68 Perpetuities
1. A nonvested interest in property is not valid unless it must vest, if at all, within twenty-one years after one or more lives in being at the creation of the interest and any relevant period of gestation.

A sample clause in a will that contains the rule is the following:

All the remainder of my estate, I give to the Fourth Western Bank to hold in trust, invest, reinvest, and distribute the net income accruing from the date of my death, for the benefit of my son, Jeremy, for life, and the remainder to such child or children of him who reach the age of 18 years.

To avoid a violation of the Rule Against Perpetuities when a will is drafted is difficult, as evidenced by the great number of lawsuits brought by persons who allege that certain trust provisions violate the rule. For this reason, you must go over the perpetuities statute of the state where the trust is to take effect in detail to ensure the trust harmonizes with it.

The above-quoted Iowa statute, for example, holds the effective term of a trust to be the remaining length of the lives of persons named in the instrument, plus 21 years, plus nine months (the "usual period of gestation"—this provision provides for persons not yet born at the time of the trust execution). The trust set up in the sample clause could last for the rest of the life of Jeremy (the life in being) and continue for 21 years and nine months. The clause falls within the limits set by the Rule Against Perpetuities.

Note: Since the rule does not affect charitable trusts, such trusts have an unlimited duration.

ASSIGNMENT 13.5

What is the Rule Against Perpetuities, and does it affect both private and public trusts?

Implied Trusts—Resulting and Constructive

The second major category in the classification of trusts is the *implied trust*, subdivided into *resulting trusts* and *constructive trusts*. Both types of implied trusts are also passive trusts. Implied trusts are trusts imposed on property by the equity courts when trust intent is lacking. Such trusts, also known as involuntary trusts, are said to be created by "operation of law." Unlike express trusts, implied trusts have no named settlor. The settlor who creates an express trust does so with intent, even though the details (i.e., the language of the trust instrument or identities of the trustee or beneficiaries) might be vague enough to require court interpretation. It is impossible, however, for any person in the capacity of settlor to create an implied trust since they, by definition, are involuntary trusts imposed by the equity court.

Resulting Trusts

A **resulting trust** is created by operation of law under circumstances in which one person becomes the possessor or holder of property with the legal title but is obligated by the equity court to hold "in trust" the title and property for another person's benefit even though there is no stated declaration to create a trust and fraud is not involved. The argument for the creation or use of the resulting trust is that property is always held for the *true owner*. Frequently, the courts use a resulting trust to settle legal disputes. There are three common situations in which implied, resulting trusts are created.

Situation One

The purchase-money resulting trust. When one person pays for land or personal property, but the legal title of the property is conveyed to another person, the law presumes that a resulting trust, called a **purchase-money resulting trust**, has been created for the benefit of the person who paid the money. That person receives

resulting trust
A trust created by operation of law from circumstances implied from the intentions of the parties that the person who holds legal title is obligated to hold it "in trust" for another person's benefit, even though there is no stated intention to create a trust and no fraud is involved. Resulting trusts often occur when an attempt to create a valid express trust fails for lack of one or more of the essential elements.

purchase-money resulting trust
A resulting trust in which property is purchased and paid for by one person, and at his direction, the seller transfers possession and title to another person.

equitable title to the property. The person to whom the property was conveyed, i.e., the holder of legal title to the property, is considered the trustee (Restatement [Third] of Trusts § 9).

Since a purchase-money resulting trust is created by implication and operation of law, it need not be in writing. However, if there is a conflict later, it may be difficult to prove whether the conveyor intended to make a gift to the alleged trustee instead of allowing a resulting trust to be created by implication.

parol evidence
Oral testimony or written evidence.

Generally, courts require clear and convincing proof to establish a resulting trust. The evidence must be strong and unmistakable, and the burden of proof rests on the party who seeks to establish the trust. To establish proof, the court allows **parol evidence**, i.e., oral testimony or written evidence, to be used in these cases. Although a person who makes a gratuitous conveyance most likely intends to make a gift, the grounds for the court's presumption that a purchase-money resulting trust is created are that a person who furnishes consideration, pays for a conveyance to another, probably does so for reasons other than a gift. The person may intend to facilitate resale of the property, repay a debt, obtain services of management from the transferee, or seek to avoid creditors. Due to these difficulties and uncertainties, several states have abolished or modified purchase-money resulting trusts by statute.

> **EXAMPLE:** Keith Andrews, age 75, buys 500 shares of Honeywell, Inc., stock with money that he needs to live. He instructs the corporation's agent to issue the certificates in the name of Carole Ann Heglin. Carole Ann is not related by blood or marriage to Keith. In the absence of further evidence, Carol Ann holds the shares as trustee in a *resulting trust* for Keith.

Situation Two

The failed trust. When a settlor creates a private express trust gratuitously (without requiring payment of the beneficiary) and the trust fails or is declared void for any reason except that it has an illegal objective, a resulting trust arises for the benefit of the settlor or the settlor's successors (Restatement [Third] of Trusts § 8). In other words, the trust arrangement no longer exists, but the trust property does, and so does the problem of disposing of it. Should the settlor be allowed to recover the property? In general, the law considers such recovery to be the only fair solution. However, if the court rules the private express trust was created for an illegal purpose, it generally does not decree (order) a resulting trust for the benefit of the settlor but instead declares the trust void. In such cases, the settlor of an illegal trust is generally not allowed to recover the trust property from the trustee since equity discourages such transactions and will not be a party to their enforcement.

> **EXAMPLE:** Angelo Rossi conveys his farm, Oakburne, by deed to Hunter Jennings in trust for Lance Anderson. Unknown to Angelo, Lance is dead at the time of the conveyance. The trust property now reverts to Angelo, but until Angelo takes possession of it, Hunter holds Oakburne in a resulting trust for Angelo.

A resulting trust also arises when a charitable trust fails in an instance where the court cannot apply the *cy-pres* doctrine. The trust property is held by the trustee for the benefit of the original settlor or the settlor's successors.

ASSIGNMENT 13.6

Allen Greenfield gratuitously transfers by deed his lakeshore cottage to Nancy Morris in trust for the benefit of Allen's son. Unknown to Nancy, Allen makes the transfer to avoid claims of his creditors. The creditors seek to have the trust set aside so they can attach the property in payment of their claims. Nancy agrees the trust should be declared void because of its illegal purpose, but she claims, as an innocent party, she should be entitled to keep the property since equity should not return it to the fraudulent settlor. Who wins? Answer the question according to the laws of your state.

Situation Three

The excessive endowment trust. When the property of a private express trust exceeds what is needed for the purpose intended by the settlor, or some part of the trust property remains after the trust has ended, the court may establish a resulting trust for the benefit of the settlor or the settlor's successors (Restatement [Third] of Trusts § 8).

> **EXAMPLE:** Regina Latessa provides in her will, "I give my shares of Highly Successful, Inc., stock to Whitney Ramos in trust to pay the income to James Mathews for life." The will does not mention who will receive the remainder. After James dies, there is a resulting trust for Regina's successors of the remaining principal in the trust fund.

ASSIGNMENT 13.7

In 2013, Bailey gives by deed all the land she owns in Pike County to the Westside State Bank for the benefit of her children and grandchildren. Her children, Trenton and Zoe, die in 2014 without children or wills. Two months later, Bailey dies.

1. What kind of trust, if any, did Bailey create in 2013?

2. What kind of trust, if any, is formed in 2013?

3. Zoe's cousin, Laverne, claims the land because she is Zoe's next of kin. Is she entitled to it?

4. Who receives the equitable and the legal titles, respectively?

Constructive Trusts

A **constructive trust** is *not* created by written agreement or the stated intent of the settlor. That is an express trust. Nor is a constructive trust created by the implied or presumed intent of a property holder of legal title whose acts cause the equity court to enforce a trust established by operation of law. That is a resulting trust. The point of similarity between a constructive trust and a resulting trust is that both are implied, passive trusts. Resulting trusts arise by implication of law or by an equity court decree that declares the property holder to be a trustee either as a result of implied intent or because of presumed intent of the parties based on the consequences of their acts. Constructive trusts are not based on express or even implied or presumed intent. A constructive trust is exclusively a creation of the

constructive trust
An involuntary trust created by operation of law to recover property from a person who has improperly obtained possession of or legal rights to property by fraud, duress, abuse of confidence, or other unconscionable conduct.

equity court and is established for the purpose of rectifying a serious wrong such as fraud, duress, unconscionable conduct, or preventing unjust enrichment of the wrongdoer.

Case One

In the case of *Wait v. Cornette*, 259 Neb. 850, 612 N.W.2d 905 (2000), the court stated, "A constructive trust is imposed when one has acquired legal title to property under such circumstances that he or she may not in good conscience retain the beneficial interest [and] equity converts the legal title holder into a trustee holding the title for the benefit of those entitled to the ownership."

When a person has acquired title to property by unlawful or unfair means or by breach of duty as trustee, the court will construct a trust for the benefit of the person rightfully entitled to that property. In such cases, the court declares that the person who has acquired or retained property wrongfully holds the property as "constructive trustee" for the person who has been unjustly deprived of the property. Therefore, a constructive trust is imposed to remedy a wrong and to prevent unjust enrichment by the person who acquired title at the expense of another. The constructive trustee has no administrative duty other than the obligation to transfer the title and possession of the property to the proper person.

Case Two

The case of *Sharp v. Kosmalski*, 40 N.Y.2d 119, 386 N.Y.S.2d 72, 351 N.E.2d 721 (1976), illustrates the creation of a constructive trust. Rodney Sharp was a 56-year-old farmer whose education did not go beyond the eighth grade. On the death of his wife of 32 years, he developed a very close relationship with Jean Kosmalski, 16 years his junior. Sharp proposed marriage to her, but she refused. He continued to make substantial gifts to her that included the execution of a deed that named her a joint owner of the farm. Later, Sharp transferred his remaining joint interest in the farm to Kosmalski. She ordered Sharp to move out of the house and vacate the farm. Sharp brought this action to impose a constructive trust on the property transferred to Kosmalski. The court ruled that a person may be determined to be unjustly enriched if that person has received a benefit, the retention of which would be unjust, as in this case; therefore, the court decided in favor of Sharp.

The court may also construct a trust for the benefit of the rightful owner when a person obtains property by fraud or willfully converts another's personal property for his own use.

EXAMPLE: Cheyenne French works for the Benedict Corporation. She embezzles $10,000 from the corporation and uses the money to buy a speedboat. Under these circumstances, the equity court could decree Cheyenne to be a constructive trustee for the corporation with the duty to transfer possession and title of the speedboat to the company.

See Exhibit 13.2 for a summary of the types of trusts.

EXHIBIT 13.2	An Outline Summary of the Main Types of Trusts

A. Two main types of trusts
  1. **Express trust** A trust intentionally created or declared in express terms either by oral declaration or by a written instrument. Express trusts may be—
     a. Private or public (charitable) trusts.
     b. Active or passive trusts.
     c. *Inter vivos* (living) trusts or testamentary trusts.
  2. **Implied trust** A trust imposed on property by the court when trust intent is lacking but the acts of the parties make the imposition necessary. Implied trusts may be—
     a. Resulting trusts.
     b. Constructive trusts.
B. **Express trusts**
  1. Private or public (charitable) trusts
     a. **Private trust** An oral or written trust created for the financial benefit of a certain named individual or individuals.
     b. **Public trust** An express trust created for the social benefit of the public, or specific groups within the public; often called a charitable trust.
  2. Active or passive trusts
     a. **Active trust** A trust that gives the trustee the power and duty to perform discretionary acts of management or administration.
     b. **Passive trust** A trust in which the trustee is a mere holder of the legal title and has no duties of administration or only minor duties that are of a mechanical or formal nature. All implied trusts are passive trusts.
  3. *Inter vivos* or testamentary trusts
     a. *Inter vivos* **(living) trust** An express active trust, either private or public, created during the settlor's lifetime.
     b. **Testamentary trust** An express active trust, either public or private, created in a decedent's will.
C. **Implied trusts**
  1. **Resulting trust** An implied trust created by the equity court to carry out the true intent of a property holder of legal title or settlor in cases where the intent of such person is inadequately expressed.
  2. **Constructive trust** An implied trust imposed by courts of equity as a means of accomplishing justice and preventing unjust enrichment. Such trusts are not based on either actual or presumed intent of the parties.

ASSIGNMENT 13.8

1. Russell Haberman owned a tract of land he believed was practically worthless. His brother-in-law, Francis Holgate, offered to buy the land for one dollar an acre. Francis knew it contained valuable mineral deposits of which Russell was unaware. Russell sold the land and, subsequently, discovered its true value. Has Francis been unjustly enriched by the transaction? What should Russell do?

2. In a will dated June 6, 2014, Misty Bohman named her nephew, Teddy Wilson, beneficiary of a substantial portion of her estate. In 2015, Misty wrote a new will in which Teddy was left nothing; later that year Misty died. Teddy discovered the second (2015) will but concealed its existence until the probate of the first (2014) will was completed. A beneficiary of the second will uncovered the truth. Some states hold that a constructive trust may be created in this case. How would your state decide this matter?

Miscellaneous Trusts

A number of special trust forms need to be discussed. These include the spend-thrift, Totten, sprinkling trusts, and a new type of revocable trust known as a digital asset protection trusts. Charitable remainder trusts and other tax-saving trusts are discussed in Chapter 14.

Spendthrift Trusts

Spendthrift trusts are commonly created by parents for children they feel are financially irresponsible. A spendthrift is a person who spends money improvidently, compulsively, and foolishly and thereby wastes the funds. As defined in the *Matter of Sowers' Estate*, 1 Kan.App.2d 675, 574 P.2d 224 (1977), *spendthrift trusts* are trusts created to provide a fund for the maintenance of a beneficiary while safeguarding the fund against the beneficiary's own extravagance or inexperience in spending money. In such trusts, only a certain portion of the total amount of the funds is given to the spendthrift beneficiary at any one time. The trustee is given discretion to decide the amount of income given to the beneficiary. The settlor provides that the beneficiary cannot assign (transfer) to anyone the right to receive future payments of income or principal from the trust (which the settlor believes the beneficiary would do in times of financial difficulty). At the same time, the settlor declares that creditors of the spendthrift beneficiary cannot reach the trust benefits by obtaining a court order that awards the trust benefits to the creditors. In this way, settlors seek to protect the beneficiary who cannot or will not handle money wisely. This protection ends once the beneficiary actually receives the distribution of the trust income from the trustee.

Spendthrift trusts do not place limitations on income once it is received by the beneficiary, who may spend it, give it away at will, or use it to satisfy creditors' claims; however, the beneficiary cannot pledge future trust income as security for a loan. The trust only guarantees that the beneficiary will not lose the income before receiving it. Principal or income is subject to creditors' claims only after it is received by the beneficiary; see N.H. Rev. Stat. Ann. § 498:8 and 9. A majority of states allows settlors to create a spendthrift trust and prohibits creditors from attaching the trust in order to obtain a beneficiary's interest. However, if there is no spendthrift provision, the creditors can enforce their claims. State statutes and case law do allow creditors to reach the beneficiary's trust income despite a spendthrift clause if they have supplied "**necessaries**" to the beneficiary. See Ky. Rev. Stat. Ann. § 381.180(6) (b), and *Matter of Dodge's Estate*, 281 N.W.2d 447 (Iowa 1979). Necessaries include necessary services a creditor performs for a beneficiary or necessary supplies a creditor delivers to the beneficiary. See *Department of Mental Health and Developmental Disabilities v. First Natl. Bank of Chicago*, 104 I11.App.3rd 461, 432 N.E.2d 1086 (1982).

necessaries
Necessary items that supply the personal needs of an individual or family, such as food, clothing, or shelter.

EXAMPLE: Lenny Demarest, a resident of Nevada, wishes to leave a considerable amount of property to his son, Scott, although he knows Scott is irresponsible and wastes his money. He fears that Scott may go into debt and pledge the income received from the trust to pay his creditors. Lenny could enable Scott to keep the right to the trust income by inserting the following "spendthrift trust" clause in his will: "It is the purpose of this trust to protect Scott Demarest from want or his own mismanagement and improvidence and to provide him with a reasonable means of support free from claims or interest of any other person. The beneficiary, Scott Demarest, of this trust shall not have the power to transfer, pledge, or assign his interest in the principal or the income of this trust in any manner, nor shall such interest be subject to the claims of his creditors, attachment, garnishment, execution, or other process of law. All payments from the trust shall be paid directly to Scott Demarest and to no other person or entity."

ASSIGNMENT 13.9

Tyler Kincaid wishes to make a gift of his utility company stocks to his daughter, Alice, who is about to be married. He knows Alice, who is inexperienced in handling securities, might sell them at a loss, and being headstrong, she would not listen to sound advice. Would a gift of the property be wise? Is it advisable for Tyler to establish a spendthrift trust for her? Explain.

Totten Trusts

A *Totten trust*, similar to a POD (payable or pay-on-death) account, is a savings account in a bank in which money is deposited in the depositor's name as trustee for another person named as beneficiary. The name derives from the first case in which such trusts were upheld—*In re Totten*, 179 N.Y. 112, 71 N.E. 748 (1904). Commonly, the trust is created by A, the depositor, in the name of "A, in trust (or as trustee) for B," or in the name of "A, payable on death to B." Such deposits permit the depositor-trustee to withdraw money while alive and allow any remaining balance of the funds to be transferred to the beneficiary after the depositor's death. If the named beneficiary dies before the depositor, the trust terminates, and the money passes into the depositor's probate estate on his death. In addition, some courts hold the depositor may revoke the "trust" by withdrawing the entire fund or changing the form of the account. The requirements for the creation and distribution of funds in such trusts vary from state to state. Therefore, the individual state statutes must be checked to determine how Totten trusts will be administered. Sections 6-212 and 6-223 of the UPC states that a bank account, such as a Totten trust, belongs to the beneficiary when the trustee dies. In the case of *Hall's Estate v. Father Flanagan's Boys' Home*, 30 Colo.App. 296, 491 P.2d 614 (1971), the court ruled that a Totten trust was created, and the beneficiary, "Boys Town, Nebraska," actually known as Father Flanagan's Boys' Home, was entitled to the trust funds. The money in a Totten trust is a nonprobate asset and is, therefore, not part of the depositor's estate, i.e., not subject to probate or to creditors' claims of the depositor.

> **EXAMPLE:** Cadence Sweeney changes a savings account in her name to "Cadence, in trust for Jeanetta Sweeney." Cadence has converted her account into a Totten trust, which is allowed in her state. She has the option of withdrawing any or all of the money as she wishes during her lifetime because the Totten trust is revocable until the settlor's death. On Cadence's death, Jeanetta, the beneficiary, will own the remaining funds in the savings account. If Jeanetta dies before Cadence, however, the Totten trust ends, and the money in the savings account belongs to Cadence. If no change is made in this savings account and Cadence dies after Jeanetta, the money will be transferred to Cadence's estate and will be subject to probate.

Sprinkling Trusts

A **sprinkling trust** gives the trustee the authority and power to accumulate or distribute the income of the trust or the principal, or both, among the trust beneficiaries in varying amounts. The financial needs of family members named as beneficiaries constantly change, and a trustee with sprinkling powers has the opportunity to change distributions from the trust to meet the needs of the beneficiaries.

> **EXAMPLE:** Destiny is a single parent with three adult children. Destiny dies with a testamentary trust in her will that gives the trustee discretionary power to "sprinkle" income to the beneficiaries (the three children) in greatest need. Destiny's youngest child, Desiree, is permanently injured in an accident and is obviously in greater financial need than Destiny's other two children, Jada and Trinity, both of whom are married and financially secure. The trustee accomplishes what Destiny herself would have wanted by giving the trust's income to Desiree.

> **EXAMPLE:** Destiny's testamentary trust in the above example would also allow her trustee to save income tax dollars since any distribution to the daughters, Jada and Trinity, would be taxed at a higher rate because of their family income.

A sprinkling trust also offers two other advantages: the trust funds are more difficult for creditors of the beneficiaries to reach since the trustee alone decides how much to give each beneficiary; and such trusts may help to reduce estate taxes.

> **EXAMPLE:** Nguyen sets up a sprinkling trust for her husband, Grover, for life, then to their children. Grover spends his own estate funds, and the trustee allows Nguyen's trust funds to accumulate. The trust funds pass to the children on Grover's death free of estate tax.

A disadvantage of a sprinkling trust is that if the trust is intended to qualify for the marital deduction on the decedent's estate tax return, the surviving spouse must receive all the income during the spouse's lifetime.

Since the trustee is given the authority to make important family financial decisions, the person selected must be someone the settlor knows is reliable, experienced, and reasonable. The following is an example of a sprinkling trust provision from West's McKinney's Forms, ESP, § 10:601(a).

> It is desired that, while the underlying principle of equality shall be followed in making distributions of net income or principal to or for the benefit of any beneficiary, the Trustee is to be entirely free to pay out either more or less to or for the benefit of any particular beneficiary as it deems advisable because of variations in health, character, education, or other requirements, and the Trustee may use both net income and principal in disproportionate amounts to provide security and opportunities for higher education for each beneficiary during the term of the trust.... The judgment of the Trustee shall be final and conclusive upon all persons.

Digital Asset Protection Trusts (DAP)

Digital asset protection trusts allow the trust creator to place existing digital rights and property into a trust for the trust beneficiaries' use, especially if the value of the assets is substantial. (See Chapter 1 for a discussion of digital assets). The trust's ownership of the assets survives the trust creator's death or incapacitation.

> **EXAMPLE:** Abe McGowen operated his own small business. He recently suffered a stroke, which left him incapacitated. Abe's only method of contact with his customers and suppliers was through his email account. Unfortunately, due to the effects of the stroke, Abe was unable to provide his family or business partners

with access to his email account. His email provider refused to provide the information without documentation of his death or a court order. Subsequently, Abe's business lost a significant amount of income.

The DAP trust may be a safer place for ownership and account information than a will because it does not become part of the public record. Moreover, trusts can be amended more easily than wills. The trust document grants the Trustee the authority to manage digital licenses on behalf of the trust beneficiaries. Digital assets often take the form of licenses that may be, by their own terms, nontransferable and expire at the owner's death. A trust can provide for orderly transfer and management. Trust beneficiaries cannot directly control the licenses, but they are entitled to the financial benefits. These trusts can also eliminate allegations of misuse of funds under such situations as a beneficiary being provided access to an incapacitated client's online banking information, or a dishonest family member emptying bank accounts.

Online companies are offering their services to eliminate potential problems with digital assets through the use of proprietary software. They allow an individual to establish a digital asset trust, to register assets with the company to be included in the trust, and to appoint the company as a successor trustee. These online services offer a high level of security and permit clients to easily store passwords and assign beneficiary designations whenever they desire. However, many estate planning attorneys are not yet confident that these sites appropriately safeguard the information or whether they will still be in existence when needed. As with many problems created by technological advances, hopefully, further technological solutions will soon be developed to provide a solution to this problem.

THE PURPOSES OF TRUSTS

A trust can be created for any lawful purpose, but it must not contravene common or statutory law (Restatement [Third] of Trusts § 27). Most trusts are created to distribute the income from the trust property to family members, friends, or a charity and/or to preserve the trust property for later distribution to such persons on termination of the trust. This can be accomplished during the settlor's lifetime by a living trust or at death by a testamentary trust.

A trust is a practical way to manage and transfer property in the best interests of a beneficiary. On the creation of a trust, the trustee assumes the duty to administer the trust, and relieves, if desired, both the settlor (grantor) and the beneficiary from the responsibility of managing and conserving the property. Numerous advantages of trusts become obvious. A living trust is created in each of the following examples. By means of such a device, the settlor can provide the following:

- Funds for the support of dependent family members, e.g., parents, spouse, children

EXAMPLE: Clinton McBride supports his elderly mother, Frieda. Due to her age and frail health, Frieda will most likely predecease Clinton. The transfer of income-producing property by outright gift in order to have the income taxed in Frieda's lower tax bracket would be illogical, since gift taxes would be owed and on her death the property would return to Clinton, reduced by his mother's estate and administration expenses. If Clinton places the property in a living trust for his mother for life, with the remainder to his only child, Madelyn, the income would be taxed to Frieda without her receiving legal title to the property. When Frieda dies, the property will pass to Madelyn, if she survives Frieda.

- Funds for the college education of children

  EXAMPLE: Sadie McIntosh, a widow, has been a homemaker and mother all her adult life. Her husband died two years ago and left her a substantial life insurance benefit. She wants to establish a fund for the college education of her two children. Since she lacks business experience and the children are minors, the creation of a living trust and the selection of an experienced trustee to invest the trust property would be good decisions.

- Professional financial management for those inexperienced in handling large sums of money, which relieves a spouse or children from this responsibility and spares a settlor the burden of property management

  EXAMPLE: Nash Burke, a single parent, age 55, has recovered from a series of mild heart attacks. He owns property that he wants to transfer by will to his children, Skylar and Asher. Since Nash is concerned about the way the property may be used or spent by his children, he would prefer to transfer it now, while he is alive, in order to determine how well the property is managed. A living trust with a spendthrift clause under experienced and expert corporate management could relieve the children of this administration responsibility, benefit them immediately, and continue after Nash's death.

- A method to avoid probate

  EXAMPLE: Wesley Parker wants to avoid the expense of probate, ancillary proceedings, and the publicity of probate. He may, therefore, choose to create, as a will substitute, a revocable living trust to continue after his death. A will is probated; a living trust is not.

- A public, charitable trust for an educational, health, scientific, or religious institution

  EXAMPLE: Priscilla wants to give a substantial amount of money to St. Mary's Hospital, but she wants to control the way the money will be used. She could establish a living trust and name herself as trustee with such powers.

ASSIGNMENT 13.10

Sonya dies testate. She gives her farm, Longacre, "to Marco in trust for my husband, Gerard, for his lifetime, and at his death, to our two children, Ursula and Eduardo, in equal shares as tenants in common." At the time of Sonya's death, all other parties mentioned are living. Does this provision of the will create a trust? Classify it. Ursula and Eduardo are remaindermen. What does the term mean?

ASSIGNMENT 13.11

Jean-Luc Bernadois, a naturalized citizen, wishes to set up a trust for the benefit of his sister, Lenore, who has recently arrived from Martinique and has little knowledge of financial matters. He has government bonds valued at $25,000.

1. Assuming that Jean-Luc does set up a trust, identify the settlor, the beneficiary, and the trust property.

2. Whom might the settlor appoint trustee? Why?

3. Would it be advisable to make a gift of the bonds rather than a transfer of them in trust? Why or why not?

Legal Restrictions

Generally, a trust can be created for any purpose that is legal; however, the law has imposed some restrictions on what constitutes a legal purpose (Restatement [Third] of Trusts §§ 27, 29). Restrictions on purposes of trusts fall into several categories. There are restrictions on purposes contrary to public policy, such as imposing total restraint on marriage or attempting to encourage divorce (Restatement [Third] of Trusts § 29).

> **EXAMPLE:** Otto Lindberg tells his son, Tobias, that he will transfer his ski resort, Arrowhead, to Rupert Maulkin in a living trust for Tobias's benefit if Tobias will divorce his wife, Matilda. Such a condition is against public policy and would invalidate the trust. In this case, Otto would retain the trust property.

Some restrictions are imposed by statute. Statutes restricting trusts are usually framed in general language; e.g., N.Y. EPTL § 7-1.4 states, "An express trust may be created for any lawful purpose." The definition of what is "lawful" is then subject to interpretation by the New York courts. Some statutes contain further restrictions, usually in the area of real property trusts.

> **EXAMPLE:** Hermann Pfaltzgraff lives in South Dakota. As a gift to his daughter, Beatrix, he transfers to her in a living trust a part of his wheat acreage. Hermann's gift must be in writing to be valid, according to S.D. Cod. Laws Ann. § 43-10-4.

Some restrictions are imposed on private noncharitable trusts by the Rule Against Perpetuities, which prohibits indefinite accumulations of wealth or property. The perpetuation of a trust that effectively prohibits all but those members of a certain class from possessing the trust property beyond an extended statutory period contravenes public policy and the Rule Against Perpetuities.

> **EXAMPLE:** In his will, Blaine Noonan gives $100,000 in trust to Investors, Inc., to hold and invest, to accumulate the income of the trust property for the next 100 years, and then to transfer the trust estate to the heirs of Blaine equally. The testamentary trust is invalid because the rule against perpetual interests in trust property requires that the period be no greater than the continuance of *lives in being* at the time the trust instrument takes effect and 21 years thereafter plus the period of gestation.

Another restriction is a valid trust cannot be formed if it is based on an illegal contract or agreement. Where a trust is created and income is to be paid to the beneficiary on condition the beneficiary aids in the commission of criminal acts, the purpose is illegal and the trust is invalid. Any illegal purpose, such as inducing the beneficiary to live in adultery with the settlor or defrauding the settlor's creditors, will invalidate the trust. Any trust designed to induce criminal acts is invalid, e.g., a trust set up to reward a beneficiary for committing perjury or to pay legal costs and fines for a beneficiary who commits a crime (Restatement [Third] of Trusts § 29).

ASSIGNMENT 13.12

Sherman Aldrich, retired president of a paper products firm, creates the Northwest Environmental Trust to preserve valuable forest land in the Pacific Northwest. He endows the trust with $500,000 and, in the trust instrument, directs the trustees to invest and reinvest the money for the cultivation and reforestation of certain tracts of land and to encourage legislation favorable to the continuation of these aims.

1. Is this trust legal or illegal? Why? (See Restatement [Third] of Trusts § 30.)

2. Under what circumstances, if any, might this trust be declared invalid?

3. In the event that one of the purposes of the trust becomes or is declared to be illegal, could the remainder of the trust be enforced?

Just as a trust may not violate statutory law, it may not violate public policy. A provision in a trust imposing total restraint on a beneficiary to marry is generally invalid (but see *Young v. Kraeling*, 134 N.Y.S.2d 109 [1954], in which the court held a remarriage caused the widower to lose his trust fund). For instance, if the trust provides that a beneficiary will be divested of an interest if the beneficiary should *ever* marry anyone, the provision is invalid since it is against public policy to prevent a person from marrying, having children, and a normal family life (Restatement [Third] of Trusts § 29). A trust that provides income payments to a person whose spouse has died until the person remarries, does not oppose public policy however, since it restrains not marriage but remarriage. Courts have generally upheld trusts that provide that the beneficiary will lose his interest if he

- marries a particular person.
- marries before reaching majority.
- marries before reaching majority without the consent of the trustee (or someone else).
- marries a person of a particular religious faith.
- marries a person of a faith different from that of the beneficiary.

These restrictions are not considered to "unduly" restrain marriage and are referred to as "reasonable restraints." In determining the validity or invalidity of a partially illegal trust, the court will likely declare the trust valid if it determines that the settlor's intent was not to restrain marriage but merely to provide support to the beneficiary as long as the beneficiary remains single. The facts, in particular the settlor's intent, are crucial to the court's decision.

If a testamentary trust provides that a beneficiary will be divested for marrying without the consent of executors and trustees, and, if under provisions of the will those persons will profit by refusing to consent to the beneficiary's marriage, the provision is invalid. Provisions that are designed to prevent hasty or imprudent marriages and that subject a minor to the restraint of parents or friends during minority are allowed. The reasoning is that the law should uphold such a provision because it protects the minor from unscrupulous persons who could dissipate the proceeds established for the minor's benefit.

Likewise, a provision in a trust that divests beneficiaries of their interests if they communicate or have social relations with certain other family members is invalid as being against public policy and disruptive of family relations (Restatement [Third] of Trusts § 29).

Another invalid provision is one that constitutes an inducement to change the religious faith of the beneficiary (Restatement [Third] of Trusts § 29). For example, if a trust provides that Maureen O'Shannahan is to receive her interest only if she changes her religious faith or that her interest ceases if she does not change her religious faith, the courts hold as a general rule that enforcement of such provisions restrains the religious freedom of the beneficiary by improperly inducing her to change or not to change her faith.

INFORMAL AND INCOMPLETE CREATION OF A TRUST

When competent legal advice is not sought, a private express living or testamentary trust might be drafted improperly, and litigation could result. The following are some of the major mistakes made in an improperly drafted trust.

- A testator-settlor, in a hand-drawn will, indicates that he wants certain testamentary trust objectives accomplished but expresses this using **precatory words** such as *hope, desire, request,* or *wish* rather than expressing it as a mandate.
- The trust document does not sufficiently identify the beneficiary or fails to name a beneficiary.
- The trust instrument fails to name a trustee or fails to name a successor when the named trustee does not want to serve.
- The document names the trustee and describes the beneficiaries but does not specify the duties of the trustee.
- Although the trust instrument purports to be transferring legal title, the trust terms are not specified, or they have only been implied in an informal oral agreement.

precatory words
Words such as *hope, desire, request, ask, beseech, wish,* or *recommend*, which are ineffective to dispose of property.

Failure to Make Intentions Clear

It is possible to create a trust without actually using the words *trustee* or *in trust*. However, in a hand-drawn instrument the use of these words is not conclusive evidence of the intent to create a trust. In order to create an express trust, the court must be satisfied that the settlor manifested an intention to impose enforceable duties on the trustee to manage the property for the benefit of others. When a testator uses precatory words such as *hope, wish, desire,* or *recommend* to devise the property of his estate, the court must determine whether he intended an absolute gift or a trust (Restatement [Third] of Trusts § 13). It will consider all relevant factors before reaching a conclusion.

> **EXAMPLE:** Rhine Cormick's will provides, in part: "I give to my wife in the event of my death all my interest in the farm we own as tenants in common and all the stock, farm implements, etc., after my debts are paid. To have and to hold the same in fee simple and to dispose of the same among the children as she may think best." An argument could be made that the will establishes a testamentary trust in the property for the benefit of the children, but another view is the devisee (the wife) is given an estate in fee simple.

> **EXAMPLE:** Brockton Vanderhaavn's will gives property to his wife "to be her absolute estate forever." He added the words, "It is my request that on her death, my said wife shall give, devise, and bequeath the real property given her to persons named in the fourth clause of this will." An ambiguity is created because the testator cannot create a fee simple estate for his wife and then request the same property be transferred to others on her death. That right belongs to the fee owner, i.e., the testator's wife. The court held the wife took the property in fee simple and not in trust.

These examples illustrate the effects that unclear terms may have on an intended trust. In some cases, inclusion of these precatory words results in the undoing of the would-be settlor's intentions.

The early English view held that the use of such words as *request, desire, hope,* and *wish* was a courteous means of creating duties enforceable by the courts. Some courts hold that the use of such *precatory words* does *not* create a trust. The intent to create a trust containing such words must be proven by other sections of the trust instrument or by extrinsic circumstances (Restatement [Third] of Trusts § 13). Other courts hold that the words create a **precatory trust** and allow the trust to be performed.

precatory trust
A trust created by precatory words, e.g., "*wish and request,*" or *have fullest confidence,* which the courts have held sufficient to constitute a trust.

EXAMPLE: Suppose a testator, Artemis Kontopos, wills all his property to his wife, and adds, "I recommend to her the care and protection of my mother and sister, and request her to make such provision for them as in her judgment will be best." Both mother and sister are invalids and in need, and the testator had supported them for some time before his death. A court could hold that his wife takes the property in trust with the obligation to make a reasonable provision for the continual care of the testator's mother and sister. Such a testamentary trust is poorly drafted because it creates an ambiguity, i.e., a conveyance of the estate property to the testator's spouse but with a request that the spouse "care and protect" the testator's invalid mother and sister. A court's decision to call this will provision a testamentary trust could be based on the circumstances, i.e., the fact that the mother and sister are invalids, and that the testator had previously cared for them. However, consider and compare the case of *In re Lubenow's Estate*, 146 N.W.2d 166 (N.D. 1966), in which the testator left his estate to his nephew with directions "to see to it that my brothers are provided for." The court held that "these [precatory] words do no more than express a wish or desire on the part of the testator." Therefore, no testamentary trust was created. The nephew received the entire estate.

When drafting wills and trusts, it is best to avoid these precatory words altogether.

Failure to Name or Identify the Beneficiary

When the trust instrument fails to name a beneficiary, a few cases give the trustee absolute ownership. However, the general rule is a "resulting trust" arises in favor of the decedent's estate if the trust instrument was testamentary (Restatement [Third] of Trusts § 24). If a living trust is created and it fails to name a beneficiary, the attempt to create a trust fails.

EXAMPLE: If Melvin Bowles sets aside money for a living trust, executes the instrument, and directs the trustee to distribute the income to persons the trustee considers deserving, the trust fails since Melvin did not clearly identify the beneficiaries. Had he augmented the description, e.g., "to be distributed to my nieces and nephews" or "to the descendants of my sister, Vanessa," the beneficiaries would at least be identifiable.

Failure to Name a Trustee or a Successor Trustee

A valid trust will not fail for want of a trustee or successor trustee. Lack of a trustee to administer the trust may come about in any of the following ways.

- If the settlor does not name a trustee in the trust instrument or fails to name a successor trustee to resolve the problem of the original trustee's death, resignation, or nonacceptance, i.e., the trustee's unwillingness or inability to serve
- If the named trustee does not qualify, e.g., refuses to accept the duty, dies before the effective date of the trust, or is refused confirmation of the office by the court because of incompetence
- If the named trustee does not have legal capacity to hold property in trust, e.g., in some states an unincorporated association
- If the named trustee is removed or resigns after the effective date of the trust

Courts will preserve trusts. Normally, the court will not allow a trust to fail for any of the above reasons and will appoint a new trustee as long as the trust is otherwise valid. Where a trustee is needed to execute and manage a trust, state statutes authorize the court to appoint the following: (1) an original trustee where the trust document or will creating the trust has not nominated a trustee or the nominee is unable or unwilling to serve; and (2) a successor trustee, when the original trustee has ceased to act and a replacement is required to finish the administration of the trust. The trust will fail only if it can be shown that the settlor intended only the named person and no one else could be the trustee.

Although the laws of a few states prohibit the creation of joint tenancy, this prohibition does not apply to property held in trust. Co-trustees generally hold title to trust property as joint tenants with the right of survivorship, so if one dies, disclaims, resigns, or is removed by a court, legal title passes to the remaining co-trustee(s) by operation of law (Restatement [Third] of Trusts § 34).

> **EXAMPLE:** Takahiro Fujii places 500 shares of Behl, Inc., in trust for the benefit of his son, Yuki, and names Takahiro's three brothers trustees as joint tenants. Later, one brother resigns due to ill health. The court decides two trustees will suffice since the settlor did not specify there must be three at all times. Therefore, the court does not appoint a new trustee. At the annual stockholders' meeting of Behl, the two trustees vote in the name of the trust. Another major stockholder contends that the Fujii trust votes were invalid because they were cast by two, not three, trustees. The votes are valid. The two trustees hold the entire legal title to the trust by right of survivorship.

LIVING (INTER VIVOS) TRUSTS

A living trust is one of the two ways property can be placed in a trust; the other is a testamentary trust. A living trust is created by a settlor and operates during the settlor's lifetime. The trust property is a nonprobate asset; therefore, it is not part of the decedent's probate estate and is not under the jurisdiction or supervision of the probate court.

A living trust can be created by either of the following:

1. A *declaration of trust* in which the settlor retains the legal title to the trust property and is, therefore, also the trustee and, thereafter, names another person or persons to be the beneficiaries. The declaration of trust must be signed by the settlor and at least two witnesses or notarized (see Exhibit 13.3 for a sample declaration of trust illustrating the introductory clause).

2. A *trust agreement* in which the settlor transfers legal title to another party, the trustee, who manages or administers the property in trust for the beneficiary who holds the equitable title and receives the benefits of the trust (see the Durham Trust in Exhibit 13.2).

A settlor's *declaration of trust* or a conveyance of trust that uses a *trust agreement* are simple methods of establishing a living trust. In the former, the owner of property, i.e., the settlor, simply declares himself trustee of the property for the benefit of another person. The conveyance of trust method requires the settlor to sign a *trust agreement* with a trustee and a successor trustee and transfer property to create the trust. As mentioned previously, the settlor and the trustee or the settlor and the beneficiary may be the same person depending on the type of trust selected. A trust is not created, however, until the declaration or the transfer of

Exhibit 13.3	Sample Declaration of Trust

Declaration of Trust

This declaration of trust is made on _____ [date],
by _____, of _____ [address], _____
[city], _____ [county], _____ [state], referred to as trustor.

Section One

Declaration of Trust

I _____ as trustor, have assigned myself as trustee and declare that I hold in trust the securities described in the attached Schedule A, which is incorporated by reference. I declare that I and my successor trustee will hold the described securities, and all substitutions and additions, as the trust estate for the use and benefit of _____, of _____ [address], _____ [city], _____ [county], _____ [state], referred to as beneficiary, for the following purposes and on the following terms and conditions: [see 17A Am. Jur. Legal Forms 2d § 251:6 for complete text.]

* * *

the trust property takes place. If the conveyance is a transfer of personal property to a living trust, no formalities are required for the declaration of trust except that the settlor-trustee must manifest an intention to hold or place the property in trust. If the trust property is realty, the settlor must put the declaration of trust or trust agreement in writing to satisfy the requirements of the Statute of Frauds (Restatement [Third] of Trusts § 22). Likewise, delivery requirements are simple. For example, if the conveyance is a gift of land, the settlor must deliver the deed to the trustee; if the gift is personal property, usually delivery of the gift itself is necessary.

EXAMPLE: Morgan St. John, a widow with four children, received her father's resort, Edgewater, from his estate. If Morgan wishes to create a living trust using this property, she will have to put the trust agreement in writing. She will also have to deliver the deed to Edgewater to the trustee.

Revocable Living Trusts

A living trust is either revocable or irrevocable. In a revocable trust, the settlor reserves the right to amend, revoke, or cancel the trust at any time while living. On the death of the settlor, the living trust becomes *irrevocable* and the trust property is disposed of or distributed according to the terms of the trust. Since revocable trusts avoid the need for and cost of probate or estate administration, they are commonly used in estate planning (see Chapter 14). A revocable living trust is not a device for saving estate taxes, however; only an irrevocable trust offers that additional tax benefit (see the discussion below). Many people today are using a revocable living trust as a substitute for a will. The trust allows the settlor to transfer the entire estate to the trust, manage and retain full control over the assets of the trust, receive the income from the trust during his or her lifetime, distribute the trust property after death to the named beneficiaries (usually children), and avoid the often substantial costs and delays of probate. The trust becomes the legal owner of the property both before and after the settlor's death and is responsible for the payments of all outstanding debts and taxes.

When a revocable living trust is created a trustee must be named to manage and control the trust. Frequently, the settlor will name himself trustee, or, if married, the settlor and the settlor's spouse will act as co-trustees or joint-trustees, which grants either spouse the legal authority to act as trustee. If one spouse becomes disabled or dies, the other spouse automatically has control of the trust without the delays and expense of the probate process or the intervention of the probate court. Even though a settlor no longer owns the trust property, the revocable living trust enables the settlor-trustee to retain complete control of the property and to avoid paying any management fees. As trustee, the settlor can invest, buy, and sell the trust property, distribute the income from the trust to himself or to whomever the settlor chooses, change the trust beneficiaries, or, because it is revocable, cancel the trust at any time. The former owner (settlor) of the trust property who is now the trustee is obligated to preserve, maintain, and insure the property and file the annual income tax returns. If the settlor appoints someone else trustee, the trust agreement usually provides the trustee is to manage and invest the trust property for the benefit of the settlor-beneficiary for life, and pay to the settlor-beneficiary all the income and as much of the principal of the trust as the trustee determines is required for the settlor-beneficiary's care. Problems that arise due to the disability, incompetence, or death of the settlor are discussed below.

In the past, the revocable living trust was most commonly used for the primary benefit of an elderly settlor who owned a substantial amount of income-producing property (assets) and desired to be relieved of the responsibility of managing the property. Today, many people of all income brackets are substituting revocable living trusts for wills.

Transfer of Trust Property to a Living Trust

If a revocable living trust is to act as a will substitute, all assets (real and personal property) owned by the settlor or in which the settlor has or acquires an interest must be transferred to the living trust. When property is transferred into a revocable living trust, a gift is not made by the settlor. Therefore, no federal or state gift taxes are due. No matter in which state it is located and whether or not it is income producing, *all real estate* including rental units such as apartment buildings, duplexes, rooming houses, and commercial buildings plus residential property including the settlor's house, vacation home, cottage, or condominium *must be* transferred to the trustee (s) of the trust. When asked to assist the settlor with these transfers, you will most likely use a quitclaim deed (Exhibit 13.4) or a trust transfer deed (Exhibit 13.5) as the document to correct or change title (ownership) of real property either from an individual or from spouses holding title as joint tenants to the trustee (s) of the living trust. This is just a change of title, not a transfer of title. The executed deed must be delivered to the trustee(s) but does not necessarily need to be recorded. However, if the deed is recorded, the legal forms required by the local county tax assessors in the county the real property is located must be executed to establish that the property is now trust property. In addition, some states have statutes or rules of procedure that ensure the transfer of the settlor's domiciliary residence (homestead) into the trust does

homestead exemption
Property tax reductions or exemptions available in some states for homestead property. A formal declaration is recorded to establish the homestead or whenever the property changes owners.

not cause the loss of the **homestead exemption** for property tax purposes. *Caveat:* Permission must be obtained from the bank that holds the mortgage on real property that the settlor intends to transfer to the trust, since the transfer may trigger a clause (provision) in the mortgage loan agreement that requires immediate repayment of the loan. This approval must be obtained *before* recording any transfer of the property.

> **EXAMPLE:** To change the title to his real property, Dexter J. Hoffman, a single person, would sign the trust transfer deed from "Dexter J. Hoffman, single" to "Dexter J. Hoffman, as Trustee of the Dexter J. Hoffman Revocable Living Trust, under trust dated August 1, 2014."

> **EXAMPLE:** If Damian E. Bradford and his wife, Hillary S. Bradford, own real property as joint tenants, they could change the title by both signing the deed from "Damian E. Bradford and Hillary S. Bradford, husband and wife as joint tenants" to "Damian E. Bradford and Hillary S. Bradford, as Trustees of the [name of trust], under trust dated August 1, 2014."

You must also change (reregister) title to personal property such as checking and savings accounts, stocks, bonds, certificates of deposit, money market and mutual funds, partnerships, cars, boats, and any other titled property to the name of the trustee(s) using the designated language as shown in the Dexter J. Hoffman example above. Untitled personal property such as clothing, furs, jewelry, art objects, antiques, stamp and coin collections, and household furnishings can easily be transferred into the trust by a written assignment from the settlor to the trustee(s) that states the property is to be added to the trust. You must also have the assignment document in which the property is listed, signed and notarized. Some states have an assignment form that transfers all untitled personal property to the trustee (s) of the living trust (see N.Y. EPTL § 7-1.18). A copy of the assignment should be attached to the trust document. Any future untitled personal property should also be assigned to the trustee (s). In addition, all property that allows the settlor to name a beneficiary (such as life insurance policies, annuities, IRAs [traditional or Roth], 401(k), pension, profit-sharing, and self-employed retirement plans) may be changed so that the primary beneficiary is the spouse or children and the secondary or successor beneficiary is the trustee(s) of the revocable living trust. Although the above property items that name a beneficiary already avoid probate, it is helpful to change the secondary or successor beneficiary to the trustee(s) of the revocable living trust to consolidate these assets, resulting in a more efficient and better coordinated administration, *and* to avoid the possible dilemma that may occur if the current owner and primary beneficiary die simultaneously. *Caveat:* Title or ownership of all retirement benefits, e.g., annuities, IRAs, and all the other retirement plans listed above **MUST NOT BE CHANGED** or **TRANSFERRED** to the living trust but should remain in the settlor's name. The change of ownership to the trustee would constitute a withdrawal and become a taxable event. Ownership of these benefits should and must *not* be transferred to the trust. *However*, the decision to name (1) the trustee (s) of the revocable living trust or (2) nonspouse individuals or charities as secondary or successor beneficiaries should only be made after receiving the necessary professional advice to maximize tax savings for the estate. Also, if the settlor is the insured person and the owner of a life insurance policy, the only change required is to name the trustee(s) the beneficiary. The settlor retains all ownership rights and should *not* transfer ownership or title to the name of the trustee(s).

EXHIBIT 13.4	Sample Quitclaim Deed

Recording Requested By

And when recorded mail to:

Name

Street
Address

City
State
Zip

Space above this line for recorder's use _____

WOLCOTTS FORMS, INC.   WWW.WOLCOTTSFORMS.COM   *SINCE 1893*

QUITCLAIM DEED

DOCUMENTARY TRANSFER TAX $ _____.
☐ computed on full value of property conveyed, or
☐ computed on full value less liens and
   encumbrances remaining at time of sale.

Autograph of Declarant or Agent Determining Tax   Firm Name

I/We, _____,
(Name of grantor(s))
the undersigned grantor(s), for a valuable consideration, receipt of which is hereby acknowledged, do hereby remise, release, convey and forever quitclaim to _____
(Name of grantee(s))
the following described real property In the City of _____, County of _____, State of _____:

Assessor's parcel No. _____

Executed on _____, _____, in the City of _____, State of _____.

_____

_____

STATE OF _____

COUNTY OF _____

On _____ before me, _____ personally appeared
_____
personally known to me (or proved to me on the basis of satisfactory evidence) to be the person(s) whose name(s) is/are subscribed to the within instrument and acknowledged to me that he/she/they executed the same in his/her/their authorized capacity(ies), and that by his/her/their signature(s) on the instrument the person(s), or the entity upon behalf of which the person(s) acted, executed the instrument

WITNESS my hand and official seal.

_____
Signature of Notary   (seal)

MAIL TAX_____

STATEMENTS TO: _____

CAPACITY CLAIMED BY SIGNER(S)
☐ Individual(s)
☐ Corporate
   Officer(s) _____
☐ Partner(s)   Limited   General
☐ Attorney in Fact
☐ Trustee
☐ Guardian/Conservator

RIGHT THUMBPRINT (Optional)

7 67775 00790 9

FORM 790   REV. 1-04A

Exhibit 13.5   Sample Trust Transfer Deed

RECORDING REQUESTED BY:

WHEN RECORDED MAIL TO:

Name

Street
Address

City

State

Zip

Space above this line for recorder's use

WOLCOTTS FORMS, INC.   *SINCE 1893*

CALIFORNIA TRUST TRANSFER DEED

Grant Deed, excluded from Reassessment under Proposition 13, California Constitution Article 13 A §1 et seq. The undersigned Grantor(s) declare(s) under penalty of perjury that the following is true and correct:

1. There is no consideration for this transfer.

2. The Documentary Transfer Tax is $ _____.
    - ❏ Computed on full value on property conveyed, or
    - ❏ Computed on full value less value of liens and encumbrances remaining at time of sale or transfer.
    - ❏ There is no Documentary Transfer Tax due because _____
    _____
    GIVE CODE PARAGRAPH OR ORDINANCE NUMBER

3. ❏ Property is in an unincorporated area of _____ County.
    ❏ Property is in the City of _____.

4. This is a Trust Transfer under §62 of the Revenue and Taxation Code. Grantor must check the applicable exclusion.
    - ❏ Transfer is to a revocable trust.
    - ❏ Transfer is to a short-term trust not exceeding 12 years with Trustor holding the reversion.
    - ❏ Transfer is to a trust where the Trustor or the Trustor's spouse is the sole beneficiary.
    - ❏ This is a change of Trustee holding title.
    - ❏ Transfer is from Trust to Trustor or Trustor's spouse where prior transfer was excluded from reappraisal and for a valuable consideration, receipt of which is acknowledged.
    - ❏ Other _____
    _____

I/We, _____, Grantor(s),

hereby grant(s) to _____

the following described real property in the City of _____, or unincorporated area of,

_____ County, State of California:

_____   _____
DATE   AUTOGRAPH

                                                                              _____
                                                                              AUTOGRAPH

Wolcotts Forms, our resellers and agents make no representations or warranty, express or implied, as to the fitness of this form for any specific use or purpose. If you have any question, it is always best to consult a qualified attorney before using this or any legal document.

©2005 WOLCOTTS FORMS, INC.

#551   REV. 10-05

EXHIBIT 13.5 (Continued)

STATE OF _____)

COUNTY OF _____)

On _____ before me, _____, Notary Public,

personally appeared _____

_____

personally known to me (or proved to me on the basis of satisfactory evidence) to be the person(s) whose name(s) is/are subscribed to the within instrument and acknowledged to me that he/she/they executed the same in his/her/their authorized capacity(ies), and that by his/her/their signature(s) on the instrument the person(s), or the entity upon behalf of which the person(s) acted, executed the instrument.

WITNESS my hand and official seal.

_____
    Signature   (Seal)

Advantages of a Revocable Living Trust as a Substitute for a Will

The following are some of the advantages of a revocable living trust.

- It avoids probate since trust property is a nonprobate asset, and it avoids probate expense—the costs of probating the estate of a decedent who dies with a will or intestate may include filing fees, court costs, publication and advertising expenses, appraisal and auction fees, bond expense, costs of will contests, expenses of challenges to creditors' claims, expenses of establishing guardianships for minor children, and, most expensive of all, the fees for attorneys and personal representatives. It is estimated that the average total probate expense ranges from 5 to 15 percent of an estate's gross value. Also, the smaller the gross estate, the higher the percentage cost. In comparison, the cost of establishing a living trust generally averages $1,500 to $3,000 depending on the complexity of the settlor's estate. Wills and trusts both need to be updated, which adds another expense.

- It avoids the lengthy delays often associated with estate administration— even if a testamentary trust is included in a decedent's will, it takes time to have a trustee appointed whenever beneficiaries of the will are minors, disabled, or incompetent persons.

Other routine problems that delay probate include locating assets, finding beneficiaries, and simply waiting for a court calendar date. It is not unusual for the final distribution of the estate property to beneficiaries and the closing of the probate process to take a year or more.

- It can also diminish the cost and delays caused by will contests or invalid creditors' claims. *Note:* A living trust can be contested but not as easily as a will. Time is also a factor when a will is contested by disgruntled family members who are not included as named beneficiaries of the decedent or who are disappointed in the amount of property left to them. Since the settlor creates and often administers the trust while living, it is in operation while the settlor can personally alter it; thus, the trust establishes persuasive evidence of the settlor's competence and clearly reflects the settlor's true wishes. Consequently, the probate court is reluctant to change it. However, where a will exists, all persons who would inherit from the decedent if the decedent died intestate must be notified of the petition to probate the will. This allows, even invites, the disinherited or dissatisfied family members to challenge the will's validity. Even if this will contest is unfounded, delays and expense are the result. Creditors may also make unsubstantiated claims against the decedent's estate, which the personal representative must challenge in a court hearing. All of these concerns take time and cost money. If a living trust is already in operation, the delays and added costs described above are usually avoided.

- It avoids publicity—the will, its contents, and the probate file and documents are public records (i.e., they are open to the public). This means anyone can examine these records to determine what property the decedent owned at the time of death and who the beneficiaries are. Vulnerable family members, especially elderly surviving spouses, may possibly be exploited by individuals who obtain information from these public records and offer to sell investments, worthless and unsolicited merchandise, unnecessary or expensive insurance, or management services. Business competitors may attempt to take advantage of an owner-manager's death by offering to buy the business at unfavorable prices or other terms. The use of a revocable living trust can assure the settlor-decedent of complete privacy in the distribution of the trust property and enable surviving family members to avoid the potential problem of dishonest opportunists.

- It is not under the control or supervision of the probate court. Instead, it enables the settlor, while living, or the settlor's trustee, to continue to control and manage the property; and after the settlor's death, the family members can retain control of the trust property. Whereas with a will, the family may find they must obtain court approval before any assets of the deceased can be distributed to named beneficiaries or sold. As noted above, this process is time-consuming and expensive.

- It also affords the settlor, while living, an opportunity to view the operation of the trust, verify its performance, and make necessary and appropriate changes, such as granting more or less power to trustees, changing beneficiaries, or selling and giving away trust property. Settlors can even cancel the revocable trust whenever they wish.

- It provides lifetime or longer management of trust assets by experienced professional corporate trustees for the benefit of the settlor, the settlor's spouse and family, or other named beneficiaries. A will, however, obviously takes effect only after death.

- It allows the settlor who owns real estate in other states to avoid the time and expense of an ancillary administration normally required to pass the title to such real estate to beneficiaries of the trust. An ancillary administration is required since only the state in which the real estate is located has jurisdiction to convey (transfer) title to the property. A will necessitates the ancillary procedures, a living trust avoids them.

- It avoids the need, expense, and delay of appointing a guardian or conservator required under state law if the settlor becomes disabled or is declared incompetent. A living trust provides a convenient, reviewable, and private administration of the settlor's affairs by a trustee who can control all of the settlor's property, wherever located, with much more flexible powers of investment and property management than a court-appointed guardian or conservator, who must report to the probate court and whose functions and duties can be restricted by both the court and state statutes. In addition, the trustee may continue to administer trust assets after the settlor's death, whereas a guardian or conservator's authority to act terminates at death.

- It also eliminates the need, expense, and delay of court-appointed guardians for minors or conservators for dependents with special needs due to physical or mental incapacity. A living trust can provide for these individuals specifically and also reassure the settlor, while living, that they are properly cared for and will continue to be cared for after the settlor's death. A will cannot verify such matters for a testator, who must die before the will takes effect.

- It may allow the settlor to save on death taxes, e.g., the federal estate tax, the state inheritance tax, and the state estate tax, but only if it is an irrevocable living trust. However, wills containing testamentary trusts may also limit these taxes. Either a testamentary or a living trust makes it possible to pass the decedent's estate tax-free to a surviving spouse; however, the testamentary trust must go through probate.

Disadvantages of a Revocable Living Trust

The following are some of the disadvantages of a revocable living trust.

- It may be more costly to create the trust than to draft a will depending on the amount of assets the settlor-testator owns or the complexity of the estate, and the trustee's management and administration fees are a continual expense throughout the life of the trust. However, wills are frequently changed and redrawn, often many times, and the total cost of many wills plus the probate costs will most likely exceed the cost of a living trust.

- It requires all of the settlor's assets, except for life insurance and retirement benefits previously discussed, to be transferred into the living trust by changing titles to real property, reregistering titled personal property, assigning untitled personal property, and placing all newly acquired property in the name of the trustee(s) of the trust. This makes the trust and not the settlor the owner of the assets. If this is not done because the settlor forgets or procrastinates, the property whose title is unchanged must go through the probate process.

Pour-Over Wills

If a revocable living trust is substituted for a will as the legal document of choice to avoid the probate process and to transfer and distribute the settlor's property after death, a **pour-over will** should also be executed. The pour-over will allows the testator to direct or pass the residue of the estate into an existing living trust. The will ensures that property acquired by the settlor after the revocable living trust was established or property the settlor forgot to transfer into the trust will be distributed according to the terms of the trust rather than pass by intestate succession.

pour-over will
A will provision in which the testator directs (passes) the residue of the estate into an existing living trust.

As a companion to the revocable living trust, the pour-over will can perform the following important functions.

1. It can dispose of property the testator neglected to add to the trust before death.

2. It can dispose of property acquired through gifts, inheritance, or good fortune shortly before death.

3. It can allow the testator to specifically disinherit family members, e.g., children and other heirs, which can only be done by a clear and expressed statement in the will.

4. It can allow the testator to name a personal and/or property guardian (conservator) for minor children.

5. It can allow the testator to name the same person as trustee of the living trust and personal representative of the will.

Irrevocable Living Trusts

An irrevocable living trust may not be amended, revoked, or canceled after its creation. Living trusts are generally irrevocable unless the trust instrument contains a provision stating it is revocable. To avoid any confusion concerning a settlor's intent, the trust should include a provision such as "The settlor hereby declares this trust agreement and all its provisions shall be irrevocable and not subject to any amendment or modification by the settlor or any other person." An irrevocable living trust not only has the advantages of avoiding probate and its expense, but also can be used as a tax-saving device.

- Although a living trust cannot save on income taxes, it can save on federal estate tax, in appropriate trusts, by excluding the trust property from the decedent-settlor's gross estate, thereby reducing or avoiding the federal estate tax. This is commonly accomplished using an irrevocable life insurance trust.

   EXAMPLE: Paulette Pittinger is a single parent with two teenage children. The total value of her gross estate including the face amount (proceeds) of her life insurance exceeds her applicable estate tax exclusion. If Paulette wishes to avoid probate and completely control her property, she can create two trusts: a revocable trust, into which she would place all of her property except her life insurance; and an irrevocable life insurance trust, into which she would place her life insurance polices and the ownership of them. By funding the irrevocable trust with an amount of money sufficient to pay the annual life insurance premiums, the amount of the life insurance will be paid to the trust when Paulette dies and will not be added to Paulette's gross estate. This will keep the estate value within her applicable exclusion amount and thereby avoid the United States (federal) estate tax (see the discussion and details in Chapter 14).

   EXAMPLE: Spouses such as Arnold and Irene Mayer, who have three children, can also take advantage of a revocable trust with an A-B trust option and an irrevocable life insurance trust to preserve both of their applicable exclusion amounts. Using a revocable trust, they can control their property during their lifetime and avoid probate at death. Using one or more irrevocable life insurance trusts as appropriate, they can eliminate the value of their life insurance from their gross estate(s) and thereby pass to their children the maximum amount of their estate by avoiding the federal estate tax (see the discussion of estate planning in Chapter 14).

Caveat: For up-to-date changes in the estate, gift, and generation-skipping transfer taxes, go to *http://www.irs.gov.*

DRAFTING A LIVING TRUST

It is important for the settlor to delegate the drafting of a trust instrument to counsel knowledgeable in this area. Often, you, as the paralegal, will be asked to prepare a preliminary draft for the settlor. The instrument must conform to the requirements of the Internal Revenue Code and to state law. Therefore, before preparing the preliminary draft of a revocable or irrevocable living trust under the attorney's supervision, you must have a clear understanding of the settlor's purpose and desire for creation of the trust as well as the applicable federal and state tax consequences.

Revocable Living Trust

As previously discussed, the popular revocable living trust is used in estate planning to avoid probate and the costs associated therewith.

The hypothetical case below describes the settlor's purpose for establishing a trust and provides a sample checklist of information you need to prepare a preliminary draft (Exhibit 13.6). On the basis of the checklist data, a sample agreement is drawn, creating a private express revocable living trust (Exhibit 13.7) and accompanying pour-over will (Exhibit 13.8).

The Facts

Landon J. Kreger, age 65, lives at 53 Lake Drive, Alexandria, Douglas County, Minnesota. Landon is a widower with two adult children, Tanner W. Kreger, who lives at 1704 Jonathon Place, Maple Grove, Hennepin County, Minnesota, and Avery M. Kreger, who lives at 2613 Dove Street, Alexandria, Douglas County, Minnesota. Tanner is divorced and has two children, Chase and Aubrey. Avery is single with one child, Annika. Landon is a retired teacher with assets amounting to $800,000. They consist of $450,000 in real property (residence and vacation home); $150,000 of personal property (stocks, bank accounts, household furnishings, personal effects, and automobile); and an IRA valued at $200,000. Landon wants to place all of the assets, except the IRA, in a revocable living trust so they will not be subject to probate when he dies. He has named Tanner and Avery beneficiaries of his IRA. Landon wants the net income from the trust property paid to him annually and as much of the principal as necessary for his living expenses during his lifetime. Unless disabled, he wants to retain the right to remove and appoint trustees and add or dispose of trust property without approval of the other trustees. At his death, the tangible personal property is to go to Tanner, or to Avery if Tanner predeceases Landon, to be distributed as provided in a separate memorandum. The remainder of the trust property goes to Tanner and Avery equally. If either Tanner or Avery predeceases Landon, their share is to be distributed to their children per stirpes. The trustees are Landon, Tanner, and Avery. If Landon is disabled, he will cease to be a trustee. Landon names Tanner to be personal representative of his will and Avery his successor personal representative.

EXHIBIT 13.6 Sample Checklist for Drafting a Private Express Revocable Living Trust

Names and Addresses of Necessary Parties

Settlor and trustee:	Landon J. Kreger	53 Lake Drive
		Alexandria, Douglas
		County, Minnesota
Trustee:	Tanner W. Kreger	1704 Jonathon Place
		Maple Grove, Hennepin
		County, Minnesota
Trustee:	Avery M. Kreger	2613 Dove Street
		Alexandria, Douglas
		County, Minnesota

Relationship of trustee(s)
to settlor: Self, son and daughter

Beneficiaries:
  Income beneficiary: Landon J. Kreger   53 Lake Drive
                                                   Alexandria, Douglas
                                                   County, Minnesota

Remainderman: Tanner W. and Avery M. Kreger
  Successor: Chase, Aubrey, and Annika Kreger

Relationship of
  beneficiaries to
  settlor: Children and grandchildren of
                               Landon J. Kreger

Trust Property

Real property
  Residence: 53 Lake Drive, Alexandria, Minnesota
  Vacation home: 1305 10th Street, Naples, Florida
Personal property
  Stocks: 500 shares of preferred stock, Ace Capital
                               450 shares of preferred stock, Upham, Inc.
  Bank accounts: Minnesota State Bank, Alexandria, MN
                               Checking Account 217463335012
                               Savings Account 217463333723
  Automobile: 2014 Buick La Crosse, VIN 1D7CG8272K3135875
  Household furnishings: Located at residence and vacation home
  Personal effects: Located at residence and vacation home

Other Assets

Insurance: None
Retirement plans: 1) IRA-Primary beneficiaries are Tanner
                               and Avery
                               2) Recommend naming trust as secondary
                               beneficiary

Revocability of Trust   Trust is revocable

Trustee's Powers and Duties

Payment of income: Net income annually to Landon
Payment (transfer)
  of principal: 1) To Landon for necessary living expenses
                               2) As necessary for Landon's care, comfort,
                               support, and maintenance if disabled

EXHIBIT 13.6   (Continued)

Powers:	Retain, acquire, or dispose of trust property and other general powers
Term of Trustee	
Removal and appointment:	Removal and appointment may be by settlor or by Tanner if Landon becomes disabled
Successor in office:	None named
Trustee 's Rights	
Acceptance or rejection (determine trustee's intention):	Trustees agree to serve
Compensation:	Trustees agree to serve without charge
Termination of Trust	
Duration of trust:	Lifetime of Landon
Distribution of principal on termination of trust:	1) Remainder transferred in equal shares to Tanner and Avery upon Landon's death 2) If either Tanner or Avery predeceases Landon, remainder transferred to their children per stirpes

Using a Checklist

A checklist similar to the one in Exhibit 13.6 should be used to gather the information necessary for drafting the Kreger trust. This checklist is for illustrative purposes only. It reflects details to be included in the prospective trust instrument based on the fact situation previously outlined. Drafters of trust instruments would not and should not use this checklist in every situation.

ASSIGNMENT 13.13

From the completed checklist in Exhibit 13.6, draft a private express revocable living trust with the appropriate provisions based on the facts in the Kreger case. Compare your draft with the annotated sample trust in Exhibit 13.7 and point out the similarities and differences in the two drafts.

ASSIGNMENT 13.14

George Conover decides to create a living trust for his children, Melissa and Gary, with his wife, Grace, as trustee and trust property consisting of real estate in your state that he operates as a summer residence for tourists. Using this information, and supplying more, as necessary, to indicate the settlor's intention, compile a checklist similar to the one in Exhibit 13.6 and draft a revocable living trust for the Conover Trust.

Exhibit 13.7   Annotated Sample Revocable Living Trust

William T. Brown Trust Agreement

This trust agreement is made on July 1, 2014, between Landon J. Kreger of Alexandria, Douglas County, Minnesota, hereinafter called Settlor, and Landon J. Kreer of Alexandria, Douglas County, Minnesota, Tanner W. Krefer of Maple Grove, Hennepin County, Minnesota, and Avery M. Kreger of Alexandria, Douglas County, Minnesota, hereinafter collectively called Trustees.

Comment: The major purpose of the introductory clause is to identify the parties involved. Always include addresses to assist in proper identification.

Recitals

I have transferred certain property to the trustees contemporaneously with signing this trust agreement, the receipt of which they acknowledge and which is described in Exhibit A attached hereto; and the parties to this agreement acknowledge that all property transferred or devised to the trust now or in the future is to be administered and distributed according to the terms of this trust agreement.

Comment: This section identifies the property of the trust. It also establishes the willingness of the person nominated to act as trustee and to accept the responsibilities outlined in later articles. Use of the words "described in Exhibit A" enables the drafter to define the trust estate without making the trust instrument unduly long.

Article I
Reservation of Rights

During my life I reserve the following rights, to be exercised without the consent or participation of any other person

1. to amend, in whole or in part, or to revoke this agreement by a written declaration.
2. to add any other real or personal property to the trust by transferring such property to the trustees, and to add any other property by my will. The trustees shall administer and distribute such property as though it had been a part of the original trust property.
3. to make payable to the trustees death benefits from insurance on my life, annuities, retirement plans, or other sources. If I do so, I reserve all incidents of ownership, and I shall have the duties of safekeeping all documents, of giving any necessary notices, of obtaining proper beneficiary designations, of paying premiums, contributions, assessments or other charges, and of maintaining any litigation.
4. to receive annual written accounts from all trustees (or the personal representative of any deceased trustee). My approval of these accounts by writings delivered to another trustee shall cover all transactions disclosed in these accounts and shall be binding and conclusive as to all persons.
5. to direct the trustees as to the retention, acquisition, or disposition of any trust assets by a writing delivered to the trustees. Any assets retained or acquired pursuant to such directions shall be retained as a part of the trust assets unless I otherwise direct in writing. The trustees shall not be liable to anyone for any loss resulting from any action taken in accordance with any such direction of mine.
6. to examine at all reasonable times the books and records of the trustees insofar as they relate to the trust.

Comment: This article identifies certain rights retained by the settlor to act independently of consent or consultation with other trustees. The right to amend or revoke the agreement confirms that the trust is revocable.

Article II
Disposition of Trust Assets

Unless I am disabled, the trustees, after paying the proper charges and expenses of the trust, shall pay to me during my lifetime the entire net income from the trust property annually, and the trustees shall also pay to me and any other person who is a financial dependent of mine, in accordance with my written instructions, such portions of the principal of the trust property as I direct. If I become disabled by reason of illness, accident, or other emergency, or I am adjudicated incompetent, the trustees, other than myself, are authorized and directed to pay to me or for my benefit such portions of the trust income or principal as the trustees deem necessary to provide for my care, comfort, support, and maintenance.

On my death, the trustees, if requested by the personal representative of my estate shall, or in their own discretion may, directly or through the personal representative of my estate, pay the expenses of my last illness and funeral, my valid debts, the expenses of administering my estate, including nonprobate assets; and pay all estate, inheritance, generation-skipping, or other death taxes that become due because of my death, including any interest and penalties.

Also, on my death, I give all my tangible personal property to Tanner W. Kreger, my son, if he survives me, or if he does not survive me, to Avery M. Kreger, my daughter. (I request the recipient of any such tangible personal property

EXHIBIT 13.7   (Continued)

to distribute the same as I may have indicated informally by memorandum or otherwise.) The trustees shall distribute all the trust property not effectively disposed of by the preceding provisions of this agreement in equal shares to the persons named below. If any person named below does not survive me, such person's share shall be distributed per stirpes to such person's descendants who survive me.

Tanner J. Kreger, my son
Avery M. Kreger, my daughter

Comment: This article describes in detail the way income and principal of the trust property are to be distributed during the settlor's lifetime. It provides for the payment of last illness and funeral expenses, debts, administration expenses, and taxes and names the beneficiaries of the remaining trust property on the settlor's death.

Article III
Selection of Trustees

Trustees shall be appointed, removed, and replaced as follows: unless I am disabled, I reserve the right and power to remove any trustee and to appoint successor or additional trustees. If I become disabled, I shall cease to be a trustee. On my death or disability, my son, Tanner W. Kreger, may at any time appoint an individual or corporate trustee and may remove any individual or corporate trustee so appointed.

Comment: Unless disabled by illness, accident, or other emergency, or adjudicated incompetent, the settlor retains the right to remove and appoint trustees. This article provides for Tanner W. Kreger, as trustee, to exercise this power if Landon J. Kreger is disabled or dies.

Article IV
Trustee Powers and Provisions

The powers granted to my trustees may be exercised during the term of this trust and after the termination of the trust as is reasonably necessary to distribute the trust assets. All of the powers are to be discharged without the authorization or approval of any court. I hereby give to my trustees the following powers

(a) To retain the property described in Exhibit A and to receive property added to the trust estate from any person, provided such property is acceptable to the trustee

(b) To sell at private or public sale, exchange, lease, and mortgage or pledge any and all of the real or personal property of the estate

(c) To repair, improve, and protect (insure) trust property

(d) To invest and reinvest, to sell or exchange the principal of this trust in such securities as trustee shall in his discretion deem to be reasonable, expedient, or proper

(e) To vote in person or by proxy all stocks or other securities held by the trustee

(f) To pay income and necessary principal to the beneficiary or directly for the care, comfort, support, and maintenance of the settlor should he become disabled by reason of illness, accident, or other emergency, or be adjudicated incompetent

(g) To pay reasonable fees for professional services regarding the trust

(h) To settle, contest, compromise, submit to arbitration or litigate claims in favor of or against the estate

(i) To exercise, with respect to the trust property held by the trustee, all rights, powers, and privileges as are lawfully exercised by any person owning similar property in his or her own right

Comment: All powers that a settlor wishes to grant to the trustee should be included in the trust instrument and clearly defined. Limitations should also be specifically enumerated.

Among the administrative provisions of this trust, I request no bond or other indemnity shall be required of any trustee nominated or appointed in this trust. I expressly waive any requirement that this trust be submitted to the jurisdiction of any court, or that the trustees be appointed or confirmed, that their actions be authorized, or that their accounts be allowed, by any court. This waiver shall not prevent any trustee or beneficiary from requesting any of these procedures.

Comment: The settlor is waiving the requirement for a bond or court approval of the trustee and his or her actions. However, the waiver does not extend to other trustees or beneficiaries who retain the right to make such a request at their discretion.

Article V
General Governing Provision

The validity of the trust and the construction of its provisions shall be governed solely by the laws of the State of Minnesota as they now exist or may exist in the future.

Exhibit 13.7   (Continued)

Comment: Each state may have certain restrictions on trusts that may affect the purpose of the trust. Such restrictions must be determined before a workable instrument can be drafted.

The settlor and the trustees have signed this agreement in duplicate on or as of the date appearing at the beginning of this agreement and the trustees accept their appointments as trustees by signing this agreement.

_____
(Settlor and Trustee)
_____
(Trustee)
_____
(Trustee)

State of Minnesota)
) SS.
County of Douglas)

The foregoing instrument was acknowledged before me this 1st day of July, 2014, by Landon J. Kreger as settlor and trustee and Tanner W. Kreger and Avery M. Kreger, as trustees.

[Notarial Seal]   _____
                                                              Notary Public

EXHIBIT A

ASSETS

Residence: $250,000
53 Lake Drive
Alexandria, Douglas County, Minnesota
Legal Description
Lot 3, South Shore Addition

Vacation Home: 200,000
1305 10th Street
Naples, Collier County, Florida
Legal Description
Everglades 4th Addition

Automobile: 14,000
2014 Buick La Crosse
VIN 1D7CG8272K3135875

Bank Accounts:
Minnesota State Bank
Checking Account 217463335012   5,000
Savings Account 217463333723   15,000
Stock:

Ace Capital, Certificate 10562   40,000
500 preferred shares
Upham, Inc., Certificate 4118   35,000
450 preferred shares

Exhibit 13.7 (Continued)	
Household Furnishings:	
53 Lake Drive, Alexandria, Minnesota	20,000
1305 10th Street, Naples, Florida	15,000
Personal Effects:	
53 Lake Drive, Alexandria, Minnesota	3,000
1305 10th Street, Naples, Florida	3,000

ASSIGNMENT 13.15

In Assignment 13.14, George Conover created a revocable living trust. Draft a self-proved pour-over will to accompany the Conover Trust.

Irrevocable Living Trust

An irrevocable living trust is a convenient device to transfer assets out of a settlor's estate. Its greatest advantage is its flexibility, its adaptability to many purposes.

Using the hypothetical case below and the sample checklist of information you need to prepare a preliminary draft (Exhibit 13.9), a sample agreement is drawn, creating a private express irrevocable living trust (Exhibit 13.9).

The Facts

Geraldine Bass, age 60, lives at 1520 Holly Drive, Flowertown, Apple County, State A. Geraldine is a widow with two adult children, Larry Bass, residing at 1402 Oak Drive, Flowertown, and Rhonda Bass, living at home with her mother. Geraldine has been a very successful businesswoman. She has also been a wise investor. Geraldine wants to transfer 10,000 shares of common stock of Golden Harvest, Inc., to an irrevocable living trust for her son's benefit (to be designated Trust I). The annual income produced by the stock varies. Larry has had serious business reverses, and his mother wants to help him overcome these problems. Geraldine wants the income produced from the stock paid to Larry annually for the next five years. At the end of the period, Geraldine instructs the trustee to transfer the trust property into two separate, equal trusts, Trust II and Trust III, for the benefit of her two children, as successor beneficiaries, for their respective lifetimes. On the death of Rhonda and Larry, Geraldine wants the trusts to terminate and the principal of the trust (stock) to pass into their respective estates. Therefore, Rhonda and Larry will have the opportunity to determine through their individual wills to whom the stock will eventually be transferred.

Geraldine names her close friend and financial adviser, Dolores Evans, trustee. Dolores lives at 1040 Merry Lane, in Flowertown. Geraldine names Dolores's husband, Herbert, successor trustee. He would take over Dolores's duties, e.g., pay trust income to the beneficiaries, should Dolores become legally unable to perform. Dolores and Herbert agree to serve without compensation. The powers and duties granted by Geraldine to her trustee include the trustee's right to vote

EXHIBIT 13.8   Sample Pour-Over Will

**WILL
OF
LANDON J. KREGER**

I, Landon J. Kreger, of Alexandria, Douglas County, Minnesota, revoke any prior wills and codicils and make this my last will.

Article I
Payment of Taxes and Expenses

I direct my personal representative to pay from my estate or to direct the trustee of the Landon J. Kreger Trust under Agreement dated July 1, 2014 (referred to hereafter as the "Landon J. Kreger Trust") to pay, or both, as determined in the sole discretion of my personal representative all expenses of my last illness and funeral, my valid debts, the expenses of administering my estate, including nonprobate assets; and to pay all estate, inheritance, generation-skipping, or other death taxes that become due because of my death, including any interest and penalties.

Article II
Special Gifts

I give all my tangible personal property to Tanner W. Kreger, my son, if he survives me, or if he does not survive me, to Avery M. Kreger, my daughter. (I request the recipient of any such tangible personal property to distribute the same as I may have indicated informally by memorandum or otherwise.)

Article III
Residue

I give the rest, residue, and remainder of my estate consisting of all the real, personal, or mixed property whatsoever and wheresoever located, that I can dispose of by will and not effectively disposed of by preceding articles of this will to the trustee or trustees of the Landon J. Kreger Trust, executed by me on July 1, 2014, at Alexandria, Minnesota, as amended and existing at my death, to be added to the remaining assets of that trust and disposed of according to the terms and provisions of that trust.

Article IV
Personal Representative

I nominate and appoint Tanner W. Kreger, my son, as my personal representative. If Tanner W. Kreger fails or ceases to act or is unable or unwilling to serve as personal representative I nominate and appoint Avery M. Kreger, my daughter, as successor personal representative.

Article V
Personal Representative and Trustee Provisions

My personal representative, in addition to all other powers conferred by law that are not inconsistent with those contained in this will, shall have the power, exercisable without authorization of any court, to sell at private or public sale, to retain, to lease, and to mortgage or pledge any or all of the real or personal property of my estate; and to settle, contest, compromise, submit to arbitration or litigate claims in favor of or against my estate. I request that my estate be administrated as an Informal Administration and that no bond or other indemnity shall be required of my personal representative. I expressly waive any requirement that the Landon J. Kreger Trust be submitted to the jurisdiction of any court, or that the trustees be appointed or confirmed, or that their actions be authorized, or that their accounts be allowed, by any court. This waiver shall not prevent any trustee or beneficiary from requesting any of these procedures.

I have signed this will consisting of two pages, including this page, on July 1, 2014.

_____
Landon J. Kreger—Testator

On the date shown above, Landon J. Kreger, known to us to be the person whose signature appears at the end of the will, declared to us, the undersigned, that the foregoing instrument was his will. He then signed the will in our presence and, at his request, we now sign our names in his presence and the presence of each other.

_____   _____
Witness   Address
_____   _____
Witness   Address

Exhibit 13.8 (Continued)

State of Minnesota)
)SS.
County of Douglas)

We,_____, and _____, the testator and the witnesses, respectively, whose names are signed to the foregoing instrument, being first duly sworn, do hereby declare to the undersigned authority that the testator signed and executed the instrument as his last will and that he had signed willingly, and that he executed it as his free and voluntary act for the purposes therein expressed; and that each of the witnesses in the presence and hearing of the testator, signed the will as witness and that to the best of his knowledge the testator was at that time eighteen (18) or more years of age, of sound mind, and under no constraint or undue influence.

_____
(Testator)
_____
(Witness)
_____
(Witness)

Subscribed, sworn and acknowledged before me by _____, the testator, and subscribed and sworn before me by _____ and _____, witnesses, this 1st day of July, 2014.

[Notarial Seal]

_____
Notary Public

the stock, to sell and reinvest in other stocks or bonds when in the best interests of the beneficiaries, and to distribute the income and principal as outlined in the trust agreement. Also, Geraldine wants to retain the right to remove any trustee she selects or to allow the beneficiaries to remove the trustee.

TRUST ADMINISTRATION

In discussing the advantages of a trust, much has been said about the fact that it is private and not under the control and supervision of the courts. Used as a substitute for a will, it avoids the probate process since the trust property is a nonprobate asset. However, trusts do require administration and this is the function of the trustee. Given the authority to act within the parameters of the trust agreement, the trustee, as fiduciary, is obligated to act prudently and loyally for the sole benefit of the beneficiary. This section will address the pre-death and post-death administration of a revocable living trust.

Pre-Death Administration

The revocable living trust, with settlor as trustee or settlor as beneficiary, requires the least amount of administration. Generally, after the trust is created and funded, the administration includes the following:

1. *Manage the trust property.* The settlor-trustee has the power and right to invest and reinvest, buy, sell, lease, exchange, and mortgage or pledge the

EXHIBIT 13.9   Sample Checklist for Drafting a Private Express Irrevocable Living Trust

Names and Addresses of Necessary Parties

Settlor:	Geraldine Bass	1520 Holly Drive, Flowertown
		Apple County, State A
Trustee:	Dolores Evans	1040 Merry Lane Flowertown
		Apple County, State A
Successor trustee:	Herbert Evans	1040 Merry Lane Flowertown
		Apple County, State A
Relationship of trustee(s) to settlor:	Financial adviser and friend	
Beneficiaries:		
Income beneficiary:	Larry Bass, son	1402 Oak Drive, Flowertown
		Apple County, State A
Successor beneficiary:	Larry Bass and	Same as above
	Rhonda Bass, daughter	Same as Geraldine (mother)
Remainderman:	Respective estates of Larry and Rhonda Bass	
Relationship of beneficiaries to settlor:	Beneficiaries (Larry and Rhonda) are the children of settlor (Geraldine)	

Trust Property

Stocks:	10,000 shares of common stock, Golden Harvest, Inc.
Location:	Stock shares—transferred to trustee on acceptance

Revocability of Trust   Trust is irrevocable

Trustee's Powers and Duties

Payment of income (Trust I):	Annually to Larry for five years
Payment to successor beneficiaries (Trusts II & III):	After five years, income to be paid equally to Rhonda and Larry for life
Payment (transfer) of principal:	Principal transferred in equal shares to the respective estates of Rhonda and Larry on their deaths
Investment powers:	Invest and reinvest the securities and other general powers

Term of Trustee

Removal:	Removal may be by either settlor or both beneficiaries acting jointly
Successor in office:	Herbert Evans, husband of proposed trustee

EXHIBIT 13.9   (Continued)

Trustee's Rights

Acceptance or rejection (determine trustee's intention):	Trustees agree to serve
Compensation:	Trustees agree to serve without charge

Termination of Trust

Duration of trust:	Settlor intends to transfer income to son for five years (Trust I); then in equal shares (Trusts II and III) to both children for life. Remainder to the children's estates
Distribution of principal of Trust I on termination of trust:	Transferred in equal shares to Trusts II and III
Distribution of principal and income of Trusts II and III on termination of said trusts:	Transferred in equal shares to respective estates of Rhonda and Larry on their deaths

trust property; vote stock and give proxies; distribute the income from the trust to himself or others; change trust beneficiaries; grant more or fewer powers to trustees; or cancel the trust at any time. If the settlor appoints another person trustee, the trustee is to manage and invest the trust property for the benefit of the settlor-beneficiary for life; pay the settlor-beneficiary all of the income and as much of the principal of the trust as the trustee determines is required for the settlor-beneficiary's care; and keep accurate records of trust administration.

2. *Preserve, maintain (repair), and protect (insure) the trust property.* The trustee has the power and right to perform all tasks routinely performed by any person owing similar property.

3. *File the annual individual income tax returns (Form 1040).* These returns are filed using the settlor's social security number.

Post-Death Administration

Irrevocable trusts require more administration with the assistance of the attorney and paralegal. *Remember:* Revocable living trusts become irrevocable on the death of the settlor. Generally, administration includes the following:

1. *File for a federal employer identification number.* The irrevocable trust is a legal entity like the decedent's estate, and, as such, will be taxed on income produced by the trust (after the death of the settlor in the case of a revocable living trust).

2. *File a Notice Concerning Fiduciary Relationship.* The filing enables the Internal Revenue Service to mail the notices and tax forms to the new fiduciary.

EXHIBIT 13.10 Annotated Sample Irrevocable Living Trust

GERALDINE P. BASS
TRUST AGREEMENT

This trust agreement is made June 1, 2014, between Geraldine P. Bass of 1520 Holly Drive, City of Flower town, County of Apple, State of A, hereinafter referred to as Settlor, Dolores L. Evans of 1040 Merry Lane, City of Flowertown, County of Apple, State of A, hereinafter referred to as Trustee, and Herbert N. Evans of 1040 Merry Lane, City of Flowertown, County of Apple, State of A, hereinafter referred to as Successor Trustee.

COMMENT: The major purpose of the introductory clause in a trust is to identify the parties involved. Always include addresses to assist in proper identification.

Settlor and trustees agree to the following:

Article I
Settlor hereby transfers to trustee 10,000 shares of common corporate stock of Golden Harvest, Inc., described in Schedule A, annexed hereto and made a part hereof by this reference, the receipt of which property is hereby acknowledged by trustee, to be held in trust based on the terms herein set forth.

COMMENT: This article identifies the property of the trust. It also establishes the willingness of the person nominated to act as trustee and to accept the responsibilities outlined in later articles. Incorporation by reference, i.e., use of the words "Schedule A, annexed hereto" enables the drafter to define the trust estate without making the trust instrument unduly long.

Article II
Trustee is authorized to receive property added to the trust estate from any person, provided such property is acceptable to the trustee.

COMMENT: If the trustee is to care for property added to the trust throughout its duration, such as stock resulting from a split, this must be stipulated. Generally, property can be added to the trust throughout its existence.

Article III
Trustee shall hold, invest, and reinvest the trust property; collect the dividends, interest, and other income thereof; and, after deducting all necessary administration expenses, dispose and distribute the net income and principal as follows:

First: The net income from the trust estate shall be placed in a trust, Trust I, and shall be paid annually to Larry Bass, son of the settlor, of 1402 Oak Drive, Flowertown, Apple County, State A, for five (5) years commencing from the date of this agreement.

Second: At the end of the five-year period, the trustee shall divide the trust principal and income into equal amounts and place them into two separate trusts, Trust II and Trust III. Trust II shall be established for the benefit of Larry Bass and Trust III for Rhonda Bass, daughter of settlor, currently residing at settlor's address. The net incomes of Trust II and Trust III shall be paid annually to the respective beneficiaries, Larry and Rhonda, until their deaths. The death of each beneficiary named herein shall terminate the respective trust created for his or her benefit, and the principal and remaining income of the trust shall become part of the decedent beneficiary's estate and shall be distributed to the beneficiary's personal representative.

COMMENT: This article describes in detail the way income and principal of the trust estate shall be distributed. The settlor's directions for payment should be clear, specific, and complete. Ambiguities should be avoided. For example, the instrument should not recite "The settlor wishes the trustee to manage and invest the trust estate and pay the income to Larry Bass for five years, and thereafter to Larry Bass and Rhonda Bass in equal shares. "Perhaps the settlor knows exactly what she intends the trust to accomplish, but the trust instrument does not convey this. The lack of definiteness leads to questions concerning the implementation of the trust. Is the trustee obliged to reinvest the trust funds? May she deduct administrative expenses? Could the trust continue indefinitely? Spelling out the powers and duties of the trustee will lessen the risk of injured feelings and litigation.

EXHIBIT 13.10   (Continued)

Article IV

The trustee shall have the following powers and discretions in addition to those conferred by law.

(a) To retain the property described in "Schedule A," and any other property added to the trust estate

(b) To invest and reinvest, to sell or exchange the principal of this trust in such stocks or bonds as trustee shall in her discretion deem to be reasonable, expedient or proper regardless of whether such stocks, bonds, or other property shall be legal investments for trusts under the laws of State A

(c) To vote in person or by proxy all stocks or other securities held by trustee

(d) To exchange the securities of any corporation or company for other securities issued by the same, or by any other corporation or company at such times and upon such terms, as trustee shall deem proper and

(e) To exercise with respect to all stock, bonds, and other investments held by trustee, all rights, powers, and privileges as are lawfully exercised by any person owning similar property in his/her own right

COMMENT: All powers that a settlor wishes to grant to the trustee should be included in the trust instrument and clearly defined. Limitations, if desired, should also be specifically enumerated. The settlor of this trust has definite ideas about what she wants the trustee to do. Section *b* above, for example, states that the trustee shall decide what investments shall be made on behalf of the trust, despite the statutes of State A, which declare and enumerate permissible trust investments. It is possible, and perfectly legal, for settlors to include such provisions in trust agreements. It is only when the settlor fails to mention the type of investments the trustee may make that such statutes go into effect. The intent of these statutes is benevolent rather than restrictive. They are designed to help inexperienced investors to invest prudently.

Article V

The settlor hereby declares that this agreement and the trusts hereby created shall be irrevocable and not subject to modification by the settlor or any other person and the settlor further declares that no trustee shall be required to furnish bond or other security to any court.

COMMENT: Placing property in trust saves estate tax only if the trust is irrevocable and not included in the settlor's estate. The settlor is taxed on the income and capital gains of the trust property if:

1. the settlor retains the right to revoke the trust (IRC § 676).

2. the settlor or the settlor's spouse currently or at any time in the future receive or "may receive" the trust income (IRC § 677 [a]).

3. the settlor retains certain dispositions or administrative powers (IRC §§ 674 and 675). It is common today that trustees can serve without bond.

Article VI

Both trustee and successor trustee have agreed to waive compensation for their services.

COMMENT: The trust instrument should expressly provide for the trustee's compensation or its waiver. In the absence of such a provision, statutes in many states fix or limit the rates of the commission. Unless the settlor indicates whether the trustee shall receive or forgo compensation as agreed, the court may order the statutory amount paid from the trust income.

Article VII

The settlor hereby appoints as successor trustee, Herbert N. Evans of 1040 Merry Lane, Flowertown, Apple County, State A. In the event that trustee or successor trustee shall die, resign, become incapacitated, or for any reason fail or refuse to act as trustee, settlor shall have the power to appoint a successor. Any successor trustee shall have all the powers and obligations of the trustee named herein.

COMMENT: It is important for the settlor to name a successor in case the original trustee is unable or unwilling to serve. Because of their fiduciary responsibilities, all trustees should be selected with care, keeping in mind the specific purposes for which the trust is created.

Article VIII

The validity of this trust and the construction of its provisions shall be governed solely by the laws of the State of A as they now exist or may exist in the future.

EXHIBIT 13.10 (Continued)

COMMENT: Each state may have certain restrictions on trusts that may affect the purpose of the trust. Such restrictions must be determined before a workable instrument can be drafted. A clause similar to this may prove more valuable than it would appear. For example, Geraldine P. Bass, the settlor, lives in State A, as does Dolores L. Evans, the trustee. At the inception of the trust, at least, it will be governed by the laws of A because that is the place where it is to be administered (carried out by the trustee), according to Article VIII. However, this situation can change. Suppose Dolores moves to the State of N and transacts business there. The laws of N regarding trusts might be quite different from the laws of A, with the result that new limitations are placed on Dolores and the trust does not achieve what Geraldine had intended. Or suppose that a year from now state A enacts a special tax on living trusts. Does the Bass Trust have to pay the tax since such a law was not in existence at the time of the trust creation? A court could resolve such problems, but the process would be both time- and money-consuming (e.g., the question involving the laws of two states, A and N, might require a federal action). It is advisable to include a clause that prevents such questions from arising.

IN WITNESS WHEREOF, settlor and trustees have executed this agreement at Flowertown, the day and year written above.

IN PRESENCE OF:

_____   _____
                        (Witness)   (Settlor)

_____   _____
                        (Witness)   (Trustee)

                                           _____
                                                         (Successor Trustee)

STATE OF <u>A</u>   ⎫
                        ⎬ ss.
County of <u>Apple</u>   ⎭

   The foregoing instrument was acknowledged before me this <u>1st</u> day of <u>June</u>, 2014, by <u>Geraldine P. Bass</u> as settlor and <u>Dolores L. Evans</u> and <u>Herbert N. Evans</u>, as trustees.

[*Notarial Seal*]   _____
                                                         Notary Public

3. *Open a checking account for the trust.* This will enable the trustee to deposit and disburse funds for the trust and keep complete and accurate records of all financial transactions during the administration of the trust.

4. *Transfer funds to the new checking account.* Inform the banking institutions that maintain any of the settlor's trust checking accounts of the death, close the accounts, and transfer the funds to the new checking account.

5. *Notify beneficiaries of the settlor's death.* Keep them informed of the status of the trust administration on a frequent basis. This may forestall a complaint in the future by an upset beneficiary. They are entitled to an annual accounting of the income and expenses of the trust.

6. *Collect, preserve, and value (appraise) the trust property as of the decedent's date of death.* It is necessary to identify and inventory the trust property for the filing of death tax returns.

7. *Prepare a schedule of property held outside the trust.* Participate with the personal representative to collect and inventory this property as of the decedent's date of death. This property may include life insurance, retirement plans, and property held in joint tenancy necessary for the filing of death tax returns.

8. *Determine the investment and disbursement of trust property, and any other obligations as provided in the trust agreement.* This is part of the duty of the trustee to manage the trust property in a prudent manner for the benefit of the beneficiary and any other requirements of the trust.

9. *Pursue or defend any claims in favor of or against the trust estate.* The trustee is required to pursue or defend litigation for the benefit of the beneficiaries.

10. *Pay creditors' claims.* Participate with the personal representative to pay approved creditors' claims of the decedent and trust estate.

11. *Make income and principal payments as provided in the trust agreement.* Examples of such payments are those to the surviving spouse.

12. *Establish and fund any additional trusts provided for in the original trust after the death of the settlor.* This includes trusts that may continue for several years, such as: Trust A (marital) and Trust B (bypass) (see Chapter 10); trusts for minor or disabled children; and charitable trusts.

13. *Obtain professional management and investment services.* Hire a trust company or investment adviser to provide professional expertise in the management of the trust and/or additional trusts as permitted by the trust agreement.

14. *File the trust (fiduciary) annual income tax return (Form 1041).* This is a requirement for the trustee of any irrevocable trust if gross income exceeds $600 for a taxable year.

15. *Prepare an annual Schedule K-1 (Form 1041) for each beneficiary who receives a distribution from the trust.* This form must be given to the beneficiary and a copy attached to Form 1041.

16. *Pay expenses of the decedent and trust.* Participate with the personal representative to pay the last illness and funeral expenses, debts of the estate and trust, administration expenses, and death taxes. This is routinely a provision in the trust agreement and pour-over will.

17. *Prepare federal and state income, gift, and death tax returns.* Participate with the personal representative in the preparation of the decedent's final tax returns.

18. *Apportion and disburse the beneficiaries' shares as provided for in the trust agreement.* This will end the obligation of the trustee to the beneficiaries and terminate the trust. This can occur after the decedent's death and filing of the estate tax return or after the termination of any additional trusts established by the original trust. To protect the trustee from claims by a beneficiary, a release should be signed by the beneficiary approving the trustee's acts and distribution and receipt of their share.

19. *File the final trust (fiduciary) income tax return (Form 1041).* The trustee should retain sufficient funds to pay any tax due on the final return.

20. *Request discharge as trustee.* The trustee can resign before termination of the trust or resign after completion of all obligations under the trust agreement by petitioning the court or the beneficiaries to be discharged. State statutes determine the procedure. If the trustee resigns before completing the administration of the trust, it will be necessary for a successor trustee to be named before being discharged.

Review Duties of the Trustee in Chapter 12. The trustee can be personally liable for mismanagement of the trust in several ways, such as failure to file required tax returns and nonpayment of tax due; failure to protect (insure) trust property causing loss to the trust value; self-dealing; and improper investments. The attorney and you, as the paralegal, must remind the trustee of the duty to follow the directions of the trust and act in the best interests of the beneficiary with loyalty, reasonable skill, prudence, and diligence.

Key Terms

express trust	passive trust	necessaries
implied trust	Rule Against Perpetuities	sprinkling trust
indefinite class	resulting trust	precatory words
cy-pres	purchase-money resulting trust	precatory trust
cy-pres doctrine	parol evidence	homestead exemption
active trust	constructive trust	pour-over will

Review Questions

1. What are the differences between the following kinds or classes of trusts: express versus implied, private versus public, active versus passive, *inter vivos* (living) versus testamentary, and resulting versus constructive?

2. What elements are necessary to create an express private trust? How do they differ from the elements needed to create an express public trust?

3. Does the *cy-pres* doctrine apply to all trusts? Explain.

4. What is meant by the phrase "the law allows resulting trusts to be proved by parol evidence"?

5. What are spendthrift and sprinkling trusts, and why would a settlor create them?

6. What is the proper way of creating a Totten trust, and can it be used to disinherit a surviving spouse? Explain.

7. What are some of the most common reasons or purposes for creating trusts?

8. Give three examples of trust restrictions that are "reasonable restraints" and do not violate public policy.

9. When is a precatory trust declared valid?

10. What is the court's position on a trust that has all its required elements but lacks a trustee? Explain.

11. Why are living trusts today often considered to be more desirable than wills? Which do you prefer? Why?

12. What are the major disadvantages of revocable living trusts?

13. How are real and personal property transferred into a living trust?

14. What is the purpose of a pour-over will? Do assets included in such a will have to be probated? Explain.

15. What are some of the uses of an irrevocable living trust?

Case Problems

Problem 1

Duncan Bennett, a single parent, wants to leave his entire estate to his only child, Asia. He knows Asia is extravagant and often spends her money foolishly; therefore, he establishes a trust with a spendthrift provision "to protect Asia from her own mismanagement and wasteful habits in spending money." The trust also provides that Asia cannot transfer, pledge, or assign her interest in the trust income or principal in any manner and that such interest is not to be subject to any of Asia's creditors' claims by attachment, garnishment, execution, or other process of law. Answer the following:

A. Are spendthrift trusts valid in all states?

B. Would this trust be valid in your state? If so, cite the statute.

C. If one of Asia's creditors supplies her with property items that are obviously "necessaries," can that creditor reach (obtain) Asia's trust income despite the spendthrift clause? See *Erickson v. Bank of California*, 97 Wash.2d 246, 643 P.2d 670 (1982).

Problem 2

Zari purchased 20 acres of land from Deon. Since Zari was immediately leaving the country to serve in the Peace Corps for two years and was unable to attend the closing, she asked Deon to deed the property to her close friend, Kaleehja. Deon conveyed the property by deed to Kaleehja in her name. When Zari returns, Kaleehja refuses to turn over the property and claims the property was a gift to her from Zari. Zari denies the property was a gift and demands that Kaleehja return the property. Answer and explain the following:

A. Since real property (land) is involved in this case, does the Statute of Frauds apply?

B. In this case, can parol evidence be used to determine whether or not a resulting trust is established?

C. If Zari and Kaleehja go to court, what methods might a court use to decide whether Kaleehja's claim is correct?

D. If it goes to court, in your opinion, which party would win this case? See *Rainey v. Rainey*, 795 S.W.2d 139 (Tenn.App. 1990).

E. If Zari had died while in the Peace Corps, would the property belong to Kaleehja?

Practical Assignments

1. You were recently informed that Landon Kreger is deceased. Your supervising attorney has asked that you complete IRS Form 56 -Notice Concerning Fiduciary Relationship, with the exception of Part I. Section B. The form can be found on the IRS website, www.irs/gov. Assume the trust is in your state and county of residency. Relevant information to complete the form can be found in Exhibits 13.6 and 13.7. Mr. Kreger's Social Security Number is 111-22-3333.

2. Find two online companies that offer their services to manage your digital assets. Compare and contrast the services offered by both companies. Which would you recommend to your client and why?

3. Draft a clause to be include in a digital asset trust that grants the trustee the power to access, modify, delete, control, and transfer your digital assets.

Outline

Objectives

After completing this chapter, you should be able to:

- Explain the components of estate planning.

- Understand the adverse factors that diminish an estate's value and how to minimize them.

- Utilize the knowledge acquired from earlier chapters to draft appropriate wills and trusts necessary for an estate plan.

- Identify and incorporate into an estate plan the tax-saving devices that increase the deductions from the gross estate or reduce the gross estate, thereby reducing or possibly eliminating federal and/or state death taxes.

SCOPE OF THE CHAPTER

This chapter examines the fundamentals of estate planning. A review of the legal documents, e.g., wills and trusts, is followed by discussions on the devices that save estate tax either by reducing the decedent's gross estate or by increasing the deductions from the estate. The chapter concludes with a section on postmortem estate planning.

ESTATE PLANNING

As previously discussed, the development of an estate plan for the client commences once the client reaches a "comfort level" with the supervising attorney and paralegal that allows the paralegal to accumulate the personal and financial data. To help the client create an appropriate estate plan, you will use all of the same techniques (interviewing, negotiating, drafting, and counseling skills) and professional conduct that were described earlier in the discussion of drafts of wills and trusts.

ASSIGNMENT 14.1

1. A new client has come to your office to discuss a will. You have not met the client, but your supervising attorney has told you that the client is shy, reserved, and reluctant to discuss private family and financial matters with "strangers." Explain some of the things you might do or say to establish a "comfort level" between you and the client so you can obtain the requisite information to draft the will.

2. Review the checklists in Chapter 5 (Exhibits 5.1 through 5.6), and determine if they are adequate to elicit the necessary information to develop and draft an estate plan. What is missing? What could you add?

Before the utilization of the data and information accumulated through the interview, checklists, worksheets, and questionnaires is discussed, it will be helpful to summarize the potential adverse factors that will diminish any estate. It is necessary to identify and understand these factors so measures can be included in the estate plan to diminish their effect. Five factors in particular require attention: federal and state death and gift taxes; administration expenses; losses resulting from the forced liquidation (sale) of assets to raise funds to pay debts of the deceased; and financial losses due to the termination of the decedent's employment.

1. *Federal gift and estate taxes*. These taxes are imposed on the transfer of property while living by gift and at death whether to beneficiaries of a will or to heirs by the intestate succession statutes (IRC § 2001 et seq.). The death and gift tax exclusion amounts may vary annually due to federal legislation. *This requires the paralegal to be knowledgeable of the tax laws affecting a specific tax year.* With proper planning, a married couple can use devices, such as trusts, to transfer significant assets free of estate tax after the deaths of both spouses. Any procedure that can diminish the tax must be included in the estate plan. *Caveat:* For updated information on how the current tax laws affect a client's estate plan, see *http://www.irs.gov.*

⚖ *Ethical Issue*

2. *State death taxes*. The taxes imposed by the states vary considerably. Some states have completely eliminated estate taxes. Other state taxes may include stand-alone estate taxes: a "credit estate tax" that "picks up" or absorbs the amount of the federal estate tax credit allowed for taxes paid to the state. A form of state taxation includes inheritance taxes, which is a tax on the beneficiaries of property received from a decedent's estate. The inheritance tax is determined by the value of property received and the relationship of the beneficiaries to the decedent.

3. *Administration expenses*. The commission (fee) of the personal representative, attorney's fee, court costs and filings, and costs of administering the estate, including the decedent's funeral and burial expenses, are incurred during an estate administration. All of these expenses must be paid from the assets of the decedent's estate and may substantially lessen its value. If the decedent owned property in more than one state, ancillary administration expense will add to these costs. Obviously, any method that reduces the decedent's gross estate, e.g., by making lifetime gifts, also reduces the probate fees and administration expenses, which are commonly computed as a percentage of the probate estate. The personal representative may elect to take the administration expenses as a deduction on the decedent's federal estate tax return (IRC § 2053) or as a deduction on the estate's fiduciary income tax return (IRC § 642[g]).

4. *Forced liquidation*. The personal representative may be forced to sell (at a sacrifice) assets of the estate in order to obtain the cash needed to pay legitimate and approved creditors' claims, federal and state taxes, and administration expenses. After reviewing the potential property to be sold with the beneficiaries, the personal representative will select and sell, according to statutory guidelines, the assets that cause the least shrinkage from their fair market value and consequently from the estate.

5. *Termination of employment*. A substantial loss of income to the estate may result for many reasons, including the direct consequence of the employee's untimely and unexpected death.

The adverse effects of some or all of these factors cannot be entirely eliminated, but a well-designed estate plan can help to minimize them.

The next sections discuss the role the following components play in the development of an estate plan.

- Documents
  - Wills and trusts
- Estate tax-saving devices that increase the deductions from the gross estate
  - The marital deduction
  - The charitable deduction
- Estate tax-saving devices that reduce the gross estate
  - Gifts
- Powers of appointment
- Trusts
- Life insurance

Earlier chapters describe in detail the plans, drafts, and uses of wills and trusts; therefore, this chapter emphasizes the tax-saving devices.

Periodic Review

No matter how well an estate plan is designed to meet the objectives of a client, changes in tax laws, domicile, family relationships (including marital status, birth or death of a child or other beneficiaries and heirs), and accumulated assets necessitate periodic review of the plan. *An ethical issue could result if the attorney or paralegal openly solicits clients to conduct this review.* Therefore, it must be made clear that the client is responsible for initiating a review when changes occur that mandate modification of the estate plan.

⚖ *Ethical Issue*

DOCUMENTS USED TO CREATE THE ESTATE PLAN

Wills

A will is one of the most common and important estate planning documents. As part of an estate plan, a will allows the testator to

- leave the entire estate to a surviving spouse *or* limit the spouse's interest to the share required by state statute since the surviving spouse cannot be disinherited (see the discussions of elective or forced share of a surviving spouse and the method used in community property states in Chapters 1 and 3).
- leave the estate to children, e.g., natural, adopted, or nonmarital, *or* disinherit one or more or all of them.
- leave the estate to anyone, such as friends or faithful employees, whether or not they are family members.
- leave the entire estate to charity or other public institutions, except for the surviving spouse's elective share.
- identify the estate assets and the beneficiaries who are to receive them, thereby minimizing confusion and the possibility of costly will contests.
- appoint both personal and property guardians for minor children. One person may serve as both types of guardian, or a financial institution, e.g., a bank, may be the property guardian, while a relative or friend is the personal guardian.
- establish testamentary trusts within the will to reduce or even avoid estate taxes and select the trustee who will administer the trusts.
- appoint an executor or executrix or, using the UPC term, a personal representative to carry out the terms of the will and administer the estate.

A will can be changed throughout the testator's lifetime since the will takes effect only on death. It should be reviewed periodically and, when necessary, updated.

Trusts

Trusts are the other key planning documents. As previously discussed, a trust can be created *inter vivos*, the living trust, or placed in a will, the testamentary trust. A living trust can be revocable or irrevocable. If it is irrevocable, the income produced by the trust property is taxable to the trust as a legal entity, or to the beneficiaries, if they receive the income, but in either case, the trust property is no longer part of the settlor's assets. Estate planners can use trusts to benefit family members in numerous other ways.

- Provide lifetime income for a surviving spouse and then pass the property to children and grandchildren.
- Protect a spendthrift child.
- Preserve privacy, since, unlike a will, a trust is not a public document.
- Obtain professional management of the trust property to maximize its income potential.
- Spread or sprinkle trust income or principal to family members years after the testator's death when their needs are better known.
- Enable the trust property to be controlled by the settlor-trustee while living and, after the settlor's death, by the successor trustee for the benefit of the beneficiary.
- Avoid the lengthy delays and expense of probate, including ancillary administration expense.
- Diminish problems such as will contests.
- Eliminate the need for the probate court to appoint a guardian or conservator for minors or for oneself due to declining health.
- Reduce federal and state death taxes by using trusts to increase the marital and charitable deductions and allow a married couple to make maximum use of their estate tax exclusions after their deaths (see the discussion of estate tax-saving devices in the next sections).

ESTATE TAX-SAVING DEVICES THAT INCREASE DEDUCTIONS FROM THE GROSS ESTATE

Two types of deductions are frequently used to produce a lower net estate subject to the federal estate tax. They are (1) the marital deduction and (2) the charitable deduction.

The Marital Deduction

marital deduction
An unlimited amount of the decedent's gross estate, which may be given to the surviving spouse without being subject to federal estate tax levied against the decedent's estate.

The **marital deduction** is an unlimited federal tax deduction allowed on the transfer of property from one spouse to another; Not all gifts to surviving spouses qualify for the marital deduction. If the gift is a terminable interest—one that ends or fails because of the occurrence of an event or lapse of time—it will not qualify for the marital deduction. Life estates and property given to a surviving spouse that would revert to the children if the surviving spouse remarries will not qualify. Under some circumstances, bequests made to spouses who are not United States citizens also may not qualify.

Section 2056 of the IRC establishes that a "qualifying" marital deduction is not limited to gifts through a will or to transfers made at the time of the decedent's death. The following transfers all qualify as part of the marital deduction from the gross estate of the decedent spouse for property that passes to the surviving spouse:

bequests and inheritances; joint tenancy property; *inter vivos* gifts; trust transfers; pension plan benefits; life insurance proceeds; and transfers made through the exercise of powers of appointment.

The unlimited deduction is allowed under the federal gift tax for *inter vivos* (lifetime) transfers between spouses (IRC § 2523) and also under the federal estate tax for property passing from a decedent to a surviving spouse by will or inheritance (IRC § 2056). The unlimited marital deduction is an essential consideration in estate tax planning for a married couple since spouses frequently leave their estates to the surviving spouse. *Note:* Without an appropriate estate tax plan, however, considerable federal estate tax that could have been avoided may be owed on the death of the second spouse.

> **EXAMPLE:** Hazim and Francesca are married. Hazim dies, leaving assets valued at 7 million dollars to Francesca. Francesca is not required to pay any federal estate taxes as a result of the unlimited marital deduction. Likewise, most states allow a marital deduction from any state estate or inheritance equal to the federal marital deduction. Therefore, Francesca will not owe any state estate or inheritance taxes either.

Based on the value of the estate, estate planners may consider rearranging property ownership. The total estate assets of each spouse's estate are rearranged so that each person has approximately the same value. This enables each spouse to take the maximum advantage of the unified credit amount, and is referred to as **estate equalization**. *The attorney and paralegal must be especially careful when acting for and advising both spouses about interspousal gifts because serious ethical problems can result when the attorney advises one spouse to make substantial gifts to the other spouse.* The ethical concern of the attorney is that the marriage might subsequently be dissolved. The solution for the attorney and paralegal is to explain the dilemma and make sure that both spouses understand the situation, acknowledge their awareness of the potential problem, and indicate their consent to this estate plan, in writing. An estate planning device that might be considered is a **bypass trust**. In a bypass trust, a deceased spouse's estate passes to a trust (bypass trust) rather than to the surviving spouse. The bypass trust is established with the assets from Hazim's estate. The trust will pay the income to the surviving spouse for life, but then pass the remainder to the couple's children without being taxed when the surviving spouse dies. The surviving spouse can then pass her estate, free of estate tax, to their children, assuming that the value of the estate is under the current estate tax exclusion.

The Charitable Deduction

To be a **charitable deduction**, a gift must be made for religious, scientific, charitable, literary, or educational purposes (IRC § 170[c]). A charitable deduction is also applicable to trusts (IRC § 512[b][11]). If a trust is to qualify and be approved as a charitable trust, it must be established for one of these purposes. A charity cannot be an individual.

Gifts made to qualified charities during the donor's lifetime can be used to reduce both estate and income taxes. The value of real or personal property given by a will or trust to certain kinds of qualified charities is deductible from the donor's gross estate for federal estate tax purposes (IRC § 2055). A lifetime donor or a testator often makes a direct, outright charitable gift of cash; alternatively, the

---

⚖️ *Ethical Issue*

estate equalization
Rearranging property ownership of total estate assets owned by the spouses so that each spouse's individual estate has approximately the same value.

bypass trust
This trust, also called Trust B of an A-B trust, credit shelter trust, residuary trust, or family trust, is an estate planning device whereby a portion of a deceased spouse's estate passes to a trust rather than directly to the surviving spouse, hence reducing the likelihood that the surviving spouse's subsequent estate will exceed the federal estate tax threshold. Typically, the surviving spouse is given a life estate in the trust.

charitable deduction
Under tax law IRC § 170(c), a charitable deduction is any contribution by a person to a qualified charity or other tax-exempt institution for which the taxpayer can claim an income tax deduction.

capital gains tax
An income tax on profits from the sale or exchange of a capital asset at a lower rate than the rates applied to ordinary income. Capital assets are all property held by a taxpayer, e.g., house, car, and stocks, except for assets listed in IRC § 1221.

charitable remainder
A gift to a qualified charity after an intervening estate that qualifies as a tax deduction under certain circumstances.

donor may give highly appreciated securities and real estate since doing so can reduce both estate taxes and **capital gains tax**. In addition, a settlor-donor can establish a trust with a gift called a **charitable remainder** (see discussion below).

Charitable Remainder Trusts

A charitable remainder trust allows a settlor or the named beneficiary to retain the income from the trust, generally for life; after death, the trust property is given to a "qualified" charity. Charitable remainder trusts can provide the following benefits.

- Reduce income tax by allowing the settlor-donor an income tax deduction for the gift in the year the contribution is made to the trust.

- Increase current income by providing a life income for the settlor or other named beneficiaries by using property that currently does not provide income (real estate such as the settlor's home or other residential property).

- Avoid capital gains tax on gifts of long-term appreciated property (securities or real estate).

- Reduce federal estate tax liability. Gifts to charities, in general, are exempt from federal estate tax as long as the recipient of the gift qualifies as a charity (IRC § 2055). If real estate is given to the charity, the value would not be included in the gross estate of the settlor-decedent, thereby decreasing the federal estate tax on the decedent's estate.

- Provide funds from lower taxes and increased income to the settlor that can be used to purchase life insurance through an irrevocable life insurance trust to replace the value of the donation (e.g., real estate) and pass the insurance proceeds through the trust to the heirs (children, etc.).

- Allow the settlor-donors to make substantial gifts to charities of their choice.

Two types of irrevocable charitable remainder trusts are the Charitable Remainder Unitrust and the Charitable Remainder Annuity Trust.

Charitable Remainder Unitrust
A trust that specifies the noncharitable income beneficiary or beneficiaries are to receive annual payments for life based on a fixed percentage (at least 5 percent) of the net fair market value of the trust's assets as determined each year.

Charitable Remainder Annuity Trust
A trust that must pay the noncharitable income beneficiary or beneficiaries a sum certain annually for life, or more frequently if desired, that is not less than 5 percent of the initial net fair market value of all property placed in the trust as determined for federal tax purposes.

Charitable Remainder Unitrust

In a **charitable remainder unitrust**, the settlor places cash or property in the trust, which pays an annual distribution of a fixed percentage of not less than 5 percent of the fair market value of the trust property (determined annually) to a non-charitable beneficiary for life (IRC § 664[d] [2] & [3]). The noncharitable income beneficiary may be the settlor-donor or other named beneficiaries. When the life beneficiary dies, the trust property passes to the qualified charity. The settlor-donor and the charitable organization negotiate the specific percentage to be paid (at least 5 percent) at the time the trust is established. Additional assets can be contributed to the trust at any time. Once the fixed percentage is agreed on by the settlor and charity, it cannot be changed. However, payments to the beneficiary will vary annually depending on the increase in the value of the trust property. If the property's value increases, so does the beneficiary's income. The unitrust provides for this potential income growth and thereby counteracts the effects of inflation.

Charitable Remainder Annuity Trust

In a **charitable remainder annuity trust**, the settlor places property in the trust, which must pay a fixed amount (sum certain) of income at least annually to a non-charitable beneficiary for life. When the beneficiary dies, the trust property passes to the qualified charity. Under Section 664(d)(1) of the IRC, the fixed annual income given to the noncharitable life beneficiary must be at least 5 percent of the initial net fair market value of all property placed in the trust. This annual income amount can never change. The court in the case *of In re Danforth's Will*, 81 Misc.2d 452, 366 N.Y.S.2d 329 (1975), upheld this definition of a Charitable Remainder Annuity Trust. If the trust property's income diminishes for some reason such as a slump in the economy, the annual fixed payment must come from the principal of the trust. But if the economy flourishes, the excess income, after the fixed payment is paid, remains in the trust. Therefore, this trust is primarily for individuals who want a guaranteed fixed income. Unlike the unitrust, the annuity trust does not allow additional contributions to be made to the trust property.

If a client does not have enough property to set up one of these charitable remainder trusts, the property can be contributed to a public "pooled income" fund such as the American Cancer Society or the March of Dimes. All individual gifts are placed in the larger "pooled" fund, and each donor receives annual income based on the contribution compared to the value of the entire fund. When the client dies, the property passes to the charity.

ESTATE TAX-SAVING DEVICES THAT REDUCE THE GROSS ESTATE

When preparing an estate plan, one of the most important goals is to identify and incorporate into the plan various ways to reduce or eliminate federal and state estate taxes. Among the most common methods used to reduce these death taxes are the following:

- Gifts made during the donor's lifetime
- Powers of appointment
- Trusts that qualify for the marital deduction or avoid multiple taxation
- Life insurance

Gifts Made during the Donor's Lifetime: The Gift Tax Annual Exclusion

According to tax law (IRC § 2503 [b]), any **donor** can make a gift of up to $14,000 beginning in 2013 to *any number* of recipients (**donees**) *each year* during the donor's life without being required to pay gift tax. Since 1999, the amount has been indexed annually for inflation (cost of living) rounded to the closest thousand dollars; i.e., the total increase must exceed $1,000 before the annual exclusion is increased. In addition, spouses may join in the annual gift to the donees and combine their individual gifts so as to give $28,000 to each donee free of gift tax ($28,000 in 2013 or after). This practice is called **gift splitting**, and it is only available between spouses (IRC § 2513). In such cases, a gift tax return for each spouse must be filed with the Internal Revenue Service. In appropriate family situations, lifetime gifts are important tax-saving devices that are essential to a well-designed estate plan. Whenever donors are looking for a method to reduce their estates in order to diminish their potential federal estate tax liability as well as to reduce the cost of probate administration of their estate, gift giving is an obvious solution.

donor
A person who makes a gift.

donee
A person who receives a gift.

gift splitting
For gift tax purposes, an election by spouses to make a gift by one of them to a third party as being made one-half by each spouse.

EXAMPLE: Trung and Seiko have five children. To reduce their estate and the corresponding federal estate tax, they can give each of their five children $28,000 (adjusted for inflation) each year for a total of $140,000 or more. If they make these same gifts for 10 years, Trung and Seiko will reduce their estate by $1,400,000 or more.

Assuming that a donor has not made any previous gifts that year to the donees, he can give them each $14,000 (indexed annually for inflation) on his deathbed to diminish his federal estate tax. Such gifts would qualify for the annual exclusion.

The annual gift tax exclusion is available only for **present interests**, i.e., unrestricted rights to the immediate possession, use, or enjoyment of property (or the income of property). A gift of a present interest results whenever the donor makes a direct transfer of property to a donee. Donors may be individuals during life or may act through wills, trusts, estates, or guardianships. An unrestricted right to receive trust income, a **legal life estate**, and a gift to a **custodian** under the Uniform Transfers (Gifts) to Minors Act are all examples of a present interest. This act allows any kind of real or personal property to be transferred to a custodian for the benefit of a minor. The **custodianship**, however, must end and all property must be transferred to the minor at age 18, 21, or, in a few states, 25 (see the discussion of this act in Chapter 11).

Gifts of **future interests**, such as gifts of remainder interests and gifts in trust subject to a preceding life estate, do *not* qualify for the annual gift tax exclusion. Sometimes clients must be cautioned not to become too eager to part with their property to reduce federal tax liability since the gifts, once executed, transfer title to the property and its control. Once clients have gifted away their property, unforeseen and disastrous financial circumstances could cause them to become dependent on others for support.

In addition to the annual exclusion, no gift tax is owed for gifts made directly to a college or university to pay for a student's tuition and gifts made directly to a hospital or doctor for another person's medical care regardless of the relationship of the donor to the donee (IRC § 2503[e]). *Remember:* Other examples of gifts that are excluded from federal gift and estate tax are property to a tax-exempt charity (IRC §§ 2522 and 2055) and gifts to spouses (IRC §§ 2523 and 2056).

All lifetime gifts made to a donee in a given year that exceed the annual exclusion must be reported on Form 709. Such lifetime gifts are taxed by the federal government as part of the estate tax law. However, no tax is owed or paid for gifts over the $14,000 annual exclusion (indexed annually for inflation) until the applicable credit amount (unified credit) based on the lifetime gift tax applicable exclusion amount of is exceeded. Any gift tax owed is assessed against the donor who is primarily obligated to pay it.

A donor who plans to make gifts to children should leave them highly appreciated property, such as real estate (e.g., a house, cottage, condominium, apartment building, or securities) in a will or trust and give them other property during his lifetime. The problem with making a gift of highly appreciated property while living is that the advantage of the "**stepped-up basis**" of the property is lost. Property "basis" is the value that is used to determine loss or gain for income tax purposes. The difference (loss or gain) between what the donor paid for the property and the amount received when the property is sold is taxable. If the donor, while alive, gives the property to his children, the property retains the donor's basis.

---

present interests
An immediate and unrestricted interest in real or personal property including the privilege of possession or enjoyment of the property.

legal life estate
A life estate created by operation of law and not directly by the parties themselves.

custodian
A person who has charge or custody of property for the benefit of another, usually for the benefit of another, usually for a minor.

custodianship
An alternative to a trust or guardianship that allows a person (called a custodian) to be appointed by the court to manage property for the benefit of a minor.

future interests
Any fixed estate or interest, except a reversion, in which the privilege of possession or enjoyment is future and not present.

stepped-up basis
An increase in the income tax basis of appreciated (increase in value) property. The property is valued on the date of death or the alternate valuation date.

However, if the donor passes the property to his children through a will or trust when he dies, the property takes a new "stepped-up basis," which is the current value of the property on the date of the donor-testator's death or **alternate valuation date**.

> **EXAMPLE** Kenya, the donor, purchased a lakeshore cottage in Minnesota in 1950 for $10,000. In her will, Kenya leaves the cottage to her two children. When Kenya dies in 2015, the property is worth $500,000. The children receive the property with the stepped-up basis of $500,000. If they sell the property for $500,000 in 2015, they will owe no federal income tax on the sale because there was no income gain. (*Note:* The stepped-up basis of $500,000 would be included in Kenya's gross estate for estate tax purposes and could result in an estate tax liability if her gross estate exceeds $5,000,000.) However, if the property had been given to the children while Kenya was alive, the basis for the property when it was sold would be Kenya's basis of $10,000. There is *no* stepped-up basis when property is passed by gift while the donor is alive. Therefore, if the basis is $10,000 and the children sell the cottage for $500,000 in 2015, the gain of $490,000 would be subject to income tax.

Powers of Appointment

A power of appointment is created by will or in a trust when one person (a testator or settlor, now also called the **donor**) confers a power or authority upon another (called the **donee**) to appoint (i.e., to select and nominate) the person who is to receive and enjoy an estate, or an income therefrom, or receive a trust fund after the donee's death. The purpose of a power of appointment is to enable the persons (called the **appointees**) who will receive the estate or trust fund to be named later when their needs are better known.

Section 2041 of the IRC identifies two types of powers.

1. A **general power of appointment**, which the Code defines as follows.

   > The term general power of appointment means a power which is exercisable in favor of the decedent, his estate, his creditors, or the creditors of his estate....

   > **EXAMPLE** In her will, Carley Juno creates a testamentary trust naming her daughter, Isabella Juno, beneficiary of the trust and provides that all income of the trust will be distributed to Isabella during her lifetime. On Isabella's death, she will be given the power to "appoint" the principal of the trust to anyone she selects.

   - Carley Juno is the testatrix and donor who creates the power of appointment.
   - Isabella is the beneficiary of the testamentary trust and donee who holds the power of appointment. She has the right to exercise the power during her life or after death in her own will by naming anyone, including herself or her estate, her creditors, or the creditors of her estate, as the beneficiaries of the trust principal.
   - The person appointed by Isabella is the appointee.
   - Isabella has a general power of appointment.

   Note: Only a general power of appointment causes the value of the property appointed to be included in the gross estate of the person who possesses the power of appointment for federal estate tax purposes. For further discussion of general power of appointment trusts, see below.

2. A **special or limited power of appointment** in which the donor limits the donee's right of appointment to an identified person or persons, other than the donee, to whom the property can be distributed.

---

alternate valuation date
A date six months from the date of death or the date the property is disposed by the estate, whichever comes first.

donor (of a power of appointment)
The testator or settlor who creates and confers a power or authority upon another (called the donee) to appoint; that is, to select the person(s) (called the appointee) to receive an estate or an income therefrom after the testator's or donee's death.

donee (of a power of appointment)
The person to whom a power of appointment is given, also called the holder, who selects the appointee to receive an estate or an income therefrom.

appointee
The person who is to receive the benefit of the power of appointment.

general power of appointment
The right to pass on an interest in property to whomever a donee chooses, including himself, his estate, his creditors, or creditors of his estate.

special or limited power of appointment
A power of appointment that cannot be exercised in favor of the donee or his estate but only in favor of identifiable person(s) other than the donee.

EXAMPLE: In the above example, Carley, in the testamentary trust, gives Isabella the power to "appoint" the principal only to Isabella's brother, Henry, or only to any siblings who survive Isabella.

- Carley is still the testatrix and donor.
- Isabella is still the beneficiary and donee who holds the power of appointment.
- Henry, or Isabella's siblings, are the appointee(s).
- Isabella has a special power of appointment.

A common use of a special power of appointment occurs between spouses whenever one spouse, e.g., the husband in a trust or will, names his wife as his beneficiary and gives her a power to appoint the principal only to their children. This special power of appointment does *not* cause the value of the property appointed to be included in the gross estate of the wife, who is the beneficiary (donee).

Trusts That Qualify for the Marital Deduction or Avoid Multiple Taxation

Transfers of property that qualify for the gift or estate tax marital deduction include the following: (1) outright transfers between spouses by gift or trust; (2) life estate with general power of appointment trusts; (3) qualified terminable interest property (QTIP) trusts; and (4) bypass trusts, which are also known as Trust B of A-B trusts, credit shelter trusts, residuary trusts, or family trusts.

Outright Transfers between Spouses by Gift or Trust

Direct transfer of ownership from one spouse to the other spouse by a gift, will, or operation of law is the simplest and most common form of a marital deduction transfer. Due to the unlimited marital deduction for these direct transfers between spouses, no federal gift or estate tax is owed. A transfer in trust may be more appropriate, however, if the recipient spouse is unable to manage the trust property properly or if the settlor-donor wants to determine and select the ultimate beneficiaries of the property at the spouse's death instead of allowing the surviving spouse to make that decision. Consider the following trust examples.

EXAMPLE: Maria establishes a trust that states, "on Maria's death, the trustee shall distribute all principal and income directly to Maria's surviving spouse, Harrison." This is an outright transfer by trust of property that qualifies for the marital deduction from Maria's gross estate.

The major tax problem created by an outright transfer to a spouse is that the entire trust property is now part of the surviving spouse's estate and may be liable for estate taxes on that spouse's death if the value of the estate is greater than the estate tax applicable exclusion amount available for the year of death (see Exhibit 11.2).

Life Estate with General Power of Appointment Trusts

A common alternative to an outright transfer that also qualifies trust property for the marital deduction is the general power of appointment trust. This living or testamentary trust alternative established by the settlor spouse requires the trustee to distribute trust income at least annually to the surviving spouse *for life*, gives *only* the spouse an unqualified general power to appoint the trust property to "anyone," including himself, his estate, his creditors, or the creditors of his estate, that he names in his will, and no other person has the power to appoint property to anyone but the surviving spouse (IRC § 2056[b][5]). Since no limitations exist on the spouse's exercise of the power of appointment, this is a general power of appointment. When the general power is given to the surviving spouse, it causes the trust property to be included in the gross estate of the "person who possesses the power," i.e., the surviving spouse (IRC § 2041 [a][2]).

> **EXAMPLE:** In his will, Sherman creates a trust transferring property to his spouse, Roxanne, for life and giving Roxanne on her death the power to appoint the balance of the trust principal to "such beneficiaries as she may designate in her will." Since there are no limitations on the power of appointment, and Roxanne can appoint the remaining principal at her death to "herself, her estate, her creditors, or the creditors of her estate," this is a general power of appointment, and the trust property will be added to Roxanne's estate and is subject to federal estate tax when she dies.

If the surviving spouse fails to exercise the power of appointment in his own will, the trust assets pass as directed in the trust document. An advantage of this trust is that it may permit the surviving spouse to make gifts of trust property to children that may qualify for the gift tax annual exclusion, which, in turn, reduces estate taxes at the surviving spouse's death. However, the general power of appointment trust fails to protect the estate of the settlor-spouse, who creates the trust, from the surviving spouse's power to change who will ultimately receive the trust property. The QTIP trust, discussed below, eliminates this problem.

A general power of appointment also occurs when a decedent spouse in a testamentary trust gives property for life to the surviving spouse and gives that spouse an unrestricted right to withdraw all or any part of the principal at any time. This would give the surviving spouse the power to appoint the principal to anyone at any time and thus becomes a general power of appointment.

As mentioned previously, to avoid the unfavorable estate tax consequences of the general power of appointment trust, a special power of appointment trust can be created instead, if appropriate. Such trusts limit the surviving spouse to appointing only an identifiable person or class of persons designated in the trust document creating the power. The appointee(s) cannot be the spouse or the spouse's estate or creditors. When special powers of appointment are created, the trust property is not included in the surviving spouse's estate on death.

QTIP Trusts

Since its creation in 1982, the **qualified terminable interest property (QTIP) trust** has been very popular. This type of trust, which can be a testamentary or living trust, allows a settlor-spouse to transfer the income from trust property to a surviving spouse for life, and then pass the remainder (principal) to someone else, usually children.

Generally, the marital deduction (for federal gift and estate tax purposes) is not available if the property transferred by one spouse (transferor) will terminate on the death of the surviving spouse (transferee) and pass to someone else. For example, if a husband places property in trust for his wife for life and passes the

qualified terminable interest property (QTIP) trust
A type of trust that will qualify for the marital deduction in which the surviving spouse receives all the income for life but is not given a general power of appointment.

terminable interest
An interest in property that terminates on the death of the holder or on the occurrence of some other specified event. The transfer of a terminable interest from one spouse to the other spouse does not qualify for the marital deduction.

remainder to their children when his wife dies, this is a **terminable interest** that does *not qualify* as a marital deduction for the husband or the husband's estate since it does not give the wife sufficient control over the trust property and is not considered a transfer to her. A QTIP trust resolves this problem because "qualified terminable interest property" is excluded from the terminable interest rule, and, therefore, the QTIP qualifies for the unlimited marital deduction.

To qualify as QTIP and thereby make possible the QTIP election, as explained below, the settlor-spouse of a QTIP trust must

- give the surviving spouse the right to all the income from the trust property for life, payable at least annually (IRC § 2056 [b] [7] [B] [ii] [I]). *Note:* This also gives the surviving spouse the right to use the trust property, e.g., to live in the family home or vacation home for life.
- not allow any person, including the surviving spouse, to have a power to appoint any part of the property to any person other than the surviving spouse for the spouse's lifetime (IRC § 2056 [b] [7] [B] [ii] [II]).

In a QTIP trust, the trustee may be allowed to use some of the trust principal, but usually only when necessary for the surviving spouse's "health, education, support, or maintenance" (IRC § 2041 [b] [1] [A]). *Note:* Although the surviving spouse in a QTIP trust receives all the income for life, the settlor-spouse can designate and pass the principal (remainder) of the trust to someone other than the surviving spouse, e.g., children. Therefore, the surviving spouse is *not* given a *general power of appointment*, and the settlor-spouse, even though the first to die, determines the trust property distribution after the death of the surviving spouse through the trust.

Caveat: For property to qualify as QTIP for the marital deduction, an election (called the QTIP election) must be made on Schedule M of Form 706, the U.S. Estate (and Generation-Skipping Transfer) Tax Return (IRC § 2056 [b] [7] [B] [v]). The election is irrevocable. If the property is transferred as a gift through a living trust, the settlor-spouse (donor) is the person who makes the QTIP election, which results in the property qualifying for the gift tax marital deduction. If the trust property is transferred after the settlor-spouse's (testator's) death through a testamentary trust, the personal representative (executor) of the estate makes the election on Form 706. The executor (or the settlor-donor in the case of the living trust) may elect to qualify all or any portion of the QTIP trust assets for the marital deduction based on the most advantageous tax strategy and benefits to the recipients. Once the QTIP election is made, the property transferred into the trust is treated as qualified terminable interest property, which causes the terminable interest restriction to be waived, with the result that the marital deduction is allowed. *Note:* In exchange for this earlier marital deduction for the settlor-spouse, the surviving spouse's gross estate must include the value of the QTIP election assets (remaining principal) of the trust property at the surviving spouse's death for federal estate tax purposes even though the surviving spouse has no control over the ultimate disposition of these assets (IRC § 2044).

Thus, the QTIP trust offers two unique advantages. First, the settlor-spouse (testator) of a testamentary trust or the settlor-spouse (donor) of an irrevocable living QTIP trust is allowed to direct the disposition (distribution) of the trust principal at the death of the surviving spouse. This ensures that the testator's or settlor's children or other intended family members will be the ultimate beneficiaries of the trust. The second advantage is the trust's flexibility for purposes of the gift or estate tax marital deduction. The testator of a testamentary trust can direct the personal representative (executor) or the settlor-donor can direct the trustee (who may be the settlor) in the irrevocable living trust to elect on the estate or gift tax return to qualify all or any part of the trust principal for the marital deduction. The portion of the trust for which the election is made must be included in the surviving spouse's gross estate for federal estate tax purposes. The result is that the federal estate tax is not avoided, but is postponed, which is another reason for the use of the QTIP trust since the postponement of paying federal estate tax when the settlor-spouse dies makes more property assets available to the surviving spouse and ultimate heirs. Another advantage is that QTIP assets are not probated after the surviving spouse's death. QTIP trusts are primarily used by spouses whose estates exceed their combined personal federal estate tax applicable exclusions. The QTIP trust is particularly useful when creating estates for spouses who have children from earlier marriages.

> **EXAMPLE:** Xavier and Mona are married. Mona has two children by a previous marriage, and Xavier has three children by a previous marriage. If Mona dies leaving all her property to Xavier in her will, no federal estate tax will be owed on her death because of the marital deduction. When Xavier dies, however, he may pass all the property he inherited from Mona to only his children. Using a QTIP trust, Mona can create a testamentary trust that pays all the trust income annually to Xavier for life; on his death, the trust principal passes to *her* children. In addition, Mona can direct her personal representative to elect on her federal estate tax return, Form 706, that all or part of the trust property be treated as QTIP property and therefore qualify for the marital deduction. *Note:* The decision to make the QTIP election by the personal representative (executor) is after the first spouse (Mona) dies, which makes important postmortem estate planning possible. On Xavier's death, the value of the QTIP election assets, which qualified for the marital deduction on Mona's death and now pass to her children, must be included in Xavier's gross estate and may be subject to federal estate tax. If Xavier remarries after Mona's death, the QTIP trust prevents him from transferring trust property to his new spouse.

The major disadvantage of the QTIP trust is that the surviving spouse is not permitted to make gifts to children from the trust principal.

Bypass Trusts

As discussed, a bypass trust (also called Trust B of an A-B trust, credit shelter trust, residuary trust, or family trust) is an estate planning device whereby a deceased spouse's estate passes to a trust rather than directly to the surviving spouse, thereby reducing the likelihood that the surviving spouse's subsequent estate will exceed the federal estate tax threshold and be taxed. In the trust, the surviving spouse is given a life estate that ends at the spouse's death and passes the remainder of the estate to named beneficiaries, usually children. This trust allows spouses with substantial estates to transfer their property, after both have died, to their children and avoid paying any federal estate tax by appropriately planning and using the marital deduction and their individual applicable exclusions. For example, as long as each spouse holds up to $5,430,000 (for 2015) in separately owned assets, and they do not use the marital deduction exclusively for those assets, the couple can use a marital deduction trust (Trust A) and a bypass trust (Trust B) to retain combined total assets worth up to $10,860,000 ($5,430,000 per spouse) that will avoid federal tax liability. See an example bypass trust within a testamentary trust in Appendix B.

As explained earlier, the process of rearranging the spouses' assets so that each spouse's estate takes maximum advantage of its unified credit is known as estate equalization. Harmony between the spouses is essential to this strategy. Marital friction and discord may make this sound estate planning device impossible.

ASSIGNMENT 14.2

Draft a revocable living trust with an A-B trust provision. Refer to the Sample Marital Deduction Testamentary Trust in Appendix B for comparison.

Life Insurance

When designing an estate plan, one of the important planning devices available to conserve the value of the estate is *life insurance*. Life insurance is a contract between the *policyholder*, in most cases, the owner of the policy and the person whose life is insured, and an insurance company whereby the company agrees, in return for annual *premium* payments, to pay a specific sum of money, i.e., the *face value*, to the designated *beneficiary* upon the death of the policyholder. The insurance company is called the *insurer* or *carrier*; the policyholder is the owner and can also be the *insured*.

> **EXAMPLE:** Sahar contracts with Metro Life Insurance Company to buy a $200,000 term life insurance policy. Sahar pays an annual *premium* of $600 to the company. She has named her son, Kareem, as her primary *beneficiary*. When Sahar dies, the insurance company must pay Kareem $200,000.

Sahar is the *policyholder* or *insured*. Metro Life Insurance Company is the *insurer* or *carrier*. Kareem is the *beneficiary*. The *premium* is $50 per month or $600 per year, and the *face value* or *amount* of the policy or contract is $200,000 (Exhibit 14.1).

Types of Life Insurance

The three major types of life insurance are ordinary, straight, or whole life insurance; term life insurance; and universal life insurance.

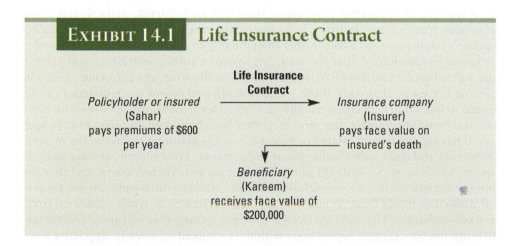

EXHIBIT 14.1   Life Insurance Contract

Life Insurance Contract

Policyholder or insured
(Sahar)
pays premiums of $600
per year
→
Insurance company
(Insurer)
pays face value on
insured's death

Beneficiary
(Kareem)
receives face value of
$200,000

1. *Ordinary, straight, or whole life insurance.* Whole or straight life insurance combines lifetime protection with a minimum savings feature called *cash surrender value* or, more commonly, *cash value.* Premium payments remain the same during the contract and are required throughout the policyholder's lifetime. After the first few years, the cash value slowly increases throughout the duration of the contract. The policyholder may *surrender* (cash in) the policy at any time and take out the cash value (money) for his own use or retain the policy until death for the benefit of the named beneficiary.

   EXAMPLE: Phyllis buys a $50,000 policy of straight life insurance, naming her daughter, Anne, *beneficiary.* Each year, Phyllis pays the *premium* for the policy. If Phyllis desires, she may at any point withdraw for her own use the *cash value* (savings) accumulated, but she must *surrender* (terminate) the policy to obtain the cash value. If Phyllis dies before the policy is terminated, Anne will receive the proceeds ($50,000).

2. *Term life insurance.* Term insurance is life insurance that is pure protection without savings *(cash surrender* or *loan value).* It is by far the least expensive insurance. It requires the insurance company to pay the face value (amount) of insurance, i.e., the proceeds, to the beneficiary if the policyholder dies within a given time (term). It is generally renewable from term to term without an additional medical examination. The cost to renew term insurance increases with the age of the insured.

   EXAMPLE: If, in the above example, Phyllis had bought a 10-year policy of term insurance in the amount of $50,000 and died within that period, Anne would receive the proceeds.

3. *Universal life insurance.* Universal life insurance is life insurance that covers a specific period and builds *cash value* for the policyholder over that time. This coverage emphasizes the separation of the portion of the premium that is used to cover the insurance protection from the portion of the premium allocated to an investment that is used to build the policy's cash value. Investments are usually flexible and selected with a view to maximize the rate of return.

Tax Consequences of Life Insurance

Regardless of the type of life insurance, the entire proceeds, i.e., the face amount of the policy, are included in the decedent-policyholder's estate if (1) the proceeds are payable to the decedent's estate or (2) the proceeds are payable to other beneficiaries and the decedent retained any "incidents of ownership" in the life insurance policy prior to death. An **incident of ownership** is an element or right of ownership or degree of control over a life insurance contract. The following are examples of incidents or rights of ownership.

incident of ownership
An element or right of ownership or degree of control over a life insurance contract.

- The right to change the named beneficiary of the policy
- The right to cancel or surrender (cash in) the policy
- The right to transfer or assign ownership of the policy to another person or to a trust
- The right to pledge the policy as collateral for a loan
- The right to obtain a loan against the cash value of the policy from the insurer (insurance company)

Caveat: The retention by the policyholder of any *incident of ownership* in a life insurance policy will cause the policy proceeds (face amount) to be included in the policyholder's gross estate on death and be subject to federal estate tax; see IRC § 2042(2). In the case *of In re Lumpkin's Estate*, 474 F.2d 1092 (1973), the U.S. Court of Appeals ruled that the decedent taxpayer (Lumpkin), under the provisions of a group term life insurance policy, had the right to alter the time and manner of the benefits of the policy and thereby possessed an incident of ownership with respect to the policy. Therefore, the court decided that the value of the insurance proceeds must be included in Lumpkin's gross estate and be subject to federal estate tax. *Note:* The policyholder and owner can avoid this detrimental tax consequence to his estate in one of three ways.

1. Transfer the ownership of an existing policy to a trust or to another person (but not to a spouse since there is no tax advantage because of the unlimited marital deduction).

2. In a written statement given to the insurance company, formally relinquish (give up) all incidents of ownership in an existing policy.

In both cases above, however, the Internal Revenue Code also requires the policyholder to *live three more years* after the date of the transfer or the date of the formal relinquishment in order for the proceeds of the policy to *not* be included in the decedent's gross estate and thus *not* be subject to federal estate tax.

3. When the insurance policy is purchased, another person (not the insured) pays the premiums and, thereby, is the owner of the policy and possessor of the incidents of ownership instead of the insured. When the insured dies, the beneficiary receives the face value (amount) of the policy, but the proceeds are *not* included in the insured's gross estate and, therefore, are *not* subject to federal estate tax.

Another important tax outcome associated with life insurance is the payment of the proceeds to the named beneficiary. Generally, when the proceeds are paid to the beneficiary on the death of the policyholder, they are exempt from federal and state income tax (IRC § 101[a]).

Life insurance proceeds are distributed by various methods. If the policyholder's *estate is the beneficiary*, the proceeds are normally distributed as a lump sum since it provides immediate cash for the family and a source of funds to pay creditors' claims and administration expenses. As noted above, however, the proceeds are subject to federal estate tax; since they enlarge the gross estate, they also increase the probate costs. When the *beneficiary is an individual*, several settlement options are available under most policies, including the following:

- The company holds the proceeds and interest accumulates.
- The company pays the beneficiaries the proceeds and interest in installments over a specific period.
- The company uses the proceeds to purchase an annuity for lifetime payments to the beneficiary.
- The company pays the beneficiary a lump sum to be invested or used as the beneficiary wishes.

Life insurance proceeds can be used for many purposes besides the payment of the decedent's debts, taxes, and administration expenses. The proceeds can supply a source of funds to replace the lost income of the decedent wage earner, maintain a family's lifestyle, pay for the college education of children, help to cover the ongoing expenses of an elderly parent or handicapped child, and provide for the financial security of future generations of family members.

Life Insurance Trusts

One method often used by families to conserve wealth is the **irrevocable life insurance trust**, a common device used in estate planning to pass proceeds of a life insurance policy to heirs tax-free. A settlor establishes an irrevocable life insurance trust by assigning the ownership of an existing policy to the trust or the trustee can purchase a new policy on the settlor's life. Each year while alive, the settlor gives the trust a certain amount of money with which the trustee pays the existing or new policy premiums. The life insurance policy is owned by the trust. When the settlor dies, the proceeds of the policy are paid to the trust, which is the named beneficiary of the policy. This process enables the settlor to direct the trustee to pass the proceeds to the trust's named beneficiaries (usually children) and keeps the proceeds from being included in the settlor's taxable estate for federal estate tax purposes. *Note:* If the settlor transfers an existing policy to the trust, thereby relinquishing the incidents of ownership, the settlor must live for three years from the date of the establishment of the irrevocable life insurance trust for the proceeds to avoid federal estate tax. In addition, depending on the replacement value of the existing policy, i.e., the amount of money it would cost to buy the policy at the present time, gift tax may be due, unless the cost was under the annual gift tax exclusion.

If the life insurance trust is designed properly, it can take advantage of an important decision on tax law that establishes the opportunity for the annual gift tax exclusion to be allowed for transfers into trusts. The decision came in the case of *Crummey v. Commissioner*, 397 F.2d 82 (9th Cir. 1968). The money the settlor contributes each year to pay the insurance premiums is not given to the beneficiaries (the children) directly but goes instead to the trustee of the trust. The trustee must give each beneficiary (child) a written notice, called a Crummey letter, indicating that the gift from the settlor has been delivered and that each beneficiary may elect (demand) to receive the gift at this time. If the demand is not made, the trustee will invest the money by paying the premiums due on the policy. Since the settlor's annual gift to the trust can be acquired by the beneficiaries each year, it constitutes a *present interest* and, therefore, qualifies for the annual gift tax exclusion. See Exhibit 14.2 for an illustration of an irrevocable life insurance trust.

irrevocable life insurance trust
A living trust that cannot be revoked or amended that is established by a settlor who assigns the ownership of a new or existing life insurance policy on the settlor's life to the trust and contributes money annually to the trust to pay the premiums. The policy proceeds are payable to the trust on the death of the settlor.

POSTMORTEM ESTATE PLANNING

Important estate planning opportunities are available even after the testator's death. This estate planning is called **postmortem** planning, and it is often used for tax-saving purposes. Disclaiming an inheritance is an example of such planning.

> **EXAMPLE:** At age 82, Barney dies, leaving half of his estate to his wife, Jana, who is 86, and the other half to their only child, Shelley. Either Jana or Shelley could reject the testamentary gifts from Barney by a disclaimer.

postmortem
After death; pertaining to matters occurring after death.

EXHIBIT 14.2   Irrevocable Life Insurance Trust Illustration

Settlor
Annually gives money to trustee in trust. The trust is the owner and beneficiary of the life insurance policy.

→ **Trustee**
Annually gives written notice of the gift and right to elect by the beneficiaries of the trust.

→ **Beneficiaries**
Refuse the gift.

→ **Trustee**
Uses gift to pay annual life insurance premium.

→ When settlor dies, the face amount of the policy is paid to the trust.

→ **Trustee**
Distributes life insurance proceeds to beneficiaries as directed by settlor.

ASSIGNMENT 14.3

In the chart below, fill in the missing Yes or No for each estate planning device (document).

This Document Can:	Documents		
	Will (without a testamentary trust)	Revocable Living Trust	Irrevocable Living Trust (if funded)
1. Be private	No	_____	Yes
2. Avoid probate	_____	Yes	Yes
3. Avoid court appointment of fiduciaries	_____	Yes	Yes
4. Use professional management	Yes	_____	Yes
5. Protect a spendthrift child	No	_____	Yes
6. Avoid ancillary administration	No	_____	Yes
7. Allow maker to control assets while alive	Yes	Yes	_____
8. Delay inheritance	_____	Yes	Yes
9. Avoid federal estate tax	No	No	_____
10. Diminish contests of the document	No	Yes	_____
11. Be revoked	Yes	Yes	_____
12. Provide for the maker's disability	_____	Yes	Yes

A **disclaimer** is a refusal to accept a bequest, inheritance, or gift acquired through a will, trust, or the law of intestate succession or to accept proceeds from life insurance or other gratuitous transfers. Named beneficiaries disclaim gifts primarily because of their age, health, and financial security and because disclaimers offer the opportunity to make sound tax-saving decisions. The following are some examples of how disclaimers and other strategies can be used to save on taxes after the testator's death.

disclaimer
The right of a beneficiary or heir to refuse a gift by will, trust, or inheritance without any adverse tax consequences.

- *Gift and estate tax savings.* When a beneficiary or donee disclaims a gift of an estate that results in a transfer of the property from the disclaimant to another person, the question arises whether the transfer is subject to gift or estate tax. The case *of Estate of Boyd v. C. I. R.*, 819 F. 2nd 170 (1987) addressed the issue whether a disclaimer of a forgiveness of a debt is subject to either tax. In ruling that the rejection of a forgiveness of a debt exercised by the donee of the forgiveness was not a taxable transfer under Internal Revenue Code Section 2518, the court stated, "the forgiveness of a debt owed to the testator [was] as much a bequest as an outright gift" [and when the] intended recipient disclaims it, [the] disclaimer is effective under Section 2518. The types of disclaimers that qualify to avoid gift and estate tax are found in state statutes and in Section 2518 of the Internal Revenue Code, which provides

1. the disclaimant must make an irrevocable and unqualified refusal to accept an interest in property.

2. the refusal must be in writing.

3. the written instrument of disclaimer must be received by the transferor of the interest, his legal representative, or the holder of the legal title to the property no later than 9 months after the later of either the date of the transfer or the day on which a minor disclaimant reaches age 21. See Exhibit 14.3 for a sample written disclaimer.

4. the disclaimant must not accept an interest or any of its benefits.

5. the refusal must be legally effective to pass the specific gift to another person without direction from the disclaimant.

As a result of the disclaimer, the interest does not pass to the disclaimant and therefore is not subject to gift or estate tax.

EXAMPLE: Kyle's will leaves a majority of his estate to Jolene, his wife. Jolene is financially secure, so she executes a written disclaimer and gives it to the personal representative and files a copy with the probate court. The disclaimer keeps the property out of Jolene's estate and is not subject to gift or estate tax. It also allows the property to pass directly to their children, which, although not specified by Jolene, is actually what she wishes.

A disclaimer is accomplished by delivering the written disclaimer to the personal representative and filing a copy with the probate court. In the case of a trust, the disclaimer would be given to the trustee. Estate tax reduction after death can also be achieved by purposely allowing the personal representative to transfer the amount of the property disclaimed to a charity or spouse. This strategy can substantially increase the charitable and marital deductions and thereby lower the gross estate of the decedent and correspondingly the estate tax. A surviving spouse's elective rights against a will can also be used to increase the marital deduction if the elective share is greater than the amount the spouse receives through the will.

- *State inheritance tax savings.* Inheritance taxes levied by some states are based on the amount of the property given to the recipient and the relationship of the person to the testator. Assuming a bequest to a child in the testator's will would be taxed at a lower rate than a bequest to a surviving spouse, the testator-decedent's spouse, by a disclaimer, may cause the property to pass to the child and be taxed at a lower rate for inheritance tax purposes. See *Matter of Wisely's Estate*, 402 N.E.2d 14 (Ind.App. 1980), in which the court held the beneficiary's renunciation of her interest in the decedent's estate under the will related back to the time of the decedent's death. Consequently, none of the estate had been transferred to her under the will, and, therefore, there was no basis for assessment of inheritance tax to her.

- *Federal and state income tax savings.* The decedent's estate as a taxable entity and the beneficiaries' income taxes may be affected by controlling the timing and amount of property distributed to the beneficiaries or prolonging the time of the estate administration into a second taxable year if this procedure is economically sound.

- *Deduction for administration expenses.* As a final postmortem tax-saving method, the personal representative can also elect to use estate administration expenses as a deduction for either estate tax or income tax purposes.

EXHIBIT 14.3   Sample Disclaimer

STATE OF NEW YORK
SURROGATE'S COURT: COUNTY OF _____

In the Matter of the Administration
of the Estate of _____, Deceased.

RENUNCIATION OF INTEREST IN ESTATE
PURSUANT TO EPTL 2-1.11
File No. _____

TO THE SURROGATE'S COURT OF THE COUNTY OF_____:
    I, the undersigned, _____, domiciled at _____, New York, pursuant to Section 2-1.11 of the New York Estates, Powers and Trusts Law, irrevocably renounce wholly all of the right, title, and interest in and to any portion of the estate of _____, deceased, to which I may be or become entitled under the laws of the State of New York.

_____ [L.S]

[Notary]

Key Terms

marital deduction	gift splitting	appointee
estate equalization	present interest	general power of appointment
bypass trust	legal life estate	special or limited power of appointment
charitable deduction	custodian	qualified terminable interest property
capital gains tax	custodianship	(QTIP) trust
charitable remainder	future interests	terminable interest
Charitable Remainder Unitrust	stepped-up basis	incident of ownership
Charitable Remainder Annuity Trust	alternate valuation date	irrevocable life insurance trust
donor	donor (of a power of appointment)	postmortem
donee	donee (of a power of appointment)	disclaimer

Review Questions

1. Who are the individuals you would choose to help you prepare an estate plan for a client?

2. What is the purpose of an estate plan? Methods for reducing or avoiding taxes are part of every estate plan. Such tax avoidance methods may be legal, but are they ethical?

3. How do potential adverse factors diminish the value of an estate? List at least three such factors.

4. What are the two key documents used to prepare an estate plan? How does each document benefit a decedent's surviving family members?

5. How is the marital deduction used to lower the net estate that is subject to federal estate tax?

6. Under what circumstances does estate equalization between spouses become important?

7. How does the charitable deduction reduce both federal estate and income taxes?

8. How does a Charitable Remainder Unitrust differ from a Charitable Remainder Annuity Trust? What function does each charitable trust serve?

9. What are the most common methods used to reduce federal and state death taxes? List four methods and explain how each reduces these taxes.

10. According to current federal tax law, what are the gift tax annual exclusion, the marital deduction, and the unified transfer tax credit (applicable credit) for gifts and estates? Explain how each is used to reduce federal taxes.

11. What is the distinction between a general and a special power of appointment? Why is a power of appointment used in a will or a trust?

12. What are four methods of transferring property that qualify for the gift or estate tax marital deduction? Explain each one.

13. What is a QTIP trust? Explain its function and advantages.

14. Why is life insurance such an important planning device for an estate plan? What is the function of an irrevocable life insurance trust?

15. What are the incidents of ownership of a life insurance policy? What effect do they have on a decedent-policyholder's potential federal estate tax?

Case Problems

Problem 1

Marsha Thompson, age 34, is a single parent who divorced her husband, Ben Thompson, three years ago. Marsha has custody of their two children, Andrea, age 12, and Jonas, age 8. Marsha is a marketing manager for a local retail store. She earns $35,000 per year. The company provides Marsha and her dependents with a health insurance plan; a group term life insurance policy worth $20,000; and a 401(k) employee benefit plan to which the company annually contributes 3 percent of her salary. Marsha makes contributions of $200 per month to the 401(k) plan, and she has named her two children the beneficiaries of the plan and her life insurance. Marsha has a checking account of $1,200; owns a 2011 Ford; and, after the divorce, has title to a house worth $85,000 with equity of $15,000. She has no other savings or investments.

Marsha's former husband, Ben, is a salesman who has difficulty keeping a job because of his dependency on alcohol. Currently, he sells new and used cars. He has visitation rights with the children, but he frequently fails to show up. Ben has been ordered to pay monthly child support of $300, which he has paid sporadically depending on whether he has a job. He is now $4,500 behind in support payments, and Marsha has little hope of enforcing payment. According to your state statutes, answer and explain the following:

A. As part of an estate plan for Marsha, would you recommend a will, a will with a testamentary trust, or a revocable living trust?

B. Name the fiduciaries who would need to be appointed as part of Marsha's estate plan.

C. If Marsha were to die first, can she exclude her former husband, Ben, from becoming the guardian of the person of her minor children? What about the guardian of the property?

D. Are the children old enough to voice their preference for a guardian?

E. What other kinds of insurance, if any, would you recommend Marsha buy, e.g., homeowners, car, life, disability, health, or long-term care?

F. What kinds of investments, if any, would you recommend, e.g., stocks, bonds, certificates of deposit, and IRAs?

Problem 2

Jake Costello, a confirmed bachelor, has been a workaholic his entire life. Financially, he has been immensely successful. Jake's net worth is over $10 million. Now 86 years of age and in failing health, Jake has outlived his immediate family members and has no surviving relatives. Realizing "you can't take it with you," Jake decides the one beneficiary he does not want to receive any death benefits, i.e., federal taxes, from his estate is the government. What options could you suggest to Jake to accomplish his wish (or is it a fantasy)?

Practical Assignments

1. Your client provides you with a copy of his life insurance policy. In reviewing the policy, you discover the following information: it has a face amount of $25,000, and the base plan states that it is a 30-year renewable and convertible term life insurance policy. Your client wants your advice on whether this policy has any current cash value. What is the answer?

2. Buford gives his girlfriend, Loretta, $20,000 in 2014. How much of this gift is excluded from federal gift taxes?

3. Determine whether your state of residency currently has state inheritance taxes.

LONG-TERM CARE

15

Outline

Objectives

After completing this chapter, you should be able to:

- Identify the users and their need for long-term care. Explain how the cost of such care is financed by individual assets, state and federal sources, and long-term care insurance.

- Determine the segment of the population that should consider the purchase of long-term care insurance.

- Interpret the options available for a long-term care insurance policy.

- Analyze different policies and determine the appropriate coverage and premium for specific situations.

- Evaluate the insurance companies for their financial strength, size, and history for payment of claims.

SCOPE OF THE CHAPTER

This chapter addresses the need for financial planning for future disability and long-term care as part of the estate plan. After an introduction to the history and development of long-term care, the resources available for this expense (Social Security, Supplemental Security Income, Medicare, and Medicaid) are examined. The chapter closes with a discussion on long-term care insurance.

LONG-TERM CARE

History and Development of Long-Term Care

During the past 40 years, health and medical advances have increased the lifespan of our nation's population, thereby creating a new field of law. It is called **elder law**, i.e., specialized legal services for our aging population. All elder law attorneys and paralegals recognize that wills and/or trusts are an essential part of a client's *estate plan*. Today, such a plan should also include financial planning for future disability and long-term care needs. While assisting your supervising attorney and the client, you will need to familiarize yourself with the new or revised federal and state programs' eligibility rules, benefits, forms, and procedures for the practice of elder law according to federal and your state statutes. This constant updating is especially needed if you work with attorneys in state-administered public legal aid clinics (offices) for low-income individuals. Coordination and utilization of legal documents (wills, trusts, and advance directives), federal and your state programs, local legal services, and public housing and benefit programs are essential to competently alleviate the aging client's long-term care concerns.

For its predominant impact on how people lived, the last half of the 20th century has been considered the "Age of the Computer." Subsequently, the first half of the 21st century is destined to be the "Era of the Seniors." In the new millennium, the *baby boomers*, those born between 1946 and 1964, will reach their senior years and cause a dramatic increase in the number of elderly persons who will require special housing and long-term medical care. According to the U.S. Census Bureau, the baby boom accounted for the largest percentage increase of any age group during the 1990–2000 decade. Although most of the aging baby boomers will initially stay in their homes, by the year 2030 (when they begin to reach the age of 85), other housing, especially nursing homes, will likely be their option.

Definition and Goal

Long-term care is the support people need when they can no longer care for themselves because of disability, frailty, or a lingering illness. This support can range from assistance with daily activities at home, such as bathing or dressing, to highly skilled care in a nursing home. Unlike traditional medical care performed by doctors, nurses, and other medical staff to cure the sick and heal the injured, long-term care provides a wide variety of services for elderly people with a chronic illness, disability, or **cognitive disorder impairment**, e.g., Alzheimer's disease. These medical problems limit the person's ability to function independently and perform the six

---

elder law
Specialized legal services for our aging population.

long-term care
The support that disabled, frail, or chronically ill people need when they can no longer care for themselves.

cognitive disorder impairment
A mental incapacity that causes disorientation, loss of memory, and lack of safety awareness, e.g., Alzheimer's disease.

activities of daily living (ADLs)
Six everyday functions and activities people do without help: bathing, eating, dressing, toileting, continence, and transferring.

toileting
Getting to and from, on and off the toilet, and performing personal hygiene.

"**activities of daily living (ADLs),**" which include bathing, dressing, eating, **toileting,** **continence**, and **transferring** (see discussion below). The *goal* of long-term care is to help the elderly maintain their level of functioning as opposed to curing or correcting specific medical problems.

Users and Costs of Long-Term Care

In most cases, the elderly receive long-term care services in their home, but they are also cared for in nursing homes, **adult day care center**, or in **assisted living facility**, such as a **continuing care retirement community**. In the United States, more than 1.4 million elderly people live in nursing *homes*.[1]

Although the numbers vary among the states, approximately 70 percent of individuals who live to age 65 will need long-term care services and support sometime in their lifetime. The average length of stay in a nursing home is two and one-half years. As each year passes for the elderly, the need for **nursing home care** increases, e.g., while slightly over 1 percent of seniors age 65 to 74 live in nursing homes, nearly 25 percent of individuals over 85 live in a nursing home, and women outnumber men by more than three to one.

The annual cost of nursing home care averages over $77,380, for a shared room and upward of $87,000 for a private room, with much higher expenses reported in some states. These costs are projected to increase approximately 3.91 percent annually.[2] A U.S. government study by the House of Representatives Select Committee on Aging found that 66 percent of all single elderly patients who enter nursing homes depleted their entire savings to pay for just one year of care. Most long-term care is provided at home by family and friends with the part-time assistance of **home health care** and **respite** caregivers, but even those cost an average of $20 per hour,[2] and there is an associated emotional expense. Caring at home for an aging family member with a chronic illness or disability can be physically and emotionally exhausting, especially for the inexperienced caregiver. It has been projected by the American Council of Life Insurance that, depending on the type of care, the annual cost of nursing home care will exceed $190,000 by the year 2030.

Need for Long-Term Care

The need for and financing of long-term care has become one of the most serious concerns of our nation's aging population. The questions each person must answer are the following:

- How soon must I plan for long-term care before the actual need arises?
- How much inheritance, if any, do I want to leave my family?
- How will I pay for housing, health, and medical expenses during the last years of my life?

For some people these expenses will be enormous. Without proper financial planning, the costs of housing and medical care may eliminate all potential inheritance to family and friends, deplete the individual's assets, impoverish the person, and make him or her a ward of the state. The sad fact is the majority of Americans over 65 do not make plans for long-term care.

continence
The ability to control bowel and bladder function.

transferring
Moving in or out of bed, a chair, or wheelchair.

adult day care center
Senior service centers that are community-based group programs that give care during the day for adults with functional or cognitive impairments and provide assistance to caregivers.

assisted living facility
A community residential living arrangement that provides individual personal care and health services for a person who requires help with activities of daily living (ADLs).

continuing care retirement community
A campus-style community that provides a combination of housing, services, and nursing care, at one location, to meet the various needs of residents as they grow older. The community generally charges a standard fee to enter and a flexible fee for a package of contract-specified services that vary as the resident's needs change.

nursing home care
A residential institution that provides care and services for the elderly or infirmed.

home health care
Medical and nonmedical (including household) services provided by doctors, nurses, therapists, home health aides, and homemakers for sick, disabled, or infirmed persons in their homes.

respite care
Care offered to relieve family caregivers for a few hours or up to several days.

Financing Long-Term Care

Many people continue to believe that when they need long-term care, our government will pay their expenses. This belief, of course, is a fantasy. The reality is that the resources (income and assets) of each person combined with federal and state government sources (e.g., Social Security, Supplemental Security Income, Medicare, and Medicaid) will determine the person's ability to pay for necessary long-term care and also will identify the need and appropriateness of adding another resource: *long-term care insurance*. Choices for financing long-term care will vary according to each person's level of income and assets. There are three levels: (1) low, (2) moderate, or (3) high. The need for long-term care and methods of paying for it by a person in each of the three levels of income are discussed next.

Resources Available to Help Pay Long-Term Care Expenses

Obviously, personal resources available to pay the cost of long-term care include an individual's income and assets from employment, home ownership, investments (stocks and bonds), and retirement plans including pension and profit-sharing plans, IRAs, 401(k) plans, and retirement plans for self-employed taxpayers. Federal programs such as Social Security, Medicare, and Medicaid also are sources that provide income, hospital and medical insurance, and medical assistance for people who are aged or whose income falls below a certain minimum standard. *Note:* Since the programs discussed below annually change their statistical information, e.g., percentages, monetary amounts, and income limits, you must refer to the Research Boxes to learn how to obtain updated information (Exhibit 15.1 and 15.2).

Social Security

The official name for Social Security is the Federal Old Age, Survivor's, and Disability Insurance (OASDI) Benefits Program, which clearly identifies its purpose. For many Americans, Social Security is the main and, in some cases, sole resource for their retirement.

EXHIBIT 15.1   Research Box

RESEARCH BOX
To obtain information about Social Security programs, call this toll-free number
1-800-772-1213 and order the following publications any time any day:
A "Snapshot" (Publication 05–10006)
Understanding the Benefits (Publication 05–10024)
Retirement Benefits (Publication 05–10035)
Survivors Benefits (Publication 05–10084)
Disability Benefits (Publication 05–10029)
Supplemental Security Income (Publication 05–11000)
Access information and numerous publications on the Internet at:
http://www.socialsecurity.gov

Social Security is funded through taxes paid by workers, employers, and self-employed people. The law that authorizes taxes for Social Security and Medicare is the Federal Insurance Contributions Act (FICA).

Social Security benefits paid to eligible workers are based on the worker's earnings while employed at a job covered by this federal program. Most self-employed persons also receive benefits based on their earnings. In 2003, the full benefit retirement age began to rise from 65; it will continue rising until the end of 2027, when the retirement age with full benefits will be 67. Age 62 remains the age for early retirement with reduced benefits. *Note:* Social Security is not a program that pays benefits based on financial need. All eligible workers and self-employed persons regardless of their personal wealth receive benefits.

Social Security benefits, subject to certain age and other conditions, are paid to the following:

- Retired workers, starting at age 62, and their dependents
- Disabled workers (any age) who have qualified for disability and their dependents
- Surviving dependents of deceased workers
- Surviving dependents of deceased disabled workers
- Former spouses, if married for at least 10 years. *Note:* If a former spouse receives benefits on the worker's account, it does not affect the amount of any benefits payable to other survivors of the worker who are also on the worker's account.

Finally

- every qualified worker is also entitled to a special one-time death benefit payment of $255.
- some higher income taxpayers may have to pay income tax on a portion of their Social Security benefits.

Supplemental Security Income (SSI)

Both Social Security and SSI are administered by the Social Security Administration. However, SSI is financed from the general revenue funds of the U.S. Treasury and not from Social Security taxes. The program makes monthly payments based on need to low-income people who have few assets. To receive the SSI basic monthly benefit you must be a U.S. citizen; live in the United States; and be 65 or older, blind, and/or disabled. The SSI payment amounts increase with the cost-of-living increases that apply to Social Security benefits.

Children can also receive SSI benefits due to blindness or disability. Most individuals receiving SSI benefits are eligible for food stamps and Medicaid (see discussion below).

SSI sets the income and asset limits for benefit eligibility. Some states add funds to the basic federal SSI monthly benefit, so you must check the local Social Security office in your state for the income limits and amount of the benefit. The asset limits, unlike the income limits, do not vary from state to state. If eligible, people may receive both Social Security and SSI benefits subject to a maximum combined benefit (see Exhibit 15.2).

ASSIGNMENT 15.1

Assume you are a paralegal working in a legal aid clinic for low-income individuals. Determine whether your state adds funds to the federal SSI monthly benefit. What are your state's income limits for eligibility, and what is the maximum amount of the benefit your state allows?

Medicare

Medicare is a federal program that provides hospital and medical insurance for people age 65 and older, certain disabled persons under 65 who qualify under Social Security, and people with permanent kidney failure treated with dialysis or a transplant. The Centers for Medicare and Medicaid Services is the federal agency within the U.S. Department of Health and Human Services that administers the Medicare and Medicaid programs. These two programs benefit approximately 109 million Americans. Medicare has four parts: A, B, C, and D.[3]

Part A is a hospital insurance program that helps pay for the following medically necessary care.

- Inpatient hospital care
- Home health care
- **Hospice care**
- Inpatient care in a skilled nursing facility following a required three-day hospital stay (not custodial or long-term care)
- Inpatient care in a religious nonmedical health care institution

hospice care
A public agency or private organization that provides supportive care at home or in an institution (e.g., hospital) for the terminally ill, i.e., persons certified by their doctor to have a life expectancy of six months or less.

ASSIGNMENT 15.2

After obtaining a current Medicare handbook, which is updated each year, list the services covered and *not* covered under Part A for inpatient hospital care.

skilled nursing facility
A Medicare qualified facility that specializes in skilled nursing or rehabilitation services under the supervision of licensed nursing personnel and based on a doctor's orders.

To be eligible for coverage under Part A for inpatient care in a **skilled nursing facility**, the patient, based on a physician's orders, must require daily skilled nursing or skilled rehabilitation services performed by, or under the supervision of, licensed nursing personnel. In the United States, many nursing homes provide custodial or personal care only and are *not* skilled nursing facilities.

EXHIBIT 15.2   Research Box

RESEARCH BOX
To obtain annual updated statistical information and the current publications, Medicare & You (CMS–10050), Your Medicare Benefits (CMS–10116), and Your Guide to Medicare Prescription Drug Coverage (CMS–11109), call this Medicare helpline toll-free number **1-800-633-4227** or visit Internet sites:

http://www.medicare.gov
http://www.cms.hhs.gov

Custodial (personal) care consists of helping the patient with daily living and personal needs provided by people lacking professional skills or training. It includes assistance in walking, bathing, dressing, eating, and taking medicines. Much of the care for the elderly that allows them to stay in their own homes is also custodial care. When workers and their spouses who are eligible for Social Security benefits reach the age of 65, they are automatically covered under Part A even if the worker has not retired. In addition, workers, regardless of age, who qualify for disability under Social Security and receive benefits for two years are also eligible for Medicare.

Part B is a medical insurance program that helps pay for the following:

- Doctor's services
- Outpatient hospital care
- Diagnostic tests
- Durable medical equipment
- Necessary ambulance services
- Home health visits needed after an injury, illness, or surgery

custodial (personal) care
Care that consists of helping the patient with daily living and personal needs provided by people lacking professional skills or training.

ASSIGNMENT 15.3

Using your Medicare handbook, list the doctor and outpatient hospital services covered and *not* covered by Medicare Part B.

Medicare has consistently expanded its services so that relevant diagnostic tests and treatments are now covered, including yearly mammograms (breast cancer); Pap smears (cervical and vaginal cancer); colorectal cancer screening; diabetes monitoring and self-management; bone mass measurements; flu, pneumonia, and hepatitis B shots; and prostate cancer screening, which includes a prostate-specific antigen (PSA) test. In summary, Medicare pays for approximately 80 percent of the Medicare-approved medical expenses for eligible recipients.

Medicare participants have health plan choices. The original Medicare Plan is the traditional fee-for-service plan and covers most hospital and doctor bills. To pay for the remainder and some other expenses Medicare does not cover, many participants buy Medicare Supplement Insurance, also known as Medigap policies.

Part C provides for Medicare Advantage Plans. In addition to the traditional plan, participants can choose Medicare Advantage Plans, which include Health Maintenance Organization (HMO) Plans, Preferred Provider Organization (PPO) Plans, Private Fee-for-Service Plans, and Special Needs Plans for a limited membership. Participants must have Medicare Parts A and B to join these plans. Generally, providers (doctors and hospitals) are part of plan networks that have agreed to accept set amounts from Medicare in payment for participants' care and in turn administer Medicare-covered benefits through these plans. Participants need to evaluate the plans carefully as the following will vary: availability of plans, choice of doctors, out-of-pocket costs, health care outside the service area of the plans, the right of providers to leave the plan network, and the right of plans to leave the Medicare program or change their benefits and premiums.

Other Medicare Health Plans include Medicare Cost Plans available in limited parts of the country, Demonstrations (special projects that test future improvements in Medicare coverage, costs, and quality of care), and Programs of All-inclusive Care for the Elderly (PACE) as an option under Medicaid.

Note: Part A and Part B of the Medicare program do not pay for long-term care expenses in a nursing home, or at home, and neither does any Medicare Supplement Insurance policy nor Medicare Advantage Plans. In most states Medicare pays for less than 5 percent of all nursing home care. To recap: Medicare only pays for a limited amount of nursing home and at-home care called skilled nursing care, which is not the same as custodial or personal care. The latter is the kind of long-term care most elderly people need, but it is not paid for by Medicare.

ASSIGNMENT 15.4

Using your Medicare handbook, list the advantages and disadvantages of the Medicare Advantage Plans compared to the Original Medicare Plan.

Part D provides prescription drug coverage that helps pay for prescription drug costs through Medicare prescription drug plans and other health plan options. This coverage is optional and available if Medicare coverage is in effect.

Medicaid

Medicaid is a form of public assistance, sponsored and funded jointly by the federal and state governments, which provides medical aid for people whose income and assets fall below a certain level. The federal government sets the guidelines for the Medicaid program, which the individual states administer, but some states have substantially modified the rules within the limits of the federal statutes and regulations. In most states the list of medical care covered by Medicaid includes the following:

- Physician services
- Most prescription drugs
- Dental care
- Medical tests
- Home health care
- Physical therapy
- Eyeglasses
- Hearing aids
- Hospital and long-term nursing home care

Requirements for Medicaid Eligibility

The amount of money and assets a person eligible for Medicaid is allowed to keep differs among the states.

ASSIGNMENT 15.5

List the eligibility requirements for nursing home residents in your state. *Note.* Each state has a toll-free 800 number for state residents to obtain this information.

Medicaid pays the medical treatment and housing expenses for nursing home or in-home care not only for those individuals who have little or no resources (income and assets) but also for some middle-income individuals who may become unable to continue to pay unexpected, catastrophic long-term nursing home expenses. Once they have spent most of their financial resources, they, too, become eligible for Medicaid. The result is that nearly 60 percent of all nursing home care expenses in the United States are paid by Medicaid and Medicare. Furthermore, nursing homes cannot discriminate between Medicaid patients and other patients; i.e., the Medicaid patients must be given services and care that are equal to the care received by patients who pay their own expenses.

Other middle-income spouses (parents) who wish to leave their children an inheritance, but realize one of them (husband or wife) faces a debilitating illness that will wipe out their resources, will attempt to use a method, often referred to as the **spend-down procedure**, to qualify for Medicaid but pass on the inheritance without impoverishing the healthy spouse. The parents' procedure is to pass on by gift (spend down) enough of their assets to their children to qualify the parents for Medicaid. However, Medicaid has a restriction that prohibits spouses (parents) and others in such cases from becoming eligible for medical assistance if any transfer of assets is done for less than fair market value during a five-year period immediately preceding an application for Medicaid. In addition to the five-year window, the disqualification (waiting) period begins when the application is made, *not* when the assets are transferred. Disqualification is based on the value of assets transferred and the monthly cost of long-term care in each state.

spend-down procedure
A procedure that requires an individual to spend enough income and resources to qualify for Medicaid eligibility.

EXAMPLE: In 2010, Gladys transfers by gift $10,000 to each of her five children and five grandchildren for a total of $100,000. In 2015, following a year of illness, Gladys enters a nursing home and applies for Medicaid assistance, having depleted her remaining assets on in-home health care. Gladys is disqualified for approximately 20 months ($100,000 divided by $5,000, the monthly cost of nursing home care in her state). Gladys and her family are now faced with the dilemma of how to pay for the 20-month waiting period, assuming Gladys did not have long-term care insurance. *Caution:* Before contemplating a spend-down procedure, consideration must be given to the source of funding for any potential disqualification (waiting) period.

As the example illustrates, you must familiarize yourself with the statutes and administrative rules of your state concerning Medicaid's procedures since they may become an increasingly important and essential part of your client's estate plan. For local advice, a directory of lawyers who specialize in elder law can be found at *http://www.naela.org*. Common financial advice for clients facing Medicaid's eligibility rules and restrictions is to convert liquid assets into exempt assets, such as a home. When spouses own a home, it is good tax and estate planning advice for them to pay off any existing mortgage so the "community spouse" (using Medicaid terminology) can continue to live there without mortgage payments. Another possible tax advantage is for spouses to buy a home, such as a condominium, so if one spouse (the "institutional spouse") moves into a nursing home covered by Medicaid, the "community spouse" will have an exempt home. *Caveat:* A homeowner with more than $500,000 in home equity may not qualify for Medicaid. A carefully created trust for a disabled child covered by Medicaid is a third potential financial consideration.

Need for Long-Term Care Insurance

Now that the sources of income and the federal and state public assistance programs available to the elderly and disabled have been identified, the methods of paying for long-term care expenses for individuals included in each of the three levels of income and assets can be discussed.

Low Income and Assets

Low-income individuals often receive nominal Social Security benefits, generally qualify for SSI, and, therefore, are eligible for Medicaid in most states. Consequently, they *cannot* afford and have no need for long-term care insurance.

High Income and Assets

High-income individuals, including married couples, with comfortable assets and income, have sufficient resources to pay for any possible long-term care expenses. Consequently, they *can* afford but have no need for long-term care insurance.

Caveat: Dr. Benjamin Spock, author of the 1946 classic *Baby and Child Care*, sold over 50 million copies of the book and was very wealthy. However, he never considered purchasing insurance to cover the cost of long-term nursing care. Before his death in 1998 at the age of 94, his family needed financial assistance to help pay for his in-home nursing care expenses. Dr. Spock's legacy: Sometimes, even with the best of intentions and thoughtful planning, a savings plan for retirement may not be sufficient if you unexpectedly need long-term round-the-clock care in a nursing home or even at home (as in the doctor's case).

Moderate Income and Assets

Moderate-income individuals are generally considered to have assets of approximately $92,114, not including a home or car, a median annual taxable income of $54,000 for an individual, and up to $83,740 for a married couple filing jointly. It is this group of individuals who can afford to buy long-term care insurance and thereby protect their estate assets.

Caveat: Unfortunately, even those who purchase long-term care insurance, because of spiraling inflation costs and the underestimated magnitude of long-term care expenses, especially those in nursing homes, may be forced to participate, as mentioned earlier, in the Medicaid spend-down program. In all states, the majority of nursing home residents are on Medicaid, and over half a million people in America become eligible for Medicaid each year. Many members of the baby boomer generation recognize that the cost of their parents' long-term nursing home care may ultimately become their responsibility. To cover the considerable expense of long-term care for their parents, some have purchased the insurance for them. At the present time, however, statistics show that the boomers need to be more concerned about their own long-term care needs. A survey by the American Health Care Association found that 68 percent of them are not financially prepared for long-term health care. In addition, 50 percent admitted that they had not given any thought as to how they will finance the costs of long-term care.

Long-Term Care Insurance

Definition

Long-term care insurance pays a fixed monetary amount (benefit) usually per day or per month for a designated period (benefit period) during which the insured can receive long-term care services in an assisted living facility, a nursing home, or at home. Long-term care insurance is not a typical health and medical insurance program. Instead, its purpose is to provide the insured with funds to maintain estate assets. These funds (benefits) are paid by the insurance company in one of two ways: (1) either it pays the insured or the provider for services up to the policy limits, or (2) it pays the insured only the amount stated in the policy regardless of the services received.

long-term care insurance
Insurance that pays a fixed monetary benefit, usually per day, for a designated benefit period during which the insured generally receives care at home or in a nursing home.

Goals of Long-Term Care Insurance

The goals of long-term care insurance are to enable the insured to

- identify the need and qualifications for long-term care insurance while factoring into the decision to buy the insurance the concern that future health restrictions or accident injuries may disqualify the applicant.
- pay the expenses of long-term care.
- maintain and protect estate assets.
- leave an inheritance to family (the most common incentive and justification for the purchase of this insurance).
- select the location (facility) where long-term care is received (assisted living facility, adult day care center, continuing care retirement community, nursing home, or at home—where this care is given most often).
- select caregivers (doctors, nurses, home care providers, etc.) and care facilities (hospital, clinic, etc.).
- receive federal income tax benefits, including allowing policy premiums to be deductible as medical expenses (subject to qualification and limits) and permitting all or most of the policy benefits to be tax-free (see the discussion on tax advantages below).
- most importantly, maintain independence and dignity without having to rely on the generosity of others.

Tax Advantages Associated with Long-Term Care Insurance

Since the passage of the Health Insurance Portability and Accountability Act of 1996, two important tax benefits are available to policyholders with tax-qualified long-term care insurance.

- Benefit payments from long-term care insurance policies are treated as tax-free income and are not subject to federal taxation.
- Premium payments for a **tax-qualified long-term care insurance policy** are deductible as personal medical expenses if the policyholders itemize their deductions and their total medical expenses (including the long-term care insurance premiums) exceed 7.5 percent of their adjusted gross income. Deductions are available for individuals, their spouses, and tax dependents,

tax-qualified long-term care insurance policy
A policy that conforms to specific standards under federal law and offers certain federal tax advantages.

e.g., parents. The deductible amount is subject to dollar limits based on the individual taxpayer's attained age before the close of the tax year. These limits are indexed annually for inflation.

Long-Term Care Insurance Policy Options

Before purchasing a long-term care insurance policy, the available and affordable contract options from competing companies must be carefully compared. These options include the following items.

1. *Amount of the maximum benefit.* Most companies will clearly list the maximum benefit they will pay over the period set in the policy. Other companies limit the maximum benefit to a total dollar amount. Benefits are usually paid on a daily, monthly, or annual basis. The amounts offered range from $50 to $350 per day or $1,500 to $10,500 per month for care in nursing homes. Coverage approved for in-home care services is usually $50 to $350 per day.

2. *Duration of the coverage.* Choosing the length of time for coverage is a difficult decision. Since the average stay in a nursing home, as noted earlier, is two and one-half years, and the vast majority of patients stay less than five years, five years may be the maximum period needed versus unnecessary and more expensive lifetime coverage, which, according to statistics, the majority of Americans will never need.

3. *Types of coverage.* Types of coverage include coverage only in a nursing home, only at home, or a combination covering both. Since insurers estimate that 9 of 10 people who live past age 65 will use home care,[1] buying coverage for home care only is a viable option since the average need is three to five years. It is the place where most people want to stay, and it is also less expensive than nursing home coverage. The only downside of home coverage is that anybody frail enough to need this care may also need nursing home care in the near future. However, buying only nursing home care could be a regrettable mistake since the buyer may never need it. The best choice may be the combined home and nursing home policy, but it is more expensive. You must prepare and consistently update a comparison of the available insurance policies in your state to enable your client to make the best and most appropriate personal selection. Some policies pay benefits that include care and services in any or all facilities.

4. *Cost of the policy.* The average annual premium, including inflation protection for a person age 45, ranges from $1,200 to $2,200; age 65 from $2,200 to $4,300; and age 70 from $3,000 to $6,100. Obviously, the younger a buyer is when the policy is purchased, the cheaper the cost. If buyers wait until they are older, they run the risk that their health will deteriorate, and they will not be able to qualify at any price. The premium cost of a long-term care insurance policy is determined by the policyholder's choice of the amount of the benefit, the length of time of the policy, and the insurance company selected. The quality and coverage of nursing home care and the costs vary among the states, but the average cost is approximately $212 per day for a shared room and $240 for a private room.[2] To determine how much coverage prospective buyers need, they should research and compare the average daily cost of care in their state in local nursing homes

and at home, if that location is a viable option. Subsequently, they should obtain quotes from at least three insurance companies comparing the same levels of coverage and benefits. The final choice should at least cover the average cost of the daily benefit plus the cost of some inflation protection (see discussion below). Each of the following can add to the cost of the premium of a long-term care insurance policy: (1) the age of the person when the policy is purchased; (2) the amount of the maximum benefit and length of the benefit period; (3) the addition of home health care coverage to a nursing home policy or the reverse; (4) the addition of nonforfeiture benefits; (5) the shortening of the waiting (elimination) period; and (6) the addition of inflation protection that, by itself, can increase the premium by 40 to more than 100 percent.[1] *Note:* AARP reported in 2004 that long-term care insurance sold in the 1990s was underpriced, resulting in significant premium increases.

5. *Housing facilities and services provided.* It is essential that the person seeking long-term care insurance be aware of which housing facilities are covered by the selected policy. If the insured is placed in a facility that is not covered by the policy, generally, the insurance company is not obligated to pay for the services provided. For example, some policies may require the insured to reside in a state-licensed facility (such as a licensed nursing home); therefore, such policies would not cover an unlicensed rest home or homes for the aged. Long-term care insurance policies may cover the following:

- Nursing home care
- Home health care (skilled nursing care)
- Personal care in your home (home health aides)
- Services in assisted living facilities
- Services in adult day care centers
- Services in other community facilities

Today, almost all policies cover Alzheimer's disease but only if the policy is purchased before the disease is diagnosed.

Check the policies that cover home health care very thoroughly. Some policies pay for home care only by licensed home health agencies. Others pay for care from licensed health care providers such as practical nurses; speech, physical, or occupational therapists; and/or home health care aides who may help with custodial (personal) care needs. *Note:* Family members who take care of a loved one at home are not paid benefits by most insurance companies.

ASSIGNMENT 15.6

Which of the following services are not covered by long-term care insurance policies?

- Alcohol or drug addiction
- Illness or injury caused by an act of war
- Attempted suicide
- Intentional self-inflicted injuries

6. **Waiting (elimination) period**. The waiting period is the amount of time the insureds must wait from the date they are certified as chronically ill until the date benefit payments for covered services begin. In other words, the insured patients will not receive benefits the first day they arrive and receive care at the nursing home nor when they begin receiving services at home. Most companies have a waiting or elimination period during which time benefits do not begin until a set number of days (30, 60, 90, or 100 days) have passed after the start and use of qualifying long-term care services. Premiums can be reduced by choosing a longer elimination period.

The insured becomes **chronically ill** when he or she is incapable of performing, without substantial assistance from another person, two or more of the ADLs for a period of at least 90 consecutive days or the person requires constant supervision because of his or her severe cognitive impairment that threatens the person's health and safety. To recap: The six ADLs include bathing, eating, dressing, continence, toileting, and transferring. Before the insured can receive benefit payments under a long-term care insurance policy, most companies require that the insured must be unable to perform any two of these activities.

7. **Inflation protection**. Due to inflation, the insured must recognize the need for increasing insurance protection. If the inflation rate is 5 percent per year, nursing home care that might currently cost $198 per day will cost $552 per day in 20 years. Although the cost for inflation protection increases the premium each year, it is recommended the insured purchase at least some inflation protection. A policy that a person age 55 buys today may not pay benefits until the person enters a nursing home at age 80. Unless the policy benefit is compounded annually to help keep up with inflation, the amount of the benefit will fall far short of the actual costs. Some states require that inflation protection be compounded, but this also increases the cost of the policy premium. *Caveat:* Long-term care insurance should not be purchased if the buyer cannot realistically expect to be able to afford the substantial increases in premiums in future years due to inflation. A buyer could waste thousands of dollars on a policy that lapses before it is needed.

8. **Preexisting condition limitation**. If a buyer of long-term care insurance had a medical problem (preexisting condition) that was diagnosed and treated prior to an application for the insurance, the policy, if acquired, may not cover the expense for the condition or may delay coverage for a stated period before payments begin. For example, almost all long-term care insurance policies cover Alzheimer's disease if the disease occurs after the policy is in effect. However, as a preexisting condition, many companies do not offer insurance to patients who already have Alzheimer's disease when they apply. *Note:* Long-term care insurance policies that contain an exclusion for Alzheimer's disease are prohibited in many states.

9. **Nonforfeiture benefit**. A provision in a long-term care insurance policy that refunds at least part of the premium if the insured cancels the policy or lets it lapse for nonpayment.

10. **Waiver of premium payment**. A provision in a long-term care insurance policy that allows insureds to stop paying the premium once they enter a nursing home, and the company begins to pay benefits. The waiver of premium payments may not apply to insureds receiving home health care.

11. *Third-party notification.* The third-party notification option allows the insured to name a third person who is to be notified if the policy is about to lapse for nonpayment of the premium.

12. *Premium refund on death.* After paying premiums for a set number of years or if death occurs before a specific age, an insured may be entitled to a refund payable on death to the estate.

Methods of Purchasing Long-Term Care Insurance

Long-term care insurance policies are sold by approximately 100 private insurance companies. Policies may be purchased in many ways through

- agents.
- the mail or by phone without an agent.
- senior citizen organizations and fraternal associations.
- employers who may offer a group insurance policy.
- continuing care retirement communities that offer or require residents to pass a physical and enroll in group policies.
- a combination of life insurance and long-term care insurance using an "accelerated benefit," a benefit of life insurance the insured uses while living.
- long-term care "partnerships" that exist between four states, i.e., California, Connecticut, Indiana, and New York, and their Medicaid agencies that allow resident purchasers of a long-term care insurance policy to go on Medicaid when the policy benefits are exhausted without first having to deplete (spend down) their own assets to become eligible.

Insurance Selection—Rating Services

Since a long-term care insurance policy may last for many years, the insured, before buying the policy, should select a company that has an established history of prompt payments and excellent service. Several private companies, called rating services, investigate and analyze the financial strength of long-term care insurance companies and rate them. Ratings from the services are available free at most public libraries. Some of these rating services include

- A.M. Best Company on the Internet at *http://www.ambest.com*
- Standard & Poor's Insurance Rating Services on the Internet at *http://www.standardandpoors.com*

Recommendation: If a person has decided to buy long-term care insurance, the following is suggested.

- Buy a policy that covers both in-home and nursing home care and lasts for at least five years.
- Buy a policy with 100 percent of the average daily benefit in your area for nursing home care and 100 percent for home care with a minimum of five visits per week.
- Buy some inflation protection.
- Keep your existing policy and change it only for a good reason.

Caution: A realistic approach to the purchase of long-term care insurance options should include consideration of a policy that will *help* defray the expense of long-term care rather than an *all-inclusive* policy that will incur prohibitive premiums to maintain.

Alternatives to Long-Term Care Insurance

Instead of buying insurance, a person might pay for long-term care by the following:

- Borrow from the cash value of a whole-life insurance policy.
- Accelerate death benefits from life insurance while the insured is still living.
- Use a reverse mortgage on the home owned by the person to help pay for long-term care.

Reverse mortgages, although intriguing, are complicated and require special counseling for retirees at HUD-approved agencies. To begin with, a person must be at least age 62 and own the home mortgage-free or be able to pay off any existing mortgage balance with funds from the reverse mortgage loan. The loan will accrue interest, which becomes due with the loan when the owner moves or dies. On the owner's death, heirs or beneficiaries have two options: (1) sell the house, pay off the loan balance, and keep the remainder if the sales price is greater than the loan; or (2) pay off the loan balance with their own funds and keep the house.

Limitations, imposed by the Federal Housing Administration (FHA), exist on the amount that can be mortgaged; e.g., if the limit in your area is $200,000 and the property is valued at $275,000, the mortgage will be based on $200,000. The most common reverse mortgage is a home equity conversion mortgage (HECM) insured by the FHA.

Choosing the method of payout is determined by the particular circumstances in each case. The owner can take a lump sum, which can be advantageous if an existing mortgage balance must be paid off. Another option is a payment schedule similar to an annuity, which provides income payments for life. The remaining option is a credit line allowing the owner to withdraw money as needed. The lump sum and credit line balances may earn interest until withdrawn.

Lastly, an important consideration before deciding on this type of loan is the fees. They will range from 6 to 8 percent on the value of the home.

Since reverse mortgages can be complicated, carrying certain costs and risks, special care must be taken in considering this option. With the homeowner spending-down home equity without having to make monthly loan repayments, debt increases as the loan payments are made to the homeowner over time with closing costs and interest added to the loan balance. With debt growing, financial problems might arise if the home's value is either growing at a slow rate or actually declining. When the reverse mortgage becomes due, the loan balance might be greater than the homeowner's equity, especially when reverse mortgage payments have been made over a long time and the home's value has not kept pace with the increasing debt. This possible problem of "rising debt and falling equity" will not occur when the home increases in value at a pace near to the growing loan balance or if only a few loan advances have been made. However, the majority of reverse mortgages usually end up as "rising debt, falling equity" loans.

Reverse mortgages are not financially suitable or appropriate for all homeowners because of various cost and risk factors. The terms and conditions of reverse mortgage options, how they work, and their related risks, must be carefully considered in light of a homeowner's current and future financial condition and needs. To effectively determine whether a reverse mortgage is a financially sound choice, homeowners are best advised to seek financial counseling from competent, knowledgeable, and trustworthy family members, friends, or professionals. Various financial institutions, senior citizen advocacy groups, and credit-counseling bureaus offer such services.

ASSIGNMENT 15.7

Using hypothetical facts for a reverse mortgage, determine the effect age, home value, and interest rates will have on the amount you can borrow at *http://www.reversemortgage.org*.

When deciding whether to purchase long-term care insurance, consider this fact: No matter what a person's current age, the cost of the total premiums for long-term care insurance over the required years of payments will be less than the amount the person would pay for one year living in a nursing home. It is estimated that only 10 percent of Americans over 65 purchase long-term care insurance.

Current Trends

The general dissatisfaction with the nursing home option for long-term care housing needs of the elderly and infirmed has established almost a universal mindset in our nation: No one wants to live in a nursing home. However, many have no alternative.

During the 1990s, a transition began that changed the housing system from a domination of highly state-regulated nursing homes to one of broader consumer choices in housing and health services that can be delivered in homes, apartments, and specialized nursing homes. With the help of family, home health aides, and other available assistance, the first choice of the elderly is usually to stay in their own homes if it is physically, mentally, and financially possible. For those who cannot or choose not to stay in their homes, the second housing option is independent assisted living, which is rapidly increasing in demand for those who can afford it.

The change occurring within the long-term care housing system is due to the combination of market forces, i.e., the baby boomers who want options other than nursing homes, and the general agreement of the need for new options among care providers, advocates for the elderly who use the services, and state and federal regulators who oversee their long-term care housing needs.

Although baby boomers will be wealthier and better educated than their counterparts of today, careful financial planning will be necessary for them to attain the goals for their long-term care housing needs. Remaining in their homes with family and other help, in assisted living apartments, and in specialized nursing homes will surely be options. However, the ever-increasing cost of long-term care housing will continue to dictate and severely limit the housing options of low- and moderate-income people.

As an added incentive for the purchase of long-term care insurance, look for legislation in the coming years that offers new or increased tax deductions for insurance premiums.

Key Terms

elder law

long-term care

cognitive disorder impairment

activities of daily living (ADLs)

toileting

continence

transferring

adult day care center

assisted living facility

continuing care retirement community

nursing home care

home health care

respite care

hospice care

skilled nursing facility

custodial (personal) care

spend-down procedure

long-term care insurance

tax-qualified long-term care insurance policy

waiting (elimination) period

chronically ill

inflation protection

preexisting condition limitation

nonforfeiture benefit

waiver of premium payment

Review Questions

1. Explain the effect the baby boomer generation will have on long-term care.

2. Who will be responsible for most of the long-term care of our seniors?

3. What federal programs are available to defray the cost of long-term care?

4. Using your Medicare handbook, list the services covered and not covered under Medicare Part A for each of the following: services provided by a skilled nursing facility, home health care, and a hospice.

5. Describe the prescription drug benefit provided by Medicare (see the Medicare handbook).

6. Explain the spend-down procedure.

7. Explain the tax advantage of a tax-qualified long-term care insurance policy under current law. How can the law be improved so there is more incentive for people to purchase long-term care insurance?

8. What should you look for when evaluating long-term care insurance companies?

9. What are the options you consider most important in selecting a long-term care insurance policy and why?

10. What are long-term care partnerships? Which states participate in these partnerships?

Case Problems

Problem 1

Mary Olson, a widow, is age 62. Her husband, George, died last year of lung cancer. Due to George's poor health for the past 20 years, Mary had been the sole breadwinner of the family. She has two adult children and one grandchild who live in a neighboring state. Mary's mother, Alice, who is 88, lives in a nearby nursing home. All of Alice's assets were used to pay for her health care and living expenses. She is now supported by Social Security and Medicaid. Mary's only sibling, a sister, died two years ago at age 52 of breast cancer. Mary plans to leave her estate to her children and grandchild. Mary's assets consist of the following:

- Home (no mortgage), current value $285,000

- 401(k) plan, current value $315,000

- Savings, investments, IRA, and miscellaneous personal property, current value $165,000

Should Mary purchase long-term care insurance? Explain.

Problem 2

Nursing home care costs are steadily increasing each year. Research these costs on the Internet and prepare a chart showing the average annual cost for a private and semiprivate room for the last five years. To get a picture of future costs, apply a 5 percent inflation rate for 20 years to the annual cost of the most recent year on your chart in each of the two categories.

As the paralegal, what would you recommend to your supervising attorney to prepare a client for this long-term care expense?

Practical Assignments

1. Search the Internet to find two insurance companies that provide long-term insurance coverage. Compare the two companies using Standard & Poor's ratings (http://www.standardandpoors.com) to determine if one would be a better choice. (To complete this exercise, you will be required to register with the Standard & Poor's site).

2. Otis Mannington created a trust for his assets approximately three years ago, on July 12. He is now seriously ill and requiring round-the-clock care. His wife, Delores Mannington, asks your office for help with obtaining Medicaid benefits for Otis. Prepare a letter to Mrs. Mannington, at her address of 499 Oak Street in your city and state, explaining why Otis is not currently eligible for the benefits and when the benefits will become available.

3. Assume that Mrs. Mannington is qualified to receive the one-time death benefit payment of $255 under Social Security as a result of her husband's death. Prepare a list of the documents that Social Security may ask her to produce in order to receive the death benefit payment.

Notes

1. Long-Term Care Services in the United States: 2013 Overview by the Centers for Disease Control & Prevention; Vital & Health Statistics, Series 3, Number 37 December 2013.

2. Genworth Cost of Care Survey (2014).

3. *2014 Medicare & You*, National Medicare Handbook, Centers for Medicare & Medicaid Services (September 2013).

APPENDIX A

SAMPLE FORMS

Form*

---

* These forms are for purposes of illustration only. They represent the types of documents that might be used in particular situations and jurisdictions.

FORM | 1 | **Petition for Formal Probate of Will and for Formal Appointment of Personal Representative**

STATE OF MINNESOTA

COUNTY OF RAMSEY

DISTRICT COURT

PROBATE DIVISION

<u>SECOND</u> JUDICIAL DISTRICT

Court File No. <u>999999</u>

Estate of

<u>Shelley Mertens</u>

Decedent

PETITION FOR FORMAL PROBATE OF WILL
AND FOR FORMAL APPOINTMENT
OF PERSONAL REPRESENTATIVE

I, <u>Christopher Mertens,</u> state:

1. My address is: <u>1005 Elm St., St. Paul, MN., 55102</u>

2. I am an interested person as defined by Minnesota law because I am: <u>spouse, heir, devisee, nominated personal rep. of the deceased</u>

3. Decedent was born on <u>11/6/30</u> , at <u>Detroit, Mich.</u>

4. Decedent died on <u>9/20/14</u>, at <u>St. Paul, MN.</u>

5. Decedent at the time of death resided in <u>Ramsey County, State of Minnesota</u>, at (address): <u>1005 Elm St.</u>

6. The names and addresses of Decedent's spouse, children, heirs, devisees and other persons interested in this proceeding so far as known or ascertainable with reasonable diligence by the Petitioner are:

Name and Mailing Address	Relationship and Interest (list all)	Birthdate of Minors
Christopher Mertens, 1005 Elm St. St. Paul, MN. Spouse, heir, devisee, nominated personal rep.		
Lindsay Mertens, 1005 Elm St. St. Paul, MN. Daughter, heir, devisee		
American Cancer Society, 222 Glen Acre Dr., St. Paul, MN.		

(attach separate schedule, if necessary)

7. Negative Allegation Statement (see Minn. Gen. R. Prac. 408(a)):
Decedent left no surviving spouse, children, or parents other than those herein named and no issue of deceased children.

8. All persons identified as heirs have survived the Decedent by at least 120 hours.

9. ☐ Decedent left no surviving spouse.

☐ Decedent left no surviving issue.

☒ All issue of Decedent are issue of Decedent's surviving spouse except for:

☐ There are issue of the surviving spouse who are not issue of the Decedent.

10. Venue for this proceeding is in this County of the State of Minnesota because:

☒ The Decedent was domiciled in this County at the time of death and was the owner of property located in the State of Minnesota.

or

☐ Though not domiciled in the State of Minnesota, the Decedent was the owner of property located in this County at the time of death.

FORM [**1**] **Petition for Formal Probate of Will and for Formal Appointment of Personal Representative – (*Continued*)**

11. I estimate the Decedent's assets and indebtedness are as follows:

Probate Assets		Non-Probate Assets	
Homestead	$450,000	Joint Tenancy	$ 80,000
Other real estate	$ 50,000	Insurance	$200,000
Cash	$ 76,350	Other	$ 35,000
Securities	$ 33,000		
Other	$345,000		
Approximate Indebtedness	$ 2,250		

12. There is no personal representative of the Decedent appointed in Minnesota or elsewhere whose appointment has not been terminated, except (state any exceptions):

13. ☒ I have not received a demand for notice and am not aware of any demand for notice of any probate or appointment proceeding concerning the Decedent that may have been filed in Minnesota or elsewhere.

    or

    ☐ Proper notice has been given to those persons who have filed a demand for notice.

14. Decedent's Will is comprised of the following:

    ☒ Last will dated June 2, 1994.

    ☐ Codicil(s) dated_____.

    ☐ Separate writing(s) under Minn. Stat. 524.2–513 dated _____.

    ☐ (check if applicable) The Will refers to a separate writing, but none has been found.

15. To the best of my knowledge and belief, the Will has been validly executed.

16. Having conducted a reasonably diligent search, I am unaware of any instrument revoking the Will or of any other unrevoked testamentary instrument.

17. The documents comprising the Will:

    ☒ accompany this Application.

    ☐ are in the Court's possession.

    ☐ have been probated elsewhere and an authenticated copy of the Will and statement or order probating the same accompany this Application.

18. The Will nominates Christopher Mertens as personal representative.

    ☒ The nominated personal representative is willing to serve and is not disqualified.

    or

    ☐ The nominated personal representative is unable or has declined to serve.

    ☐ _____ has priority to serve as personal representative because: and is willing to serve and is not disqualified.

19. The Will specifies:

    Bond: ☒ No bond   Administration: ☐ Undesignated

    　　　　☐ Minimum bond　　　　　　　　　　　　☐ Unsupervised

    　　　　☐ $_____ bond　　　　　　　　　☒ Supervised

    　　　　☐ Unspecified

20. At least 120 hours, but not more than 3 years (except as permitted by Minn. Stat. 524.3–108), have elapsed since Decedent's death.

(continued)

FORM [1] **Petition for Formal Probate of Will and for Formal Appointment of Personal Representative – (*Continued*)**

WHEREFORE, I request the Court fix a time and place for a hearing on this Petition and enter an order formally:

1. Finding the Decedent is dead.

2. Finding venue is proper.

3. Finding the proceeding was commenced within the time limitation prescribed by Minnesota law.

4. Determining Decedent's domicile at death.

5. Determining Decedent's heirs.

6. Determining Decedent's testacy status.

7. Determining the Will is valid and unrevoked and should be probated.

8. Determining John C. Doe is entitled to appointment as personal representative and should be appointed.

9. Enter an John C. Doe order appointing as personal representative, with no bond, in ☐ an unsupervised ☒ a supervised administration.

10. Authorizing issuance of letters testamentary upon qualification and acceptance.

11. Grant such other relief as may be proper.

Under penalties for perjury, I declare or affirm that I have read this document and I know or believe its representations are true and complete.

Dated: 26 September, 2014

/s/ Christopher Mertens
Christopher Mertens
Petitioner

Attorney for Petitioner: Allan J.Jaycox
Name: Allan J.Jaycox
Firm: Jaycox and Jackson, P.A.
Street: First State Bank Bldg.
City, State, ZIP: Mpls, MN., 55455
Attorney License No.: 5692103
Telephone: (612)823-1469   Fax: (612)823-1470

FORM   **2**   **Notice and Order for Hearing on Petition for Probate of Will and Appointment of Personal Representative and Notice to Creditors**

STATE OF MINNESOTA
COUNTY OF <u>RAMSEY</u>

Estate of

<u>Shelley Mertens</u>
Decedent

DISTRICT COURT
PROBATE DIVISION
<u>SECOND</u> JUDICIAL DISTRICT
Court File No. <u>999999</u>

NOTICE AND ORDER FOR HEARING
ON PETITION FOR PROBATE OF WILL AND APPOINTMENT
OF PERSONAL REPRESENTATIVE AND NOTICE
TO CREDITORS

It is Ordered and Notice is given that on <u>October 31, 2014 at 10:00 a.m.</u> (a.m.)(p.m.), a hearing will be held in this Court at Room 102A, Municipal Courthouse, <u>St. Paul</u>, Minnesota, for the formal probate of an instrument purporting to be the will of the <u>Decedent, June 2, 1994</u> dated , and codicil dated <u>   </u>, and separate writing under Minn. Stat. 524.2 513 ("Will"), and for the appointment of <u>Christopher Mertens</u> whose address is: <u>1005 Elm St., St. Paul, MN., 55102</u>.

as personal representative of the Estate of the Decedent in a/an ☒ SUPERVISED ☐ UNSUPERVISED administration. Any objections to the petition must be filed with the Court prior to or raised at the hearing. If proper and if no objections are filed or raised, the personal representative will be appointed with full power to administer the Estate including the power to collect all assets, to pay all legal debts, claims, taxes and expenses, to sell real and personal property, and to do all necessary acts for the Estate.

    Notice is also given that (subject to Minn. Stat. 524.3 801) all creditors having claims against the Estate are required to present the claims to the personal representative or to the Court Administrator within four months after the date of this Notice or the claims will be barred.

<u>/s/ Richard B. Evans</u>

District Court Judge, Probate Division

DATED: <u>September 30, 2014</u>

Court Administrator
By: <u>/s/ Thomas T. Malone</u>
Deputy Court Administrator _____   Date _____

Attorney for Applicant: <u>Allan J. Jaycox</u>
Name: <u>Allan J. Jaycox</u>
Firm: <u>Jaycox and Jackson, P.A.</u>
Street: <u>First State Bank Bldg.</u>
City, State, ZIP: <u>Mpls., MN, 55455</u>
Attorney License No.: <u>5692103</u>
Telephone: <u>(612) 823-1469</u>   FAX: <u>(612) 823-1470</u>

FORM   **3**   **Proof of Placing Order for Publication**

STATE OF MINNESOTA   PROBATE COURT
COUNTY OF <u>RAMSEY</u>   COURT FILE NO. <u>999999</u>

In Re: Estate of _____   <u>PROOF OF PLACING ORDER</u>

                                                     <u>FOR PUBLICATION</u>

_____ <u>Shelley Mertens</u> _____
                <u>Decedent</u>

_____

_____

TO THE CLERK OF PROBATE COURT:

That is to verify that <u>Christopher Mertens, whose address is 1005 Elm St.,</u>
<u>St.Paul,MN 55102</u>   , applicant(s)

has made arrangements for the publication of:

☐   NOTICE OF INFORMAL APPOINTMENT OF PERSONAL
     REPRESENTATIVE(S) AND NOTICE TO CREDITORS

☒   NOTICE OF FORMAL PROBATE OF WILL AND APPOINTMENT OF
     PERSONAL REPRESENTATIVE(S) AND NOTICE TO CREDITORS

☐

once a week for two consecutive weeks in the <u>FINANCE AND COMMERCE</u>

                                                     Daily Newspaper
_____
and this is to confirm that the same will be published accordingly commencing in the next available
issue, and that arrangements for payment of the cost of said publication have been made.
Dated: <u>September 30, 2014</u>

                              <u>FINANCE AND COMMERCE Daily Newspaper</u>
                                                     Publisher

                              By: <u>/s/ Dorothy L.Wolf</u>

FORM 4 — Affidavit of Publication

COURT FILE NO. 999999

ORDER AND NOTICE OF
HEARING ON PETITION FOR
PROBATE OF WILL
, AND
APPOINTMENT OF
PERSONAL REPRESENTATIVES
IN SUPERVISED
ADMINISTRATION AND NOTICE
TO CREDITORS

STATE OF MINNESOTA
COUNTY OF Ramsey
PROBATE COURT

In Re: Estate of
Jane M. Doe,
Deceased.

TO ALL INTERESTED PERSONS
AND CREDITORS:

It is ordered and notice is herby given that on Monday, the 31st day of October, 2014, at ten o'clock A.M., a hearing will be held in the above named Court at C-4 Ramsey County Court House, St. Paul, Minnesota, for the probate of an instrument purporting to be the Will of the above decedent and for the appointment of Christopher Mertens, whose address is 1005 Elm St., St. Paul, Minnesota 55102

, as personal representative of the estate of the above named decedent in supervised administration. That, if proper, and no objections are filed, said personal representative will be appointed to administer the estate, to collect all assets, pay all legal debts, claims, taxes, and expenses, and sell real and personal property, and do all necessary acts for the estate. upon completion of the administration, the representatives shall file a final account for allowance and shall distribute the estate to the person thereunto entitled as ordered by the Court, and close the estate.

Notice is further given that ALL CREDITORS having claims against said estate are required to present the same to said personal representatives or to the Clerk of Probate Court within four months after the date of this notice or said claims will be barred.

Dated: October 30th, 2014,
HON, Richard B. Evans,
Judge of Probate Court.
Thomas Malone,
Clerk of Probate Court.

(COURT SEAL)

By: John Cranwall,
Attorney,
First Trust Bldg.
St. Paul, MN 55101

AFFIDAVIT OF PUBLICATION

State of Minnesota,
} ss

County of Ramsey

Warren E. Maul , *being duly sworn, on oath says: that ...he now is, and during all the times herein stated has been the editor and publisher of the newspaper known as* Finance and Commerce *, and has full knowledge of the facts hereinafter stated.*

(1) *That said newspaper is printed in the English language in newspaper format and in column and sheet form equivalent in printed space to at least 1200 square inches;*

(2) *That said newspaper, if a weekly, be distributed at least once each week for 50 weeks each year, or if a daily, at least five days each week; but in any week in which a legal holiday is included, not more than four issues of a daily paper are necessary;*

(3) *That said newspaper has 25 percent, if published more often than weekly, or 50 percent, if a weekly, of its news columns devoted to news of local interest to the community which it purports to serve, and it may contain general news, comment, and miscellany, but not wholly duplicate any other publication, or be made up entirely of patents, plate matter, and advertisements;*

(4) *That said newspaper is circulated in and near the municipality which it purports to serve, has at least 500 copies regularly delivered to paying subscribers, has an average of at least 75% of its total circulation currently paid or no more than three months in arrears, and has entry as second-class matter in its local postoffice;*

(5) *That said newspaper has its known office of issue in the County of* Ramsey *in which lies, in whole or in part, the municipality which the newspaper purports to serve;*

(6) *That said newspaper files a copy of each issue immediately with the State Historical Society;*

(6a) *Be made available at single or subscription prices to any person, corporation, partnership or other unincorporated association requesting the newspaper and making the applicable payment.*

(7) *That said newspaper has complied with all the foregoing conditions of this subdivision for at least one year last past.*

(8) *That said newspaper has filed with the Secretary of State of Minnesota prior to January 1, of each year, an affidavit in the form prescribed by the Secretary of State and signed by the publisher or managing officer and sworn to before a Notary Public stating that the newspaper is a legal newspaper.*

That the printed Probate Notice hereto attached as a part hereof was cut from the columns of said newspaper; was published therein in the English Language once each week for 2 *successive weeks; that it was first so published on the...* 30th ... *day of* October *, 2009 and thereafter on* Wednesday *of each week to and including the* 11th *day of* October *, 2014; and that the following is a copy of the lower case alphabet which is acknowledged as the size and kind of type used in the printed publication of said notice.*

abcdefghijklmnopqrstuvwxyz

/s/ Warren E. Maul

Subscribed and sworn to before me this 30th *day of* October *,* 2014,

/s/ Dorothy L. Wolf

Notary Public Ramsey *County, Minnesota*

My Commission Expires September 23 *,* 2014

FORM   **5**   Affidavit of Mailing Order or Notice of Hearing for Formal Probate Will and Notice to Spouse and Children and Affidavit of Mailing

---

STATE OF MINNESOTA
COUNTY OF <u>RAMSEY</u>

DISTRICT COURT
<u>SECOND</u> JUDICIAL DISTRICT
PROBATE COURT DIVISION
Court File No. <u>999999</u>

In the Matter of the Estate of

<u>Shelley Mertens</u>
Decedent

AFFIDAVIT OF MAILING
ORDER OR NOTICE

STATE OF MINNESOTA   )
) ss
COUNTY OF RAMSEY   )

I, J.M. Golden, being first duly sworn on oath, state that on <u>5 October, 2014</u>, at <u>St. Paul</u>, Minnesota, I mailed a copy of the attached Order or Notice to each person or entity named below by mailing a copy in a sealed envelope, postage prepaid, with the U.S. Postal Service as follows:

NAME & MAILING ADDRESS:

```
Christopher Mertens      1005 Elm St., St. Paul, MN., 55102
Lindsay Mertens          1005 Elm St., St. Paul, MN., 55102
American Cancer Society   222 Glen Acre Dr., St. Paul, MN., 55102
```

<u>/s/ J.M. Golden   5 October, 2014</u>

Affiant   Date

Signed and sworn to (or affirmed) before me on
(date) 5 October, 2014 by

NOTORIAL STAMP OR SEAL (OR OTHER TITLE OR RANK)	(name of affiant) J.M. Golden, <u>/s/ Judith Harris</u>
	SIGNATURE OF NOTARY PUBLIC OR OTHER OFFICIAL

INSTRUCTIONS: (1) A copy of the Order or Notice must be mailed to each heir, devisee, personal representative, the foreign consul pursuant to Minn. Stat. 524.3-306 and 524.3-403, lawyers representing interested parties pursuant to Minn. Stat. 524.1-401(a), and the Minnesota Attorney General, if a devisee is a charitable organization or if the decedent left no devisees or heirs. In determining the persons or entities entitled to receive this order or notice, see Minn. Stats. 501B.41(5), 524.1-201(19), 524.1-403 and 524.1-404 and Minn. Gen. Rules of Practice 404(b) and 408(d). If the Decedent is survived by a spouse or minor child, also use Notice to Spouse and Children. (2) Attach to this affidavit another copy of the Order or Notice which was sent. (3) It may be necessary to give notice to creditors. See Minn. Stat. 524.3-801(3) and Supplementary Notice to Known and Identified Creditors form.

Source: Minnesota Probate Court.

FORM **6** **Order of Formal Probate of Will and Formal Appointment of Personal Representative**

STATE OF MINNESOTA
COUNTY OF <u>RAMSEY</u>

DISTRICT COURT
PROBATE DIVISION
<u>SECOND</u> JUDICIAL DISTRICT
Court File No. <u>999999</u>

Estate of

<u>Shelley Mertens</u>
Decedent

ORDER OF FORMAL PROBATE OF WILL
AND FORMAL APPOINTMENT
OF PERSONAL REPRESENTATIVE

The Petition for Formal Probate of Will and Formal Appointment of Personal Representative, <u>Christopher Mertens</u> signed <u>September 26, 2014</u> by <u>John C. Doe</u>, came before the Court on <u>31 October, 2014</u>. The Court, having heard and considered the Petition, determines the following:

1. The Court has jurisdiction and venue in this County is proper.
2. The Petition is complete.
3. The Petitioner has declared or affirmed that the representations contained in the Petition are true to the best of Petitioner's knowledge or belief.
4. The Petitioner is an interested person as defined by Minnesota law.
5. Any notice required by Minnesota law has been given.
6. Decedent died on September 20, 2014 at St. Paul, Minnesota.
7. Decedent's Will is comprised of the following:
    ☒ Last will dated June 2, 1994.
    ☐ Codicil(s) dated _____.
    ☐ Separate writing(s) under Minn. Stat. 524.2 513 dated _____.
    ☐ (check if applicable) The Will refers to a separate writing, but none has been found.
8. The documents comprising the Will:
    ☒ are in the Court's possession.
    ☐ have been probated elsewhere, and an authenticated copy of the Will and statement or order probating the same are on file with this Court.
    ☐ are unavailable, but a Statement of Contents of Lost, Destroyed or Otherwise Unavailable Will is in the Court's possession.
9. It appears from the Petition that the proceeding was commenced within the time limitation prescribed by Minn. Stat. 524.3-108.
10. The Petition indicates that there is no personal representative appointed in this or any other county of Minnesota whose appointment has not been terminated, except:
11. The Petition does not indicate the existence of a possible unrevoked testamentary instrument which may relate to property subject to Minnesota law, and which is not filed for probate in this Court.
12. The person appointed below has priority and is entitled to be appointed personal representative, and is not disqualified to serve as personal representative.

(continued)

FORM [**6**] **Order of Formal Probate of Will and Formal Appointment of Personal Representative – (*Continued*)**

---

13. The Will specifies:

    Bond: ☒ No bond   Administration: ☐ Unsupervised
        ☐ Minimum bond   ☐ Undesignated
        ☐ $ _____ bond   ☒ Supervised
        ☐ Unspecified

14. Decedent's heirs under Minnesota law are:
    ☒ as identified in the Petition commencing this proceeding;
    or
    ☐ as follows:

15. All persons identified as heirs have survived the Decedent by at least 120 hours.

16. (Check appropriate boxes)
    ☐ Decedent left no surviving spouse.
    ☐ Decedent left no surviving issue.
    ☒ All issue of Decedent are issue of Decedent's surviving spouse except for:

    ☐ There are issue of the surviving spouse who are not issue of the Decedent.

17. No objections to the Petition have been asserted.

IT IS ORDERED:

1. The Petition is granted.
2. The Will is formally probated.
3. John C. Doe is formally appointed as the personal representative of the Decedent's Estate, with no bond, in
   ☐ an unsupervised ☒ a supervised administration.
4. Upon filing any required bond and statement of acceptance and oath, letters testamentary will be issued.

         /s/ Richard B. Evans October 31, 2014
         _____ _____
         Judge of District Court   Date

FORM **7** **Letters Testamentary**

STATE OF MINNESOTA
COUNTY OF RAMSEY

DISTRICT COURT
PROBATE DIVISION
SECOND JUDICIAL DISTRICT
Court File No. 999999

Estate of

Shelley Mertens
Decedent

LETTERS ☒ TESTAMENTARY
☐ OF GENERAL ADMINISTRATION

1. The Decedent died on September 20, 2014.

2. John C. Doe has been appointed Personal Representative of Decedent's Estate in

   ☐ an unsupervised
   ☒ a supervised administration

   and is now qualified to act as Personal Representative of the Estate and has authority to administer the Estate according to law.

(COURT SEAL)

/s/ Richard B. Evans   October 31, 2014
_____
Judge   Date

Source: Minnesota Probate Court.

FORM `8` **Inventory**

STATE OF MINNESOTA
COUNTY OF <u>RAMSEY</u>

DISTRICT COURT
PROBATE DIVISION
<u>SECOND</u> JUDICIAL DISTRICT
Court File No. <u>999999</u>
INVENTORY
☒ ORIGINAL
☐ AMENDED
☐ SUPPLEMENTAL

Estate of

<u>Shelley Mertens</u>
Decedent

Date of Death: <u>September 20, 2014</u>
Social Security No.: <u>321-54-9876</u>

John C. Doe, the Personal Representative of the Estate, states:

1. The following is a true and correct inventory at date of death values of all the property of the Estate, both real and personal, which has come into my possession as Personal Representative. If an appraisal of any asset has been made, the name and address of each appraiser used is included. After diligent search and inquiry concerning the assets of the Estate, the following is a list of the Estate assets by category:

SCHEDULE		VALUE
Schedule A:	Real Estate	$ 575,000
Schedule B:	Stocks, Bonds, and Other Securities	$ 33,000
Schedule C:	Bank Accounts, Mortgages, Contracts for Deed, Notes and Cash	$ 76,350
Schedule D:	Other Personal Property	$ 729,000
	SUBTOTAL	$ 1,413,350
Less Schedule E: Mortgages and Liens—miscellaneous, unsecured indebtedness		($ 3,300)
	TOTAL	$ 1,410,050

2. A copy of this Inventory, including all schedules, has been mailed to the surviving spouse, if any, and to all residuary distributees of the Decedent and to interested persons and creditors who have requested a copy of the Inventory.

    Under penalties for perjury, I declare or affirm that I have read the Inventory and I know or believe its representations are true and complete.

/s/ Christopher Mertens 21 Dec. 2014
Personal Representative   Date

Attorney for Personal Representative: Allan J. Jaycox
Name: Allan J. Jaycox
Firm: Jaycox and Jackson, P.A.
Street: First State Bank Bldg.
City, State, ZIP: Mpls., MN 55455
Attorney License No.: 5692103
Telephone: (612) 823-1469   FAX: (612) 823-1470

GENERAL INSTRUCTIONS for all Schedules.

1. Values reported should be as of date of death.

2. The appointment of an appraiser is not always necessary.

3. Each asset of a Schedule is to be given its own "Item Number."

4. DO NOT list any joint tenancy property unless the Decedent did not intend to create a true joint tenancy, but rather created for convenience a nominal joint tenancy which is subject to probate. Joint tenancy with right of survivorship property listed in this inventory may be converted to probate property with the consent of the surviving joint tenant(s).

5. List the gross fair market value of each item without subtracting for mortgages or liens.

6. List all mortgages and liens for which decedent was liable on Schedule E.

7. Blank schedules need not be attached.

(_continued_)

FORM   **8**   Inventory – (*Continued*)

ESTATE OF Shelley Mertens   Court File No. 999999

SCHEDULE A: REAL ESTATE

INSTRUCTIONS for Schedule A:

1. Include both the legal description and the street address. If rural property also include acreage.
2. For Contracts for Deed: If Decedent owned a Vendor/Seller's interest describe the land on Schedule A, valuing it at zero and show the remaining contract balance on Schedule C. If Decedent owned a Vendee/Buyer's interest, describe the property on Schedule A valuing it at its fair market value.
3. County Assessor's market value can be obtained from the County Assessor or department of taxation.
4. List only Minnesota real estate. DO NOT list real estate located in other states.

Item Number	Description of Property	County Assessor's Market Value	Fair Market Value
1	Homestead in the County of Ramsey, 1005 Elm St., St. Paul, MN., 55102 Legal Description: Lot 615, Block 42, Reiser Addition to St. Paul, (Plat #22760, Parcel #7600)	$ 475,000	$ 500,000
2	Other Real Estate: County of Ramsey, State of Minnesota Undivided 1/4 interest in duplex located at 776 Cliff Rd., St. Paul, MN., Legal Description: Lots 16 & 17, Block 20, Lovey Addition to St. Paul (Plat #32689, Parcel #5562)	$ 285,000 71,250 (1/4)	$ 300,000 75,000 (1/4)
	Schedule A: Real Estate	TOTAL	$ 575,000

FORM 8 **Inventory – (*Continued*)**

ESTATE OF <u>Shelley Mertens</u>   Court File No. <u>999999</u>

SCHEDULE B: STOCKS, BONDS, AND OTHER SECURITIES

INSTRUCTIONS for Schedule B:

1 Specify face value of bonds, number of shares of stock, stock certificate number, and CUSIP number, if available.

2 List each bond issue, stock, or certificate separately.

Item Number	Description of Property	Unit Value	Fair Market Value
1	Stocks: 500 Shrs. Innovative Software Common Stock, CUSIP #674322189, Cert. #C068297, dated 12/31/92 NYSE	$40/shr.	$20,000
2	1000 Shrs. Minnesota Co-Op, Common Stock, Cert. #D2289663, dated 12/31/89	$10/shr.	$10,000
3	United States Savings Bonds: Series I Bond #R4502363, 4/90	$1,000	$ 1,500
4	Series II Bond #R4502364, 4/90	$1,000	$ 1,500
	Schedule B: Stocks, Bonds and Other Securities	TOTAL	$ 33,000

(*continued*)

FORM   **8**   **Inventory – (*Continued*)**

ESTATE OF <u>Shelley Mertens</u>   Court File No. <u>999999</u>

SCHEDULE C: BANK ACCOUNTS, MORTGAGES, CONTRACTS FOR DEED, NOTES AND CASH

INSTRUCTIONS for Schedule C:

1. List Vendor/Seller's interest in Contract for Deed on this Schedule. Also include the date of the contract, name of Vendee/Buyer, interest rate and unpaid balance at date of death, and accrued interest, if any.

2. List Mortgages owned by Decedent as assets, NOT mortgages for which Decedent is liable or mortgages secured by property in the Estate.

Item Number	Description of Property	Unit Value	Fair Market Value
1	10 American Express Traveler's Checks #1008-17	$100/ea	$ 1,000
2	Checking Account, St. Paul National City Bank, #55-5555		$50,000
3	Savings Certificate, St. Paul, American National Bank, #44-4444 5.5%/yr.		$15,000
4	Promissory Note, Johnson Furriers, St. Paul, MN dated 3/20/2008, payable 3/20/2010 7% interest/yr.		$10,000
5	Accrued Item #4 interest from 3/20/14 to 9/20/14		$ 350
	Schedule C: Bank Accounts, Mortgages, Contracts for Deed, Notes and Cash	TOTAL	$ 76,350

ESTATE OF Shelley Mertens   Court File No. 999999

SCHEDULE D: OTHER PERSONAL PROPERTY

INSTRUCTIONS for Schedule D:

1. List on this schedule, any personal property owned by Decedent and not reported on other schedules. Examples of property to be listed on this schedule include: refunds, wearing apparel, household goods, automobiles, furniture, business interests, and insurance payable to the Estate.
2. Where appropriate, specify the location of the property.
3. Use actual value or specify if asset has no pecuniary value.
4. DO NOT list non-probate property.

Item Number	Description of Property	Unit Value	Fair Market Value
1	Household goods, furniture		$ 50,000
2	Clothing, personal effects		$ 16,000
3	2013 Mazda VIN 6778899926, Title #03618957		$ 12,000
4	Minnesota Life Ins. Co. Policy #J566622 accumulated dividend $1000, Estate of Shelley Mertens beneficiary	$600,000	$601,000
5	Power of Appointment Trust created under agreement dated 12/02/75 by father of decedent for decedent's benefit under which decedent had a general power of appointment (to distribute income and/or principal) which power had not been exercised during decedent's lifetime, but which decedent exercised under her will. The assets remaining in this trust and subject to this power are 500 shares of Green Giant common stock and undistributed earnings (dividends) thereon.	$100/shr.	$ 50,000
	Schedule D: Other Property	TOTAL	$ 729,000

(*continued*)

FORM   **8**   Inventory – (*Continued*)

ESTATE OF Shelley Mertens   Court File No. 999999

SCHEDULE E: MORTGAGES AND LIENS

INSTRUCTIONS for Schedule E:

1. Show any mortgages and liens secured by property in the Estate. Detail the date of the installment, names of the parties, interest rate, payment terms, and any other relevant data. Indicate the Schedule and Item Number of the secured property from prior schedule. The remaining balance of Contracts for Deed in which Decedent was the Vendee/Buyer or was the mortgage debtor should be listed on this Schedule. Also include interest and taxes due at date of death.

Item Number	Description of Property	Unit Value	Fair Market Value
	None		
	Schedule E: Mortgages and Liens	TOTAL	$

FORM **9** **Final Account**

STATE OF MINNESOTA   DISTRICT COURT
COUNTY OF RAMSEY   PROBATE DIVISION
                                                     SECOND JUDICIAL DISTRICT
                                                     Court File No. 999999

Estate of   FINAL ACCOUNT
Shelley Mertens   ☒ ORIGINAL
_____,   ☐ AMENDED
                  Decedent   ☐ SUPPLEMENTAL
S.S.# 321-54-9876
READ INSTRUCTIONS AT END OF FORM

		DEBITS	CREDITS
DEBITS			
Schedule A: Real Estate	$ 575,000		
Schedule B: Securities	$ 33,000		
Schedule C: Bank Accounts/Cash	$ 76,350		
Schedule D: Other Personal Property	$ 729,000		
SUBTOTAL	$1,413,350		
Less Schedule E: Mortgages/Liens— Miscellaneous Debts	($ 3,300)		
TOTAL		$1,410,050	
(For Form Foundry Use)			
(For Form Foundry Use)			
Increases:			
Assets Omitted from Inventory	$_____		
Advances to Estate	$_____		
Interest	$ 23,230		
Dividends	$ 2,460		
Dividend Reinvestment	$_____		
Refunds	$_____		
Gain on Sale of Property	$_____		
TOTAL		$ 5,690	
ASSET ADJUSTMENTS (see Instruction A and attach schedule)		$_____	$_____

(continued)

FORM | **9** | **Final Account – (Continued)**

	DEBITS	CREDITS
CREDITS-DISBURSEMENTS		
Decrease in Estate:		
Loss on sale of property	$ _____	
Other	$ _____	
TOTAL Decrease		$ _____
MAINTENANCE AND SELECTION		
Family maintenance	$ 4,800	
Statutory selection	$ 10,000	
Other _____	$ _____	
Other _____	$ _____	
TOTAL Maintenance and Selection	.	$ 14,800
EXPENSES OF ADMINISTRATION		
Probate Court Filing Fees	$ 20	
Publication Fees	$ 50	
Bond Premiums	$ _____	
Copy Fees	$ 30	
Appraiser Fees	$ 500	
Compensation of Personal Representative	$ 10,000	
Expenses of Personal Representative (explain)	$ _____	
Attorneys' Fees to Date	$ 15,000	
Estimated Future Fees to Be Charged	$ _____	
Repayment of Advances to Estate	$ _____	
Other Accounting Fees Tax Returns	$ 1,500	
Other Miscellaneous	$ 450	
TOTAL Expenses of Administration		$ 27,550
FUNERAL EXPENSES		
Mortician	$ 9,500	
Marker	$ 1,000	
Flowers	$ 200	
Cemetary	$ 1,000	
TOTAL Funeral Expenses		$ 11,700

FORM **9** **Final Account – (*Continued*)**

	DEBITS	CREDITS
EXPENSES OF LAST ILLNESS		
Hospital	$ 850	
Medical Attendance	$ 1,250	
	$	
TOTAL Expenses of Last Illness		$ 2,100
TAXES		
Real Estate Taxes:		
Homestead	$ 3,650	
Other Real Estate	$ 750	
Income Taxes of Decedent:		
Minnesota	$_____	
Federal	$_____	
Fiduciary Income Taxes:		
Minnesota	$_____	
Federal	$_____	
Estate Taxes:		
Minnesota	$_____	
Federal	$_____	
Other Taxes:		
_____	$_____	
_____	$_____	
TOTAL Taxes		$ 4,400
PAYMENTS MADE ON MORTGAGE, CONTRACT FOR DEED, AND OTHER LIENS		
Principal	$_____	
Interest	$_____	
Other	$_____	
TOTAL Payments		$_____

(*continued*)

FORM | **9** | **Final Account – (*Continued*)**

	DEBITS	CREDITS
OTHER CLAIMS ALLOWED AND PAID		
Ace Plumbing $ 300		
Xcel Energy $ 150		
Acme Rental $ 150		
Dr. Norma J. Dennison $ 600		
$ _____		
$ _____		
$ _____		
$ _____		
$ _____		
$ _____		
$ _____		
$ _____		
$ _____		
$ _____		
TOTAL Claims Paid		$ 1,200
CLAIMS ALLOWED AND NOT PAID		
(See Instruction E)		
$ _____		
$ _____		
$ _____		
$ _____		
$ _____		
$ _____		
$ _____		
$ _____		
$ _____		
$ _____		
$ _____		
$ _____		
$ _____		
$ _____		
$ _____		
TOTAL Claims Allowed Not Paid		$ _____

FORM ⬜**9**   **Final Account – (*Continued*)**

	DEBITS	CREDITS
PRIOR DISTRIBUTION TO DEVISEES AND HEIRS		
(See Instruction F)		
_____ $_____		
_____ $_____		
_____ $_____		
_____ $_____		
_____ $_____		
_____ $_____		
_____ $_____		
_____ $_____		
_____ $_____		
_____ $_____		
_____ $_____		
_____ $_____		
TOTAL Devisees /Heirs Paid and Distributed		$_____
SUBTOTAL DEBITS AND CREDITS	$ 1,435,740	$ 61,750
PLUS: TOTAL PROPERTY ON HAND FOR DISTRIBUTION (from last line of form)		$ 1,373,990
TOTAL (Debits should equal Credits)	$ 1,435,740	$ 1,435,740

PERSONAL PROPERTY ON HAND FOR DISTRIBUTION

	DEBITS	CREDITS
Stocks, Bonds, and Other Securities		
500 Shs. Innovative Software Common Stock Cert. #C068297	$ 20,000	
1000 Shs. Minnesota Co-Op Common Stock Cert. #D2289663	$ 10,000	
	$_____	$ 30,000
Mortgages, Notes, Contracts for Deed, Etc.		
$1,000 U.S. Savings Bonds Series I #R4502363	$ 1,500	
$1,000 U.S. Savings Bonds Series I #R45002364	$ 1,500	
Johnson Furriers Promissory Note dated 3/20/2008 due 3/20/2015 to 9/20/2015	$ 10,350	$ 13,350
Cash on Hand.		$ 649,290

(*continued*)

All Other Personal Property (Describe):
2013 Mazda VIN 6778899926 Title #03618957	$ 12,000	
Power of Appointment Trust	$ 50,000	
Household Goods/Furnishings	$ 66,000	$ 128,000

Less: Amounts reserved for future payments	$ (_____)
Less: Liens on Personal Property.	$ (_____)
Less Other:	$ (_____)
TOTAL Personal Property.	$ 820,640

REAL ESTATE ON HAND FOR DISTRIBUTION
(Legal Descriptions; attach schedule, if necessary)

Homestead:	$ 500,000
Other Real Estate: Undivided 1/4 interest in duplex located in Ramsey County Legal Description: Lots #16 & 17, Bl. 20, Lovey's Add. to St. Paul (Plat #32689 Parcel #5562)	$ 75,000
Less: Mortgages, Contracts for Deed & Liens Unpaid (See Instruction H)	$ (_____)
TOTAL Real Estate	$ 575,000
	$ 1,395,640

TOTAL PROPERTY ON HAND FOR DISTRIBUTION

Under penalties for perjury, I declare or affirm that I have read this Final Account, and that I know or believe its representations are true and complete.

Christopher Mertens   June 3, 2015
Personal Representative   Date

Attorney for Personal Representative: Allan J. Jaycox
Name: Allan J. Jaycox
Firm: Jaycox and Jackson, P.A.
Street: First State Bank Bldg.
City, State, ZIP: Mpls., MN 55455
Attorney License No.: 5692103
Telephone: (612) 823-1469   FAX: (612) 823-1470

FORM **9** **Final Account – (*Continued*)**

INSTRUCTIONS—Please Read Carefully

A. Principal Adjustment entries should be used to report changes in the composition of assets, e.g., use of estate cash to purchase an investment; exchanges of assets, such as stock splits or swaps. Note that debits should equal credits. Principal payment on mortgages or contracts for deed are shown later in the Final Account (see Instruction H, below). Attach schedule showing full details of transactions.

B. Attach additional explanation as needed, for example, payments on mortgages or contracts for deeds; omissions in inventory, rent, increases, decreases, etc.

C. The Court may require vouchers for all amounts paid and distributed. In an informal administration, check with the Court.

D. The property on hand for distribution must be adequately described, and any variance from the Inventory should be explained.

E. For insolvent estates, check with the Court for its preferred format of accounting for claims allowed but unpaid.

F. In a supervised administration, interim distributions to residuary distributees must have prior approval of the Court. Distribution of specific devises in testate estates may be made without prior Court order in solvent estates.

G. A vendor's/seller's interest in a contract for deed is personal property. All contracts for deed must be fully described, including terms, parties, and legal descriptions of the real estate. Balances on all contracts as of the Final Account date should be used to value the personal property shown on hand for distribution.

H. When describing liens, mortgages, etc., show the date for which the amount was calculated.
To calculate the remaining unpaid balances on real estate on hand for distribution, reduce the total lien/mortgage by the amount of principal and interest paid on the lien/mortgage.

ORDER OF COMPLETE SETTLEMENT OF ESTATE AND DECREE OF DISTRIBUTION

STATE OF MINNESOTA   DISTRICT COURT
COUNTY OF <u>RAMSEY</u>   <u>SECOND</u> Judicial District
In Re: Estate of <u>Shelley Mertens</u>   PROBATE DIVISION
                                                                Court File No. <u>999999</u>

ORDER OF COMPLETE SETTLEMENT OF THE ESTATE AND DECREE OF DISTRIBUTION

The petition of <u>Christopher Mertens</u> dated <u>June 3, 2015,</u> for an order of complete settlement of the estate and decree of distribution in the estate of the above named decedent having duly come on for hearing before the above named Court on <u>June 18, 2015,</u> the undersigned Judge having heard and considered such petition, being fully advised in the premises, makes the following findings and determinations:

1. That the petition for order of complete settlement of the estate and decree of distribution is complete.
2. That the time for any notice has expired and any notice as required by the laws of this state has been given and proved.
3. That the petitioner(s) (has) (have) declared or affirmed that the representations contained in the petition are true, correct and complete to the best knowledge or information of petitioner(s).
4. That the petitioner(s) appear(s) from the petition to be (an) interested person(s) as defined by the laws of this State.
5. That the decedent died testate at the age of 79 years on <u>September 20, 2014</u> at <u>St. Paul.</u>
6. That venue for this proceeding is in the above named County of the State of Minnesota, because the decedent was domiciled in such County at the time of death, and was the owner of property located in the State of Minnesota, or because, though not domiciled in the State of Minnesota, the decedent was the owner of property located in the above named County at the time of death.
7. That this Court has jurisdiction of this estate, proceeding, and subject matter.
8. That the said estate has been in all respects fully administered, and all expenses, debts, valid charges, and all claims allowed against said estate have been paid.
9. That a final account has been filed herein by the personal representative(s) for consideration and approval.
10. That decedent's last will duly executed on <u>June 2, 1994</u> and codicil or codicils thereto duly executed on, 20, (was) (were) probated by the order of this Court dated <u>Oct 31, 2015</u> or (is) (are) formally probated by this order, and should be construed to provide that under the provisions thereof, the estate of decedent is devised as follows:

(State actual legal relationship of each devisee to decedent)

American Cancer Society, Charitable Devisee $10,000

<u>Christopher Mertens,</u> all the rest, residue, and remainder of the real and personal property of the deceased's estate <u>$1,295,640</u>

FORM | **10** | **Order of Complete Settlement of the Estate and Decree of Distribution – (*Continued*)**

11. That the following named persons are all the heirs of the decedent and their actual relationship to decedent is as stated (If decedent died testate, do not list heirs unless all heirs are ascertained):

```
Christopher Mertens       Spouse/heir/devisee/personal representative
1005 Elm St.
St. Paul, MN 55102

Lindsay Mertens           Daughter/heir
1005 Elm St.
St. Paul, MN 55102
```

12. That the property of the decedent on hand for distribution consists of the following:

(A) Personal property of the value of $ 820,640 described as follows:

```
Household Goods and Wearing Apparel      $ 66,000
Stock: 500 Shs Innovative Softwear,
   Common, Cert C068297                    20,000
1000 Shs Minnesota Co-Op, Common,
   Cert D2289663                           10,000
U.S. Savings Bonds: Series I, # R4502363    1,500
                    Series I, # R4502364    1,500
Promissory Note: Johnson Furriers,
   Note dated 03/20/2008 due 09/20/2015    10,350
Cash on hand                              649,290
2013 Mazda, VIN 6778899926                 12,000
Power of Appointment Trust                 50,000
                                          820,640
```

(B) Real property described as follows:

(1) The homestead of the decedent situated in the County of Ramsey, State of Minnesota, described as follows:

```
Lot 615, Block 42, Reiser's Addition to St. Paul, MN
(Plat #22760 Parcel #7600)
$ 500,000
```

(2) Other real property situated in the County of Ramsey, State of Minnesota, described as follows: Lots 16 and 17, Block 20, Lovey Addition to St. Paul, MN
```
(Plat #32689 Parcel #5562)
$75,000
```

13. That the inheritance taxes on the herein described property have been paid or waived.

14. That any previous order determining testacy should be confirmed as it affects any previously omitted or unnotified persons and other interested persons.

(*continued*)

FORM | **10** | **Order of Complete Settlement of the Estate and Decree of Distribution – (*Continued*)**

NOW, THEREFORE, it is ORDERED ADJUDGED, and DECREED by the Court as follows:

1. That the petition is hereby granted.
2. That the final account of the personal representative(s) herein is approved.
3. That decedent's last will duly executed on June 2, 1994, and codicil or codicils thereto duly executed on, 20, (is) (are) (hereby) (has or have been) formally probated and (is) (are) construed as above stated.
4. That the heirs of the decedent are determined to be as set forth above.
5. That the property of the decedent on hand for distribution is as above stated.
6. That title to the personal and real property described herein, subject to any lawful disposition heretofore made, is hereby assigned to and vested in the following named persons in the following proportions or parts:

    The whole thereof to decedent's spouse, Christopher Mertens

7. That the lien of inheritance taxes, if any, on the above described property is hereby waived.
8. That any previous order determining testacy is hereby confirmed as it affects any previously omitted or unnotified persons and other interested persons.

Dated: June 18, 2015   /s/ Richard B. Evans
                                                        Judge

        (COURT SEAL)

                              FILED:

Source: Minnesota Probate Court.

FORM | **11** | **Petition for Discharge of Personal Representative**

STATE OF MINNESOTA   **DISTRICT COURT**
COUNTY OF <u>RAMSEY</u>   **PROBATE DIVISION**
                                               <u>SECOND</u> **JUDICIAL DISTRICT**
                                               Court File No. <u>999999</u>

Estate of

     <u>Shelley Mertens</u>   Date of Death: <u>September 20, 2014</u>
     Decedent   Social Security No.: <u>321-54-9876</u>

PETITION FOR DISCHARGE OF

<u>Christopher Mertens</u>   ,

                               **PERSONAL REPRESENTATIVE of NAMED
DECEASED**

1. Petitioner has the following interest in the estate: spouse, heir, devisee, personal representative of deceased
2. <u>Christopher Mertens</u>, the Personal Representative of this estate, should be discharged to Minnesota Code 524.3-611 for the following reasons:

   - Petitioner has fully administered the estate of the decedent, has paid all debts, charges and expenses owed by the decedent at death and the estate

   - Petitioner's final account of said estate has been presented to and allowed by this Court, a decree or order of distribution has been made and all required taxes have been paid and receipts therefore properly filed

   - Petitioner has paid out and distributed the balance of the estate remaining in his hands for distribution pursuant to the order allowing the final account in accordance with the decree or order of distribution

   - Petitioner has filed with the Court proper receipts from all named parties for their respective legacies and/or distributive shares pursuant to decedent's will

WHEREFORE Petitioner requests that this Court, after notice and hearing, issue an Order which:

A. Discharges John C. Doe as Personal Representative.

B. Directs the disposition of the estate assets remaining in the name of, or under the control of, the Personal Representative.

FURTHER, under penalty for perjury, I declare and affirm that I have read the foregoing Petition and attest to the best of my knowledge or information, that its contents are complete, accurate and true.

DATED : <u>June 29, 2015</u>

                            <u>/s/ Christopher Mertens</u>
                            Signature of Petitioner

<u>/s/ Allan J. Jaycox</u>
Attorney for Petitioner
Jaycox and Jackson, P.A.
First State Bank Bldg.
Mpls., MN 55455
License # 5692103
Telephone: (612)823-1469   FAX: (612)823-1470

FORM **12** **Order of Discharge of Personal Representative**

STATE OF MINNESOTA   DISTRICT COURT
COUNTY OF RAMSEY   PROBATE DIVISION
                                                      SECOND JUDICIAL DISTRICT
                                                      Court File No. 999999

Estate of

        Shelley Mertens   Date of Death: September 20, 2014
             Decedent   Social Security No.: 321-54-9876

ORDER FOR DISCHARGE OF PERSONAL
REPRESENTATIVE

Christopher Mertens filed a Petition for Discharge of Personal Representative, Conservator or Guardian on June 29, 2015.

This Court having considered that Petition finds that Christopher Mertens has fully discharged the responsibilities under formal, supervised probate.

Personal Representative and has fully distributed the property of this estate to the persons entitled thereto;

IT IS ORDERED that:

Christopher Mertens is discharged from further demand as personal representative

of any interested person in regard to this estate.

Personal Representative.

[ ] Releases _____ from any bond given in the form of cash or lien on real property or any surety which may have been arranged.

DATED : July 20, 2015

                        /s/ Richard B. Evans
                                  Judge

(COURT SEAL)

Source: Minnesota Probate Court.

FORM | 13 | **Application for Informal Probate of Will and for Informal Appointment of Personal Representative**

STATE OF MINNESOTA
COUNTY OF <u>HENNEPIN</u>

DISTRICT COURT
PROBATE DIVISION
<u>FOURTH</u> JUDICIAL DISTRICT
Court File No. <u>19850</u>

Estate of

<u>Cheryl Ann Kennedy</u>
Decedent

APPLICATION FOR INFORMAL PROBATE
OF WILL AND FOR INFORMAL APPOINTMENT
OF PERSONAL REPRESENTATIVE

I, <u>Charles Michael Kennedy</u>, state:

1. My address is: <u>1010 Willow Ln., Mpls., MN 55409</u>
2. I am an interested person as defined by Minnesota law because I am: <u>spouse, heir, devisee, nominated personal representative of the decedent.</u>
3. Decedent was born on <u>January 13, 1971,</u> at <u>Minneapolis, MN.</u>
4. Decedent died on <u>August 1, 2015,</u> at <u>Minneapolis, MN.</u>
5. Decedent at the time of death resided in Hennepin County, at (address): <u>1010 Willow Ln., Mpls., MN 55409</u>
6. Decedent's Social Security number is 217-48-4307.
7. The names and addresses of Decedent's spouse, children, heirs, devisees, and other persons interested in this proceeding so far as known or ascertainable with reasonable diligence by the Applicant are:

Name	Relationship and Interest (list all)	Address
Charles Michael Kennedy	Spouse/heir/devisee	1010 Willow Ln., Mpls., MN 55409
Cindy Ann Kennedy	Daughter/heir/devisee	Same as above
Carl Lee Kennedy	Son/heir/devisee	Same as above
Corey Thomas Kennedy	Son/heir/devisee	Same as above
Catherine Betty Kelly	Mother/heir/devisee	1452 21st St. So. Mpls., MN 55409
Karen Lea Kennedy	Sister/heir/devisee	Same as above

(attach separate schedule, if necessary)

8. Negative Allegation Statement (see Minn. Gen. R. Prac. 408(a)):
   Decedent left no surviving spouse, children, parents, or siblings other than those herein named, and no issue of any predeceased children
9. All persons identified as heirs have survived the Decedent by at least 120 hours and not more than 3 years (except as permitted by Minn. Stat. Ann § 524.3-108) has elapsed since Decedent's death.

(continued)

10. ☐ Decedent left no surviving spouse.

☐ Decedent left no surviving issue.

☒ All issue of Decedent are issue of Decedent's surviving spouse except for:

☐ There are issue of the surviving spouse who are not issue of the Decedent.

11. Venue for this proceeding is in this County of the State of Minnesota because:

☒ The Decedent was domiciled in this County at the time of death and was the owner of property located in the State of Minnesota.

or

☐ Though not domiciled in the State of Minnesota, the Decedent was the owner of property located in this County at the time of death.

12. I estimate the Decedent's assets and indebtedness are as follows:

Probate Assets		Non-Probate Assets	
Homestead	$ 195,000	Joint Tenancy	$ 72,000
Other real estate	$ –	Insurance	$ 5,000
Cash	$ 2,000	Other	$
Securities	$ 4,000		
Other	$ 29,300		

Approximate Indebtedness $ 3,500

13. There is no personal representative of the Decedent appointed in Minnesota or elsewhere whose appointment has not been terminated.

14. ☒ I have not received a demand for notice and am not aware of any demand for notice of any probate or appointment proceeding concerning the Decedent that may have been filed in Minnesota or elsewhere.

or

☐ Proper notice has been given to those persons who have filed a demand for notice.

15. Decedent's Will is comprised of the following:

☒ Last will dated November 21, 2010.

☐ Codicil(s) dated_____.

☐ Separate writing(s) under Minn. Stat. 524.2 513 dated _____.

☐ (check if applicable) The Will refers to a separate writing, but none has been found.

16. To the best of my knowledge and belief, the Will has been validly executed.

17. Having conducted a reasonably diligent search, I am unaware of any instrument revoking the Will or of any other unrevoked testamentary instrument.

18. The documents comprising the Will:

☒ accompany this Application.

☐ are in the Court's possession.

☐ have been probated elsewhere and an authenticated copy of the Will and statement or order probating the same accompany this Application.

FORM | **13** | Application for Informal Probate of Will and for Informal Appointment of Personal Representative – (*Continued*)

19. The Will nominates <u>Charles Michael Kennedy</u> as personal representative.

 ☒ The nominated personal representative is willing to serve and is not disqualified.

 or

 ☐ The nominated personal representative is unable or has declined to serve.

 ☐ _____ has priority to serve as personal representative because:

 and is willing to serve and is not disqualified.

20. The Will specifies:

 Bond: ☒ No bond Administration: ☐ Undesignated
 ☐ Minimum bond ☒ Unsupervised
 ☐ $_____ bond ☐ Supervised
 ☐ Unspecified

21. At least 120 hours, but not more than 3 years (except as permitted by Minn. Stat. 524.3 108), have elapsed since Decedent's death.

 WHEREFORE, I request the Registrar informally:

1. Enter a statement probating the Will;

2. Enter an order appointing <u>Charles Michael Kennedy</u> as personal representative, with no bond, in an unsupervised administration;

3. Issue letters testamentary to <u>Charles Michael Kennedy</u>; and

4. Grant such other relief as may be proper.

 Under penalties for perjury, I declare or affirm that I have read this document and I know or believe its representations are true and complete.

<u>Charles Michael Kennedy</u>	<u>August 30, 2015</u>
Applicant	Date

Name: <u>Susan G. Brown</u>
Firm: <u>Brown and Smith</u>
Street: <u>1400 Main St. S.E.</u>
City, State, ZIP: <u>Mpls., MN 55455</u>
Attorney License No.: <u>9865743</u>
Telephone: <u>(612)775-3777</u> FAX: <u>(612)775-3778</u>

FORM **14** **Statement of Informal Probate of Will and Order of Informal Appointment of Personal Representative**

STATE OF MINNESOTA
COUNTY OF <u>HENNEPIN</u>

DISTRICT COURT
PROBATE DIVISION
<u>FOURTH</u> JUDICIAL DISTRICT
Court File No. <u>19850</u>

Estate of

<u>Cheryl Ann Kennedy</u>
Decedent

STATEMENT OF INFORMAL PROBATE OF WILL
AND ORDER OF INFORMAL APPOINTMENT
OF PERSONAL REPRESENTATIVE

The Application for the Informal Probate of Will and Informal Appointment of Personal Representative, signed by <u>Charles Michael Kennedy,</u> came before the Registrar on <u>August 30, 2015.</u> The Registrar, having considered the Application, determines the following:

1. The Application is complete.
2. The Applicant has declared or affirmed that the representations contained in the Application are true to the best of Applicant's knowledge or belief.
3. The Applicant appears from the Application to be an interested person as defined by Minnesota law.
4. On the basis of the statements in the Application, venue in this County is proper.
5. Any notice required by Minnesota law has been given.
6. Decedent's Will is comprised of the following:
   - ☒ Last will dated <u>November 21, 2010.</u>
   - ☐ Codicil(s) dated _____.
   - ☐ Separate writing(s) under Minn. Stat. 524.2 513 dated _____.
   - ☐ (check if applicable) The Will refers to a separate writing, but none has been found.
7. The documents comprising the Will:
   - ☒ are in the Registrar's possession.
   - ☐ have been probated elsewhere, and an authenticated copy of the Will and statement or order probating the same accompany this Statement.
8. Decedent died on <u>August 1, 2015</u> and at least 120 hours, but not more than 3 years, (except as permitted by Minn. Stat. 524.3 108) have elapsed since the Decedent's death.
9. (Check appropriate boxes)
   - ☐ Decedent left no surviving spouse.
   - ☐ Decedent left no surviving issue.
   - ☒ All issue of Decedent are issue of Decedent's surviving spouse except for:
   - ☐ There are issue of the surviving spouse who are not issue of the Decedent.
10. From the statements in the Application, the person appointed below has priority and is entitled to be appointed personal representative, and is not disqualified to serve as personal representative.

FORM | **14** | **Statement of Informal Probate of Will and Order of Informal Appointment of Personal Representative – (*Continued*)**

---

11. The Will specifies:

Bond: ☒ No bond   Administration: ☐ Undesignated
☐ Minimum bond   ☒ Unsupervised
☐ $_____ bond   ☐ Supervised
☐ Unspecified

12. The Application indicates that there is no personal representative appointed in this or another county of Minnesota whose appointment has not been terminated.

IT IS ORDERED:

1. The Application is granted.

2. The Will is informally probated.

3. <u>Charles Michael Kennedy</u> is informally appointed as the personal representative of the Decedent's Estate, with no bond.

4. Upon filing any required bond and statement of acceptance and oath, letters testamentary will be issued.

/s/ Lorina B. Arneson   September 8, 2015

Registrar   **Date**

STATE OF MINNESOTA
COUNTY OF <u>HENNEPIN</u>

DISTRICT COURT
PROBATE DIVISION
<u>FOURTH</u> JUDICIAL DISTRICT

Court File No. <u>19850</u>

Estate of

<u>Cheryl Ann Kennedy</u>
Decedent

NOTICE OF INFORMAL PROBATE OF WILL AND
APPOINTMENT OF PERSONAL REPRESENTATIVE
AND NOTICE TO CREDITORS

Notice is given that an application for informal probate of the Decedent's will dated <u>November 21,</u> <u>2010,</u> and codicil(s) to the will, dated _____, and separate writing(s) under Minn. Stat. 524.2 513 dated _____ ("Will"), has been filed with the Registrar. The application has been granted.

Notice is also given that the Registrar has informally appointed <u>Charles Michael Kennedy</u>, whose address is:

<u>1010 Willow Ln., Mpls., MN 55409</u>

as personal representative of the Estate of the Decedent. Any heir, devisee, or other interested person may be entitled to appointment as personal representative or may object to the appointment of the personal representative. Unless objections are filed with the Court (pursuant to Minn. Stat. 524.3 607) and the Court otherwise orders, the personal representative has full power to administer the Estate including, after 30 days from the date of issuance of letters, the power to sell, encumber, lease, or distribute real estate.

Any objections to the probate of the will or appointment of the Personal Representative must be filed with this Court and will be heard by the Court after the filing of an appropriate petition and proper notice of hearing.

Notice is also given that (subject to Minn. Stat. 524.3 801) all creditors having claims against the Estate are required to present the claims to the personal representative or to the Court Administrator within four months after the date of this Notice or the claims will be barred.

<u>/s/ Lorina B. Arneson</u>   <u>September 8, 2015</u>
Registrar   Date

<u>/s/ Bradford R. Mitlar</u>   <u>September 9, 2015</u>
Court Administrator   Date

Attorney for Applicant: <u>Susan G. Brown</u>
Name: <u>Susan G. Brown</u>
Firm: <u>Brown and Smith</u>
Street: <u>1400 Main St. S.E.</u>
City, State, ZIP: <u>Mpls., MN 55455</u>
Attorney License No.: <u>9865743</u>
Telephone: <u>(612) 775-3777</u>   FAX: <u>(612) 775-3778</u>

FORM **16** **Proof of Placing Order for Publication**

STATE OF MINNESOTA
COUNTY OF <u>HENNEPIN</u>

PROBATE COURT—UNSUPERVISED
COURT FILE NO. <u>19850</u>

In Re:Estate of

PROOF OF PLACING ORDER

<u>Cheryl Ann Kennedy</u>
<u>Decedent</u>

<u>FOR PUBLICATION</u>

_____
_____

TO THE CLERK OF PROBATE COURT:

That is to verify that <u>Susan G.Brown</u>

_____ <u>Attorney for</u> , applicant(s)

has <s>have</s> made arrangements for the publication of:

☐ **NOTICE OF INFORMAL APPOINTMENT OF PERSONAL REPRESENTATIVE(S) AND NOTICE TO CREDITORS**

☒ **NOTICE OF INFORMAL PROBATE OF WILL AND APPOINTMENT OF PERSONAL REPRESENTATIVE(S) AND NOTICE TO CREDITORS**

☐

once a week for two consecutive weeks in th<u>e FINANCE AND COMMERCE</u>

Daily Newspaper

and this is to confirm that the same will be published accordingly commencing in the next available issue, and that arrangements for payment of the cost of said publication have been made.

Dated: <u>September 9,2015</u>

/s/ D.C.Morrison
_____
Publisher

Source: Minnesota Probate Court.

FORM `17` **Inventory**

STATE OF MINNESOTA
COUNTY OF HENNEPIN

DISTRICT COURT
PROBATE DIVISION
FOURTH JUDICIAL DISTRICT
Court File No. 19850
INVENTORY
☒ ORIGINAL
☐ AMENDED
☐ SUPPLEMENTAL

Estate of

Date of Death: August 1, 2015
Social Security No.: 217-48-4307

Cheryl Ann Kennedy
Decedent

Charles Michael Kennedy, the Personal Representative of the Estate, states:

1. The following is a true and correct inventory at date of death values of all the property of the Estate, both real and personal, which has come into my possession as Personal Representative. If an appraisal of any asset has been made, the name and address of each appraiser used is included. After diligent search and inquiry concerning the assets of the Estate, the following is a list of the Estate assets by category:

SCHEDULE		VALUE
Schedule A:	Real Estate	$ 195,000
Schedule B:	Stocks, Bonds, and Other Securities	$ 4,000
Schedule C:	Bank Accounts, Mortgages, Contracts for Deed, Notes and Cash	$ 2,000
Schedule D:	Other Personal Property	$ 29,300
SUBTOTAL		$ 230,300
Less Schedule E: Mortgages and Liens—Miscellaneous Indebtedness		($ 3,500)
TOTAL NET APPRAISEMENT		$ 226,800

2. A copy of this Inventory, including all schedules, has been mailed to the surviving spouse, if any, and to all residuary distributees of the Decedent and to interested persons and creditors who have requested a copy of the Inventory.

    Under penalties for perjury, I declare or affirm that I have read the Inventory and I know or believe its representations are true and complete.

Charles Michael Kennedy   September 17, 2015
Personal Representative   Date

Attorney for Personal Representative: Susan G. Brown
Name: Susan G. Brown
Firm: Brown and Smith
Street: 1400 Main St. S.E.
City, State, ZIP: Mpls., MN 55455
Attorney License No.: 9865743
Telephone: (612)775-3777 **FAX:** (612)775-3778

FORM **17** **Inventory – (Continued)**

GENERAL INSTRUCTIONS for all Schedules.

1. Values reported should be as of date of death.
2. The appointment of an appraiser is not always necessary.
3. Each asset of a Schedule is to be given its own "Item Number."
4. DO NOT list any joint tenancy property unless the Decedent did not intend to create a true joint tenancy, but rather created for convenience a nominal joint tenancy which is subject to probate. Joint tenancy with right of survivorship property listed in this inventory may be converted to probate property with the consent of the surviving joint tenant(s).
5. List the gross fair market value of each item without subtracting for mortgages or liens.
6. List all mortgages and liens for which decedent was liable on Schedule E.
7. Blank schedules need not be attached.

(continued)

FORM | 17 | **Inventory – (*Continued*)**

ESTATE OF Cheryl Ann Kennedy   Court File No. 19850

SCHEDULE A: REAL ESTATE

INSTRUCTIONS for Schedule A:

1. Include both the legal description and the street address. If rural property also include acreage.
2. For Contracts for Deed: If Decedent owned a Vendor/Seller's interest describe the land on Schedule A, valuing it at zero and show the remaining contract balance on Schedule C. If Decedent owned a Vendee/Buyer's interest, describe the property on Schedule A valuing it at its fair market value.
3. County Assessor's market value can be obtained from the County Assessor or department of taxation.
4. List only Minnesota real estate. DO NOT list real estate located in other states.

Item Number	Description of Property	County Assessor's Market Value	Fair Market Value
1	Homestead in the County of Hennepin 1010 Willow Ln., Mpls. MN Legal Description: Lot 3, Block 1, Loring Park Addition to Mpls., (Plat #17068 Parcel #3196)	$ 185,000	$ 195,000
2	Other Real Estate:	$	$

Schedule A: Real Estate	TOTAL	$ 195,000

FORM **17** *Inventory – (Continued)*

ESTATE OF Cheryl Ann Kennedy   Court File No. 19850

SCHEDULE B: STOCKS, BONDS, AND OTHER SECURITIES

INSTRUCTIONS for Schedule B:

1 Specify face value of bonds, number of shares of stock, stock certificate number, and CUSIP number, if available.
2 List each bond issue, stock, or certificate separately.

Item Number	Description of Property	Unit Value	Fair Market Value
1	Stock: 100 Shrs. Users Inc., Common Stock, Certificate #U0556484, dated 1/13/96	$ 40/shr.	$ 4,000

Schedule B: Stocks, Bonds, and Other Securities		TOTAL	$ 4,000

(continued)

FORM | **17** | Inventory – (*Continued*)

ESTATE OF <u>Cheryl Ann Kennedy</u>   Court File No. <u>19850</u>

SCHEDULE C: BANK ACCOUNTS, MORTGAGES, CONTRACTS FOR DEED, NOTES, AND CASH

INSTRUCTIONS for Schedule C:

1. List Vendor/Seller's interest in Contract for Deed on this Schedule. Also include the date of the contract, name of Vendee/Buyer, interest rate and unpaid balance at date of death, and accrued interest, if any.

2. List Mortgages owned by Decedent as assets, NOT mortgages for which Decedent is liable or mortgages secured by property in the Estate.

Item Number	Description of Property	Unit Value	Fair Market Value
1	Allied 1st Bank of Mpls., MN Acct. #201-3285-48		$ 2,000

Schedule C: Bank Accounts, Mortgages, Contracts for Deed, Notes and Cash	TOTAL	$ 2,000

FORM **17** **Inventory – (*Continued*)**

ESTATE OF <u>Cheryl Ann Kennedy</u>   Court File No. <u>19850</u>

SCHEDULE D: OTHER PERSONAL PROPERTY

INSTRUCTIONS for Schedule D:

1. List on this schedule, any personal property owned by Decedent and not reported on other schedules. Examples of property to be listed on this schedule include: refunds, wearing apparel, household goods, automobiles, furniture, business interests, and insurance payable to the Estate.
2. Where appropriate, specify the location of the property.
3. Use actual value or specify if asset has no pecuniary value.
4. DO NOT list non-probate property.

Item Number	Description of Property	Unit Value	Fair Market Value
1	Household Goods and Furnishings		$ 15,000
2	Wearing Apparel, Jewelry, etc.		$ 8,800
3	2010 Ford, VIN 5342718653 Title #04142313		$ 5,500

Schedule D: Other Property	TOTAL	$ 29,300

(*continued*)

ESTATE OF Cheryl Ann Kennedy   Court File No. 19850

SCHEDULE E: MORTGAGES AND LIENS

INSTRUCTIONS for Schedule E:

1. Show any mortgages and liens secured by property in the Estate. Detail the date of the installment, names of the parties, interest rate, payment terms, and any other relevant data. Indicate the Schedule and Item Number of the secured property from prior schedule. The remaining balance of Contracts for Deed in which Decedent was the Vendee/Buyer or was the mortgage debtor should be listed on this Schedule. Also include interest and taxes due at date of death.

Item Number	Description of Property	Unit Value	Fair Market Value
	None		

Schedule E: Mortgages and Liens	TOTAL	$

FORM | **18** | **Notice of Informal Appointment of Personal Representative and Notice to Creditors (Intestate)**

STATE OF MINNESOTA
COUNTY OF <u>HENNEPIN</u>

DISTRICT COURT
PROBATE DIVISION
<u>FOURTH</u> JUDICIAL DISTRICT
Court File No. <u>19850</u>

Estate of

<u>Cheryl Ann Kennedy</u>
Decedent

NOTICE OF INFORMAL APPOINTMENT
OF PERSONAL REPRESENTATIVE AND
NOTICE TO CREDITORS (INTESTATE)

Notice is given that an application for informal appointment of personal representative has been filed with the registrar. No will has been presented for probate. The application has been granted.

Notice is also given that the Registrar has informally appointed <u>Charles Michael Kennedy,</u> whose address is: <u>1010 Willow Ln., Mpls., MN 55409</u>

as personal representative of the Estate of the Decedent. Any heir, devisee, or other interested person may be entitled to appointment as personal representative or may object to the appointment of the personal representative. Unless objections are filed with the Court (pursuant to Minn. Stat. 524.3 607) and the Court otherwise orders, the personal representative has full power to administer the Estate including, after 30 days from the date of issuance of letters, the power to sell, encumber, lease, or distribute real estate.

Any objections to the probate of the will or appointment of the Personal Representative must be filed with this Court and will be heard by the Court after the filing of an appropriate petition and proper notice of hearing.

Notice is also given that (subject to Minn. Stat. 524.3 801) all creditors having claims against the Estate are required to present the claims to the personal representative or to the Court Administrator within four months after the date of this Notice or the claims will be barred.

<u>/s/ Lorina B. Arneson</u> <u>September 8, 2015</u>
Registrar   Date

<u>/s/ Bradford R. Mitlar</u> <u>September 9, 2015</u>
Court Administrator   Date

Attorney for Personal Representative: <u>Susan G. Brown</u>
Name: <u>Susan G. Brown</u>
Firm: <u>Brown and Smith</u>
Street: <u>1400 Main St. S.E.</u>
City, State, ZIP: <u>Mpls., MN 55455</u>
Attorney License No.: <u>9865743</u>
Telephone: <u>(612) 775-3777</u>   FAX: <u>(612) 775-3778</u>

FORM **19** **Proof of Placing Order for Publication**

STATE OF MINNESOTA
COUNTY OF <u>HENNEPIN</u>

PROBATE COURT—UNSUPERVISED
COURT FILE NO. <u>19850</u>

In Re: Estate of

<u>   Cheryl Ann Kennedy   </u>
<u>Decedent</u>

PROOF OF PLACING ORDER
FOR PUBLICATION

_____

_____

TO THE CLERK OF PROBATE COURT:

That is to verify that <u> Susan G.Brown </u>

_____ <u>Attorney for </u> , applicant(s)

has ~~have~~ made arrangements for the publication of:

☐ NOTICE OF INFORMAL APPOINTMENT OF PERSONAL
    REPRESENTATIVE(S) AND NOTICE TO CREDITORS

☒ NOTICE OF INFORMAL PROBATE OF WILL AND APPOINTMENT OF
    PERSONAL REPRESENTATIVE(S) AND NOTICE TO CREDITORS

☐

once a week for two consecutive weeks in the <u> FINANCE AND COMMERCE </u>

_____
                                        Daily Newspaper

and this is to confirm that the same will be published accordingly commencing in the next available issue,
and that arrangements for payment of the cost of said publication have been made.
Dated: <u>September 9,2015</u>

                          <u>/s/   D.C.Morrison</u>
                                        Publisher

FORM | **20** | **Letters of General Administration**

STATE OF MINNESOTA
COUNTY OF <u>HENNEPIN</u>

DISTRICT COURT
PROBATE DIVISION
<u>FOURTH</u> JUDICIAL DISTRICT
Court File No. <u>19850</u>

Estate of

<u>Cheryl Ann Kennedy</u>
Decedent

LETTERS
☒ TESTAMENTARY
☐ OF GENERAL ADMINISTRATION

1. The Decedent died on <u>August 1, 2015.</u>
2. <u>Charles Michael Kennedy</u> has been appointed Personal Representative of Decedent's Estate in

   ☒ an unsupervised
   ☐ a supervised administration

   and is now qualified to act as Personal Representative of the Estate and has authority to administer the Estate according to law.

(COURT SEAL)

/s/ Harold R. Carlins September 10, 2015
Judge   Date

FORM | **21** | Application for Employer Identification Number (Form SS-4)

Form **SS-4**
(Rev. January 2010)
Department of the Treasury
Internal Revenue Service

Application for Employer Identification Number

(For use by employers, corporations, partnerships, trusts, estates, churches, government agencies, Indian tribal entities, certain individuals, and others.)
▶ See separate instructions for each line.   ▶ Keep a copy for your records.

OMB No. 1545-0003

EIN

Type or print clearly.

1 Legal name of entity (or individual) for whom the EIN is being requested
Estate of Shelley Mertens

2 Trade name of business (if different from name on line 1)

3 Executor, administrator, trustee, "care of" name
Christopher Mertens, Personal Representative

4a Mailing address (room, apt., suite no. and street, or P.O. box)
1005 Elm Street

5a Street address (if different) (Do not enter a P.O. box.)

4b City, state, and ZIP code (if foreign, see instructions)
St. Paul, MN 55102

5b City, state, and ZIP code (if foreign, see instructions)

6 County and state where principal business is located

7a Name of responsible party

7b SSN, ITIN, or EIN
321-54-9876

8a Is this application for a limited liability company (LLC) (or a foreign equivalent)? . . . . ☐ Yes ☐ No

8b If 8a is "Yes," enter the number of LLC members . . . ▶

8c If 8a is "Yes," was the LLC organized in the United States? . . . . ☐ Yes ☐ No

9a **Type of entity** (check only one box). **Caution.** If 8a is "Yes," see the instructions for the correct box to check.

☐ Sole proprietor (SSN) _____
☐ Partnership
☐ Corporation (enter form number to be filed) ▶_____
☐ Personal service corporation
☐ Church or church-controlled organization
☐ Other nonprofit organization (specify) ▶_____
☐ Other (specify) ▶

☑ Estate (SSN of decedent) 321 54 9876
☐ Plan administrator (TIN) _____
☐ Trust (TIN of grantor) _____
☐ National Guard   ☐ State/local government
☐ Farmers' cooperative   ☐ Federal government/military
☐ REMIC   ☐ Indian tribal governments/enterprises
Group Exemption Number (GEN) if any ▶

9b If a corporation, name the state or foreign country (if applicable) where incorporated

State | Foreign country

10 **Reason for applying** (check only one box)
☐ Started new business (specify type) ▶ _____
_____
☐ Hired employees (Check the box and see line 13.)
☐ Compliance with IRS withholding regulations
☑ Other (specify) ▶ Fiduciary - Death

☐ Banking purpose (specify purpose) ▶_____
☐ Changed type of organization (specify new type) ▶_____
☐ Purchased going business
☐ Created a trust (specify type) ▶_____
☐ Created a pension plan (specify type) ▶_____

11 Date business started or acquired (month, day, year). See instructions.

12 Closing month of accounting year

13 Highest number of employees expected in the next 12 months (enter -0- if none).

If no employees expected, skip line 14.

Agricultural	Household	Other

14 If you expect your employment tax liability to be $1,000 or less in a full calendar year **and** want to file Form 944 annually instead of Forms 941 quarterly, check here. (Your employment tax liability generally will be $1,000 or less if you expect to pay $4,000 or less in total wages.) If you do not check this box, you must file Form 941 for every quarter. ☐

15 First date wages or annuities were paid (month, day, year). **Note.** If applicant is a withholding agent, enter date income will first be paid to nonresident alien (month, day, year) . . . . ▶

16 Check **one** box that best describes the principal activity of your business.
☐ Construction ☐ Rental & leasing ☐ Transportation & warehousing ☐ Health care & social assistance ☐ Wholesale-agent/broker
☐ Real estate ☐ Manufacturing ☐ Finance & insurance ☐ Accommodation & food service ☐ Wholesale-other ☐ Retail
☐ Other (specify)

17 Indicate principal line of merchandise sold, specific construction work done, products produced, or services provided.

18 Has the applicant entity shown on line 1 ever applied for and received an EIN? ☐ Yes ☑ No
If "Yes," write previous EIN here ▶

Third Party Designee

Complete this section **only** if you want to authorize the named individual to receive the entity's EIN and answer questions about the completion of this form.

Designee's name

Designee's telephone number (include area code)
(   )

Address and ZIP code

Designee's fax number (include area code)
(   )

Under penalties of perjury, I declare that I have examined this application, and to the best of my knowledge and belief, it is true, correct, and complete.

Name and title (type or print clearly) ▶ Christopher Mertens   Personal Representative

Applicant's telephone number (include area code)
(612) 345-5000

Signature ▶ /s/ Christopher Mertens   Date ▶ 10-31/2014

Applicant's fax number (include area code)
(612) 345-4712

For Privacy Act and Paperwork Reduction Act Notice, see separate instructions.   Cat. No. 16055N   Form **SS-4** (Rev. 1-2010)

FORM | **21** | **Application for Employer Identification Number (Form SS-4) – (*Continued*)**

Form SS-4 (Rev. 1-2010)   Page **2**

Do I Need an EIN?

File Form SS-4 if the applicant entity does not already have an EIN but is required to show an EIN on any return, statement, or other document.[1] See also the separate instructions for each line on Form SS-4.

IF the applicant...	AND...	THEN...
Started a new business	Does not currently have (nor expect to have) employees	Complete lines 1, 2, 4a–8a, 8b–c (if applicable), 9a, 9b (if applicable), and 10–14 and 16–18.
Hired (or will hire) employees, including household employees	Does not already have an EIN	Complete lines 1, 2, 4a–6, 7a–b (if applicable), 8a, 8b–c (if applicable), 9a, 9b (if applicable), 10–18.
Opened a bank account	Needs an EIN for banking purposes only	Complete lines 1–5b, 7a–b (if applicable), 8a, 8b–c (if applicable), 9a, 9b (if applicable), 10, and 18.
Changed type of organization	Either the legal character of the organization or its ownership changed (for example, you incorporate a sole proprietorship or form a partnership)[2]	Complete lines 1–18 (as applicable).
Purchased a going business[3]	Does not already have an EIN	Complete lines 1–18 (as applicable).
Created a trust	The trust is other than a grantor trust or an IRA trust[4]	Complete lines 1–18 (as applicable).
Created a pension plan as a plan administrator[5]	Needs an EIN for reporting purposes	Complete lines 1, 3, 4a–5b, 9a, 10, and 18.
Is a foreign person needing an EIN to comply with IRS withholding regulations	Needs an EIN to complete a Form W-8 (other than Form W-8ECI), avoid withholding on portfolio assets, or claim tax treaty benefits[6]	Complete lines 1–5b, 7a–b (SSN or ITIN optional), 8a, 8b–c (if applicable), 9a, 9b (if applicable), 10, and 18.
Is administering an estate	Needs an EIN to report estate income on Form 1041	Complete lines 1–6, 9a, 10–12, 13–17 (if applicable), and 18.
Is a withholding agent for taxes on non-wage income paid to an alien (i.e., individual, corporation, or partnership, etc.)	Is an agent, broker, fiduciary, manager, tenant, or spouse who is required to file Form 1042, Annual Withholding Tax Return for U.S. Source Income of Foreign Persons	Complete lines 1, 2, 3 (if applicable), 4a–5b, 7a–b (if applicable), 8a, 8b–c (if applicable), 9a, 9b (if applicable), 10, and 18.
Is a state or local agency	Serves as a tax reporting agent for public assistance recipients under Rev. Proc. 80-4, 1980-1 C.B. 581[7]	Complete lines 1, 2, 4a–5b, 9a, 10, and 18.
Is a single-member LLC	Needs an EIN to file Form 8832, Classification Election, for filing employment tax returns and excise tax returns, or for state reporting purposes[8]	Complete lines 1–18 (as applicable).
Is an S corporation	Needs an EIN to file Form 2553, Election by a Small Business Corporation[9]	Complete lines 1–18 (as applicable).

[1] For example, a sole proprietorship or self-employed farmer who establishes a qualified retirement plan, or is required to file excise, employment, alcohol, tobacco, or firearms returns, must have an EIN. A partnership, corporation, REMIC (real estate mortgage investment conduit), nonprofit organization (church, club, etc.), or farmers' cooperative must use an EIN for any tax-related purpose even if the entity does not have employees.

[2] However, do not apply for a new EIN if the existing entity only (a) changed its business name, (b) elected on Form 8832 to change the way it is taxed (or is covered by the default rules), or (c) terminated its partnership status because at least 50% of the total interests in partnership capital and profits were sold or exchanged within a 12-month period. The EIN of the terminated partnership should continue to be used. See Regulations section 301.6109-1(d)(2)(iii).

[3] Do not use the EIN of the prior business unless you became the "owner" of a corporation by acquiring its stock.

[4] However, grantor trusts that do not file using Optional Method 1 and IRA trusts that are required to file Form 990-T, Exempt Organization Business Income Tax Return, must have an EIN. For more information on grantor trusts, see the Instructions for Form 1041.

[5] A plan administrator is the person or group of persons specified as the administrator by the instrument under which the plan is operated.

[6] Entities applying to be a Qualified Intermediary (QI) need a QI-EIN even if they already have an EIN. See Rev. Proc. 2000-12.

[7] See also *Household employer* on page 4 of the instructions. **Note.** State or local agencies may need an EIN for other reasons, for example, hired employees.

[8] See *Disregarded entities* on page 4 of the instructions for details on completing Form SS-4 for an LLC.

[9] An existing corporation that is electing or revoking S corporation status should use its previously-assigned EIN.

Form **56**
(Rev. December 2011)
Department of the Treasury
Internal Revenue Service

Notice Concerning Fiduciary Relationship

(Internal Revenue Code sections 6036 and 6903)

OMB No. 1545-0013

Part I   Identification

Name of person for whom you are acting (as shown on the tax return)	Identifying number	Decedent's social security no.
Estate of Shelley Mertens	41-6246975	321-54-9876

Address of person for whom you are acting (number, street, and room or suite no.)
1005 Elm Street

City or town, state, and ZIP code (If a foreign address, see instructions.)
St. Paul, MN 55102

Fiduciary's name
Christopher Mertens

Address of fiduciary (number, street, and room or suite no.)
1005 Elm Street

City or town, state, and ZIP code
St. Paul, MN 55102

Telephone number (optional)
(612) 345-5000

Section A. Authority

1 Authority for fiduciary relationship. Check applicable box:

a ☑ Court appointment of testate estate (valid will exists)
b ☐ Court appointment of intestate estate (no valid will exists)
c ☐ Court appointment as guardian or conservator
d ☐ Valid trust instrument and amendments
e ☐ Bankruptcy or assignment for the benefit or creditors
f ☐ Other. Describe ▶ _____

2a If box 1a or 1b is checked, enter the date of death ▶ ____09/20/2014____
2b If box 1c—1f is checked, enter the date of appointment, taking office, or assignment or transfer of assets ▶ _____

Section B. Nature of Liability and Tax Notices

3 Type of taxes (check all that apply): ☑ Income   ☑ Gift   ☑ Estate   ☐ Generation-skipping transfer   ☐ Employment
☐ Excise   ☐ Other (describe) ▶ _____

4 Federal tax form number (check all that apply): **a** ☑ 706 series **b** ☑ 709 **c** ☐ 940 **d** ☐ 941, 943, 944
e ☐ 1040, 1040-A, or 1040-EZ **f** ☑ 1041 **g** ☐ 1120 **h** ☐ Other (list) ▶ _____

5 If your authority as a fiduciary does not cover all years or tax periods, check here . . . . ▶ ☐
and list the specific years or periods ▶ _____

6 If the fiduciary listed wants a copy of notices or other written communications (see the instructions) check this box . . . . ▶ ☑
and enter the year(s) or period(s) for the corresponding line 4 item checked. If more than 1 form entered on line 4h, enter the
form number.

Complete only if the line 6 box is checked.

If this item is checked:	Enter year(s) or period(s)	If this item is checked:	Enter year(s) or period(s)
4a 706	2014	**4b** 709	2014
4c		**4d**	
4e		**4f** 1041	2014
4g		**4h:**	
4h:		**4h:**	

For Paperwork Reduction Act and Privacy Act Notice, see the separate instructions.   Cat. No. 16375I   Form **56** (Rev. 12-2011)

FORM   **22**   Notice Concerning Fiduciary Relationship (Form 56) – (*Continued*)

Form 56 (Rev. 12-2011)   Page **2**

Part II	**Court and Administrative Proceedings**	
Name of court (if other than a court proceeding, identify the type of proceeding and name of agency)		Date proceeding initiated
Ramsey County, Minnesota District Court Probate Division 2nd Judicial District		09/26/2014
Address of court		Docket number of proceeding
65 West Kellogg Blvd.		999999

City or town, state, and ZIP code	Date	Time		a.m.	Place of other proceedings
St. Paul, Minnesota 55102	10/31/2014	10:00	☑ p.m.		N/A

Part III	**Signature**	

Please Sign Here	I certify that I have the authority to execute this notice concerning fiduciary relationship on behalf of the taxpayer.		
	▶ _____ Fiduciary's signature	Personal Representative _____ Title, if applicable	_____ Date

Form **56** (Rev. 12-2011)

Source: Department of the Treasury—Internal Revenue Service.

FORM **23**   U.S. (Fiduciary) Income Tax Return for Estates and Trusts (Form 1041)

Form **1041**   Department of the Treasury—Internal Revenue Service
U.S. Income Tax Return for Estates and Trusts   20**14**   OMB No. 1545-0092

▶ Information about Form 1041 and its separate instructions is at *www.irs.gov/form1041.*

A Check all that apply: For calendar year 2014 or fiscal year beginning   Sept. 20   , 2014, and ending   May 10   , 2015

☐ Decedent's estate
☐ Simple trust
☐ Complex trust
☐ Qualified disability trust
☐ ESBT (S portion only)
☐ Grantor type trust
☐ Bankruptcy estate-Ch. 7
☐ Bankruptcy estate-Ch. 11
☐ Pooled income fund

Name of estate or trust (If a grantor type trust, see the instructions.)
Estate of Shelley Mertens

Name and title of fiduciary
Christopher Mertens, Personal Representative

Number, street, and room or suite no. (If a P.O. box, see the instructions.)
1005 Elm Street

City or town, state or province, country, and ZIP or foreign postal code
St. Paul, MN 55102

C Employer identification number
41-6246975

D Date entity created
9/20/2014

E Nonexempt charitable and split-interest trusts, check applicable box(es), see instructions.
☐ Described in sec. 4947(a)(1). Check here if not a private foundation . . . ▶ ☐
☐ Described in sec. 4947(a)(2)

B Number of Schedules K-1 attached (see instructions) ▶ 0

F Check applicable boxes: ☑ Initial return   ☑ Final return   ☐ Amended return
☐ Change in trust's name   ☐ Change in fiduciary   ☐ Change in fiduciary's name
☐ Net operating loss carryback
☐ Change in fiduciary's address

G Check here if the estate or filing trust made a section 645 election . . . . . . ▶ ☐ Trust TIN ▶

Income	1	Interest income	1	23,230 00
	2a	Total ordinary dividends	2a	2460 00
	b	Qualified dividends allocable to: (1) Beneficiaries _____ (2) Estate or trust _____		
	3	Business income or (loss). Attach Schedule C or C-EZ (Form 1040)	3	
	4	Capital gain or (loss). Attach Schedule D (Form 1041)	4	
	5	Rents, royalties, partnerships, other estates and trusts, etc. Attach Schedule E (Form 1040) .	5	1,100 00
	6	Farm income or (loss). Attach Schedule F (Form 1040)	6	
	7	Ordinary gain or (loss). Attach Form 4797	7	
	8	Other income. List type and amount _____	8	
	9	**Total income.** Combine lines 1, 2a, and 3 through 8 . . . . ▶	9	26,790
Deductions	10	Interest. Check if Form 4952 is attached ▶ ☐	10	3,900
	11	Taxes	11	4,400
	12	Fiduciary fees	12	10,000
	13	Charitable deduction (from Schedule A, line 7)	13	
	14	Attorney, accountant, and return preparer fees	14	7,890
	15a	Other deductions **not** subject to the 2% floor (attach schedule)	15a	
	b	Net operating loss deduction (see instructions)	15b	
	c	Allowable miscellaneous itemized deductions subject to the 2% floor	15c	
	16	Add lines 10 through 15c . . . . ▶	16	26,190
	17	Adjusted total income or (loss). Subtract line 16 from line 9 . . . **17** 600 00		
	18	Income distribution deduction (from Schedule B, line 15). Attach Schedules K-1 (Form 1041)	18	
	19	Estate tax deduction including certain generation-skipping taxes (attach computation) . .	19	
	20	Exemption	20	600
	21	Add lines 18 through 20 . . . . ▶	21	600
Tax and Payments	22	Taxable income. Subtract line 21 from line 17. If a loss, see instructions	22	0
	23	**Total tax** (from Schedule G, line 7)	23	0
	24	**Payments: a** 2014 estimated tax payments and amount applied from 2013 return	24a	
	b	Estimated tax payments allocated to beneficiaries (from Form 1041-T)	24b	
	c	Subtract line 24b from line 24a	24c	
	d	Tax paid with Form 7004 (see instructions)	24d	
	e	Federal income tax withheld. If any is from Form(s) 1099, check ▶ ☐	24e	
		Other payments: **f** Form 2439 _____ ; **g** Form 4136 _____ ; Total ▶	24h	
	25	**Total payments.** Add lines 24c through 24e, and 24h . . . . ▶	25	
	26	Estimated tax penalty (see instructions)	26	
	27	**Tax due.** If line 25 is smaller than the total of lines 23 and 26, enter amount owed . .	27	0
	28	**Overpayment.** If line 25 is larger than the total of lines 23 and 26, enter amount overpaid .	28	
	29	Amount of line 28 to be: **a** Credited to 2015 estimated tax ▶ _____ ; **b** Refunded ▶	29	

Sign Here
Under penalties of perjury, I declare that I have examined this return, including accompanying schedules and statements, and to the best of my knowledge and belief, it is true, correct, and complete. Declaration of preparer (other than taxpayer) is based on all information of which preparer has any knowledge.

▶ _____ Signature of fiduciary or officer representing fiduciary   Date   ▶ 6/3/2015   EIN of fiduciary if a financial institution

May the IRS discuss this return with the preparer shown below (see instr.)? ☐ Yes ☐ No

Paid Preparer Use Only
Print/Type preparer's name	Preparer's signature	Date	Check ☐ if self-employed	PTIN
Firm's name ▶			Firm's EIN ▶	
Firm's address ▶			Phone no.	

For Paperwork Reduction Act Notice, see the separate instructions.   Cat. No. 11370H   Form **1041** (2014)

FORM 23

U.S. (Fiduciary) Income Tax Return for Estates and Trusts (Form 1041)

Form 1041 (2014)   Page **2**

Schedule A — Charitable Deduction. Do not complete for a simple trust or a pooled income fund.

1	Amounts paid or permanently set aside for charitable purposes from gross income (see instructions)	1	
2	Tax-exempt income allocable to charitable contributions (see instructions)	2	
3	Subtract line 2 from line 1	3	
4	Capital gains for the tax year allocated to corpus and paid or permanently set aside for charitable purposes	4	
5	Add lines 3 and 4	5	
6	Section 1202 exclusion allocable to capital gains paid or permanently set aside for charitable purposes (see instructions)	6	
7	**Charitable deduction.** Subtract line 6 from line 5. Enter here and on page 1, line 13	7	

Schedule B — Income Distribution Deduction

1	Adjusted total income (see instructions)	1	
2	Adjusted tax-exempt interest	2	
3	Total net gain from Schedule D (Form 1041), line 19, column (1) (see instructions)	3	
4	Enter amount from Schedule A, line 4 (minus any allocable section 1202 exclusion)	4	
5	Capital gains for the tax year included on Schedule A, line 1 (see instructions)	5	
6	Enter any gain from page 1, line 4, as a negative number. If page 1, line 4, is a loss, enter the loss as a positive number	6	
7	**Distributable net income.** Combine lines 1 through 6. If zero or less, enter -0-	7	
8	If a complex trust, enter accounting income for the tax year as determined under the governing instrument and applicable local law **8**		
9	Income required to be distributed currently	9	
10	Other amounts paid, credited, or otherwise required to be distributed	10	
11	Total distributions. Add lines 9 and 10. If greater than line 8, see instructions	11	
12	Enter the amount of tax-exempt income included on line 11	12	
13	Tentative income distribution deduction. Subtract line 12 from line 11	13	
14	Tentative income distribution deduction. Subtract line 2 from line 7. If zero or less, enter -0-	14	
15	**Income distribution deduction.** Enter the smaller of line 13 or line 14 here and on page 1, line 18	15	

Schedule G — Tax Computation (see instructions)

1	**Tax: a** Tax on taxable income (see instructions)	1a		
	b Tax on lump-sum distributions. Attach Form 4972	1b		
	c Alternative minimum tax (from Schedule I (Form 1041), line 56)	1c		
	d Total. Add lines 1a through 1c	▶	1d	
2a	Foreign tax credit. Attach Form 1116	2a		
b	General business credit. Attach Form 3800	2b		
c	Credit for prior year minimum tax. Attach Form 8801	2c		
d	Bond credits. Attach Form 8912	2d		
e	**Total credits.** Add lines 2a through 2d	▶	2e	
3	Subtract line 2e from line 1d. If zero or less, enter -0-		3	
4	Net investment income tax from Form 8960, line 21		4	
5	Recapture taxes. Check if from: ☐ Form 4255 ☐ Form 8611		5	
6	Household employment taxes. Attach Schedule H (Form 1040)		6	
7	**Total tax.** Add lines 3 through 6. Enter here and on page 1, line 23	▶	7	

Other Information

		Yes	No
1	Did the estate or trust receive tax-exempt income? If "Yes," attach a computation of the allocation of expenses. Enter the amount of tax-exempt interest income and exempt-interest dividends ▶ $		
2	Did the estate or trust receive all or any part of the earnings (salary, wages, and other compensation) of any individual by reason of a contract assignment or similar arrangement?		
3	At any time during calendar year 2014, did the estate or trust have an interest in or a signature or other authority over a bank, securities, or other financial account in a foreign country?		
	See the instructions for exceptions and filing requirements for FinCEN Form 114. If "Yes," enter the name of the foreign country ▶		
4	During the tax year, did the estate or trust receive a distribution from, or was it the grantor of, or transferor to, a foreign trust? If "Yes," the estate or trust may have to file Form 3520. See instructions		
5	Did the estate or trust receive, or pay, any qualified residence interest on seller-provided financing? If "Yes," see the instructions for required attachment		
6	If this is an estate or a complex trust making the section 663(b) election, check here (see instructions) ▶ ☐		
7	To make a section 643(e)(3) election, attach Schedule D (Form 1041), and check here (see instructions) ▶ ☐		
8	If the decedent's estate has been open for more than 2 years, attach an explanation for the delay in closing the estate, and check here ▶ ☐		
9	Are any present or future trust beneficiaries skip persons? See instructions		

Form **1041** (2014)

APPENDIX B

SAMPLE MARITAL DEDUCTION TESTAMENTARY TRUST

LAST WILL AND TESTAMENT OF JOHN P. DOE

I, John P. Doe, a/k/a _____, of _____, City of _____, County of _____, State of _____, being of sound and disposing mind and memory, and not acting under undue influence of any person, do make, publish, and declare this document to be my last will and testament, and do hereby expressly revoke all wills and codicils previously made by me.

Article I

I hereby direct my personal representative, herein after named, to pay all my just debts, administrative expenses, and expenses for my last illness, funeral, and burial out of my estate.

Article II

I give my homestead legally described as _____, which I own in _____ County, State of _____, to my wife _____, in fee simple, if she survives me.

Article III

I give my diamond ring to my son, _____, and my (name and address) collection of guns and rifles to my son, _____. (name and address)

Article IV

I give all my other personal property, including my automobiles, household furnishings, clothing, jewelry, ornaments, books, and personal effects of every kind used about my home or person to my wife, _____, to do with as she sees fit, if she survives me.

Article V

If my wife, _____, survives me, I give to the _____ of _____ as trustee (name of individual of corporate trustee, e.g., a bank) (address), (city), and (state) of a trust to be known as "TRUST A," assets of my estate to be selected by my personal representative and having a value which, when added to the value of all interests in property that pass or have passed to my wife, either by this will or by other means, in a manner that qualifies for and will be equal to the maximum marital deduction allowable in my estate under the provisions of the United States Internal Revenue Code in effect at the time of my death. Only assets qualifying for the marital deduction shall be allocated to Trust A. My personal representative shall satisfy the foregoing transfer (devise) with such assets as will qualify for said marital deduction and shall compute all values of assets for these purposes in accordance with the Federal Estate Tax values finally computed in my estate except the assets allocated to "TRUST A" shall have an aggregate market value that fairly represents the net appreciation or depreciation of the available property on the date or dates of distribution.

TRUST A shall be administered and distributed by my trustee as follows:

1. Beginning on the date of my death, the net income from TRUST A shall be paid to my wife, _____, in convenient installments to be determined by my trustee, but at least annually, during her life.

2. My trustee shall pay to my wife or apply for her benefit such amounts from the principal of TRUST A as she shall request at any time

585

in writing. In addition, my trustee may pay to my wife or apply for her benefit amounts of the principal of TRUST A as it determines is necessary or advisable for her care, comfort, support, maintenance, and welfare, including reasonable luxuries.

3. Upon the death of my wife, my trustee shall distribute the entire assets in TRUST A, including income, to appointee or appointees in the manner and proportions as my wife may designate by her last will, which shall expressly refer to this general power of appointment; included in the power shall be her right to appoint free of any other trust provisions hereunder. This general power of appointment conferred upon my wife shall exist immediately upon my death and shall be exercisable by my wife exclusively and in all events.

4. If, under the above provisions, any portion of TRUST A is not disposed of, it shall be added to TRUST B of ARTICLE VII and administered and distributed as a part of TRUST B.

5. It is my intention that TRUST A shall qualify for the marital deduction that is allowed under the Federal Estate Tax provisions of the Internal Revenue Code in effect at the time of my death. Any provisions of this will that relate to TRUST A shall be so construed and questions pertaining to TRUST A shall be resolved accordingly.

6. If my wife predeceases me or the creation of TRUST A does not effectively reduce the Federal Estate Tax payable by reason of my death, the devise and bequest of this ARTICLE V shall lapse and no TRUST A shall be established.

Article VI

I hereby direct my personal representative to pay out of my residuary estate (and not from TRUST A) all estate and inheritance taxes assessed against my taxable estate or the recipients thereof, whether passing by this will or by other means, without contribution or reimbursement from any person.

Article VII

I give the residue of my estate to _____ of (name of individual or corporate trustee) _____, as trustee of a separate trust, which (address, city, state) shall be known as "TRUST B," the bypass trust, and which shall be administered and distributed by my trustee as follows:

1. During the life of my wife, _____.
   a. Beginning on the date of my death, the net income from TRUST B shall be paid to my wife, _____, in convenient installments to be determined by my trustee, but at least annually, during her life.
   b. If there are not sufficient principal funds readily available in TRUST A, then in addition to the net income from TRUST B, my trustee may pay to my wife or apply for her benefit sums from the principal of TRUST B as my trustee determines to be necessary or advisable to provide for her proper care, support, and maintenance.
   c. My trustee may also pay to or apply for the benefit of any child or other issue of mine sums from the principal of TRUST B as my trustee determines to be necessary in order to provide for their proper care, support, maintenance, and education. It is not required that such payments be for the equal benefit of my children and other issue.

2. After the death of my wife, _____, or in the event she does not survive me, then upon my death, my trustee shall administer and distribute TRUST B as follows:
   a. Until my youngest living child reaches the age of twenty-five (25) years, my trustee may pay to or apply directly for the benefit of my children and other issue sums from the net income and principal of TRUST B as my trustee determines necessary to provide for their proper care, support, maintenance, and education. It is not required that such payments be for the equal benefit of my children and other issue.
   b. When my youngest living child has reached the age of twenty-five (25) years, my trustee shall divide TRUST B into equal shares and shall provide one share for each of my then living children, and one share to be divided equally among the living issue, collectively, of each deceased child of mine. In making such division, my trustee shall take into account all advances of principal to a child made after such child reached the age of twenty-five (25) years. It shall be within the discretion of my trustee to take into account some, none, or all advances of principal to a child made before such child had reached the age of twenty-five

(25) years. After such division has been made, said shares shall be distributed outright to such children and to the issue of deceased children by right of representation.

Article VIII

If at any time before final distribution of my estate or trust estate, it happens that there not be in existence anyone who is or might become entitled to receive benefits therefrom as hereinabove provided, then upon the occurrence of such event, all of my estate and trust estate then remaining shall be paid over and distributed outright to my heirs at law, in such proportions as though I had at that time died without a will, a resident of the State of _____, in accordance with the intestate succession laws of personal property of the State of _____ now/then in effect.

Article IX

It is an express condition of this will, which shall control over all other provisions, that in no event shall the duration of any trust created herein continue for a period longer than the lives of all of: my wife, _____, and of any of my issue who may be living at the time of my death, and the survivor of all of them and twenty-one (21) years thereafter, and at the end of such time the trustee shall distribute the entire trust estate, principal, and any undistributed income outright to the persons then entitled to receive the income therefrom or to have it accumulated for their benefit, in shares that shall be the same as those in which such income is then being distributed to, or accumulated for, them.

Article X

My trustee shall have all powers and authority necessary or advisable to ensure the proper administration and distribution of each trust created by my will. Except as I may otherwise expressly direct or require in my will and in extension but not in limitation of the powers provided by applicable _____
(state)
law, I hereby grant to my trustee as to any properties, real, personal, or mixed, at any time constituting a part of any trust hereunder and without the necessity of notice to or license or approval of any court or person, full power and authority during the term of such and in the continuing sole discretion of my trustee:

1. To retain any assets, including cash, for so long as it deems advisable, whether or not such assets are hereinafter authorized for investment; to sell, exchange, mortgage, lease, or otherwise dispose of any assets of my trust estate for terms within and extending beyond the term of such trust; and to receive any additional properties acceptable to the trustee, from whatever source.

2. Within the trustee's discretion, to invest, reinvest, or exchange assets for, any securities and properties, including but not limited to common and preferred stocks, and no statutes, rules of law, custom, or usage shall limit the selection of investments; and to commingle for the purpose of investment all or any part of the funds of said trust in any common trust fund or funds now or hereafter maintained by the trustee.

3. To collect, receive, and obtain receipts for any principal or income; to enforce, defend against, compromise or settle any claim by or against the trust; and to vote or issue proxies to vote, oppose or join in any plans for reorganization, and to exercise any other rights incident to the ownership of any stocks, bonds, or other properties that constitute all or a part of the trust estate.

4. To hold assets in bearer form, in the name of the trustee, or in the name of the trustee's nominee or nominees without being required to disclose any fiduciary relationship; and to deposit cash assets as a general deposit in a special bank account without liability for interest thereon; provided that, at all times, such cash and assets shall be shown to be a part of the trust on the books of the trustee.

5. To charge premiums on bonds and other similar investments against principal. The trustee shall not be required to charge any depreciation or depletion against income from any real estate or personal property.

6. To make, without the necessity of intervention or consent of any legal guardian, any payments by the terms of this will be payable to or for the benefit of any minor person in any or all of the following ways: (1) directly for the maintenance, education, and welfare of any such minor beneficiary; (2) to the parent or

natural guardian of such minor beneficiary; or (3) to any person at that time having custody and care of the person of said minor beneficiary. The receipt of such person shall be full acquittance of the trustee and the trustee shall have no responsibility to oversee the application of the funds so paid.

7. To hold or make division or distribution whenever herein required in whole or in part in money, securities, or other property, and in undivided interests therein, and to continue to hold any such undivided interest in any trust hereunder, and in such division or distribution the judgment of the trustee concerning the propriety thereof and the valuation of the properties and securities concerned shall be binding and conclusive on all persons in interest.

8. To charge against the trust principal and to receive on behalf of the trustee reasonable compensation for services hereunder and payment for all reasonable expenses and charges of the trust.

Article XI

In the event that my said wife, _____, predeceases me or should we both die under such circumstances that it cannot be established by sufficient evidence that we died other than simultaneously, then my wife shall be deemed to have survived me with regard to all dispositive provisions for her benefit in this, my last will and testament. In the event that one or more of my children does not survive me, then I hereby give, devise, and bequeath the share of my property that that child would normally have taken under this will, to the living issue, collectively, of each deceased child of mine.

Article XII

If assets of my estate are to become a part of any trust by the terms of this will, and if such assets will immediately distribute upon receipt thereof by the trustee, the trustee may distribute such assets in exactly the same manner as provided in such trust without requiring such trust to be established.

Article XIII

Except for the income and general testamentary power of appointment reserved to my wife in TRUST A or ARTICLE V, no title in the trusts created by this will, or in the income from said trusts shall vest in any beneficiary and neither the principal nor the income of said trusts shall be liable for the debts of any beneficiary, and none of the beneficiaries herein shall have any power to sell, assign, transfer, encumber, or in any other manner to dispose of his or her interest in any such trust, or the income produced by such trust, prior to the actual distribution in fact, by the trustee to said beneficiary.

Article XIV

As used in this will, the singular includes the plural and the masculine includes the feminine, and the terms "issue" and "child" are defined as follows:

> "**issue**" means all persons who are descended from the persons referred to, either by legitimate birth to or legally adopted by him or any of his legitimately born or legally adopted descendants.
> "**child**" means an issue of the first generation.

Article XV

I hereby waive any and all requirements that any trust herein created be submitted to the jurisdiction of any court, that the trustee be appointed or confirmed by any court, that evidence of such appointment or confirmation be filed in any court, and that the trustee's accounts be examined, heard, filed with, or allowed by any court. This provision shall be overridden by a request by any trust beneficiaries, trustees, or executors to require the procedures waived in this article.

Article XVI

Any trusts herein created shall terminate if the trustee shall determine that the continued administration of such trusts could be unduly expensive or burdensome to the beneficiaries, and if such event should occur the assets of any such trusts shall be distributed to the beneficiaries then entitled to receive the net income of said trusts in such proportions as they are entitled to receive said net income.

Article XVII

If my estate includes any business, I hereby expressly authorize my personal representative and trustee to retain and carry on any such business regardless of the fact that such business may constitute a large or major portion of my estate or trust estate. My personal representative and trustee shall have all necessary powers to enable them to do any and all things deemed appropriate by them for the carrying on of such business, including the power to incorporate and reorganize the business, to put in additional capital, and to hire a business manager or other such employees as they shall deem necessary. My estate and trust estate shall bear the sole risk of any business interest so retained, and my personal representative and trustee shall not be liable for any loss incurred thereby except when such loss is caused by their own negligence. Since the desirability of retaining any such business interests may be affected by many factors, any powers given in this Article to my personal representative and trustee shall not be mandatory. My personal representative and trustee shall have the power to close out and liquidate or sell such business interests upon such terms as they in their sole discretion shall deem best.

Article XVIII

In the event that my trustee under this will is the beneficiary of proceeds of any pension, profit-sharing, or stock bonus plans that qualify under applicable provisions of the Internal Revenue Code, said trustee shall not use any of such proceeds to pay any taxes, debts, or other obligations enforceable against my estate, including both probate and non-probate assets. All such funds shall be allocated to "TRUST B."

Article XIX

The payment by an insurance company of the proceeds of any policy of insurance to my trustee under this will as beneficiary shall fully discharge all obligation of such insurance company on account of such policy and such insurance company shall bear no responsibility for the proper discharge of my trust or any part thereof. I direct my trustee to administer and distribute such insurance proceeds as follows:

1. If my wife survives me, my trustee shall allocate said insurance proceeds between "TRUST A" and "TRUST B," according to provisions in this will and as directed by my personal representative.

2. When acting under this will with respect to insurance proceeds as insurance beneficiary, rather than as distributee of my probate estate, my trustee shall have all duties, powers, rights, privileges, and discretions given to my personal representative, and I direct that my trustee shall cooperate with my personal representative

to ensure the most efficient and economical administration of my total gross estate.

Article XX

In the event my wife, _____, does not survive me, I hereby nominate and appoint _____(name and address) as guardian of the person for my minor child or children. The guardian may use the income from "TRUST B" for the support, education, and well-being of said child or children. In the event _____ is unable or unwilling to act as personal guardian, I hereby appoint _____ to serve in his place as personal guardian.

Article XXI

I hereby nominate _____ of _____ as the personal representative of this my last will and testament, and I give and grant unto my personal representative with respect to my estate and to each and every portion thereof, real, personal, or mixed, all such duties, powers, and discretions herein given and granted to my trustee hereof with respect to my trust estate, all of which duties, powers, and discretions shall be in addition to and not in limitation of those that normally my personal representative would possess.

If at any time after my death, my wife shall file a request in writing with the herein named personal representative and trustee that she wishes to become a co-personal representative and/or co-trustee hereunder, I hereby nominate her as co-personal representative and/or co-trustee. Until such request is filed, the personal representative herein named shall be the sole personal representative and trustee.

Any trustee herein named may at any time after my death, resign by giving notice in writing to the then income beneficiary. The date of delivery shall be specified in such instrument of resignation, and such resignation shall take effect no earlier than thirty (30) days after delivery of such written resignation. Upon such effective resignation the resigning trustee shall be relieved of all further duties and responsibilities and shall bear no liability or responsibility for the acts of any successor trustee.

I hereby direct that my personal representative or trustee shall have custody and possession of all assets, shall bear the responsibility for all receipts and disbursements, and all accounting. I direct that bond shall not be required of my personal representative and trustee.

In witness whereof, I have hereunto set my hand to this my last will and testament, consisting of _____ typewritten pages, including this page and each bearing my signature, on this _____ day of _____, _____ at _____, _____, in the presence of each and
(city) (address)
all the subscribing witnesses, each of whom I have requested in the presence of the others to subscribe his/her name, with his/her address written opposite thereto, as an attesting witness, in my presence and in the presence of all the others. _____

The above and foregoing instrument was on the date thereof, signed, published, sealed, and declared by the testator, _____, to be his last will and testament in our presence, and we at his request and in his presence and in the presence of each other, have hereunto subscribed our names as witnesses thereto.

_____ Residing at _____

_____ Residing at _____

[Notary]

GLOSSARY

A

abatement The process that determines the order in which gifts made by the testator in the will shall be applied to the payment of the decedent-testator's debts, taxes, and expenses.

active trust A trust in which a trustee performs active duties of management for the benefit of the beneficiary.

activities of daily living (ADLs) Six everyday functions and activities people do without help: Bathing, eating, dressing, toileting, continence, and transferring.

adeem To take away, extinguish, revoke, or satisfy a legacy or devise by delivery of the gift or a substitute to the beneficiary by the testator before death.

ademption The intentional act of the testator, while alive, to revoke, recall, or cancel a gift made through the will or deliver the gift or a substitute to the beneficiary.

administrator/administratrix The man or woman appointed by the probate court to administer the decedent's estate when there is no will.

adopted child The person (child) adopted.

adoption The legal process by statute that establishes a relationship of parent and child between persons who are not so related by nature.

adoptive parent A person who legally adopts another individual, usually a child.

adult day care center Senior service centers that are community-based group programs that give care during the day for adults with functional or cognitive impairments and provide assistance to caregivers.

advance medical directives Various legal documents individuals execute and use to ensure their wishes for medical care and treatment are followed after they become terminally ill and can no longer make their own decisions.

advancement Money or property given by a parent while living to a child in anticipation of the share the child will inherit from the parent's estate and in advance of the proper time for receipt of such property.

affiant The person who makes, subscribes, and files an affidavit.

affidavit A printed declaration made voluntarily under oath or affirmed before a notary public.

agent A person authorized by another person (principal) to act in place of the principal.

alternate valuation date A date six months from the date of death or the date the property is disposed by the estate, whichever comes first.

ambulatory Subject to change and revocation anytime before death; e.g., a will is ambulatory.

ancillary administration Additional administration used to dispose of and distribute that portion of the decedent's estate located in a state other than the decedent's domiciliary state.

ancillary administrator (administratrix) The personal representative appointed by the court to distribute that part of a decedent's estate located in a state other than the decedent's domiciliary state.

antenuptial (premarital) agreement A contract made by a man and woman before their marriage or in contemplation of that marriage whereby the property rights of either or both the prospective husband or wife are determined.

antilapse statute A statute that prevents a lapse (termination) of a clause in a will that would otherwise occur if the beneficiary who was to receive property under the clause dies before the testator.

applicable credit amount (unified credit) A credit against the federal unified transfer tax on gifts (prior to death) and estates (after death).

applicable exclusion amount The maximum value of property that can be transferred to others without incurring any federal gift or estate tax because of the application of the applicable credit amount (unified credit).

appointee The person who is to receive the benefit of the power of appointment.

apportionment clause A clause in a will that allocates the tax burden among the residuary estate and the beneficiaries of the will.

appraisal (appraisement) A market-based valuation of the decedent's real or personal property by a recognized expert (appraiser).

assisted living facility A community residential living arrangement that provides individual personal care

591

and health services for a person who requires help with activities of daily living (ADLs).

attest (a will) To bear witness; to affirm or verify a will as genuine.

attestation clause Witnesses to a will state that they have attested the maker's signature and that they have subscribed (signed) a clause in the will to this effect.

attorney in fact An agent, not necessarily an attorney, who is given authority by the principal in a written document called a power of attorney to perform certain specific acts on behalf of the principal.

B

beneficiary (of a trust) The person or institution who holds equitable title and to whom the trustee distributes the income earned from the trust property and, depending on the terms of the trust, even the trust property itself.

beneficiary (of a will) A person who is entitled to receive property under a will or to whom the decedent's property is given or distributed.

bond A certificate whereby a surety company promises to pay money if the personal representative of a deceased fails to faithfully perform the duties of administering the decedent's estate. The bond is the contract that binds the surety.

bypass trust This trust, also called Trust B of an A-B trust, credit shelter trust, residuary trust, or family trust, is an estate planning device whereby a portion of a deceased spouse's estate passes to a trust rather than directly to the surviving spouse, hence reducing the likelihood that the surviving spouse's subsequent estate will exceed the federal estate tax threshold. Typically, the surviving spouse is given a life estate in the trust.

C

capital gains tax An income tax on profits from the sale or exchange of a capital asset at a lower rate than the rates applied to ordinary income. Capital assets are all property held by a taxpayer, e.g., house, car, and stocks, except for assets listed in IRC § 1221.

case law Law made by judges' decisions.

cause of action The right of a person to commence a lawsuit.

charitable deduction Under tax law, a contribution to a qualified charity or other tax exempt institution for which a taxpayer may claim an income tax deduction (IRC § 170[c]). Also applicable to trusts (IRC § 512[b][11]).

charitable remainder A gift to a qualified charity after an intervening estate that qualifies as a tax deduction under certain circumstances.

Charitable Remainder Annuity Trust A trust that must pay the noncharitable income beneficiary or beneficiaries

a sum certain annually for life, or more frequently if desired, that is not less than 5 percent of the initial net fair market value of all property placed in the trust as determined for federal tax purposes.

Charitable Remainder Unitrust A trust that specifies the noncharitable income beneficiary or beneficiaries are to receive annual payments for life based on a fixed percentage (at least 5 percent) of the net fair market value of the trust's assets as determined each year.

chattel Generally, any item of personal property.

chose in action A right to bring a civil lawsuit to recover money damages or possession of personal property.

chronically ill A continuing or recurring illness that prevents the person from performing activities of daily living or requires supervision because of a cognitive impairment.

citation The legal form, used in some states, that is the court's order fixing a date, time, and place for hearing the petition to prove a will or for administration; the petitioner is required to give notice of the hearing to all interested persons.

civil union A legal union between same-sex couples offering many of the same rights and responsibilities associated with legal marriage.

claimant A creditor who files a claim against the decedent's estate.

clerk An administrative assistant to the court who receives and files documents and keeps records of court proceedings.

closing statement An affidavit signed by the personal representative at the end of informal probate proceedings to close the estate and to be discharged.

codicil A written amendment to the will that changes but does not invalidate it.

cognitive disorder impairment A mental incapacity that causes disorientation, loss of memory, and lack of safety awareness, e.g., Alzheimer's disease.

collateral heirs (relatives) Heirs who do not ascend or descend from each other but descend from the same ancestor, e.g., sisters, aunts, nephews, cousins.

commingling Combining community and separate property, e.g., into the same account or by using both to acquire a different item of property.

common probate Informal probate proceedings that involve limited court supervision, if any, and are primarily used for smaller estates.

community property All property, other than property received by gift, will, or inheritance, acquired by either spouse during marriage is considered to belong to both spouses equally in the nine community property states and Alaska if community property is elected.

competent witness A person who is legally capable and suitable to act as a witness to a will.

condition precedent A condition or specific event that must occur before an agreement or obligation becomes binding.

condition subsequent A condition that will continue or terminate an existing agreement or duty if the condition does or does not occur.

conflict of interest Divided loyalties (it would be a conflict of interest for an attorney to represent both sides in a dispute).

conservator A fiduciary; an individual or trust institution appointed by a court to care for and manage property of an incompetent person.

constructive trust An involuntary trust created by operation of law to recover property from a person who has improperly obtained possession of or legal rights to property by fraud, duress, abuse of confidence, or other unconscionable conduct.

continence The ability to control bowel and bladder function.

continuing care retirement community A campus-style community that provides a combination of housing, services, and nursing care, at one location, to meet the various needs of residents as they grow older. The community generally charges a standard fee to enter and a flexible fee for a package of contract-specified services that vary as the resident's needs change.

curtesy The right of the surviving husband to a life estate in all of his wife's real property owned during the marriage, but only if the married couple had a child born alive.

custodial (personal) care Care that consists of helping the patient with daily living and personal needs provided by people lacking professional skills or training.

custodian A person who has charge or custody of property for the benefit of another, usually for the benefit of another, usually for a minor.

custodianship An alternative to a trust or guardianship that allows a person (called a custodian) to be appointed by the court to manage property for the benefit of a minor.

cy-pres As near as possible.

cy-pres **doctrine** The equity court may order a gift intended for a charity, or for a charitable purpose, that is now nonexistent be given or applied to another charity whose purpose is as near as possible to the one originally chosen by the settlor.

D

damages The monetary remedy from a court of law that can be recovered by the person who has suffered loss or injury to person, property, or rights by the unlawful act, omission, or negligence of another.

declaration of trust A document that creates a trust in which the settlor is also the trustee.

deed A writing signed by the grantor whereby title to real property is transferred or conveyed to the grantee.

defeasance The termination of a vested estate by the happening or nonhappening of an event (condition subsequent).

defeasible Capable of being defeated, annulled, revoked, or undone upon the happening of a future event or the performance of a condition subsequent, or by a conditional limitation, as a defeasible title to property.

degree of relationship A method of determining which collateral relatives or heirs will inherit from an intestate.

degrees of kindred The relationship between a decedent and his or her survivors that governs descent and distribution. A genealogy chart.

demand To assert and file a claim for payment based on a legal right.

demandant Any person who has a financial or property interest in a decedent's estate and who files with the court a demand for notice of any order or filing pertaining to the estate.

demonstrative legacy A gift or bequest of a specific monetary amount to be paid from the sale of a particular item of property or from some identifiable fund.

deposition A written statement signed under oath by a witness that may serve to validate a will in place of testimony given in open court.

descent and distribution Refers to the distribution by intestate succession statutes.

designated or reciprocal beneficiaries Same-sex couples who have entered into a valid reciprocal beneficiary relationship offering limited benefits associated with legal marriage.

digital executor The representative of an estate who is responsible to manage the digital assets of the estate.

direct skip A generation-skipping transfer of an interest in property to a skip person; a direct skip is subject to the federal generation-skipping transfer tax and also the federal gift or estate tax.

disclaimer The right of a beneficiary or heir to refuse a gift by will, trust, or inheritance without any adverse tax consequences.

disposition The parting with, transfer of, or conveyance of property.

domestic partnership A legal arrangement between same-sex couples offering limited benefits to broad rights and responsibilities associated with legal marriage.

domicile The legal home where a person has a true, fixed, and permanent place of dwelling and to which the person intends to return when absent.

domiciliary administration The administration of an estate in the state where the decedent was domiciled at the time of death.

domiciliary state The state in which the decedent's domicile (legal home) is located.

donee [of a power of appointment] The person to whom a power of appointment is given, also called the holder, who selects the appointee to receive an estate or an income therefrom.

donee A person who receives a gift.

donor [of a power of appointment] The testator or settlor who creates and confers a power or authority upon another (called the donee) to appoint; that is, to select the person(s) (called the appointee) to receive an estate or an income therefrom after the testator's or donee's death.

donor A person who makes a gift.

dower At common law, the right of the surviving wife to a life estate in one-third of all real property her husband owned during the marriage.

E

ejectment An action (a lawsuit brought in a court) for the recovery of the possession of land.

elder law Specialized legal services for our aging population.

elective or forced share statute The statute that grants the surviving spouse the election or choice. Also called statutory share.

equitable title (of a trust) The right of the party who holds the equitable title or beneficial interest to the benefits of the trust.

escheat The passage of an intestate's property to the state when there are no surviving blood relatives or a spouse.

estate All property owned by a person while alive or at the time of death. Also called gross estate, probate estate, probate assets, or probate property.

estate equalization Rearranging property ownership of total estate assets owned by the spouses so that each spouse's individual estate has approximately the same value.

estate plan An arrangement of a person's estate using the laws of various disciplines, e.g., wills, trusts, taxes, insurance, and property, to gain maximum financial benefit of all the laws for the disposition of a person's assets during life and after death.

execution of a valid will The acts of the testator who writes and signs the will and the two or more witnesses who attest and sign it to establish the will's validity.

executor/executrix A man or woman named in the will by the maker to be the personal representative of the decedent's estate and to carry out the provisions of the will.

exempt property The decedent's personal property up to a specific dollar amount that is given to the surviving spouse and/or minor children and is exempt from creditors' claims.

exordium clause The beginning or introductory clause of a will.

express trust A trust created or declared in explicit terms for specific purposes by a written document (deed or will) or an oral declaration.

F

"family" allowance A statute that allows the court to award to the surviving spouse and/or minor children a monthly cash allowance for their maintenance and support.

federal estate tax A tax imposed on the transfer of property at death.

fee simple estate An estate in real property that is the largest, best, and most extensive estate possible. Also known as a fee simple absolute, an estate in fee, or simply a fee.

fiduciary A person, such as a personal representative, guardian, conservator, or trustee, who is appointed to serve in a position of trust and confidence and controls and manages property exclusively for the benefit of others. By law the fiduciary's conduct is held to the highest ethical standard.

fiduciary duty A duty or responsibility required of a fiduciary to act solely for another's benefit that arises out of a position of loyalty and trust.

fixture Something so attached to land as to be deemed a part of it, e.g., real property that may have once been personal property but now is permanently attached to land or buildings.

foreign state Any state other than the decedent's domiciliary state.

formal probate A court-supervised administration of a decedent's estate.

freehold estate An estate in real property of uncertain duration. Examples include fee simple and life estates.

future interest Any fixed estate or interest, except a reversion, in which the privilege of possession or enjoyment is future and not present.

G

garnish Make a claim against.

garnishment A three-party statutory proceeding in which a judgment creditor may demand that someone who owes money to or possesses property of a judgement debtor pay the money or transfer the property to the creditor to satisfy the creditors claim against the debtor.

general legacy A gift of a fixed amount of money from the general assets of the estate.

general power of appointment The right to pass on an interest in property to whomever a donee chooses, including himself, his estate, his creditors, or creditors of his estate.

general power of attorney A written document in which a principal appoints and authorizes an agent or attorney in fact to perform a variety of acts on behalf of the principal.

generation-skipping transfer A transfer of assets to a person two or more generations below the transferor, e.g., from a grandparent to a grandchild.

generation-skipping transfer tax A federal tax on the transfer of property when its value exceeds the lifetime exemption to a person two or more generations below the generation of the transferor (donor or decedent), e.g., a grandparent who transfers property to a grandchild, thereby skipping a child.

generation-skipping transfer trust A trust that partially avoids federal gift and estate taxes on transfers of large sums of money or other valuable assets established to transfer these assets to a beneficiary two or more generations below the transferor.

gift splitting For gift tax purposes, an election by spouses to make a gift by one of them to a third party as being made one-half by each spouse.

grantee The person to whom a conveyance of real or personal property is made.

grantor The person who makes a conveyance (transfer) of real or personal property to another.

guardian The person or institution named by the maker of a will or appointed by the court when there is no will to care for the person and/or property of a minor or a handicapped or incompetent person.

H

heir Traditionally, a person, including a spouse, who is entitled by statute to the real property of an intestate. Today, a person entitled to any gift (real or personal property) of the intestate or in the decedent's will.

holographic will A completely handwritten, signed, and usually dated will that often requires no witnesses.

home health care Medical and nonmedical (including household) services provided by doctors, nurses, therapists, home health aides, and homemakers for sick, disabled, or infirmed persons in their homes.

homestead allowance A statute that provides a modest cash award for the benefit of a surviving spouse or minor children; it is a priority payment to them and is not subject to creditors' claims.

homestead The house and adjoining land occupied by the owner as a home.

homestead exemption Property tax reductions or exemptions available in some states for homestead property. A formal declaration is recorded to establish the homestead or whenever the property changes owners.

hospice care A public agency or private organization that provides supportive care at home or in an institution (e.g., hospital) for the terminally ill, i.e., persons certified by their doctor to have a life expectancy of six months or less.

householder The head of the household or family who is entitled to the homestead exemption.

I

implied trust A trust created by operation of law or the equity court based on the implied or presumed intent of the person who holds legal title and, generally, to prevent fraud.

***in rem* jurisdiction** The authority of the court over the decedent's property.

"in terrorem" clause A clause in a will that if a beneficiary of the will objects to probate or challenges the will's distributions, that contestant forfeits all benefits of the will.

incidents of ownership An element or right of ownership or degree of control over a life insurance policy.

income Interest, dividends, or other return from invested capital.

incompetent person A person under legal disability, e.g., a mentally incapacitated person.

indefinite class A group of persons within the public whose number is not specified and are unknown to the settlor of the trust.

inflation protection A policy option that provides for increases in benefit amounts to help pay for expected increases in the costs of long-term care services due to inflation.

informal probate A court proceeding of a decedent's estate with limited or no court supervision.

inheritance Property that descends (passes) to an heir when an ancestor dies intestate.

insane delusions A person with a disordered mind imagines facts to exist for which there is no evidence.

insolvent estate An estate where the debts are greater than the assets.

***intervivos* or living trust** A trust created by a maker (settlor) during the maker's lifetime. It becomes operational immediately after the trust is created.

interested party [person] A person including heirs, devisees, beneficiaries, personal representatives, creditors, and any others having a property right to or claim against the estate of a decedent.

interested witness A person who is a beneficiary and a witness of the same will.

interlineations The act of writing between the lines of an instrument.

intestacy Death without a valid will.

intestate succession statutes Laws passed in each state establishing the manner in which a decedent's property will be distributed when death occurs without a valid will.

inventory A detailed list of property and other assets containing a description or designation of each specific item and its value at the time of the decedent's death.

irrevocable life insurance trust A living trust that cannot be revoked or amended that is established by a settlor who assigns the ownership of a new or existing life insurance policy on the settlor's life to the trust and contributes money annually to the trust to pay the premiums. The policy proceeds are payable to the trust on the death of the settlor.

irrevocable trust A trust that may not be revoked by the settlor after its creation.

issue All persons who have descended from a common ancestor.

J

joint tenancy Ownership of real or personal property by two or more persons with the right of survivorship.

joint tenants Two or more persons who own or hold equal, undivided interests in property with the right of survivorship.

joint will A will for spouses that consists of a single document signed by them as their will.

jurisdiction The authority by which a particular court is empowered by statute to decide a certain kind of case and to have its decision enforced.

L

lapse Failure to distribute a gift in a will because the beneficiary or devisee dies before the testator.

leasehold estate An estate in real property held under a lease.

legal capacity Age at which a person acquires capacity to make a valid will, usually 18.

legal life estate A life estate created by operation of law and not directly by the parties themselves.

legal title (of a trust) The form of ownership of trust property held by the trustee, giving the trustee the right to control and manage the property for another's benefit, i.e., the holder of the equitable title.

legatee A person who receives a gift of personal property under a will.

letter of instructions A document that specifies the testator's instructions for organ donation and funeral and burial plans. It can also be an all-inclusive checklist of various personal and estate information to help the family and personal representative locate and identify property and documents necessary to administer the estate.

Letters of Administration The formal document of authority and appointment given to a personal representative (administrator) by the proper court to carry out the administration of the decedent's estate according to the proper state intestate succession statute.

Letters of Authority Certificates of appointment called either Letters Testamentary, when there is a will, or Letters of Administration, when there is no will.

Letters Testamentary The formal document of authority and appointment given to a personal representative (executor) by the proper court to carry out the administration of the decedent's estate according to the terms of a will.

life estate A freehold estate in which a person, called the life tenant, holds an interest in real property during his own or someone else's lifetime.

life tenant The person holding a life estate.

limited power of attorney A written document in which a principal appoints and authorizes an agent or attorney in fact to perform a few specific acts on behalf of the principal.

living will A document, separate from a will, that expresses a person's wish to be allowed to die a natural death and not be kept alive by artificial means.

long-term care The support that disabled, frail, or chronically ill people need when they can no longer care for themselves.

long-term care insurance Insurance that pays a fixed monetary benefit, usually per day, for a designated benefit period during which the insured generally receives care at home or in a nursing home.

lucid interval A temporary restoration to sanity during which an incompetent person has sufficient intelligence and judgment to make a valid will.

M

marital deduction An unlimited amount of the decedent's gross estate, which may be given to the surviving spouse without being subject to federal estate tax levied against the decedent's estate.

marshaling of assets The arrangement or ranking of testamentary gifts into a certain order to be used for the payment of debts.

memorandum A written list of the testator's personal property and the name of the beneficiary who receives each item. It is signed by the testator but is not a legally enforceable document.

mutual (reciprocal) wills Separate and identical wills made by spouses that contain reciprocal provisions and agree that neither spouse will change his or her will after the death of the first spouse.

N

natural objects of the testator's bounty Family members and other persons (friends) and institutions (charitable or religious organizations) for whom the testator has affection.

necessaries Necessary items that supply the personal needs of an individual or family, such as food, clothing, or shelter.

nonforfeiture benefit A policy feature that returns a portion of the premiums if the insured cancels the insurance policy or allows it to lapse.

nonmarital child A child born to parents who are not married.

notary public A person authorized by the state whose function is to administer oaths, certify documents and deeds, and attest to the authenticity of signatures.

nuncupative will An oral will.

nursing home care A residential institution that provides care and services for the elderly or infirmed.

O

operation of law Rights pass automatically to a person by the application of the established rules of law, without the act, knowledge, or cooperation of the person.

P

parol evidence Oral testimony or written evidence.

partition The division of real property held by joint tenants or tenants in common into separate portions so that the individuals may hold the property in severalty, i.e., in single ownership.

passive trust A trust in which the trustee has no active duties to perform.

per capita by representation A method of dividing an intestate estate; if the members of the identified group are not of the same generation, then the younger generation will only be entitled to the that portion of the estate that the older generation would have received had they survived.

per capita distribution A method of dividing an intestate estate; if a member of the identified group predeceases the decedent, then his or her share would pass to the other members of the group rather than to his descendants.

per stirpes distribution A distribution of property that depends on the relationship to the intestate of those entitled to the estate. Distribution by representation.

personal guardian An individual or trust institution appointed by a court to take custody of and care for a minor or an incompetent person.

personal representative The person who administers and distributes a decedent's estate according to the will or the appropriate intestate succession statute. It includes executor and executrix when there is a will and administrator and administratrix when there is no will.

POLST A dying individual's statement specifying the type of care wanted in end-of-life situations, directing family and medical professionals to follow the stated wishes.

portability Surviving spouse's right to carry over the unused portion of a predeceased spouse's estate or gift tax exemption and combine it with his or her own exemptions at death.

posthumous child A child born after the death of his or her father.

postmortem After death; pertaining to matters occurring after death.

postnuptial agreement A contract made by spouses after marriage whereby the property rights of either or both spouses are determined.

pour-over will A will provision in which the testator directs (passes) the residue of the estate into an existing living trust.

power of attorney A document, witnessed and acknowledged, authorizing another to act as one's agent or attorney in fact.

precatory trust A trust created by precatory words, e.g., "*wish and request*, "or *have fullest confidence*, which the courts have held sufficient to constitute a trust.

precatory words Words such as *hope, desire, request, ask, beseech, wish*, or *recommend*, which are ineffective to dispose of property.

preexisting condition limitation An illness or disability for which the insured was diagnosed or treated during a period before applying for a long-term care insurance policy.

present interest An immediate and unrestricted interest in real or personal property including the privilege of possession or enjoyment of the property.

pretermitted (omitted) child A child omitted in a parent's will.

prima facie At first sight; on the face of it. A fact presumed to be true unless disproved by evidence to the contrary.

principal In trust law, the capital or property of a trust, as opposed to the income, which is the product of the capital. Also, a person who authorizes another (agent) to act on the person's behalf.

pro rata According to a certain rate or percentage.

probate [of a will] The procedure by which a document is presented to the court to confirm it is a valid will.

probate court The court that has jurisdiction (authority) over the probate of wills and the administration of the decedent's estate.

probate proceedings The process of distributing the estate of a person who died testate or intestate; includes all other matters over which probate courts have jurisdiction.

probate property Decedent's property that is subject to estate administration by the personal representative.

property guardian An individual or trust institution appointed by a court to care for and manage the property of a minor or an incompetent person.

public (charitable) trust A trust established for the social benefit either of the public at large or the community.

publication In the law of wills, the formal declaration made by a testator at the time of signing a will that it is his last will and testament.

purautre vie An estate lasting for the life of a person other than the life tenant.

purchase-money resulting trust A resulting trust in which property is purchased and paid for by one person, and at his direction, the seller transfers possession and title to another person.

Q

qualified small estate A decedent's estate that consists entirely of statutory exempt property or allowances and funeral and administration expenses, and is within a certain limited monetary value.

qualified terminable interest property (QTIP) trust A type of trust that will qualify for the marital deduction in which the surviving spouse receives all the income for life but is not given a general power of appointment.

quasi-community property Property that is acquired in a common law state and then moved into a community property state or that is owned by spouses who have moved into a community property state.

R

real property Land, buildings, and things permanently attached to them.

registrar (aka surrogate) A person designated by the judge to perform the functions of the court in informal proceedings.

remainder A future estate in real property that takes effect on the termination of a prior estate created by the same instrument at the same time.

remainderman A person entitled to the future fee simple estate after a particular smaller estate, e.g., a life estate, has expired.

residence The dwelling in which one temporarily lives or resides.

residuary clause A clause in a will that disposes of the remaining assets (residue) of the decedent's estate after all debts and gifts in the will are satisfied.

residuary estate The remaining assets (residue) of the decedent's estate after all debts have been paid and all other gifts in the will are distributed.

residuary legacy or devise A gift of all the testator's personal property not otherwise effectively disposed of by a will is a residuary legacy, and a gift of all the real property not disposed of is a residuary devise.

respite [care] Care offered to relieve family caregivers for a few hours or up to several days.

resulting trust A trust created by operation of law from circumstances implied from the intentions of the parties that the person who holds legal title is obligated to hold it "in trust" for another person's benefit, even though there is no stated intention to create a trust and no fraud is involved. Resulting trusts often occur when an attempt to create a valid express trust fails for lack of one or more of the essential elements.

reversion or reversionary interest The interest in real property that a grantor retains when a conveyance of the property by deed or by will transfers an estate smaller than what the grantor owns, e.g., when the grantor has a fee simple estate and conveys to the grantee a life estate. At some future time the real property reverts back to the grantor.

revocable trust A trust that the settlor has a right or power to cancel or revoke.

revocation clause A clause or statement in a will that revokes all prior wills and codicils.

right of election The right of a surviving husband or wife to choose to take, under the decedent's state law, his or her statutory share in preference to the provision made in the deceased spouse's will.

right of representation The right of a child to receive the share of an intestate's property the child's deceased parent would have received if the parent were still living.

right of survivorship Passes the decedent joint tenant's interest in property automatically to the surviving joint tenant(s) by operation of law without the need for probate.

right to die The right of a dying person to refuse extraordinary medical treatment to prolong life.

right-to-die laws Cases and statutes that recognize the right to die and the right of a dying person's guardian to ask the court to substitute its judgment for that of the dying person who no longer has the mental capacity to make such a judgment.

Rule Against Perpetuities The principle that no interest in property is good (valid) unless it must vest (take effect), if at all, not later than 21 years, plus the period of gestation, after some life or lives in being at the time of the creation of the interest. The rule fixes the time within which a future interest must vest. The period of gestation is included to cover cases of posthumous birth.

S

self-proved will A will that replaces the traditional attestation clause with another state statute clause that contains a self-proving affidavit signed by the testator and witnesses in the presence of a notary public who also signs and seals it, thereby creating the self-proved will.

self-proving affidavit (clause) A clause at the end of a will that contains an acknowledgment or affidavit of the testator and affidavits of witnesses signed by them in the presence of a notary public who also signs and seals it. This clause is used to replace the traditional attestation clause.

separate property Property that the husband or wife owned prior to their marriage or acquired during marriage by gift, will, or inheritance.

settler A person who creates a trust; also called donor, grantor, creator, or trustor.

severalty (tenancy in severalty) Ownership of property held by one person only.

severance The destruction of a joint tenancy by one of the joint tenants transferring while alive his interest in real property to another person by deed, thereby creating a tenancy in common with the new owner and the other remaining joint tenant(s).

simultaneous death clause A clause in a will that determines the distribution of property in the event there is no evidence as to the priority of time of death of the testator and another, usually the testator's spouse.

skilled nursing facility A Medicare qualified facility that specializes in skilled nursing or rehabilitation services under the supervision of licensed nursing personnel and based on a doctor's orders.

skip person An individual (such as a grandchild) who receives the property in a generation-skipping transfer and is two or more generations below the generation of the transferor.

small estate A decedent's estate with few assets and a limited monetary value.

solemn probate Formal probate proceedings that require court supervision throughout the administration of the decedent's estate.

sound mind To have the mental ability to make a valid will. The normal condition of the human mind, not impaired by insanity or other mental disorders.

special or limited power of appointment A power of appointment that cannot be exercised in favor of the donee or his estate but only in favor of identifiable person(s) other than the donee.

specific devise A gift of real property in a will. Under the UPC, a gift of real or personal property in a will.

specific legacy or bequest A gift of a particular item or class of personal property in a will.

spend-down A procedure that requires an individual to spend enough income and resources to qualify for Medicaid eligibility.

spouse's statutory, forced or elective share The spouse's statutory right to choose a share of the decedent spouse's estate instead of inheriting under the provisions of the decedent's will.

sprinkling trust The trustee has the authority and discretion to accumulate or distribute trust income or principal, or both, among the trust beneficiaries in varying amounts.

standing The requirement that a person stands to lose a pecuniary interest in a decedent's estate if a will is allowed.

Statute of Frauds State laws that provide that no lawsuit or civil action shall be maintained on certain classes of oral contracts unless the agreement is put in writing in a note or memorandum and signed by the party to be charged, i.e., the person being sued, or an authorized agent of the person.

statutes Laws passed by state and federal legislatures.

statutory will A fill-in-the-blank will that is created and authorized by statute in a few states.

stepped-up basis An increase in the income tax basis of appreciated (increase in value) property. The property is valued on the date of death or the alternate valuation date.

stock dividend A dividend of shares of stock distributed to stockholders.

stock split One share of stock is split into a larger number of shares resulting in a proportional change in the number of shares owned by each stockholder.

straw man A person used to create a joint tenancy of real property between the existing owner of the property and one or more other persons.

subscribe (a will) To sign one's name at the end of a will.

succession The act of acquiring property of a decedent by will or by operation of law when the person dies intestate.

successor An all-inclusive UPC term meaning any person, other than a creditor, who is entitled to real or personal property of a decedent either under the will or through intestate succession.

surcharge An overcharge beyond what is just and right, e.g., an amount the fiduciary is required by court order to make good because of negligence or other failure of duty.

surety An individual or insurance company that, at the request of a personal representative, agrees to pay money up to the amount of a bond in the event that the personal representative fails to faithfully perform his duties.

surviving spouse The traditional meaning/usage of wife or husband based on legal marriage and expanded in some states to include same-sex conjugal couples.

T

taxable distribution Any distribution of income or principal from a trust to a skip person that is not a taxable termination or direct skip.

taxable termination Any termination of an interest in property held in trust.

tax-qualified long-term care insurance policy A policy that conforms to specific standards under federal law and offers certain federal tax advantages.

tenancy by the entirety A form of joint tenancy available only to a husband and wife; it also has the right of survivorship.

tenancy in common The ownership of an undivided interest of real or personal property by two or more persons without the right of survivorship, which allows each owner's interest to be passed to his or her beneficiaries or heirs upon death.

terminable interest An interest in property that terminates on the death of the holder or on the occurrence of some other specified event. The transfer of a terminable interest from one spouse to the other spouse does not qualify for the marital deduction.

testacy Death with a valid will.

testament Another name for a will.

testamentary capacity The sanity (sound mind) requirement for a person to make a valid will.

testamentary intent Requirement for a valid will that the testator must intend the instrument to operate as his/her last will.

testamentary trust A trust created in a will. It becomes operational only after death.

testator/testatrix A man or a woman who makes and/or dies with a valid will.

testimonium clause A clause in a will in which the maker states that he or she has freely signed and dated the will and requests the proper number of witnesses to do the same.

tickler system A chronological list of all the important steps and dates in the stages of the administration of the decedent's estate.

toileting Getting to and from, on and off the toilet, and performing personal hygiene.

Totten trust A bank deposit of a person's money in the name of the account holder as trustee for another person.

transferee The beneficiary who receives the benefits of a generation-skipping transfer trust.

transfer-on-death deed or beneficiary deed A type of deed, properly executed and recorded, that allows the transfer of real property to a designated beneficiary without probate. The transfer does not take effect until the death of the owner.

transferor The decedent or donor who creates a generation-skipping transfer trust.

transferring Moving in or out of bed, a chair, or wheelchair.

trust A right of property, real or personal, held by one person (trustee) for the benefit of another (beneficiary).

trust agreement A written agreement (contract) between the settlor and trustee(s) that creates the trust and is signed by them.

trustee The person or institution named by the maker of a will or a settlor of a trust to administer property for the benefit of another (the beneficiary) according to provisions in a testamentary trust or an *inter vivos* trust.

U

undivided interest A right to an undivided portion of property that is owned by one of two or more joint tenants or tenants in common before the property is divided (partitioned).

Uniform Health Care Decisions Act (UHCDA) Uniform law issued by National Conference of Commissioners on Uniform State Laws intended to give increased consistency and stability for individuals making end-of-life medical decisions.

Uniform International Wills Act A section of the UPC intended to streamline probating wills in American courts that were drafted in a foreign country and vice-versa.

Uniform Probate Code (UPC) A uniform law available for adoption by the states to modernize and improve the efficiency of the administration of a decedent's estate.

Uniform Trust Code (UTC) A uniform law available for adoption by the states to provide a uniform codified law on trusts.

V

venue The particular place, city or county, where a court having jurisdiction may hear and decide a case.

W

waiting (elimination) period The amount of time in calendar or benefit days after the initial use of qualifying long-term care services in a nursing home or at home before benefits are paid.

waiver of premium payment A provision in a long-term care insurance policy that allows the insured to stop paying premiums once benefits are received.

ward A minor or incompetent person placed under the care and supervision of a guardian by the probate court.

waste Any act or omission that does permanent damage to real property or unreasonably changes its character or value.

will contest Litigation to overturn a decedent's will.

will The legally enforceable written declaration of a person's intended distribution of property after death.

INDEX